The Complete Book of Ground Covers

THE COMPLETE BOOK OF GROUND COVERS

**4000 Plants That
Reduce Maintenance,
Control Erosion, and
Beautify the Landscape**

GARY LEWIS

TIMBER PRESS
Portland, Oregon

For my mom, Kitty Lewis, who started it all.
And for Randy Rae, for his love, support, and patience!

Published in 2022 by Timber Press, Inc.
The Haseltine Building
133 S.W. Second Avenue, Suite 450
Portland, Oregon 97204-3527
timberpress.com

Printed in China on paper from responsible resources
Text design by Laura Shaw Design
Cover design by Richard Ljoenes

ISBN 978-1-60469-460-4

Catalog records for this book are available from the
Library of Congress and the British Library.

Frontispiece: Stonecrops (*Sedum* spp.) grow well together, as
their trailing stems easily intermingle and they require the
same growing conditions. Opposite: *Epimedium* sp. with new
spring foliage.

Page 6 (clockwise from top left): *Lysimachia nummularia* 'Aurea'
cascades over and softens the hard surface of a wall at Wisley
Gardens, UK. / A mass planting of *Brunnera macrophylla* 'Jack
Frost' provides an effective shady ground cover. / The spring
ephemeral *Ficaria verna* 'Coppernob' provides seasonal coverage with this primrose before later perennials emerge at the
Miller Garden, Seattle.

Contents

GROUND COVERS are widely considered a utilitarian group of low-growing plants held to a narrow set of expectations: cover dirt and outcompete weeds. Certainly they can reliably provide these valuable services and become the negative space—much like a lawn—that enables the rest of the garden hardscape and softscape to shine. Ground covers do not play an exciting role in our garden plans, and they normally exist outside the limelight we shine on their larger, more inspiring compatriots. We think of ground covers when we have a problem that needs a solution: How fast will it fill an area? Can we insert it into the tight spaces between pavers? How much foot traffic can it withstand?

Nevertheless, these small but tough and useful plants punch above their weight, so to speak—not just in function, but also in beauty—and, like Napoleon, or Tinker Bell, or Frodo, ground covers are small but mighty and deserve a little respect. These resilient plants are not just "doers"; they offer a diverse range of beautiful and intriguing options with a great variety of colors, textures, and forms for the garden. They are both sprinters and marathoners that quickly cover ground and keep it covered for the long haul, horticultural bouncers that muscle out weeds, and heavy lifting garden Atlases that hold up slopes and prevent erosion. They can also be design imperatives that can unify a garden; knit together plantings and hardscape; add extra layers of beauty, dynamism, and surprise; and take a garden to the next level.

Continued introductions, either from the intrepid travels of plant explorers or the deft work of plant breeders, have greatly expanded the diverse and intriguing palette of ground cover options over the years. Their diversity and ease of cultivation also make them useful for more modern applications in containers and hanging baskets and on living walls and green roofs.

Ground covers also have an important role as we consider the state of our environment and its

A toad takes refuge among *Ajuga reptans* 'Binblasca' Black Scallop, *A. reptans* 'Burgundy Glow', and *Phlox glaberrima* subsp. *triflora* 'Triple Play'.

stewardship. When used as an alternative to lawns, they can reduce our use of water, fertilizer, pesticides, herbicides, carbon-based fuels, and electricity, not to mention time and money. We can also transform wide swaths of grass into a diverse landscape of habitat and food for native insects, birds, and other wildlife. As a replacement for hardscape such as concrete, asphalt, gravel, and pavers, ground covers can reduce stormwater runoff, improve the health of our natural waterways, enhance groundwater replenishment, and reduce the heat island effect of our urban environments.

This compendium seeks to bring ground covers out of the utilitarian shadows and into the spotlight, to build for them a pedestal in the pantheon of the best and most valuable garden plants.

Stachys byzantina 'Big Ears' and *Artemisia versicolor* 'Sea Foam' set the stage for white alliums, backed with Mexican feather grass (*Nassella tenuissima*) at the Denver Botanic Gardens.

Acknowledgments

Thank you to the following people for their encouragement and expertise: Janet Anderson, Tony Avent, Evan Bean, Todd Boland, Paul Bonine, Angie Clelan, John Friel, Dan Heims, Dan Hinkley, John Hoffman, Sean Hogan, Brent Horvath, Brad Jalbert, Panayoti Kelaidis, Karla Lortz, Ewan MacKenzie, Jody Nolin, Kelly Norris, Steve Schreiner, Greg Shepherd, Ritchie Steffen, Ross Shrigley, Mary Vaananen, David Victor, Rob Wein, and Dave Wilson.

Thank you to my staff at Phoenix Perennials, the Phoenicians, for their support and patience when writing and photography trips took me away from the nursery. And to Valerie Wilmot for early organizational help.

Thank you to Cyndi Henderson and Lochaus for a place to hide and work.

Thank you to Andrew Beckman, Mike Dempsey, Sarah Milhollin, Lisa Theobald, and the entire team at Timber Press for their dedication to this project. A very special thank you to Tom Fischer for his quiet confidence, calm reassurance, and seemingly inexhaustible patience over the eight long years it took to write this book!

Sedum spurium and *Thymus pseudolanuginosus* can cover large expanses, offer alternatives to turf, and provide interesting contrast to specimen plants such as these globe blue spruce.

Introduction to Ground Covers

GROUND COVERS include any plant that can be used reliably to cover the ground. Typically, the term refers to low-growing and wide-spreading species, especially those that are rhizomatous or stoloniferous or that have trailing or arching stems. Clumping plants, if they have good foliage and branch spread relative to their height, can also be mass-planted to form a ground cover. Ground covers can also be perennials or shrubs that are evergreen, semi-evergreen, deciduous, or herbaceous.

This book focuses primarily on ground covers up to 12–18 in. (30–45 cm) tall with a spread at least double the height. Some taller plants of 18–36 in. (45–90 cm) in height are also included, especially if they offer significant spread. Much taller plants, especially shrubs 3–6 ft. (1–1.8 m) tall, can function as ground covers in large settings such as parks, estates, and institutional plantings. These are sometimes mentioned, especially when they represent larger options of plants that fit the book's main size criteria.

Ground covers spread via different growth habits that offer opportunities and drawbacks related to their rate of spread, interaction with other plants and hardscape, and propagation. Most plants have just one mode of spread, but some employ multiple strategies, such as *Ajuga reptans*, which spreads both by short rhizomes and by long stolons.

Types of Ground Covers

Rhizomatous Plants

A rhizome, sometimes referred to as a creeping rootstalk, is a horizontally spreading modified stem that usually emerges at or below the soil surface. Nodes are usually closely spaced and branching, also producing roots and aboveground growth. In rhizomatous plants, the rhizome is the main stem of the plant. Rhizomes can be long and thin, as in lily of the valley (*Convallaria majalis*); somewhat thick and woody, as in barrenwort (*Epimedium* spp.); or thickened into fleshy storage organs, as in the dwarf bearded iris (*Iris pumila*). Rhizomatous plants usually spread more slowly than stoloniferous ones, creating a denser cover that is often better suited for small spaces and where a controlled spread is desired. Some rhizomatous ground covers, however, can be fast spreading, such as bishop's weed (*Aegopodium podagraria*) and chameleon plant (*Houttuynia cordata*).

Rhizomatous ground covers are useful for "respecting" the boundaries of hardscape in that their rhizomes are usually stopped by stone pathways, patios, driveways, and sidewalks, creating a cleaner line of division as compared with stoloniferous or trailing ground covers, which can spread across hardscape surfaces. Rhizomes tend to be long-lived and, because they are usually below ground, are more difficult to remove should that become necessary.

Stoloniferous and Running Plants

The terms "stolon" and "runner" are often confused and used interchangeably because the resulting plant habits are functionally similar in horticulture. Differentiating the two habits is sometimes confusing and generally unnecessary in horticulture, so the term "stolon" is used broadly here to describe both habits. Both stoloniferous and running ground covers have long, primarily aboveground stems, usually with widely spaced internodes. Both are useful for quickly growing around perennials, shrubs, rocks, and other hardscape features and intermingling with other ground covers, though it may take time to achieve full coverage.

The ice plants, in this case *Delosperma* 'Pwwg02s' Red Mountain Flame, produce verdant and colorful carpets in full sun, especially on slopes.

Rhizomatous plants can form a large, dense cover. ↓

The stolons of *Saxifraga stolonifera* and sempervivum are somewhat short-lived, while the runners of strawberries (*Fragaria* spp.) and *Ajuga reptans* are more persistant. ↓

Aegopodium podagraria 'Variegatum'

Saxifraga stolonifera

Convallaria majalis with *Galium odoratum*

Sempervivum and *Jovibarba globifera*

Barrenwort (*Epimedium* sp.)

Fragaria spp. with *Ophiopogon planiscapus* 'Nigrescens'

Houttuynia cordata

Ajuga reptans 'Binblasca' Black Scallop

A true stolon grows from the main stem, producing a rooting plantlet at its tip. Once mature, the daughter plant can produce additional stolons radiating in any direction. True stoloniferous plants tend to produce intersecting networks of temporarily connected plants, since stolons are generally short-lived. Examples include strawberry begonia (*Saxifraga stolonifera*) and hen and chicks (*Sempervivum* spp.).

Thin aboveground rhizomes, stoloniferous rhizomes, or prostrate stems are sometimes considered to be runners. They are usually indeterminate in growth and travel in straight lines that root and produce plants at the internodes. Daughter plants can then grow more runners in any direction, which tend to be more persistent than stolons. Examples include strawberries (*Fragaria* spp.) and bugleweed (*Ajuga reptans*).

Suckering Plants

Suckers usually arise from adventitious buds on the crown of a plant or nearby roots, though some plants can produce suckers at some distance from the mother plant. Suckers are usually produced by woody ground covers and tend to arise from the soil, with upright stems forming a sort of thicket. Examples include Japanese anemone (*Anemone hupehensis*), trumpet creeper (*Campsis radicans*), Himalayan sweet box (*Sarcococca hookeriana*), and fragrant sumac (*Rhus aromatica*). Suckering ground covers tend not to spread much during establishment and at a slow to moderate rate thereafter. They usually form a dense cover good for small spaces and slope stabilization.

(ABOVE) The vertical, suckering stems of *Sarcococca hookeriana* will form a closed cover over time. (BELOW) Japanese anemone (*Anemone hupehensis*) spreads along a wall.

Trailing or Creeping Plants

Many ground covers have horizontally trailing or creeping stems that can be fully prostrate, prostrate with ascending tips (decumbent), arching, or weeping. Examples include most ground cover *Sedum* spp., periwinkle (*Vinca minor*), carmel creeper (*Ceanothus griseus* var. *horizontalis*), and creeping juniper (*Juniperus horizontalis*). Some have readily to occasionally rooting stems, while others, especially shrubs, produce procumbent stems that do not grow roots. Trailing ground covers spread at varied rates depending on the species. Prostrate shrubs can take time to reach mature size but can be interplanted with faster growing ground covers to provide interim coverage. Trailing or creeping ground covers are useful for filling in around perennials, shrubs, and hardscape features such as rocks and concrete work. They can also grow across pathways, paving stones, and patios, which may not be desirable.

Vinca minor forms dense mats of interweaving stems that can root where they touch the ground.

This extremely low-growing *Juniperus horizontalis* 'Pancake' can spread to 4 ft. (1.2 m) wide with nonrooting stems.

Vines

In the wild, vines usually clamber across the ground until they find a vertical plant or natural structure to climb. Without vertical garden supports such as woody plants, pergolas, fences, or trellises, vines can be used as rambling, billowing ground covers. In general, they can be expected to reach 6–24 in. (15–60 cm) tall and spread widely over a medium-sized to large area. Most vines would quickly overwhelm small spaces unless pruned hard each year.

Trailing, flexible, and widely spreading stems make vines effective on slopes, over walls, and across and around rough, uneven ground. They are also useful in obscuring unsightly landscape features such as rocks, boulders, rubble, hardscape, stumps, or other undesirable topography. Some have rooting stems. Because vines can spread widely, they can be strategically planted in favorable soil conditions and encouraged, directed, or pinned to grow into problem areas such as dry shade or rocky, poor soils. Also, a single ground-covering vine can be allowed to grow upward when it finds vertical support, which also makes it more likely to flower. Examples include English ivy (*Hedera helix*), Virginia creeper (*Parthenocissus* spp.), honeysuckle (*Lonicera* spp.), trumpet creeper (*Campsis* spp.), jasmine (*Jasminum* spp.), star jasmine (*Trachelospermum* spp.), most *Clematis* species, deciduous and evergreen climbing hydrangeas (*Hydrangea anomala* subsp. *petiolaris* and *H. seemannii*), and Japanese hydrangea vine (*Schizophragma hydrangeoides*).

Clumping Perennials and Shrubs

Any clumping, mounding, arching, or wide-spreading perennial or shrub can be mass-planted to cover the ground. In general, good candidates are plants that grow at least twice as wide as tall. Examples include heartleaf brunnera (*Brunnera macrophylla*), Japanese sedge (*Carex oshimensis*), *Hosta* spp., and California lilac (*Ceanothus* spp.).

Though some ferns, grasses, and grasslike plants spread rhizomatously, most are clumping or, at best, very slowly spreading. When mass-planted, their arching, textural foliage can form closed, dynamic covers of subtle greens or bold, colorful statements from selections of genera *Acorus*, *Athyrium*, *Carex*, *Hakonechloa*, and *Liriope*, often contributing movement and sound in the wind. They are valuable for their informal and textural aesthetic and for connecting or transitioning between cultivated and naturalistic areas. Many grasses also "die well,"

Without vertical support, vines can serve as ground covers.

Virginia creeper (*Parthenocissus* spp.) with *Lamium galeobdolon* 'Florentinum'

Clematis as a ground cover with *Miscanthus ×giganteus*

Jasminum nudiflorum trailing over and softening a wall

Hydrangea anomala subsp. *petiolaris* as both ground cover and vine

Many wide-spreading, clumping, or mainly clumping perennials can be mass-planted to form a closed cover.

Podophyllum 'Spotty Dotty' forms a closed cover in a shady garden.

Mass-planted *Hakonechloa macra* 'All Gold' can act as a ground cover.

Lavandula angustifolia covers the ground at Nymans Garden, England.

Japanese painted fern (*Athyrium niponicum* var. *pictum*) forms a silvery closed cover in this woodland.

Hostas provide excellent ground covers for shade.

providing interest with straw-colored stems, leaves, and flowers over the winter months, while many grass-like plants and some ferns are evergreen.

Clumping plants should be spaced on center so that mature plants will touch and form a closed cover. A fast-spreading, trailing, or stoloniferous ground cover can be interplanted to provide quick interim coverage, or clumping plants can be spaced widely and interplanted with spreading plants for an open and varied aesthetic of mounds rising from a contrasting carpet.

Self-Seeding Plants

Some clumping plants can readily self-seed into colonies, including celandine poppy (*Stylophorum diphyllum*), Mexican fleabane (*Erigeron karvinskianus*), violets such as *Viola odorata* and *V. riviniana* Purpurea Group, and the white- or yellow-flowered *Corydalis lutea* and *C. ochroleuca*. Seed dispersal and germination success can be dependent on garden conditions and produce variably closed to open colonies, though seedlings can be moved to more desired locations and seed collected and sown to enhance coverage. Self-seeding ground covers can also be used to fill in around other perennials and shrubs or planted in combination with other ground covers.

Functional and Economic Benefits of Ground Covers

Tough and adaptable, ground covers offer many solutions for problem spots, including areas affected by drought, areas of deep shade, hell strips, and areas with salt-affected soils. Ground covers can control and outcompete self-seeding and rhizomatous weeds, thereby reducing maintenance time and costs. They improve the health of the garden and benefit nearby perennials, shrubs, and trees by shading the ground, reducing soil temperature and moisture loss; increasing soil porosity, resulting in better oxygenation and water penetration; and improving fertility by preventing erosion from wind and rain (especially on slopes) and capturing organic matter so it can decompose and return nutrients to the soil.

Strategically planted in islands around trees and large shrubs, ground covers reduce the time and difficulty of mowing under low-hanging branches; protect trunks from the mechanical damage of mowers, whipper snippers (string trimmers), and other tools; and reduce soil compaction from foot traffic in root zones,

The seeds of yellow-flowering *Corydalis lutea* can sprout from any nook and cranny, producing surprising garden moments.

The purple-infused foliage of self-seeding *Viola riviniana* Purpurea Group infiltrates *Acaena saccaticupula*.

At Great Dixter, Mexican fleabane (*Erigeron karvinskianus*) has self-seeded to cover a wall.

Liriope spicata covers the exposed roots of several large trees at Longue Vue House and Gardens, New Orleans.

which can stunt woody plant growth. They can also stabilize snow and reduce drifting in winter, and they are less expensive than installing hardscape surfaces such as pavers, stone, and concrete and don't require annual cleaning.

Environmental benefits

Because they can help reduce our environmental impact and carbon footprint and enhance spaces for wildlife, ground covers offer many environmental benefits. Their ability to capture and compost fallen leaves, fruits, branches, and seeds from nearby plants helps create a better natural system in the garden that is similar to how plants grow in the wild; this not only reduces maintenance and increases fertility and garden health, but it also saves on the cost to individuals and municipalities of transporting organic matter to composting facilities or to a landfill.

As lawn replacements, ground covers can offer significant benefits. They do not require mowing, trimming, or edging or the requisite gas or electricity to perform these tasks on turf. They require little in the way of fertilizers, herbicides, and pesticides and demand far less water than a grassy expanse.

As alternatives to hardscape surfaces such as pavers and concrete, ground covers can improve the livability of the urban environment. They can keep the ground cool and prevent the absorption and storage of summer heat, thus helping to reduce the urban heat island effect of our cities. They can also significantly reduce noise pollution. When used in place of hard surfaces, ground covers reduce stormwater runoff, improving the health and stability of our waterways and increasing rainwater infiltration and groundwater replenishment.

As alternatives to lawns, hardscape, and bare soil, ground covers can help increase the biodiversity of garden wildlife, especially when a variety of ground covers are used to diversify habitat structure and provide a range of food sources such as nectar, pollen, fruit, seeds, and foliage. With the continued loss of natural spaces to urbanization, agriculture, and industry, human-created green spaces can become important refugia for a diversity of invertebrates, such as native bees and other beneficial and pollinating insects, and vertebrates, including birds and small mammals. Greater plant diversity will also help support more robust and diverse populations of beneficial soil fungi and bacteria, which contribute to overall garden health and resilience.

A hybrid swarm of wild manzanita (*Arctostaphylos ×media*) in Desolation Sound, British Columbia, enhances fertility, minimizes erosion, and cools the soil for Douglas fir (*Pseudotsuga menziesii*) and madrona (*Arbutus menziesii*) trees.

Mats of acaenas help build and protect precious alpine soils in the Remarkables mountain range, Otago, New Zealand.

Liriope spicata, Pachysandra terminalis, and *Hakonechloa macra* 'Albovariegata' offer a beautiful, low-maintenance alternative to turf or hard-scape surfaces.

(BELOW) In this New Orleans garden, a patio is surrounded by ground covers, including *Ophiopogon japonicus* 'Nanus'.

Aesthetic benefits

The functional and economic benefits of ground covers tend to be the main drivers in their use. However, their aesthetic benefits are diverse and make them indispensable in garden spaces.

Ground covers soften the edges of hardscape features such as driveways and sidewalks. They help mitigate the transition between hardscape and softscape plantings in the wider garden by connecting these disparate components. They cover bare, unattractive soil and can often do so in tough conditions. They help to delineate spaces, direct garden traffic, accentuate focal point plants and garden art, and contribute to the experience and emotional impact of a garden space. Their small size, diversity, versatility, and ease of growth also allows for creative, surprising, and whimsical plantings in garden nooks and crannies.

Though the flowers may garner more attention in this study in yellow at Chanticleer Garden in Pennsylvania, the gold foliage of the *Hedera helix* that festoons the container and the *Lysimachia nummularia* 'Aurea' and *Salvia officinalis* 'Icterina' at its base set and hold the theme.

Planning for Success

Selection, Planting, Care, Maintenance, and Propagation

CHOOSING A PLANT that will thrive in particular site conditions is the secret to a successful, long-lived, low maintenance planting. A species suited to its site will require less intervention to maintain performance such as watering, fertilizing, replanting, and pest control. The converse is to attempt to alter a site to suit a specific ground cover. Adding small amendments or changes to a site could be successful if those alterations remain stable over time, such as adding drainage with sand or gravel. However, other changes that require ongoing input such as irrigation for dry soils or the addition of organic matter to clay soils could lead to reduced vigor and eventual failure if the needed care or inputs cease. It is easier at the outset to choose the right ground cover for the conditions already present.

Evaluating the Site

To develop a shortlist of suitable species and cultivars, evaluate the various and potentially variable site conditions and how those may change through the year. Choosing the right ground cover, especially for large plantings, is not a decision to be taken lightly, because mistakes can be costly, they can detract from the beauty of a space, and they take time to remedy. Should time allow, start with test plantings, and then evaluate and compare results for a season before making final decisions.

Light intensity and seasonal patterns

Light intensity is usually measured in horticulture as the number of hours of direct sunlight received. Plants that need full sun require six or more hours of direct

European wild ginger (*Asarum europaeum*) grows luxuriantly in dappled shade.

sun a day. Some, such as succulents and species from open, sunny habitats, may require eight to ten hours a day and prefer the light at the hottest part of the day. Plants that thrive in part sun require three to six hours of direct sun, with a preference for the higher end of the range and a tolerance for sun during the hotter part of the day. Plants that require part shade also need three to six hours of direct sun, preferring the lower end of the range, such as the softer morning or evening sun or dappled shade throughout the day. Shade plants require about three hours of direct sun, the equivalent in dappled shade throughout the day or reflected light from nearby structures. Few plants will grow well in deep shade, though some can tolerate such conditions.

In addition, diurnal and seasonal patterns should be closely monitored in different areas of the garden. Beneath deciduous trees and shrubs, light intensity will be highest from autumn to spring once leaves have fallen and before they emerge again. From spring

A juniper ground cover surrounds a statue at the Denver Botanic Gardens.

Access to ample soil moisture suits *Lysimachia nummularia* 'Aurea'.

to autumn when plants are in leaf, the same area could experience part to full or even deep shade. Similarly, some garden spaces may be shaded by structures or evergreen trees in winter but may receive more direct sunlight during the growing season, with longer days and a higher sun angle, especially gardens in more northerly regions.

Plants also vary in their seasonal needs for light. Most obviously, herbaceous and deciduous plants need no light in winter when dormant. Spring ephemerals need light from early spring when they come into growth until late spring or early summer when they go dormant. Even evergreen plants need much less light in winter, especially in climate zones where they are dormant or semidormant during cold periods.

Moisture availability

Available moisture is also of paramount importance for plants, as are seasonal variations of moisture in different climates resulting from rainfall patterns and heat. Mediterranean type climates experience cool, wet winters and dry, hot summers. Other climates may offer similar amounts of rainfall year-round, though summer heat may reduce the availability of moisture through evaporation. Also important are low-lying sites that experience seasonal flooding and soil characteristics that can influence moisture retention. Of course, the presence or lack of summer irrigation will also affect available moisture.

Soil characteristics

Soil texture, structure, porosity and compaction, fertility, and pH are important considerations in any garden. Soil comprises inorganic and organic components, water, and air, plus living organisms including insects and other invertebrates such as worms, fungi, and bacteria.

TEXTURE The relative proportion of inorganic sand, silt, and clay in the soil influence the soil's water-holding capacity and the rate that water penetrates and moves through the soil profile, along with soil fertility. Coarsely textured sandy soils will drain well and have good air volume (important for root health) but can be nutrient poor and dry without regular rainfall or irrigation. Fine-textured clay-rich

Most stonecrops (*Sedum* spp.) are well suited to thin, gravelly, or sandy soils.

soils hold moisture and can be relatively fertile but are wet and cold in spring, sometimes experiencing poor drainage and less air volume, and they can become dry, hard, compacted, and resistant to rewetting in summer. Medium-textured loamy soils have more balanced proportions of sand, silt, and clay and offer the best overall growing conditions to the widest range of species. Many ground covers are tough and resilient and can grow in a range of soil textures.

STRUCTURE The arrangement of inorganic soil components and the resultant porosity of the soil influence the soil structure. The volume and size of pores will determine the soil's water- and air-holding capacities, which in turn will affect root growth and health. Soil structure can be reduced by soil compaction, often caused by foot or vehicular traffic. Compacted soils will hold less water and air and will drain more slowly after rainfall, factors that can negatively impact root and plant health. Compacted soils also resist root penetration, which will slow establishment and spread.

ORGANIC MATTER The organic components of soil consist of dead plant and animal matter. Organic matter is important for garden soil because it increases water retention, especially in sandy soils, and porosity, especially in clay soils. It increases soil fertility as it breaks down, making nutrients available to plants. It also supports more plentiful and diverse populations of beneficial fungi and bacteria that play an important role in plant health by making water and nutrients more available to plants and protecting against pathogens.

FERTILITY Soil fertility is generally higher in medium- and fine-textured soils, in soils with abundant organic matter, and in soils with a healthy and diverse complement of beneficial fungi and bacteria. Coarse-textured sandy soils tend to have the lowest fertility. Some species are tolerant of low soil fertility, though all plants will establish and spread more quickly with denser coverage in adequately fertile soils.

SOIL PH The relative acidity or alkalinity of a soil, measured using a numeric scale of 0 (highly acidic) to 14 (highly alkaline), affects the availability of nutrients to plants. A range of 6 to 7, with 7 representing neutral soil, is the opportune range for most garden plants; however, many plants are tolerant of soils with a fairly wide range of pH values. Some plants prefer more acidic soils, including members of the Ericaceae such as blueberries (*Vaccinium* spp.), while others, such as hellebores (*Helleborus* spp.), prefer slightly alkaline soils. Within their perfect pH range, these plants may

Hebe anomala 'Purpurea Nana' leaves are outlined in frost.

be somewhat more robust but will usually grow well in other conditions. Soils in areas with high rainfall, such as the Pacific Northwest, are usually slightly acidic because rain is slightly acidic. Soils in the Midwest and prairie regions of North America tend to be neutral. Dry western regions, such as the U.S. Southwest, and areas with calcareous soils, such as those derived from limestone, are usually alkaline. In general, soil pH need not be tested unless a concern arises. In such a case, a soil pH testing kit or pH meter can be used.

Climatic zone and plant hardiness

The cold tolerance, or hardiness, of plant species in winter is of prime importance in determining the plant palette that will thrive in a given region. This book uses the United States Department of Agriculture (USDA) plant hardiness zone system, which delineates the climate zones across a map of North America based on the average annual minimum winter temperatures. The USDA zones are numbered from the coldest zone, zone 1, to the warmest zone, zone 13.

Plants are classified as hardy within a range of zones. The lowest zone represents the absolute coldest temperatures a species can withstand with little to no winter damage. The highest zone is less important, less studied, and less reliable, but it attempts to quantify a plant's tolerance to heat and humidity and its requirement for sufficient time in dormancy and vernalization for proper flowering, fruiting, and overall growth.

The hardiness zone rating for each species and cultivar is developed over time through testing in trial gardens and by breeders, but also through the collective experience of the horticultural industry and gardeners. Over time, the hardiness zone rating of each plant becomes increasingly reliable as more observations are made and general agreement is achieved. Still, reported plant hardiness ratings in books, magazines, and websites can vary because of differences in local climates and because of reporting errors. Also, new or rare plants do not benefit from years of collective experience. Breeders often publish a conservative hardiness rating when a plant is introduced, even though greater hardiness is often suspected and later proven. The hardiness ratings of rare plants can sometimes be unreliable, though they often prove to be hardier than first suspected.

Plant hardiness is affected by factors other than minimum air temperature. Reliable snow cover has an insulating effect that can enable plants to survive in regions colder than their rating. Other factors such as high soil moisture, desiccating winds, freeze and thaw cycles, and unexpected early or late cold snaps can

The insulating effect of snow cover can increase plant hardiness.

Although the light and moisture conditions of this south-facing slope are perfect for *Dicentra formosa* in the spring, by summer these plants will go dormant, revealing the underlying, year-round carpet of ivy (*Hedera helix*).

cause damage or death even when air temperatures remain within the hardiness range of a given species.

Since the USDA plant hardiness zones are based on minimum temperatures, they do not account for climatic or diurnal temperature differences in different regions with the same zone rating. For instance, zone 8 of the Pacific Northwest, with its cool, rainy winters and small daily temperature range, is very different from zone 8 of the Carolinas, where nighttime lows may be the same as the Pacific Northwest but higher daytime temperatures and sunnier conditions offer a very different overwintering environment.

For large plantings, it is advisable to choose plants that are reliably hardy for your region. Choosing borderline hardy plants in a fit of "zonal denial" could result in outright failure or winter damage, followed by a slow, unattractive recovery and vulnerability to weed establishment. Choose ground covers that are strongly hardy, perhaps hardier to one zone colder than your own.

Other environmental stresses

Different sites may present additional stressors for plants. Windy sites can desiccate plants in both summer and winter. Reflected heat and light from structures, roads, and other built features can sunburn leaves and overheat plants. Coastal soils affected by salt spray or soils along winter-salted roadways can inhibit plant roots' water uptake ability and damage leaf cells during transpiration. Damage from too much foot traffic can overwhelm a ground cover's ability to recover.

The criteria for characterizing the conditions of a site can also vary within a site where difficult areas and microclimates can exist.

- Dry shade can occur under the eaves of a house or beneath evergreen trees. These areas may receive little to no rainfall, and tree roots represent significant moisture competition.

- Sunny slopes will present more intense sun exposure, higher temperatures, sharper drainage, and drought.

- Low-lying areas or areas with clay soils will present wetter soils with slow drainage.

- Hell strips, the space between the sidewalk and the street, will present infertile soils of poor texture, structure, and fertility following construction; saline conditions from winter road salt; reflected heat and light from asphalt and concrete; and potential mechanical damage from snow plows, piled snow, and vehicle and foot traffic.

- In cold winter climates where snow is important for insulating plants, shaded and protected sites will maintain a good protective layer, whereas windy sites can easily be divested of snow cover.

- Houses, walls, outbuildings, and other structures can create warmer microclimates that can benefit heat-loving plants and protect borderline hardy plants in winter.

Finally, there is sometimes no better clue to which plants will best grow in an area than to consider the plants already growing and flourishing (or not flourishing) there. By understanding the cultural requirements of these plants and considering their performance, you can narrow down the list of suitable ground covers.

Plant Selection

The sum of important site characteristics will help you determine a shortlist of potential ground covers. Your next step becomes selecting species and cultivars to meet the goals and aesthetics of the project based on several considerations.

Growth habit, mature size, and growth rate

The strategy by which a ground cover spreads— rhizomes or stolons/runners, suckering, trailing, clumping, vining, or self-seeding—determines how it interacts with other plants and the hardscape. The type of growth habit may also influence the rate of spread and time to full coverage.

Mature height and spread will help determine the quantity of plants required for an area. Growth rate or vigor will determine how quickly a ground cover will reach mature size and provide complete coverage. Vigor should be matched to the size of the space, with less vigorous ground covers planted in smaller spaces and more vigorous, fast-spreading ground covers used in larger gardens. Planting an overly vigorous ground cover could overwhelm a space. Conversely, less vigorous ground covers planted at low densities may take too much time to fill in, leaving garden spaces vulnerable to weed establishment.

Budget

Ground covers are generally inexpensive and offered at fairly uniform prices but are often required in large quantities. Most plants are available in 3.5 in. (9 cm) pots but can sometimes be found in smaller 2 in. (5 cm) plugs or larger containers. Ground covers in larger containers can sometimes be divided to increase numbers and save money. In most cases, price is determined by the ease and cost of propagation by seed, cuttings, or tissue culture. Lower prices may correspond with more vigorous ground covers, while more expensive plants may be more difficult to propagate, newer cultivars, or those with a slower growth rate.

Maintenance requirements

If a ground cover of suitable size, vigor, and growth habit is selected, what remains is the basic care required by the plant itself. Ground covers generally require little maintenance, but some may benefit from or require shearing, deadheading, pruning, and fall cleanup.

Aggressive or invasive nature

Of the thousands of ground covers, most are well-behaved and respectful if well chosen for their space, but others can become overly aggressive, quickly overtaking the landscape and growing into and outcompeting other plants while often being difficult to remove. The perception of aggressivity can be relative to the size of the space. Some vigorous ground covers such as English ivy (*Hedera helix*), bishop's weed (*Aegopodium podagraria*), and St. John's wort (*Hypericum calycinum*) may overwhelm small spaces but may be appreciated for large applications. An aggressive ground cover could also be appropriate in a smaller space where hardscape features can control its spread or less favorable light or moisture conditions reduce its vigor.

Although the term "aggressive" can refer to native and nonnative plants, the term "invasive" refers only to nonnative plants that may or may not be aggressive in the garden but that can escape to invade and

Donkeytail spurge (*Euphorbia myrsinites*) is potentially invasive in dry habitats of western North America but seemingly benign in other regions.

degrade natural areas. Invasive plants can spread vegetatively or via seed or berries. They can occupy and overrun natural spaces, outcompeting native plants, reducing biodiversity, changing habitat structure, altering ecosystem services, and reducing food for wildlife. Invasive plants can be a serious threat and should generally be avoided, especially in gardens near natural spaces. However, invasivity can depend on a species' response to the regional climate and other local factors. A species that is invasive in one region may not be invasive in another, or it may exhibit varying degrees of invasivity. Also, not all nonnative species that grow in natural areas are considered invasive; some may be chance escapees from nearby gardens that pose little threat or plants that persist from gardens around old homesteads. Some nonnative plants can become "naturalized" in wild spaces, where they operate like a native species without deleterious effects.

To avoid planting invasive species, consult local or regional organizations that focus on controlling these species, such as agricultural extension offices. They will identify invasive plants in your region and will often offer lists of better behaved alternatives. Some

invasive plants that spread only vegetatively may present a low risk in urban or suburban settings far from natural spaces. However, considering the propensity of gardeners to share plants and of garden centers to stock plants for which there is demand, it remains best to avoid potentially invasive species. There are always other options that won't negatively impact the natural environment.

Integrating native plants

Consider integrating native plants and "nativars"— cultivars of native plants—into the garden. Native plants are adapted to the rainfall and temperature patterns of their home region and offer many benefits of habitat and food resources to wildlife. They are also beautiful and connect the garden to its place in the world. Many are easily adaptable to average garden conditions in urban and suburban environments. Being native does not guarantee success, however; closer attention to their growing requirements may be necessary. For instance, urban and suburban soil conditions can differ greatly from those of native habitats.

Planting for Success

Good site preparation, proper planting, and reliable aftercare are vital for the success of any new planting to ensure better establishment, minimal losses, enhanced growth rates, and reduced time to achieve full coverage.

Preparing the site

Even if you choose the right plants for the conditions, plantings will benefit greatly from good site preparation. If the area is covered with weeds, sod, or other plants that are no longer desired, these must be removed before you plant ground covers. Removal can be achieved mechanically by hand and with hand tools or with a rototiller or sod cutter; by smothering the area with newspaper and compost or smothering and baking the area with black plastic or landscape fabric over a summer season, followed by digging in or roto-tilling; or by using a herbicide (the choice of last resort, because herbicides can injure humans and beneficial organisms and damage nearby plants). Let soils sit and settle for a time to enable any remaining weed seeds to germinate or bits of broken roots to regenerate so they can be removed before planting. If the area is already covered with bark mulch, shrubby ground covers can be planted directly. For smaller ground covers, the mulch can be dug into the soil before planting.

If soils are compacted, they should be loosened with a spade or rototiller. Most ground covers will appreciate the addition of well-rotted organic matter such as compost, manure, or leaf mold, which will increase water retention and fertility and enhance populations of beneficial microorganisms. This is also the time to make other amendments as needed, such as adding sand or gravel for increased drainage. Water soil thoroughly by hand or with a sprinkler before planting.

Planting from containers

Herbaceous and small ground covers are most commonly sold in 3.5 in. (9 cm), 4.5 in. (11 cm), or 6.5 in. (16.5 cm) "gallon" pots, which actually contain about 2 qts. (2 l) of soil. They can occasionally be found in smaller plugs and larger pots and sometimes in open flats and can be planted as is or divided into smaller pieces. Ground cover shrubs are usually available in 1-gallon, 2-gallon, and 3-gallon pots. Larger pot sizes will be more expensive, but these plants will reach full coverage more quickly.

Before planting, remove the plants from their pots and inspect their roots. If the plants are pot-bound with roots densely covering the entire surface of the root ball, gently use your fingers or a garden tool to lightly scour the edges of the root ball, which will encourage roots to spread and establish in the soil. Install plants at a depth equal to the level of soil in the pot: planting too high can result in quick desiccation of the root ball, and planting too deeply can result in rotted stems.

Planting density and spacing patterns

To determine the quantity of plants you'll need, consider the size of the area to be planted, the vigor and mature size of the plants selected, your level of patience as you wait for full coverage, and your budget. Full coverage will be attained more quickly by planting a greater density of plants but will require a larger budget.

To ensure full coverage, the maximum distance on center between ground covers should be no greater than the mature width of a single plant. A rule of thumb is to plant at a distance on center equal to between half the mature width to the full mature width of the plant. In general, common ground covers in 3.5 in. (9 cm) pots that grow at a moderate to fast rate would be planted at a distance of 6–12 in. (15–30 cm) on center.

Once planted, ground covers will tend to grow in all directions. Planting in triangular patterns or in staggered rows will ensure that plants are placed at the same distance in all directions, resulting in faster, more even coverage and often a more natural look after full coverage is achieved. In a grid layout, plants are placed farther apart on the diagonal, and more time will be required to cover the centers of each square.

Applying fertilizer

Apply a transplant fertilizer and/or a slow-release fertilizer at the time of planting. Transplant fertilizers are specially formulated to encourage quick establishment by helping to minimize transplant shock and encourage vigorous root growth. They contain a ratio of N-P-K (nitrogen, phosphorous, potassium) needed by new plantings and a rooting hormone that enhances root growth. Some also contain kelp, a natural rooting stimulant.

Slow-release fertilizers are designed to release nutrients over a predetermined period, depending

Because it will take a few years for these *Acorus gramineus* 'Minimus Aureus' to fill in, other complementary, fast-spreading, or trailing plants could be interplanted to provide interim coverage.

on the type of fertilizer. Choose one that releases for a period of three to six months—a longer period if you're planting in the spring and a shorter period if you're planting in the fall. These fertilizers release nutrients at a rate that meets the needs of plants but that is slow enough to reduce leaching, runoff, and the contamination of groundwater, and they need to be applied only once per season. Use a fertilizer with a balanced N-P-K ratio of 1:1:1 or 2:1:2, or one with a higher nitrogen number to maximize vegetative growth.

Organic fertilizers can also be used. However, they are usually not available in slow-release formulas and have lower concentrations of N-P-K, so regular applications will be required.

Choosing when to plant

In cooler summer climates, spring and fall are the best times to plant, but summer planting can be successful with proper irrigation. Less hardy or borderline hardy ground covers should be planted in spring to allow for a full season of root establishment, which will increase overwintering success. If planting in fall in cold winter climates, do so well before the ground freezes to allow for good root establishment, better overwintering success, and less risk of frost heaving. Mulch with fallen leaves and cover with extra snow to insulate plants from the cold and protect from freeze-thaw cycles. In hot summer and arid climates, fall, winter, and spring are good times for planting.

Care and Maintenance After Planting

For the first few years, new plantings should be monitored to evaluate performance and identify any care or maintenance that may be required. Although proper site preparation will minimize the need for weeding, weeds can still germinate between plants before full coverage is achieved. Mulching after planting with wood chips, pine needles, or fine bark helps to control weeds during establishment, and the mulch helps retain soil moisture.

Watering

Water thoroughly after planting to settle the plants into the soil and provide moisture for root growth.

Monitor the plants' water needs regularly over the first few months while they establish. As with lawns, water in the morning and as deeply and as infrequently as possible to encourage a deeper root system that can withstand dry periods. Occasional summer watering may be required during dry periods in subsequent years, but overall water needs should be low if ground covers are well selected for their site. In cold winter regions that experience summer and fall droughts, a few deep waterings can be helpful for overwintering success.

Making adjustments

Ground covers are generally low maintenance plants, but they are not maintenance-free. If a planting is not performing to expectations, you can make adjustments to correct the situation.

New plantings will first focus on establishing strong root systems before beginning to spread aboveground. If plants are not spreading as quickly as desired over the first season or two, apply more fertilizer or plant more of the same species or cultivar to help the planting fill in more quickly. If it seems that the existing planting may not perform well in the long term and the plants are not fully covering the intended area, you can interplant with a different ground cover to create a combination planting with a better chance of success. If the original planting looks to be establishing well but is naturally slow growing, interplant a smaller and more vigorous ground cover to provide fast interim coverage while the desired species fills in and slowly outcompetes it. Some clumping ground covers, on the other hand, can become overcrowded with time, reducing vigor, flowering, and disease resistance. If vigor decreases, they can benefit from periodic division and replanting.

Trimming or shearing

Most ground covers require little to no trimming, though some may need to be trimmed back if they are spreading across hardscape surfaces. Others may benefit from a light shearing, deadheading, or mowing to refresh tired foliage, especially after a hot summer or to clean up spent flower stalks. Use selective pruning to control the growth or shape of woody ground covers. In later years, a hard prune may be required to renew plantings. Spring-flowering ground covers should be pruned after flowering. Summer- and fall-flowering species should be pruned in early spring. Ground cover combinations can be evaluated for overly vigorous members that can be selectively trimmed.

Feeding

Given good site preparation and reasonably good soils, ground covers don't require much fertilizer or feeding once established. However, plants will grow more robustly and will benefit by feeding at the start of each growing season. In spring, spread compost or manure on top of herbaceous ground covers before they emerge, to a depth of ½–1 in. (1.3–2.5 cm). Or sprinkle it into evergreen or woody ground covers if the material will easily infiltrate the plant growth and reach the soil surface—as long as it does not cover up leaves or smother stems. Slow-release fertilizers can be easily broadcast in spring when new growth begins.

Dealing with pests and diseases

Ground covers that are well matched to their site conditions should grow vigorously and be resistant to insects and disease pressures. Ground covers experiencing regular insect attack such as from aphids, weevils, or mites, or from slugs or snails, or those experiencing fungal attack are likely not suited to the site. Evaluate the soil fertility and moisture conditions, light, air circulation, and irrigation timing for possible adjustments. Treating ongoing insect or disease damage can be expensive and time consuming. If you cannot easily rectify the issues, consider replacing the existing ground cover.

Falling leaves

Ground covers can trap fallen leaves in autumn, which may settle into the canopy of evergreen and shrubby ground covers, slowly decomposing to provide nutrients. Leaves that remain trapped in the canopy can be gently raked up or left in place if they cannot be seen. Leaves that collect among herbaceous ground covers can remain in place over the winter as a protective mulch and either left to decompose if they are not impeding new growth or cleaned up in spring. Leaving fallen leaves in place has the added benefit of providing overwintering habitat for beneficial insects, which help to enhance the overall health of the garden.

Propagation

Ground covers tend to be relatively easy to propagate. Industrious gardeners who want to save money can propagate their own, especially if many plants are required for large projects. The best methods of propagation for each species are listed in individual plant descriptions. Consult any number of books on plant propagation for more detailed instructions.

CUTTINGS Both woody and herbaceous plants can be grown from cuttings with the use of a rooting hormone and in an environment where humidity can be maintained at or close to 100 percent, such as under a covered tray or in a small plastic tent. Success is often determined by taking cuttings at the right time of year and at the appropriate level of maturity of the mother plant. Softwood, semi-hardwood, hardwood, and basal cuttings are all options.

LAYERING This process involves rooting a stem while it is still attached to the mother plant. After a section of the stem is pressed into the ground and held in place with a rock or metal pin, the section is lightly covered with soil. Once roots have formed, the cutting can be removed and planted.

DIVISION Dividing ground covers is a quick and easy way to propagate. Rhizomatous species can be dug, the rhizome divided or cut into pieces, and the sections replanted. Trailing, mat-forming ground covers tend to root into the ground as they spread. They can be dug, divided, and replanted. In addition, many stoloniferous and running ground covers such as strawberries (*Fragaria* spp.) and hen and chicks (*Sempervivum* spp.) produce young plants along or at the end of spreading horizontal stems. Once the plantlets are large enough to be viable and have begun to form roots, they can be separated from the mother plant and replanted.

SEED Growing from seed is the fastest way to produce the largest number of plants at the lowest cost. Seed propagation can be relatively easy, though some species are difficult to grow from seed. Remember that named cultivars will not come true from seed unless those seeds are from a uniform seed strain. Vegetative propagation is sometimes the only way to guarantee plants of identical characteristics.

Geranium 'Brempat' Patricia can be lightly trimmed of spent flower heads or sheared hard to the ground, and the mounds will reflush within a few weeks.

Designing with Ground Covers

AS WE CREATE a design for a garden space, we naturally progress through a list of priorities. First is to plan the hardscape and the locations of pots and garden art. Next comes selection of the trees and shrubs. Vines can then be layered in and perennial plantings designed, including any large applications of ground covers. With the shape of the project set and the larger components in place, we can add the finishing touches such as bulbs and more detailed use of ground covers. At the end of a project, however, we sometimes forget the importance and opportunity of such finishing touches. After installing mass plantings of ground covers for large areas, we may miss the smaller, more refined, and creative flourishes that are possible with ground covers as well as the opportunities to accent the larger plants, soften the hardscape, and enhance the overall design.

Ground covers contribute to the beauty, diversity, dynamism, and cohesiveness of any garden design. As you select ground covers from a list of species appropriate to the site, consider several general aesthetic considerations.

- **PLANT FORM** Choose plants with shapes and forms that are appropriate for the site, such as mats, mounds, clumps, or dense and upright thickets.

- **GROWTH HABIT** Choose between perennials or shrubs and ground covers that spread via rhizomes, stolons, suckers, trailing stems, or seeds.

- **PLANT SIZE** Decide on the height and spread required. Small sites will require smaller growing ground covers, and larger sites can accommodate more substantial plants. A larger plant in a small space, especially a shrub, may serve as a good specimen plant. Conversely, very low or slow-spreading ground covers may become lost in large spaces, when a more distinctive planting of larger plants may be more aesthetically engaging.

- **FOLIAGE** In most situations, foliage is more important than flowers.

  > **TYPE** The seasonal behavior of foliage is important to consider. Choose between herbaceous or evergreen perennials or deciduous, semi-evergreen, or evergreen shrubs.

  > **SHAPE, SIZE, AND TEXTURE** Depending on your design goals, smaller, finer leaves are often better for small spaces, while larger, bolder foliage usually fits the scale of larger sites. The foliage creates the textural effect.

  > **COLOR** Foliage color can range from subtle to bold and have a sizeable impact. Ground covers offer virtually every foliage color, including diverse shades of green, gray, silver, blue, purple, burgundy, red, orange, and gold, plus variegated forms.

- **FLOWERS** Considerations for flowers include color, size, bloom season, length of bloom, and pollinator value.

- **FRUIT** Some ground covers produce attractive fruit that can also be valuable for wildlife.

- **QUANTITY** Determining the number of different ground covers to plant in an area is important. Planting a single species will create simplicity and cohesion throughout a space. Planting two to three complementary species can also create cohesion with repetition but will produce a more interesting and dynamic display. Although the use of more species may sacrifice cohesion and harmony, it may provide a colorful counterpoint to uniform mass plantings of shrubs or large perennials or make a more dynamic garden.

Sedum spurium, S. rupestre 'Angelina', *Thymus* sp., and *Bergenia* sp. make for a dynamic combination of leaf shape, size, color, and texture.

Carpets of thyme contrast in both flower and foliage at Government House in Victoria, British Columbia.

Sedum rupestre cultivars 'Blue Spruce' and 'Angelina' combine with *S. spurium* 'Voodoo' for a colorful, highly textured design.

Design and Style Enhancement

Ground covers can enhance a design or help to emphasize a garden style in many ways. They can be the component that takes the design to the next level. Use them to create a more dynamic, surprising, and whimsical garden by tucking them into surprising places, such as in pathways and on steps; popping out between pavers, bricks, and other stonework; tumbling over or growing out of walls; tucked beneath benches; and covering bare, boring, or unsightly soil. Their diversity and versatility offer limitless creativity, playfulness, and flexibility. They can be the finishing touch that takes advantage of every opportunity to enhance the garden space and create a truly magical garden.

In large, open spaces, a finely textured, small-leaved, low-growing mat can create space and openness and offer a sense of calm and tranquility. The use of moss and mosslike or grasslike plants in Japanese Zen gardens is a good example. Combinations of two or three ground covers in a space can be more interesting and dynamic, especially with contrasting shades of green, blue, gray, or purple. For example, consider a mix of *Sempervivum* cultivars with leaves of varying shades of green, gray-green, and perhaps burgundy, or use bolder combinations such as the muted purple *Acaena inermis* 'Purpurea' with the grayish powder-blue of *A. saccaticupula* 'Blue Haze'.

A choice of brighter foliage colors such as gold, lime-green, orange, burgundy, and red, plus variegated forms, will create excitement and energy, especially combinations of bold, contrasting colors. Consider adding the bright gold foliage of *Sedum rupestre* 'Angelina's Teacup' to blue and purple *Acaena* spp., or add golden *Sempervivum* 'Gold Nugget' and burgundy-red *Sedum spurium* 'Voodoo' to a hen and chicks (*Sempervivum* spp.) combination. Variegated cultivars offer bold contrasts of green and gold or green and white in a single plant.

To add more energy and movement to cool- or hot-colored combos, vary plant heights by adding the mounding, deep green leaves of *Beesia deltophylla* to other quiet colors or the vibrant red leaves of *Heuchera* 'Fire Alarm' to an energetic combination. Other ground covers could contribute to other moods. *Erigeron karvinskianus* 'Profusion', with its masses of white and lavender-pink, narrow-petaled daisies, contribute a lush, romantic feel. Large-leaved and billowy ground covers can make a space seem smaller and create intimacy. Succulent combinations will create drama, while ferny combinations, such as *Anthemis* or *Adiantum* species and cultivars, are more textured and quietly inspiring.

Ground covers can contribute to and build on themes. A hot-colored perennial border with red, orange, and yellow flowers can be supported thematically by edging ground covers with flowers or foliage in similar hot colors. A pastel border meant to be calm and relaxing can be filled in with ground covers in soft flower tones and foliage in shades of green, blue, gray, and purple with occasional variegated flourishes.

Garden styles

Ground covers can contribute to garden styles to create a fully immersive garden experience.

FORMAL GARDENS Choose a limited palette of ground covers with refined (or sometimes bold) textures that have uniform, controlled shapes, especially those growing as mats, mounds, and clumps, such as mat-forming rupturewort (*Herniaria glabra*) or blue star creeper (*Pratia pedunculata*), mounds of English lavender (*Lavandula angustifolia*) or the *Sedum* Sun-Sparkler Series cultivars, and clumping *Hosta* cultivars or *Carex oshimensis* EverColor Series selections. They can be used in mass plantings of a single or several cultivars planted in grids or other patterns. For instance, try grid-planted *Festuca glauca* 'Cascall' Beyond Blue, with its finely textured, powder-blue mounds interplanted with muted purple *Acaena inermis* 'Purpurea' or gray-green *Thymus pseudolanuginosus*. If the design has strong formal lines from hardscape such as walls and pathways or from softscape such as box hedging (*Buxus sempervirens*), more informal ground cover plantings or combinations could be used to counter or enhance these features.

INFORMAL OR COTTAGE GARDENS Anything goes in a cottage garden, especially if the ground cover is lush and leafy and produces lots of flowers. Plant in drifts of multiple species and use combinations. Designs would benefit from repetition of the same or similar plants or ground covers that echo traits of color or texture to create cohesion in the design and add counterpoint to the rambunctious nature of the perennial beds. *Geranium* 'Gerwat' Rozanne and *G. macrorrhizum* are naturals, as are *Erigeron*

Blooming lamb's ears (*Stachys byzantina*) line the boxwood hedging and emphasize the formal design at Drummond Castle, Scotland.

Lamium maculatum and *Omphalodes cappadocica* are planted with *Astilbe* and *Epimedium* spp. at the foreground of this bed.

Donkeytail spurge (*Euphorbia myrsinites*), New Zealand moss (*Scleranthus uniflorus*), New Zealand burr (*Acaena inermis* 'Purpurea'), New Zealand scab plant (*Raoulia australis*), sedge (*Carex* spp.), treasure flower (*Gazania* spp.), and *Coprosma* spp. fill in among dramatic agaves, spiral aloe (*Aloe polyphylla*), and lichen-covered rocks at Larnach Castle, New Zealand.

karvinskianus 'Profusion', candytuft (*Iberis semper-virens*), basket of gold (*Aurinia saxatilis*), spotted dead nettle (*Lamium maculatum*), and *Lithodora diffusa*.

SUBTROPICAL GARDENS A subtropical design is based on large, bold, colorful foliage. Ground covers could include bugleweed, especially *Ajuga reptans* 'Burgundy Glow' and *A. reptans* 'Binblasca' Black Scallop, heart-leaved bergenia (*Bergenia cordifolia*), *Saxifraga* London Pride Group, redwood sorrel (*Oxalis oregana* 'Klamath Ruby'), New Zealand iris (*Libertia peregrinans*), and the holly ferns (*Cyrtomium* spp.). Fine-textured, small-leaved ground covers such as ice plants (*Delosperma* spp.), brass buttons (*Leptinella* spp.), and Berggren's sedge (*Carex berggrenii*) could also

Ground covers including *Lithodora diffusa*, black mondo grass (*Ophiopogon planiscapus* 'Nigrescens'), sedges (*Carex* spp.), blue chalksticks (*Senecio serpens*), and blue fescue (*Festuca glauca*) soften the hardscape and help emphasize the nikau palms (*Rhopalostylis sapida*) and other subtropical elements at Larnach Castle, New Zealand.

be used to enhance large-leaved specimen plants such as selections of *Canna*, *Ligularia*, and *Yucca*.

DESERT OR XERISCAPE GARDENS Hardy succulents are the backbone to any desert garden and are important in xeriscapes, especially stonecrops (*Sedum* spp.), hen and chicks (*Sempervivum* spp.), and ice plants (*Delosperma* spp.). Other plants with silver foliage, good structure, and drought tolerance can also serve as important components, such as filigree daisy (*Anthemis marschalliana*), manzanita (*Arctostaphylos* spp.), California fuchsia (*Epilobium* spp.), lamb's ears (*Stachys byzantina*), and grasses such as blue fescue (*Festuca glauca*) and Mexican feather grass (*Nassella tenuissima*).

MODERN GARDENS Like formal designs, modern designs feature a limited palette of plants focused on foliage with controlled forms but with bolder textures, colors, and leaf shapes. Ground covers may include New Zealand burr (*Acaena* spp.), cushion bolax (*Azorella trifurcata*), grassy leaved sweet flag (*Acorus gramineus*), brass buttons (*Leptinella squalida* 'Platt's

This modern planting in the Smithsonian Gardens in Washington, DC, includes a mat of *Juniperus rigida* subsp. *conferta* 'Silver Mist' providing a base for *Sedum* 'Maestro', *Schizachyrium scoparium* 'The Blues', and *Cotinus coggygria* 'Royal Purple'.

Pachysandra terminalis creates a simple, textured open space for this stone water feature.

Black'), lilyturf (*Liriope* spp.), and black mondo grass (*Ophiopogon planiscapus* 'Nigrescens').

JAPANESE, CHINESE, AND CONTEMPLATIVE GARDENS This style requires simple ground covers, especially those that are mosslike, that support a controlled, spacious feeling. Ground covers are often used in Japanese gardens to emphasize specimen conifers and rocks and to contrast with expanses of gravel or stone. Plants with good texture, controlled mat-forming habits, and nonshowy flowers include rupturewort (*Herniaria glabra*), brass buttons (*Leptinella squalida* and *L. gruveri*), baby's tears (*Soleirolia soleirolii*), New Zealand moss (*Scleranthus uniflorus*), and Irish moss (*Sagina subulata*).

MEDITERRANEAN GARDENS Evergreen shrubs are the dominant vegetation type of Mediterranean climate zones, so ground covers to enhance this style would include woody, mounding or horizontally spreading shrubs such as manzanita (*Arctostaphylos*

spp.), California lilac (*Ceanothus* spp.), rock rose (*Cistus* spp.), lavender (*Lavandula* spp.), trailing rosemary (*Rosmarinus officinalis* 'Renzels' Irene), and common sage (*Salvia officinalis*). Subshrubs or herbaceous plants such as California fuchsia (*Epilobium* spp.), lavender cotton (*Santolina* spp.), and thyme (*Thymus* spp.) would also contribute well.

ROCK AND ALPINE GARDENS Gardens designed to grow alpine plants emulate high-elevation mountainous areas. Ground covers to enhance this style would be small, slow-growing species forming mats, buns, or small mounds such as rock cress (*Arabis* and *Aubrieta* spp.), pinks (*Dianthus* spp.), mountain avens (*Dryas* spp.), moss phlox (*Phlox subulata*), European pasque flower (*Pulsatilla vulgaris*), stonecrops (*Sedum* spp.), and hen and chicks (*Sempervivum* spp.).

PRAIRIE, MEADOW, AND WILDLIFE GARDENS These informal gardens focus on supporting pollinators including beneficial insects such as bees and

(ABOVE) Diverse ground covers form the maze in the Lavender Garden at Chatfield Farms, Denver Botanic Gardens.

Clouds of white flowers of *Calamintha nepeta* subsp. *nepeta* in the Lurie Garden, Chicago, continue to attract a range of pollinators long after the purple coneflowers (*Echinacea purpurea*) have finished in late summer.

A carpet of pink-flowered *Cardamine quinquefolia* emerges amid mounds of winter-growing *Arum italicum* to be followed later by clumps of *Hakonechloa macra* 'Aureola' in this woodland-like setting at the Miller Garden, Seattle.

butterflies, and birds and hummingbirds. Flowering ground covers that produce nectar, pollen, seeds, or fruit would help to add more food and habitat complexity beneath and around taller perennials.

WOODLAND GARDENS These gardens provide a relaxed and informal aura reminiscent of a natural setting. Unlike a shade garden, which takes its design cues from traditional borders, the plantings in woodland gardens are more randomized and naturalistic, and they resemble a forest floor more than a garden. Woodland gardens would make use of seasonal or ephemeral ground covers such as *Cardamine* spp., *Cyclamen* spp., *Arum italicum*, *Ficaria verna*, and *Anemone nemorosa*, while depending on plants such as hellebores, barrenwort (*Epimedium* spp.), Japanese forest grass (*Hakonechloa macra*), and ferns for interest throughout the rest of the year.

Design Strategies

Most simply, and perhaps most obviously, ground covers are valuable for covering bare soil. This makes sense from a functional and environmental viewpoint, but it is also imperative from an aesthetic perspective. Too much bare soil can create a forlorn scene of isolated shrubs and perennials, which can suggest emptiness and disinterest, especially if weeds become established. Bare soil also represents the missed opportunity for more creative, complex, unified, and inspiring plantings.

Ground covers can do much more than just cover bare soil. They can be used as transitional elements or focal points to direct movement through the garden, enhance the visual experience, and emphasize garden features.

Create smooth transitions

Ground covers are indispensable for edging and transitioning. They can soften and mitigate the physical and aesthetic transition from one space to another or draw attention to and celebrate the point of transition.

They can provide a transition from softscape to softscape, such as from a garden bed to a lawn. A lawn is an evenly textured, homogenous, horizontal surface of negative space. A garden bed, however, is usually a dynamic and complex space of many tall, mounding, and upright perennials and shrubs. The visual move from lawn to garden bed, negative to positive space, can thus be an abrupt experience unless mitigated by ground covers. Ground covers can occupy the transitional space and connect the two disparate forms by minimizing the abrupt change in plant size and habit and by softening the transition with various shapes, textures, and colors.

They can provide a transition from softscape to hardscape, such as from a garden bed to a flat driveway or patio. The contrast is even more stark in this case because the negative space of the asphalt, concrete, gravel, or stone is very different in color, texture, and shape from a green lawn. Ground covers can also be chosen to cross the border between these two different areas by billowing or trailing over the

The repetition of the heart-shaped leaves of *Brunnera macrophylla* and the fine texture of *Hakonechloa macra* and its cultivar 'Aureola' unifies this patio area at Swarthmore College, Pennsylvania.

Stachys byzantina softens the edges of a stone pathway at Chanticleer Gardens, Pennsylvania.

edge of the hardscape. For a hardscape comprising flagstones, slate, brick, or paving stones, with planting spaces between the pieces, ground covers used in the edge of the border can be repeated between the stonework to create even more integration. This can be extended vertically to use ground covers to minimize or cover ugly or stark features such as walls, boulders, or stumps. Spreading ground covers can trail over walls to soften the vertical hardscape, and vines can ramble over ugly rocks or stumps.

Ground covers can provide a transition from hardscape to hardscape, such as the transition from a concrete or asphalt driveway to a stone or brick front walkway or a gravel path arriving at a flagstone patio. The contrast between different types of hardscape with different textures and colors can be stark. Ground covers can be used at these places of contact to help ease the transition from one surface to another.

Gardens can be filled with many unrelated and disparate elements beyond flat hardscape surfaces. Other built elements could include a house, garage, pool, pond, water feature or fountain, garden art, barbecue area or outdoor kitchen, fire pit, children's play area, vegetable garden, greenhouse, workshop/shed, garden studio, pergola, and gazebo, among other possibilities. Without unifying plantings to create a relationship between these many components and other prominent planted elements such as trees or shrubs, the overall space can seem like a disjointed collection of unrelated elements.

Ground covers can visually define, connect, transition, and unify a space or an entire property, such as a single repeated ground cover or a selection of a few different contrasting ground covers around and within the space. They can also be used to connect spaces by planting the same species in adjacent areas or where these areas transition from one to the other.

Influence and enhance the visual experience

The diversity of ground covers and their amenability and versatility for creating patterns makes them useful for guiding the eye through a designed space and for enhancing or manipulating the visual experience and perspective of the garden. Ground covers can be used in strategic patterns such as large mats, drifts, lines, and repeated plantings alone or in combination with other plants.

Large mats of ground covers create a sense of openness and space and provide the eye a place to rest. Drifts can draw attention to a desired direction, while also creating a sense of dynamism and movement, especially with two or three different interacting ground covers. When planted in linear patterns, they will provide a sense of formality and control and lengthen or widen a space. Their repetition through a garden can provide a sense of cohesion. Even plant collectors who eschew the mantra of planting perennials in groups of three, five, or seven in preference for "drifts of one" can achieve a more cohesive display by repeating a distinctive ground cover at the front of the border to unify the whole.

Use these planting patterns to break up the monotony of wide, flat spaces such as lawns, driveways, or other open areas. A large expanse of lawn, for instance, can be sectioned by creating a low-maintenance raised bed of mat-forming or mounding ground covers. This adds interest to the landscape and maintains the sense of openness and space without increasing maintenance requirements. A driveway may need only two tracks for vehicle tires: the middle area can host a linear bed filled with ground covers that breaks up the space and adds beauty to an otherwise stark, utilitarian feature.

Ground covers can also be used to alter the perception of space in a garden and create or support optical illusions through strategic use of their forms, sizes, colors, and textures. Shrubby ground covers with horizontal branching or mounding habits can soften the visual severity of a steep slope, making it seem less steep. In small gardens, large and/or tall plants can overwhelm the space and make it seem smaller. Using a diversity of ground covers with a variety of heights instead can create interesting plantings that don't diminish a small space.

To change the perception of space, ground covers can be used to create visual lines or, if a line is part of the hardscape or other softscape, to accentuate them. In a deep and narrow garden, they can be planted in lines that cross the axis on the perpendicular to make the space seem wider. In a shallow and wide back yard, lines stretching from the house to the back offer the illusion of length and depth. This could include the facing edges of a double border separated by lawn or a meandering pathway that gets narrower as it extends farther from view. A curving pathway or garden bed edge will also create a greater sense of distance and depth than a straight pathway. Ground covers can be used strategically to achieve these visual tricks or used in conjunction with other features.

Still other illusions can be created. Using large-leaved ground covers in the foreground with

A river of *Geranium ×cantabrigiense* 'Karmina' separates two large stones and divides this space, making it seem smaller and more intimate.

small-leaved cultivars in the distance will make a space seem larger. The opposite arrangement will make the space seem smaller. The same holds true for large versus small mats or mounds. If these grow smaller into the distance, the space will seem larger.

Hot- and bold-colored flowers and foliage in shades of red, orange, yellow, magenta, and bright pink will also seem closer than they really are, while cooler, more muted colors such as purples, blues, burgundies, and pale pinks will seem farther away. Hot colors in the foreground with cooler colors in the distance will make a space seem larger, while hot colors in the distance will pull the space in, making it seem smaller.

Guide physical movement through the garden

Just as ground covers can draw the eye to various areas of the garden and play with the perception of space, they can also help to direct physical movement and to emphasize or even create thoroughfares in the garden.

Pachysandra terminalis creates a wide open space in front of a statue in the gardens at Newfields in Indianapolis.

Golden creeping Jenny (*Lysimachia nummularia* 'Aurea') lights the way along a dark, shady path.

Spaces usually used for gathering or moving through the garden can become inviting and intriguing areas that refocus visitors on the journey and experience, not just the destination.

When planted along the edges of hardscape walkways, ground covers can emphasize the direction of travel, make the path more interesting, and perhaps slow the viewer's pace. Use them without hardscape to create informal pathways of soil, gravel, or bark chips to suggest a route through a woodland, a front yard planted entirely without turf, or even an alpine garden.

To delineate space for stopping and resting, plantings of a single ground cover or a small selection of different ground covers can make the area's purpose clear and inviting. For instance, a mass planting of fragrant thyme or Corsican mint (*Mentha requienii*) beneath and around a garden bench or between flagstones on a patio add an olfactory dimension to the experience, inviting a visitor to linger or take a seat.

Emphasize garden features

A particular strength of ground covers is their ability to emphasize garden features, especially when planted as mats or drifts. Use them to create an area of negative space around a focal point to give it prominence and pride of place. Plant focal points could include dramatic succulents such as agave or yucca, bold perennials such as Mediterranean spurge or pineapple lily, trees with beautiful bark, or trees or shrubs with structural forms. Other features supported by ground covers could include garden art and structures. Ground covers will also protect plant and hardscape features from rain-splattered soil.

Two maidenhair ferns, *Adiantum aleuticum* and *A. venustum*, frame a tall pot converted into a fountain.

Black mondo grass (*Ophiopogon planiscapus* 'Nigrescens') frames the trunk of a sprawling pine at the Miller Garden, Seattle.

Ground covers take center stage in this installation at Phoenix Perennials in Richmond, British Columbia.

Create focal points

Although ground covers are often used in functional or supporting roles, they need not play second fiddle. Instead, they can be stars in their own right. Their range of textures, flower and foliage colors, and sizes and shapes offer many aesthetic options. Their diversity can be used to create dynamic patterns and combinations, making a ground cover garden just as interesting as any other, especially for small spaces, in large planters, atop walls, for hell strips and boulevard plantings, and for green roofs and living walls.

Unique Design Opportunities

Ground covers are uniquely suited and can make important contributions to many garden designs. For example, larger plants will not fit in the tight spaces between flagstones; nor will they grow robustly on green roofs or in living walls. Although other plants are important for wildlife, edible, and rain gardens, ground covers can contribute extra function and diversity to these spaces.

Add multiseason interest

Winter-growing ground covers and spring ephemeral species, such as Italian arum (*Arum italicum*) and hardy cyclamen (*Cyclamen coum* and *C. hederifolium*), offer interesting opportunities, especially for gardens in milder climates, when planted on their own or in combination with species with other seasons of interest. Winter-growing ground covers emerge from dormancy in fall and winter, and they are in leaf and flower in fall, winter, and spring before going dormant again before summer. Plant winter growers where they can be enjoyed during the colder months of the year. Spring ephemerals usually emerge in late winter and early spring, not long after the snow has melted. Plants bloom in early to midspring, set seed, and then go fully dormant by summer.

These unique plants make wonderful winter and early spring ground covers when planted in clumps or drifts between herbaceous perennials, under deciduous shrubs and trees, and among spring-flowering bulbs, where they can outcompete weed seeds that germinate in winter and early spring. Spring

WINTER-GROWING AND SPRING EPHEMERAL GROUND COVERS FOR MULTISEASON INTEREST

Anemone blanda	*Cyclamen hederifolium*
Anemone nemorosa	*Dicentra canadensis*
Arum italicum	*Dicentra cucullaria*
Cardamine spp.	*Ficaria verna*
Corydalis solida	*Hepatica nobilis*
Cyclamen coum	*Sanguinaria canadensis*

Cyclamen hederifolium emerges en masse in Bordeaux, France, in early October; after flowering, it forms dense mats of mottled, ivylike foliage until it goes dormant in late spring.

ephemerals help to add an extra layer of spring color when most other plants are just beginning to stir. Though most are considered shade plants, they perform well in full, early season sun soon to be shaded when larger plants break dormancy. Winter growers and spring ephemerals are also partial solutions to cover areas of deep shade beneath deciduous trees and shrubs where conventional ground covers may not grow well. They can bask in the full sun beneath winter-bare branches, provide their show in the offseason, and go dormant just as the foliage above emerges.

Enliven tight spaces

Ground covers are often considered only for mass plantings, large displays, or smaller uniform applications, but individual plants are extremely versatile and can be inserted into all manner of small spaces, such as at the base of or between larger plants, including between exposed tree roots, in cracks and crevices, along pathways, in stairs and patios, in containers and planter boxes, and in any manner of other surprising places. This flexibility allows for more opportunities to enhance a design with finishing touches.

To fit within tight spaces, ground covers should be shortly rhizomatous, trailing, or clumping. Trailing ground covers, unlike rhizomatous and clumping plants, will grow across hardscape and require trimming. If planted between pavers or stepping stones, they must also be tolerant of sand or poor or thin soils that usually underlay these elements. On patios and pathways, they should be low-growing to avoid tripping hazards and tolerant of a degree of foot traffic.

Mexican feather grass (*Nassella tenuissima*) fills in spaces between pavers at the High Line in New York City.

GROUND COVERS FOR TIGHT SPACES

Acaena spp.	*Ophiopogon japonicus* 'Nanus'
Ajuga reptans	*Oxalis magellanica*
Alchemilla ellenbeckii	*Phlox subulata*
Anemone blanda	*Pratia* spp.
Anemone nemorosa	*Rosularia* spp.
Antennaria dioica	*Sagina subulata*
Arabis spp.	*Saxifraga* spp.
Arenaria spp.	*Sedum* spp.
Armeria maritima	*Selaginella kraussiana*
Aubrieta spp.	*Sempervivum* spp.
Campanula spp.	*Soleirolia soleirolii*
Cardamine trifolia	*Thymus* spp.
Carex berggrenii	*Trifolium repens*
Cymbalaria muralis	*Umbilicus oppositifolius*
Delosperma spp.	*Veronica* spp.
Gaultheria procumbens	*Viola riviniana* Purpurea Group
Herniaria glabra	*Viola walteri* 'Silver Gem'
Jovibarba spp.	
Leptinella spp.	
Mazus spp.	
Mentha requienii	

Asarum europaeum, *Carex siderosticta* 'Variegata', *Vancouveria hexandra*, and *Soleirolia soleirolii* are tucked around stepping stones.

Plant throughout the perennial border

Ground covers are commonly used to edge borders, which helps integrate taller perennials and shrubs with the facing lawn or hardscape, but ground covers can also be used both aesthetically and functionally within the border.

Perennial borders are usually filled primarily with herbaceous plants, most of which lack winter interest. Winter-growing, spring ephemeral, and evergreen, shade-tolerant ground covers can be planted between existing perennials and shrubs to provide coverage and beauty in the winter and spring border.

Should weeds be a problem in a newly planted border, a low, vigorous ground cover can be interplanted with larger perennials and shrubs to exert quick control. It should be a species that is easy to remove once its services are no longer required or that will eventually be outcompeted by the expanding border plants and increasing shade. Typically a sun-loving, stoloniferous or trailing ground cover will meet these criteria. Avoid most rhizomatous species. Equally, should weeds be a problem within an existing border, a fast-growing, shade-tolerant ground cover can be planted between existing plants.

Add "green mulch" under shrubs and trees

A common practice in shrub borders and under trees is to apply mulches of bark chips, sawdust, pine needles, or other organic material to control weeds and help maintain soil moisture. However, this abundant organic matter can over-encourage microbes such as bacteria and fungi, which can steal nitrogen, reduce growth, and act as hiding places for damaging insects such as earwigs and vine weevils. This uninspired practice also foregoes all of the beauty and benefits that can be provided by a green mulch of ground covers.

Conditions can vary widely beneath woody plants. Soils can be dry or thin at the base of shrubs and trees but rich and of good moisture between them. Light can abruptly change from full sun to shade. Choose ground covers with a wide range of light and moisture tolerances; use trailing, running, or rhizomatous ground covers that can spread from favorable to less favorable conditions; or use different ground covers for different conditions within the border. A well-chosen ground cover or selection of ground covers that flourish in a site will provide additional beauty and benefits to wildlife, and it will save you the time and money required to reapply mulch as it breaks down.

Replace lawns

Lawns are a near ubiquitous component of gardens with many uses and benefits. Most importantly, they offer negative space to counterpoint borders and other plantings and areas for recreation and leisure that are tolerant of foot traffic. However, their surprising scale and impact begs a reevaluation of their role in our landscapes.

In the continental United States, turf grass is the most common of all ground covers, occupying about 40 million acres (16 million hectares), or 2 percent of the total land base—three times more than corn and more than any other irrigated crop. Though lawns are cheap and easy to install by seed or sod, the installation cost of lawns belies the ongoing maintenance costs of time and money. Americans spend about $30 billion a year on lawn care, which is also one of the most time-consuming household chores from spring through fall. Lawns require regular mowing, trimming, edging, raking, and removal or composting of grass clippings. They must be watered and fertilized regularly and, in the spring, often reseeded, dethatched, and aerated. Herbicides and pesticides are also frequently used.

The environmental impact of lawns is immense considering the water required to keep them lush, the carbon footprint of the gasoline and electricity to run the machines to maintain them, the noise pollution made by those machines, and the environmental impact of herbicides and pesticides on beneficial insects, birds, and other wildlife. Lawns are also a lost opportunity for environmental benefit. They are a green desert for most wildlife, providing little food or habitat. Yet the same space could grow a diversity of ground covers and other garden plants that could have significant benefit.

If a lawn is not used for recreation and not important for aesthetic reasons, there is no reason it cannot be partially or completely replaced with ground covers. Where a flat negative space is aesthetically desirable, lawns can be reduced in size or replaced with carpeting ground covers to provide a similar effect. Recreationally, no ground cover is as tolerant of foot traffic as a conventional lawn, but the scale of these areas can often be reduced.

Ground covers can replace lawns in problem spots such as in shaded areas where turf grows poorly or in hot, dry locations where lawn dries out too quickly. Ground covers can also be valuable on hard-to-maintain steep slopes, in wet areas with soft soil, in

Liriope spicata flanks the walkway and front door of a house to provide a similar aesthetic to turf grass without the maintenance costs, plus its flowers are valued by bees.

Adjacent drifts of *Sedum spurium, Herniaria glabra,* and *Thymus pseudolanuginosus* can spread across large expanses of ground and provide a more interesting display than turf grass.

GROUND COVER ALTERNATIVES TO LAWNS

Acaena spp.
Achillea millefolium
Ajuga reptans
Alchemilla ellenbeckii
Antennaria spp.
Arctostaphylos uva-ursi
Arenaria montana
Artemisia rupestris subsp. *viridis*
Carex pansa
Carex pensylvanica
Carex praegracilis
Cerastium tomentosum
Chamaemelum nobile
Cotula hispida
Dichondra repens
Duchesnea indica
Eleocharis radicans
Euonymus fortunei 'Coloratus', 'Kewensis', 'Minimus', and 'Wolong Ghost'
Fragaria spp.
Hedera spp.
Herniaria glabra
Leptinella spp.

Lindernia grandiflora
Liriope minor
Liriope spicata
Lysimachia nummularia
Mazus spp.
Mentha requienii
Muehlenbeckia axillaris
Ophiopogon japonicus 'Nanus'
Ophiopogon planiscapus 'Nigrescens'
Oxalis magellanica
Phlox subulata
Pleioblastus pygmaeus
Pratia spp.
Rubus rolfei
Rubus tricolor
Sagina subulata
Selaginella kraussiana
Thymus spp.
Trifolium repens
Vaccinium macrocarpon
Veronica spp.
Vinca minor
Waldsteinia spp.

drainage ditches, under low-hanging tree branches, among exposed tree roots, and where landscape features require awkward repositioning of the mower.

Lawn alternatives can be planted as a single species monoculture, as adjacent drifts of different ground covers, or as interplanted combinations of multiple cultivars. Careful research can help you identify the right ground cover(s) for a particular site's conditions and proposed uses. If the area will need to be traversed more than a ground cover can withstand, a path or stepping stones could also be installed. Because mistakes can be costly when converting large areas, consider preparing and planting a test plot to evaluate a short list of ground covers before moving forward with the project.

Many other ground covers can replace lawns but are generally not tolerant of foot traffic, including *Aegopodium podagraria, Cotoneaster* spp., *Delosperma* spp., *Juniper* spp., *Lamium galeobdolon* and *L. maculatum, Oxalis oregana, Pachysandra procumbens* and *P. terminalis, Persicaria affinis, Sedum* spp., *Stachys byzantina,* and climbers such as *Clematis* spp., Boston ivy and Virginia creeper (*Parthenocissus* spp.), and *Trachelospermum asiaticum.*

Replace hardscape elements

The urban environment is rife with concrete, asphalt, brick, and stone. Though immensely practical for transportation and other urban uses, hardscape elements can also be problematic. Rainwater that would normally percolate slowly into the soil to replenish groundwater and slowly feed our creeks, rivers, lakes, and oceans is instead diverted into stormwater systems that can overwhelm our water courses and their wildlife with blasts of warmer water that can carry garbage and residues of oils, chemicals, herbicides, and pesticides.

These dark, hard surfaces absorb sunlight and hold heat, creating an urban heat island effect that raises the air temperatures of cities significantly above those of the surrounding countryside. Low plant cover also means less evapotranspiration and shade, both of which cool the air. Hotter cities reduce the quality of life and increase electricity usage for air conditioners. Hard surfaces also create more uncomfortable glare and reflection than plant foliage.

It is beneficial to build or retain only the hardscape that is required for the good functioning of yards and cities and to turn over the rest to plants. Ground covers can be low maintenance and used similarly to hardscape while providing many other benefits. Where the openness of a flat surface is required or preferred aesthetically, ground covers can be grown across and over hardscape or can replace it altogether. Driveways or laneways require only two strips of hardscape for the wheels of a car. The rest of the asphalt or concrete is never or rarely used and could become a low, linear garden bed.

The replacement of hardscape with ground covers also benefits the overall health of the garden. Ground covers enable rain to replenish soil moisture and make it available to other plants, and they reduce soil compaction for better soil aeration for healthy roots and stronger, healthier, more disease- and stress-resistant plants.

Support wildlife

Many gardens are designed with the goal of attracting charismatic and beneficial garden visitors such as beneficial insects (native bees, butterflies, beetles, other pollinators, and spiders), birds (especially hummingbirds), and other wildlife. Ground covers can play a role in increasing habitat structural diversity and plant biodiversity that will attract a variety of wildlife

Dianthus 'First Love' is a popular nectar source for butterflies and has edible flowers for humans.

into the garden, especially if they replace lawn or hardscape.

Native plants and their "nativars" (cultivars of native plants) are important for habitat and food, including nectar, pollen, leaves, berries, and seeds, for garden wildlife. They are especially important as larval hosts for native butterfly and moth species, which often have specific plant associations, the relationship between the milkweeds (*Asclepias* spp.) and monarch butterflies being one of the most celebrated. Nonnative plants also provide habitat and are excellent for producing nectar and pollen, especially long-blooming cultivars. A diverse selection of native and nonnative ground covers will usually be the most effective in supporting the most diverse range of wildlife with food and habitat. Greater biodiversity is also supported by greater habitat complexity, which means using diverse ground cover habits such as mats, mounds, vines, and woody forms.

Food production

The interest in and resurgence of local foods and edible gardening continues to grow. Ground covers that produce fruit and edible leaves and flowers can help increase the variety of a garden's edible bounty, especially from spaces beyond the veggie plot or herb garden, such as pathways, patios, and border edges. They can also help beautify conventional edible plots or can be integrated with ornamental plants throughout the garden.

Before eating any plant you do not know, make sure to identify it carefully and research its edible (and

EDIBLE GROUND COVERS

Akebia spp.
Calamintha spp.
Chamaemelum nobile
Dianthus spp.
Fragaria spp.
Galium odoratum
Gaultheria procumbens
Gaultheria shallon
Glechoma hederacea
Houttuynia cordata
Humulus lupulus
Jasminum officinale
Juniperus communis
Lavandula angustifolia
Lavandula ×intermedia
Mentha spp.
Nepeta spp.
Origanum vulgare

Passiflora incarnata
Petasites japonicus
Polypodium glycyrrhiza
Primula vulgaris
Rosa spp.
Rosmarinus officinalis (trailing cultivars)
Rubus arcticus
Rumex sanguineus var. *sanguineus*
Salvia officinalis
Satureja spp.
Thymus citriodorus
Thymus vulgaris
Trifolium repens
Vaccinium spp.
Viola spp.

TRAILING GROUND COVERS

Acaena spp.
Ajuga spp.
Akebia spp.
Alchemilla ellenbeckii
Ampelopsis spp.
Arctostaphylos spp. (especially *A. uva-ursi*)
Arenaria montana
Aurinia saxatilis
Aubrieta cultivars
Arabis spp.
Azorella trifurcata
Cerastium tomentosum
Clematis spp.
Convolvulus sabatius
Cotoneaster spp.
Cymbalaria spp.
Delosperma spp.
Dianthus spp.
Ellisiophyllum pinnatum
Euonymus fortunei
Gypsophila repens
Hedera spp.
Helianthemum spp.
Jasminum spp.
Lamium galeobdolon

Lithodora diffusa
Lonicera spp.
Mentha requienii
Muehlenbeckia spp.
Parthenocissus spp.
Phlox subulata
Rosmarinus officinalis (trailing cultivars)
Rubus rolfei
Saponaria spp.
Scleranthus uniflorus
Sedum spp.
Silene uniflora
Soleirolia soleirolii
Symphoricarpos ×chenaultii 'Hancock'
Tanacetum densum subsp. *amani*
Thymus spp.
Tiarella cordifolia (running cultivars)
Trachelospermum spp.
Trifolium repens
Verbena canadensis
Veronica spp.
Vinca spp.

Ground covers such as the alpine strawberry, *Fragaria vesca* 'Improved Rügen', can be beautiful, functional, and edible.

inedible) parts and how they should be prepared and eaten. Also, it is best to eat only small quantities at first and to grow these edibles organically to avoid pesticide and fungicide residues.

Cover walls and hardscape

The built urban and suburban environments present many hard and austere surfaces that create glare, absorb heat, and contribute to the urban heat island effect, not to mention their unappealing appearance.

Azorella trifurcata 'Nana' flows like green lava through aeoniums, softening a rock wall at Larnach Castle, New Zealand.

Sedum spathulifolium planted between the rocks of a stone wall provide a colorful focal point.

Trailing or vining ground covers can be invaluable for softening hard landscape features. They can be planted atop a wall and allowed to trail over the edge, encouraged to grow over uneven ground, and used to obscure unsightly landscape features such as rocks, boulders, rubble, stumps, and other undesirable topography.

Green roofs and living walls

Most green roofs and living walls are planted primarily, if not exclusively, with ground covers, which adapt well to the shallow soil depth and small soil volume of the planting space and help bind the soil. They are tolerant of exposure to the elements, have low nutrient needs, require little maintenance, and are usually long-lived or self-propagating. The growing popularity of green roofs and living walls has helped to expand the availability of certain groups of ground covers, especially stonecrops.

Rain gardens

Rain gardens are usually shallow depressions that are designed to slow, collect, and hold rainwater runoff from hard, flat surfaces such as roofs, patios, driveways, and parking areas. The collected water can then percolate slowly into the ground, replenishing soil

GROUND COVERS FOR GREEN ROOFS AND LIVING WALLS

Achillea spp.	*Nepeta* spp.
Antennaria spp.	*Ophiopogon japonicus*
Armeria spp.	*Opuntia* spp.
Calamintha nepeta	*Origanum laevigatum*
Campanula spp.	*Origanum vulgare*
Carex spp.	*Orostachys* spp.
Cerastium tomentosum	*Pennisetum* spp.
Coreopsis verticillata	*Penstemon* spp.
Delosperma spp.	*Phemeranthus calycinus*
Dianthus spp.	*Phlox* spp.
Festuca spp.	*Potentilla* spp.
Fragaria spp.	*Pulsatilla vulgaris*
Geranium ×*cantabrigiense*	*Rhus aromatica* 'Gro-Low'
Geranium sanguineum	*Saponaria ocymoides*
Gypsophila repens	*Saxifraga* spp.
Helianthemum spp.	*Sedum* spp.
Heuchera americana	*Sempervivum* spp.
Jovibarba spp.	*Teucrium chamaedrys*
Juniperus spp.	*Thymus* spp.
Nassella tenuissima	*Veronica* spp.

Most plants on this living wall on the Semiahmoo Library, Surrey, British Columbia, are ground covers.

Acorus gramineus, an excellent ground cover for a rain garden, is tolerant of variable moisture conditions from average to wet.

GROUND COVERS FOR RAIN GARDENS

Acorus gramineus	*Iris cristata*
Ajuga reptans	*Liriope spicata*
Alchemilla spp.	*Luzula* spp.
Anemone canadensis	*Lysimachia nummularia*
Arctostaphylos uva-ursi	*Onoclea sensibilis*
Armeria maritima	*Packera aurea*
Asarum spp.	*Parathelypteris*
Aster spp.	*novae-boracensis*
Caltha palustris	*Pennisetum* spp.
Carex spp.	*Phlox divaricata*
Chrysogonum	*Polygonatum* spp.
virginianum	*Polystichum* spp.
Convallaria majalis	*Pratia* spp.
Coreopsis verticillata	*Salix* spp.
Dryopteris spp.	*Sanguinaria canadensis*
Eurybia spp.	*Symphyotrichum* spp.
Geum spp.	*Tiarella cordifolia*
Hosta spp.	*Vaccinium* spp.
Hypericum calycinum	

moisture, reducing pressure on the stormwater drainage system, and mitigating the environmental impacts of stormwater drainage into the environment. Rain garden plants are tolerant of inundation after rainfall and dry periods between rain events. They beautify the landscape, slow the flow of water, reduce erosion, create wildlife habitat, and help to remove the water through evapotranspiration. Native plants are often recommended because they are adapted to the rainfall patterns of their native region, but a mix of native and nonnative plants can be used. Most rain gardens will present a variety of different moisture conditions, with some species preferring wetter or drier positions.

Ground Cover Combinations

Ground covers are often planted as a single cultivar; certainly a large, uniform drift can have impact or offer an effective simplicity. But ground covers can also be planted side by side in contrasting mounds or drifts, or interplanted to intermingle in dynamic carpets of mixed colors and textures. These combinations can range from a quiet study of texture and green tones to bold combinations of foliage and flower.

Careful selection of small groups of complementary ground covers can offer dynamic displays and year-round interest. Effective combinations require that all plants have similar cultural requirements and rates of growth, compatible sizes, and modes of spread suited to the purpose of the plantings. For instance, mounding ground covers that reach a maximum size may be best for drifts that maintain their shape over time, whereas indeterminately spreading ground covers may be best for intermingled combinations where change over time is desirable. Given so many ground cover options, you may find that some trial and error is required, with ongoing monitoring, maintenance, and adjustments should species perform differently than expected.

Same species, different cultivars

Cultivars of the same species usually have similar overall sizes, growth rates, and cultural requirements, making them natural partners. Consider a combination of green *Lysimachia nummularia* or *Sagina subulata* with their golden forms. Green-leaved and pink-flowering *Sedum spurium* 'John Creech' contrasts nicely with burgundy-leaved and deep red-flowering 'Voodoo'. Try a fine-textured combination of gold and blue with *Sedum rupestre* 'Angelina' and 'Blue Spruce'.

Mounding and spreading species

Combine taller mounding or more upright ground covers with rhizomatous, stoloniferous, and trailing ones. This strategy provides a more topographic display of mounds or clumps sitting on a low-growing carpet. It's also practical, because clumps or mounds can sometimes leave spaces of bare soil where weeds can grow. A vast number of combinations are possible but here are a few ideas.

- Interplant any medium-sized hosta with *Tiarella cordifolia* 'Running Tapestry', with its lobed, light green, burgundy-veined leaves and showy white flower spikes in spring, and *Rubus rolfei* 'Emerald Carpet', with its lobed, textured, dark, evergreen leaves.

Helleborus ×*hybridus*, surrounded by a carpet of *Omphalodes verna* 'Alba', will soon flush a new mound of foliage.

- Combine finely textured, powder-blue *Festuca glauca* 'Casca11' Beyond Blue with the dark green leaves and cobalt-blue flowers of *Veronica* 'Tidal Pool' and the reddish pink flowers of *Thymus* Coccineus Group or its variegated counterpart, *T.* 'Hartington Silver'.

- Use *Brunnera macrophylla* 'Silver Heart', with its mounds of silver, heart-shaped leaves, with the large-leaved, burgundy-infused *Ajuga reptans* 'Catlin's Giant' and the bright gold, rounded foliage of *Lysimachia nummularia* 'Aurea'.

- Combine the golden, spiky fans of sweet flag, *Acorus gramineus* 'Ogon', with the bright green mats and pale blue flowers of blue star creeper (*Pratia pedunculata*), and the gray-green, pink, and white leaves of *Ajuga reptans* 'Burgundy Glow', with its spikes of purple-blue flowers.

- Plant *Mukdenia rossii* 'Karasuba', with its fan-shaped, light green leaves that become reddish in summer, with the dark green, succulent rosettes of *Saxifraga* London Pride Group and the gray-green succulent *Sedum spathulifolium*.

- Use *Beesia deltophylla*, with its mounds of dark green, heart-shaped, evergreen leaves, with *Omphalodes verna* 'Alba' and *Maianthemum dilatatum*, both with lighter green leaves and white flowers.

- Combine *Origanum* 'Kent Beauty', with its mounds of blue-green leaves and pink-bracted inflorescences, with the succulent ice plant *Delosperma* Hot Cakes 'Tangerine Tango'.

- Interplant *Carex oshimensis* 'Everillo', with its fountains of golden, evergreen, linear foliage, with the dense mats of powder-blue foliage and pink flowers of *Dianthus* 'Feuerhexe' and the burgundy-flushed blue-gray rosettes of *Sempervivum* 'Lavender and Old Lace'.

- Combine hellebores (*Helleborus* ×*hybridus*), with their nodding early spring flowers and mounds of leathery foliage, with the spring ephemeral wood anemone (*Anemone nemorosa*), followed later in the season by the pink flowers and silvered leaves of *Lamium maculatum* 'Beacon Silver'.

- Use the rich purple, ruffled foliage of *Heuchera* 'Tnheufp' Forever Purple with low mats of feathery gray-green and lavender-gray *Leptinella squalida* 'Platt's Black' and golden, succulent teardrops of *Sedum makinoi* 'Ogon'.

Mounds of a silver-foliaged cultivar of *Brunnera macrophylla* meet mats of golden *Lysimachia nummularia* 'Aurea'.

Fast growers for cover while slow plants fill in

If a desired ground cover is slow to establish and fill in, a fast-spreading species can be planted to provide quick coverage, either to form an interesting, long-term interplanting or to be eventually outcompeted or pushed to the edge of the colony once its job is done. Combine black mondo grass (*Ophiopogon planiscapus* 'Nigrescens') with mossy *Sagina subulata* and *S. subulata* var. *glabrata* 'Aurea'. Or use sweet box (*Sarcococca hookeriana* var. *humilis*) with the redwood sorrel (*Oxalis oregana* 'Klamath Ruby'). Combine *Pachysandra terminalis* with white star creeper (*Pratia angulata*). Or try the mounding *Salvia officinalis* 'Purpurea' with *Thymus pseudolanuginosus*. Finally, combine trailing *Ceanothus griseus* var. *horizontalis* 'Yankee Point' with *Sedum rupestre* 'Angelina' or 'Blue Spruce'

Fragrant and Aromatic Ground Covers

Fragrance is an important component of the garden experience, and like many other plants, some ground covers offer fragrant flowers and aromatic foliage. To bring the flowers' fragrance to garden visitors, mass plant them or add them to raised positions, such as hanging over walls, in raised planters, or along stairways.

Dianthus 'Frosty Fire', like most pinks, has an intense sweet and spicy fragrance.

FRAGRANT AND AROMATIC GROUND COVERS

Achillea spp.
Achlys triphylla
Acinos alpinus
Acorus gramineus
Akebia spp.
Alyssum spp.
Androsace spp.
Anemone sylvestris
Anthemis spp.
Arabis spp.
Artemisia spp.
Aurinia saxatilis
Calamintha spp.
Ceanothus spp.
Chamaemelum nobile
Chrysanthemum weyrichii
Clematis armandii
Clematis Herbaceous
    Group (C. 'Mrs.
    Robert Brydon' and C.
    'Praecox')
Clematis koreana var.
    fragrans
Clematis terniflora
Convallaria majalis
Corydalis spp.

Cotoneaster dammeri
Dianthus spp.
Dicentra canadensis
Erysimum spp.
Filipendula spp.
Galium odoratum
Gaultheria procumbens
Gelsemium sempervirens
Geranium
    ×cantabrigiense
Geranium dalmaticum
Geranium macrorrhizum
Glechoma hederacea
Gypsophila repens
Hedera colchica
Helleborus niger 'Coseh
    210' HGC Joel, 'HGC
    Jacob', and 'HGC
    Joshua'
Heuchera sanguinea
Hosta plantaginea
Houttuynia cordata
Hydrangea anomala
    subsp. petiolaris
Hydrangea seemannii
Iris japonica

Iris pumila
Jasminum officinale
Juniperus spp.
Lavandula angustifolia
Lavandula ×intermedia
Libertia peregrinans
Linnaea borealis
Lonicera spp.
Magnolia laevifolia
    'Free Spirit'
Mahonia spp.
Mentha spp.
Mitchella repens
Monardella macrantha
Nepeta spp.
Oenothera spp.
Origanum spp.
Osteospermum barberae
    var. compactum
Pachysandra spp.
Passiflora incarnata
Paxistima myrsinites
Peucedanum ostruthium
Phlomis russeliana
Phlox spp.
Phuopsis stylosa

Podophyllum peltatum
Polygala chamaebuxus
Polygonatum odoratum
Polygonum aubertii
Primula spp.
Prostanthera cuneata
Reineckea carnea
Rhus aromatica
Rosa spp.
Rosmarinus officinalis
    (trailing cultivars)
Rubus arcticus
Salvia officinalis
Santolina spp.
Saponaria ocymoides
Sarcococca hookeriana
Satureja spp.
Schizophragma spp.
Speirantha gardenii
Tellima grandiflora
Teucrium spp.
Thymus spp.
Trachelospermum spp.
Valeriana supina
Verbena canadensis
Viola spp.

Ground covers with aromatic foliage can be planted along pathways, on stairways, and around patios, where visitors may brush against or lightly bruise the leaves to release their aromas for an immersive olfactory experience. Plant Corsican mint (*Mentha requienii*) or creeping thyme (*Thymus serpyllum*) between stepping or patio stones. Line a front walkway with common thyme (*Thymus vulgaris*), lemon thyme (*T. citriodorus*), lavender, or rosemary (*Rosmarinus officinalis*).

Ground Covers and Bulbs

Ground covers and bulbs make natural companions. In fact, every drift of ground covers should be underplanted with bulbs. Bulbs are easy to plant and care for, cost effective, and long-lived. They can share space with most ground covers, doubling the floral display when they rise up through mats or mounds during their season of growth and bloom. Bulbs can be

Snowdrops (*Galanthus nivalis*), covered in raindrops, rise through a mat of cotoneaster in late winter.

SPRING BULB GROUND COVER COMPANIONS

Anemone blanda	*Hyacinthus* spp.
Anemone coronaria De Caen Group	*Iris reticulata*
	Leucojum aestivum
Brodiaea spp.	*Muscari* spp.
Chionodoxa spp.	*Narcissus* spp.
Crocus spp.	*Puschkinia scilloides*
Eranthis hyemalis	*Scilla siberica*
Fritillaria spp.	*Triteleia* spp.
Galanthus spp.	*Tulipa* spp.
Hyacinthoides hispanica	
Hyacinthoides non-scripta	

SUMMER AND FALL BULB GROUND COVER COMPANIONS

Allium spp.	*Gladiolus* spp.
Arisaema spp.	*Lycoris* spp.
Colchicum spp.	*Nerine bowdenii*
Crocus cartwrightianus	*Roscoea* spp.
Crocus ochroleucus	*Sternbergia lutea*
Crocus sativus	

An autumn crocus (*Colchicum* sp.) rises through a bed of redwood sorrel (*Oxalis oregana*) in fall.

selected to bloom simultaneously with ground covers, or they may bloom at a different time to create multiple seasons of interest from the same patch of ground. In small city gardens with limited space, this strategy is all the more valuable.

This combination is also practical because bulbs are hard to keep track of when dormant. Planted under ground covers, their place is easily marked and protected from the marauding shovels of gardeners attempting to shoehorn yet another treasure into the border. Practically any small to medium-sized bulb makes a suitable companion for ground covers, and even large bulbs can be used.

As bulbs begin to enter dormancy, allow them to die back naturally, removing the spent foliage only after it has turned completely yellow. Though this stage is not attractive, it is important for the ongoing health of the bulbs. In combination with ground covers, the yellowing leaves will be less prominent.

Ground Covers for Challenging Situations

Many tough ground covers can offer solutions for problem spots in the garden.

Dry shade

Dry shade usually occurs in two kinds of situations— beneath trees, especially coniferous or broadleaf evergreen species, and under the eaves of buildings, where rainfall is reduced or prevented from reaching the ground. Under trees, the soil can also be dry from shallow tree roots that outcompete smaller plants for moisture and space.

The palette of plants for dry shade is limited, because most shade plants are adapted to the rich, moist soils of forest floors, wooded ravines, and shaded slopes. No ground cover will grow in powder-dry soils, but some can tolerate dry shade with limited moisture and others can be used in strategic ways to achieve coverage.

Trailing, running, rhizomatous, or vining ground covers can be planted outside of the drip line of a tree canopy or out from under the eaves of a building in more favorable soil conditions and then encouraged to grow into areas of dry shade, a task made easier if they are growing toward more light. Trailing or rhizomatous plants can be used for smaller areas, whereas vining plants, such as English ivy (*Hedera helix*) and

Virginia creeper (*Parthenocissus* spp.), provide some of the only hope for coverage in larger areas of dry soils if planted in more favorable soils nearby.

GROUND COVERS FOR DRY SHADE

Arrhenatherum elatius var. bulbosum	Lamium galeobdolon
Asplenium scolopendrium	Lamium maculatum
Bergenia cordifolia	Liriope spp.
Carex appalachica	Maianthemum dilatatum
Carex flacca	Maianthemum stellatum
Carex oshimensis	Pachysandra procumbens
Carex pensylvanica	Pachysandra terminalis
Ceratostigma plumbaginoides	Parthenocissus spp.
Convallaria majalis	Polypodium glycyrrhiza
Cyclamen coum	Polypodium scouleri
Cyclamen hederifolium	Polypodium vulgare
Dryopteris filix-mas	Polystichum acrostichoides
Dryopteris marginalis	Polystichum aculeatum
Epimedium spp.	Polystichum munitum
Euphorbia amygdaloides var. robbiae	Polystichum setiferum
Geranium macrorrhizum	Pulmonaria spp.
Geranium nodosum	Sedum oreganum
Hedera helix	Sedum ternatum
Helleborus ×hybridus	Vinca major
Hypericum calycinum	Vinca minor
	Waldsteinia spp.

Euphorbia amygdaloides var. *robbiae* and *Lamium galeobdolon* are both tolerant of dry shade.

Sunny slopes

The angle and exposure of sunny slopes can result in intense sunlight and heat, which is made more challenging by dry soils. Because rainfall is shed quickly before it can be absorbed into the ground, conditions are often too extreme for turf grass and many perennials and shrubs. However, many tough, drought-tolerant ground covers are adapted to these conditions. They can also help stabilize a slope and reduce erosion.

GROUND COVERS FOR SUNNY SLOPES

Acaena spp.	Lonicera pileata
Achillea spp.	Marrubium spp.
Acinos alpinus	Muehlenbeckia spp.
Alyssum spp.	Nepeta spp.
Anaphalis spp.	Oenothera spp.
Anthemis spp.	Opuntia spp.
Arabis spp.	Origanum spp.
Arctostaphylos spp.	Orostachys spp.
Arenaria spp.	Pennisetum spp.
Armeria spp.	Phlox subulata
Artemisia spp.	Prostanthera cuneata
Aurinia saxatilis	Rhodiola spp.
Baccharis spp.	Rosmarinus officinalis (trailing cultivars)
Calamintha spp.	Ruschia pulvinaris
Ceanothus spp.	Salvia officinalis
Cerastium tomentosum	Saponaria ocymoides
Chamaemelum nobile	Scutellaria spp.
Cistus spp.	Sedum spp.
Convolvulus spp.	Sempervivum spp.
Cotoneaster spp.	Stachys byzantina
Delosperma spp.	Stephanandra incisa
Dryas spp.	Symphoricarpos ×chenaultii 'Hancock'
Epilobium spp.	Symphyotrichum ericoides
Euphorbia myrsinites	
Euphorbia rigida	Tanacetum densum subsp. amani
Festuca spp.	Teucrium spp.
Gazania linearis	Thymus spp.
Genista spp.	Vaccinium spp.
Gypsophila spp.	Verbena spp.
Hypericum calycinum	Veronica spp.
Iberis spp.	
Juniperus spp.	
Lavandula spp.	

Stachys byzantina and *Origanum vulgare* 'Aureum Crispum' are both tolerant of dry soils on sunny slopes.

California fuchsias (*Epilobium* spp.) and prickly pear cactus (*Opuntia* spp.) are extremely tolerant of tough conditions such as hell strips.

Hell strips

The usually narrow, linear spaces between sidewalks and roads have thin, poorly structured soils as a result of road and sidewalk construction, with a high salt content from snow control in cold winter regions and with low soil moisture because irrigation is rarely available. They experience intense heat and light, including that reflected by asphalt and concrete, and they suffer from damage from foot traffic and the indignities delivered by passing dogs and smokers. Though challenging, a successful hell strip planting can enhance curb appeal, beautify the neighborhood, and help create community.

A certain amount of trial and error may be required to identify the best plants for a particular site and regional climate. Many plants suitable for hell strips are also salt tolerant, a trait that becomes less important in mild regions with little snowfall. Hell strips that receive shade from street trees could support additional species.

Saline soils

Saline soils result from salt spray and saltwater inundation of coastal sites, low precipitation in arid and semiarid regions, and salt applications on roads and sidewalks in cold winter areas. These soils affect the water uptake efficiency of roots, and salt spray can burn leaves. Salty sites often present other challenges including wind, heat, and thin, rocky, or sandy soils.

Many salt-tolerant ground covers are also adapted to sunny, exposed sites, while others will appreciate

GROUND COVERS FOR HELL STRIPS

Achillea spp.	*Geranium sanguineum*
Ajuga spp.	*Gypsophila repens*
Anaphalis spp.	*Hebe* spp.
Antennaria spp.	*Helianthemum* spp.
Anthemis tinctoria	*Helictotrichon*
Arabis spp.	*sempervirens*
Arctostaphylos spp.	*Hypericum calycinum*
Arenaria montana	*Iberis sempervirens*
Armeria maritima	*Juniperus* spp.
Armeria pseudarmeria	*Lavandula* spp.
Artemisia pycnocephala	*Leymus arenarius*
Artemisia stelleriana	*Lithodora diffusa*
Callirhoe involucrata	*Muehlenbeckia* spp.
Carex testacea	*Nassella tenuissima*
Ceanothus spp.	*Nepeta* spp.
Cerastium tomentosum	*Opuntia* spp.
Cistus spp.	*Penstemon* spp.
Cotoneaster spp.	*Phlox subulata*
Delosperma spp.	*Pinus mugo*
Dianthus spp.	*Rhus aromatica*
Epilobium spp.	*Rosmarinus officinalis*
Erigeron spp.	*Santolina* spp.
Eryngium spp.	*Sedum* spp.
Erysimum spp.	*Sempervivum* spp.
Euphorbia myrsinites	*Silene uniflora*
Festuca glauca	*Stachys byzantina*
Fragaria chiloensis	*Thymus* spp.
Geranium 'Gerwat'	*Veronica* spp.
Rozanne and other hybrids	

Basket of gold (*Aurinia saxatilis*) is salt and drought tolerant.

GROUND COVERS FOR SALINE SOILS

Achillea spp.
Anaphalis spp.
Anemone canadensis
Anemone hupehensis
Anemone ×*hybrida*
Anemone tomentosa
Anthemis tinctoria
Arctostaphylos spp.
Armeria maritima
Armeria pseudarmeria
Artemisia pycnocephala
Artemisia stelleriana
Aurinia saxatilis
Baccharis spp.
Calluna spp.
Carex testacea
Ceanothus spp.
Cistus spp.
Cornus canadensis
Cotoneaster spp.
Delosperma spp.
Dianthus spp.
Erica spp.
Erigeron spp.
Eryngium spp.
Euphorbia myrsinites
Festuca glauca
Fragaria chiloensis
Gypsophila repens
Hebe spp.
Hedera helix
Helianthemum spp.
Helictotrichon sempervirens
Hydrangea anomala subsp. *petiolaris*
Hypericum calycinum

Iberis sempervirens
Juniperus spp.
Lavandula spp.
Leymus arenarius
Liriope spicata
Lonicera spp.
Maianthemum spp.
Muehlenbeckia spp.
Nassella tenuissima
Nepeta spp.
Opuntia spp.
Pachysandra terminalis
Parthenocissus spp.
Paxistima canbyi
Phlox douglasii
Phlox ×*procumbens*
Phlox subulata
Picea abies
Picea pungens
Pinus mugo
Pinus nigra
Pinus thunbergii
Rhus aromatica
Rosmarinus officinalis
Santolina spp.
Schizophragma hydrangeoides
Sedum spp.
Sempervivum spp.
Silene uniflora
Stachys byzantina
Thymus serpyllum
Vaccinium angustifolium
Vaccinium vitis-idaea
Veronica spp.
Waldsteinia spp.

more soil moisture and less sun. Saline soils occur in diverse climatic zones. Observe the plants already in use in your region or enquire at reputable garden centers for additional options.

Soils with challenging pH

Soil pH is the measure of its acidity, neutrality, or alkalinity, measured on a scale of 0–14, with 7 being neutral. The soils in average to high rainfall regions tend to be slightly acidic because rain is slightly acidic. The soils in semiarid regions or atop calcareous bedrock tend toward alkalinity. The soil's pH affects plants' ability to absorb nutrients. In soils of challenging pH, plants may exhibit reduced vigor, less flowering and fruiting, and signs of nutrient deficiency.

Most cultivated plants thrive in somewhat acidic to neutral soils (pH of 6–7), though many are adaptable to a range of pH values. Consequently, although soil pH is an important factor in plant health, it is secondary to climate zone, light, soil moisture, soil structure, and soil fertility. Most gardeners need not worry about soil pH unless they live in a region with particularly acidic or alkaline conditions. Numerous local and regional plant lists are available online, or enquire at reputable garden centers. In other cases, you may want to grow species with a strong preference for a certain pH. For instance, ericaceous plants such as heaths, heathers, and blueberries will produce more flowers and fruit in acidic soils. Conversely, hellebores, though tolerant of various soil pH levels, seem more robust in neutral to alkaline soils that more closely match the pH of their native habitats atop limestone.

Many plants that either prefer or are tolerant of alkaline soils are native to calcareous soils that have a high pH. Most of these plants will also grow well in neutral and slightly acidic soils.

GROUND COVERS FOR ACIDIC SOILS

Andromeda polifolia	*Linnaea borealis*
Calluna spp.	*Luzula* spp.
Cornus canadensis	*Mahonia* spp.
Daboecia cantabrica	*Mitchella repens*
Dennstaedtia punctilobula	*Pachysandra* spp.
Erica spp.	*Paxistima myrsinites*
Galium odoratum	*Picea* spp.
Gaultheria procumbens	*Potentilla tridentata*
Gaultheria shallon	*Rubus arcticus*
Gaylussacia brachycera	*Vaccinium* spp.
	Woodwardia spp.

GROUND COVERS FOR ALKALINE SOILS

Achillea spp.	*Gypsophila repens*
Adiantum capillus-veneris	*Hakonechloa macra*
Akebia spp.	*Helianthus salicifolius*
Amsonia spp.	*Helleborus* spp.
Antennaria dioica	*Houttuynia cordata*
Anthemis spp.	*Iberis sempervirens*
Arabis spp.	*Iris cristata*
Armeria maritima	*Jovibarba* spp.
Artemisia spp.	*Juniperus* spp.
Asarum europaeum	*Lavandula* spp.
Astrantia major	*Lonicera* spp.
Baccharis spp.	*Marrubium rotundifolium*
Bergenia spp.	*Mazus reptans*
Calamintha nepeta	*Oenothera macrocarpa*
Campanula cochlearifolia	*Ophiopogon* spp.
Campanula portenschlagiana	*Origanum vulgare*
Cardamine trifolia	*Parthenocissus* spp.
Carex flacca	*Paxistima canbyi*
Carex flaccosperma	*Persicaria affinis*
Cerastium tomentosum	*Phlox subulata*
Ceratostigma plumbaginoides	*Polypodium cambricum*
Chamaemelum nobile	*Potentilla crantzii*
Clematis texensis	*Pratia* spp.
Convallaria majalis	*Pulsatilla vulgaris*
Convolvulus spp.	*Rosmarinus officinalis* (trailing cultivars)
Coreopsis auriculata	*Salvia officinalis*
Cotoneaster spp.	*Santolina* spp.
Cymbalaria muralis	*Saponaria ocymoides*
Cyrtomium spp.	*Sedum* spp.
Dianthus spp.	*Sempervivum* spp.
Dryas spp.	*Stachys byzantina*
Erodium spp.	*Teucrium chamaedrys*
Euphorbia spp.	*Thymus* spp.
Filipendula vulgaris	*Valeriana supina*
Genista spp.	*Verbena canadensis*
Geum triflorum	*Viola odorata*
Globularia cordifolia	

Eastern hay-scented fern (*Dennstaedtia punctilobula*) is frequently found in acidic soils across its range in eastern North America.

GROUND COVERS FOR MOIST OR WET SOILS

Acorus gramineus	*Leptinella* spp.
Ajuga reptans	*Lindernia grandiflora*
Andromeda polifolia	*Luzula sylvatica*
Anemone canadensis	*Lysimachia japonica*
Anemone rivularis	var. *minutissima*
Arenaria balearica	*Lysimachia nummularia*
Asarum caudatum	*Mazus* spp.
Blechnum spp.	*Mentha pulegium*
Caltha palustris	*Mentha requienii*
Carex berggrenii	*Parathelypteris*
Carex flaccosperma	*novae-boracensis*
Carex laxiculmis	*Persicaria* spp.
Carex muskingumensis	*Petasites frigidus* var.
Carex praegracilis	*palmatus*
Carex tenuiculmis	*Pratia* spp.
Cymbalaria spp.	*Primula* spp.
Decumaria barbara	*Sagina subulata*
Eleocharis radicans	*Selaginella* spp.
Equisetum spp.	*Soleirolia soleirolii*
Ficaria verna	*Tellima grandiflora*
Geum rivale	*Tolmiea menziesii*
Gunnera spp.	*Vaccinium macrocarpon*
Houttuynia cordata	*Veronica repens*
Hydrocotyle	*Viola* spp.
sibthorpioides	*Woodwardia* spp.
Iris japonica	

Luzula sylvatica thrives on a moist, shaded hillside in Scotland.

Though no plant is 100 percent resistant to browsing by hungry herbivores, hellebores are pretty close.

Moist or wet soils

Excessively moist or wet soils present their own set of challenges for plants, particularly a lack of soil aeration for proper root health. Because it can be difficult to garden in these areas, a low-maintenance ground cover offers a useful solution.

Deer and rabbits

Many suburban and rural gardeners must contend with hungry deer and rabbits. Luckily, many ground covers are resistant to herbivory. Plants that are fully herbivore resistant are rare. Herbivores can vary in their preferences from individual to individual, population to population, and region to region. Deer and rabbits, both adult and juvenile, are inquisitive and may often sample a new plant before finding it unpalatable. They may also browse on the delicate young shoots and leaves of species that become unpalatable when they mature. When there is a shortage of browsing material during the winter or during a drought, they may eat anything.

All of the listed plants are considered deer resistant, and those marked with an asterisk (*) are also considered rabbit resistant. Because deer resistance is better documented than for rabbits, some of the unmarked species may also be rabbit resistant. Conversely, some plants listed here may not be resistant to herbivory in some regions—it depends on the culinary preferences of your local populations of deer and rabbits.

GROUND COVERS RESISTANT TO DEER AND RABBITS

Acaena spp.
Achillea spp.*
Achlys triphylla
Acorus gramineus
Adiantum spp.*
Aegopodium podagraria*
Ajania pacifica
Ajuga spp.*
Akebia spp.
Alchemilla spp.*
Alyssum spp.
Ampelopsis
   brevipedunculata
Amsonia spp.
Anacyclus pyrethrum var.
   depressus*
Anaphalis spp.*
Andromeda polifolia
Anemone spp.*
Antennaria spp.*
Anthemis spp.
Arabis spp.
Arctostaphylos spp.
Arenaria spp.
Armeria spp.*
Arrhenatherum elatius var.
   bulbosum
Artemisia spp.*
Arum italicum
Aruncus aethusifolius*
Asarum spp.*
Asplenium scolopendrium*
Astilbe spp.*
Athyrium spp.*
Aubrieta spp.
Aurinia saxatilis*
Azorella trifurcata
Baccharis spp.*
Bergenia spp.*
Blechnum spp.*
Brunnera spp.*
Calamintha spp.*
Calluna spp.*
Campanula spp.*
Campsis spp.*
Cardamine trifolia
Carex spp.
Ceanothus spp.
Cerastium tomentosum*
Ceratostigma spp.*
Chamaemelum nobile
Chrysanthemum weyrichii
Chrysogonum virginianum
Cistus spp.
Clematis spp.*
Convallaria majalis*

Convolvulus spp.
Coreopsis spp.*
Cornus canadensis*
Corydalis spp.*
Cotoneaster spp.*
Cyclamen spp.*
Cyrtomium spp.*
Daboecia cantabrica
Delosperma spp.
Dennstaedtia punctilobula*
Dianthus spp.
Dicentra spp.*
Dryopteris spp.*
Duchesnea indica*
Epilobium spp.
Epimedium spp.
Equisetum scirpoides
Erica spp.*
Erigeron spp.
Eriogonum spp.*
Eryngium spp.*
Erysimum spp.*
Euphorbia spp.*
Eurybia spp.
Festuca spp.
Filipendula spp.*
Fragaria spp.*
Galium odoratum*
Gaultheria procumbens*
Gaura spp.*
Gelsemium sempervirens*
Genista spp.*
Geranium spp.*
Geum spp.*
Glechoma hederacea
Gymnocarpium dryopteris*
Gypsophila spp.
Hakonechloa macra
Hedera spp.*
Helianthemum spp.*
Helleborus spp.*
Herniaria glabra
Heuchera spp.*
Heuchera spp.*
×Heucherella spp.*
Houttuynia cordata*
Hypericum calycinum*
Iberis sempervirens*
Imperata cylindrica*
Iris spp.*
Jasminum spp.
Jovibarba spp.*
Juniperus spp.*
Lamium spp.*
Lavandula spp.*

Leptinella spp.
Leymus arenarius*
Libertia peregrinans*
Linnaea borealis
Liriope spp.*
Lithodora diffusa
Lonicera spp.*
Luzula spp.*
Lysimachia spp.*
Mahonia spp.*
Marrubium spp.*
Mazus spp.
Mentha spp.*
Microbiota decussata*
Mitchella repens*
Monardella macrantha*
Muehlenbeckia spp.*
Nassella tenuissima*
Nepeta racemosa*
Oenothera spp.*
Omphalodes spp.*
Onoclea sensibilis*
Ophiopogon spp.*
Opuntia spp.*
Origanum spp.*
Osteospermum barberae
   var. compactum*
Oxalis spp.*
Pachysandra spp.*
Packera spp.*
Parathelypteris
   novae-boracensis*
Parthenocissus spp.*
Pennisetum spp.
Penstemon spp.
Persicaria spp.*
Peucedanum ostruthium
Phegopteris
   decursive-pinnata*
Phlomis russeliana*
Phlox spp.*
Phuopsis stylosa*
Physalis alkekengi var.
   franchetii
Picea spp.*
Pinus spp.*
Pleioblastus pygmaeus
Podophyllum peltatum*
Polygala chamaebuxus
Polygonatum spp.*
Polygonum aubertii*
Polypodium spp.
Polystichum spp.*
Potentilla spp.
Pratia spp.*
Primula spp.

Prostanthera cuneata
Prunella grandiflora*
Pterocephalus depressus
Pulmonaria spp.*
Pulsatilla vulgaris*
Ranunculus repens
Rhodiola spp.*
Rhus aromatica*
Rohdea japonica
Rosmarinus officinalis*
Rosularia chrysantha*
Rubus rolfei
Rubus tricolor
Rumex sanguineus var.
   sanguineus
Ruschia pulvinaris
Sagina subulata*
Salvia officinalis*
Sanguinaria canadensis*
Santolina spp.*
Saponaria ocymoides*
Sarcoccoca hookeriana*
Satureja douglasii
Saxifraga spp.*
Scleranthus uniflorus
Scutellaria spp.*
Sedum spp.*
Selaginella spp.*
Sempervivum spp.*
Speirantha gardenii*
Stachys spp.*
Stephanandra incisa*
Stylophorum spp.*
Symphoricarpos
   ×chenaultii
Symphyotrichum ericoides
Symphytum grandiflorum
Tanacetum densum subsp.
   amani*
Tellima grandiflora*
Teucrium spp.*
Thymus spp.*
Tiarella cordifolia*
Tolmiea menziesii*
Trachelospermum spp.
Trachystemon orientalis
Vaccinium vitis-idaea
Vancouveria spp.*
Verbena spp.
Veronica spp.*
Vinca spp.*
Viola spp.
Waldsteinia spp.*
Woodwardia spp.*

Ground Covers A–Z

T HIS COMPENDIUM includes the vast majority of ground cover species and their cultivars grown in the temperate gardening world, with an emphasis on North America, but with attention paid to the United Kingdom and continental Europe. The included species are either readily or somewhat available as plants or seed from nurseries or mail-order sources. Some rarer species have been included to encourage their cultivation. If a species offers a large number of cultivars, the most commonly grown selections or those best suited for use as ground covers are included.

ORGANIZATION AND NOMENCLATURE The plants are arranged alphabetically by scientific name. Nomenclature mostly follows the Royal Horticultural Society (RHS) Plant Finder, with additional references made to the Catalogue of Life and various regional floras, including Flora of North America, Euro+Med Plant-Base, Flora of China, and others. Where disagreement exists, the RHS is usually followed, though sometimes a more authoritative source is used. In most cases, the most up-to-date nomenclature is used. Occasionally, though, older nomenclature may be used for clarity, either because the new nomenclature seems not yet fully accepted within plant taxonomy or it is not yet often used in the horticultural world.

COMMON NAMES AND PLANT FAMILY The most frequently used common names for each species are included. Plant family name is included, because knowledge about plant families gives you a structured understanding of the plant world and can offer clues for use in horticulture especially related to morphology, habit, flowering, overall performance, cultural requirements, faunal associations, and other benefits.

ZONE HARDINESS The United States Department of Agriculture (USDA) plant hardiness zones are used. This system classifies geographical regions based on their average minimum winter temperatures, with zone 1 being the coldest zone and zone 13 the warmest. Plant hardiness is designated by the zonal range in which a plant will normally survive the winter. The lower zone in the range designates the coldest temperatures a species can withstand. The upper zone in the range refers to the warmest zone where a species can be successfully grown. Whereas the lowest zone is related to cold hardiness, the upper zone is usually related to heat (and humidity) tolerance and to the needs of the plant for sufficient time in dormancy and vernalization for proper flowering, fruiting, and overall growth. The cold hardiness ratings of species in temperate horticulture are fairly reliable, but some disagreement is common and some species may still prove hardier than the current general consensus. The main hardiness range of a species is provided. If it may possibly be hardier in a zone outside this range, the zone value is displayed in parentheses.

ORIGIN AND HABITAT Geographic origin and native habitat are included if this information is available. This information summarizes the climatic and habitat conditions to which a species is adapted and informs how it can be successfully cultivated in a garden setting.

GENUS DESCRIPTION A general description of each genus is provided, often with discussion of its use and value as a ground cover, plus other pertinent information.

CULTURE/CARE The general culture and care of the genus is included, beginning with general growing and maintenance instructions, followed by any species or cultivar specific instructions.

USES The locations and best uses for the particular ground cover, any additional benefits such as pollinator value, and tolerances are described.

PROPAGATION The general methods of propagation are included, but detailed instructions are not provided. Diverse books and online resources can provide detailed instructions on propagation.

SPECIES AND HORTICULTURAL SELECTIONS The discussion of each genus is followed by relevant species and horticultural selections that include subspecies, varieties, forms, cultivars, and strains. For cultivars with trademark names, the trademark name follows the cultivar name. In some cases, all of the relevant and reasonably available plants are included. For genera with many species and/or cultivars, the most relevant plants are discussed, while others may be listed in the genus or species description. Some very rare or mostly unavailable taxa may not be included. If a description includes the acronym "AGM," this indicates that the plant has earned the Award of Garden Merit from the Royal Horticultural Society. The AGM is granted based on a plant's reliable performance in the garden, including its stability in form and color, pest and disease resistance, and other considerations. Some descriptions also include a plant's selection as Perennial Plant of the Year, an annual award granted by the Perennial Plant Association for perennials that satisfy similar criteria.

(ABOVE) *Parthenocissus* sp. and *Lamium galeobdolon* intermingle in a woodland setting.

A

Acaena
ROSACEAE

This peculiar, mainly Southern Hemisphere, rose family genus forms low-growing, rhizomatous or stoloniferous, spreading mats of small, pinnate, ferny textured, olive-green, glaucous, or reddish leaves topped with ½–1 in. (1.3–2.5 cm) spheres of apetalous, white, wind-pollinated summer flowers that become long-lasting, prickly, burrlike seed heads, aging to pink, copper, burgundy, or red. Evergreen in milder climates but often deciduous in colder zones. All of horticultural merit hail from New Zealand.

CULTURE/CARE Full sun to part shade in well-drained, moist to dry soils of average to low fertility. More light encourages tighter, denser growth and bolder foliage color. Drought tolerant once established. Easy to grow and adaptable. Clip the leading edge to control spread.

USES Indefinitely spreading for border edges, between paving stones, in rock gardens, and tumbling from walls and planters. Use fast-spreading stoloniferous species for larger areas and rhizomatous species for controlled mats, especially between pavers. Some species have barbed burrs that can adhere to shoes, socks, and pet fur. Tolerant of light to moderate foot traffic. Deer resistant.

PROPAGATION Division of clumps or rooted stems, softwood cuttings, seed

Acaena buchananii
NEW ZEALAND BURR

Zones (5)6–9
Lowland to montane riverbeds and short, dry tussock grassland on the South Island, New Zealand, east of the Main Divide.
Tight, evergreen, strong-growing, rhizomatous mats 2 in. (5 cm) tall with glaucous, gray-green or milky green leaves ½–4 in. (1.3–10 cm) long, each with 11–13 toothed leaflets. Burrs age through yellow and crimson to reddish brown on 2–4 in. (5–10 cm) stems.

Acaena caesiiglauca
GLAUCOUS BIDIBID,
SILVER-LEAFED NEW ZEALAND BURR

Zones 5–9
Montane and subalpine tussock grassland and open ground on the South Island, New Zealand.
Stoloniferous, evergreen, blue-gray to bluish green, slower growing mats, 2 in. (5 cm) tall, with leaves ¾–4 in. (2–10 cm) long, each with 7–11 toothed leaflets. Red-brown burrs on stems 2–4 in. (5–10 cm) tall.

Acaena inermis
SPINELESS BIDIBID, BLUE MOUNTAIN BIDIBID

Zones 5–9
Montane riverbeds and tussock grasslands throughout New Zealand.
Rhizomatous, olive-green, blue-gray, or purplish brown evergreen mats 2 in. (5 cm) tall, with leaves 1–2 in. (2.5–5 cm) long, each with 11–15 toothed leaflets. Red-brown, nonbarbed burrs on 2–4 in. (5–10 cm) stems.

'Purpurea': amethyst to warm purple foliage, darkest in full sun

Acaena microphylla
SCARLET BIDIBID, ROSY-SPINED NEW ZEALAND BURR

Zones 5–9
Grasslands, riverbeds, and herbfields throughout New Zealand, especially the Volcanic Plateau on the North Island.
Rhizomatous, bluish to bronzy to olive-green, evergreen mats 1–2 in. (2.5–5 cm) tall, with small, ¼–1¼ in. (6–30 mm) long leaves, each with 9–15 toothed leaflets and boldly contrasting, glowing, rosy red to scarlet burrs on 2 in. (5 cm) stems. AGM

'Kupferteppich' (syn. 'Copper Carpet'): deeper red-brown foliage, especially in full sun

Acaena novae-zelandiae
NEW ZEALAND BURR, RED BIDIBID

Zones 5–9
Lowland to montane grasslands and open places in New Zealand, Southeast Australia, and New Guinea. Invasive in the United Kingdom, California, Oregon, and Hawaii.

Acaena inermis 'Purpurea'

Vigorous, stoloniferous, shiny, evergreen mats 3–4 in. (7.5–10 cm) tall, with 2–4 in. (5–10 cm) long leaves, each with 9–15 toothed leaflets. Red burrs with barbed spines on 4–6 in. (10–15 cm) stems.

Acaena saccaticupula
NEW ZEALAND BURR, BIDIBID

Zones (5)6–9

Montane to alpine herbfields and stony ground on the South Island, New Zealand.

Stoloniferous, evergreen, vigorous, glaucous mats 1–2 in. (2.5–5 cm) tall, with leaves up to 2 in. (5 cm) long, each with 11–15 toothed leaflets. Red burrs with barbed spines on 2–4 in. (5–10 cm) stems.

'Blue Haze': powder-blue foliage, mahogany-red burrs

Achillea
Asteraceae

Achillea millefolium and its cultivars and the taller *A. filipendulina* are long-beloved garden plants sporting colorful, flat-topped heads of tiny flowers on upright stems. Named for the Greek hero Achilles, who used yarrow to heal the wounds of his soldiers, they can make effective taller ground covers with spreading mats of aromatic, ferny foliage. Lesser known options include *A. clavennae*, *A. nobilis* subsp. *neilreichii*, *A. umbellata*, *A.* ×*huteri*, and *A.* ×*kellereri*.

CULTURE/CARE Easy to grow in full sun in free-draining soils of average to low moisture and fertility. Tolerant of alkaline soils and drought. Stems can flop over with excessive moisture and fertility. Shear after flowering to encourage rebloom. Divide and replant if vigor decreases. *Achillea millefolium* is tolerant of various soils, including dry to moist locations and sandy, clay, and salt-influenced sites.

USES Small to medium-sized applications as an edger for borders and walkways and in rock gardens. Mass plant to achieve faster coverage. Some are tolerant of foot traffic. The straight species *A. millefolium*, which usually spreads well rhizomatously, can be planted or seeded as a lawn alternative. Deer and rabbit resistant. Attractive to pollinators, especially bees and butterflies.

PROPAGATION Division in early spring or fall, cuttings in summer, seed

Acaena saccaticupula 'Blue Haze'

Achillea ageratifolia

GREEK YARROW

Zones 3–9

Mountains of the Balkan Peninsula on limestone cliffs and outcrops.

Low-growing, aromatic, silver, toothed to nearly smooth-edged foliage forms low mats 18 in. (45 cm) or more wide. Solitary (rather than clustered) summer flowers resemble daisies, with bright white petals and yellowish centers on 4–10 in. (10–25 cm) tall stems. Evergreen in milder climates. AGM

Achillea clypeolata

YELLOW YARROW

Zones 4–8

Endemic to Bulgaria and Romania in grasslands, pastures, scrubland, and hillsides.

Semi-evergreen, frosty silver to gray-green, ferny foliage forming small mats or clumps. Bright yellow flowers in flat-topped corymbs 18–26 in. (45–66 cm) tall in summer. Similar to but shorter than A. *filipendulina*. Best in dry borders, rock gardens, and containers.

'Anblo' Anthea: hybrid with A. 'Moonshine' with similar foliage, a more upright habit, paler yellow flowers, and a nonwoody base

'Moonshine': canary-yellow, flat-topped clusters on silver stems 12–24 in. (30–60 cm) tall over silver foliage; likely a chance hybrid of A. *clypeolata* and A. 'Taygetea', itself a hybrid of A. *millefolium* and A. *clypeolata*, zones 3–9

Achillea millefolium

COMMON YARROW, MILFOIL

Zones (2)3–10

North America and Eurasia in pastures and meadows, roadsides, streamsides, woodlands, waste ground, and a variety of wet and dry soil types, including saline soils, from sea level to high elevations.

Rhizomatous (sometimes stoloniferous), evergreen to herbaceous perennial with finely dissected, fern-like, green to gray-green, aromatic foliage forming ever-expanding (some may say aggressive) textural mats. Tiny, white, daisy-like flowers are borne in 2–3 in. (5–7.5 cm) wide, flat-topped inflorescences, 12–24 in. (30–60 cm) tall, from early summer until late summer or fall. The species is useful as a lawn alternative, whereas selected forms and hybrids with clumping or less spreading habits, a wide range of flower colors, and more strongly upright flower stalks are used in gardens or for smaller ground cover applications.

This list includes common spreading selections of A. *millefolium*, hybrids involving it, or cultivars presumed to be derived from it. Clumpers are not listed but could be mass-planted to achieve a closed cover.

'Cassis': cherry red flowers, 18–28 in. (45–71 cm) tall

'Cerise Queen': cherry-pink to magenta flowers, 18–30 in. (45–75 cm) tall

Colorado Mix/Group: hybrid seed blend offering red, pink, yellow, white, and apricot flower colors, 18–24 in. (45–60 cm) tall

'Fanal' (syn. 'The Beacon'): hybrid, bright red flowers, 18–28 in. (45–71 cm) tall

'Feuerland' (syn. 'Fire Land'): hybrid, bright red flowers, 24–36 in. (60–90 cm) tall

'Fire King': deep red to magenta-red flowers, 18–30 in. (45–75 cm) tall

'Forncett Fletton' (Forncett Series): hybrid, salmon-red to salmon-orange flowers, 18–24 in. (45–60 cm) tall

Galaxy Series: hybrids with A. 'Taygetea'

'Apfelblüte' (syn. 'Appleblossom'): lavender-pink flowers, 18–30 in. (45–75 cm) tall

'Heidi': hybrid, cherry-pink to pale pink flowers, 18–24 in. (45–60 cm) tall, AGM

'Lachsschönheit' (syn. 'Salmon Beauty'): salmon-pink to peach flowers, 24–36 in. (60–90 cm) tall

'Lilac Beauty': lavender-pink flowers, 18–24 in (45–60 cm) tall

'Oertel's Rose': vivid rose-pink flowers, 12–24 in. (30–60 cm) tall

'Paprika': red flowers, 18–30 in. (45–75 cm) tall

'Red Beauty': crimson-red flowers, 18–28 in. (45–71 cm) tall

'Red Velvet': red to rose-red flowers, slow to fade, 18–24 in. (45–60 cm) tall

'Snow Sport': white flowers, 18–24 in. (45–60 cm) tall

Song Siren Series: strong stems, slow-fading flowers

'Angie': deep rose-pink flowers, 22 in. (56 cm) tall

'Laura': strawberry-red flowers, 16 in. (40 cm) tall

'Layla': deep pink flowers, 22 in. (56 cm) tall

'Little Susie': rose-pink flowers, 16 in. (40 cm) tall

'Pretty Woman': red flowers, 24 in. (60 cm) tall

Achillea 'Moonshine'

Achillea millefolium 'Cerise Queen'

Achillea ptarmica 'Perry's White'

Summer Pastels Group (syn. 'Summer Pastels'): spreading seed strain 12–24 in. (30–60 cm) tall, with cream, yellow, pink, salmon, mauve, and red flowers

'Summerwine': hybrid, crimson-red flowers, 18–24 in. (45–60 cm) tall

'Terracotta': hybrid, orange to orange-yellow flowers, 24–36 in. (60–90 cm) tall

'Walther Funcke': hybrid, fiery red to orange flowers, strong stems, 16–24 in. (40–60 cm) tall

'Wesersandstein' (syn. 'Weser River Sandstone'): hybrid, salmon to pink flowers, 18–24 in. (45–60 cm) or more tall

'White Beauty': white flowers, 18–24 in. (45–60 cm) tall

Achillea ptarmica
SNEEZEWORT YARROW, SNEEZEWEED

Zones 3–9

Meadows, ditches, banks, fields, shores, and waste places throughout Europe (excluding the Mediterranean) east to Siberia and Western Asia.

A vigorous, old-fashioned perennial with loose clusters of white, buttonlike flowers with yellowish centers resembling daisies, on stems 24–36 in. (60–90 cm) tall from early to late summer. Dark green, finely serrated, aromatic leaves are held in mounds or spreading clumps. Double-flowered and dwarf forms are the most commonly grown.

'Angel's Breath': double flowers, 18–24 in. (45–60 cm) tall

'Ballerina': double flowers, 12–18 in. (30–45 cm) tall

'Double Diamond': seed strain of double flowers on stems 24–32 in. (60–80 cm) tall

'Nana Compacta': single flowers on bushy, compact plants, 10–12 in. (25–30 cm) tall

The Pearl Group: variable seed strain with semidouble to double flowers on stems 24 in. (60 cm) tall

> 'Boule de Neige': clonal selection with double flowers, 18–24 in. (45–60cm) tall

> 'The Pearl': clonal selection from the seed strain with semidouble to double flowers on stems 24 in. (60 cm) tall

'Perry's White': double flowers on stems 32–40 in. (80–100 cm) tall

'Peter Cottontail': larger flowers, good habit, 18–24 in. (45–60 cm) tall

Achillea tomentosa

WOOLLY YARROW, DWARF YARROW

Zones 2–10

Arid, stony slopes, prairies, meadows, and pastures in the hills and mountains of Southern Europe and Western Asia.

A dwarf species to 6–8 in. (15–20 cm) tall when in flower over a tight, low-growing, soft-textured mat, to 18 in. (45 cm) or more wide, of gray-green, aromatic, fuzzy leaves. Golden yellow flowers. Extremely drought tolerant. Evergreen in milder climates. Tolerant of occasional foot traffic. AGM

'Aurea' (syn. 'Maynard's Gold'): vigorous selection with large heads of lemon-yellow flowers

Golden Fleece: uniform, compact seed strain

'Goldie': shorter and earlier to bloom than 'Aurea'

'Lemon': lemon-yellow flowers

A. ×lewisii 'King Edward': drought-tolerant hybrid with A. clavennae, with gray-green, semi-evergreen foliage in low, spreading mats, 1–2 in. (2.5–5 cm) tall, with primrose-yellow flowers on short stems, 3–6 in. (7.5–15 cm) tall, zones 3–8, AGM

Achlys triphylla

VANILLA LEAF, DEER FOOT

Berberidaceae

Zones 7–9

Mesic to moist coniferous mountain forests and shaded streambanks from low elevations up to 5000 ft. (1500 m), from British Columbia to Northern California.

An unusual, herbaceous, barberry relative, the midgreen, palmately divided, tripartite leaves resemble trios of scalloped butterfly wings, on thin stems from branching rhizomes. Flowering stems also originate from the rhizome, rising through the foliage in mid- to late spring with short, white, bottlebrush-like flowers, 1–2 in. (2.5–5 cm) long, of showy stamens. Seeds form within mahogany-colored follicles. Grows 12–18 in. (30–45 cm) tall, spreading indefinitely. Dried leaves smell like vanilla and were hung in doorways by native peoples as an insect repellent. Deer resistant.

CULTURE/CARE Quickly forms colonies in full to part shade and rich, evenly moist soils. Colonies become denser over time as rhizomes crisscross into an underground network.

Achillea tomentosa 'Aurea'

Achlys triphylla in the wild on Vancouver Island, BC

USES Small to medium-sized areas in shade and woodland gardens, along pathways, and at the base of shrubs and trees. Not tolerant of foot traffic.

PROPAGATION Division of dormant rhizomes, seed

Acinos alpinus
ALPINE ROCK THYME, ALPINE CALAMINT

Lamiaceae

Zones 4–9

Dry, sunny habitats including cliffs and rocky places in the mountains of Central and Southern Europe and Northern Africa.

A small genus of mounding subshrubs forming low, aromatic cushions with small, tubular flowers. Small, elliptic to rounded, sometimes toothed and hairy, mid- to deep-green leaves, evergreen in milder zones, on mounds 4–6 in. (10–15 cm) tall and 8–12 in. (20–30 cm) wide. Flowers are held on short, spikelike whorls over a long period from early to late summer. They are purple to lavender-pink and sometimes hairy with white and purple markings on the lower lips. Recently moved into genus *Clinopodium*, a change not yet adopted in horticulture.

CULTURE/CARE Easy to grow in average to dry, rocky soils in full sun. Drought tolerant once established. Good winter drainage is important for longevity.

USES Small applications as a border edger, along pathways, in rock gardens, and overhanging walls and troughs. Mass plant to achieve a solid cover for larger areas. Slow to moderate growth rate. Not tolerant of foot traffic. Attractive to pollinators, especially bees and butterflies.

PROPAGATION Seed, cuttings

Acorus gramineus
GRASSY LEAVED SWEET FLAG, JAPANESE SWEET FLAG

Acoraceae

Zones 5–9

Shaded to open habitats including dense forests, moist and rocky streambanks, and meadows below 8500 ft. (2590 m) from northeast India and Southeast Asia, through China, Japan, and Korea to eastern Siberia.

Thought to be possibly the oldest living lineage of monocotyledons, these rhizomatous plants of wet places have attractive fans of narrow, swordlike or

Acorus gramineus 'Ogon', Gibbs Gardens, Georgia

grasslike foliage. Three species are used in horticulture: *A. gramineus*, and the much taller American and Asian species, *A. americanus* and *A. calamus*, which can be useful as tall ground covers on a landscape scale in wet places, where their vigorous rhizomes and dense foliage can retain soil and outcompete weeds.

Acorus gramineus forms dense, grasslike, spreading, evergreen to semi-evergreen clumps of narrow, arching, rich green foliage in tightly packed fans more reminiscent of irises than grasses or sedges, from slowly spreading rhizomes at or just below the soil surface. Leaves are narrow, ¼ in. (6 mm) wide and 6–12 in. (15–30 cm) or more long. Rhizomes, and sometimes foliage, can emit the scent of citrus, licorice, and baking spices when crushed. Inconspicuous flower spikes are sometimes produced in midspring with 3 in. (7.5 cm) long spadices densely packed with tiny greenish yellow florets that can form tiny, fleshy, yellowish berries aging to brownish red.

CULTURE/CARE Easily grown in full sun to light shade in average, moist, wet, and even submerged soils. Prefers rich, acidic to neutral conditions. In hot summer climates, provide more moisture or shade to maintain lush foliage. After winter, lightly trim browned tips or cut plants to the ground just before spring growth begins. The outward-spreading, sometimes partially prostrate or arching fans may leave bald spots in the middle of old clumps. If unsightly, dig up the clump, divide, and replant or interplant with a trailing ground cover.

USES Spreads slowly but indefinitely into spiky mats for small to medium-sized applications as a border edger, along pathways, at the edges of ponds and streams, and in containers. Not tolerant of foot traffic.

Dwarf cultivars are useful between stepping stones and in miniature gardens. Deer resistant.

PROPAGATION Division, seed

'Hakuro-nishiki': dwarf, 2–6 in. (5–15 cm) tall with golden foliage flecked with green

'Licorice': green foliage and rhizomes smell of sweet anise when crushed

'Masamune': old Japanese dwarf form of 'Variegatus', 6 in. (15 cm) tall

'Minimus Aureus': miniature or dwarf golden sweet flag, with striking, chartreuse to gold, narrow foliage, 2–6 in. (5–15 cm) long

'Oborozuki': confused in the trade; many professionals see no difference from 'Ogon', while others describe 'Oborozuki' as more gold with less or no green and slightly shorter with narrower leaves

'Ogon': most popular cultivar with gold and green–striped foliage producing an overall gold appearance

var. *pusillus*: miniature or dwarf sweet flag with rich green, very narrow foliage, 2–6 in. (5–15 cm) long

'Variegatus': green leaf blades with one side variegated white to creamy white

Adiantum
Pteridaceae

Among the most beautiful, delicate, and unique ferns in temperate horticulture, *Adiantum* species have deep brown, dark purple, or black stems; fronds that are either lance-shaped, ovate, or fan-shaped; and pinnae (leaflets) that are round, oblong, or fan-shaped and thin like green rice paper. With their palmate frond structure, *A. aleuticum* and *A. pedatum* are the classics of the genus, but other species also make effective and distinctive ground covers.

CULTURE/CARE Part to full shade or morning sun in rich, evenly moist soil. Tolerant of more sun with good moisture. *Adiantum aleuticum* is best grown in gardens within its natural range along the West Coast of North America, while the similar *A. pedatum* is best in the east. *Adiantum capillus-veneris* prefers neutral to alkaline soils. The less hardy *A. hispidulum* is tolerant of part sun and drier conditions but should be planted in a more protected microclimate, and *A. venustum* is tolerant of periods of drought and is evergreen in milder climates. Shear to the ground after winter to refresh.

USES Small to medium-sized applications in woodland and shade gardens, along pathways, atop walls, along stairways, and in living walls. *Adiantum aleuticum* and *A. pedatum* are effective on slopes. Both *A. capillus-veneris* and *A. venustum* can be planted around larger perennials, ferns, shrubs, or trees, in shaded rock gardens or as a border edger. *Adiantum hispidulum* can be grown outdoors in mild climates or in containers at the base of house plants and brought indoors for winter. All spread at a slow rate. None are tolerant of foot traffic. Deer and rabbit resistant.

PROPAGATION Division, spores

Adiantum aleuticum
WESTERN MAIDENHAIR FERN,
ALEUTIAN MAIDENHAIR FERN

Zones (3)4–9

Wooded ravines and moist cliffs, shaded banks, talus slopes, serpentine barrens, and coastal headlands in soil or as a lithophyte or epiphyte from sea level to 10,500 ft. (3200 m), from Alaska to California, mostly west of the Coast, Cascade, and Sierra Nevada mountains, but with disjunct populations at elevation in wet rock fissures in most of the western United States and on serpentine outcrops in eastern North America, from Newfoundland to Pennsylvania.

Western maidenhair and its close relative the northern maidenhair fern (*A. pedatum*) are two of the most distinctive of all temperate ferns. Clumping or very slowly creeping herbaceous mounds of thin black stems hold light green, palmate fronds in a fan or funnel shape. *Adiantum aleuticum* typically forms clumps 12–24 in. (30–60 cm) tall and 24 in. (60 cm) wide but can grow up to 3 ft. (1 m) tall in rich, moist conditions. Fronds are normally arching but are more upright in increasing light. Previously treated as a variety or subspecies of *A. pedatum*, but now considered a separate species based on taxonomic features of little interest to gardeners. *Adiantum aleuticum* can be large, with fronds that are arching to stiffly erect, whereas *A. pedatum* fronds are usually lax or arching. AGM

'Imbricatum': dwarf, 6–12 in. (15–30 cm) tall, with overlapping pinnae possibly with a bluish cast and more erect habit in some conditions

'Japonicum': new fronds emerge pinkish red to burgundy, turning green

Adiantum aleuticum 'Subpumilum'

'Miss Sharples': more compact with lighter green to yellow-green foliage and broader pinnae

'Subpumilum': compact, dwarf, 4–6 in. (10–15 cm) tall, with close-packed pinnae, AGM

different cultivars have been selected, including 'Alabama Lace', 'Bermuda Run', 'Falling Waters', 'Fan Dance', 'Mt. Ida', and 'Rock Springs', though none of these is widely available.

Adiantum capillus-veneris
SOUTHERN MAIDENHAIR FERN,
BLACK MAIDENHAIR FERN

Zones 7–10

Moist calcareous cliffs, banks, and ledges along streams and rivers. Cosmopolitan on most continents, occurring in North America, across the southern half of the United States, disjunct in the Black Hills of South Dakota and at Fairmont Hot Springs, British Columbia.

Delicate, lacy, herbaceous fern with plum-black, wiry stems and branched, triangular fronds of elegant, light green, fan-shaped pinnules. Plants spread slowly by creeping rhizomes, eventually forming large, textured mats of billowing foliage 6–18 in. (15–45 cm) tall.

Owing to its extensive range, *A. capillus-veneris* shows much morphological variation from which

Adiantum hispidulum
ROSY MAIDENHAIR FERN,
ROUGH MAIDENHAIR FERN

Zones (7)8–11

Among rocks in open or shaded areas, along rivers and streambanks, in rainforests or open forests in Africa, Southeast Asia, Australia, New Zealand, and the Pacific Islands including Hawaii.

Resembles the northern and western maidenhair ferns, but smaller, 12–18 in. (30–45 cm) tall, with beautiful, shiny, pink new growth. Herbaceous. Can spread slowly by rhizomes. Less hardy than other species. Slow to emerge in a cool spring.

'Bronze Venus': deep pink to bronzy new growth

'Mt. Halealkala': possibly hardier selection from 5000 ft. (1500 m), near the top of Maui's Mount Halealkala volcano

Adiantum ×mairisii

MAIRIS'S MAIDENHAIR FERN

Zones (6)7–10

Garden origin.

Forms vigorous, rounded, slowly spreading, evergreen mounds, 12–18 in. (30–45 cm) tall and 36 in. (90 cm) wide, of light green, delicate foliage that looks like clouds of tiny green leaves, held on black stems. Slow to emerge in spring. May be herbaceous in colder zones but will hold foliage into late autumn. This sterile hybrid of A. capillus-veneris and an unknown, likely tropical, maidenhair (A. aethiopicum, A. cuneatum, or A. raddianum) was discovered at the height of Pteridomania (the Victorian era fern craze) at Britain's Mairis and Company nursery sometime before 1885. Surprisingly hardier, more vigorous, taller, and more erect than either of its parents but with smaller pinnules. AGM

Adiantum pedatum

NORTHERN MAIDENHAIR FERN,
FIVE-FINGERED FERN

Zones (2)3–8

Rich, deciduous woodland, often on humus-covered talus slopes and moist, limestone-derived soils in eastern North America, from Nova Scotia to Minnesota south to Louisiana, from sea level to 2300 ft. (700 m).

Quite similar to its close relative, A. aleuticum, but hardier, possibly to zone 2. Forms gorgeous clumps of thin, black stems topped with arching to lax, light green, palmate fronds. Typically grows 12–24 in. (30–60 cm) tall and wide, sometimes larger.

Adiantum ×tracyi

TRACY'S MAIDENHAIR FERN

Zones (6)7–10

Shady banks, along rivers, and in moist, shady habitats in Northern California at 1000–1500 ft. (300–455 m).

Naturally occurring sterile hybrid between winter-herbaceous A. aleuticum and summer-herbaceous California maidenhair (A. jordanii), found where the species' ranges overlap. Its form and hardiness are intermediate; however, unlike either parent, it is evergreen except perhaps in colder zones, reaching 12–24 in. (30–60 cm) tall and wide and spreading slowly by underground rhizomes.

Adiantum pedatum

Adiantum venustum

Adiantum venustum

HIMALAYAN MAIDENHAIR FERN

Zones 5–9

Rock crevices and mountain slopes at 6600–9600 ft. (2000–2925 m) in the Himalayas.

The best maidenhair for use as a ground cover, *A. venustum* is a gorgeous evergreen creeping fern, spreading slowly but indefinitely into dense, light green, textural carpets 4–6 in. (10–15 cm) tall. Unlike *A. capillus-veneris*, which produces a billowy mass of maidenhair foliage, the pinnules lay flat and in line with the triangular blades, which layer one atop the other. Tiny new fiddleheads are tinged in a rich salmon-rose color in spring, unfurling to copper-yellow and then to light green on black stems. Semi-evergreen to herbaceous in colder climates. AGM

Aegopodium podagraria

BISHOP'S WEED, GOUTWEED

Apiaceae

Zones 3–9

Broadleaf forests, streambanks, forest margins, pastures, gardens, parks, and waste places from Europe to Siberia.

Much scorned by gardeners and professionals alike for its vigorous, frequently overly aggressive nature, bishop's weed can be a useful ground cover where its spread can be controlled by hardscape or competition from other plants. If you're attracted to bishop's weed, just be sure in your heart that you want it. You will be together till (your) death do you part! This herbaceous perennial has long, vigorous, white, branching rhizomes spreading indefinitely into masses of attractive mid- to dark green foliage on upright stems, 6–24 in. (15–60 cm) tall. Leaves are twice-divided into threes, resembling the foliage of ash or elderberry. Domed inflorescences of white flowers resembling Queen Anne's lace in early summer on 12–24 in. (30–60 cm) tall stems.

CULTURE/CARE Moist, well-drained soils in sun to part shade and adaptable to a wide range of soil types including infertile or compacted sites. Spreads rapidly in good conditions, more slowly in drier or infertile soils. Resilient to dry periods but may wilt at midday. 'Variegatum' may scorch in full sun during prolonged droughts. Mow to the ground to encourage a quick reflush if needed, especially after or to avoid flowering.

USES Always plant where its spread can be controlled. 'Variegatum' is useful for illuminating shaded areas beneath trees and shrubs. Though its name can inspire fear and loathing, bishop's weed is useful in

Aegopodium podagraria 'Variegatum'

deep shade and dry shade. Not tolerant of foot traffic but will recover quickly from occasional disturbance. Potentially invasive in some regions. Deer and rabbit resistant.

PROPAGATION Division, seed

'Variegatum': slower growing and shorter, to 6–10 in. (15–25 cm) tall; a better-behaved alternative for small applications is *Peucedanum ostruthium* 'Daphnis'

Ajania pacifica
SILVER AND GOLD, PACIFIC CHRYSANTHEMUM

Asteraceae

Zones 5–9
Endemic to seashore habitats of Honshu, Japan.
Unusual, spreading, rhizomatous perennial or subshrub sure to excite foliage lovers with lobed, egg-shaped, 2 in. (5 cm) long leaves, green to silver-green above and silver-fuzzy beneath, the fuzz of the undersides extending beyond the leaf margin to outline each leaf with a distinctive silver edge. Plants form attractive, dense mounds, 12–24 in. (30–60 cm) tall and 24–36 in. (60–90 cm) wide. Clusters of rayless yellow button flowers appear in mid- to late fall though may not form in cool summer climates. Evergreen in milder climates, herbaceous in colder zones with foliage turning to reds, oranges, and yellows prior to dormancy. Has been crossed with *Chrysanthemum* species to create "petaled" cultivars, including 'Pink Ice' and 'Snow Dome', though these are uncommon.

CULTURE/CARE Full sun to part shade in average to moist soils with good drainage. Tolerant of high heat, humidity, and some drought once established. Avoid full sun in hot summer climates. Pinch stem tips in late spring to maintain compactness, or, where plants are evergreen, shear to 3 in. (7.5 cm) in early spring. Provide winter mulch in zone 5.

USES Mass plant to achieve a closed, mounded cover for small to large applications, spreading at a moderate rate. Not tolerant of foot traffic. Deer resistant.

PROPAGATION Division, stem and root cuttings, seed

Ajuga
Lamiaceae

Ajuga is among the most popular and useful of all perennial ground covers thanks to its hardiness

Ajania pacifica

and vigor, its versatility in the garden, and its many horticultural forms—especially from *A. reptans*. Three mainly European species, *A. genevensis*, *A. pyramidalis*, and *A. reptans*, make useful low-growing ground covers with their stoloniferous and/or rhizomatous growth habits. In spring they are covered in short, vertical spikes of blue, blue-purple, pink, or white flowers.

CULTURE/CARE Easy to grow in well-drained, evenly moist soils in full sun to shade. Tolerant of drier conditions in cooler climates or shade. Protect from full sun in hot summer climates or provide more moisture to improve sun tolerance. Burgundy foliage is more intense in younger leaves and in higher light. After flowering, the spikes can be removed, mowed, or left to break down.

USES Use *A. reptans* for small to large applications as border edgers, along pathways, between pavers or stepping stones, and hanging over walls. The non-stoloniferous *A. genevensis* and *A. pyramidalis* can be used for small applications, where their more compact habits are useful as edgers, between stonework, and in rock gardens. Tolerant of light to moderate foot traffic. Deer and rabbit resistant. Attractive to pollinators, especially bees, butterflies, and hummingbirds.

PROPAGATION Division, separation of stoloniferous plantlets

Ajuga genevensis
GENEVA BUGLEWEED, BLUE BUGLEWEED

Zones 3–10

Edges of dry woods, in thickets, and in grasslands in temperate Eurasia from southern Sweden to Central Europe east to the Caucasus.

Infrequently grown but much appreciated by those who know it, with gentian blue flowers on spikes up to 12 in. (30 cm) tall, from light green to midgreen, lobed or toothed, somewhat coarse-textured foliage, forming dense mats with time. Plants are rhizomatous, not stoloniferous, expanding much more slowly than *A. reptans*.

Pink forms such as 'Pink Beauty' and 'Tottenham' and white forms such as 'Alba' are rarely encountered.

Ajuga pyramidalis
PYRAMIDAL BUGLEWEED, NORTHERN BUGLEWEED

Zones 3–9

Dry or rich meadows, pasture and grazing land, forest margins, and woods across most of Europe.

Uncommon except for its few cultivars that do not much resemble the wild species, with pyramid-shaped inflorescences with large, purple-tinted, hairy bracts that become smaller and taper up the stem. Leaves are also hairy. Plants are not stoloniferous, bulking up slowly from short rhizomes. Various "crisped" cultivars exist uncommonly in cultivation with some confusion in naming.

'Metallica Crispa' (syn. 'Mini Crispa Red'): tightly growing miniature, with heavily crinkled, shiny, green and burgundy foliage

Ajuga reptans
CARPET BUGLEWEED, COMMON BUGLEWEED

Zones 3–9

Damp fields and woods from Northern and Central Europe south to North Africa and east to Asia Minor.

Unendingly useful, small, mat-forming rosettes, 2 in. (5 cm) tall and spreading indefinitely, with green to burgundy, scalloped, thumb print–sized leaves, 1–2 in (2.5–5 cm) long and up to 1 in. (2.5 cm) wide, on fast-spreading plants expanding by short underground rhizomes and 4–12 in. (10–30 cm) long, aboveground runners producing plantlets at their tips. Blooms in early to midspring, with 4–6 in. (10–15 cm) tall spikes of tubular, lightly fragrant flowers in shades of purple, blue, pink, or white, subtended by leafy bracts. Plants are semi-evergreen to evergreen in milder climates, herbaceous in colder climates. Can be overly aggressive in some regions, spreading vegetatively or by seed through borders or into lawns, a phenomenon referred to as "buglelawn."

Some burgundy cultivars may be confused in horticulture.

'Alba': white flowers, green leaves

'Arctic Fox': variable foliage with gray-green to cream centers with dark green edges

'Atropurpurea': vigorous cultivar with green leaves flushed coppery bronze

'Binblasca' Black Scallop: lustrous, puckered, burgundy-black foliage with highly scalloped margins, a tight habit, and violet-blue flowers

Ajuga reptans 'Binblasca' Black Scallop

Ajuga reptans 'Chocolate Chip'

Ajuga reptans 'Dixie Chip'

Ajuga reptans 'Burgundy Glow'

Ajuga reptans 'Golden Glow'

'Binsugplu' Sugar Plum: gray-green and cream-colored leaves flushed with plum-purple when young

'Blueberry Muffin': vigorous with small, thick, smooth-margined leaves emerging burgundy flushed and aging to green, with densely packed, purple-blue flower spikes

'Braunherz': dark reddish bronze leaves highlighted with coppery hues

'Bronze Beauty': purple-bronze, shiny foliage

'Burgundy Glow': less vigorous grower with tricolor foliage of white and gray-green, flushed pink when young

'Catlin's Giant': large-growing and vigorous with metallic, bronzy, puckered foliage and flower spikes up to 8 in. (20 cm) tall, AGM

'Dixie Chip': sport of 'Valfredda', with variegated white, green, and pink foliage

Feathered Friends Series

> 'Cordial Canary': gold version of 'Valfredda'
>
> 'Fancy Finch': narrow leaves in shades of light green, gold, and orange-bronze
>
> 'Fierce Falcon': shiny, puckered, burgundy leaves
>
> 'Noble Nightingale': narrow burgundy leaves
>
> 'Parrot Paradise': gold, orange, and bronze leaves
>
> 'Petite Parakeet': small golden leaves with orange veins
>
> 'Tropical Toucan': gold leaves

'Golden Glow': slower growing, with green leaves edged in creamy yellow, flushed burgundy and pink when young

'Mahogany': young dark burgundy leaves age to a rich reddish burgundy

'Multicolor': bronze and green foliage with irregular margins of creams and pinks

'Pink Lightning': crinkled, mint-green foliage edged with white, with pink flowers

'Purple Brocade': purple to maroon foliage with deeply furrowed leaf veins

'Silver Beauty': sage-green foliage with irregular white margins

'Silver Queen': gray-green foliage variably edged with cream, pink flushed in cool weather

'Valfredda' Chocolate Chip: dwarf cultivar with small, linear, smooth-margined burgundy leaves

'Variegata': white to creamy yellow leaf edges flushed pink when young, with blue flowers

Akebia
Lardizabalaceae

Fairly hardy vines from Asia with attractive, compound foliage, vanilla- or chocolate-scented flowers, and weird, edible fruit. Without vertical support, they will grow as vigorous ground covers. In addition to the species treated here, the rare, evergreen, blue-fruited *A. longeracemosa* and its cultivar 'Victor's Secret' could also be useful.

CULTURE/CARE Easy to grow in average to moist soils in full sun to part shade. Tolerant of periods of drought and full shade. Good pollination and fruit production may require full sun and the presence of two different clones. Can be pruned hard to control spread. Can be invasive in some regions, including parts of the eastern United States, where its shade tolerance allows for dense growth across the forest floor.

USES Medium-sized to large applications including on slopes for erosion control and to cover unsightly landscape features. Not tolerant of foot traffic. Deer resistant.

PROPAGATION Cuttings, layering, seed

Akebia quinata
CHOCOLATE VINE, FIVE-LEAF AKEBIA

Zones 4–8

Forest margins, especially along streams, and in scrub on mountain slopes from low to moderate elevations in China, Korea, and Japan.

Vigorous, deciduous to evergreen, twining, woody vine with leathery, palmately compound leaves of five elliptic to oblong leaflets, 1–3 in. (2.5–7.5 cm) long, green above and bluish beneath. Clusters of small, drooping, deep purple and pink, cupped flowers smell of chocolate and appear in early to midspring with separate male and female flowers on the same raceme. Edible, sausage-shaped, 4 in. (10 cm) long, purple fruit contain small black seeds and a sweet, whitish pulp. Vines can quickly grow 20–40 ft. (6–12 m) long and, used as a ground cover, about 6–12 in. (15–30 cm) tall. A naturally occurring hybrid with *A. trifoliata*, *A.* ×*pentaphylla* also has five-parted leaves.

'Alba': white flowers with pale, dusty purple stamens and white fruit

'Amethyst Glow': UK selection, male flowers have pale pink petals and purple stamens and female flowers are purple

'Cultivar No. 2' Silver Bells: male flowers have white petals and lavender stamens, female flowers are pink to dusty lavender with purple pistils

'Kohin Nishiki': rare variegated form with variable creamy white mottling

'Purple Rose': floriferous with reddish purple flowers

'Shirobana': white flowers with white to nearly white centers

'Variegata': foliage variably white variegated

A. ×*pentaphylla* 'Akebia Hybrid #1' Purple Incense: dark purple hybrid with fragrant flowers and exceptionally large fruit

Akebia trifoliata
THREE-LEAF AKEBIA

Zones 5–8

Forest margins and openings, hillside scrub, and along streams from low to moderately high elevations in China and Japan.

Similar in habit and flowers to *A. quinata* but with less leathery leaves comprising three oblong to egg-shaped leaflets, dark green above and light green beneath, with smooth, rippled, or lobed margins.

Deep Purple: deep purple flowers

'Murasaki' Purple Haze: warm purple and pink flowers and large, flavorful fruit

'Shikin' Purple Kimono: deep purple flowers and large, flavorful fruit

Alchemilla
Rosaceae

Famous for the magic of water droplets that rest like shining, spherical jewels upon its leaves, lady's mantles, like lotuses, nasturtiums, taro, and the wings of certain insects, exhibit the "lotus effect," or super-hydrophobicity. Alchemists, for whom the genus is named, believed these droplets to be the purest form of water and collected them for their experiments to turn base metal into gold. If this history doesn't impress, try lady's mantle's taxonomy: these species with airy sprays of tiny chartreuse flowers are members of the rose family.

The genus *Alchemilla* includes approximately 300 species, with only a handful in common cultivation. They are mostly clump-forming from woody rhizomes or sometimes creeping with unusual, gray-green to green, fan-shaped leaves with scalloped or deeply lobed, sometimes finely hairy margins with small, white, serrated teeth. The apetalous flowers are tiny, yellow to electric green, and held in loose sprays in late spring and summer. In addition to those treated here, other more uncommon species may also be useful, including *A. epipsila, A. faeroensis* and *A. faeroensis* var. *pumila, A. saxatilis,* and *A. xanthochlora* (syn. *A. vulgaris*).

CULTURE/CARE Full sun to part shade in average to moist soils. Avoid full sun in hot summer climates. Some species such as *A. mollis* and *A. erythropoda* can self-seed in some situations. Deadhead before seed set to avoid unwanted plants, or shear back plants entirely after blooming to rejuvenate foliage.

USES Mass plant clumping species to form a dense cover. Gentle self-seeding can help fill in gaps. Use both clumping and stoloniferous species as border edgers, along pathways, in the rock garden, and on walls. *Alchemilla ellenbeckii* is tolerant of light foot traffic. Deer and rabbit resistant.

PROPAGATION Division, seed

Alchemilla alpina
ALPINE LADY'S MANTLE, MOUNTAIN LADY'S MANTLE

Zones 3–9

Moorland, alpine meadows, pastureland, cliffs, streambanks, and woodland clearings, mainly on acid soils, in mountainous areas of Western and Northern Europe and southern Greenland.

Low mounds 4–8 in. (10–20 cm) tall and 12 in. (30 cm) wide of small, deeply lobed, emerald-green leaves, somewhat shiny on top and densely silky/hairy beneath, edged with a distinctive, silver-white, toothed margin. Chartreuse-yellow flowers in early summer.

Alchemilla conjuncta
SILVER LADY'S MANTLE

Zones 3–8

Rocky, high mountain pastures in the western European Alps.

Similar to *A. alpina* but somewhat larger. Deeply lobed, green to blue-green leaves are hairy underneath, edged with silver teeth, in clumps, 12–18 in. (30–45 cm) tall and 12 in. (30 cm) wide. Scented flowers bloom from early summer to fall.

Alchemilla alpina

Alchemilla ellenbeckii

Alchemilla mollis

Alchemilla ellenbeckii
CREEPING LADY'S MANTLE, AFRICAN LADY'S MANTLE

Zones 6–9

Mountainous regions of Ethiopia and Kenya.

Unusual carpeting species with cherry-red creeping stems and tiny, green, kidney-shaped, evergreen leaves with lobed margins. Flowers are tiny, greenish yellow, and sometimes obscured by the foliage. Grows in mats 1–4 in. (2.5–10 cm) tall, spreading indefinitely.

Alchemilla erythropoda
DWARF LADY'S MANTLE

Zones 3–9

Eastern Europe from the Carpathian and Balkan Mountains to Turkey and the Caucasus.

Half-sized version of *A. mollis*, 6 in. (15 cm) tall and 8–12 in. (20–30 cm) wide, with small grayish green leaves. Flowers emerge electric-green, developing peachy orange tones on reddish stems. AGM

Alchemilla mollis
LADY'S MANTLE

Zones 3–9

Streambanks, meadows, open plains, and mountainous areas from northern Greece through the Carpathian and Caucasus Mountains into northern Iran.

A cottage garden favorite, with large, softly hairy, scalloped and serrated, grayish green leaves perfect for catching droplets of water, 12–18 in. (30–45 cm) tall, spreading slowly by short rhizomes to 18–24 in. (45–60 cm) wide. Masses of airy chartreuse flowers create an electric-green froth. AGM

'Auslese': said to be more restrained, compact, and upright

'Robustica': more vigorous and larger, to 24 in. (60 cm) tall and wide, often reblooming in autumn

'Senior': to 16 in. (40 cm) tall, may rebloom

'Thriller': slightly larger, 18–24 in. (45–60 cm) tall, with larger leaves and more profuse flowering

Alchemilla sericata
LADY'S MANTLE

Zones 3–8

Dry meadows and grasslands in subalpine and alpine areas from the Mediterranean to the Caucasus.

Similar to *A. mollis*, but leaves are more deeply lobed, in compact mounds of gray-green, scalloped foliage to 14 in. (36 cm) tall and 16 in. (40 cm) wide. Evergreen in milder climates.

'Gold Strike': seed strain with consistent habit and performance

Alyssum
Brassicaceae

Madworts are low-growing, mounding or spreading subshrubs with gray-green foliage and fragrant flowers in yellow, white, or pink. They are closely related and similar to the more common basket of gold (*Aurinia* spp.) and the annual sweet alyssum (*Lobularia* spp.). Some can be short-lived, especially if not planted in full sun and dry conditions.

CULTURE/CARE Full sun and good to excellent drainage, especially in winter. Drought tolerant once established. Trim plants lightly after blooming to maintain a compact, bushy habit and to remove old flowering stems and unattractive seed heads.

USES Rock gardens, green roofs, gravel beds, walls, and as edgers for dry borders. Not tolerant of foot traffic. Attractive to pollinators, especially bees and butterflies. Deer resistant.

PROPAGATION Seed, cuttings

Alyssum montanum
MOUNTAIN MADWORT, CREEPING BASKET OF GOLD

Zones 3–9

Ledges, rocky slopes, scree, dry grassy areas, and sandy habitats from middle to high elevations in the Mediterranean Basin.

Perennial subshrub forming spreading mats from a woody base, with gray-green stems and linear, hairy, evergreen foliage. Fragrant golden yellow flowers on racemes in spring. More compact and better for smaller spaces than the related basket of gold (*Aurinia saxatilis*).

'Berggold' (syn. 'Mountain Gold'): seed strain, 4–6 in. (10–15 cm) tall and 12–18 in. (30–45 cm) or more wide

'Luna': heavy-flowering seed strain blooms 1–2 weeks earlier than 'Berggold'

'Tekara': seed strain producing uniform, flat, spreading cushions, 4 in. (10 cm) tall and 12 in. (30 cm) wide

Alyssum spinosum
SPINY ALYSSUM, MADWORT

Zones 6–10

Open rocky sites including gravel slopes and cliffs from Southern France to southeastern Spain.

Unusual, low-growing dwarf shrub with wiry stems and hairy, silver-gray leaves and spines. Resembles and offers a good perennial alternative to the annual sweet alyssum (*Lobularia maritima*), with honey-scented, white, pink, or dark pink flowers in mid- to late spring on plants 12 in. (30 cm) tall and 12–18 in. (30–45 cm) wide. Now known scientifically as *Hormathophylla spinosa*.

'Roseum': rosy-pink flowers, AGM

Alyssum wulfenianum
ALPINE ALYSSUM, MADWORT

Zones 3–9

Open sunny sites in the southeastern European Alps.

Low, spreading mounds or cushions of gray-green foliage with fragrant, golden yellow flowers in mid- to late spring or early summer. Longer lived and more compact than *A. montanum*, 6–8 in. (15–20 cm) tall and 12–14 in (30–36 cm) wide.

'Golden Spring': larger flowers, propagated vegetatively

Ampelopsis brevipedunculata
PORCELAIN VINE, PORCELAIN BERRY

Vitaceae

Zones 4–9

Thickets and forested hills and valleys in China, Japan, Korea, and eastern Russia.

Although there are numerous Asian *Ampelopsis* species, only *A. brevipedunculata*, with its attractive, deeply lobed, grapelike leaves and intriguing fruit, is commonly available. Some others, such as *A. aconitifolia* and its cultivar 'Chinese Lace', are occasionally cultivated. Normally grown as a self-clinging vine, with no vertical support, it can make a

Ampelopsis brevipedunculata 'Elegans'

good, low-growing, deciduous ground cover, 4–8 in. (10–20 cm) tall and 10–25 ft. (3–7.5 m) or more wide. The loose clusters of shiny, multicolored green, pink, purple, sky-blue, and royal-blue berries are produced in fall from insignificant greenish white flowers.

CULTURE/CARE Easy to grow in any well-drained soil in full sun to part shade.

USES Somewhat slow growing for medium-sized to large areas including slopes. Considered invasive in the eastern United States. Not tolerant of foot traffic. Deer resistant.

PROPAGATION Seed, cuttings

'Elegans': foliage variably splashed with white and gray-green, flushed pink when young, with bright pink leaf petioles; more likely to flower and fruit in brighter conditions

Amsonia
Apocynaceae

The primarily North American bluestars are clumping, upright to arching perennials and, though not traditional ground covers, can be mass-planted to form beautiful and effective drifts of blue flowers atop textural foliage that turns gold in autumn. Taller species, such as *A. ciliata*, *A. tabernaemontana*, and *A. hubrichtii* and their cultivars, make beautiful mass-planted ground covers in landscape settings. Shorter selections and hybrids are better for smaller scale garden settings.

CULTURE/CARE Sun to part shade in dry, average, or evenly moist, well-drained soils, performing best in sun with good moisture.

USES Mass plant to achieve a closed cover. Not tolerant of foot traffic. Deer resistant.

PROPAGATION Division, seed

Amsonia ciliata
FRINGED BLUESTAR

Zones 5–9

Sandy areas, rocky shores, limestone glades, bald knobs, streambanks, and limestone bluff escarpments in the southeastern United States into Mexico.

Narrow, lance-shaped foliage and sky-blue flowers in spring on plants 2–3 ft. (60–90 cm) tall. The dwarf *A. ciliata* var. *tenuifolia* (syn. var. *filifolia*) is shorter growing, to 12 in. (30 cm) tall and wide, with narrower needlelike foliage.

'Spring Sky': larger, more prominent, and longer lasting flowers on plants 24 in. (60 cm) tall and wide, with narrow foliage that turns gold to bronze in fall

var. *tenuifolia* 'Georgia Pancake, unique prostrate habit, 5 in. (12 cm) tall but spreading to 24 in. (60 cm) wide, with pale blue flowers in spring on upturned stems and foliage that turns golden yellow in fall

Amsonia tabernaemontana
EASTERN BLUESTAR

Zones 3–9

Rocky woodlands, shaded rocky ravines, gravelly seeps, stream edges, limestone glades, and moist, sandy meadows across the central and eastern United States from Texas to Kansas and Florida to New York.

Perennial, 2–4 ft. (0.6–1.2 m) tall and wide, with clusters of pale blue, starlike flowers in spring above mid- to dark green, lance-shaped foliage turning gold in fall.

'Blue Ice': likely a hybrid, possibly with A. *orientalis*, that offers the best (and darkest) flowers of the genus with a two-toned spring display of dark blue buds and sky-blue flowers on vigorous plants, 12–16 in. (30–40 cm) tall and 18–24 in. (45–60 cm) wide, with midgreen, lance-shaped foliage that turns bright yellow in fall, zones 4–9

'Short Stack': dwarf selection, 10 in. (25 cm) tall and 18 in. (45 cm) wide, may be less hardy, zones 5–9

Amsonia 'Blue Ice'

Anacyclus pyrethrum var. depressus
MOUNT ATLAS DAISY, FLATTENED ALEXANDER'S FOOT

Asteraceae

Zones 5–10

Dry, sunny sites from the Mediterranean Basin to the Himalayas.

Prostrate with finely textured, fernlike, grayish green to silver leaves on plants 4 in. (10 cm) tall and 8–16 in. (20–40 cm) wide, with solitary daisies that are reddish pink in bud, opening to white ray florets with deep pink to red reverses around yellow centers. Flowers bloom from spring into summer, opening during the day and closing at night.

CULTURE/CARE Full sun in well-drained soils. Can be short lived, especially where soils are too wet. May reseed.

USES Slow to moderate grower for small applications in containers, rock gardens, gravel areas, dry pathways, walls, garden stairs, and other arid sites. Tolerant of occasional foot traffic. Deer and rabbit resistant. Attractive to pollinators, especially bees and butterflies.

PROPAGATION Seed, cuttings

f. *compactum* 'Silberkissen' (syns. 'Silver Kisses', 'Silver Cushion'): compact seed strain with shorter side branches

'Garden Gnome': more compact and less sprawling

'Spring Carpet': shorter side branches than 'Garden Gnome' with a denser, more compact habit

Anacyclus pyrethrum var. depressus

Anaphalis
Asteraceae

An old-fashioned garden plant with flowers that feature dull yellow centers surrounded by dry, pure white (sometimes pink tinged), papery bracts, popular for drying and indoor decoration. Species are primarily dioecious with separate male and female plants. Of the approximately 110 species, most are Asian with only a single species, *A. margaritacea*, venturing into North America, though it is fairly ubiquitous in almost every state, province, and territory from the south to the very north and from sea level to high mountains.

CULTURE/CARE *Anaphalis alpicola* requires full sun and dry to average soils with good drainage, while *A. margaritacea* and *A. triplinervis* can be grown in full sun to part shade, offering uncommon silver foliage for shadier locations. Although *A. margaritacea* is tolerant of a wide range of soil types, including salty sites and moist to dry conditions, *A. triplinervis* is best with consistent moisture in average to moist soils and is humidity tolerant. Both are tolerant of poor soil fertility.

USES Borders, naturalistic plantings, meadows, green roofs, rock gardens, and as edgers. Use *A. alpicola* between flagstones, spreading at a reasonable but not aggressive rate. Both *A. margaritacea* and *A. triplinervis* can spread at slow to fast rates, depending on soil fertility and moisture. Attractive to pollinators, especially butterflies and bees. Deer and rabbit resistant. Not tolerant of foot traffic.

PROPAGATION Division, seed

Anaphalis alpicola
ALPINE EVERLASTING, SILVER ANAPHALIS

Zones 4–9
Alpine slopes of Japan.
Rhizomatous perennial reminiscent of *Antennaria dioica*, forming spreading mats of silver, lance-shaped, woolly foliage. White, pink, and yellow flowers occur in dense corymbs on stems 4–8 in. (10–20 cm) tall from early to late summer.

Anaphalis margaritacea
PEARLY EVERLASTING

Zones 2–9
Widespread across most of North America into Northeast Asia in moist meadows, riversides, roadsides, woods, subalpine grasslands, and shrublands, and in sandy, gravelly, or disturbed sites from sea level to high elevations. Naturalized in Northern Europe.

Rhizomatous perennial with silver-white stems and felted, linear to lance-shaped leaves, often becoming grayish green with age, forming spreading colonies of upright stems 12–24 in. (30–60 cm) or more tall. Blooms from summer into fall with long-lasting clusters of papery, yellow and white, buttonlike flowers. Basal foliage often begins to fade as flowering begins. *Anaphalis margaritacea* var. *yedoensis*, the Japanese or Yedoan pearly everlasting, is similar but may have larger flowers.

'Neuschnee' (syn. 'New Snow'): compact seed strain

Anaphalis triplinervis
THREE-VEINED EVERLASTING,
TRIPLE-NERVED PEARLY EVERLASTING

Zones 3–9
Open habitats, including clearings in oak forests, rocky areas, and grassy slopes at moderately high to high elevations from Afghanistan through the Himalayas to Southwest China.

Creeping, rhizomatous perennial, 12–24 in. (30–60 cm) tall and wide, with white to gray-green, felted, elliptic foliage. Leaves are somewhat broader than *A. margaritacea* and have three or five lengthwise veins, producing a lusher, more textured mound. Typical flowers bloom from summer into fall. AGM

'Sommerschnee' (syn. 'Summer Snow'): more compact, 10–12 in. (25–30 cm) tall, AGM

Anaphalis triplinervis

Andromeda polifolia
BOG ROSEMARY

Ericaceae

Zones 2–9

Circumboreal and circumpolar in open wet sites such as bogs, fens, pool margins, and along boggy shores from low to middle elevations.

A monotypic heath family genus with a single, extremely hardy, widespread species divided into two varieties in North America: A. *polifolia* var. *polifolia* is found mainly across Northern Canada, whereas A. *polifolia* var. *latifolia* occurs farther south and east in Canada and the United States. The latter, with its hairy to velvety white undersides, larger flowers, and higher flower count per cluster, is the source of our garden cultivars. They are low-growing, evergreen shrubs from creeping rootstocks, typically 12–18 in. (30–45 cm) tall in cultivation and wider than tall with small, narrow, leathery, green to blue-green foliage with white undersides and downward curled margins, resembling the unrelated culinary rosemary (*Rosmarinus officinalis*). Foliage can develop purple tints in winter. Clusters of small, pink, sometimes white, nodding, urn-shaped flowers are borne in spring.

CULTURE/CARE Moist, acidic soils with high organic matter. Adapts well to average to evenly moist garden soils in sun to part shade. Amend with peat moss to keep pH low and organic matter and moisture high. Prefers cooler climates. Requires more shade in hotter summer regions.

USES Slow to moderate grower useful as an alternative to heaths (*Erica* spp.) and heathers (*Calluna* spp.) for small to moderate-scale plantings and in wetter sites or as an accent. Not tolerant of foot traffic. Deer resistant.

PROPAGATION Division, stem cuttings

Andromeda polifolia 'Blue Ice'

'Alba': white flowers, green to blue-green foliage, 6–12 in. (15–30 cm) tall

'Blue Ice': striking, icy blue foliage and midpink flowers, 12–18 in. (30–45 cm) tall and 24–36 in. (60–90 cm) wide

'Blue Lagoon': branch sport of 'Blue Ice', with icier blue foliage described as being more grayish blue than greenish blue

'Compacta': pale pink flowers on compact, dense plants 12 in. (30 cm) tall, AGM

'Kirigamine' (syn. 'Kiri-Kaming'): dwarf form with shorter, narrower leaves and pale pink flowers on plants 8 in. (20 cm) tall and 18 in (45 cm) wide

'Macrophylla': larger, broader green leaves with light pink flowers, to 8 in. (20 cm) tall by 24 in. (60 cm) wide, AGM

Androsace
Primulaceae

The genus *Androsace* includes more than 100 species of small, cushion-forming or spreading, evergreen perennials from Arctic and Northern Hemisphere alpine habitats, especially in Europe and Asia. It first arose in the Himalayas about 35 million years ago, likely as an annual, and then independently evolved its perennial cushion habit twice, in Asia and in Europe. The stoloniferous and strongly rhizomatous species make for good small-scale ground covers.

CULTURE/CARE Full sun in cool climates and part shade in hotter climates, always with excellent drainage.

USES Small applications in rock and gravel gardens, as border edgers, between large stones, on walls, along pathways, and between cracks and crevices. Not tolerant of foot traffic.

PROPAGATION Seed, division, cuttings

Androsace carnea
ROCK JASMINE

Zones 4–8

Turf, rubble, rocky pastures, and slopes in the high mountains of Spain, France, Switzerland, and Italy.

Narrow, linear, pointed leaves, forming tightly clustered rosettes, 2–5 in. (5–12.5 cm) tall, slowly spreading by rhizomes into small mats. Numerous, short, reddish stems hold small clusters of fragrant flowers—pink in A. *carnea* subsp. *rosea* (AGM) and subsp. *laggeri* (AGM), and white in subsp. *brigantiaca*—with yellow eyes in late spring or summer.

Androsace lanuginosa
WOOLLY ROCK JASMINE

Zones 4–9

Mountain habitats of the Western Himalayas of Pakistan and northwestern India.

Carpets of small, silvery gray to blue-gray, hairy, evergreen foliage on low, spreading, reddish stems, 3–4 in. (7.5–10 cm) tall and 12–24 in. (30–60 cm) wide, topped by clusters of fragrant, pale pink to mauve flowers that fade to white as the centers transition from green through yellow, orange, and red in late spring or summer. AGM

Androsace sarmentosa
ROCK JASMINE

Zones 3–9

Sandy, mountain habitats in mixed forests, in open woodlands, and on rocky or grassy slopes at high elevations in the Himalayas, from Sikkim to Kashmir, India.

Compact, midgreen, evergreen rosettes of short leaves covered in white hairs, spreads vigorously via red stolons into interlacing mats, 12–24 in. (30–60 cm) or more wide. Flowering stems 4–10 in. (10–25 cm) tall, topped with clusters of bright pink to purple, fragrant spring flowers with yellow centers aging to orange and then red.

'Sherriffii': easy to grow and vigorous, with taller flowering stems

Androsace sempervivoides
SEMPERVIVUM-LEAVED ROCK JASMINE

Zones 4–9

Mountain habitats of the northwest Himalayas.

Small, tight, green to blue-green, evergreen rosettes resembling hen and chicks (Sempervivum spp.), multiplying from red stolons. Foliage develops red tints with sun or drought stress. Fragrant pink flowers in spring with yellow, orange, and then red eyes. Vigorous grower can quickly spread into relatively large mats up to 12 in. (30 cm) or more wide. AGM

'Susan Joan': slightly more vigorous

Androsace lanuginosa

Androsace sempervivoides

Androsace studiosorum
ROCK JASMINE

Zones 5–8

Mountain habitats of the Western Himalayas of Kashmir and northwest India.

Tight, evergreen, stoloniferous mats of crisscrossing, reddish runners, quickly expanding to 12 in. (30 cm) or more wide, with dense rosettes of short, hairy to woolly leaves. Fragrant pink flowers have yellow eyes that age to orange and red on stems 3–8 in. (7.5–20 cm) tall. Closely related to and often confused with *A. sarmentosa*. AGM

'Chumbyi': easy grower with darker pink flowers

'Doksa': flowers opening very pale mauve, fading to white

'Salmon's Variety': deep pink flowers

Anemone
Ranunculaceae

Poetic windflowers—*anemone* is Greek for daughter of the wind—have yellow-centered flowers with radiating linear, elliptic, or rounded petals in shades of white, pink, yellow, purple, and blue, with species suitable for sun or shade with some tolerant of a wide range of light conditions. An important horticultural genus, *Anemone* is beloved for the Japanese and wood anemones but offers other useful yet lesser known ground covers. All are deer and rabbit resistant.

PROPAGATION Division, rhizome cuttings, seed

Anemone blanda
GRECIAN WINDFLOWER, WINTER WINDFLOWER

Zones 5–10

Forest edges and openings, rocky places, scrub areas, and mountain habitats from southeastern Europe to the Middle East.

Ephemeral ground cover with starlike or daisylike blue, purple, pink, or white flowers with 10–20 linear tepals around yellow centers in early to midspring on plants 6 in. (15 cm) tall, with finely cut, compound foliage. Similar in habit to its typically six-petaled cousin, *A. nemorosa*. Black rhizomatous tubers can spread quickly into clumps and drifts in the right conditions. Plants go completely dormant before summer. AGM

CULTURE/CARE Full sun to part shade in rich, evenly moist spring soils that are dry or well-drained in summer during dormancy.

USES Provides seasonal coverage and weed suppression in early to midspring under deciduous trees or shrubs, around late-emerging perennials, or intermixed with other evergreen or herbaceous ground covers. Not tolerant of foot traffic.

'Blue Shades': pale blue, dark blue, and purple-blue flowers

'Blue Star': blue flowers

'Charmer': deep pink tepals with white bases

var. *rosea* 'Pink Star': bright pink tepals with white bases

var. *rosea* 'Radar': magenta tepals with white bases, AGM

'Violet Star': deep lavender-pink tepals with white bases

'White Splendour': pure white flowers, AGM

Anemone canadensis
CANADA ANEMONE, MEADOW ANEMONE

Zones 3–8

Moist meadows, damp thickets, wet prairies, streambanks, ditches, clearings, sandy lakeshores, and occasionally swampy areas across much of Canada and the North Central and northeastern United States.

Vigorous, rhizomatously spreading perennial topped with mostly solitary, five-petaled white flowers with yellow centers, from midspring into summer, on stems 12–18 in. (30–45 cm) tall, each with an attractive whorl of dissected, veined, leafy bracts that resemble the divided basal foliage.

CULTURE/CARE Full sun to part shade in rich, moist to average soils. Flowering may decrease with crowding. Divide in fall as needed. Can spread rapidly by underground rhizomes and be overly aggressive in moist conditions. Spreads more slowly in dry soils. Tolerant of salt.

USES Fast-spreader for medium-sized to large applications where its vigorous nature is an asset, or in small spaces where plants can be contained by hardscape features. Not tolerant of foot traffic.

Anemone canadensis

Anemone hupehensis var. *japonica* 'Pamina'

Anemone hupehensis
JAPANESE ANEMONE, CHINESE ANEMONE

Zones (4)5–10

Scrub, grassy slopes, and streamsides in hilly regions of Central and Southwest China. Naturalized in Japan for hundreds of years. *Anemone hupehensis* var. *japonica* is native to southern China.

Midsummer to fall bloomer, popular in the border for its white, light pink, or dark pink, 2–3 in. (5–7.5 cm) wide flowers with 5–7 rounded, often cupped tepals of varying sizes surrounding the central yellow stamens on narrow, branching stems up to 30 in. (75 cm) tall. Attractive seed heads resemble white strawberries, with black seeds that break apart in early winter to reveal white cotton. Midgreen leaves of three leaflets form mounds 12–18 in. (30–45 cm) tall and wide, spreading in good conditions from fibrous, suckering roots into large colonies. *Anemone hupehensis* var. *japonica* typically produces taller flowering stems of 2–5 ft. (0.6–1.5 m). Flowers are typically semidouble (7–10 tepals per flower) to double (20–30 narrow tepals per flower) and bloom a few weeks later than the species.

Anemone hupehensis has been crossed with *A. vitifolia* to form *A.* ×*hybrida*. Both *A. hupehensis* and *A.* ×*hybrida* have borne numerous cultivars, many of which are frequently confused in horticulture as to their parental origins.

CULTURE/CARE Full sun to part shade in fertile, consistently moist, well-drained, average to alkaline soils. Salt tolerant. Foliage can burn in full sun in hot summer climates especially if soils are dry. Flowering stems can become leggy if grown in too much shade. Avoid wet winter soils that can cause rot.

USES Mass plant in small to large areas and enable plants to fill in over time into a low, dense mass of foliage topped with nearly leafless, see-through flower stems, 18 in. (45 cm) to 5 ft. (1.5 m) tall, depending on cultivar. Not tolerant of foot traffic.

'Bowles's Pink': light pink to rose-pink blooms on stems 18–30 in. (45–75 cm) tall, AGM

'Curtain Call Deep Rose' and 'Curtain Call Pink': hybrids of *A. hupehensis* var. *japonica* 'Pamina' and *A.* ×*hybrida*

'Hadspen Abundance': deep pink single flowers edged in light pink over a medium bloom period on stems 24–36 in. (60–90 cm) tall, AGM

'Little Princess': compact, 24 in. (60 cm) stems with pink and dark pink flowers

'Pink Saucer': earlier flowering seed strain with pink flowers on stems 24–36 in. (60–90 cm) tall, hardy to zone 4a

'Praecox': earlier flowering in midsummer, at 24 in. (60 cm) tall with small, deep pink, single, long-lasting flowers

A. hupehensis var. japonica cultivars

'Bodnant Burgundy': large, deep pink semidouble to double flowers on stems up to 36 in. (90 cm) tall

'Bressingham Glow': large, deep pink semidouble to double flowers over a medium to long period on plants 24 in. (60 cm) tall

'Pamina': popular cultivar with deep pink semidouble to double flowers on stems up to 36 in. (90 cm) tall over a medium bloom period, AGM

'Prinz Heinrich' (syn. 'Prince Henry'): popular cultivar with large, rose-pink to rose-mauve semidouble to double flowers atop 12–36 in. (60–90 cm) stems over a long period

'Rotkäppchen': deep pink semidouble flowers on stems 24–36 in. (60–90 cm) tall

'Splendens': deep pink, single to semidouble flowers on stems 24–36 in. (60–90 cm) tall over a long period

'Sweetly' Fall in Love: hybrid of 'Pamina' and A. ×hybrida 'Pretty Lady Emily' with deep pink semidouble flowers atop 24 in. (60 cm) stems, spreads slowly by rhizomes

Anemone ×hybrida
JAPANESE ANEMONE

Zones 5–10

Hybrid of two Asian species, A. hupehensis var. japonica from southern China, and the grape-leaved anemone, A. vitifolia from the Himalayas, though plants may also include A. tomentosa. Cultivars of A. ×hybrida and A. hupehensis are often confused in horticulture and are frequently attributed to the wrong parentage, which is understandable, because hybrid plants are very similar to, if not indistinguishable from, their A. hupehensis parent. Anenome ×hybrida cultivars generally produce taller stems than A. hupehensis, to 4–5 ft. (1.2–1.5 m), though dwarf cultivars exist.

CULTURE/CARE Full sun to part shade in fertile, consistently moist, well-drained, average to alkaline soils. Salt tolerant. Foliage can burn in full sun in hot summer climates especially if soils are dry. Flowering stems can become leggy if grown in too much shade. Avoid wet winter soils that can cause rot.

USES Mass plant in small to large areas and enable plants to fill in over time into a low, dense mass of foliage topped with nearly leafless, see-through flower stems, 18 in. (45 cm) to 5 ft. (1.5 m) tall, depending on cultivar. Not tolerant of foot traffic.

'Andrea Atkinson': pure white single to semidouble flowers on 3–4 ft. (1–1.2 m) tall stems, usually shorter than 'Honorine Jobert' with smaller flowers over a longer period

Fantasy Series: dwarf cultivars 12–18 in (30–45 cm) tall by 18–24 in. (45–60 cm) wide

'Belle': double midpink flowers, darker than 'Pocahontas'

'Cinderella': single midpink flowers

'Jasmine': single midpink flowers, darker than 'Cinderella'

'Pocahontas': ruffled, midpink double flowers

'Red Riding Hood': single deep rose-pink flowers

'Snow Angel': double white flowers

'Honorine Jobert': large, pure white single to semidouble flowers on 3–4 ft. (1–1.2 m) tall stems over a medium bloom period, AGM, Perennial Plant of the Year 2016

'Königin Charlotte' (syn 'Queen Charlotte'): pale pink semidouble flowers on stems to about 36 in. (90 cm) tall, with a shorter bloom period, AGM

'Lady Gilmour' (syn. A. hupehensis 'Crispa'): single pink flowers with a short bloom period on 24 in. (60 cm) stems, crinkled foliage resembles light green parsley

'Margarete': deep pink semidouble to double flowers on 24–36 in. (60–90 cm) stems over a medium bloom period

'Montrose': pale lavender-pink double flowers on 24–36 in. (60–90 cm) stems over a medium bloom period

'Party Dress': extra large, double pink, ruffled flowers on 24–36 in. (60–90 cm) stems

'Pkan' Pink Cloud (syn. Pink Kiss): single rose-pink flowers on stems 12–14 in. (30–36 cm) tall

Pretty Lady Series: dwarf cultivars to 16 in. (40 cm) tall by 24 in. (60 cm) wide

'Pretty Lady Diana': dark pink single flowers

'Pretty Lady Emily': light to midpink double flowers

'Pretty Lady Julia': midpink double flowers

'Pretty Lady Maria': single white flowers

'Pretty Lady Susan': mid- to dark pink single flowers

Anemone ×hybrida 'Margarete'

Anemone leveillei
WINDFLOWER

Zones 5–9

Damp meadows, ditches, open woodlands, grassy slopes, streamsides, and lakesides in Central China.

Delicate yet long-lived woodland species similar to *A. rivularis* (of which it is sometimes considered a synonym), with single, white, starlike flowers with broad, rounded petals that are mauve-blue on their reverses, centered with green pistils and deep purple-blue stamens. Stems are 15–18 in. (38–45 cm) tall, branching at 45-degree angles, presenting an open, interlaced cloud of flowers in midspring to early summer atop low mounds of dark green, deeply divided, softly hairy, tripartite foliage.

CULTURE/CARE Part shade and evenly moist, fertile, woodland soils.

USES Mass plant to achieve a closed cover. Not tolerant of foot traffic.

Anemone ×hybrida 'Robustissima'

'Richard Ahrens': pale pink single to semidouble flowers on 24–36 in. (60–90 cm) stems over a medium bloom period

'Robustissima': pink single flowers on 3–4 ft. (1–1.2 m) tall stems over a long bloom period

'September Charm': small to medium-sized rose-pink flowers on 24–36 in. (60–90 cm) stems over a medium bloom period, AGM

'Serenade': pink semidouble flowers on 24 in. (60 cm) stems over a long bloom period

'Whirlwind': pure white semidouble flowers on 24–36 in. (60–90 cm) stems over a medium bloom period

Anemone nemorosa

WOOD ANEMONE, WINDFLOWER

Zones (3)4–9

Woodland and shady hillsides throughout most of Europe (though rare in the Mediterranean) into Western Asia.

Early to midspring-flowering, ephemeral ground cover, 4–6 in. (10–15 cm) tall, producing starlike blue, mauve, pink, or white flowers of 6–7, or sometimes 8–10 tepals, around yellow centers. Attractive textured mats of deeply cut, compound, tripartite foliage is said to have a musky smell. Brown or black rhizomes can spread indefinately at a reasonable pace into large colonies. Similar in habit, form, and summer dormancy to its more heavily petaled cousin, *A. blanda*, and to yellow *A. ranunculoides*. AGM

CULTURE/CARE Woodland or shaded gardens in rich, evenly moist soils. Full sun is tolerated in early spring if colonies are shaded during summer dormancy.

USES Provides seasonal coverage and weed suppression in early to midspring under deciduous trees or shrubs, around late-emerging perennials, or intermixed with other evergreen or herbaceous ground covers. Not tolerant of foot traffic.

'Alba Plena': pure white flowers with a base of 6–7 normal tepals, topped with a central mound of petal-like staminodes over a long bloom period

'Allenii': lavender-blue tepals with pink- or purple-streaked reverses, AGM

'Blue Eyes': double white flowers with a central blue corona around yellow stamens, newly established plants may produce single flowers

'Bracteata Pleniflora': double white flowers with long, narrow tepals atop a ruff of leafy, green bracts

'Green Fingers': single white anemone, white tepals centered with leafy green staminodes

'Leed's Variety': vigorous with large white flowers flushed in pink

'Lychette': large white flowers, similar to 'Leed's Variety'

'Robinsoniana': lavender-blue flowers, AGM

'Royal Blue': one of the bluest cultivars with lavender-blue flowers with purple reverses

'Stammerberg': large, 3 in. (7.5 cm) wide, pale pink double flowers

Anemone nemorosa 'Green Fingers'

Anemone nemorosa 'Royal Blue'

Anemone nemorosa

Anemone ranunculoides 'Pleniflora'

'Stars in the Night': white flowers, purple-tinted spring foliage turns dark green

'Vestal': pure white flowers with a base of six or seven normal tepals, topped with a central mound of petal-like staminodes over a long period; similar to 'Alba Plena' but said to have larger flowers with a smaller central ruff, AGM

'Virescens': peculiar, mounding flowers of finely divided, leafy green tepals, sometimes centered with white and purple, AGM

Anemone ranunculoides
YELLOW ANEMONE, YELLOW WOOD ANEMONE

Zones 4–8

Forest, woodland, and scrub areas across most of continental Europe though less frequent in the Mediterranean region.

Similar in habit and form to *A. nemorosa* and *A. blanda* but with smaller, dark yellow flowers with 5–8 tepals in early to midspring. Forms spreading mats 2–6 in. (5–15 cm) tall (sometimes taller) from brown, underground rhizomes. Blooms in early spring and goes dormant by summer. The leaves are more fernlike than *A. nemorosa* with 3–5 multilobed leaflets. AGM

CULTURE/CARE Woodland or shaded gardens in rich, evenly moist soils. Full sun is tolerated in early spring if colonies are shaded during summer dormancy.

USES Provides seasonal coverage and weed suppression in early to midspring under deciduous trees or shrubs, around late-emerging perennials, or intermixed with other evergreen or herbaceous ground covers. Not tolerant of foot traffic.

'Pleniflora': dark yellow double flowers, AGM

A. ×*lipsiensis*, naturally occurring hybrid where the ranges of *A. ranunculoides* and *A. nemorosa* overlap, with pale yellow flowers and foliage intermediate in character between the parent species; cultivars 'Pallida' (AGM) and 'Vindobonensis' have lemon-yellow flowers

Anemone rivularis
RIVERSIDE WINDFLOWER

Zones 5–9

Forest margins, grassy slopes, streamsides, lakesides, and grazed places from moderate to very high elevations in Southwest China, Bhutan, India, Indonesia, Nepal, and Sri Lanka.

Long-lived and similar to *A. leveillei* (which is sometimes considered a form of *A. rivularis*), with single, white, starlike flowers with broad, rounded petals, with mauve to blue reverses and deep purple-blue stamens around green pistils. Reddish flower stems are 18–24 in. (45–60 cm) or more tall with highly dissected bracts and branches angled at 45 degrees, presenting an open, interlaced cloud of flowers in midspring to early summer. Plants form low mounds of dark green, deeply divided, softly hairy, tripartite foliage.

CULTURE/CARE Sun to part shade and evenly moist to damp, fertile soils.

USES Mass plant to achieve a closed cover. Not tolerant of foot traffic.

'Glacier': white flowers with bold metallic blue reverses

Anemone Swan Series
Zones (4)5–8

Garden origin.

The Swan Series began with 'Macane001' Wild Swan—a chance seedling likely involving *A. rupicola* and up to five or six other parents—winning the Chelsea Flower Show Plant of the Year. The large, five-petaled, 3–4 in. (7.5–10 cm) wide, white flowers are similar to Japanese anemone (*A.* ×*hybrida*) but with light bluish purple reverses. It blooms from early summer to fall and forms clumping mounds of thick, dark green foliage. Further crosses with *A.* ×*hybrida* have yielded similar cultivars.

CULTURE/CARE Rich, fertile, evenly moist soil in full sun to part shade.

USES Mass plant to achieve a closed cover. Deer and rabbit resistant.

'Macane001' Wild Swan: large, pure white flowers with golden centers and purple reverses on 18–24 in. (45–60 cm) tall stems

'Macane004' Dreaming Swan: semidouble, ruffled white flowers with purple reverses on 24 in. (60 cm) tall stems

'Macane005' Dainty Swan: slightly shorter version of Wild Swan with pink reverses

'Macane007' Ruffled Swan: semidouble, ruffled white flowers with purple reverses on 32 in. (80 cm) tall stems

'Macane017' Elfin Swan: dwarf form of 'Macane001' Wild Swan, 10–18 in. (25–45 cm) tall

Anemone sylvestris
SNOWDROP ANEMONE, SNOWDROP WINDFLOWER

Zones 4–8

Forest margins and grassy or sandy slopes in Central and Eastern Europe through Russia to China and Mongolia.

Pure white, lightly fragrant, cupped flowers with 5–6 tepals around golden yellow centers, on stems 12–18 in. (30–45 cm) tall in spring, sometimes reblooming in fall. Seed heads eventually release brown to black seeds covered in dense, white, woolly hairs. Deep green compound leaves are divided into three-lobed leaflets that form attractive mounds. Vigorously spreads by branching rhizomes.

CULTURE/CARE Part sun to part shade. Tolerant of full shade and of full sun in cooler climates. Average to moist, fertile soils. Can spread aggressively in loose soils or more slowly in heavier clay soils or in drier conditions.

USES Fast spreader for medium-sized to large applications where its vigorous nature is an asset, or in small spaces where plants can be contained by hardscape features. Not tolerant of foot traffic.

'Elise Fellmann' (syn. 'Elise Feldman'): pure white, double pom-pom flowers with greenish yellow centers

'Madonna': larger, 2–3 in. (5–7.5 cm) wide flowers

Anemone 'Macane001' Wild Swan

Anemone sylvestris

Antennaria dioica
COMMON PUSSYTOES, MOUNTAIN EVERLASTING

Asteraceae

Zones 3–8

Dry slopes, tundra, forest heaths, rocky outcrops, meadows, mountain grasslands, woodland edges, pastures, and banks, often on calcareous soils, across Europe and Asia to the Aleutian Islands in Alaska.

A tough, ground-hugging, stoloniferous, mat-forming ground cover with small, spoon-shaped, semi-evergreen to evergreen leaves, grayish green above and silver-hairy beneath, with vertical, 2–8 in. (5–20 cm) stems topped with small clusters of 3–7 white and/or pink heads, surrounded by papery bracts resembling a cat's paw. The species is dioecious with separate male and female plants. However, lone female plants can produce seed through apomixis.

Ironically, this Eurasian species is by far the most commonly cultivated, yet North America is the center of diversity for the genus with 53 taxa. Some, such as *A. microphylla*, *A. neglecta*, *A. parlinii*, *A. parvifolia*, *A. plantaginifolia*, and *A. rosea*, are slowly entering cultivation with interest in native plants and through green roof projects, in part because of the importance of various species as larval hosts for some species of butterflies and moths. Another Eurasian species, *A. carpatica*, is occasionally grown.

CULTURE/CARE Dry, infertile sites with rocky or sandy soils. Drought tolerant. Sun to light shade. Prefers cooler summer climates. May not perform well in hot, humid regions.

USES Border edger, in rock gardens, between rocks or stepping stones, on green roofs or rock walls, and as a small-scale lawn alternative, spreading at a slow to moderate rate. Tolerates occasional foot traffic when not in bloom. Deer and rabbit resistant.

PROPAGATION Division, seed, propagation of stolons

'Alex Duguid': bright pink flowers

'Minima': half-size dwarf form

'Rotes Wunder' (syn. 'Red Wonder'): dark pink to cherry-red flowers

'Roy Davidson': half-size dwarf with pink to lavender-pink flowers, possibly a hybrid, may not belong to *A. dioica*

'Rubra': glowing pink to red-pink flowers

Anthemis
Asteraceae

These tough, drought-tolerant daisies are closely related to chamomile (*Chamaemelum* spp.), with mounds of intricate, fernlike, aromatic foliage and white or yellow flowers with golden yellow centers.

CULTURE/CARE Full to part sun in average to dry, rocky soils. Tolerant of drought and infertile soil. Provide excellent drainage, especially in winter; otherwise, plants can be short-lived. Deadhead or lightly shear after flowering to encourage rebloom and maintain tidy mounds. Some species are tolerant of salt, particularly *A. tinctoria*.

USES *Anthemis carpatica* and *A. marschalliana* are good as edgers for borders and pathways and for rock gardens and walls. Tolerant of occasional foot traffic. Mass plant mounding *A. punctata* and *A. tinctoria* to achieve closed covers for borders, slopes, xeriscapes, and larger rock gardens as one would use *Artemisia* 'Powis Castle' or 'Silver Mound', two aster family species with similar foliage but insignificant flowers. Neither are tolerant of foot traffic. All species are deer resistant and attractive to pollinators, especially bees and butterflies.

PROPAGATION Seed, cuttings, division

Anthemis carpatica
SNOWY MARGUERITE, WHITE MAT CHAMOMILE

Zones 3–9

Open rocky habitats in mountainous regions of Southern Europe, including the Pyrenees, the eastern Alps, the Carpathians, and the mountains of the Balkan Peninsula.

Tufted, mounding to mat-forming, woody-based perennial, 4–12 in. (10–30 cm) tall, with green to greenish gray to silvery, smooth to densely hairy, highly dissected, fernlike foliage. Classic, 1.5 in. (4 cm) wide, yellow-centered, white daisies are borne singly on short stems from late spring into midsummer. May rebloom. Moderately spreads into mats.

'Karpatenschnee' (syn. 'Snow Carpet'): uniform seed strain of midsized plants, 6–8 in. (15–20 cm) tall and up to 24 in. (60 cm) wide with silver-gray foliage

Anthemis marschalliana
FILIGREE DAISY, ALPINE MARGUERITE

Zones 4–9
Scree, rock crevices, and mountain turf from 6200–10,200 ft. (1890–3110 m) in the southern Caucasus Mountains of Turkey.

Tufted or slowly mat-forming perennial growing 4–6 in. (10–15 cm) tall and 24 in. (60 cm) wide from a woody base with fernlike, highly dissected, densely hairy, aromatic, silver leaves. Flowers are 1 in. (2.5 cm) wide with dark yellow centers and golden yellow ray florets borne singly on bare, 6–10 in. (15–25 cm) stems.

Anthemis marschalliana

Anthemis punctata subsp. cupaniana
SICILIAN CHAMOMILE

Zones 7–9
Sunny, dry habitats of Sicily, Malta, and northwestern Africa.

Woody-based evergreen perennial with finely dissected, pungent, silvery foliage reminiscent of some *Artemisia* species, forming a moderately spreading mound, 12 in. (30 cm) tall by 24–36 in. (60–90 cm) wide. Classic daisy flowers are up to 2.5 in. (6 cm) wide, with yellow centers and white ray florets produced over a long period from midspring to midsummer. AGM

Anthemis punctata subsp. *cupaniana*

Anthemis tinctoria
GOLDEN MARGUERITE, DYER'S CHAMOMILE

Zones 3–9
Sunny slopes, rocky areas, railway tracks, roadsides, steppe, waste places, scrub, and walls, often on limestone, throughout the Mediterranean to Turkey, the Caucasus, Syria, and Iran.

Previously used to produce yellow and orange dyes, hence its species and common names. Now more valued as an ornamental forming large, evergreen mounds, 24 in. (60 cm) tall by 24–36 in. (60–90 cm) wide, of pungent, mid- to grayish green, feathery foliage topped with 1–2 in. (2.5–5 cm) wide daisies with yellow, cream, or white ray florets around deep yellow centers on long stems in summer. Moderate grower.

CULTURE/CARE Shear to 6 in. (15 cm) after flowering to encourage basal shoots for the subsequent year.

'Alba': creamy white flowers

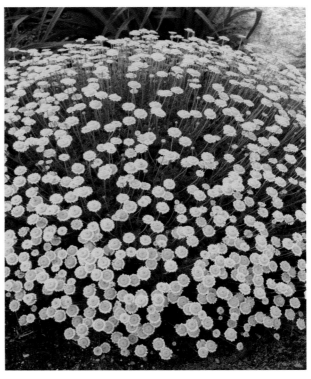
Anthemis tinctoria 'Charme'

Anthemis tinctoria 'Sauce Hollandaise'

Arabis alpina subsp. *caucasica*

'Blomit' Susanna Mitchell: chance cross with *A. punctata* subsp. *cupaniana* with the size and form of *A. tinctoria* but with silver foliage and creamy white to palest yellow flowers with bright yellow centers, blooming earlier than *A. tinctoria*

'Charme': dwarf cultivar, 12–16 in. (30–40 cm) tall by 20–24 in. (50–60 cm) wide, with 1 in. (2.5 cm) wide bright yellow daisies with large centers and short ray florets

'E.C. Buxton': lemon-yellow petals surrounding yellow-orange centers, introduced in 1910

'Kelwayi': bright yellow daisies with yellow-orange centers, introduced in 1891

'Sauce Hollandaise': pale yellow to creamy white flowers

'Tetworth': cross between 'E.C. Buxton' and *A. punctata* subsp. *cupaniana*, with silvery foliage and white to creamy white flowers with yellow centers, blooming earlier than *A. tinctoria*

'Wargrave Variety': lemon-yellow to creamy yellow flowers around deeper yellow centers

Arabis
Brassicaceae

Plants of the genus *Arabis* and its more familiar cousin *Aubrieta* are common, old-fashioned, mat-forming ground covers that are almost completely covered in four-petaled flowers in spring. They are often used to accentuate spring-flowering bulbs such as tulips and daffodils.

CULTURE/CARE Sun to part sun in average to moist, free-draining soils. Good winter drainage is important. Drought tolerant once established. Shear lightly after blooming to remove spent flower heads and encourage a tight, compact habit.

USES Rock gardens, on slopes, as a border edger, or spilling over walls, spreading at a moderate rate. Usually experiences a tired, semi-dormant period after blooming. Shear lightly and combine with later blooming ground covers with good foliage such as *Sedum* and *Veronica* spp. Not tolerant of foot traffic. Deer resistant. Attractive to pollinators, especially butterflies.

PROPAGATION Seed, cuttings, layering, division

Arabis alpina
ALPINE ROCK CRESS, WALL CRESS

Zones 3–9

Screes, rocky areas, rock ledges, streambanks, and other moist sites in the mountains of Europe, North and East Africa, and Central and Eastern Asia.

Evergreen ground cover (semi-evergreen in colder climates) forming spreading mounds, 4–6 in. (10–15 cm) tall and 12–24 in. (30–60 cm) or more wide, with gray-green, felted, spatulate leaves with shallowly serrated or lobed edges. Four-petaled, sweetly fragrant, white or sometimes pink flowers are held in small, open clusters just above the foliage.

A. alpina subsp. caucasica cultivars

'Deep Rose' and 'White' (Little Treasure Series): heavy flowering cultivars

'Douler Angevine': cream to pale yellow-edged leaves, pink flowers

'Flore Pleno': white double flowers

'Pixie Cream': cream to pale yellow flowers

'Rosea': pink flowers

'Schneehaube' (syn. 'Snow Cap'): white flowers

'Snowball': white flowers

'Snowfix': compact habit, white flowers, first year flowering from seed

'Variegata': cream to pale yellow-edged leaves, white flowers, sometimes reverts to green

A. ×*arendsii* cultivars: crosses with A. *aubrietioides*

'Compinkie': rich midpink flowers

'La Fraîcheur': midpink flowers

'Rosabella': light pink flowers fading with age

Arabis blepharophylla
COAST ROCK CRESS, ROSE ROCK CRESS

Zones 5–9
Endemic to rocky, grassy hillsides and bluffs at low elevations in the San Francisco Bay Area and Coast Ranges, California.
Slowly spreading basal cushions, 4–6 in. (10–15 cm) tall by 6–8 in. (15–20 cm) wide, with dark green, evergreen, fuzzy, shallowly serrated, spatulate leaves in clustered rosettes. Spring flowers are fragrant, rose- to purplish pink, and clustered on short stems.

'Alfa' Rose Delight: early flowering, rose-pink to glowing magenta blooms

'Frühlingszauber' (syn. 'Spring Charm'): magenta buds open to lavender-pink flowers

'Rote Sensation' (syn. 'Red Sensation'): reddish pink flowers

Arabis ferdinandi-coburgi
ALPINE ROCK CRESS, ALPINE WALL CRESS

Zones 3–9
Calcareous rocky and stony habitats and high elevation grasslands in the mountains of Southeast Europe.
Rosettes of spatulate, slightly waxy leaves spreading via short stolons to 2–4 in. (5–10 cm) tall by 6–8 in. (15–20 cm) wide. Evergreen foliage is tinted red in winter. Thin stems produce clusters of white flowers in early to midspring.

'Old Gold': deep green leaves with yellow edges

Arabis procurrens 'Variegata'

Arabis procurrens
SPREADING ROCK CRESS, RUNNING ROCK CRESS

Zones 4–9
Calcareous screes and other rocky habitats of Central and Eastern Europe.
Rosettes of spatulate, slightly waxy leaves spreading via short stolons to 2–4 in. (5–10 cm) tall by 12–18 in. (30–45 cm) wide. Evergreen foliage tinted red in winter. Thin stems produce clusters of white flowers in early to midspring on stems 4–8 in. (10–20 cm) tall. Similar but more compact A. ×*sturii* is a hybrid of obscure origin but similar habit that forms quick-spreading mounds or mats of green leaves topped with white flowers in spring.

'Glacier': green leaves

'Variegata' (syn. A. *ferdinandi-coburgi* 'Variegata'): variegated white to cream-edged green leaves

Arctostaphylos
Ericaceae

Manzanitas are shrubs or small trees mainly of western North America, from British Columbia to Mexico. However, three species called bearberries, A. *uva-ursi,* A. *rubra,* and A. *alpina,* are low-growing, woody ground covers of temperate, subarctic, and arctic habitats. Kinnikinnick (A. *uva-ursi*) has become a widespread and useful ground cover in temperate horticulture.
Other western North American species and their cultivars and hybrids are commonly cultivated in California, with interest expanding into the Pacific

Northwest. They are appreciated for their attractive evergreen foliage, charming and scented flowers, exfoliating bark, and toughness. Some have low-growing, ground-covering habits. In addition to those treated here, others with potential are *A. nummularia* 'Select Form' (zone 7), *A. nevadensis* and its cultivar 'Chipeta' (zone 5), and *A. edmundsii* and its cultivars 'Bert Johnson', 'Carmel Sur', and 'Rosy Dawn' (zone 8).

CULTURE/CARE The western natives are best grown in full to part sun in lean, dry soils, especially on slopes, and require excellent drainage, particularly in winter. Some may be prone to leaf spotting in rainy winter climates. Grow *A. uva-ursi* in full sun to part shade in average to dry or rocky soils. In good conditions, it will be lush and dense; in drier, poorer sites it will be more open. May resent the heat and humidity of hot summer regions unless grown in part shade to shade. All are drought and salt tolerant.

USES Use *A. uva-ursi* in small to large applications in varied light conditions. Useful on slopes, as a lawn alternative, and on green roofs and living walls. The West Coast species and cultivars are taller and spreading or mounding. Use as edgers, on slopes, or as mass-planted mounds over medium-sized to large areas. Growth is slow to moderate. Tolerant of some foot traffic. Deer resistant.

PROPAGATION Cuttings, layering, seed

Arctostaphylos hookeri
HOOKER'S MANZANITA, MONTEREY MANZANITA

Zones 7–11

Maritime chaparral, in conifer forests over stable dunes, and on sandstone uplands at lower elevations around Monterey Bay, California.

Variable, evergreen shrub with prostrate or erect, smooth, reddish branches forming mats or mounds from 4 in. to 5 ft. (10 cm to 1.5 m) tall, with shiny, bright green, narrowly to broadly elliptic leaves, to about 1 in. (2.5 cm) long. White to pink, urn-shaped, early spring flowers in small terminal clusters are followed by small, spherical red fruit. Stems can root where they touch the ground.

'Buena Vista': dense habit, 18 in. (45 cm) tall and 5 ft. (1.5 m) wide, with glossy, bright green leaves and pale pink flowers

'Ken Taylor': bright green leaves on maroon branches with pink-flushed, white flowers, 24 in. (60 cm) tall and 8 ft. (2.4 m) wide

'Mills': small, shiny, pointed leaves and pale pink flowers, 12–24 in. (30–60 cm) tall and 3–4 ft. (1–1.2 m) or more wide

'Monterey Carpet': small, deep green leaves and white flowers, up to 12 in. (30 cm) or more tall and 4–8 ft. (1.2–2.4 m) wide

'Wayside': vigorous grower with deep green, pointed leaves and white flowers, 24 in. (60 cm) tall and 6–8 ft. (1.8–2.4 m) wide

Arctostaphylos hybrids
MANZANITA

Zones: See cultivar information
Dry, sunny habitats of western North America.

Hybridization within the genus is common and a valuable source of new forms. For instance, *A. columbiana* and *A. uva-ursi* readily cross where their ranges overlap from British Columbia to California, creating hybrid swarms of quite variable *A. ×media* plants. These and other crosses offer a number of low-growing cultivars useful for their evergreen foliage, dense habits, and attractive flowers, fruit, and bark.

×*coloradensis*: naturally occurring hybrid from western Colorado, the panchito or mock bearberry manzanita has deep to bright green leaves and white to pale pink flowers, 12–24 in. (30–60 cm) tall and 3–5 ft. (1–1.5 m) wide; 'Chieftain' is a vigorous selection, zone 4 or 5

'Game Lake': dusty blue foliage and pale pink flowers, 6 in. (15 cm) tall and up to 10 ft. (3 m) wide, zone 6

Arctostaphylos ×*coloradensis* 'Chieftain'

×*media* 'Martha Ewan': dense habit with deep green leaves and white flowers, 24 in. (60 cm) tall and 6 ft. (1.8 m) wide, zone 6

×*media* 'Xera Pacific': light green leaves, white flowers, and exfoliating, mahogany-colored bark, 24 in. (60 cm) tall and 5 ft. (1.5 m) or more wide, zone 6

'Pacific Mist': gray-green to blue-green leaves and pale pink flowers, 24 in. (60 cm) tall and 6–10 ft. (1.8–3 m) wide, zone 7

Arctostaphylos uva-ursi
KINNIKINNICK, COMMON BEARBERRY

Zones 3–8

Circumboreal across northern North America, Europe, and Asia in cool temperate to Arctic habitats, including gravelly or sandy soils, exposed dry slopes and outcrops, open forest, and forest margins.

Tough, reliable, versatile, low-growing, prostrate, woody ground cover, 1–12 in. (2.5–30 cm) tall, depending on cultivar, with small, glossy, 1 in. (2.5 cm) long, evergreen leaves with bronze to red winter tints. Young stems are reddish. Old, woody stems are cinnamon-colored with flaking bark. Small clusters of white to pale pink, urn-shaped flowers occur in spring, darkening toward the mouth. Persistent scarlet berries ripen in summer, lasting into winter. Spreads indefinitely, rooting where it touches the ground.

'Big Bear': larger grower with larger leaves and fruit

'Emerald Carpet': hybrid, presumably with A. *nummularia*, 10–16 in. (25–40 cm) tall and 3–6 ft. (1–1.8 m) wide, with rich green foliage on dense, compact plants, zones 6–9

'Little Leaf Massachusetts': similar to 'Massachusetts' but with half-size leaves held more closely together

'Massachusetts': disease resistant, with small leaves and abundant flowers and fruit

'Microphylla': small leaves

'Point Reyes': rounded leaves, dense habit, vigorous growth, and a potentially larger size, with more heat and drought tolerance

'Radiant': heavy flowers and fruit, lighter green leaves

'Thymifolia': Arctic form with small leaves

'Vancouver Jade': fast spreading, with flowers on semi-upright stems, disease resistant

'Wood's Compact': denser and more compact

'Wood's Red': large fruits, excellent red fall color

Arctostaphylos uva-ursi in the wild, Desolation Sound, BC

Arctostaphylos uva-ursi berries

Arenaria
Caryophyllaceae

Arenaria is Latin for sand-loving, which suits this Old World genus native to rocky and sandy habitats. Mountain sandwort (A. *montana*) is most commonly cultivated, but other species can be useful, including A. *alfacarensis* and A. *purpurascens*, which are good ground covers for troughs and crevice gardens.

CULTURE/CARE Full sun to part shade, especially in hotter climates or in drier soils. Well-drained soils with reasonable moisture is best. Somewhat drought tolerant once established. Shear spent flower heads to avoid reseeding.

USES Small applications in rock gardens, walls, troughs, or pots; as border edgers; between flagstones; and as a lawn alternative (especially A. *montana*). Spreads slowly. Tolerant of light foot traffic. Deer resistant.

PROPAGATION Seed, division, layering

Arenaria balearica
CORSICAN SANDWORT, MOSSY SANDWORT

Zones 4–9

Endemic to shaded, humid, rocky slopes and terraces of the western Mediterranean islands including Corsica, Sardinia, and Mallorca.

Compact, evergreen, mosslike mats, 1–2 in. (2.5–5 cm) tall by 12–18 in. (30–45 cm) or more wide, with tiny green leaves and small, pure white flowers with green centers held on green to black stems in late spring or summer. The compact, prostrate growth will accentuate the contours of uneven ground, growing across soil and cascading over stones.

Arenaria ledebouriana
SANDWORT

Zones 5–8

Stony or sandy places in sun and shade at high elevations in Turkey and Iran.

Cushion- or mat-forming plant of just a few inches in height with evergreen, bristle-like foliage, resembling its cousin, Irish moss (*Sagina subulata*), or a miniature dianthus, but green to bluish green and even purple tinged. Small, white, five-petaled flowers with a greenish yellow eye are held a few inches above the foliage in summer.

Arenaria montana
MOUNTAIN SANDWORT, MOUNTAIN DAISY

Zones 2–9

Rocky and stony mountain habitats of southwestern Europe, primarily the Iberian Peninsula.

Low-growing, evergreen, spreading, rooting mats up to 12 in. (30 cm) or more wide with small, elliptic, rich-green to grayish green leaves. Upright, 4 in. (10 cm) stems bear small, pure white, slightly cupped, five-petaled flowers with green and yellow centers in late spring or early summer.

'Avalanche': larger flowers over a longer period on compact plants

'Blizzard': heavily flowering

'Sapare' Flurry: compact with large, white flowers

'Lemon Ice': sport of 'Avalanche' with large, lemon-yellow flowers

Arenaria montana

Arenaria 'Wallowa Mountains'

Arenaria **'Wallowa Mountains'**
WALLOWA MOUNTAINS SANDWORT

Zones 4–8

High elevations in the Wallowa Mountains of Oregon.

Compact, evergreen, mosslike buns or mats, ½–1 in. (1.3–2.5 cm) tall by 10–14 in. (25–36 cm) or more wide, with tiny, lance-shaped, bright green leaves and occasional small, pure white flowers. Reminiscent of *Scleranthus uniflorus* following the contours of uneven ground. Of mysterious orgins. Sometimes attributed to *A. speciosa*, itself seemingly not a valid species.

Arisarum proboscideum
MOUSE PLANT, MOUSE TAIL PLANT

Araceae

Zones (6)7–9
Shady woodlands and moist slopes of Italy
and Spain.

Tuberous, winter- and spring-growing, summer-
dormant aroid with small, glossy, midgreen, arrow-
shaped leaves resembling *Arum italicum* in miniature,
growing 4–6 in. (10–15 cm) tall and spreading indefinitely. Densely packed leaves emerge in early spring
followed (or sometimes preceded) by peculiar inflorescences consisting of a hooded spathe, white below
and burgundy above, with a long, burgundy, tail-like
appendage up to 6 in. (15 cm) long, resembling the
hind quarters and tails of little mice poking from the
greenery. A mushroomy aroma attracts pollinating
fungus gnats.

CULTURE/CARE Part to full shade in evenly moist,
well-drained soils. Spreads quickly in loose, fria-
ble soils. Avoid heavy clay. Drought tolerant once
established and when dormant. Will go prematurely
dormant in drier soils.

USES Ephemeral ground cover for shade. Useful in
combination with evergreen ground covers, planted
around large and late-emerging perennials or beneath
deciduous shrubs, and as a green foil for early spring
bulbs. Not tolerant of foot traffic.

PROPAGATION Division of rhizomatous tubers, seed

Armeria
Plumbaginaceae

Large genus of more than 100 species offering a
handful of garden-worthy plants that have long had a
place in the perennial border and rock garden, particularly the sea thrift, *A. maritima*. Their delicate, pink
or white, lollipop inflorescences and thin, grasslike
foliage belie their toughness against drought, wind,
salt, and cold.

CULTURE/CARE Full to part sun in average to dry
soils. Avoid heavy and wet soils. *Armeria maritima* and
A. pseudarmeria are salt tolerant.

USES Mass plant for small applications along
pathways, garden stairways, seaside beds, or in rock
gardens, troughs, or wall crevices. Slowly spreads into
mats, clumps, or cushions. Not tolerant of foot traffic.
Deer and rabbit resistant. Attractive to pollinators,
especially bees and butterflies.

PROPAGATION Seed, division

Armeria juniperifolia
JUNIPER-LEAVED THRIFT, SPANISH THRIFT

Zones 3–9
Mountain pastures and rock crevices of
Central Spain.

Short, dark green, needlelike leaves less than
1 in. (2.5 cm) long resemble those of juniper. Forms
dense buns or slowly spreading cushions, 8–16 in.
(20–40 cm) wide and only a few inches tall. Clusters of
soft pink spring flowers on stems 3–5 in. (7.5–12.5 cm)
tall may rebloom in summer and fall. Requires excellent drainage. AGM

'Alba': white flowers

'Bevan's Variety': deeper pink flowers, AGM

Armeria maritima
SEA THRIFT, COMMON THRIFT

Zones (2)3–9
Coastal salt marshes, meadows, grassy slopes,
maritime cliffs, crevices, rocky embankments, and dry,
sandy soils in temperate coastal areas of the Northern
Hemisphere, especially in the United Kingdom and
Western Europe, but also in Asia, North America, and
parts of South America.

A familiar, beloved, and tough wildflower of northwestern Europe, especially in the British Isles, and
commonly grown in temperate gardens. Forms slowly
spreading tufts of narrow, grasslike, evergreen foliage,
4 in. (10 cm) tall and 8–12 in. (20–30 cm) or more wide.
Densely covered in pom-poms of white, pink, or bright
pink, somewhat papery flowers on short, leafless
stems, 4–10 in. (10–25 cm) tall, in midspring with
intermittent reblooming in summer and fall.

'Alba': white flowers

Armada Series: early flowering with shorter stems

'Armada Rose': magenta-pink flowers

'Armada White': white flowers

'Bloodstone': glowing pink flowers

'Cotton Tail': white flowers

'Düsseldorfer Stolz' (syn. 'Dusseldorf Pride'): glowing,
deep pink flowers

'In the Red': smaller clusters of deep pink flowers and
compact, reddish to purple-infused foliage

Armeria maritima 'Bloodstone'

Morning Star Series: first-year flowering from seed

　'Morning Star Deep Rose': glowing deep pink flowers

　'Morning Star White': white flowers

'Nifty Thrifty': creamy white to pale yellow and green variegated foliage that sometimes reverts to green, with glowing pink flower clusters, less plentiful than other cultivars

'Rosa Stolz': lavender-pink flowers

'Rubrifolia': deep pink flowers and reddish burgundy foliage, darker in cool weather

'Splendens': glowing rose-pink flowers

'Varretu': very short flower stems with pink flowers held within or just above the foliage

'Vesuvius': deep pink flowers atop smoky purple foliage, darker in cool weather

'Victor Reiter': lavender-pink flowers

Armeria pseudarmeria
FALSE SEA THRIFT

Zones 5–9

Narrowly endemic to the region around Lisbon and Sintra, Portugal, on vegetated sea cliffs, rocky slopes, rock walls, and in low intensity agricultural fields.

Larger, less hardy, and clumping with additional colors and larger flower clusters up to 1 in. (2.5 cm) wide, with broader, lusher foliage, and taller, stiffer flower stems. Plants bloom at 12–16 in. (30–40 cm) tall, with clusters of white, pink, or near red flowers in mid- to late spring, reblooming through summer and fall atop lush, lance-shaped, evergreen foliage.

Ballerina Series: first-year flowering

　'Ballerina Lilac': lilac to lilac-pink flowers

　'Ballerina Red': unusual rose-red flowers

　'Ballerina White': white flowers

Dreameria Series: may bloom continuously from early spring to late fall

> 'Daydream': light salmon-pink flowers
>
> 'Dream Clouds': white flowers
>
> 'Dream Weaver': deep pink flowers
>
> 'Dreamland': bright salmon-pink flowers
>
> 'Sweet Dreams': pink flowers

Joystick Series: tall and first-year flowering to 16–20 in. (40–50 cm), originally developed for cut flower production; attributed to *A. pseudarmeria* but actually a hybrid cross

> 'Joystick Lilac Shades': lavender to lavender-pink flowers
>
> 'Joystick Red': rose-red flowers
>
> 'Joystick White': white flowers

Arrhenatherum elatius var. bulbosum
BULBOUS OAT GRASS, TUBER OAT GRASS

Poaceae

> Zones (3)4–9
> Grasslands, road verges, along hedgerows, and on riverbanks throughout Europe.
> Cool-season grass with active growth in spring and fall, forming slowly spreading clumps of narrow foliage, 8–12 in. (20–30 cm) tall. Insignificant summer flowers rise just above the foliage in cooler climate regions. In regions with hot summer nights, plants tend not to bloom and to go semidormant in summer.

Arrhenatherum elatius var. *bulbosum* 'Variegatum'

CULTURE/CARE Full sun to part shade in a variety of soils with dry, average, or even moisture. Tolerant of dry shade. Cut foliage if it goes partially or completely summer dormant.

USES Small to medium-sized applications as a border edger and along pathways. Not tolerant of foot traffic. Deer resistant.

PROPAGATION Division

'Variegatum': the only cultivated form, with nearly white foliage with thin green centers

Artemisia
Asteraceae

Hundreds of species of *Artemisia* offer no floral beauty, with insignificant, wind-pollinated flowers, but their origins in mostly dry, temperate habitats has resulted in a range of aromatic, dissected, often silver foliage that can be highly ornamental. Additionally, the genus brings us tarragon (*A. dracunculus*); the absinthe wormwood (*A. absinthium*) used to flavor absinthe, vermouth, wormwood wine, and beer; and tree wormwood (*A. arborescens*), which is combined with mint to flavor Middle Eastern teas. In addition to the low-growing species, ground covers for larger spaces include the hybrid *A.* 'Powis Castle', which can quickly reach 24–36 in. (60–90 cm) tall and wide, eventually spreading to 6 ft. (1.8 m) wide. *Artemisia ludoviciana* and its cultivars 'Silver Queen' and 'Valerie Finnis' can spread quickly by rhizome into large, weed-smothering, silver-white colonies, 18–36 in. (45–90 cm) tall.

CULTURE/CARE Full sun in average to dry soils of average to low fertility. Shear plants in spring to maintain form or to remove unattractive inflorescences. Some species, such as *A. schmidtiana*, may not appreciate humidity in hot summer climates.

USES Borders, pathways, and slopes, especially in dry, sunny sites. *Artemisia pycnocephala* and *A. stelleriana* are salt and drought tolerant. *Artemisia caucasica*, *A. viridis*, and *A. versicolor* can be useful on retaining walls and in crevice or rock gardens, and *A. viridis* can be used as a lawn alternative for small applications. Deer and rabbit resistant. Not tolerant of foot traffic.

PROPAGATION Cuttings, division

Artemisia alba
MUGWORT

Zones 7–9 (perhaps hardier)
Open sites in Southern Europe from Spain and France to Bulgaria.
Semi-evergreen subshrub with dissected, silvery gray leaves, forming bushy, spreading mounds, 4–20 in. (10–50 cm) tall and wide.

'Canescens': superb selection with intricately dissected, filigree, silver-white foliage on bushy plants, 8–12 in. (20–30 cm) tall and 24 in. (60 cm) wide, AGM

Artemisia caucasica
CAUCASIAN ARTEMISIA, SILVER SPREADER

Zones 4–8
Plains, plateaus, and hills of the Caucasus.
Silvery, dissected, evergreen, silky haired foliage on sturdy mats, 3–6 in. (7.5–15 cm) tall and 24 in. (60 cm) wide. Somewhat ornamental silvery flower stems are produced in summer with insignificant flowers. Also known as *A. alpina*.

Artemisia pontica
ROMAN WORMWOOD, OLD WARRIOR

Zones 2–9
Rocky slopes, dry valleys, steppes, hills, disturbed areas, and shaded thickets from low to middle elevations from Central and Eastern Europe to China.
Finely dissected, lightly aromatic, gray-green foliage on upright, 12–18 in. (30–45 cm) tall, suckering stems, spreading indefinitely and quickly into large colonies. Plant where it can be contained by hardscape features.

Artemisia pycnocephala
COASTAL SAGEWORT, SANDHILL SAGE

Zones 7–10
Rocky or sandy soils along coastal beaches and dunes in California and Oregon.
Finely dissected, faintly aromatic, evergreen, silver foliage growing at a moderate to fast rate into mounds 12–28 in. (30–71 cm) tall and wide.

'David's Choice': selected from a population at the lighthouse at Point Reyes, California, forming dense mounds, 12 in. (30 cm) tall and 36 in. (90 cm) wide, finer and more compact than *A. arborescens* 'Powis Castle'

Artemisia rupestris subsp. viridis
CREEPING ARTEMISIA, MINIATURE WORMWOOD

Zones 3–9
Unknown origin.
Often listed as *A. viridis*, this unusual, low-growing, semi-evergreen species forms a dense, aromatic, olive-green, textured mat, 3 in. (7.5 cm) tall and 18 in. (45 cm) or more wide.

'Tiny Green': seemingly the only cultivated form, possibly a hybrid

Artemisia schmidtiana
SILVERMOUND, SATINY WORMWOOD

Zones 1–9
Grassy slopes and bare soil, from sea level to the high mountains of Central and Northern Japan.
Extremely hardy, evergreen perennial with soft, finely dissected, aromatic, silky-hairy, silver foliage forming small, symmetrical mounds or mats, 12–24 in. (30–60 cm) tall and wide. Spreads at a moderate rate by creeping underground stems. Prefers cool summer climates. Resents heat and humidity.

'Ever Goldy': golden form of 'Nana'

'Nana': compact mounds, 4–12 in. (10–30 cm) tall and 12–18 in. (30–45 cm) wide, AGM

Artemisia schmidtiana 'Nana'

Artemisia stelleriana

DUSTY MILLER, BEACH WORMWOOD

Zones 3–9

Maritime dunes of Japan, China, eastern Russia, and the Aleutian Islands. Naturalized in parts of North America and Europe.

Evergreen, rhizomatous, and stoloniferous species with a prostrate habit growing at a moderate rate to 12–24 in. (30–60 cm) tall and 36 in. (90 cm) wide. Foliage is densely white-felted and faintly aromatic with lusher, more broadly dissected and lobed leaves than other species.

'Boughton Silver' (syn. 'Silver Brocade'): somewhat shorter, more compact, and more prostrate form, 6–12 in. (15–30 cm) tall, with infrequent flowers

'Silver Cascade': shorter selection, 4–8 in. (10–20 cm) tall

Artemisia versicolor

CURLICUE SAGE

Zones 4–9

Unknown origin.

Distinctive, highly textured, evergreen species with finely dissected, lacy, downward-curling, silver-white foliage forming clumps of upright, ascending, and prostrate stems, 8–12 in. (20–30 cm) tall and 24 in. (60 cm) wide. Grows at a moderate rate. Listed in horticulture but may not be a true species.

'Sea Foam': the only horticultural form

Arum italicum subsp. italicum

ITALIAN ARUM, LORDS AND LADIES

Araceae

Zones 5–9

Ditches, fields, wooded areas, stony ground, and hedgerows from Great Britain to the Mediterranean Basin and Madeira, the Azores, and the Canary Islands.

This Old World relative of the South African calla lily (Zantedeschia aethiopica) and the North American Jack in the pulpit (Arisaema triphyllum) is an intriguing and easy garden plant with a valuable seasonal growth pattern. In mild winter regions, new, glossy, arrow-shaped foliage with pale green to white veins emerges in fall, remaining evergreen through winter. In cold winter areas, new foliage is produced in fall until freezing weather forces dormancy. New foliage is produced again in spring. Large, green-spathed inflorescences with yellow spadices are produced among the leaves in mid- to late spring. As stems develop fleshy green fruits, the foliage goes summer dormant. Fruits turn orange-red by midsummer, lasting into fall. Leaves are 8–12 in. (20–30 cm) long on plants 12–18 in. (30–45 cm) tall and wide. In the wild, populations can exhibit considerable variation of leaf mottling, from green leaves with faint lighter green veins to boldly mottled forms.

CULTURE/CARE Rich, evenly moist soil in part sun to shade.

USES Mass plant as a winter ground cover or interplant around winter-dormant herbaceous perennials, especially hostas and ferns, to maintain year-round coverage. Not tolerant of foot traffic. Deer resistant.

PROPAGATION Seed, division

'Marmoratum': bold white to mint-green veining, AGM

'Spotted Jack': good veining with random black specks

'White Winter': extremely bold, silver-white mottling

Aruncus aethusifolius

DWARF KOREAN GOAT'S BEARD,
DWARF GOAT'S BEARD

Rosaceae

Zones 3–9

Endemic to moist habitats, including volcanic crevices and creek banks, on Jeju Island, South Korea, at 1300–5900 ft. (400–1800 m).

Best known of the genus is the tall, circumboreal species A. dioicus, which resembles a giant white astilbe. Less known are the textural dwarf Korean goat's beard and its hybrids, valuable as mass-planted ground covers. This slow-growing, clump-forming, herbaceous perennial with dense, much dissected, fernlike, midgreen leaves forms mounds up to 6 in. (15 cm) tall and 12–18 in. (30–45 cm) wide, sporting yellow, orange, and red fall color. Open, upright, astilbe-like plumes resembling fireworks rise to 12 in. (30 cm), with ivory-white flowers in the spring. AGM

CULTURE/CARE Part sun to part shade in average to moist, fertile soils. Avoid dry soils. Most selections do not like heat and humidity.

USES Mass plant to achieve a closed cover. Somewhat slow growing. Remove spent flower stems. Not tolerant of foot traffic. Deer and rabbit resistant.

PROPAGATION Division, seed

Artemisia stelleriana 'Boughton Silver'

Arum italicum subsp. *italicum*

Artemisia versicolor 'Sea Foam'

Aruncus aethusifolius

'Noble Spirit': compact, floriferous, less than 12 in. (30 cm) tall with orange to red fall color, may be a hybrid

Hybrids with A. dioicus

'Guinea Fowl': foliage to 12 in. (30 cm), flowers to 18 in. (45 cm) on red stems

'Horatio': red stems, 30–40 in. (75–100 cm) tall

'Johannifest': foliage with reddish tints, dark stems to 24 in. (60 cm) or taller

'Misty Lace': more heat and humidity tolerant, 24–36 in. (60–90 cm) tall with dark red stems

Asarum
Aristolochiaceae

Many *Asarum* species are excellent ground covers, with beautiful evergreen foliage, intriguing flowers, and dense mounds or mats of arrow- or kidney-shaped leaves. The best species belong to three aesthetically different groups: those with often mottled, arrow-shaped or heart-shaped leaves endemic to the southeastern United States (*A. arifolium* and *A. shuttleworthii* often listed as a *Hexastylis* spp.); those with all green, heart- or kidney-shaped leaves found in more northerly areas of North America and Europe (*A. canadense*, *A. caudatum*, and *A. europaeum*); and those Asian species with larger, bolder, often shiny or mottled, arrow-shaped foliage (*A. delavayi*, *A. maximum*, and *A. splendens*). All bloom at ground level from early spring to summer, depending on the species, with flowers often hidden by or peaking out from the foliage.

CULTURE/CARE Part to full shade in evenly moist, humus-rich soil. Young leaves can be susceptible to slug damage, especially the Asian species. Apply an environmentally friendly slug bait in early spring when new leaves emerge.

USES Small to medium-sized applications along pathways, as shady border edgers, and under trees and shrubs. None are fast spreading. Most take some time to establish before expanding. For quicker coverage, plant as densely as possible. Not tolerant of foot traffic. Deer and rabbit resistant.

PROPAGATION Division

Asarum arifolium
JUG PLANT, LITTLE BROWN JUG

Zones 5–9
Upland deciduous and mixed deciduous–coniferous forests from sea level to 2000 ft. (600 m) in the southeastern United States from Virginia, Tennessee, and Louisiana, to Florida.

Evergreen, heart- or arrow-shaped, anise-scented leaves are 4–6 in. (10–15 cm) long, dark green, and beautifully mottled in silver or light green, in dense, slowly spreading clumps, 6–8 in. (15–20 cm) tall and 12–18 in. (30–45 cm) wide, from underground rhizomes. Jug- or urn-shaped, burgundy-brown flowers bloom in early to midspring. Also known as *Hexastylis arifolia*.

'Silver Spreader': boldly silvered, more stoloniferous, and faster spreading

Asarum canadense
CANADA WILD GINGER, CANADIAN SNAKEROOT

Zones 3–9
Moist, rich soils in woodlands and deciduous (occasionally coniferous) forests from sea level to 4300 ft. (1300 m), from Manitoba to New Brunswick, and south to North Carolina and Kansas.

Deciduous, downy textured, light green, kidney- or heart-shaped leaves, typically 2–3 in. (5–7.5 cm) long by 3–6 in. (7.5–15 cm) wide. Plants grow 4–6 in. (10–15 cm) tall and 12–18 in. (30–45 cm) or more wide from spreading rhizomes that expand faster than *A. europaeum*. Cylindrical flowers with dense, silver hairs outside and white or green inside, with spreading or reflexed, short to long, burgundy lobes, bloom from spring to early summer.

Asarum caudatum
BRITISH COLUMBIA WILD GINGER, WESTERN WILD GINGER

Zones 3–9
Understory plant of coniferous forests, usually in average to wet soils from sea level to 4000 ft. (1200 m) west of the Coast and Cascade Mountain ranges from the Alaska Panhandle to Northern California, and in the inland rainforest of the Columbia Mountains of British Columbia and Idaho.

Evergreen, kidney- or heart-shaped, slightly hairy and shiny leaves, 1–4 in. (2.5–10 cm) long by 2–5 in.

Asarum canadense

Asarum caudatum

Asarum europaeum

(5–12.5 cm) wide, that smell of ginger when rubbed or crushed. Plants grow 4–6 in. (10–15 cm) tall and 12–18 in. (30–45 cm) or more wide from spreading rhizomes, expanding more quickly than *A. europaeum*. Cup-shaped flowers are greenish, tan, or brown outside with silver hairs and white and burgundy inside, flaring into three lobes with long, tail-like appendages from spring through summer.

f. *album*: greenish white flowers

Asarum delavayi
CHINESE GINGER, WILD GINGER

Zones 7b–9b

Forests, thickets, moist and shady areas, and mountain slopes at 2600–5200 ft. (790–1585 m) in Sichuan and Yunnan, China.

Large, shiny, arrow-shaped, evergreen leaves, 3–8 in. (7.5–20 cm) long by 2–6 in. (5–15 cm) wide, sometimes larger, that are green on top, sometimes with subtle veining, and green beneath, sometimes with a reddish purple flush. Plants grow 6–8 in. (15–20 cm) tall and 12–18 in. (30–45 cm) or more wide from slowly spreading rhizomes. Fascinating, 4 in. (10 cm) wide, bell-shaped, early spring flowers are among the largest in the genus with three large, flaring, purple to burgundy-black lobes with white to pinkish picotee edges and basal triangles around the throat.

'Sichuan Splendour': large, 8 in. (20 cm) long leaves with subtle light green speckling

Asarum europaeum
EUROPEAN WILD GINGER, ASARABACCA

Zones 4–8

Moist, open woodlands, especially on calcareous soils, from Finland and northern Russia to the Mediterranean.

The most popular wild ginger ground cover and one of the best for deep shade and dry shade, with thick, evergreen, glossy, pepper-scented, rounded, kidney- or heart-shaped leaves, 2.5–5 in. (6–12.5 cm) wide. Plants grow in tight, compact mats, 4–6 in. (10–15 cm) tall and 12 in. (30 cm) or more wide, from slowly spreading rhizomes. Cup-shaped flowers are greenish and burgundy outside with silver hairs and burgundy inside, flaring into three curving lobes in early to midspring. More slug resistant.

Asarum maximum
PANDA FACE WILD GINGER

Zones 7–9

Forested areas in humus-rich soils, at 2000–2600 ft. (600–790 m), in Hubei and Sichuan, China.

Large, shiny, somewhat rounded, arrow-shaped, evergreen leaves up to 6 in. (15 cm) long and nearly as wide offer variable, attractive, light green to silver mottling and veining. Clumping to very slowly spreading plants, 4–6 in. (10–15 cm) tall and 8–12 in. (20–30 cm) or more wide. Distinctive, bell-shaped, mushroom-scented flowers are 2 in. (5 cm) or more wide, with three large, flaring, purple-black to black lobes with white basal triangles and white picotee edges in mid- to late spring.

'Green Panda': unmottled green foliage

'Ling Ling': symmetrical light green mottling on foliage

'Shell Shocked': bold, light green tortoise shell veining on foliage

'Silver Panda': bold silver-green mottling on foliage

Asarum shuttleworthii
MOTTLED WILD GINGER, SHUTTLEWORTH GINGER

Zones 5–9

Rich, deciduous or mixed deciduous–coniferous mountain forests, often along creeks and in acidic soils, at 1300–4300 ft. (400–1300 m), in the Appalachian Mountains from Alabama to Virginia.

Thick, evergreen or semi-evergreen, glossy, rounded, heart-shaped, usually silver-mottled, aromatic leaves, 2–4 in. (5–10 cm) across, on plants 8 in. (20 cm) tall and 14 in. (36 cm) wide, from slowly spreading rhizomes. Small, cup- or bell-shaped flowers taper toward the flared calyx lobes, tan or purplish brown outside and creamy inside with heavy burgundy speckling in midspring to early summer. Very slow growing. Also known as *Hexastylis shuttleworthii*.

var. *harperi* 'Callaway': dramatic silver veination and good stoloniferous habit, spreading into large mats given time

Asarum splendens
CHINESE WILD GINGER

Zones 5b–9

Thickets, grasslands, and moist mountain slopes at 2600–4300 ft. (790–1300 m) in southeastern China.

Asarum maximum 'Ling Ling'

Asarum shuttleworthii var. *harperi* 'Callaway'

Asarum splendens

Large, shiny, arrow-shaped, evergreen leaves, 4–6 in. (10–15 cm) long and nearly as wide, with bold silver-green mottling on a dark green background. Plants grow 6–8 in. (15–20 cm) tall and 12–18 in. (30–45 cm) or more wide by relatively fast-spreading rhizomes, making *A. splendens* the best of the Asian species for use as a ground cover. Bell-shaped, 2 in. (5 cm) or more wide, toadlike flowers have three large, flaring, ruffled, greenish, tan, off-white, and purple lobes with varied speckling in early spring.

'Quicksilver': excellent silver variegation and larger flowers

Asplenium scolopendrium
HART'S TONGUE FERN

Aspleniacaee

Zones 4–9

Widespread across Europe into North Africa and eastward to Japan on moist banks, damp and rocky areas, screes, shady cliffs, and walls in woodlands and open shaded sites, often in lime-rich soils. Some extremely rare populations occur in eastern North America from Ontario to Alabama. Cultivated forms are from Europe.

The decidedly "unferny," simple, undivided fronds of hart's tongue fern, also known by its synonym *Phyllitis scolopendrium*, make it one of the most distinctive for temperate gardens, with glossy, leathery, undulated, mid- to dark green, 12–24 in. (30–60 cm) long and 1–3 in. (2.5–7.5 cm) wide, strap- or tongue-like leaves. Attractive bands of rust-colored sori are reminiscent of centipede legs, which is the meaning of its species name. Plants form evergreen rosettes with upward and angled foliage from the current year and prostrate foliage from the previous year, bulking up slowly by tightly held offsets. AGM

CULTURE/CARE Part sun to full shade in evenly moist soils. Tolerant of dry shade once established.

USES Mass plant for small to large applications in woodlands, on slopes, in walls, and in living walls. Not tolerant of foot traffic. Deer and rabbit resistant.

PROPAGATION Division, spores

'Angustatum' (syn. 'Angustifolia'): narrow, dark green fronds with deeply cut and sharply undulated margins

Crispum Group: deeply frilled margins on broad, light green fronds, resembling lasagna noodles

Asplenium scolopendrium, VanDusen Botanical Garden, Vancouver, BC

Asplenium scolopendrium 'Kaye's Lacerated'

Cristatum Group: wavy margins with forked or crested frond tips

'Furcatum': wavy margins and forked tips

'Kaye's Lacerated': wide fronds with many fingered and frilled margins

'Muricatum': narrow, dark green fronds with crinkled edges and ridges across the upper surface

Undulatum Group: light green fronds with wavy margins that spread across the frond surface to the central midrib

Aster tongolensis
EAST INDIES ASTER, TONGO DAISY

Asteraceae

Zones 4–8

Alpine and open subalpine forests and thickets, streambanks, grasslands, boggy lake margins, and rocky or grassy slopes at 8200–13,100 ft. (2500–3990 m) in west-central China into India.

Most asters are upright, but a few from various genera can make good ground covers. *Aster tongolensis* is a dense, mat-forming, rhizomatous and often stoloniferous species with tight foliage, 6 in. (15 cm) tall, producing masses of solitary blue or lavender to purplish, 2 in. (5 cm) wide flowers with orange-yellow centers on short, nearly leafless stems, 6–20 in. (15–50 cm) tall, over a long period from midspring to early summer.

CULTURE/CARE Full sun in average to moist, fertile, well-drained soils.

USES Small-scale applications in rock gardens and along border edges. Not tolerant of foot traffic.

PROPAGATION Division, seed, cuttings

'Berggarten': bluish lavender daisies

'Napsbury': pinkish lavender daisies

'Wartburgstern' (syn. 'Wartburg Star'): violet-blue daisies

Astilbe
Saxifragaceae

A classic of temperate horticulture, major players in perennial borders, and great as mass-planted ground covers, false spiraea forms low mounds of textured, herbaceous foliage, usually 6–24 in. (15–60 cm) tall and wide (sometimes wider). Though most are clumping, cultivars of *A. chinensis* can spread slowly

to moderately by underground rhizomes. The upright, branching panicles of tiny red, pink, or white flowers can reach 8 in. (20 cm) in *A. chinensis* var. *pumila* and *A.* ×*crispa* 'Perkeo' and 2–4 ft. (0.6–1.2 m) for the *A.* ×*arendsii* hybrids, though the shorter species and cultivars are best as ground covers in average garden situations. Larger cultivars, including the *A. japonica* hybrids, *A. thunbergii*, *A.* ×*arendsii*, and others, are effective for larger landscape applications.

CULTURE/CARE Easy to grow and best in part sun to part shade in cool, average to moist soils. Tolerant of full sun in cooler summer climates or with good moisture. *Astilbe chinensis* is more tolerant of drought and sun than other species. Remove faded flower stems or retain for winter interest. Divide every three or four years to maintain vigor and enhance flower production.

USES Border edges, along pathways, or as a mass-planted general cover. Most cultivars reach full size and spread within a few years. Not tolerant of foot traffic. Deer and rabbit resistant.

PROPAGATION Division

Astilbe chinensis
CHINESE ASTILBE

Zones 3–9

Forests and forest margins, meadows, valleys, and riversides at 1300–11,800 ft. (400–3600 m) in China, Japan, Korea, and Russia.

Deeply incised, coarse leaves are two- or three-times compound, glossy above, dull below, with reddish pubescence on both sides, giving rise to panicles, 10–18 in. (25–45 cm) tall, with densely packed, lilac-pink to purple flowers in mid- to late summer. Spreads slowly by underground rhizomes. Moderately tolerant of drought and full sun with reasonable moisture. *Astilbe chinensis* var. *pumila* is a dwarf variety that is among the best as a ground cover. For large applications on a landscape scale, use *A. chinensis* 'Amber Moon', 'Diamonds and Pearls', 'Finale', 'Milk and Honey', and 'Purpurkerze', and *A. chinensis* var. *taquetti* 'Purpurlanze' and 'Superba', which produce large mounds of spreading foliage and inflorescences 2–4 ft. (0.6–1.2 m) tall.

'Little Vision in Pink': shorter, more compact version of 'Vision in Pink', with dark green foliage and rose-pink panicles, 14–16 in. (36–40 cm) tall

'Little Vision in Purple': similar to 'Visions' but shorter and more compact, with more dissected leaves and darker colored lavender plumes, 12–15 in. (30–38 cm) tall

var. *pumila*: late to bloom on vigorous, spreading mounds of midgreen foliage, 6 in. (15 cm) tall and 12–18 in. (30–45 cm) wide, with lilac-pink panicles, 8–12 in. (20–30 cm) tall, from midsummer into fall, AGM

'Veronica Klose': deep green foliage, purplish rose-colored flowers, 16 in. (40 cm) tall

'Vision in Pink': blue-green leaves, pink flowers, 18–20 in. (45–50 cm) tall

'Vision in Red': bronze-green foliage, panicles of deep red buds open to pinkish red flowers, 15–18 in. (38–45 cm) tall

'Vision in White': smooth, glossy, less coarse leaves, with creamy white plumes, 24 in. (60 cm) tall

'Visions': midgreen leaves and fragrant, raspberry-pink plumes, 14–18 in. (36–45 cm) tall

Astilbe ×crispa
CRISPED ASTILBE

Zones 4–9
Hybrid origin.
A group of hybrids probably involving *A. simplicifolia* and *A. chinensis* var. *pumila* that are clump-forming, with deeply toothed, "crisped," and crinkled leaf margins with stiff-stemmed panicles, 8 in. (20 cm) tall in midsummer. Somewhat tolerant of dry shade.

'Lilliput': light pink to salmon-pink flowers, with glossy, dark green leaves

'Perkeo': mid- to deep pink flowers, with glossy, dark green leaves, bronze-flushed when young, AGM

Astilbe glaberrima var. saxatilis
SMOOTH ROCK ASTILBE

Zones 4–9
Mountain habitats of Yakushima Island, Japan.
Tough miniature species resembling *A. simplicifolia* with delicate, deeply dissected foliage, green above and red beneath, growing 3–4 in. (7.5–10 cm) tall and 12–18 in. (30–45 cm) wide, with short, 8 in. (20 cm) tall panicles of pale mauve-pink to white flowers in late summer. Prefers good moisture. AGM

Astilbe chinensis var. *pumila*

Astilbe 'Sprite'

Astilbe simplicifolia

DWARF ASTILBE

Zones (3)4–9

Mountainous regions of Honshu, Japan.

Distinctive dwarf species with more open panicles of arching branches resembling a Christmas tree, typically reaching 8–12 in. (20–30 cm) tall, blooming in late spring to midsummer with white flowers, with simple, glossy leaflets once-dissected into threes. May be slower to establish, requiring longer to reach full size. More ornamental seed heads provide additional interest.

'Darwin's Snow Sprite': open, arching plumes of white flowers, 10–12 in. (25–30 cm) tall, and bronze-tinged foliage

'Jacqueline': pink flowers on plumes 12–18 in. (30–45 cm) or more tall

Key Series: seedlings of 'Sprite'

'Key Biscayne': fuller, light pink panicles, 14–16 in. (36–40 cm) tall, and two-tone green foliage with red edges

'Key Largo': slightly fragrant, bright raspberry-pink flowers on panicles 16–18 in. (40–45 cm) tall, with mid- to deep green foliage

'Key West': vigorous, with reddish buds opening to pink flowers on panicles 12–14 in. (30–36 cm) tall, dissected foliage emerges red fading to green with red edges

'White Sensation': white flowers on panicles 15–18 in. (38–45 cm) tall, with glossy green foliage

A. *simplicifolia* hybrids

'Aphrodite': sparkling, rose-red plumes, 16 in. (40 cm) tall, new red foliage matures to green with larger leaves

'Hennie Graafland': light pink flowers on panicles 16–18 in. (40–45 cm) tall, with attractive rusty seed heads

'Inshriach Pink': light pink flowers on red stems, 16 in. (40 cm) tall, bronzy green foliage

'Pink Lightning': full, well-branched 18 in. (45 cm) tall, rose-pink panicles fading to light pink followed by rusty seed heads, with glossy, deep green foliage with dark margins

'Sprite': among the best of the dwarf cultivars for use as a ground cover, with shell-pink flowers on drooping panicles, 12–15 in. (30–38 cm) tall, followed by attractive, rust-colored seed heads, with finely textured foliage emerging bronze and fading to deep green, AGM, Perennial Plant of the Year 1994

'White Wings': dwarf cultivar with full panicles of pink-tinged, white flowers, 12 in. (30 cm) tall, with textured, dark green foliage

'Willie Buchanan': dwarf cultivar with palest pink to creamy white flowers on panicles 9–12 in. (23–30 cm) tall, with red-tinted leaves

Astrantia
Apiaceae

Masterworts are widely grown in British gardens but have yet to achieve similar ubiquity in North America, despite their many desirable attributes and ease of cultivation. Attractive herbaceous mounds of palmate foliage, 12 in. (30 cm) tall and wide, can be mass-planted to achieve a closed cover. The see-through flower stems reach about 24 in. (60 cm) tall, with unusual pincushions of tiny florets subtended by colorful bracts over a long period from late spring to fall. Of the three cultivated species, *A. major* is most commonly grown with many cultivars, followed by *A. maxima*. *Astrantia carniolica*, usually represented by its cultivar 'Rubra', is a shorter species and occasionally grown.

CULTURE/CARE Part sun to part shade in average to evenly moist, humus-rich soils. In zone 4, provide a mulch to increase overwintering success. May gently self-seed.

USES Mass plant as a general cover for small to large areas. Not tolerant of foot traffic. Attractive to pollinators, especially bees and butterflies.

PROPAGATION Division, seed

Astrantia major
GREAT MASTERWORT

Zones 4–9

Moist woodlands and forest clearings, streambanks, grasslands, and mountain meadows, usually on calcareous soils, at 330–7550 ft. (100–2300 m), in Central and Eastern Europe and Western Asia. Naturalized in the United Kingdom.

Mounds of textured, slightly shiny, palmate, midgreen foliage with lobes and serrations, 8–12 in.

Astrantia major 'Sunningdale Variegated'

(20–30 cm) tall and 12–18 in. (30–45 cm) wide. The nearly leafless flower stems rise 24–36 in. (60–90 cm) tall, each one splitting once or twice above a green bract to produce one to a few pincushion-like inflorescences consisting of a dome of many tiny florets, subtended by a ring of ornamental bracts, about 1.5 in. (4 cm) or more wide, over a long period from late spring through summer. Florets and bracts offer colors of white through pink to deepest pink-red, fading in late summer to green but remaining ornamental. May self-seed. Hybrids with *A. maxima* are sterile and may also rebloom.

'Abbey Road': glowing purple-red, reblooming flowers, 24 in. (60 cm) tall, with glossy leaves

'Claret': wine-red flowers, 28 in. (71 cm) tall

'Florence': lavender-pink florets and bracts fading to white, 36 in. (90 cm) tall

Gill Richardson Group: seed strain with large, cherry-red flowers with purple-black–tipped bracts and purple-flushed stem bracts on dark stems, 32 in. (80 cm) tall subsp. *involucrata* 'Shaggy' (syn. 'Margery Fish'): white flowers with a subtle pink flush and green-tipped bracts, 32 in. (80 cm) tall, AGM

'Lars': lavender-pink long-blooming flowers, 24 in. (60 cm) tall

'Moulin Rouge': sterile hybrid seedling of unknown parentage, with dark burgundy-red florets with white stamens and nearly black bracts, 22 in. (56 cm) tall, reblooming

var. *rosea*: midpink florets and silver-pink bracts, 24 in. (60 cm) tall

'Rubra': rose-red flowers, 28 in. (71 cm) tall

'Ruby Cloud': red-purple flowers, 24 in. (60 cm) tall

'Ruby Star': hybrid with purple-red flowers and purple-black–tipped bracts, 24 in. (60 cm) tall

'Ruby Wedding': dark purple-red flowers, burgundy stems, 24 in. (60 cm) tall, reblooming

Star Series: vigorous and floriferous cultivars in a range of colors

> 'Star of Beauty': purple-red flowers with white centers, 30 in. (75 cm) tall
>
> 'Star of Billion': white and green flowers, 30 in. (75 cm) tall
>
> 'Star of Fire': burgundy-red flowers with white centers and dark purple stems, 30 in. (75 cm) tall
>
> 'Star of Heaven': white flowers, 24 in. (60 cm) tall
>
> 'Star of Magic': leaves boldly variegated with creamy white, flushed pink in cool weather, with deep purple-red flowers on dark stems, 24 in. (60 cm) tall
>
> 'Star of Royals': white florets and white bracts with pink reverses, 30 in. (75 cm) tall

'Sunningdale Variegated': green leaves edged in yellow and creamy white over a long period in spring, slowly deepening to green by summer, with white and green flowers flushed pink, 28 in. (70 cm) tall, AGM

'Superstar': hybrid with large white flowers with green-tipped bracts, 24 in. (60 cm) tall

'Vanilla Gorilla': blue-green leaves with wide white margins remaining variegated all season and pink-flushed in cool weather, with pale silver-pink flowers, 24 in. (60 cm) tall

'Venice': deep wine-red flowers on dark stems, 24 in. (60 cm) tall

Sterile hybrids with A. maxima

'Buckland': dusty pink florets, pale silver-pink to white bracts, 24 in. (60 cm) tall, may rebloom

'Dark Shiny Eyes': glowing purple-red flowers and white anthers, burgundy stems, 24 in. (60 cm) tall, may rebloom

'Hadspen Blood': deep red flowers and purple-black–tipped bracts on short, burgundy stems 20 in. (50 cm) tall, may rebloom

'Roma': fast growing with glowing dusty pink flowers and broad pink bracts, 28 in. (70 cm) tall, AGM

'Snow Star': white and green flowers, 24 in. (60 cm) tall

Astrantia maxima
LARGE MASTERWORT

Zones 4–9

Meadows, woodlands, among scrub, and in coniferous forests at 2300–7900 ft. (700–2400 m) in Turkey and the Caucasus.

Clumping or forming small colonies via stolons. Large, dusty rose (sometimes white) flower heads, 1.5–2.5 in. (4–6 cm) wide, with broad, overlapping, triangular bracts, are solitary or in twos or threes on stems 16–36 in. (40–90 cm) tall in late spring or summer. Hybrids with *A. major* produce desirable sterile and reblooming cultivars. AGM

Athyrium
Woodsiaceae

These easy to grow deciduous ferns can be mass-planted to achieve colorful, textural cover. In the Pacific Northwest, the native lady fern (*A. filix-femina*) can readily spread by spores into large, tall, dense colonies. Its relatives, the Japanese painted fern (*A. niponicum* var. *pictum*) and the eared lady fern (*A. otophorum*), do not have overenthusiastic tendencies and make good smaller ground covers.

CULTURE/CARE Moist, humus-rich, well-drained soils in part to full shade. Evenly moist soils are a must to encourage vigorous, long-lived plants, especially for *A. niponicum*.

USES Mass plant beneath trees and shrubs and in woodland settings for small to medium-sized applications. Not tolerant of foot traffic. Deer and rabbit resistant.

PROPAGATION Division, spores

Astrantia maxima

Athyrium niponicum var. *pictum* 'Regal Red'

Athyrium otophorum var. *okanum* with *Stachys byzantina*

Athyrium niponicum var. *pictum*

JAPANESE PAINTED FERN, JAPANESE LADY FERN

Zones 3–8

Forests, streamsides, shaded and wet mountain slopes, and shrubby and grassy slopes from near sea level to 8500 ft. (2590 m) in eastern Asia, including China, India, Korea, and Japan.

The Japanese painted fern is one of the most popular and distinctive of garden ferns. Plants typically grow 12–18 in. (30–45 cm) tall and wide from shortly creeping rhizomes, offering herbaceous, arching, lacy, twice-pinnate fronds colored with red stipes (stems) and silver-green pinnae (leaflets), usually emerging with the boldest coloration and maturing to more muted tones. Established clumps can form dense colonies. AGM, Perennial Plant of the Year 2004

'Apple Court': silver fronds with crested tips

'Branford Rambler': hybrid with A. *filix-femina*, spreading via creeping rhizomes, with green fronds with red stipes, 12–24 in. (30–60 cm) long

'Burgundy Lace': new foliage emerges burgundy-purple with silver-tipped fronds, slowly maturing to silver-green with purple stipes

'Godzilla': large hybrid with A. *filix-femina*, with the same look and habit as a painted fern, but larger, 24–36 in. (60–90 cm) tall and 4–6 ft. (1.2–1.8 m) wide

'Pewter Lace': silver-gray foliage with green edges and pinkish red stipes

'Red Beauty': silver-green fronds with brighter red stems and veins

'Regal Red': silver fronds with green tips and burgundy-red stipes, subtly twisted pinnules

'Silver Falls': bolder, more silver form that intensifies rather than fades through the season, with wine-red stipes, AGM

'Ursula's Red': new foliage emerges burgundy-red down the center of each frond, with silver tips, slowly matures to silver-green with reddish stipes

'Wildwood Twist': silver-green, twisting fronds

Athyrium otophorum

EARED LADY FERN, AURICULATE LADY FERN

Zones 4–9

Evergreen broadleaf and bamboo forests and wet areas at 1300–4600 ft. (400–1400 m) in China, Korea, and Japan.

Distinctive herbaceous, clumping fern with red stipes and triangular, bipinnate fronds. Bold new growth emerges from red fiddleheads into creamy yellow to light green fronds that slowly mature to gray-green. Plants grow 12–24 in. (30–60 cm) tall by 12–18 in. (30–45 cm) wide in an arching vase shape. The differences between the species and A. *otophorum* var. *okanum* are unclear, but the variety may have yellower new growth and redder stipes. AGM

Aubrieta

Brassicaceae

Zones 3–8

Rocky habitats in hills and mountains from Southern Europe east to Central Asia.

Popular spring-flowering mound- or mat-forming ground cover offering billowy masses of color for 3–4 weeks each spring on plants 4–6 in. (10–15 cm) tall and 12–24 in. (30–60 cm) or more wide. Four-petaled flowers, sometimes with white centers, are lavender-purple, magenta-red, pink, or white and can completely cover the evergreen to semi-evergreen, hairy, grayish green foliage when in full bloom.

Seemingly countless cultivars have been produced over time, with most attributed to A. *deltoidea* or A. ×*cultorum*, but all are now considered of hybrid origin.

CULTURE/CARE Full sun to part shade in average to dry soils, though reasonable moisture is best. Provide light shade in hot summer climates. Wet soils can cause root rot. Plants can look messy after flowering. Shear off seed heads and stem tips to encourage fresh growth.

USES Rock gardens, slopes, walls, or border edges. Grows quickly. Tolerates occasional foot traffic. Deer resistant. Attractive to pollinators, especially butterflies.

PROPAGATION Seed, cuttings, division

'Argenteovariegata': reddish purple flowers and gray-green leaves with white to creamy yellow edges

Audrey Series: early blooming, fast-growing F1 hybrid (seed grown) series, includes 'Audrey Blue', 'Audrey Red', and 'Audrey Red and Purple'

Aubrieta cv.

Aurinia saxatilis

Axcent Series: large-flowered, cutting-grown series with more uniform habit than seed strains, includes 'Audelanro' Axcent Antique Rose, 'Audelbley' Axcent Blue with Eye, 'Audeldare' Axcent Dark Red, 'Audelip' Axcent Lilac, 'Audelmag' Axcent Magenta, 'Audelpur' Axcent Deep Purple, and 'Audelvioe' Axcent Violet with Eye

'Blue Beauty': lilac-purple double flowers

Cascade Series: popular F1 seed strains, includes 'Blue Cascade', 'Lilac Cascade', 'Purple Cascade', and 'Red Cascade', AGM

'Doctor Mules Variegata': warm purple flowers with gray-green leaves with creamy white edges

Royal Series: popular seed strains, includes 'Royal Blue', 'Royal Red', and 'Royal Violet'

'Swan Red': purple-red flowers with gray-green leaves with creamy white edges

'Whitewell Gem': velvety, bluish purple flowers

Aurinia saxatilis
BASKET OF GOLD, GOLDEN ALYSSUM

Brassicaceae

Zones 3–9
Stony places among rocks, including ledges, cliffs, and rocky slopes in Southern and Central Europe and Turkey.

This popular and old-fashioned evergreen rock garden plant is a mounding or mat-forming, drought-tolerant perennial with a woody base, with 5 in. (12.5 cm) long, finely pubescent, silvery green basal foliage. Leafy stems rise 6–20 in. (15–50 cm) tall into heavily branched panicles covered in a profusion of tiny, canary-yellow, fragrant flowers in early to mid-spring. AGM

CULTURE/CARE Full sun in average to dry soils. Shear lightly after flowering.

USES Rock gardens, walls, slopes, or border edges. Often grown with *Arabis* and *Aubrieta* spp. and with spring-flowering bulbs. Not tolerant of foot traffic. Deer and rabbit resistant. Attractive to pollinators, especially bees and butterflies.

PROPAGATION Seed

'Citrina': pale lemon-yellow flowers, 8–12 in. (20–30 cm) tall and 12–24 in. (30–60 cm) wide, AGM

'Compacta': dwarf, 8–12 in. (20–30 cm) tall and 12–24 in. (30–60 cm) wide

'Dudley Nevill Variegated': variegated, cream-edged, olive-green to silvery leaves

'Goldkugel' (syn. 'Gold Ball'): compact, floriferous, 4–6 in. (10–15 cm) tall and 12–18 in. (30–45 cm) wide

'Summit': compact, 6–8 in. (15–20 cm) tall and 12–18 in. (30–45 cm) wide

Azorella trifurcata
CUSHION BOLAX, EMERALD CUSHION

Apiaceae

Zones 7–10
Coastal beaches and gravel streambanks, heath areas, and forest margins from sea level to high altitudes of at least 5000 ft. (1500 m) in southern Argentina and Chile.

Hailing from the ends of the Earth, this peculiar carrot relative forms a slowly creeping, pillowy cushion or mat, 1–2 in. (2.5–5 cm) tall and 12–24 in. (30–60 cm) or more wide, of evergreen, shiny, feathered rosettes that are surprisingly hard and plasticky to the touch. Tiny clusters of yellow flowers sit atop the foliage in summer.

CULTURE/CARE Full sun to part shade in average to dry soils with excellent drainage.

USES Alpine or rock gardens, scree areas, tucked within stairs, and between pavers. Slow growing. Tolerant of occasional foot traffic. Deer resistant.

PROPAGATION Division, seed

'Nana': dwarf, compact form

Azorella trifurcata 'Nana'

multitudes of small, red-budded, white daisies from late spring through summer. Plants grow 2–4 in. (5–10 cm) tall by 12–16 in. (30–40 cm) wide. May reseed gently.

CULTURE/CARE Full sun to part shade in evenly moist, well-drained soils.

USES Spreads at a moderate pace in the rock garden, at the front of the border, between pavers, and along stairways. Use in shady spots that will not support creeping thyme and sedums. Tolerant of moderate foot traffic. Attractive to pollinators, especially bees.

PROPAGATION Division, cuttings, seed

Bergenia
Saxifragaceae

This deservedly popular and hardy genus is primarily evergreen, even in cold climates, often with puckered or ruffled foliage, and offers a unique ground cover of large, bold leaves that contrast well with other finer textured ground covers, border perennials, and shrubs. Most cultivars have glowing maroon-red or brooding purple winter foliage, and all are topped by branching inflorescences of magenta, pink, or white flowers in early to midspring. Easy to grow, tough, and resilient, this is an indispensable ground cover. Numerous hybrids exist as well as rare species such as *B. agavifolia, B. crassifolia, B. emeiensis,* and *B. stracheyi.*

CULTURE/CARE Full sun to part shade with even moisture in organically rich soil. Plants are moderately drought tolerant, especially in shaded areas, once established. Avoid full sun in hot summer climates and full shade in cooler summer climates. Foliage may gradually incur winter damage in cold winter areas, especially with poor snow cover, and can be cleaned up in spring. Protect from slugs when leaves are young and from weevils throughout the season. Top dress with compost to cover any exposed rhizomes.

USES Slowly spreading for small to medium-sized applications such as along pathways, atop walls, and as a border edger. Mass plant for faster coverage or interplant with other smaller ground covers such as *Ajuga* spp., *Arctostaphylos uva-ursi, Fragaria* spp., or *Adiantum venustum.* Not tolerant of foot traffic. Deer and rabbit resistant. Attractive to pollinators, especially hummingbirds.

PROPAGATION Division, seed

Bergenia ciliata
FRINGED BERGENIA, HAIRY LEAF BERGENIA

Zones 5–9

Moist, rocky areas and rock ledges in forests and alpine meadows at 6500–11,500 ft. (1980–3500 m) or taller from Afghanistan to eastern Tibet, China.

Distinctive, tropical-looking species, best in shadier conditions, with large, oval to rounded, 8–12 in. (20–30 cm) diameter, fuzzy or bristly, herbaceous leaves (or evergreen in mild winter regions), often with a heart-shaped base. The upper leaf surface can be less fuzzy while the leaf margin, stem, and undersides, especially the veins, are quite fuzzy. Bell-shaped, light pink to midpink flowers produced on one side of a sturdy branching raceme or corymb in early to midspring, to 12 in. (30 cm) tall. Mounds can be 12 in. (30 cm) tall and 24 in. (60 cm) wide.

'Dumbo': fuzzy leaves on both sides are 8–12 in. (20–30 cm) long and nearly as wide, with pale pink flowers that deepen to midpink with age

'Susan Ryley': leaves with ruffled margins and white to pale pink flowers

'Wilton': pale to midpink flowers and leaves with ruffled margins may turn red in fall

Bergenia cordifolia
HEART-LEAVED BERGENIA, PIGSQUEAK

Zones 3–8

Damp forests, rock crevices, shaded slopes, and meadows at 3600–5900 ft. (1090–1800 m) in Russia, North Korea, and northern Mongolia.

This best-known species and the most important hybrid parent is an evergreen perennial spreading slowly from thick rhizomes, to 24 in. (60 cm) or more wide and 8–12 in. (20–30 cm) tall. Large, dark green, leathery, ruffled, oval-shaped leaves to 6–10 in. (15–25 cm) long and nearly as wide, with heart-shaped bases and tints of red, burgundy, and purple in winter. Flowers produced on one side of a branched cyme, 12–16 in. (30–40 cm) tall, in early spring with magenta, pink, or white flowers.

'Lunar Glow': new leaves emerge lemon-yellow, maturing to creamy yellow and then green with the veins changing first, with magenta flowers

'Purpurea': magenta flowers on red stems, leaves purplish especially in winter but also during the growing season

Bergenia ciliata, Larnach Castle, New Zealand

'Tubby Andrews': midgreen leaves variably splashed and streaked with creamy white and yellow, on red stems with midpink flowers

'Vinterglöd' (syns. 'Winter Glow', 'Winterglut'): bold, red-tinted winter foliage and magenta flowers on red stems

Several cultivars are sometimes attributed to *B. cordifolia* but are more likely hybrids involving this species. Others may be hybrids between other species.

'Abendglut' (syn. 'Evening Glow'): magenta flowers on red stems, leaves boldly maroon in winter with some color remaining throughout the year

'Angel Kiss' (Dragonfly Series): compact with small, slightly more linear, tonguelike leaves turning wine-red in winter, with semidouble, pink-flushed, white flowers

'Baby Doll': compact with smaller leaves to about 6 in. (15 cm) long, turning maroon-red in winter, with pale pink flowers on orange-red stems

'Bach': dark green foliage turning burgundy-red in winter, orange-red stems in winter hold large conical mounds of white to pale pink flowers

'Bartók': bold red winter foliage, magenta flowers

'Bressingham Ruby': deep maroon-red winter foliage, magenta flowers

'Bressingham Salmon': salmon-pink flowers, winter foliage not as bold as other cultivars

'Bressingham White': white flowers on red stems with bronzy winter foliage, AGM

'Eden's Dark Margin': large leaves with red edges turning deep maroon in winter, deep pink flowers

'Eden's Magic Giant': large, ruffled leaves, purple-tinted in winter, midpink flowers on red stems, AGM

'Eroica': glowing magenta flowers on red stems with bold red winter foliage, AGM

'Harzkristall': white flowers flushed with pink

'Morgenröte' (syn. 'Morning Red'): deep pink flowers on orange stems, often reblooms in late spring or fall, AGM

'Overture': reddish winter leaves, red stems, and magenta flowers

'Pink Dragonfly' (Dragonfly Series): compact with narrower, tonguelike foliage turning purple-red in winter, with midpink flowers

'Rosi Klose': compact grower with light to midpink flowers and lightly bronzed winter foliage

Bergenia cordifolia, Royal Botanic Garden, Edinburgh, UK

'Rotblum': seed strain with magenta flowers and good fall/winter color

'Sakura' (Dragonfly Series): compact with small, slightly more linear, tonguelike leaves turning wine-red in winter, with semidouble midpink flowers

'Silberlicht' (syn. 'Silverlight'): white flowers develop a pink flush with age atop reddish stems, with maroon-purple foliage in winter, AGM

'Sunningdale': red stems with magenta flowers and reddish winter foliage, AGM

'Wintermärchen': small leaves twist slightly to reveal red undersides, red stems and deep pink flowers, AGM

Bergenia purpurascens
PURPLE BERGENIA, CHINESE BERGENIA

Zones 4–9

Forests, scrub, open slopes, alpine meadows, and alpine rock crevices, at 8800–15,700 ft. (2680–4790 m) in western China and parts of adjacent Himalayan countries.

Evergreen perennial spreading slowly from thick rhizomes, to 24 in. (60 cm) or more wide and 12–20 in. (30–50 cm) tall, with large, dark green, leathery, ruffled, oval-shaped leaves, 6–10 in. (15–25 cm) long and nearly as wide, flushed burgundy-red in new growth, on the leaf undersides, and across the whole leaves in winter. Magenta flowers produced on one side of a branched cyme, 12–16 in. (30–40 cm) tall, in early spring with magenta, pink, or white flowers. AGM

'Irish Crimson': upright leaves, bright red to burgundy in winter, AGM

Blechnum
Blechnaceae

Though this genus offers only a few species to temperate horticulture, all are valuable and tough garden plants and ground covers, especially for moist, shady locations. Their distinctive, thick, ladderlike, linear, sterile, and fertile fronds provide a solid and substantial textural element to the garden more similar to the hart's tongue fern (*Asplenium scolopendrium*) than to the majority of other fern species that are more classically lacy and ethereal.

CULTURE/CARE Evenly moist to wet soils rich in organic matter in part to full shade, though plants will tolerate full sun with good moisture. Remove brown or damaged foliage in early spring. In areas of high humidity, the rare *B. niponicum*, which sports red new growth, is said to grow more strongly than *B. spicant* and may be worth trying.

PROPAGATION Division, spores

Blechnum penna-marina
ALPINE WATER FERN, ANTARCTIC HARD FERN

Zones (5)6–10

Mountain grasslands, heathlands, rock crevices, open forests, subalpine scrub, and moist habitats from sea level to high elevations in New Zealand, southern Australia, southern South America, and on some sub-Antarctic islands.

Now known scientifically as *Austroblechnum penna-marina*, this evergreen, colony-forming fern spreads slowly via slender, creeping rhizomes into dense mats. Leaves resemble smaller versions of the better known deer fern, *B. spicant*, with reddish brown stipes and once-pinnate blades, 2–10 in. (5–25 cm) long. These emerge vertically, flushed copper-red, maturing to greenish yellow and then deep green. Older fronds eventually lie more prostrate. Longer, narrower fertile fronds follow later in the season. AGM

USES Along stairways and paths, between rocks, at the front of the shady border, and in moist areas in sun or shade, spreading at a slow to moderate rate. Overwintered foliage can be trimmed to the ground if needed. Tolerant of occasional foot traffic. Deer and rabbit resistant.

subsp. *alpinum*: smaller and most common in horticulture, with fronds to about 4 in. (10 cm) long, possibly hardy to zone 5

'Cristatum': crested with forked tips

subsp. *penna-marina*: larger subspecies with fronds up to 10 in. (25 cm) long

Blechnum spicant
DEER FERN, HARD FERN

Zones 4–8

Wet coniferous forests, swamps, woods, heaths, moors, mountain grasslands, and rocky areas from sea level to 4600 ft. (1400 m) in coastal western North America from California to Alaska, across most of Europe to North Africa, and in Japan.

Now known scientifically as *Struthiopteris spicant*, a beautiful and tough, clumping, evergreen fern with

Blechnum penna-marina

Blechnum spicant with *Lysimachia nummularia* 'Aurea'

two types of once-pinnate fronds rising from the central rosette. The infertile fronds are lance-shaped, 12–18 in. (30–45 cm) long, emerging vertically and later becoming arching to prostrate, with reddish brown stipes becoming green toward the tips and midgreen, fingerlike, upward-curved pinnae. The longer, vertical, fertile fronds, to 18–24 in. (45–60 cm), have reddish brown to black stipes and narrower pinnae with rust-colored sporangia on the undersides. The fertile fronds wither by season's end. AGM

USES A useful textural ground cover when mass-planted for small to large applications. Clumps bulk up at a moderate pace. Not tolerant of foot traffic. Generally deer and rabbit resistant though it is sometimes browsed in the wild in British Columbia.

Bletilla striata
CHINESE GROUND ORCHID, URN ORCHID

Orchidaceae

Zones 5–9

Evergreen broadleaf and coniferous forests, grassy areas, and rocky crevices at 330–10,500 ft. (100–3200 m), in China, Japan, Korea, and Myanmar.

Easy, colony-forming, hardy, terrestrial orchid that can form an effective ground cover once clumps spread and fill in, taking about 5–7 years to reach 24 in. (60 cm) wide. Subtropical-looking, pleated, midgreen, arching leaves, 6–10 in. (15–20 cm) long and 1 in. (2.5 cm) wide, lie lightly atop one another. In spring, 12–18 in. (30–45 cm) long stems emerge with 3–7 small, 1 in. (2.5 cm) wide, magenta-lavender to white flowers. Other species such as *B. formosana* and *B. ochracea* are similar but not as hardy or vigorous.

CULTURE/CARE Part sun to part shade in evenly moist, organically rich, well-drained soil. Tolerant of deeper shade but may not flower. Provide a winter mulch in zone 5, especially if good snow cover is not assured.

USES Slowly spreading for small to medium-sized applications. Underplant with a low-growing ground cover such as *Isotoma* spp., *Leptinella* spp., *Mazus* spp., or *Selaginella* spp. to maintain coverage until *B. striata* fills in. Not tolerant of foot traffic.

PROPAGATION Division

'Alba': white flowers, lips often marked with lavender or pink and yellow

'Alba Variegata': same as 'Alba' but with white-margined leaves

'Albostriata': magenta-lavender flowers, white-margined leaves

'Big Bob': taller flower stems to 24 in. (60 cm), each with up to 20 large, 2 in. (5 cm) wide flowers

'Gotemba Stripes' (syn. 'Yellow Striped'): magenta-lavender flowers, leaves irregularly and boldly streaked with golden yellow and cream

'Junpaku': pure white flowers

'Kuchi-beni': white and pale pink flowers, lips with lavender and yellow markings

'Murasaki Shikibu': pale lavender flowers, lips darker lavender and yellow

'Peaches and Cream': hybrid of *B. striata* and *B. ochracea,* with magenta buds that open to lavender-pink flowers with deep pink and yellow markings on the lip

'Soryu': bluish lavender flowers

'Tri-Lips': magenta-lavender flowers with three lips instead of one

Yokohama 'Kate': large hybrid of *B. striata* 'Big Bob' and *B. formosana,* with pale lavender-pink flowers and lips with magenta, yellow, and white markings atop stems 40 in. (100 cm) tall

Briza media
QUAKING GRASS

Poaceae

Zones 4–10
Sloping meadows and grassy clearings in forests from Europe to China.
Loosely tufted, creeping, rhizomatous grass clumps, 12–18 in. (30–45 cm) wide, potentially forming larger colonies over time. Foliage is 6–12 in. (15–30 cm) long, bright green, and unremarkable. Flowering occurs in late spring and summer with intriguing, pendulous, heart-shaped inflorescences of green, burgundy, and tan on open-branched stems, 18–24 in. (45–60 cm) tall, that shiver and rattle in the slightest breeze.
CULTURE/CARE Fertile or infertile, well-drained soils in sun. Drought tolerant.
USES Spreads at a slow to moderate rate. Use as an accent or front of the border perennial or a mass-planted ground cover for small to large applications that will fill in over time. Not tolerant of foot traffic.
PROPAGATION Division, seed

Brunnera
Boraginaceae

One of the most popular perennials for shade, owing to the breakthrough cultivar *B. macrophylla* 'Jack Frost', with textured and heart-shaped leaves, and the true-blue flowers that resemble forget-me-nots. Plants can form a solid ground cover when mass-planted. Variegated forms offer diverse design options.
CULTURE/CARE Evenly moist, well-drained, organically rich soils in part sun to full shade. Remove spent flower stems. Divide plants if flowering decreases over time.
USES Mass plant *B. macrophylla* over small to large areas along pathways, at the front of shaded borders, and beneath trees and shrubs. Clumps bulk up at a moderate rate in good conditions. Use spreading *B. sibirica* in similar locations. Neither are tolerant of foot traffic. Deer and rabbit resistant.
PROPAGATION Division, seed, root cuttings

Brunnera macrophylla
HEARTLFEAF BRUNNERA, SIBERIAN BUGLOSS

Zones 3–9
Forests, forest edges, and stony mountain slopes into the subalpine zone in the Caucasus.
Heart-shaped, course-textured, midgreen, herbaceous foliage to 8 in. (20 cm) across, forming a long-lived mound, 12 in. (30 cm) tall and 12–24 in. (30–60 cm) wide, with airy masses of pale blue flowers, similar to forget-me-nots, in spring. Flowers can appear before, with, or after the foliage emerges. Tough and very hardy.

'Alexander's Great': giant silvered cultivar similar to 'Jack Frost' but with much larger, somewhat ruffled leaves, 8–11 in. (20–28 cm) across, forming mounds 14 in. (36 cm) tall by 30 in. (75 cm) wide

'Alexandria': size of 'Alexander's Great', with leaves fully frosted, similar to 'Looking Glass'

'Betty Bowring': green leaves and white flowers

'Dawson's White' (syn. 'Variegata'): tricolor foliage irregularly variegated with green and grayish green centers and broad ivory-white edges

'Diane's Gold': chartreuse to gold foliage, bolder color in brighter light

'Emerald Mist': green leaves with bold silver patches following the leaf edges

'Green Gold': chartreuse to gold foliage matures to light green by summer, bolder color in brighter light

Brunnera macrophylla 'Alexander's Great'

Brunnera macrophylla 'Hadspen Cream'

Brunnera macrophylla 'Jack Frost'

'Hadspen Cream': tricolor leaves with green centers edged in light green, changing to creamy yellow to creamy white

'Jack Frost': heavily silvered leaves with green veins and green edges, Perennial Plant of the Year 2012

'Jack of Diamonds': like a larger version of 'Jack Frost', to 16 in. (40 cm) tall and 32 in. (80 cm) wide, with larger, more rounded leaves up to 10 in. (25 cm) across, cordate lobes overlapping

'King's Ransom': sport of 'Jack Frost' with the same silvered foliage but with creamy yellow margins

'Langtrees': subtly variegated green leaves with small, irregular shaped silver spots following the leaf edge

'Looking Glass': leaves almost completely frosted silver except for a few thin veins and a thin green edge

'Mister Morse': like 'Jack Frost' but with white flowers

'Queen of Hearts': similar to 'Jack of Diamonds' but more heavily silvered, heart-shaped leaves, 18 in. (45 cm) tall and 36 in. (90 cm) wide

'Sea Heart' (Garden Candy Series): similar to 'Jack Frost' but with thicker leaves on earlier blooming, two-toned flowers in sky-blue and lavender-blue and more tolerance of heat and humidity

'Silver Charm': similar to 'Jack Frost' but more compact and vigorous

'Silver Heart' (Garden Candy Series): similar to 'Looking Glass' but with thicker leaves and more tolerance of heat and humidity

'Silver Wings': green to grayish green leaves with silver patches along the leaf edges

'Sterling Silver': large, heavily silvered leaves with thin green veins and good heat tolerance

'Tnbruap' Alchemy Pewter: vigorous, developing new crowns quickly, with silvered, slightly ruffled leaves with prominent green veins

'Tnbruas' Alchemy Silver: vigorous, developing new crowns quickly, with heavily silvered leaves with thin green veins, tolerant of heat and humidity

Brunnera sibirica
SIBERIAN BUGLOSS

Zones 4–9

Taiga, forest margins, and meadows in Siberia.

A rare species resembling *B. macrophylla* with typical heart-shaped, course-textured, green leaves and blue flowers in spring. Spreads moderately to vigorously via underground rhizomes.

C

Calamintha
Lamiaceae

The mint family is well loved for its aromatic foliage, but it is frequently avoided thanks to the reputation of the culinary mints (*Mentha* spp.) as spreading garden thugs. Despite their ability to spread via underground rhizomes, these related mints are much better behaved, producing airy, nectar-filled, white, pink, pale lavender, or blue flowers in great numbers over long periods on mounding to slowly spreading plants. The leaves and flowers are edible.

CULTURE/CARE Full sun to part shade in average to dry soils. Tolerant of heat and drought. Can be trimmed hard after flowering to rejuvenate foliage.

USES Use as edging for pathways, patios, and borders, or plant atop walls or as a ground cover for small to medium-sized applications. Spreads at a moderate rate. Use *C. nepeta* as an alternative to baby's breath (*Gypsophila paniculata*), which is invasive in some regions. Not tolerant of foot traffic. Deer and rabbit resistant. Attractive to pollinators, especially bees, butterflies, and hummingbirds.

PROPAGATION Division, seed, cuttings

Calamintha grandiflora
LARGE-FLOWERED CALAMINT

Zones (4)5–9

Damp woods and scrub, often on limestone, from Spain, east to Iran and the Caucasus.

Small, fragrant, fuzzy, oval leaves with serrated edges on stems 12–18 in. (30–45 cm) tall, spreading by rhizomes to form mounds 12–24 in. (30–60 cm) or more wide, though plants are not overly aggressive. Small, rose-pink flowers are tubular, relatively large for the genus, and bloom from late spring into fall.

'Variegata': variably splashed and speckled with creamy white

Calamintha grandiflora 'Variegata'

Calamintha nepeta subsp. *nepeta*

Callirhoe involucrata

Calamintha nepeta

LESSER CALAMINT, DWARF CALAMINT

Zones 4–9

Dry banks, scrub, garrigue, valley sides, and rocky places, usually on calcareous soils, throughout Europe, northwest Africa, northern Turkey, the Caucasus, and Ukraine.

Delicately textured with small, fragrant, oval leaves with fine gray hairs, subtle veining, and shallow serrations on thin stems to 12–18 in. (30–45 cm) tall, forming spreading mounds, 12–24 in. (30–60 cm) wide. Tiny, tubular, pale lilac or white flowers are produced by the hundreds, forming clouds of pollinator-attracting blooms from late spring into fall. Spreads via rhizomes but is not overly aggressive.

subsp. *glandulosa* 'White Cloud': larger, whiter flowers than the species

'Montrose White': sterile with white flowers

subsp. *nepeta*: more robust and vigorous, with larger leaves and flowers and more flowers per stem

subsp. *nepeta* 'Blue Cloud': lavender-blue flowers

Callirhoe involucrata

WINE CUPS, PURPLE POPPY MALLOW

Malvaceae

Zones 4–8

Dryish, rocky soils in prairies, fields, and along roadsides from the South Central United States into Mexico.

Attractive, midgreen, palmate, geranium-shaped leaves on sprawling, prostrate, nonrooting stems, forming textured, herbaceous mats, 4–10 in. (10–25 cm) tall and 36 in. (90 cm) or more wide from a long tap root. Upward-facing, cup-shaped, 2–3 in. (5–7.5 cm) wide, five-petaled magenta flowers with white centers resemble poppies but for the malvaceous central column of yellow stamens. Blooms occur from early summer through fall.

CULTURE/CARE Easy to grow in well-drained, average to dry soils in full sun. Tolerant of some shade though flowering will be reduced.

USES Small to medium-sized applications along pathways, at the front of borders, or as a weaving plant to spread between larger perennials, bulking up at a moderate pace. Tolerant of occasional foot traffic. Attractive to pollinators, especially butterflies and hummingbirds.

PROPAGATION Seed

var. *lineariloba* 'Logan Calhoun': white flowers

var. *tenuissima*: deeply dissected, ferny foliage and lavender to deep pink petals

Calluna vulgaris

HEATHER, LING

Ericaceae

Zones 4–8

Acidic soils in open woodlands, on slopes, in old pastures, along roadsides, on dunes, and in bogs, fens, and marshy ground from Northern Europe into northwest Morocco and Western Asia. Introduced in northeastern North America and the Pacific Northwest.

A well-known garden plant often connected with the moors of Scotland, heather is a small evergreen shrub with tiny, scalelike, clasping, overlapping, green to grayish green leaves on wiry stems, forming mounds 6–24 in. (15–60 cm) or more tall and 3–4 ft. (1–1.2 m) wide. Small white, pink, purplish pink, and pinkish red, four-petaled, urn-shaped flowers can be produced from midsummer to early winter on terminal spikes up to 10 in. (25 cm) long. Winter foliage can take on bronzy hues, especially in more exposed sites. Many cultivars offer new spring foliage in brilliant shades of cream, golden yellow, orange, coral, and pink. More reliable in colder climates than species of *Erica* or *Daboecia*.

CULTURE/CARE Full sun to light shade in acidic, average to infertile, coarse, sandy or gritty, well-drained, evenly moist soil. Tolerant of salt and some drought. Not tolerant of high humidity. Avoid hot summer climates and clay soils. Plants can become leggy in overly rich soils. Shear lightly in spring before new growth appears to maintain compactness.

USES Slopes, shrub borders, alpine and rock gardens, and other small to large applications. Can be interplanted with the similar winter and spring-blooming heaths (*Erica* spp.) for two seasons of flowering in the same bed. Spreads at a moderate rate. Not tolerant of foot traffic. Deer and rabbit resistant. Attractive to pollinators, especially bees.

PROPAGATION Cuttings

More than 800 cultivars have been selected over time, with hundreds still in cultivation. Forms with double flowers and colorful seasonal foliage displays are popular. More recently, bud bloomers have gained attention for their nonopening flowers that last for an extended period of time.

'Annemarie': rose-pink double flowers from late summer to midfall, to 20 in. (50 cm) tall and somewhat wider

Calluna vulgaris 'Firefly', RHS Garden Rosemoor, UK

Calluna vulgaris 'Sun Sprinkles'

'Blazeaway': lavender-pink flowers from late summer into fall on plants to 14 in. (36 cm) tall and 24 in. (60 cm) wide, with golden foliage with orange highlights in summer, becoming fiery red in winter

'Corbett's Red': magenta-red flowers from late summer to midfall on plants 10 in. (25 cm) tall by 16 in. (40 cm) wide

'County Wicklow': reliable grower across diverse conditions with large, pale pink double flowers from mid-summer to midfall on plants 12 in. (30 cm) tall by 18 in. (45 cm) wide

'Dark Beauty': magenta-red semidouble flowers from late summer to midfall on plants 8 in. (20 cm) tall by 14 in. (36 cm) wide

'Firefly': deep lavender-pink flowers from late summer to early fall on plants 18 in. (45 cm) tall and somewhat wider, with chartreuse to gold summer foliage with orange highlights, turning to brick-red in winter

'Flamingo': lavender-pink flowers from late summer to early fall on plants 12 in. (30 cm) tall by 20 in. (50 cm) wide, with hot-pink to pinkish red new growth atop over-wintered green foliage in spring

Garden Girls Series

'Alicia': white bud bloomer from late summer to early winter, 12 in. (30 cm) tall and somewhat wider

'Amethyst': red-purple bud bloomer from late summer to midwinter, 16 in. (40 cm) tall and somewhat wider, with dark purple winter foliage

'Anette': pink bud bloomer from late summer to late fall, 14 in. (36 cm) tall and somewhat wider

'Athene': magenta-red bud bloomer from late summer to early winter, 16 in. (40 cm) tall and wide

'Larissa': brick-red bud bloomer from late summer to late fall, 12 in. (30 cm) tall by 18 in. (45 cm) wide

'Sandy': white bud bloomer from late summer to late fall, 14 in. (36 cm) tall and somewhat wider

'Susanne': lilac-pink bud bloomer from early to late fall, 16 in. (40 cm) tall and wide

'Tessa': pink bud bloomer from early to late fall with golden foliage year-round, 18 in. (45 cm) tall and 24 in. (60 cm) wide

'Hoyerhagen': pale crimson flowers, 10 in. (25 cm) tall and 14 in. (36 cm) wide, with golden to orange summer foliage turning bright red in winter

'Jana': magenta double flowers from late summer to early fall, 14 in. (36 cm) tall by 20 in. (50 cm) wide

'Kerstin': mauve flowers in late summer to early fall, 12 in. (30 cm) tall by 18 in. (45 cm) wide, with softly textured, gray winter foliage and new spring growth of yellow, pink, and red

'Nr 5157' Lady in Pink, 'Nr 5163' Lady in Red, 'Nr 580' Lady in White: series of early bud bloomers in pink, red, and white, from late summer to midwinter, 18 in. (45 cm) tall by 24 in. (60 cm) wide

'Robert Chapman': lavender-pink flowers from late summer to midfall, 12 in. (30 cm) tall by 24 in. (60 cm) wide, with golden summer foliage turning to orange in autumn and brick-red in winter

'Silver Knight': lavender flowers from mid- to late summer, 20 in. (50 cm) tall by 24 in. (60 cm) wide, with downy, silver-gray foliage

'Spring Cream': white flowers from late summer to late fall, 14 in. (36 cm) tall by 18 in. (45 cm) wide, with yellow tips in fall and winter and cream-colored tips in spring

'Spring Torch': mauve flowers from late summer to midfall, 14 in. (36 cm) tall by 18 in. (45 cm) wide, with hot pink and red new growth, turning to pink and cream by summer

'Sun Sprinkles': white flowers from late summer to early fall, 14 in. (36 cm) tall by 18 in. (45 cm) wide, with yellow tips in spring

'Tib': deep lilac-pink double flowers from midsummer to midfall, 12 in. (30 cm) tall by 16 in. (40 cm) wide

'Wickwar Flame': mauve flowers from late summer to late fall, 20 in. (50 cm) tall by 26 in. (66 cm) wide, with gold summer foliage turning to orange and red in winter

'Winter Chocolate': lavender flowers from late summer to midfall, 8 in. (20 cm) tall by 18 in. (45 cm) wide, with gold foliage in summer tipped with pink, turning bronze in winter followed by salmon-pink new growth in spring

Caltha palustris

MARSH MARIGOLD, KINGCUP

Ranunculaceae

Zones 3–8

Circumboreal in temperate regions from Alaska to Newfoundland, into the northern United States, and across Europe and Asia in marshes, fens, swamps, ditches, and wet woods and meadows, in open to partly shaded sites from sea level to 5000 ft. (1500 m).

The large and lustrous, emerald-green foliage and big, bright yellow flowers of marsh marigold make for a surprising, almost tropical display in cooler climates. The shiny, midgreen foliage is rounded, kidney-, or

Caltha palustris

Campanula carpatica 'Rapido White'

heart-shaped, and up to 8 in. (20 cm) across, with smooth to toothed margins. It forms bold, clumping mounds, 8–18 in. (20–45 cm) tall and wide. Bright yellow buttercup flowers, to 2 in. (5 cm) wide, in clusters of 1–7 are produced in early to late spring. Plants can form colonies via seed in good conditions.

CULTURE/CARE Wet to moist, organically rich soils in full sun to part shade. Plants will go dormant in summer if soils become dry. Avoid hot summer climates.

USES Mass plantings for small to medium-sized areas along pond or stream edges or in permanently moist sites. Not tolerant of foot traffic.

PROPAGATION Seed, division, root cuttings

var. *alba*: white flowers

'Flore Pleno': double pom-pom flowers last longer than the single cultivars, AGM

'Himalayan Snow': white flowers with more petals than var. *alba*.

'Honeydew': primrose-yellow flowers

'Multiplex': similar to, if not the same as, 'Flore Pleno'

var. *palustris* (syn. *C. polypetala*): giant marsh marigold, larger variety, grows from slowly creeping rhizomes, flowers to 3 in. (7.5 cm) across, foliage to 12 in. (30 cm) across, plants growing to 24 in. (60 cm) or more tall and wide, may form plantlets after flowering from the nodes of the flowering stems

var. *palustris* 'Plena': double-flowered version of this large-growing variety

Campanula
Campanulaceae

Campanula is a large genus of the Northern Hemisphere, offering many cottage garden favorites, from the small ground-covering species to taller, upright border perennials. Though their color palette is limited to blues, purples, whites, and sometimes pink, the bellflowers are extremely hardy and reliable. Of the many diminutive species, many are too small or dainty outside of a rock garden, though some may offer promise for additional ground-covering options.

CULTURE/CARE Full sun to part shade in average, well-drained soils. Roots prefer cool soils. Plant in part shade in hot summer climates. Deadheading may extend bloom time. Division every 2–4 years may be necessary to maintain vigor.

USES Small-scale uses in rock gardens, along pathways, on walls, between pavers, and at the front of the border, spreading at a slow to moderate rate. Not tolerant of foot traffic. Deer and rabbit resistant. Attractive to pollinators, especially bees and hummingbirds.

PROPAGATION Division, seed

Campanula carpatica
CARPATHIAN BELLFLOWER, TUSSOCK BELLFLOWER

Zones 3–8
Among rocks in the Carpathian Mountains of Southeast Europe.

A tufted perennial, semi-evergreen to evergreen (herbaceous in colder regions), forming low-growing, slowly spreading clumps, 6–8 in. (15–20 cm) tall and 18 in. (45 cm) wide, of small, rounded, heart-shaped or triangular, light green leaves with serrated edges. Upward-facing, open, bell-shaped, five-lobed, 1 in. (2.5 cm) wide, blue, lilac-blue, or white solitary flowers on stems 3–12 in. (7.5–30 cm) tall can obscure the foliage from late spring to early summer. Possible rebloom in summer and fall, especially in cooler climates. The cross of *C. carpatica* var. *turbinata* and *C. pulla*, known as *C. ×pulloides*, has resulted in cultivars of similar size and creeping habit but with nodding, more closed, bell-shaped flowers. AGM

f. *alba* 'Weisse Clips' (syn. 'White Clips'): most common white form

'Blaue Clips' (syn. 'Blue Clips'): most common blue form, with midblue flowers

'Blue Uniform': lavender-blue flowers on compact plants

'Nonor' Blue Orb: *C. carpatica* hybrid arising from a branch mutation of 'Samantha', with lavender-blue, upward-facing flowers all summer long

'Pearl Deep Blue': slightly deeper blue flowers than other cultivars

'Pearl Light Blue': light blue to lavender-blue flowers

'Pearl White': white flowers

'Rapido Blue': blue flowers about 4 weeks earlier than the Clips cultivars

'Rapido White': white flowers about 4 weeks earlier than the Clips cultivars

'Samantha': *C. carpatica* hybrid with long-blooming, upward-facing, lavender-blue flowers gradually fading to white toward the center

'White Uniform': white flowers on compact plants

C. ×pulloides 'G.F. Wilson': nodding, bell-shaped, rich purple-blue flowers

C. ×pulloides 'Jelly Bells': nodding, bell-shaped, rich purple-blue to warm purple flowers, more vigorous than 'G.F. Wilson' with larger flowers

Campanula cochlearifolia
FAIRY THIMBLES, FAIRY'S THIMBLES

Zones 3–9

Rock crevices and other rocky areas in most mountainous regions of temperate Europe, often growing on limestone.

Campanula cochlearifolia

A tufted perennial forming colonies or mats a few inches tall and 12 in. (30 cm) or more wide by slender rhizomes, with tiny, glossy, bright green, lightly serrated, rounded to oval leaves. Flowering stems are 4 in. (10 cm) tall with blue, lavender-blue, or white, nodding, bell-shaped flowers like small thimbles from late spring into midsummer. AGM

'Advance Blue': blue flowers on taller, more robust plants, 6–8 in. (15–20 cm) tall

var. *alba*: white flowers

var. *alba* 'Advance White': white flowers on taller, more robust plants, 6–8 in. (15–20 cm) tall

var. *alba* 'Bavaria White': compact seed strain with white flowers

var. *alba* 'White Baby': white flowers on compact plants

'Bavaria Blue': compact seed strain with blue flowers

'Blue Baby': blue flowers on compact plants

'Elizabeth Oliver': palest blue double flowers, like nodding roses, AGM

'Tubby': blue bell-shaped flowers broader than other cultivars

Campanula garganica
ADRIATIC BELLFLOWER

Zones 4–9
Shady, rocky areas in southeastern Italy and western Greece.

Star-shaped, upward-facing blue flowers with white centers held in loose clusters from late spring through summer, atop slowly spreading mounds or mats, 4–6 in. (10–15 cm) tall and 6–18 in. (15–45 cm) wide. Foliage is rounded to heart-shaped, cupped and serrated, and evergreen in mild winter regions. Once considered a subspecies, *C. fenestrellata* is similar but more diminutive at two-thirds the size. AGM

'Birch Hybrid': hybrid, most likely with *C. poscharskyana,* similar in habit to *C. garganica* except with broader petal lobes, for a less starlike flowering display in lavender-blue

'Dickson's Gold': blue flowers, gold foliage in sun or lime-green in shade, can burn if light is too intense or soils too dry

Campanula portenschlagiana
DALMATIAN BELLFLOWER, WALL BELLFLOWER

Zones 3–9
Limestone cliffs along the Dalmatian Coast of the former Yugoslavia.

Larger growing than most of the ground cover bellflowers and similar to *C. poscharskyana,* spreading into a robust patch, 8–12 in. (20–30 cm) tall and 24–36 in. (60–90 cm) wide. Small, rounded to heart-shaped, cupped basal leaves with serrated edges give rise to cascading to prostrate, branching stems of bell-shaped, blue to purple-blue flowers with starlike reflexed lobes from midspring to late summer. Evergreen in mild winter regions. AGM

'Catharina': violet-mauve flowers

'Miss Melanie': long-blooming violet-blue flowers on compact plants

'Resholdt's Variety': slower growing, more compact, and more vibrant lavender-blue flowers

Campanula poscharskyana
SERBIAN BELLFLOWER, TRAILING BELLFLOWER

Zones 3–9
Stony places in the Dinaric Alps of the former Yugoslavia and in Italy.

Larger growing than most of the ground cover bellflowers and similar to *C. portenschlagiana,* spreading into a robust patch, 8–12 in. (20–30 cm) tall and 24–36 in. (60–90 cm) wide. Small, rounded to heart-shaped and cupped, somewhat hairy, basal leaves with serrated edges give rise to cascading to prostrate, branching stems of bell-shaped, blue to violet-blue flowers with starlike reflexed lobes and white centers from midspring to late summer. Flowers are slightly larger than *C. portenschlagiana* with narrower lobes. May rebloom in fall. Evergreen in mild winter areas.

'Camgood' Blue Waterfall: compact, floriferous plants to about 8 in. (20 cm) tall with violet-blue to blue flowers

'E.H. Frost': compact plants to about 6 in. (15 cm) tall with white flowers and lighter green foliage

'Lisduggan Variety': compact plants to about 8 in. (20 cm) tall with lavender-pink flowers

'Stella': compact plants to about 6 in. (15 cm) tall with violet-blue flowers, AGM

Campanula punctata
SPOTTED BELLFLOWER, LONG-FLOWERED HAREBELL

Zones 4–8
Forests, thickets, and grassy meadows in lowlands up to 7550 ft. (2300 m) in Japan, China, Korea, and Siberia.

Thick mounds or mats of oval- to heart-shaped, serrated, slightly hairy basal leaves with leafy, branched flowering stems, 8–30 in. (20–75 cm) tall. Buds are pleated like a folded umbrella, opening to large, pendulous, tubular bells, 1–2.5 in. (2.5–6 cm) long, in white, yellowish, or pink with purple or red spotting, mostly in the interior but sometimes on the exterior, with possible fragrance. Bloom period lasts from late spring through summer. Clump-forming but can spread by creeping rhizomes.

'Hot Lips': 10–12 in. (25–30 cm) tall, with whitish to pale pink bells with heavy burgundy-red interior spotting

'Little Punky': red stems, 8–10 in. (20–25 cm) tall, and palest pink bells with pink interior spots

Campanula 'Birch Hybrid'

Campanula poscharskyana

Campanula portenschlagiana

Campanula 'Pink Octopus'

Campanula punctata f. rubriflora 'Cherry Bells'

'Pantaloons': lavender-pink to deep pink, hose-in-hose, double bells on stems to 28 in. (71 cm) tall

'Pink Chimes': shorter with pale pink flowers on stems to 12 in. (30 cm) tall

'Pink Octopus': hybrid, corolla split into five thin petals, deep pink on the outside and white on the inside, with deep pink spots

'Plum Wine': pale pink bells on red stems atop pewter-silver foliage that emerges burgundy in spring and reverts to burgundy in winter

f. *rubriflora* (syn. 'Rubra'): midpink to deep pink bells with interior spotting on red stems, new leaves often burgundy-flushed

f. *rubriflora* 'Bowl of Cherries': mid- to deep pink bells with lighter lobes on red stems 12–18 in. (30–45 cm) tall

f. *rubriflora* 'Cherry Bells': mid- to deep pink bells with lighter lobes on stems 12–18 in. (30–45 cm) tall

'Silver Bells': pale lavender-pink bells on red stems with silvery foliage that emerges burgundy in spring and reverts to burgundy in winter

'Wedding Bells': short, somewhat plumper, white, hose-in-hose, double bells with deep pink interior spots

Campanula takesimana
KOREAN BELLFLOWER

Zones 4–8

Grassy habitats in Korea.

Similar to the closely related *C. punctata* but more vigorously spreading and potentially overly aggressive for smaller spaces. Forms mounds or mats of heart-shaped, serrated basal leaves with red, leafy, branched flowering stems, 20–30 in. (50–75 cm) tall. Buds are pleated like a folded umbrella, opening from early summer to early fall as large, white to pink, pendulous, tubular bells, 1–2.5 in. (2.5–6 cm) long, with pink to deep pink interior spotting and light fragrance.

'Alba': white flowers with interior spotting on red stems 18 in. (45 cm) tall

'Beautiful Trust': split corolla with five pure white petals on stems 24 in. (60 cm) tall, slower spreading than the species

'Elizabeth': deep pink bells lightening on the lobes and spotted with deeper pink on red stems to 30 in. (75 cm) tall

Campsis radicans
TRUMPET CREEPER, TRUMPET VINE

Bignoniaceae

Zones 4–9

Woods, thickets, fields, along streams, and in disturbed sites in the southeastern United States, but naturalized throughout much of eastern North America.

Campsis radicans is a vigorous, even aggressive, deciduous, woody, self-clinging vine that can climb 30–40 ft. (9–12 m). Grown without vertical support, it makes a vigorous, spreading ground cover, 12–18 in. (30–45 cm) tall, that can quickly cover large areas. Its shiny, midgreen, compound, pinnate leaves can be 12–16 in. (30–40 cm) long, comprising 4 in. (10 cm) long, serrated, elliptic to oblong leaflets that turn yellow in fall. The showy red, orange, or yellow trumpet-shaped flowers, usually produced at the top of the tallest stems, are 3 in. (7.5 cm) long and held in loose terminal clusters throughout the summer, followed by long, green, beanlike pods. Plants can spread readily by suckers and seed. Its Asian relative *C. grandiflora* and its cultivar 'Morning Calm' are similar yet more restrained in their size and growth rate; *C. ×tagliabuana* is a hybrid with this species.

CULTURE/CARE Easy to grow in average to lean soils with average moisture, in full sun to part shade; full sun is necessary, however, for best flowering, which occurs on new growth. Prune in early spring. Tolerant of heat, humidity, and drought.

USES For large applications, spreads at a fast rate across open ground, on slopes for erosion control, or to cover unsightly landscape features. Not tolerant of foot traffic. Deer and rabbit resistant. Attractive to pollinators, especially hummingbirds.

PROPAGATION Cuttings, division, seed

'Atropurpurea': red flowers

'Flamenco': fiery red flowers

f. *flava* (syn. 'Flava'): yellow flowers

'Monbal' Balboa Sunset: red to fiery red flowers

'Stromboli' Atomic Red: red to orange-red flowers

C. ×tagliabuana

'Kudian' Indian Summer: flowers in tones of red, peach, and orange

'Madame Galen': salmon-red and fiery orange flowers

Campsis radicans

Summer Jazz Series: grows about half the size at half the rate of other cultivars

> 'Takarazuka Fresa' Summer Jazz Fire: fiery red flowers

> 'Takarazuka Yellow' Summer Jazz Sunrise Gold: peachy yellow flowers

> 'Takarazuka Zujin' Summer Jazz Tangerine: coral-red and orange flowers

Cardamine
Brassicaceae

A woodland genus well worth integrating into shaded gardens, the majority of cultivated *Cardamine* species are spring ephemerals with early season compound foliage and white or pink flowers that go dormant by summer, with the exception of the evergreen *C. trifolia*. The ephemeral species provide opportunities for dynamic combination plantings. This genus is infamous for offering the horticultural world *C. hirsuta*, common or hairy bittercress or snapweed, but don't let this pernicious pest of nurseries and gardens prejudice you to the merits of its relatives.

A number of less common species not treated here may also be useful for those who want to explore, including *C. enneaphylla*, *C. glanduligera*, *C. heptaphylla*, *C. kitaibelii*, *C. maxima*, and *C. waldsteinii*.

CULTURE/CARE Average to evenly moist, rich soils in part shade or sun to part sun in early spring, followed by part shade to shade after flowering.

USES The ephemeral species are useful as seasonal ground covers in small to medium-sized applications beneath deciduous shrubs and trees or between later emerging perennials such as hostas and deciduous ferns or hellebores, where the foliage is removed in late winter. They will go dormant as the later emerging foliage fills in and casts shade. They could also be used in combination with other herbaceous and evergreen ground covers, such as *Ajuga* spp., *Asarum canadense*, *Bergenia* spp., *Euonymus fortunei* 'Wolong Ghost', and *Hosta venusta*, to create a seasonally dynamic vignette. *Cardamine trifolia* is good for small applications along pathways, at the front of the border, between pavers, and in shady rock gardens. None of the species is tolerant of foot traffic, though *C. trifolia* should withstand the occasional errant footstep and is deer resistant. All species may provide pollen and nectar for early season native bees, butterflies, and moths.

PROPAGATION Division, seed

Cardamine diphylla
BROADLEAF TOOTHWORT, TWO-LEAF TOOTHWORT

Zones 3–8

Moist woodlands and edge habitats, ravines, cliffs, bluffs, ledges, shaded slopes, meadows, and moist fields, at 165–4265 ft. (50–1300 m) elevation in most of eastern North America, from the Atlantic provinces west to Ontario and Wisconsin south to Georgia.

A rhizomatous spring ephemeral with foliage emerging in fall or winter at the warmer end of its range and early spring in cooler regions, going dormant by summer. Plants spread at a moderate rate into a colony of trifoliate, toothed, olive-green to green foliage, often with lighter veins and purplish reverses. White, sometimes light pink, four-petaled, bell-shaped to open flowers bloom from early to late spring in clusters at the top of 6–12 in. (15–30 cm) stems, each with two or three stem leaves.

'American Sweetheart': foliage emerges purple-flushed with bold white veins and purple reverses

'Eco Cut Leaf': shiny leaves with sharper serrations and good white veining

'Eco Moonlight': larger white flowers and white-veined leaves

Cardamine diphylla

Cardamine pentaphylla
FIVE-LEAFLET BITTERCRESS, SHOWY TOOTHWORT

Zones (4)5–9

Mountain woods and rocky places at 1300–7200 ft. (400–2200 m) in Central and Western Europe.

A rhizomatous clumping or slowly spreading perennial with densely held, palmate leaves composed of 3–5 or more lance-shaped, toothed leaflets with relatively large, nearly 1 in. (2.5 cm) wide, funnel- to bell-shaped, slightly ruffled, lavender or pink, sometimes white flowers held in slightly nodding clusters in midspring or early summer, to 12 in. (30 cm) or more in height. Foliage often goes dormant in late summer. AGM

Cardamine pentaphylla

Cardamine quinquefolia
FIVE-LEAF TOOTHWORT, CUCKOO FLOWER

Zones 6–9

Moist woodlands and riverbanks from Eastern Europe to Iran.

A rhizomatous, moderately to quickly spreading, ephemeral ground cover that will fill in the spaces

Cardamine quinquefolia

between later emerging perennials with lush colonies without becoming a pest. Midgreen, slightly shiny, palmate leaves usually with five lance-shaped, serrated leaflets emerge in late winter, soon followed by small clusters of lavender-pink, four-petaled flowers on stems to 10 in. (25 cm) tall. Often blooms with snowdrops (*Galanthus nivalis*) and hellebores. Goes dormant by early summer.

Cardamine trifolia
TRIFOLIATE BITTERCRESS,
THREE-LEAVED CUCKOO FLOWER

Zones 5–9

Moist, shady, mountain woods, especially on limestone, in Central Europe south to Italy and the former Yugoslavia.

A tough and resolute ground cover, slowly creeping by shallow rhizomes, with evergreen, dark green, three-part, toothed leaves, the segments four-sided to rounded and purplish beneath. Foliage is held densely in a tight, weed-smothering, frequently circular mound or mat to 2–4 in. (5–10 cm) tall. Small, white, four-petaled, somewhat short-lived flowers are produced in early to midspring on leafless stems, 6–12 in. (15–30 cm) tall. Appreciates evenly moist soil

Cardamine trifolia

but tolerant of dry shade once established. May not perform well in areas with high heat and humidity. Deer resistant.

Carex
Cyperaceae

The sedges are diverse and indispensable ground covers that provide texture and color. Often confused with grasses, these related monocots are taxonomically different and occupy their own family. In the garden, they make important contributions that many grasses can't, including finer textures, bolder foliage colors, evergreen foliage, arching and mounded habits, tolerance of wet soils, and a greater versatility in preferred light conditions including shade, a place where most grasses fear to tread. With more than 2000 species worldwide and additional species being grown for habitat restoration, more could enter ornamental horticulture. In addition to the species treated here, others have potential for increased use, including *C. amphibola*, *C. cherokeensis*, *C. divulsa*, *C. eburnea*, *C. nigra*, *C. petrei*, *C. radiata*, *C. speciosa* 'Velebit Humilis', and *C. texensis*.

CULTURE/CARE   Most species are tolerant of a range of light and soil conditions. In general, some tend more toward brighter conditions, from full sun to part shade, preferring drier to average soils, while others tend toward part sun to shade, preferring even moisture, though they may be tolerant of drier sites. Some typically shade-loving sedges will tolerate more sun given good moisture. More detailed care instructions are provided with each species.

Many sedges are evergreen, especially in milder regions, though they may be herbaceous in colder zones. In milder zones, even evergreen sedges can develop winter discoloration, requiring a spring clean-up with scissors, shears, or a lawn mower before new growth emerges. All sedges are cool-season growers, putting on new growth in early to midspring and sometimes again in fall.

USES   Mass plantings from small to large scales. Clumping species should be mass-planted to attain full coverage at maturity. Rhizomatous species tend not to be fast spreading so should also be planted close together to attain good coverage in a reasonable amount of time. Most sedges are not tolerant of foot traffic but will recover from occasional trodding. Those useful as lawn alternatives will tolerate light to moderate foot traffic. Deer resistant.

PROPAGATION   Seed, division

Carex appalachica
APPALACHIAN SEDGE

Zones 3–8

Deciduous or mixed deciduous–coniferous forests in dry to mesic, sandy or rocky soils at 330–3300 ft. (100–1000 m) from Ontario to Maine and south to Georgia.

Midgreen, arching, shiny, hair-thin leaves, 8–12 in. (20–30 cm) or more in length, held in tight clumps, 10–12 in. (25–30 cm) tall and 12–24 in. (30–60 cm) wide. In mass plantings, the foliage moves in the breeze and intermingles, creating beautiful effects. Insignificant flowers add texture in mid- to late spring.

CULTURE/CARE Part sun to shade in dry to average soils. Tolerant of dry shade at the base of trees but not tolerant of too much moisture.

Carex berggrenii
BERGGREN'S SEDGE, CARAMEL CARPET SEDGE

Zones (5)6–9

At the edges of wet places, including bogs and marshes, in New Zealand.

A peculiar little rhizomatous, slow-spreading sedge with stout, flattened, blunt-tipped, vertical to arching, green to gray-green to copper-brown leaves on plants 2–4 in. (5–10 cm) tall and 6–8 in. (15–20 cm) or more wide. Brown foliage forms are the most common in cultivation, resembling a burgundy-brown dwarf mondo grass (*Ophiopogon japonicus* 'Nanus'). Insignificant flowers.

CULTURE/CARE Full sun to part shade in average to moist soils. Deepest foliage color in full sun.

Carex caryophyllea
SPRING SEDGE, VERNAL SEDGE

Zones 5–9

Meadows, pastures, and heaths, often in calcareous soils, across Eurasia. Introduced in the northeastern United States.

The true species is uncommon in horticulture, instead represented by two cultivars that are more likely hybrids of this and another species or hybrids of two entirely different species, namely *C. digitata* and *C. ornithopoda*. The cultivars make excellent ground covers, forming dense, flopping, mop-top mounds, 12 in. (30 cm) wide, of narrow, curving leaves that trail on the ground. They are evergreen in milder zones and spread slowly by rhizomes.

CULTURE/CARE Full sun to part shade in average to moist soils.

'Beatlemania': green foliage with a subtle yellow edge in mounds 6 in. (15 cm) tall

'The Beatles': green foliage in mounds 8 in. (20 cm) tall

Carex ciliatomarginata
BROAD-LEAVED SEDGE

Zones 5–9

Deciduous oak forests with deep, moist soils in northeastern China.

Similar to *C. siderosticta* with broad, slightly fuzzy, green leaves, 6 in. (15 cm) long and 1 in. (2.5 cm) wide, forming a herbaceous, slowly spreading ground cover, 3–8 in. (7.5–20 cm) tall by 12–24 in. (30–60 cm) wide.

CULTURE/CARE Average to evenly moist soils in part shade to shade.

'Shima-nishiki' (syn. 'Island Brocade'): midgreen leaves with broad creamy yellow to gold edges and variable interior stripes

'Treasure Island': midgreen leaves with broad white edges and variable interior stripes

Carex comans
NEW ZEALAND HAIR SEDGE

Zones (6)7–9

Damp tussock grassland, pastures, and by rivers up to 4265 ft. (1300 m) in New Zealand.

Dense, textural, arching, evergreen mounds of hairlike, 18 in. (45 cm) long, green to brownish leaves, usually 14 in. (36 cm) or more tall and 12–24 in. (30–60 cm) wide. Leaves emerge upright, later curving downward to touch the ground. Inflorescences are insignificant.

CULTURE/CARE Full sun to part shade in moist to dryish soils.

'Amazon Mist': ColorGrass seed strain, mint-green foliage with white undersides

'Bronco': ColorGrass seed strain, bronzy brown foliage

bronze-leaved (syn. 'Bronze'): bronzy brown foliage

'Frosted Curls': green foliage with a silvery cast, more compact than the species

'Milchoc' Milk Chocolate: possibly a hybrid, with bronzy brown foliage with subtle pink highlights at the edges and orange colors in fall

Carex appalachica

Carex berggrenii in the wild, Remarkables mountain range, New Zealand

Carex ciliatomarginata 'Treasure Island'

Carex comans

Carex conica 'Snowline'

Carex conica
BIRDFOOT SEDGE

Zones 5–9

Low-elevation mountain forests of Japan and the southern Korean Peninsula.

A dainty species, evergreen in milder regions and semi-evergreen in colder regions, with narrow, shiny, arching, midgreen foliage forming slowly spreading mounds, 8–12 in. (20–30 cm) tall and 12–24 in. (30–60 cm) wide. Somewhat attractive inflorescences resemble little sparklers of pale yellow stamens.

CULTURE/CARE Light shade and evenly moist soils.

'Snowline' (syn. 'Hime-kan-suge'): slow-growing variegated cultivar with deep green leaves and white margins, 6–8 in. (15–20 cm) tall and 12 in. (30 cm) wide, possibly larger given time

Carex dolichostachya
GOLD FOUNTAIN SEDGE

Zones 5–9

Mountain woodlands in China, Japan, and the Philippines.

Narrow, arching, midgreen leaves, 6–10 in. (15–25 cm) long, forming small clumps 10–12 in. (25–30 cm) tall and 20 in. (50 cm) wide. Evergreen in mild winter regions. Insignificant flowers.

CULTURE/CARE Part sun to part shade in average to evenly moist soils. Tolerant of full shade or sun if provided good moisture. Provide shade in hot summer climates.

'Kaga-nishiki' (syn. 'Gold Fountains'): green centers with yellow to pale green borders

Carex flacca
BLUE CREEPING SEDGE, BLUE-GREEN SEDGE

Zones 4–9

Diverse habitats including grasslands, moorlands, disturbed areas, and edges of salt marshes, often on calcareous soils, in Europe and North Africa.

Attractive and versatile rhizomatous, creeping sedge, slowly forming expanding clumps of narrow, arching, evergreen foliage, blue-green above and powdery blue beneath, to 16 in. (40 cm) long, forming clumps 6–12 in. (15–30 cm) tall and 16 in. (40 cm) or more wide. Green to dark brown, pendulous, 1–2 in. (2.5–5 cm) long inflorescences are held on mostly

Carex flacca 'Blue Zinger'

Carex flaccosperma

Carex flagellifera 'Bronzita'

upright stems, 12–16 in. (30–40 cm) tall, in early to midsummer. Potentially invasive in eastern North America.

CULTURE/CARE Sun to part shade in moist to dry soils. Moist soils will encourage better lateral spreading as will shearing three or four times a year. Tolerant of dry shade.

'Blue Zinger': steel-blue leaves, slightly larger, more upright, and less spreading than the species

Carex flaccosperma
BLUE WOOD SEDGE

Zones 5–8

Wet to mesic, rich, calcareous soils in deciduous forests on flood plains, bottomlands, and in swamps up to 660 ft. (200 m), from Virginia to Kansas south to Texas and Florida.

Striking, glaucous blue, rhizomatous species with broad, puckered leaves up to ⅝ in. (1.6 cm) wide in slowly spreading mounds, 6–10 in. (15–20 cm) tall and 12 in. (30 cm) or more wide. Evergreen in milder regions. Insignificant flowers.

CULTURE/CARE Part to full shade in average to wet soils. Some drought tolerance once established. May tolerate more sun with good moisture.

Carex flagellifera
WEEPING BROWN SEDGE, ORANGE HAIR SEDGE

Zones 6–9

Moist, open habitats or along forest margins from sea level to 3300 ft. (1000 m) throughout New Zealand.

Evergreen species resembling *C. comans*, with thin, hairlike, arching, green to copper-brown leaves forming mop-top mounds, 8–12 in. (20–30 cm) tall and 12–24 in. (30–60 cm) wide. Insignificant flowers.

CULTURE/CARE Full sun to part shade in dry, average, or moist soils.

'Bronzita': ColorGrass seed strain with copper-brown foliage

'Kiwi': olive-green foliage with a slight shimmer

'Toffee Twist': coppery red-brown foliage with a subtle luster

Carex laxiculmis
CREEPING SEDGE

Zones (4)5–9
Low-lying wet places in deciduous or mixed deciduous–coniferous forests, often in clay soils along springs, seeps, and streams, from sea level to 3300 ft. (1000 m) in eastern North America.

Evergreen, green to glaucous, mainly clumping sedge with broad foliage, 12–14 in. (30–36 cm) long and ½ in. (1.3 cm) wide, forming mounds 12 in. (30 cm) tall and 18 in. (45 cm) wide that may spread slowly over time. Resembles *C. flaccosperma* but often tidier in appearance. Insignificant flowers.

CULTURE/CARE Part sun to shade in average to moist soils. May tolerate full sun with good moisture.

'Hobb' Bunny Blue: powder-blue foliage

Carex morrowii
JAPANESE SEDGE, MORROW'S SEDGE

Zones 5–9
Low elevations in mountainous areas of Japan.
Clump-forming, semi-evergreen to evergreen sedge resembling *Liriope* spp., with arching, leathery, deep green, slightly shiny leaves, 12 in. (30 cm) long, held in dense, sturdy mounds, 12 in. (30 cm) or more tall and 12–18 in. (30–45 cm) wide. Flowering stems, 12–18 in. (30–45 cm) tall, are produced in midspring with green to brown, cylindrical inflorescences.

CULTURE/CARE Sun to shade in average to moist soils. Avoid sun in hot summer climates, which can bleach the foliage.

'Fisher's Form': leaves with creamy white edges

'Ice Ballet': sport of 'Ice Dance' with broader, brighter white margins that also spreads by rhizomes

'Ice Dance': hybrid, similar to 'Variegata', with white-edged leaves but with a spreading habit

'Silver Sceptre': likely a hybrid with narrow, white-margined leaves

var. *temnolepis* 'Silk Tassel': very narrow, fine-textured foliage resembling *C. comans*, with green edges and a silvery white central stripe, giving plants a shimmering appearance from a distance

'Variegata': white-edged leaves

Carex 'Ice Dance'

Carex muskingumensis

Carex oshimensis 'Evergold'

Carex muskingumensis
PALM SEDGE

Zones 3–9

Moist to wet, deciduous flood plains and meadows and lowland, swampy woods and thickets at 330–1300 ft. (100–400 m), from Manitoba through the Great Lakes region south to Kentucky and Missouri.

Distinctive, tough, somewhat tropical-looking, rhizomatous, slowly spreading, herbaceous sedge with upright to arching stems, 12–24 in. (30–60 cm) or more tall, with whorls of bright green, narrow, 4–8 in. (10–20 cm) long leaves resembling thickets of miniature palm trees or papyrus. Produces green to brown cylindrical, upright inflorescences in terminal spikes in summer.

CULTURE/CARE Wet, moist, or average soils in full sun to part shade.

'Little Midge': dwarf form to 12 in. (30 cm) tall

'Oehme': green foliage gradually develops light green and then yellow margins, becoming brightest in midsummer

'Silberstreif': green leaves with a white central band

Carex oshimensis
JAPANESE SEDGE, OSHIMA SEDGE

Zones 5–9

Dry woods and rocky slopes of Honshu, Japan.

Among the most popular of the ornamental sedges, with thick, arching leaves, ⅛–¼ in. (3–6 mm) wide and 12–18 in. (30–45 cm) long, forming evergreen, clumping mounds up to 12 in. (30 cm) tall and 18 in. (45 cm) wide. Similar to C. morrowii but with less leathery and more pointed leaves. Tassels of pale yellow and brown flowers emerge in late spring to early summer.

CULTURE/CARE Full sun to part shade in average to dryish soils. Tolerant of dry shade. Avoid full sun in hot summer climates.

'Et Crx01' Feather Falls: hybrid, extra large mounds of thick green and white foliage

EverColor Series

'Carfit01' Everest: green leaves with crisp, white margins

'Everdi': green foliage on compact plants to 8 in. (20 cm) tall

'Everglow': cream-variegated margins in spring and summer, deepening to orange in fall and winter

'Everillo': best of the series with lime-green foliage in more shade, gold in more sun

'Everlime': deep green leaves with lime-green margins

'Everlite': green leaves with a bright white central band

'Everoro': similar to 'Evergold' but more vigorous with bolder color

'Eversheen': lime-yellow central band with dark green margins

'Ficre' Evercream: deep green leaves with cream margins

'Evergold': among the most popular of all sedges, with green leaves with a creamy yellow to gold central band

'Gold Strike': creamy white central bands mature to creamy yellow

'Ice Cream': sport of 'Evergold' with a creamy white central band

Carex pansa
SAND DUNE SEDGE, CALIFORNIA MEADOW SEDGE

Zones 7–11

Dunes, coastal prairies, and other moist, sandy, open habitats near sea level in western North America from British Columbia to Baja California, Mexico.

An evergreen, rhizomatous lawn alternative and slope stabilizer for erosion control in areas with mild climates, similar to the hardier C. pensylvanica and C. praegracilis (with which it is sometimes confused), with narrow, arching, almost hairlike, 10–12 in. (25–30 cm) long, shiny, midgreen to deep green leaves, spreading at a reasonable rate without being overly aggressive. Foliage flops over into mats 6–8 in. (15–20 cm) tall. Insignificant flowers.

CULTURE/CARE Full sun to part shade in moist to dryish soils. Can be mown to a few inches tall. Tolerant of moderate foot traffic. Evergreen with adequate moisture from rain or weekly summer irrigation during dry spells. Otherwise plantings can go summer dormant. Foliage develops bronze tones in cool weather and can go winter dormant with increased cold.

Carex pensylvanica

PENNSYLVANIA SEDGE, OAK SEDGE

Zones 4–8

Well-drained, acidic, sandy, rocky, and loamy soils in deciduous forests, forest edges, and savannahs at 500–5000 ft. (150–1500 m) from Manitoba to Maine and south to Arkansas and Georgia.

A fine-textured, semi-evergreen lawn alternative and shade ground cover with narrow, arching, almost hairlike, shiny, mid- to deep green foliage, forming mounds 8–10 in. (20–25 cm) tall and 12–18 in. (30–45 cm) or more wide. Plants spread by rhizomes at a reasonable though not overly aggressive, forming colonies of overlapping, flopping foliage resembling waves. Insignificant flowers.

CULTURE/CARE Shade to part sun in average to dryish soils. More moisture is required in sunnier positions, especially in hot summer climates. Tolerant of dry shade and occasional foot traffic. If grown as a lawn alternative, mow in spring before new growth appears.

'Straw Hat': larger, showier inflorescences

Carex plantaginea

SEERSUCKER SEDGE, PLANTAIN-LEAVED SEDGE

Zones 3–8

Rich, moist, deciduous or mixed deciduous–coniferous forests, along streams, at the edges of depressions, and in mountain gorges at 330–2000 ft. (100–600 m), across much of eastern North America.

An unusual and distinctive clumping species with broad, 1 in. (2.5 cm) wide, semi-evergreen to evergreen, somewhat shiny, midgreen leaves, 6–16 in. (15–40 cm) long, puckered along their length. Foliage is arching to prostrate in mounds 6–10 in. (15–25 cm) tall and 12 in. (30 cm) wide. Nearly black, fuzzy inflorescences with pale yellow stamens are held on short stalks in early to midspring.

CULTURE/CARE Average to moist soils in part shade to shade. Drought tolerant once established.

Carex platyphylla

SILVER SEDGE, BROAD-LEAF SEDGE

Zones 4–8

Rocky or gravelly slopes and in clay soils in rich, moist, deciduous forests at 330–3600 ft. (100–1090 m)

from Wisconsin to New Brunswick and south to Tennessee and North Carolina.

Similar to *C. plantaginea* with distinctive, broad, 2–9 in. (5–23 cm) long by 1 in. (2.5 cm) wide, pleated, evergreen leaves with a striking powder-blue cast. Plants form dense clumps, 8–12 in. (20–30 cm) tall and 12–18 in. (30–45 cm) wide. Inflorescences resemble small torches in spring.

CULTURE/CARE Part shade to shade in average to moist soils. Drought tolerant once established. May tolerate more sun with good moisture.

Carex praegracilis

CLUSTERED FIELD SEDGE

Zones 4–8

Wet to seasonally dry meadows, prairies, streambanks, lakeshores, ditches, and other wet areas, plus woodland openings and roadsides, often in alkaline and salty soils across most of North America excluding the Atlantic provinces and the U.S. Southeast.

Rhizomatous lawn alternative and slope stabilizer for erosion control, similar to but larger than *C. pansa* and *C. pensylvanica*. Clumps of narrow, arching, almost hairlike, 10–32 in. (25–80 cm) long, shiny, mid- to deep green leaves form upright, arching, and/or flopping mats, 6–24 in. (15–60 cm) tall. Spreads at a reasonable rate without becoming overly aggressive. Evergreen, at least in milder zones. Insignificant flowers.

CULTURE/CARE Full sun to part shade in moist to dryish soils. Can be mowed regularly to a few inches. Tolerant of moderate foot traffic, salt, and alkaline conditions. May go summer dormant without regular rainfall or irrigation but requires less water than a traditional lawn. Herbaceous in late summer or fall without added moisture or when temperatures drop below freezing.

Carex siderosticta

CREEPING BROADLEAVED SEDGE

Zones 5–9

Mixed deciduous–coniferous forests, forest margins, and dry grasslands at 3300–6600 ft. (1000–2000 m) in China, Japan, Korea, and the Russian Far East.

Similar to *C. ciliatomarginata* with broad, 4–8 in. (10–20 cm) long by 1¼ in. (3 cm) wide, arching to prostrate leaves in tight, herbaceous clumps, creeping slowly via rhizomes. Insignificant flowers.

Carex pensylvanica

Carex platyphylla

Carex praegracilis

Carex plantaginea

Carex siderosticta 'Variegata'

CULTURE/CARE Part shade to shade in evenly moist soils. Tolerant of dry shade.

'Banana Boat' (syn. 'Golden Falls'): golden yellow leaves with variable green edges

'Lemon Zest': golden yellow leaves

'Snow Cap': creamy to bright white leaves with variable green edges, good vigor for such a variegated plant

'Variegata': green leaves with variable white edges

Carex tenuiculmis
RED-LEAVED SEDGE

Zones (6)7–9
Wet habitats including streambanks, lake margins, and ponds from lowland to montane areas on the South Island, New Zealand.
  Similar to *C. comans* and *C. flagellifera* with narrow, hairlike, arching, evergreen foliage in intergrading shades of red-brown to copper-red, forming clumping mounds 12–16 in. (30–40 cm) tall and 18–24 in. (45–60 cm) wide. Insignificant flowers.
  CULTURE/CARE Sun to part shade in average to moist soils.

'Cappuccino': new growth emerges red-brown, turns coppery brown and develops red, orange, and yellow highlights in fall

Carex testacea
COPPER HAIR SEDGE,
ORANGE NEW ZEALAND SEDGE

Zones 6–9
Sand dunes, coastal forest and scrub, dense forests, and tussock grasslands from sea level to montane areas primarily on the North Island, New Zealand.
  Narrow, arching, evergreen foliage similar to *C. tenuiculmis* but hardier, with leaves olive-green at the base becoming bronzy orange toward the tips, in clumping mounds 12–16 in. (30–40 cm) tall and 18–24 in. (45–60 cm) wide. Orange foliage color deepens in winter and with more sun. Insignificant flowers.
  CULTURE/CARE Sun to part shade in average to moist soils. Salt tolerant.

'Prairie Fire': ColorGrass seed strain with good coloration

Ceanothus
Rhamnaceae

Genus of small to large shrubs found primarily along the U.S. West Coast, especially California, but also throughout North America. They are much loved by gardeners in milder zones for their true-blue, often fragrant flowers that are popular with bees. The low-growing, mounding, or prostrate forms, with their interlacing branches and shiny, evergreen foliage, make excellent weed-smothering ground covers. In addition to the species treated, others are worth searching out, including *C. cuneatus* var. *ramulosus* and its cultivar 'Rodeo Lagoon', *C. foliosus* and its cultivar 'Berryhill', *C. hearstiorum*, *C. maritimus*, and *C. pumilus*.
  CULTURE/CARE Full sun in cool summer climates and coastal positions to part sun or afternoon shade in hot summer climates. Commonly cultivated species and cultivars are usually tolerant of sandy or clay soils and irrigation, while other species may be more exacting in their requirements for soil type and prefer drier soils. Salt tolerant.
  USES Small to large applications in dry, hot sites, especially without irrigation; on slopes, banks, and spilling over walls; as informal ground-covering hedges; and in coastal plantings. Wide-spreading selections can be pruned to control width. Rate of growth is slow to fast, depending on the species. Not tolerant of foot traffic. Deer resistant. Attractive to pollinators, especially bees and butterflies.
  PROPAGATION Cuttings

Ceanothus gloriosus
POINT REYES CEANOTHUS, GLORY MAT

Zones 8–10
Coastal bluffs, slopes, ridges, and dunes from sea level to 2440 ft. (740 m) in Marin, Sonoma, and Mendocino counties, California.
  Excellent, dense, sprawling, prostrate species (especially var. *gloriosus* and var. *porrectus*), forming low-growing, mounding, or spreading thickets of interlacing, branching stems with small, dark green, toothed, elliptic, hollylike leaves. Copious clusters of fragrant, deep blue to lavender-blue flowers put on a bold show in spring. Provide afternoon shade in hot summer climates.

var. *exaltatus* 'Emily Brown': cultivar of Navarro ceanothus or glory bush, 24–36 in. (60–90 cm) tall and 8–10 ft. (2.4–3 m) wide

Carex testacea

Ceanothus gloriosus with *Acaena* sp.

Ceanothus griseus var. *horizontalis* 'Diamond Heights'

var. *gloriosus* 'Anchor Bay': bright blue flowers and larger leaves to 1 in. (2.5 cm) long on dense mats, 12–24 in. (30–60 cm) or more tall and 6–8 ft. (1.8–2.4 m) wide

var. *gloriosus* 'Heart's Desire': very low and dense, to 6–12 in. (15–30 cm) tall and 5 ft. (1.5 m) wide, with deep blue flowers

var. *porrectus*: Mount Vision ceanothus, 12–24 in. (30–60 cm) tall by 6 ft. (1.8 m) wide, with smaller, less toothed leaves

Ceanothus griseus var. horizontalis
CARMEL CEANOTHUS, CARMEL CREEPER

Zones 8–10

Exposed bluffs, headlands, steep canyon slopes, and dunes from sea level to 1650 ft. (500 m), from Santa Barbara to Mendocino counties, California.

Dense, lush species with large, 1–2 in. (2.5–5 cm) long, midgreen, veined and shiny, oval to elliptic leaves. Thimble-like panicles, 1–2 in. (2.5–5 cm) long, of tiny pale to dark blue flowers appear in midspring.

'Centennial': hybrid with *C. foliosus*, vigorous, shade tolerant with cobalt-blue flowers and small, glossy, dark green leaves on sprawling stems, 6–12 in. (15–30 cm) or more tall and 4–8 ft. (1.2–2.4 m) wide

'Diamond Heights': pale blue flowers atop striking chartreuse to gold foliage with variable, dark green central markings on dense, spreading plants, 6–12 in. (15–30 cm) tall by 4–6 ft. (1.2–1.8 m) wide, needs afternoon shade in hot regions

'Hurricane Point': large leaves to 2 in. (5 cm) long, with pale blue flowers on fast-growing, sprawling plants, 24–36 in. (60–90 cm) tall and up to 8–15 ft. (2.4–4.5 m) wide

'Yankee Point': popular for its fast growth rate, sprawling to 24–36 in. (60–90 cm) tall and 8–12 ft. (2.4–3.6 m) or more wide, with bright blue flowers

Ceanothus thyrsiflorus var. repens
LOW BLUE BLOSSOM, CREEPING BLUE BLOSSOM

Zones 8–10

Sandy or rocky habitats, coastal chaparral, and forest openings from sea level to 1970 ft. (600 m) from Oregon to Baja California, Mexico.

Vigorous, prostrate, mounding or sprawling shrub, 12–24 in. (30–60 cm) tall and 6–15 ft. (1.8–4.5 m) wide, with panicles of sky-blue flowers in spring against shiny, midgreen, oval foliage with indented veins and serrated edges. Similar to *C. griseus* var. *horizontalis* but with smaller leaves and a lower, denser habit. Shade tolerant. AGM

Cerastium tomentosum
SNOW IN SUMMER, DUSTY MILLER

Caryophyllaceae

Zones 2–8

Scree, rocky areas, and disturbed sites in foothills and mountains at 2000–7200 ft. (600–2200 m) from central Italy to Sicily. Naturalized across Europe.

Old-fashioned, vigorous, evergreen ground cover forms mats 6 in. (15 cm) tall and 24 in. (60 cm) or more wide, with small, 1 in. (2.5 cm) long, lance-shaped, silver-green to fully silver, woolly foliage. Masses of small, clustered, 1 in. (2.5 cm) wide, pure white, five-petaled flowers on stems to 6–12 in. (15–30 cm) tall in mid- to late spring. The similar *C. biebersteinii* or the very low carpeting *C. alpinum* var. *lanatum* are sometimes also grown.

CULTURE/CARE Full sun in light, sandy, dry soils. Short-lived without excellent drainage. May resent heat and humidity. Plants can look untidy after flowering. Shear plants to 2 in. (5 cm) to encourage fresh growth.

USES Fast spreader in full sun and poor soils, on rock walls, on steep banks, in rock gardens, at the front of dry borders, and as a small-scale lawn alternative. Not tolerant of foot traffic. Deer and rabbit resistant.

PROPAGATION Seed, division, cuttings

var. *columnae*: shorter, more compact, to 4 in. (10 cm) tall

'Silberteppich' (syn. 'Silver Carpet'): 4–6 in. (10–15 cm) tall

'Yo Yo': floriferous with a slower, more restrained habit

Ceratostigma
Plumbaginaceae

Valued for its true-blue flowers and late-season foliage color, blue leadwort is a classic, herbaceous ground cover, while the subshrub, Burmese plumbago (*C. griffithii*), can be used for a more unusual tall cover. On a landscape scale, *C. willmottianum* and its cultivars 'Lice' Forest Blue, 'My Love', and 'Palmgold' Desert Skies, though not treated here, can be mass-planted for a taller shrub cover to 3 ft. (1 m) tall.

CULTURE/CARE Full sun to part shade in all but overly moist soils. Because *C. griffithii* blooms on new wood, prune in winter or early spring. *Ceratostigma plumbaginoides* emerges in late spring and can spread aggressively in optimum conditions but is generally well behaved. Provide a winter mulch in zone 5 and

afternoon shade in hot summer climates. Drought tolerant once established and tolerant of dry shade. Deer and rabbit resistant. Attractive to pollinators, especially butterflies.

PROPAGATION Division, cuttings

Ceratostigma griffithii
BURMESE PLUMBAGO

Zones 7–10

Steppe shrublands, scrub, and grasslands on plateaus, valley floors, and lower mountain slopes in warm valleys at 7200–9200 ft. (2200–2800 m) in China, Bhutan, and other Himalayan countries.

A subshrubby to shrubby, evergreen plumbago similar to the much better known *C. plumbaginoides*, with reddish, wiry stems, 18–24 in. (45–60 cm) or more tall and 24–36 in. (60–90 cm) wide. Dull-green, thick-textured, rounded, egg-shaped leaves with purple margins are topped with clusters of light royal-blue flowers from red buds from midsummer into fall. Foliage develops red tints in late summer and fall. Semi-evergreen to deciduous in colder zones.

USES Specimen for small spaces. Mass plant in larger areas for a tall ground cover. Not tolerant of foot traffic.

Ceratostigma plumbaginoides
LEADWORT, BLUE LEADWORT

Zones 5–9

Rocky places and among low scrub in the foothills of northeastern China.

A tough, deciduous, rhizomatous, woody-based ground cover, 6–12 in. (15–30 cm) tall and 24 in. (60 cm) or more wide, with 2 in. (5 cm) long, oval to slightly egg-shaped green leaves. Clusters of 15–30 small, gentian-blue flowers from deep red buds begin to bloom on red stems in midsummer, continuing through fall as leaves turn to scarlet and then maroon-red. AGM

USES Front of the border, as a slope stabilizer for erosion control, and in rock gardens. Foliage emerges late in spring, offering space for an underplanting of early spring bulbs or interplanting with spring ephermals such as *Anemone nemorosa* and *Corydalis solida*. Not tolerant of foot traffic.

Cerastium tomentosum

Ceratostigma plumbaginoides

Chamaemelum nobile 'Flore Pleno'

Chamaemelum nobile

ROMAN CHAMOMILE

Asteraceae

Zones 4–9

Moderately acidic soils in seasonally wet grasslands, sandy pastures and fields, and in coastal grasslands and on cliffs in Western Europe from the United Kingdom to Portugal.

A ground cover and aromatic edible herb rolled into one, forming a low-spreading carpet, 3–6 in. (7.5–15 cm) tall by 12 in. (30 cm) or more wide, of small, bright-green, evergreen (in milder zones), fernlike, divided leaves with a fruity fragrance. In summer, 1 in. (2.5 cm) wide white daisies with yellow centers are produced on stems up to 12 in. (30 cm) tall.

CULTURE/CARE Full sun to light shade in sandy, well-drained, average to dry soils. Roots run deep, conferring good drought tolerance. As a lawn alternative, mow to 3 in. (7.5 cm) tall. Allowing plants to flower may sacrifice surface coverage. Provide enough irrigation to keep green and lush. Fertilize in spring and summer.

USES Excellent border or herb garden edger, ground cover for dry and sunny sites, or lawn alternative. Plants will creep together with interlocking stems at a moderate to fast rate. Tolerant of occasional foot traffic. Deer resistant.

PROPAGATION Seed, division

'Flore Pleno': double white pom-poms with yellow centers

'Treneague': nonflowering plants to 2–3 in. (5–7.5 cm) tall, best as a lawn alternative

Chrysanthemum weyrichii
WEYRICH CHRYSANTHEMUM

Asteraceae

Zones 4–9

Among seashore rocks of Hokkaido to Kamtschatka and on nearby islands in Japan.

Herbaceous, stoloniferous perennial with aromatic, lobed, palmate or pinnate leaves. Stems are 10–12 in. (25–30 cm) tall in late summer and fall, topped with 2 in. (5 cm) wide, white or lavender-pink daisies with golden centers. Known scientifically as *C. zawadskii*. Formerly known as *Dendranthema weyrichii*.

CULTURE/CARE Easy to grow in full sun to part shade in average, well-drained soils.

USES Indefinitely spreading at a moderate rate for small to large areas in borders, on banks, and along roadsides. Not tolerant of foot traffic. Deer resistant. Attractive to pollinators, especially bees and butterflies.

PROPAGATION Division, cuttings

'White Bomb': white flowers blushing pink with age on purple-flushed stems

'Pink Bomb': pale pink flowers

Chrysogonum virginianum
GREEN AND GOLD, GOLDEN STAR

Asteraceae

Zones 5–9

Moist to dry woodlands and forests, especially in clearings, edges, and rocky, open areas from sea level to 2300 ft. (700 m) from New York to Tennessee and South Carolina.

Tough, dependable, easy to grow, variably clumping to stoloniferous species with evergreen to semi-evergreen, hairy, egg-shaped to triangular leaves, 1–4 in. (2.5–10 cm) long, with scalloped edges, forming clumps or spreading mats to 4 in. (10 cm) tall. Bright yellow, starlike, daisy flowers with five notched ray florets are borne singly or in pairs in spring, sometimes intermittently thereafter and/or reblooming in fall. Three varieties are recognized: var. *australe*, with long stolons 5–24 in. (12.5–60 cm) long and short flower stems 1–4 in. (2.5–10 cm) tall; var. *brevistolon*, with short stolons 1–2 in. (2.5–5 cm) long and variable flowering stems 2–10 in. (5–25 cm) tall; and clump-forming var. *virginianum*, with flowering stems 6–14 in. (15–36 cm) tall.

Chrysogonum virginianum

CULTURE/CARE Full sun (with good moisture) to part shade in average to moist, well-drained soils. Flowers are most abundant in cooler conditions. Provide shade in hot climates, more sun in cooler regions.

USES Border edges and woodland gardens. Rate of spread depends on the variety; *C. virginianum* var. *australe* is the fastest spreader. Tolerant of occasional foot traffic. Deer and rabbit resistant.

PROPAGATION Division, seed

'Allen Bush' (likely var. *virginianum*): compact dwarf cultivar with smaller flowers

'Eco Lacquered Spider' (likely var. *australe*): blue-green, shiny foliage turns purplish in winter, with long, purplish stolons

'Golden Acres' (likely var. *virginianum*): large leaves and long bloom period

'Pierre' (likely var. *virginianum*): lighter green leaves and long bloom period

'Quinn's Gold': flowers emerge golden yellow, aging to light yellow and cream

'Superstar' (syn. 'Norman Singer's Form') (likely var. *virginianum*): vigorous, floriferous clumps, 5 in. (12.5 cm) tall and 12 in. (30 cm) wide

Chrysosplenium davidianum

Chrysosplenium macrophyllum

Chrysosplenium
Saxifragaceae

A peculiar Northern Hemisphere genus of shaded habitats with intriguing, flat-topped flower clusters subtended by leafy bracts. Those with yellow bracts are more reminiscent of *Euphorbia* species than plants of their own family. Somewhat rare in cultivation but well worth growing.

CULTURE/CARE Moist to wet, shady locations in soils with high organic content.

USES Small to medium-sized applications in shade and woodland gardens, in wet and low-lying locations, or beside ponds or streams, spreading at a moderate rate. Not tolerant of foot traffic.

PROPAGATION Division

Chrysosplenium davidianum
DAVID'S GOLDEN SAXIFRAGE

Zones 7–9

Shaded and wet, grassy areas in mountain forests, shaded rock clefts, and ravines at 5000–13,450 ft. (1500–4100 m) in Southwest China.

Rhizomatous, creeping, evergreen to semi-evergreen, mat-forming perennial, 2–8 in. (5–20 cm) tall, with indefinite spread and alternate, rounded, scalloped, hairy, mid- to dark green leaves held on reddish, silver-hairy stems. Euphorbia-like inflorescences comprise flat-topped clusters of apetalous flowers with four cupped, golden sepals and gold and green bracts, blooming from spring to early summer.

Chrysosplenium macrophyllum
GIANT GOLDEN SAXIFRAGE

Zones 7–9

Forests and shaded ravines in moist to wet soils at 3300–7200 ft. (1000–2200 m) in most of southern China.

Useful, dense, robust, evergreen ground cover with leathery, oval, deep-green leaves resembling those of *Bergenia* species, up to 8 in. (20 cm) long and half as wide, with brown upper surface hairs. Foliage emerges reddish in spring, becoming tan to reddish in winter. Plants spread via brownish red, hairy stolons, 8–12 in. (20–30 cm) long. Apetalous flowers are produced in flat-topped clusters with white sepals, long-filamented pink stamens, and white bracts on red stems to 8 in. (20 cm) tall in late winter and early spring.

Chrysosplenium oppositifolium
OPPOSITE-LEAVED GOLDEN SAXIFRAGE

Zones 4–8

Along shady streams, in wet woodlands, and in other damp or wet shaded habitats in Western and Central Europe from the United Kingdom and Norway, south to Spain and northern Italy.

Rhizomatous, creeping, evergreen to semi-evergreen, mat-forming perennial, 2–8 in. (5–20 cm) tall, spreading indefinitely with opposite, paired, rounded, scalloped, green leaves topped with flattened clusters of apetalous flowers with four spreading golden sepals and bright green bracts in early to late spring.

Cistus
Cistaceae

Zones 7 or 8–11

Dry, rocky, relatively infertile soils of the Mediterranean Basin.

Cistus, the rock rose, is a genus of evergreen, prostrate, mounded or upright, sometimes resinous shrubs with gray-green to green, elliptic to oval leaves, often with a rough or fuzzy surface. Their crinkled, papery, five-petaled flowers with a central boss of yellow stamens resemble single roses in shades of white and pink, though some have petals with dark burgundy basal spots. Individual flowers last for a short time, sometimes only a day, though plants bloom over a period of 3–4 weeks in midspring to early summer. Many are mounding shrubs 3–5 ft. (1–1.5 m) tall and wide, suitable as tall, mass-planted ground covers for large, parklike spaces. The shorter prostrate forms are suited to more conventional applications.

CULTURE/CARE Full sun in infertile, dry, free-draining, even rocky soils. In wet winter climates, plant in sharp drainage and on slopes, if possible. Salt and drought tolerant.

USES Rock gardens, sunny slopes and walls, seaside plantings, and nonirrigated beds. Not tolerant of foot traffic. Deer and rabbit resistant.

PROPAGATION Cuttings

C. ×*crispatus* 'Warley Rose': bright pink flowers, 2.5 in. (6 cm) wide, with gray-green foliage on shrubs, 18–24 in. (45–60 cm) tall and 4 ft. (1.2 m) wide, zone 7

C. ×*dansereaui* 'Decumbens': white flowers up to 3 in. (7.5 cm) wide, with dark burgundy basal blotches and dull green foliage on shrubs 18–24 in. (45–60 cm) tall and 3–4 ft. (1–1.2 m) wide, zone 8

Cistus ×*pulverulentus* 'Sunset'

C. ×*hybridus* 'McGuire's Gold': small, white flowers, 1.5 in. (4 cm) wide, atop gold to lime-green foliage on shrubs 18 in. (45 cm) tall and 30 in. (75 cm) wide, zone 7

C. ×*hybridus* 'Mickie': small, white flowers, 1.5 in. (4 cm) wide, atop gold foliage with green centers on shrubs 18 in. (45 cm) tall and 36 in. (90 cm) wide, zone 7

C. ×*pulverulentus* 'Sunset': glowing magenta flowers, 2 in. (5 cm) wide, with green leaves on shrubs 24–36 in. (60–90 cm) tall and 6–8 ft. (1.8–2.4 m) wide, zone 8

C. salviifolius 'Prostratus': white flowers, 1.5 in. (4 cm) wide, with green leaves on low-spreading shrubs 12–24 in. (30–60 cm) tall and 6–8 ft. (1.8–2.4 m) wide, zone 8

Clematis
Ranunculaceae

The "queen of the vines" is much-loved for the beauty of its flowers, including their range of colors, patterns, shapes, and sizes. The diversity of habit and plant size within the genus *Clematis* also suits it to various applications, including perhaps the least explored application as a ground cover. Few gardeners consider that vines in the wild can just as easily be found spreading across the ground, clambering over rocks, bounding down slopes, and threading through neighboring plants as are found climbing into shrubs and trees. Nature, after all, doesn't provide trellises. Only when they eventually encounter a vertical support do vines begin growing upward. In the garden and without a structure to climb, clematis plants will form billowy, informal mats, 6–24 in. (15–60 cm) tall, depending on the species or cultivar and the amount of pruning. They can also be interplanted with perennials in the border, where they can crawl and scramble between and through their neighbors, suppressing weeds across otherwise bare ground and adding whimsy and spontaneity as flowers pop up and bloom throughout the border.

Clematis species are primarily deciduous, semi-woody, twining vines, usually with midgreen, simple to compound leaves, and solitary or clustered flowers that can be small and star-shaped, bell-shaped, or large and open. Their spherical seed heads can be attractive, with feathered and often silver seed appendages. A few species are evergreen and others do not twine but grow like a semi-upright or scrambling perennial.

CULTURE/CARE Full sun to part shade in soils of average to good fertility and moisture. Provide a cool root zone shaded by other plants or mulch. Most clematis could be used as ground covers, but those that are resistant to wilt and powdery mildew are best.

USES In borders among other plants as a ground cover or "knitter," on flat ground or slopes, as an unconventional lawn alternative, and over walls. For small to large applications, depending on the species or cultivar, spreading at a moderate to fast rate. Not tolerant of foot traffic. Deer and rabbit resistant. Attractive to pollinators, especially bees and butterflies.

PROPAGATION Cuttings, seed

Clematis armandii
EVERGREEN CLEMATIS

Zones (6)7–9

Forest margins, slopes, scrub, and along streams from low to moderately high elevations in southern China.

A large, vigorous, evergreen vine with stems up to 20 ft. (6 m) long, with dark green, leathery, somewhat shiny, three-part leaves of lance-shaped leaflets with heart-shaped bases, the new growth emerging burgundy. Masses of small, starry, four-tepaled, 1 in. (2.5 cm) wide, fragrant flowers are borne in early spring. Prune lightly after flowering only if required.

'Apple Blossom': pink buds opening to white flowers with pink reverses, AGM

'Snowdrift': white flowers

Clematis armandii

Clematis Atragene Group

Zones (3)4–9

Mountainous regions, often in forests or scrub. *Clematis alpina* comes from Europe; *C. macropetala* is from northern China, Mongolia, and adjacent Russia; and *C. koreana* is from the Korean Peninsula and adjacent China.

Extremely hardy and easy to grow with early blooming, somewhat small, bell- or lantern-shaped, outward to downward facing flowers produced on old wood in a range of colors with white to yellowish centers, followed by attractive, silvery, feathered seed heads that persist into fall and winter. Plants can rebloom in summer or fall. Stems can reach 6–12 ft. (1.8–3.6 m) and do not require regular pruning.

C. alpina (alpine clematis), small, usually single flowers

'Constance': deep rose-pink flowers, AGM

'Frances Rivis': blue flowers, AGM

'Helsingborg': purple flowers, AGM

'Pamela Jackman': purple-blue flowers, AGM

'Pink Flamingo': light pink flowers, AGM

'Stolwijk Gold': light purple-blue flowers, gold foliage

'Willy': light pink flowers

C. koreana, flowers slightly larger and later blooming than *C. alpina*

var. *carunculosa* 'Lemon Bells' (syn. *C. chiisanensis*): lemon-yellow flowers with thick tepals on purple stems, usually sold under its synonym

var. *fragrans*: lightly fragrant purple flowers

C. macropetala (downy clematis), spidery, multitepaled blooms, usually larger than *C. alpina*

'Blue Bird': hybrid, pale purple-blue flowers

'Jan Lindmark': hybrid, early blooming purple flowers

'Lagoon': purple-blue flowers, AGM

'Markham's Pink': pink flowers, AGM

'Pauline': hybrid, purple-blue flowers, AGM

'Purple Spider': hybrid, dark purple flowers

'Rosy O'Grady': hybrid, light pink flowers, AGM

'White Swan': hybrid, white flowers

Clematis alpina 'Pamela Jackman'

Clematis 'Praecox'

Clematis integrifolia 'Psharlan' Mongolian Bells

Clematis Herbaceous Group
BUSH CLEMATIS, SOLITARY CLEMATIS

Zones 3 or 4–9

Plants in the Herbaceous Clematis group have an upright, leaning, and/or sprawling habit and stems that die back each winter either to the ground or to a woody base; they can be pruned when dormant.

Clematis heracleifolia occurs at forest margins and in scrub, in low to higher elevations in southern and eastern China to Korea. *Clematis integrifolia* is found on grassy slopes, scrub, and riverbanks at moderately high elevations, from Europe through Russia and Kazakhstan to western China.

Heracleifolia Group: small, starlike flowers with recurved tepals held in small clusters, woodier and bushier than Integrifolia Group

'Mrs. Robert Brydon': hybrid with small, white, fragrant flowers tinged with palest lavender or pale blue, sometimes listed as a *C.* ×*jouiniana* cultivar

'Praecox': vigorous hybrid with small, white to palest lavender, lightly fragrant flowers, likely the best ground cover of the herbaceous cultivars, often listed as a *C.* ×*jouiniana* cultivar, AGM

C. tubulosa (syn. *C. heracleifolia* var. *tubulosa*) 'Wyevale': fragrant, bluish purple flowers

Integrifolia Group: small, nodding, bell-shaped, sometimes lightly fragrant flowers with recurved tepals, can be upright and nearly self-supporting or leaning to sprawling and may best be used as a "knitter" in the perennial border

'Alba': white flowers

'Alionushka': hybrid with rose-pink flowers with deep pink reverses, AGM

'Arabella': hybrid with open-faced, blue and light purple flowers, AGM

'Cleminov 51' Saphyra Indigo (Sapphire Indigo): hybrid, excellent rambling ground cover with relatively large, open-faced, rich purple flowers

'Fascination': hybrid, lax semiclimber with purple flowers with lighter edges

'Jan Fopma': hybrid with deep pink flowers with lighter edges

'Olgae': purple flowers

'Psharlan' Mongolian Bells: pink, white, lavender, or blue flowers on plants 16 in. (40 cm) tall and wide

'Rooguchi': hybrid with dark purple flowers with lighter edges

C. ×*diversifolia*: gray-blue flowers

C. ×*durandii* (syn. *C. integrifolia* 'Durandii'): rich purple, ribbed tepals, zone 5, AGM

Clematis Tangutica Group
GOLDEN BELL CLEMATIS

Zones (3)4–9

Forests and scrub, slopes, grassy areas, and riverbanks from low to high elevations in Central and Northwest China.

Clematis tangutica is a large plant with stems 10–20 ft. (3–6 m) long, with golden yellow, bell- or lantern-shaped, downward facing flowers flaring more open with age to reveal deep purple to black stamens in summer, followed by silvery, feathered seed heads. Can be cut back hard in spring or left to develop size and spread.

'Aureolin': hybrid with bright yellow flowers

'Bill MacKenzie': bright yellow flowers, AGM

'Golden Harvest': hybrid with butter-yellow flowers

'Helios': hybrid with yellow flowers

'Kugotia' Golden Tiara: hybrid with bright golden yellow flowers, AGM

'My Angel': hybrid with yellow flowers with reddish reverses and white edges

Clematis tangutica 'Bill MacKenzie'

Clematis terniflora

SWEET AUTUMN CLEMATIS, VIRGINSBOWER

Zones 4–9

Forest margins, scrub, grassy areas, slopes, and in rocky habitats from sea level to moderate elevations in China, Mongolia, Siberia, and Japan.

A vigorous, large growing, deciduous to semi-evergreen species often listed as *C. paniculata*, with woody stems up to 25 ft. (7.5 m) long and masses of small, starry, four-tepaled, fragrant flowers in late summer and fall, followed by attractive seed heads. Can be cut back hard in spring or left to develop size and spread. Potentially invasive in the Central and eastern United States, spreading vegetatively and by seed.

Clematis texensis

SCARLET CLEMATIS, TEXAS CLEMATIS

Zones 4–9

Woodlands, calcareous cliffs, and streambanks from low to moderate elevations in the state of Texas.

A heat-tolerant and somewhat drought-tolerant species, typically with stems 6–10 ft. (1.8–3 m) long, with small, urn-, tulip-, to bell-shaped, deep pink to red summer flowers with four or more tepals, the hybrids flaring more open with age. Can be cut back hard in spring or left to develop size and spread.

'Duchess of Albany': hybrid with tulip-shaped deep pink flowers, each tepal with a darker pink central band

'Gravetye Beauty': hybrid with ruby-red tulip-shaped flowers with pale pink margins

'Princess Diana': hybrid with glowing, deep pink tulip-shaped flowers, each tepal with a red central band, AGM

'Zoprika' Princess Kate: hybrid with white tulip-shaped flowers with warm purple bases and deep purple throats

Clematis Viticella and Large Flowered Groups

ITALIAN CLEMATIS, VITICELLA CLEMATIS

Zones 3 or 4–11

Southern Europe from Portugal to the Caucasus (Viticella Group) and hybrids of a variety of Asian species (Large Flowered Groups).

Clematis 'Gravetye Beauty'

Clematis 'Alba Luxurians'

These groups contain the most popular cultivars of the genus with large, dramatic flowers often produced two to three times between mid- to late spring and fall.

Viticella Group: resemble the classic large-flowered hybrids but differ in their smaller and more numerous flowers. Tough, easy to grow, vigorous, and free-flowering, with blooms 2–5 in. (10–12.5 cm) across, and tolerant of both cool and hot climates. Less susceptible to clematis wilt. Can be cut back hard in spring or left to develop size and spread.

> 'Alba Luxurians': four white tepals with green tips
>
> 'Betty Corning': bell-shaped, lavender flowers
>
> 'Étoile Violette': royal purple flowers, AGM
>
> 'Madame Julia Correvon': magenta-red flowers, AGM
>
> 'Minuet': white flowers with lavender-pink edges, AGM
>
> 'Pagoda': bell-shaped, lavender-pink flowers with a dark pink bar
>
> 'Polish Spirit': rich purple to warm purple flowers
>
> 'Purpurea Plena Elegans': muted reddish purple to dusky magenta, congested, double flowers, AGM
>
> 'Royal Velours': magenta-red flowers
>
> 'Rubra': magenta-red to red flowers
>
> 'Venosa Violacea': lavender-purple flowers, white-frosted in the center of each tepal, AGM

Large Flowered Groups: The early and late large-flowered groups include the most commonly grown clematis vines that everyone thinks of when they consider the genus. Though they are not as good as other groups for use as ground covers, potentially being more prone to powdery mildew and wilt, they may be worth experimenting with. Additionally, a few cultivars and groups are worth trying.

Boulevard and Patio and Garden Collections: These more compact clematis are worth trying, especially in smaller gardens.

Flora Collection are quite useful as dwarf, multistemmed, mounding plants, with stems 12–18 in. (30–45 cm) long, growing in all directions.

> 'Evipo029' Filigree: lavender flowers
>
> 'Evipo030' Bijou/Thumbelina: rich, warm purple flowers
>
> 'Evipo068' Luiza: glowing, deep pink flowers

Kivistik Series: This extra hardy series (zone 3 or 4) from Estonia has many cultivars with medium-sized flowers on tough, compact plants.

Convallaria majalis
LILY OF THE VALLEY, MAY BELLS

Asparagaceae

Zones 2–9

Dry shaded woodlands, especially on calcareous soils, across much of Europe east to the Caucasus.

A classic, old-fashioned, herbaceous ground cover loved by generations of gardeners for its elegant spring flowers and delicate fragrance, which belie its toughness and extreme hardiness. Though slow at first to establish, plants eventually spread via rhizomes into an impregnable, weed-defying, ever-expanding mass of thick, upright, elliptic leaves, 4–8 in. (10–20 cm) long and 1–3 in. (2.5–7.5 cm) wide. In midspring, the upright flower scapes rise 4–9 in. (10–23 cm) within or just above the foliage, holding 5–15 flowers each. They are evenly spaced, pendulous, six-petaled, and fused into a waxy white bell with flaring tips. Plants are self-infertile, forming orange-red berries only when pollinated by a different clone. Leaves turn yellow to brown in fall. All parts are poisonous. Invasive in some regions. AGM

Three major morphologically similar populations occur on three continents, designated as either distinct species or varieties of *C. majalis*: var. *majalis* of Europe, var. *keiskei* of Asia, and var. *montana* of the southeastern United States. *Convallaria majalis* var. *majalis* is the taxon in horticulture.

CULTURE/CARE Easily grown in part to full shade in average to evenly moist soils. Plants require 1–3 years before rhizomes establish and begin to spread strongly. Tolerant of dry shade, poor soils, and sunnier

Convallaria majalis

positions in cool summer climates with good moisture, though foliage can turn more yellow-green in more light. Prefers slight alkalinity though plants are widely adaptable.

USES In borders, along pathways, under trees and shrubs, and for erosion control on shady slopes. Not tolerant of foot traffic. Deer and rabbit resistant.

PROPAGATION Division

'Albostriata': leaf blades with creamy yellow linear stripes

'Bordeaux': scapes higher above the foliage with slightly larger and more numerous flowers

'Fernwood's Golden Slippers': bright green to gold-green foliage, brightest in spring

'Flore Pleno': double flowers

'Fortin's Giant': larger in all respects than the species

'Golden Jubilee': bright green to gold-green foliage, brightest in spring

'Hardwick Hall': leaves edged with creamy green to yellow

'Prolificans': single flowers in clusters of 3–7, resembling large double flowers

var. *rosea* (syn. 'Rosea'): pale pink flowers

'Variegata' (syn. 'Aureovariegata'): foliage with variable linear stripes of creamy yellow to golden yellow

Convolvulus
Convolvulaceae

Morning glories are old-fashioned cottage garden annual vines, appreciated for their white, pink, purple, and true-blue, funnel-shaped flowers. For gardeners in mild climates with sunny gardens, two interesting related species, one a perennial and one a shrub, can be used as ground covers.

CULTURE/CARE Full sun in well-drained soils of average to low fertility and moisture. Heat and drought tolerant. Provide excellent drainage in wet winter climates. *Convolvulus cneorum* can be sheared to maintain shape, if needed.

USES On walls, along pathways, and at the front of borders for small applications or mass-planted for medium-sized sites, spreading at a slow rate. Not tolerant of foot traffic. Deer resistant. Attractive to pollinators, especially butterflies.

PROPAGATION Cuttings, seed

Convolvulus cneorum

Convolvulus sabatius

Convolvulus cneorum
SILVERBUSH, SHRUBBY BINDWEED

Zones 8–10

Rocky coastal areas, especially on calcareous substrates in Italy, the Balkans, and Tunisia.

A mounding, evergreen shrub with small, 1–2 in. (2.5–5 cm) long, narrowly oblong, silky, silver-green foliage that shimmers like metal in sunlight. Plants grow 12–24 in. (30–60 cm) tall and 2–4 ft. (0.6–1.2 m) wide. Pink buds open to funnel-shaped, yellow-throated flowers, 1–2 in. (2.5–5 cm) wide, over a long period from late spring through summer. AGM

Convolvulus sabatius
BLUE ROCK BINDWEED, GROUND MORNING GLORY

Zones 7–10

Open rocky, calcareous habitats in Italy and western North Africa.

A trailing, woody-based, herbaceous to evergreen perennial with small, soft, oval, gray-green leaves on mats 4–6 in. (10–15 cm) tall and 18–36 in. (45–90 cm) or more wide. Lavender to violet-blue, funnel-shaped, 1 in. (2.5 cm) wide flowers with white centers bloom continuously from early summer into fall. AGM

'Moroccan Beauty': more compact, lower growing, with denser foliage

Coreopsis
Asteraceae

Tickseeds are much loved in gardens for their ease of cultivation, long bloom times, and cheerful flowers shaped like daisies. The commonly cultivated species hail from eastern North America. Three are rhizomatous or stoloniferous and make good ground covers: *C. auriculata*, *C. rosea*, and *C. verticillata*.

Numerous complex hybrids have been introduced in recent years frequently involving crosses of *C. auriculata*, *C. grandiflora*, *C. rosea*, and *C. verticillata*, and occasionally *C. lanceolata* and *C. pubescens*. These cultivars typically form mounding plants that can be mass-planted for good coverage. They include the Big Bang and Li'l Bang Series, among others.

CULTURE/CARE Full to part sun in fertile, loamy soil. *Coreopsis verticillata* grows in average to dry soils and is drought tolerant, while *C. rosea* grows well in average soils with even moisture and will tolerate seasonally wet situations. Deadheading encourages rebloom.

USES Mass plant at small to medium-sized scales to spread slowly into a solid cover at the front or middle of the border or along pathways. Not tolerant of foot traffic. Deer and rabbit resistant. Attractive to pollinators, especially bees and butterflies. The seeds attract birds.

PROPAGATION Division, seed

Coreopsis auriculata
DWARF EARED TICKSEED, MOUSE-EARED TICKSEED

Zones 4–9

Roadsides, forest openings, and pine barrens at 30–1650 ft. (9–500 m) or higher, often on calcareous soils, in the southeastern United States.

Herbaceous perennial, 4–12 in. (10–30 cm) or more tall, with flower stems up to 24 in. (60 cm) tall, spreading slowly via short stolons. Midgreen leaves are broadly elliptic with one or two basal lobes, and lush—particularly compared with the threadleaf species—forming semi-evergreen mats, especially in mild winter regions. Deep yellow, 1–2 in. (2.5–5 cm) wide flowers with toothed ray florets appear one per stem from late spring into early summer, blooming intermittently through summer or reblooming in fall.

'Autumn Blush': hybrid from a cross of 'Nana' and a hybrid of *C. rosea* and *C. verticillata*, with broad, pale yellow ray florets with deep burgundy-red bases and narrower foliage than the species, to 24 in. (60 cm) tall

'Elfin Gold': seed strain resembling 'Nana', to 10 in. (25 cm) tall

'Jethro Tull': hybrid from a cross of 'Zamphir' and *C. lanceolata* 'Early Sunrise', resembling 'Zamphir' but flowers bloom longer, with broader petals and fluted ray florets, to 18 in. (45 cm) tall

'Moonlight': hybrid from a branch mutation of C. 'Autumn Blush', with pale yellow flowers

'Nana': dwarf selection, 6–9 in. (15–23 cm) tall

'Pinwheel': hybrid from a cross with C. 'Limerock Ruby', with pale yellow, fluted ray florets around red-orange centers and pointed, lance-shaped foliage

'Zamphir': flowers with fluted ray florets, to 18 in. (45 cm) tall

Coreopsis 'Jethro Tull'

Coreopsis rosea

PINK TICKSEED, PINK THREADLEAF COREOPSIS

Zones 3–8

Pine barrens, moist and open woods, sandy shores, marsh edges, and other wet, coastal sites, from sea level to 165 ft. (50 m) on the east coast of North America from Nova Scotia to South Carolina.

A threadleaf species resembling *C. verticillata*, with upright stems from spreading rhizomes, useful for its unique pink flowers. Plants grow quickly to 12–24 in. (30–60 cm) tall by 24–36 in. (60–90 cm) wide and bloom in mid- to late summer with small flowers up to 1 in. (2.5 cm) wide of pink, toothed ray florets around yellow centers.

'Alba': white flowers

'American Dream': pale- to midpink flowers, 8–16 in. (20–40 cm) tall

'Dream Catcher': sport of 'Sweet Dreams', with glowing pink ray florets with raspberry-colored bases

'Heaven's Gate': a sport of 'Sweet Dreams', with midpink ray florets and broad raspberry-pink bases

'Sweet Dreams': a sport of 'American Dream', with white ray florets blushing pink with age and raspberry-colored bases around red-orange centers

Coreopsis verticillata

THREADLEAF COREOPSIS, WHORLED TICKSEED

Zones 3–9

Sunny positions in open woods including pine and oak woodlands, often in rocky, sandy, poor soils at 30–1650 ft. (10–500 m) in eastern North America from Ontario and Quebec south to Arkansas and Florida.

A classic, tough, drought tolerant perennial spreading at a slow to moderate rate via short rhizomes. Thin, midgreen, threadlike foliage is held in whorls on upright stems topped with light to deep yellow flowers over a long period from early to late summer, on plants 12–24 in. (30–60 cm) tall and 24–36 in. (60–90 cm) wide.

These cultivars are either selections of *C. verticillata* or threadleaf hybrids involving and resembling this species.

'Bengal Tiger': golden yellow ray florets with bold burgundy-red bases around dark red centers

'Buttermilk': pale yellow ray florets with deeper yellow bases around deep red centers

'Center Stage': magenta-red flowers

'Crembru' Crème Brûlée: light yellow flowers with deep yellow centers

Cruizin' Series: often listed as *C. verticillata* but more likely hybrids

> 'Broad Street': orange-red flowers

> 'Electric Avenue': bright yellow flowers

> 'Main Street': magenta flowers with orange centers

> 'Route 66': pale yellow flowers with red bases and red highlights

> 'Sunset Strip': orange-yellow ray florets with red bases and striping

'Golden Gain': golden yellow flowers

'Grandiflora' (syn. 'Golden Shower'): larger golden yellow flowers, AGM

'Imperial Sun': golden yellow flowers with dark centers, larger than 'Zagreb' on more compact plants

'Ladybird': red flowers with yellow highlights

'Lightning Bug': ray florets with fiery red bases and yellow tips on compact plants 10 in. (25 cm) tall

'Moonbeam': classic cultivar with pale yellow flowers, Perennial Plant of the Year 1992

'Moonray': pale to creamy yellow ray florets, lighter than 'Moonbeam'

'Novcorcar' Crème Caramel: apricot-orange flowers with yellow tones

'Red Satin' (Permathread Series): deep red flowers with yellow centers

Satin & Lace Series

> 'Berry Chiffon': raspberry-red flowers with white tips

> 'Red Chiffon': light yellow ray florets with burgundy-red bases

'Show Stopper': glowing rose-pink to magenta flowers

Coreopsis verticillata 'Grandiflora' at Sissinghurst Castle Garden, UK

'Sienna Sunset': pale red-orange flowers that age to apricot

Sizzle & Spice Series

    'Crazy Cayenne': deep red-orange flowers

    'Curry Up': golden yellow ray florets with burgundy-red bases

    'Hot Paprika': glowing red flowers

'Zesty Zinger': raspberry-colored ray florets grading toward white at the tips

'Tweety': similar to 'Zagreb', with smaller, deep yellow flowers on more compact plants

'Zagreb': darker yellow counterpart to 'Moonbeam', AGM

Cornus canadensis
BUNCHBERRY, CRACKERBERRY

Cornaceae

Zones 2–9

Cool, moist soils (that can be dry in summer) at the edges of coniferous woods, on old tree stumps, in mossy areas, and in other moist habitats including marshes and bogs from boreal and montane forests to coastal areas in northern regions of eastern Asia and across Canada and the northern United States, extending south into New Mexico.

One of the most attractive of North American ground covers and a common site along hiking trails and at cabins and cottages across its range, forming lush, midgreen colonies of upright stems, 4–8 in. (10–20 cm) tall, from creeping rhizomes topped with a whorl-like cluster of shiny leaves with prominently indented veins, similar to leaves of dogwood (*C. kousa* and *C. florida*). In late spring, stems are topped with a single compound inflorescence comprising a central cluster of florets surrounded by four pure white, oval, petal-like bracts. Florets produce a cluster of shiny, long-lasting, orange-red fruits persisting well into fall. The foliage can turn brilliant shades of yellow, orange, red, and purple in late summer and fall and may be herbaceous or evergreen.

Two rare relatives are uncommonly found, but interesting. The Swedish bunchberry, *C. suecica*, is a distinctive related species of coastal heaths, bogs, and headlands, with less tightly clustered, smaller leaves and inflorescences with dark purple-black centers. It occurs in northeastern and northwestern North America (but not in between) and in Europe and Northeast Asia. The western bunchberry, *C. unalaschkensis*, is an allotetraploid hybrid of the previous two species that arose before the last glaciation, with a coastal distribution from Alaska to California. It resembles *C. canadensis* in habit but has inflorescences with purple and white centers. It occurs in forests and bogs, especially in layers of decaying matter.

CULTURE/CARE Part shade to shade with even moisture but excellent drainage. Sometimes difficult to establish. Though common on moist forest floors, close inspection reveals that the rhizomes tend to grow between the soil layer and the duff layer of decaying plant matter, in moss layers, or in other light, free-draining substrates. These conditions should be emulated in the garden. Avoid rich, heavy, compost-amended soils. Salt tolerant.

USES Shaded or woodland gardens and along pathways, especially under conifers or broadleaf evergreen shrubs. Small applications. Spreads slowly. Not tolerant of foot traffic. Deer and rabbit resistant.

PROPAGATION Division, seed

Cornus canadensis

Corydalis
Papaveraceae

A large genus whose common horticultural members are mostly shade-loving, short- to long-lived perennials, with delicate, dissected foliage and tubular, spurred flowers held in clusters that resemble the mythical hydra, a serpentine beast with multiple dragonlike heads.

CULTURE/CARE Average to moist soils in part sun to shade. Even moisture will extend the freshness of the foliage in all species and postpone the summer dormancy of *C. flexuosa* and *C. solida*. *Corydalis cheilanthifolia*, *C. lutea*, and *C. ochroleuca* can be short-lived but tend to self-seed readily. Some species, such as *C. flexuosa*, having grown into healthy clumps, can occasionally disappear without warning.

USES Borders, woodlands, walls, and pathways in small applications except for *C. scouleri*, which can cover large areas. Clumping or slowly spreading species such as *C. cheilanthifolia* and *C. shimienensis* should be mass-planted to create a solid cover. Not tolerant of foot traffic. Deer and rabbit resistant.

PROPAGATION Division, seed

Corydalis cheilanthifolia
FERN-LEAF CORYDALIS

Zones 4–9
Shaded slopes and rocky crevices at 2600–5600 ft. (790–1700 m) in Central and South Central China.

Arching, highly dissected, fernlike, evergreen to semi-evergreen foliage resembling *Cheilanthes* species, emerging bronze-tinted and becoming green to bluish in dense, finely textured, clumping mounds up to 12 in. (30 cm) tall and wide. Bright yellow flowers on upright stems from midspring into summer. Plants can be short-lived but usually reseed.

Corydalis curviflora subsp. rosthornii
CORYDALIS

Zones 6–9
Hilly grasslands and meadows at 9900–13,200 ft. (3020–4020 m) in northern and northwestern Sichuan, China.

Resembles the better known *C. flexuosa* but is generally smaller, later blooming, and more fragrant, with darker, more glaucous leaves resisting summer dormancy or avoiding it altogether. Plants typically grow

Corydalis cheilanthifolia

to 8 in. (20 cm) tall and 12 in. (30 cm) or more wide, blooming from midspring to early summer.

'Blue Heron': considered to be the best of the blue-flowered cultivars, with bluish green, dissected foliage, red leaf and flower stems, and relatively large, fragrant, rich sky-blue to royal-blue flowers with white markings

Corydalis elata
BLUE CORYDALIS, FUMEWORT

Zones 5–9
Shaded subalpine coniferous forests, among shrubs, and in sloping grasslands at 9600–13,200 ft. (2925–4020 m) in western Sichuan, China.

Similar to *C. flexuosa* with light to midgreen, fernlike, dissected foliage and clusters of fragrant, royal-blue flowers on reddish stems. Differs in being taller and more upright, to 12–24 in. (30–60 cm) tall, spreading by rhizomes to 24–36 in. (60–90 cm) wide and blooming later from midspring into summer. It is also more heat and humidity tolerant, performs better in hot summer regions, and does not go summer dormant as long as even moisture is provided.

'Blue Summit': possibly more vigorous

'Couriblue' Blue Line: hybrid with *C. flexuosa* with metallic blue flowers on red stems, to 16 in. (40 cm) tall, blooming from spring to fall

Corydalis flexuosa
BLUE CORYDALIS, FUMEWORT

Zones 5–9
Forests and forest openings, grassy slopes, riversides, and wet and rocky areas at 4300–8900 ft. (1310–2700 m) in central Sichuan, China.

Corydalis flexuosa is the best known species, prized for its dissected, fernlike foliage, often with a bluish cast and burgundy detailing, and its early to midspring clusters of fragrant, tubular, spurred flowers in shades of sky- to midblue and sometimes purple. Plants form rhizomatous spreading mats, 6–12 in. (15–30 cm) tall and 12–24 in. (30–60 cm) wide, often going semidormant to dormant in summer, especially in hot summer climates, but may reflush and rebloom in fall in warmer zones, sometimes persisting over winter. In cool summer climates, plants can remain in growth well into the summer with even moisture. Robust, established drifts of *C. flexuosa* can sometimes

Corydalis flexuosa 'Purple Leaf'

disappear inexplicably. It is unclear whether this results from changing conditions or that the species is somewhat short-lived. Where coverage is critical, establish multiple clumps as "insurance" and grow in combination with other ground covers. AGM

'Blue Panda': bright blue flowers, more clumping, and later blooming, AGM

'China Blue': taller, 12–16 in. (30–40 cm), with sky-blue flowers on reddish stems and green foliage, more heat and humidity tolerant

'Golden Panda': light green to golden foliage, bright sky-blue flowers

'Père David': taller, 12–16 in. (30–40 cm), with bright blue flowers, sometimes tinted purple, on reddish stems with bluish foliage

'Porcelain Blue': hybrid with bluish foliage and vivid light blue flowers, reblooming from spring through fall without going summer dormant

'Purple Leaf': compact plants, 6–10 in. (15–20 cm) tall, with red-flushed, olive-green foliage and red stems, flowers begin warm lavender-purple aging to blue, usually creating a bicolor effect, AGM

Corydalis leucanthema
CORYDALIS, FALSE BLEEDING HEART

Zones 5–8

Among rocks and in stony ground by running water in evergreen broadleaf forests at 3000–9900 ft. (915–3020 m) in central Sichuan, China.

A vigorous, rhizomatous, herbaceous perennial with delicate, bluish green, dissected, fernlike foliage to 10–16 in. (25–40 cm) tall, spreading into large mats. Tolerant of heat and humidity, though plants may go dormant in summer, especially if soils become dry. In milder zones, foliage can reemerge in fall, persisting over winter. Early to midspring, fragrant blooms are pale lavender with a dark purple lip.

'Silver Spectre': leaflets with attractive silver-white patches

Corydalis lutea
YELLOW CORYDALIS, YELLOW FUMITORY

Zones (3)4–9

Shaded places in forests, on cliffs, and on rocky outcrops in the southern foothills of the Italian and Swiss Alps into the Balkan states, at 1300–5600 ft. (400–1700 m).

Mounds of dissected, fernlike, green foliage, 8–16 in. (20–40 cm) tall and wide, producing clusters of bright yellow, spurred flowers from midspring into fall, sometimes pausing at the peak of summer in hot summer climates. Can self-seed, readily forming large, ground-covering colonies in garden beds, between rocks and pavers, and in the cracks and crevices of walls, especially in light shade and with good moisture. More vigorous in cool summer climates. Known scientifically as *Pseudofumaria lutea*.

Corydalis ochroleuca
WHITE CORYDALIS

Zones 4–8

Rocky woodland habitats of northern Italy and the western half of the Balkan Peninsula south to Greece.

Similar to *C. lutea*, with mounds of dissected, fernlike, light green to bluish green foliage, 12–20 in. (30–50 cm) tall and wide, producing clusters of creamy white, spurred, fragrant flowers with yellow throats. Flowering period and garden performance are the same as *C. lutea*. Known scientifically as *Pseudofumaria alba*.

Corydalis lutea

Corydalis ochroleuca

Corydalis scouleri

Corydalis scouleri
SCOULER'S FUMEWORT, SCOULER'S CORYDALIS

Zones 6–8

Moist woodlands, forests, seeps, and streambanks from sea level to 3600 ft. (1090 m), from southern Vancouver Island in British Columbia to northern Oregon.

Herbaceous, rhizomatous, long-lived perennial with bright green to bluish green, dissected, fernlike leaves, typically 24–36 in. (60–90 cm) or more tall, spreading indefinitely into large colonies. Mid- to deep pink, spurred flowers, darkest at the tips, are held in terminal spikes in midspring. Valuable as a tall ground cover for medium-sized to large applications. May go dormant in dry soils in summer.

Cotoneaster atropurpureus
ROCK COTONEASTER

Zones 5–8

Thickets, rocky slopes, and dry mountains at moderate to high elevations in China and Nepal.

Prostrate fans of small, shiny, oval, dark green leaves on mounding to spreading, deciduous shrubs, 12–36 in. (60–90 cm) tall and up to 8 ft. (2.4 m) wide. Small white to pinkish flowers become scarlet-red berries. Similar to and often treated as synonymous with *C. horizontalis*.

'Variegatus': creamy white margins, flushed pink to red in autumn, on compact plants 18 in. (45 cm) tall and 36–48 in. (90–120 cm) wide

Cotoneaster dammeri
BEARBERRY COTONEASTER

Zones 5–8

Open, mixed mountain forests and among rocks at 4300–13,500 ft. (1310–4115 m) in western China.

A dense, vigorous, prostrate, sprawling species that is evergreen in milder climates to semi-evergreen in colder climates, with stiff, branching stems, reddish when young, to several feet long, forming mats 6–18 in. (15–45 cm) tall by 6 ft. (1.8 m) wide, rooting where stems contact the soil. Small, oblong to elliptic, semiglossy, slightly textured, dark green, leathery leaves with indented veins are held roughly in the same plane as the stems and develop a bronze to purplish cast in winter. Small, bright white, fragrant flowers in mid- to late spring are followed by bright red berries from late summer into winter.

'Eichholz' (syn. 'Oakwood'): very low growing and wide spreading, 8–12 in. (20–30 cm) tall and up to 10 ft. (3 m) wide, with gold to orange-red autumn color

'Lowfast': fast growing, to 12 in. (30 cm) tall by 10 ft. (3 m) wide, with small leaves

'Moner' Canadian Creeper: very low growing, to 6 in. (15 cm) tall by 8 ft. (2.4 m) wide

'Mooncreeper': very low growing, to 6 in. (15 cm) tall by 5 ft. (1.5 m) wide

'Streib's Findling': usually attributed to *C. dammeri*, but likely a hybrid, 6–12 in. (20–30 cm) tall and up to 8 ft. (2.4 m) wide

C. ×*suecicus* 'Coral Beauty' (syn. 'Royal Beauty'): hybrid of *C. conspicuus* and *C. dammeri*, commonly attributed to *C. dammeri* with a more compact habit, shinier leaves, and more abundant fruit, to 12 in. (30 cm) tall and 6 ft. (1.8 m) wide, AGM

C. ×*suecicus* 'Juliette': gray-green leaves edged with white, flushed pink in autumn, 12 in. (30 cm) tall by 36 in. (90 cm) wide, AGM

C. ×*suecicus* 'Skogholm': 24–36 in. (60–90 cm) tall and 9 ft. (2.7 m) wide

Cotoneaster microphyllus
LITTLE-LEAF COTONEASTER

Zones 5–9

Rocky slopes, high mountain areas, and thickets in western China and the Himalayas.

A low-growing, stiff, horizontally spreading, evergreen to semi-evergreen shrub, 24–36 in. (60–90 cm) tall and 6–8 ft. (1.8–2.4 m) wide, covered in small, shiny, dark green leaves with woolly gray undersides. Clusters of small white flowers in mid- to late spring are followed by bright red berries from late summer into winter.

'Cooperi': prostrate mats up to 4 in. (10 cm) tall and 3–6 ft. (1–1.8 m) wide that hug the contours of the ground

Cotoneaster procumbens
GROUND-HUGGING COTONEASTER

Zones 4–8

Western China.

A dense, prostrate, evergreen species with branching stems, slowly forming mats 6–12 in. (15–30 cm) tall by 6 ft. (1.8 m) wide, with small, rich green, oval leaves. Small white flowers in spring are followed by bright red berries from late summer into winter.

'Gerald' Little Dipper: mats, 6–12 in. (15–30 cm) tall

'Queen of Carpets': very low growing, 2–6 in. (5–15 cm) tall, can weave and melt around hardscape features, AGM

Cotoneaster atropurpureus

Cotoneaster dammeri 'Coral Beauty'

Cotoneaster microphyllus

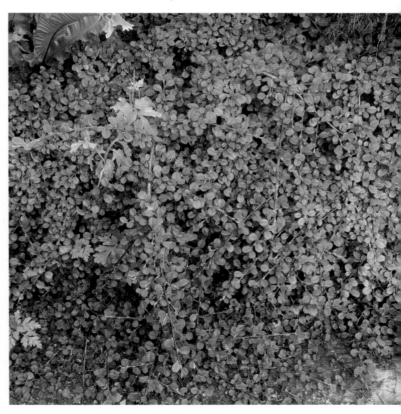

Cotoneaster procumbens 'Queen of Carpets'

Cotoneaster salicifolius
WILLOW-LEAF COTONEASTER

Zones (5)6–9

Mixed mountain forests, slopes, and open places from 1300–9800 ft. (400–3000 m) in western China.

A large-growing species, to 17 ft. (5 m) tall, offers vigorous, ground-covering, dwarf, horticultural forms. Narrow, lance-shaped, evergreen, shiny leaves lightly indented along the veins are held on reddish new stems. White spring flowers are followed by red berries from late summer into winter. Tolerant of dry shade.

'Gnom': mounding habit, 6–12 in. (15–30 cm) tall and up to 6 ft. (1.8 m) wide, AGM

'Repens': prostrate habit, 6–12 in. (15–30 cm) tall and up to 8 ft. (2.4 m) wide

'Scarlet Leader': said to be more disease and insect resistant, to 6–12 in. (15–30 cm) tall by 6–8 ft. (1.8–2.4 m) wide

Cotula hispida
SILVER COTULA

Asteraceae

Zones (5)6–9

Alpine areas of South Africa.

Low-growing mounds or tufted mats of soft, shiny, finely dissected, silver-green leaves reminiscent of *Artemisia schmidtiana* 'Silver Mound', to 2–4 in. (5–10 cm) tall and 10–12 in. (25–30 cm) wide.

Cotula hispida

Evergreen in milder climates. Unique yellow button-like flowers comprising only disc florets bloom in late spring on dark, leafless 4 in. (10 cm) stems well above the foliage. Drought tolerant once established.

CULTURE/CARE Full sun in free-draining rocky or thin soils. Avoid clay and winter wet.

USES Small applications, especially in alpine and rock gardens, gravel, screes, troughs, and between pavers. Not tolerant of foot traffic.

PROPAGATION Seed

'Tiffindell Gold': hybrid referred to as creeping gold buttons, but yet to be attributed to a particular species, 1–2 in. (2.5–5 cm) tall, spreading quickly into mats 24–36 in. (60–90 cm) wide of finely dissected, bright green foliage topped with yellow, buttonlike flowers from spring to fall on stems to 4 in. (10 cm) tall, for small to medium-sized applications and as a lawn alternative for small areas, zones 5–10

Cyclamen
Primulaceae

Hardy cyclamen are less well known than the florists's cyclamen, *C. persicum*, but they are worthy of greater use. Summer dormant, winter evergreen, and fall and winter blooming, they can add dynamism and seasonal interest, beautifying displays in the off-season when herbaceous ground covers are dormant and evergreen plants are in stasis. The easiest species to grow are *C. coum* and *C. hederifolium*, from which numerous seed strains and named forms have been selected by specialist nurseries. Adventurous gardeners who can pay closer attention to growing conditions can also try *C. cilicium*, *C. graecum*, and *C. purpurascens*.

CULTURE/CARE Part shade to part sun in well-drained or sandy soils. Appreciates some dryness when dormant.

USES Excellent winter ground cover for small areas, planted around and between winter-dormant perennials such as hostas, ferns, and other shade perennials or with hellebores and *Arum italicum*. Combine with evergreen or winter-dormant ground covers including *Ajuga* spp., *Arctostaphylos uva-ursi*, *Galium odoratum*, *Gymnocarpium dryopteris*, *Lamium* spp., *Leptinella* spp., *Mazus reptans*, *Omphalodes* spp., or *Pratia angulata*. Plant beneath coniferous and deciduous trees where they will appreciate the dry shade in summer. Not tolerant of foot traffic. Deer and rabbit resistant.

PROPAGATION Seed

Cyclamen coum

Cyclamen coum
PERSIAN VIOLET, EASTERN SOWBREAD

Zones 5–9

Deciduous or evergreen woodland and scrub, from sea level to 7100 ft. (2150 m) in Crimea and Bulgaria, south through Turkey to Israel and Jordan.

A tuberous, summer-dormant perennial emerging in leaf and/or flower in late fall or early winter, with its main floral display in late winter. Light pink to glowing magenta-pink or white, nodding, dainty flowers with five rounded, lightly twisted petals on stems to 4 in. (10 cm) tall. Leaves, which usually emerge during or after flowering, are somewhat semisucculent, heart- or kidney-shaped, and 1–2 in. (2.5–5 cm) across, ranging from nearly fully green to nearly fully silver with all manner of intermediate markings and patterns. Mature tubers can produce mounds 2–4 in. (5–10 cm) tall by 6 in. (15 cm) wide and slowly naturalize by seed, forming colonies over time. AGM

Cyclamen hederifolium
IVY-LEAVED CYCLAMEN, SOWBREAD

Zones 5–9

Woodlands, shrublands, and rocky areas from sea level to 4300 ft. (1310 m), from southern France and Switzerland to Bulgaria and southern Turkey, including many Mediterranean islands.

A tuberous, summer-dormant perennial emerging in leaf and/or flower in late summer or early fall, with deep pink to light pink or white, sometimes scented, nodding, dainty flowers with five lightly twisted petals on stems 4–6 in. (10–15 cm) tall. Leaves, which usually emerge during or after flowering in midfall, are highly variable, ranging from nearly fully green to nearly fully silver with an array of marblings and veinings in between, somewhat semisucculent and ivylike, in shield, arrow, or heart shapes, 2–6 in. (5–15 cm) long. Mature tubers can produce mounds 6 in. (15 cm) tall by 12 in. (30 cm) wide and slowly naturalize by seed, forming large colonies over time. AGM

Cymbalaria
Plantaginaceae

Cute, low-growing, prostrate ground covers closely related to snapdragons (*Antirrhinum* spp.) and toadflaxes (*Linaria* spp.) but with flowers produced singly, not in spikes, with a creeping growth habit suited to

Cyclamen hederifolium growing through moss and *Ophiopogon japonicus* 'Nanus' at the Miller Garden, Seattle

rocky crevices and walls, its favored habitat. *Cymbalaria muralis* orients its flowers toward sunlight, but once pollinated, it turns the developing seed pods away from the light and into dark crevices, where seeds can be released into hospitable conditions.

CULTURE/CARE Shade to part sun and average to evenly moist soils. May not tolerate hot, humid summer climates.

USES Between flagstones and pavers, along pathways and stairways, in rock walls or spilling over walls, and in partly shaded rock gardens. Can spread at moderate to fast rates via stolons and seed. Tolerant of occasional light foot traffic. Attractive to pollinators, especially bees and butterflies.

PROPAGATION Division, seed

Cymbalaria aequitriloba
MINI KENILWORTH IVY, DWARF KENILWORTH IVY

Zones (6)7–10
Moist, shady habitats of Corsica, Sardinia, the Balearic Islands, and mainland Spain and Italy.

A miniature version of *C. muralis*, with tiny, 3–5 lobed, scalloped, evergreen to semi-evergreen leaves growing in mosslike mats less than 1 in. (2.5 cm) tall, spreading via stolons up to 16 in. (40 cm) long. Violet, sometimes white, snapdragon-like flowers with dark markings at the throat bloom from midspring into summer.

Cymbalaria aequitriloba

Cymbalaria hepaticifolia
HEPATICA-LEAVED TOADFLAX, CORSICAN TOADFLAX

Zones 7–8
Moist, rocky areas in the mountains of Corsica and Sardinia.

A little known evergreen, stoloniferous species resembling the better-known *C. muralis* but with larger, smooth, kidney- or heart-shaped leaves reminiscent of a *Hepatica* species, with 3–5 lobes and light green veins. Plants reach 2 in. (5 cm) tall, spreading indefinitely by both 8 in. (20 cm) long stolons and seed. Blooms from midspring to autumn with larger solitary flowers resembling snapdragons, with two upper and three lower lavender to white lobes, yellow at the throat and with lavender-pink calyces.

Cymbalaria muralis
KENILWORTH IVY, IVY-LEAVED TOADFLAX

Zones 5–9
Shaded, rocky areas in woodlands of Mediterranean Europe. Commonly naturalized elsewhere including Northern Europe and North America.

A dainty, yet tough and vigorous, stoloniferous plant with small, shiny, semisucculent, smooth or slightly hairy, evergreen, ivylike leaves, typically with 5–7 lobes and up to 1 in. (2.5 cm) wide, held on reddish stems. Plants reach 2 in. (5 cm) tall, spreading indefinitely by 24 in. (60 cm) long stolons and seed. Blooms from midspring to autumn with small, solitary flowers resembling snapdragons, with two upper and three lower lavender lobes, with white, yellow, and purple markings near the throat.

'Alba': white flowers with yellow at the throat, lighter green leaves

'Alba Compacta': white flowers with yellow at the throat, lighter green leaves, compact, mounding habit, possibly the same as 'Nana Alba'

'Nana Alba': white flowers with yellow at the throat, lighter green leaves, compact, mounding habit

'Snow Wave': leaves with creamy white margins, white flowers with yellow at the throat

Cymbalaria pallida
ITALIAN TOADFLAX

Zones 3–8

Among rocks, in rock crevices, and on scree in the mountains of Central Italy.

Hardier and larger growing with evergreen to semi-evergreen, softly hairy, semisucculent, green to bluish green leaves that are round, semicircular, or 3–5 lobed, and up to 1 in. (2.5 cm) across. Plants form tight mats to 4 in. (10 cm) tall, spreading indefinitely via 8 in. (20 cm) long stolons. Flowers are lavender with yellow and white at the throat and up to twice the size of *C. muralis* blossoms.

'Alba' and 'Albiflora': both are listed in the trade and may be synonymous, with white flowers with yellow throats and lighter green leaves

Cyperus albostriatus
DWARF UMBRELLA PLANT

Cyperaceae

Zones 7–10

Shaded, rocky woodlands and forests in Southern Africa.

An unusual herbaceous ground cover for milder zones, resembling a miniature papyrus, with lightly pleated basal leaves and long-lasting inflorescences with large whorls of green, pleated bracts, subtending the airy, green, grasslike flowers. Plants reach 12 in. (30 cm) tall, spreading indefinitely and fairly quickly into large patches via rhizomes.

CULTURE/CARE Shade to part sun or full sun with ample moisture. Prefers evenly moist soils but tolerant of dry shade.

USES Versatile for shaded to part sun areas in average, moist, and evenly wet soils including pond edges or in dry shade. Not tolerant of foot traffic.

PROPAGATION Division

'Nanus': presumably smaller than the species

'Variegatus': variably streaked with white to creamy white stripes

Cypripedium formosanum

Cypripedium formosanum
FORMOSA LADY'S SLIPPER ORCHID

Orchidaceae

Zones 6–10

Shaded mountain habitats of Taiwan, China.

The easiest to grow of all lady's slippers is a rhizomatous, colony-forming ground cover, 6–8 in. (15–20 cm) tall, spreading indefinitely at a slow to moderate rate. Plants emerge from a network of thick, branching rhizomes in spring, with light green, pleated, fan-shaped, 5 in. (12.5 cm) wide leaves that persist in a semiclosed to closed cover until frost. Buds emerge with the foliage, soon opening to large, inflated, pale pink slippers with white petals spotted with dark pink.

CULTURE/CARE Part sun to part shade in evenly moist, well-drained, humus-rich soils. In good conditions, colonies can increase the number of stems and flowers by 50 to 100 percent each year.

USES Small applications beneath shrubs and trees, along pathways, and border edges. Not tolerant of foot traffic.

PROPAGATION Division

Cyrtomium
Dryopteridaceae

These are some of the most unique and striking temperate ferns—next to the hart's tongue fern (*Asplenium scolopendrium*)—owing to once-dissected fronds with broad, leathery, almost subtropical-looking pinnae. They form lush, evergreen mounds even in dry, deep shade and in colder regions to zone 5.

CULTURE/CARE Rich, evenly moist soils in full to part shade. Tolerant of deep shade, dry shade, and hot, humid conditions. Provide a winter mulch in colder zones. Remove damaged fronds in spring.

USES Mass plant so fronds overlap to create a beautiful, lush, tall ground cover under trees and shrubs and on slopes, or use as accents to punctuate areas of lower spreading ground covers. Not tolerant of foot traffic. Deer and rabbit resistant.

PROPAGATION Spores

Cyrtomium falcatum
JAPANESE HOLLY FERN

Zones 6–10
Coastal and lowland forests, crevices in coastal cliffs, along streambanks, on rocky slopes, and in other moist areas from sea level to 1650 ft. (500 m) in eastern Asia.

A lush, evergreen fern with arching, brown to black, scaly stipes and a blade once-dissected with alternating pinnae, resembling holly leaves, light to midgreen, thick and leathery with a subtle gloss, 12–24 in. (30–60 cm) long and 6 in. (15 cm) wide. Clumps are 12–24 in. (30–60 cm) tall and 24–36 in. (60–90 cm) wide, with fronds numerous enough to provide good coverage. Some salt tolerance.

'Rochfordianum': extra glossy fronds with serrated edges

Cyrtomium fortunei
FORTUNE'S HOLLY FERN

Zones 5–10
Limestone crevices in open areas or in forests at 330–7900 ft. (100–2400 m), from India through China and Japan south to Thailand.

Hardiest of the holly ferns, with evergreen foliage often holding up under the snow in zone 5, though if exposed to the vagaries of winter wind and cold, could be herbaceous. Stipes are arching with brown scales. The blade is once-dissected with alternating, lance- or sickle-shaped, leathery, dull, light to midgreen pinnae, 12–24 in. (30–60 cm) long or more and 6 in. (15 cm) wide, with wavy margins. Clumps grow 12–24 in. (30–60 cm) tall and about 24 in. (60 cm) wide, with fronds numerous enough to provide good coverage.

var. *clivicola*: more compact with narrower, lighter green, and less numerous pinnae, on more horizontal fronds

Cyrtomium macrophyllum
BIGLEAF HOLLY FERN, LARGELEAF HOLLY FERN

Zones 6–10
Forests from moderate to higher elevations from Pakistan through the Himalayas and China to Japan.

Largest fronds of the genus, to 28 in. (71 cm) long and up to 12 in. (30 cm) wide, with arching stipes with blackish brown scales and blades once-dissected with alternating, leathery, light to midgreen, glossy pinnae, rounded at the base with pointed tips and smooth margins. Clumps grow 24 in. (60 cm) tall and 36–48 in. (90–120 cm) wide.

Cyrtomium falcatum

Cyrtomium fortunei

D

Daboecia cantabrica
IRISH HEATH, ST. DABEOC'S HEATH

Ericaceae

Zones 6–8

Dry to moist, acidic, sandy soils including heath and peat bogs at low to middle elevations in coastal Europe from Ireland to Portugal and the Azores.

This uncommon, beautiful, and useful genus is related to the genera *Calluna* and *Erica*, with species similar in size and habit, forming branched, evergreen mounds, 12–18 in. (30–45 cm) tall and 12–24 in. (30–60 cm) wide, but with larger, lusher, leathery, elliptic leaves and larger, showier, nodding, urn-shaped, long-blooming flowers in shades of white, pink, lavender, and magenta, often produced twice a year in early summer and early fall. A garden hybrid with *D. azorica*, the more compact *D. ×scotica* is 8–12 in. (20–30 cm) tall, with smaller leaves, blooming from summer to fall.

CULTURE/CARE Average to evenly moist, acidic soils in full sun. Avoid standing water and alkaline soils, which can result in chlorosis. Prune lightly after flowering. Apply protective winter mulch around plants in zone 6. Plants can be damaged by spring frosts. Performs best west of the Coast and Cascade mountain ranges in North America or in warmer zones of the southern United States.

USES As with heaths and heathers, mass plant in drifts to cover small to large areas, or use in small gardens as an edger. Deer resistant.

PROPAGATION Cuttings

'Alba': white flowers, glossy green leaves, upright plants, 20 in. (50 cm) tall by 24 in. (60 cm) wide

'Arielle': glowing magenta flowers, dark green leaves, compact plants, 12 in. (30 cm) tall by 20 in. (50 cm) wide

'Atropurpurea': deep magenta-red flowers, glossy, dark green leaves, 16 in. (40 cm) tall by 28 in. (71 cm) wide

'Glamour': deep lavender-pink flowers, glossy, dark green leaves, 12 in. (30 cm) tall by 16 in. (40 cm) wide

'Hookstone Purple': soft purple-pink flowers, medium green foliage, 18 in. (45 cm) tall by 32 in. (80 cm) wide

D. ×scotica 'Silverwells': white flowers, dark green leaves, 6 in. (15 cm) tall by 16 in. (40 cm) wide, AGM

D. ×scotica 'William Buchanan': magenta-red flowers, medium green leaves, upright plant, 18 in. (45 cm) tall by 24 in. (60 cm) wide, AGM

Decumaria barbara
WOODVAMP

Hydrangeaceae

Zones 6–10

Wet bottomlands, swamps, riverbanks, and rich mesic forests in the southeastern United States.

Deciduous to semi-evergreen, self-clinging, climbing hydrangea relative, with shiny, smooth, dark green, rounded to oval leaves and 2–4 in. (5–10 cm) wide, flat-topped clusters of small, honey-scented white flowers. Stems can grow 10–30 ft. (3–9 m) long. Makes a lush ground cover but only climbing stems will bloom.

CULTURE/CARE Part sun to part shade in average to wet, fertile soils.

USES Medium-sized to large applications, especially in woodland gardens and naturalized settings. Not tolerant of foot traffic.

PROPAGATION Cuttings

Daboecia cantabrica 'Atropurpurea'

Decumaria barbara

Delosperma
Aizoaceae

Ice plants are long-blooming, carefree, mat-forming perennial succulents, similar in habit to ground-covering sedums that thrive in heat, drought, and nearly any well-drained soil. They are among the most colorful of ground covers, producing floriferous, long-lasting carpets of near-neon colors including white, yellow, orange, pink, lavender-pink, magenta, and red as well as bicolors and tricolors. Their small, daisy-shaped, upward-facing flowers have yellow stamens surrounded by multiple narrow, linear, shimmering petals. The leaves are usually three sided, narrow, and lance- or boat-shaped. The leaf surface of many species is dotted with water-storing bladder cells that reflect light as if covered in ice crystals. A number of species are quite cold hardy given excellent winter drainage.

CULTURE/CARE Full to part sun in dry, hot locations. Plants may appreciate some summer irrigation. Winter drainage must be excellent; otherwise, plants can rot, especially in wet winter regions and in colder zones. Plants are evergreen in warmer climates but may be semi-evergreen in colder regions. Salt tolerant.

USES At the front of the border, between flagstones, in rock gardens, on green roofs, in living walls, and trailing over walls. Ice plants, especially the compact species, can form beautiful mats, spreading across landforms and around larger plants and hardscape. Rate of spread can be slow to fast depending on the species. Not tolerant of foot traffic. Deer resistant. Attractive to pollinators, especially bees.

PROPAGATION Cuttings, division, seed

Delosperma ashtonii
ASHTON'S ICE PLANT

Zones 5–9
Grasslands of Free State and Mpumalanga, South Africa.

Distinctive, flattened, broadly lance-shaped, hairy, evergreen leaves cupped upward, forming a low, creeping mat, 2–4 in. (5–10 cm) tall and 18 in. (45 cm) or more wide. Summer and fall flowers are magenta with white eyes and 1 in. (2.5 cm) across. Very hardy.

'Blut': long-blooming, intense magenta flowers

Delosperma basuticum
WHITE-EYED ICE PLANT

Zones 4–9
High elevation habitats of the Drakensberg Mountains of Southern Africa.

Extremely hardy with tightly packed, boat-shaped, light green leaves and bright yellow flowers with white centers, 1.5 in. (4 cm) across, in midspring or summer. Plants are 1–2 in. (2.5–5 cm) tall, spreading to 6–8 in. (15–20 cm) or more wide.

Delosperma congestum
ICE PLANT

Zones 4–9
Wet alpine meadows at high elevations in the Drakensberg Mountains of Lesotho and South Africa.

Extremely hardy with tightly packed, light green, evergreen leaves like flattened, rounded, or pointed jelly beans, and bright yellow flowers, 1 in. (2.5 cm) wide, blooming over a long period from late spring to fall. Foliage turns maroon in fall and winter. Mats are 2–3 in. (5–7.5 cm) tall, spreading to 18–24 in. (45–60 cm) or more wide. *Delosperma congestum* has been reclassified as *Malotigena frantiskae-niederlovae*, a mouthful of a name that has yet to gain common usage. Appreciates more moisture than other species, though soils must be well-drained.

'Gold Nugget': a selection from 10,000 ft. (3000 m)

'White Nugget' (syn. 'Album'): sport of 'Gold Nugget' with white flowers flushed pale yellow at the centers

Delosperma cooperi
TRAILING ICE PLANT, PINK CARPET

Zones 6–10
Grasslands at higher altitudes in central Southern Africa.

A vigorous, quickly spreading, more open, evergreen carpet, to 3 in. (7.5 cm) tall by 24 in. (60 cm) or more wide, with light green, nearly cylindrical leaves. Large, bright magenta to pink flowers, to 2 in. (5 cm) across, bloom over a long period from early to late summer. A good choice for covering larger areas.

'Tiffindell Magenta': bright magenta flowers start blooming earlier than the species

Delosperma congestum 'White Nugget'

Delosperma nubigenum 'Basutoland'

Delosperma floribundum
ICE PLANT

Zones (5)6–9

Flat, sandy habitats and disturbed sites in Free State, South Africa.

Similar to *D. cooperi*, but forming a tighter, moderately dense to somewhat open evergreen carpet to 4 in. (10 cm) tall by 18 in. (45 cm) or more wide, with midgreen, nearly cylindrical, lance-shaped leaves. Large, lavender-pink to purple-magenta flowers, up to 2 in. (5 cm) across, with white centers, bloom over a long period from early to late summer.

'Balosquin' Sequins: rose-purple flowers with large white centers

'Starburst': lavender-pink flowers

'Stardust': seed strain with lavender-pink to bright pink flowers

Delosperma cooperi

Delosperma dyeri
ICE PLANT

Zones 5–8

Dry mountains of the Eastern Cape, South Africa.

Moderately dense, evergreen carpet, 2–3 in. (5–7.5 cm) tall by 18 in. (45 cm) or more wide, of midgreen, nearly cylindrical, lance-shaped leaves. Large, up to 2 in. (5 cm) across, reddish orange flowers aging to coral, with white centers surrounded by a faint magenta ring, blooming over a long period from mid- to late spring into fall.

'Psdold' Red Mountain: scarlet-red flowers, almost 2 in. (5 cm) across, aging to crimson-purple

Delosperma nubigenum
YELLOW ICE PLANT, CLOUD-LOVING ICE PLANT

Zones 4–9

Rocky screes and wet cliffs in the Drakensberg Mountains, eastern South Africa.

This species, likely the hardiest of ice plants, has tightly packed, light green, boat-shaped leaves and small, bright yellow flowers up to ¾ in. (2 cm) wide, from late spring into summer. Leaves turn reddish in fall, deepening to bronze in winter. Plants are vigorous, quickly reaching 2 in. (5 cm) tall and 24–36 in. (60–90 cm) wide.

'Basutoland': differences from the species are unclear

Delosperma sutherlandii
SUTHERLAND ICE PLANT, HAIRY DELOSPERMA

Zones 6–11

Higher altitude grasslands in northeastern South Africa.

Among the largest and showiest ice plants, with flowers resembling D. *cooperi*, with small, pale yellow centers and numerous glowing magenta petals, sometimes forming semidouble blooms to 2 in. (5 cm) across. Midgreen, flattened, lance- to boat-shaped, hairy leaves in fairly tight mats, 4–6 in. (10–15 cm) tall by 24 in. (60 cm) or more wide.

'Peach Star': pale apricot-pink flowers with pale yellow centers

Delosperma hybrids
ICE PLANT

Many hybrids have been introduced in recent years in a wide range of colors.

'Alan's Apricot': larger flowered seedling of 'Kelaidis' Mesa Verde, with long-blooming, apricot-orange flowers fading to pale apricot-pink, 1–2 in. (2.5–5 cm) tall, zones 4–9

'Beaufort West': very small, pale pink flowers, long-blooming, compact, near-cylindrical foliage, 1–2 in. (2.5–5 cm) tall, zones 6–10

Delmara Series: large flowers over a long season on mounding plants, 4 in. (10 cm) tall, zones (4)5–10

    'Delmara Fuchsia': reddish flowers with yellow centers

    'Delmara Orange': tangerine-orange flowers with yellow centers

    'Delmara Pink': bright candy-pink flowers with white centers

    'Delmara Red': orange-red flowers with yellow centers

    'Delmara Yellow': bright yellow flowers with white centers

Hot Cakes Series: long-blooming, compact plants with medium-sized flowers and dense flower coverage, zones 6–10

    'Banana Blast': yellow flowers with white centers

    'Coconut Crush': white flowers

    'Fig Fusion': lavender-pink flowers with white centers

Delosperma 'Alan's Apricot'

Delosperma 'John Proffitt' Table Mountain

Delosperma 'Kelaidis' Mesa Verde

Delosperma 'Osberg'

Delosperma 'P001s' Fire Spinner

'Pumpkin Perfection': deep orange and orange-red flowers with white centers

'Saucy Strawberry': red flowers with white and magenta centers

'Tangerine Tango': reddish orange flowers with white centers

Jewel of Desert Series: long-blooming, compact plants with medium-sized flowers, zones 5–10

'Jewel of Desert Amethyst': glowing magenta flowers with white centers

'Jewel of Desert Candystone': lavender-pink flowers

'Jewel of Desert Garnet': reddish tips grade inward to magenta and small white centers

'Jewel of Desert Grenade': glowing orange-red flowers with white centers

'Jewel of Desert Moon Stone': pure white flowers

'Jewel of Desert Opal': glowing magenta flowers

'Jewel of Desert Peridot': bright yellow flowers with white centers

'Jewel of Desert Rosequartz': deep lavender-pink flowers with white centers

'Jewel of Desert Ruby': reddish tips grade inward to yellow and white centers

'Jewel of Desert Sunstone': bright orange flowers with purple and white centers

'Jewel of Desert Topaz': orange flowers with white centers

'John Proffitt' Table Mountain: large, bright fuchsia-pink flowers up to 2 in. (5 cm) across on vigorous, moderately compact plants, 2–4 in. (5–10 cm) tall and 24 in. (60 cm) or more wide, zones 4–9

'Kelaidis' Mesa Verde: hybrid involving *C. cooperi*, with long-blooming, salmon-pink flowers, 3 in. (7.5 cm) tall by 24 in. (60 cm) or more wide, zones 4–9

'Lesotho Pink': large, bright magenta flowers on compact plants, 1 in. (2.5 cm) tall by 18 in. (45 cm) wide, zones 5–9

'Orange Crush': a sport of 'P001s' Fire Spinner, with light orange flowers with a central pale pink blush

'Osberg': long-blooming, white flowers, 2 in. (5 cm) tall by 18 in. (45 cm) wide, zones 5–9

'P001s' Fire Spinner: vigorous plants, 2 in. (5 cm) tall by 24 in. (60 cm) wide, with small yet dramatic multicolored flowers with white centers circled with magenta, then red, and then glowing orange, can be shy to bloom, at least in cool summer climates, zones 5–8

Delosperma 'Psfave' Lavender Ice

Delosperma 'Pwwg02s' Red Mountain Flame

'Pjs01s' Granita Raspberry: large, glowing raspberry and lavender-purple flowers, 2 in. (5 cm) tall, zones 5–10

'Pjs02s' Granita Orange: large, mandarin-orange flowers, 2 in. (5 cm) tall, zones 5–10

'Psfave' Lavender Ice: large, 2 in. (5 cm) wide, pale lavender to lavender-pink flowers, 2–4 in. (5–10 cm) tall by 18–24 in. (45–60 cm) wide, zones 4–9

'Pwwg02s' Red Mountain Flame: large, 2 in. (5 cm) wide, bright orange-red flowers, with white and magenta centers, zones (4)5–9

'Ruby Stars': small magenta-red flowers, zones 5–9

Wheels of Wonder Series: large-flowered, large-growing, sometimes rangy, long-blooming plants, 4–6 in. (10–15 cm) tall by 18–24 in. (45–60 cm) wide, shear to revitalize clumps, zones 6–10, possibly hardier

> 'P15-py-4' Salmony Pink Wonder: salmon-pink, orange, and yellow flowers
>
> 'P15r1' Purple Wonder: deep lavender-pink flowers with small white centers
>
> 'Wow312' Limoncello: yellow petals with white tips
>
> 'Wowd20111' Golden Wonder: bright yellow flowers with white centers
>
> 'Wowday2' Fire Wonder: orange-red flowers with yellow centers
>
> 'Wowdoy3' Orange Wonder: orange flowers with yellow centers
>
> 'Wowdrw5' Violet Wonder: deep lavender-pink flowers with white centers
>
> 'Wowdry1' Hot Pink Wonder: magenta flowers with yellow and white centers
>
> 'Wowdw7' White Wonder: white flowers

Dennstaedtia punctilobula
EASTERN HAY-SCENTED FERN

Dennstaedtiaceae

Zones 3–8

Rocky slopes, sandy meadows, open woods, streambanks, and roadsides, especially in acidic soils, from sea level to 4000 ft. (1200 m) in most of eastern North America.

A distinctive fern with fronds that smell like newly mown hay when brushed or bruised, hay-scented fern is an aggressive, rhizomatous, deciduous species with elegant, arching to erect, finely textured, silver-hairy, light green, triangular fronds, 16–40 in. (40–100 cm)

Dennstaedtia punctilobula

long, on plants 12–24 in. (30–60 cm) tall. Fronds turn a dramatic coppery orange in fall.

CULTURE/CARE Part sun to shade in a variety of average to evenly moist soils with good drainage. Tolerant of full sun with consistent moisture.

USES An early colonizer of disturbed sites and vigorous rhizomatous spreader. Valuable for filling medium-sized to large spaces; could overwhelm a small garden. Use on slopes for erosion control, in woodland gardens, or in informal spaces for a naturalistic, tall ground cover. Not tolerant of foot traffic. Deer and rabbit resistant.

PROPAGATION Division, spore

Dianthus
Caryophyllaceae

Cottage garden favorites in cultivation for hundreds of years, pinks are prized for their cheerful, fragrant, edible flowers and their textured, evergreen mats of green to blue, linear foliage. The common name is not a reference to the color so common in the genus, but to the serrated petal edges that resemble the work of pinking shears. In addition to the many species used in rock or alpine gardens, such as *D. alpinus*, *D. arenarius*, and *D. simulans*, and the species treated here, thousands of hybrids have been created over the years.

A considerable number of cultivars available in the United Kingdom are not available in North America and, to a lesser extent, vice versa. The species and cultivars treated here are the most commonly available in North America.

CULTURE/CARE Full sun in average to dry, well-drained soils or part sun in hot summer climates. Salt tolerant. Plants can become rangy, splaying open to bald centers, and can be short lived in overly rich, poorly drained, or wet winter soils. Shear after flowering to refresh plants and encourage rebloom.

USES Small to medium-sized areas, especially where soils are thin, gravelly, and well-drained, spreading at a slow to moderate rate. Use as an edger for pathways and borders, in rock gardens, and on walls. Not tolerant of foot traffic. Deer resistant. Attractive to pollinators, especially butterflies and hummingbirds.

PROPAGATION Division, cuttings, seed

Dianthus deltoides

Dianthus gratianopolitanus

Dianthus deltoides
MAIDEN PINK

Zones 3–9

Dry meadows, pastures, rocky ground, banks, hillsides, and roadsides, often in calcareous soils, from Western Europe to Western Asia.

Spreading mats of evergreen, narrow, lance-shaped, green to blue-green leaves, to 4–6 in. (10–15 cm) tall and 24 in. (60 cm) wide, topped in late spring with stems 8–12 in. (20–30 cm) tall, sporting single, ¾ in. (2 cm) wide, lightly fragrant, typically deep pink flowers, the petals with serrated tips and a jagged band of magenta near the base, forming a ring around the eye zone. May self-seed.

'Albus': pure white flowers with a faint off-white ring

'Arctic Fire': flowers with a pink eye zone, magenta ring, and white tips

'Brilliant': cherry-red to magenta flowers with a darker ring

Confetti Series

'Confetti Carmine Rose': deep glowing pink flowers with a deeper pink ring

'Confetti Cherry Red': glowing cherry-red flowers said to be an improvement over 'Brilliant'

'Confetti Deep Red': flowers approaching true red

'Confetti White': pure white flowers with a faint off-white ring

'Leuchtfunk' (syn. 'Flashing Light'): ruby-red flowers with a deep red ring

'Shrimp': salmon-pink flowers with a deep pink ring

'Vampire': scarlet-red flowers

'Zing Rose': rose-red flowers

Dianthus gratianopolitanus
CHEDDAR PINK

Zones 3–9

Meadows, stony places, and limestone cliffs from low elevations up to 6000 ft. (1830 m) in Western and Central Europe, occurring in Great Britain only in Cheddar Gorge, Somerset.

Cheddar pink and Cheddar cheese owe their names to the village of Cheddar and nearby Cheddar Gorge in Southwest England. This pink forms spreading mats of evergreen, narrow, lance-shaped, bluish green leaves, 6–8 in. (15–20 cm) tall and 12–24 in. (30–60 cm) wide, topped from spring into summer with 4–10 in. (10–25 cm) stems sporting single, rose-pink to pink, clove-scented flowers, 1 in. (2.5 cm) wide, with serrated, sometimes ruffled, petal tips. Tolerant of hot summer climates.

'Sternkissen' (syn. 'Star Cushion'): compact, 2–4 in. (5–10 cm) tall with midpink flowers on short stems

'Tiny Rubies': double midpink flowers resemble pom-poms atop compact cushions

Dianthus plumarius
COTTAGE PINK, FEATHERED PINK

Zones 3–9

Grasslands and open habitats in calcareous mountains of Central Europe, from Germany and Poland to Hungary.

Spreading mats of evergreen, narrow, lance-shaped, blue-green to powder-blue foliage, 8 in. (20 cm) tall and 12–18 in. (30–45 cm) wide, topped from spring into summer with stems 12–16 in. (30–40 cm) tall, sporting single, white to deep pink, highly fragrant flowers, 1–1.5 in. (2.5–4 cm) wide, the petals with highly serrated, feathered tips and the centers usually with a darker eye.

'Itsaul White': pure white, heavily ruffled, vanilla-scented semidouble flowers

'Rosish One': cherry-red double flowers with dark red markings and white, shallowly fringed margins

Scent from Heaven Series: fragrant single and double flowers in a range of colors and color patterns with good repeat bloom on compact plants

'Sweetness': seed strain offering shades from white through deep pink, with deep pink to red central eyes

Dianthus hybrids
PINKS

Zones 3, 4, 5 or 6–9

Garden origin.

The majority of pinks in common cultivation are hybrids. They vary mostly in the relative intensity of green to blue in their foliage, in having single or double flowers, in their flower colors and patterns, and in their bloom times. As ground covers, they are largely interchangeable.

Individual cultivars are hardy to zones 3–9 unless otherwise noted.

'Bath's Pink': lavender-pink, fringed flowers from purple buds

'Bewitched': sport of 'Feuerhexe', light pink flowers with a magenta ring around a white eye

'Blue Hills': glowing rose-pink flowers

'Chomley Farran': lavender-purple double flowers with irregular red striping, zones 5–9

'Dragon Fruit': rose-pink double flowers with deep red markings, zones 4–9

'Feuerhexe' (syn. 'Firewitch'): rose-pink flowers, Perennial Plant of the Year 2006

'Fire and Ice': compact and floriferous, with single, raspberry-colored flowers with pink edges, zones 4–9

'First Love': multicolor effect, with flowers emerging white, aging to pink, and then deep rose-pink, zones 4–9

'Frosty Fire': ruby-red double flowers

'Horatio': maroon, red, and white double flowers

'Inchmery': eighteenth-century heirloom with semidouble, pale pink flowers with nearly entire margins

'Little Jock': pale pink semidouble flowers with a magenta to maroon eye

'Mountain Mist': light to midpink, heavily fringed flowers, tolerant of heat and humidity

'Sangria Splash': cherry-red flowers flecked (or blotched) and edged with pink

'Spotty': cherry-red petals edged in pink, each with two circular light pink blotches

'Velvet and Lace': deepest maroon double flowers edged in white, zones 5–9

'Wicked Witch': sport of 'Feuerhexe' with cherry-red flowers

Series (hardy to zones 5–9 unless otherwise noted)

American Pie Series: single flowers of good size in simple color patterns with good fragrance, on strong stems

Beauties Series: single flowers in a range of colors, zones 4–9

Constant Beauty Series: lightly double fragrant flowers often with picotee edges in a range of colors, good heat tolerance, zones 4–9

Constant Cadence Series: highly fragrant double flowers in a range of solid colors with no patterning, zones 4–9

Constant Promise Series: fragrant, long-lasting double flowers with excellent heat tolerance in a range of colors, zones 4–9

Dessert Series: fragrant single flowers with complex patterning in a range of colors

Devon Cottage Series: later blooming, fragrant double flowers on relatively large plants in a range of colors

Early Bird Series: early flowering, fragrant double flowers in a range of colors on compact plants

Everlast Series: early flowering, fragrant, and long-blooming single or double flowers in a range of colors and color patterns

Dianthus 'Cherry Vanilla' (Fruit Punch Series)

Fruit Punch Series: fragrant double flowers in a range of colors and color patterns, good heat and humidity tolerance, zones 4–9

Kahori Series: long-blooming single flowers in pink shades, good rebloom, zones 3–9

Mountain Frost Collection: fragrant single or double flowers in a range of colors, all hybrids of alpine species bred for landscape performance, drought tolerance, and resilience in rainy and wet conditions

Olivia Series: single bicolor flowers on compact plants

Oscar Series: fragrant double flowers in a range of colors, zones 6–9

Paint the Town Series: bright colors and increased heat tolerance, zones 4–9

Pretty Poppers Series: semidouble to double flowers in a range of colors, zones 4–9

Promotional Line Series: fragrant semidouble and double flowers in a range of colors and color patterns

Scent First Series: fragrant double flowers on compact plants

Star Series: fragrant single and double flowers in a range of colors on dwarf plants

Super Trouper Series: fragrant double flowers in a wide range of colors and color patterns on strong stems, zones 6–9

Dicentra
Papaveraceae

Bleeding hearts are beloved among gardeners, thanks to the cottage garden favorite *D. spectabilis* (now *Lamprocapnos spectabilis*), with its arching stems displaying rows of pendulous pink and white heart-shaped flowers. The related species differ in having dissected, fernlike, green to bluish foliage, with clustered flowers and longer bloom periods, and a low mounding, or spreading habit.

CULTURE/CARE Evenly moist, humus-rich soils in part sun to shade. *Dicentra eximia* and *D. formosa* bloom profusely in spring, reblooming in fall in hot summer climates or continuously until fall in cool summer climates. Deadhead to encourage rebloom. *Dicentra canadensis* and *D. cucullaria* are spring ephemerals that go dormant by summer.

USES *Dicentra eximia*, *D. formosa*, and their hybrids make excellent textured ground covers. Mass plant clumping forms for full coverage. Spreading forms expand at a slow to moderate rate. Use *D. canadensis* and *D. cucullaria* around late-emerging perennials, under deciduous shrubs and trees, or combined with other ground covers. None are tolerant of foot traffic. Deer and rabbit resistant. Attractive to pollinators, especially bees, butterflies, and hummingbirds.

PROPAGATION Division

Dicentra canadensis

SQUIRREL CORN, WILD BLEEDING HEART

Zones 3–8

Deciduous woods in rich loam soils, often among rocks, from sea level to 5000 ft. (1500 m) in most of eastern North America.

A spring ephemeral emerging in early spring, blooming in midspring, and going dormant by summer, forming small to large colonies given time. Foliage is dissected, fernlike, glaucous to frosted, and 6–10 in. (15–25 cm) tall. Reddish flower stems rise just above the foliage with clusters of 3–12 heart-shaped, fragrant white flowers, sometimes with a faint hint of pink and yellow. Roots produce yellow globose bulblets resembling corn.

Dicentra cucullaria

DUTCHMAN'S BREECHES

Zones 3–8

Deciduous woods and clearings in rich loam soils from sea level to 5000 ft. (1500 m) in most of eastern North America and disjunct to the Pacific Northwest.

Similar to and often found growing with D. canadensis, but blooming 7–10 days earlier, with clusters of 3–14 white (occasionally pink), nonfragrant flowers like upside down pantaloons with a yellow and orange "waist" at the flower opening, held on reddish stems. Foliage is dissected, fernlike, glaucous, and 6–10 in. (15–25 cm) tall. Roots produce pink to white, teardrop-shaped bulblets.

'Pink Punk': soft pink flowers

Dicentra cucullaria

Dicentra eximia

Dicentra eximia

FRINGED BLEEDING HEART,
EASTERN BLEEDING HEART

Zones 3–8

Dry to moist mountainous woodlands, often among rocks and in rock crevices at 330–5600 ft. (100–1700 m), primarily in the Appalachian Mountains of eastern North America.

Deeply cut, fernlike, green to gray-green foliage in clumps or slowly spreading mounds, 8–12 in. (20–30 cm) tall by 12–18 in. (30–45 cm) wide. Clusters of five to many pale to midpink, elongated, heart-shaped flowers are held on numerous upright to arching stems, blooming profusely in spring with sporadic rebloom through summer and fall. Good moisture encourages rebloom and keeps foliage fresh through summer. More tolerant of heat and dry soils than other species.

'Snowdrift': white flowers

Dicentra formosa

WESTERN BLEEDING HEART,
PACIFIC BLEEDING HEART

Zones (2)3–9

Loamy or gravelly soils in moist woods or clearings and along streambanks, from sea level to 7400 ft. (2250 m) from British Columbia to California.

Rhizomatous mounds or mats of deeply cut, fernlike, green, gray-green, or bluish green foliage, 8–12 in. (20–30 cm) tall by 12–24 in. (30–60 cm) or more wide. Blooming profusely in spring, with sporadic rebloom

Dicentra formosa

Dicentra 'Ivory Hearts'

through summer and fall, with 2–30 pale pink to deep reddish pink, cream, or pale yellow heart-shaped flowers (more rounded than the similar *D. eximia*), held on numerous upright to arching stems. Plants may go dormant in mid- to late summer in sunnier or drier locations. Evenly moist soils help to maintain fresh foliage.

f. *alba*: white flowers

'Bacchanal': magenta-red to wine-red flowers, bluish foliage, AGM

'Langtrees': creamy to white flowers, bluish foliage, AGM

'Spring Gold': rose-pink flowers, gold to chartreuse foliage aging to light green

'Spring Magic': soft pink flowers, bluish foliage

Dicentra hybrids

Hybrids involving *D. eximia*, *D. formosa*, and their Asian cousin *D. peregrina* offer long bloom periods, persistent and attractive foliage, clumping habits, and varied flower colors.

'Adrian Bloom': deep pink to ruby-red flowers, blue-green foliage

'Amore Pink': green to bluish green foliage, midpink flowers

'Amore Rose': glowing rose-pink flowers, blue-green foliage

'Aurora': white flowers, gray-green foliage

'Burning Hearts': near red flowers with a white edge on large, reflexed petals, powder-blue foliage

'Candy Hearts': midpink flowers with blue-green foliage

'Ivory Hearts': pure white flowers with blue-green foliage

'King of Hearts': glowing rose-pink flowers with blue-green foliage

'Love Hearts': creamy white and yellow flowers with blue-green foliage

'Luxuriant': deep pink to reddish pink flowers with blue-green foliage, AGM

'Red Fountain': cherry-red flowers with blue-green to powder-blue foliage

'Stuart Boothman': mid- to deep pink flowers with blue-green foliage, AGM

'Sulphur Hearts': pale yellow flowers with blue-green foliage

Dichondra repens
LAWN LEAF, KIDNEY WEED

Convolvulaceae

Zones 7–10
Forests, woodlands, and grassland habitats in Australia and New Zealand.

Evergreen relative of the popular annual, *D. argentea* 'Silver Falls', for milder climates with small, bright green, kidney-shaped leaves less than 1 in. (2.5 cm) wide on creeping, rooting stems, forming lush, indefinitely spreading carpets, 1–2 in. (2.5–5 cm) tall. Inconspicuous flowers. May reseed.

CULTURE/CARE Full sun to part shade in average to moist, fertile soils. Can be mowed a few times a year.

USES Between pathway or patio pavers and as a lawn alternative. Tolerant of light foot traffic.

PROPAGATION Seed, division

Disporopsis pernyi

Disporum sessile 'Variegatum'

Disporopsis pernyi
EVERGREEN SOLOMON'S SEAL

Asparagaceae

Zones 6–9

Shady forested habitats, especially among rocks and along streams, at 1000–8250 ft. (300–2510 m) in southern China.

A tough yet elegant rhizomatous shade plant whose virtues, as well as those of its uncommon sister species *D. aspersa*, *D. arisanensis*, *D. fuscopicta*, and *D. undulata*, deserve to be better known. The purple-spotted, arching stems are 8–16 in. (20–40 cm) tall, with 2–5 in. (5–12.5 cm) long, alternate, evergreen, glossy, somewhat leathery, lance-shaped to elliptic leaves with rounded bases and pointed tips. Pendulous, white, bell-shaped, lightly lemon-scented flowers with pale green, flared lobes and occasional dark red markings are solitary or in clusters of twos or threes along the stem in mid- to late spring. Dark purple to brown-purple berries are produced by fall. Plants spread slowly yet indefinitely by rhizomes, eventually covering large areas with dense mats.

CULTURE/CARE Part to deep shade in evenly moist, well-drained, humus-rich soils. Drought tolerant once established. If overwintered foliage is damaged or unsightly, cut down in early spring before new growth emerges. Slugs can be a problem for new foliage.

USES Under deciduous and evergreen trees and shrubs and on slopes. Tolerant of deep shade and dry shade. Not tolerant of foot traffic.

PROPAGATION Division

'Bill Baker': flowers with inner black stripes

Disporum
Colchicaceae

Fairy bells are upright plants that, when young, act as accents for the shade garden; once established, they can form spreading, ground-covering colonies. The foliage is lush and subtly attractive with horizontal veins and a slight shine. The pendulous flowers are followed by attractive berries. In addition to those treated here, *D. smithii* is occasionally grown.

CULTURE/CARE Part to full shade in evenly moist, well-drained, humus-rich soils.

USES Mass plant or intermingle with other ground covers under trees and shrubs, along shaded pathways, or in woodland gardens. Not tolerant of foot traffic.

PROPAGATION Division

Disporum sessile
JAPANESE FAIRY BELLS

Zones 4–8

Wooded hills and foothills in Japan.

Herbaceous, rhizomatous perennial resembling a dainty Solomon's seal (*Polygonatum* spp.), with upright, sometimes branched stems, 12–24 in. (30–60 cm) tall, with 2–6 in. (5–15 cm) long, oval to lance-shaped, midgreen leaves. Spreads, sometimes vigorously, into dense colonies 24–36 in. (60–90 cm) wide, or intermingles with other perennials. Whitish green, tubular to bell-shaped flowers hang singly or in small clusters at the stem tips in spring, followed by black berries in summer and fall. Cultivars with various cream- and gold-colored leaves exist but are rare in cultivation.

'Variegatum': leaves variably streaked and edged with white, more common in cultivation than the species

Disporum smilacinum
FAIRY BELLS

Zones 4–9

Forests and woods in hills and foothills, from sea level to 1300 ft. (400 m) in Japan and Korea and adjacent regions of China and Russia.

An uncommon yet worthwhile herbaceous, rhizomatous perennial similar to *D. sessile* but shorter, to 6–12 in. (15–30 cm) tall, with one or two white, starlike, dangling flowers at the tip of each usually unbranched stem in spring, followed by black berries in summer and fall. Midgreen, oval to elliptic leaves are up to 2.5 in. (6 cm) long. Plants spread slowly by short rhizomes or long stolons into open or dense mats.

'Ki-no-tsukasa': midgreen leaves with yellow streaks toward the tips

'Kogane-tsuki': bright gold foliage with green streaks on stems to 4 in. (10 cm) tall

Disporum uniflorum
YELLOW FAIRY BELLS

Zones 4–9

Forested habitats at 330–8250 ft. (100–2510 m) in Northwest China and Korea.

Disporum uniflorum, commonly sold as *D. flavens* and sometimes as *D. flavum*, is a herbaceous, rhizomatous, and stoloniferous perennial with upright, branched or unbranched stems, 8–32 in. (20–80 cm) tall, with broad, elliptic, midgreen leaves up to 3.5 in. (9 cm) long. The cylindrical, bell-shaped, pendulous flowers are yellow and hang singly or in small clusters at the stem tips in spring, followed by black berries in summer and fall. Plants can be tightly clumping, to 24 in. (60 cm) wide, or slowly spreading. Mass plant to use as a ground cover.

Disporum viridescens
GREEN FAIRY BELLS

Zones 4–9

Woodlands and grassy slopes, from sea level to 2000 ft. (600 m) in northeastern China, eastern Russia, Japan, and Korea.

A lesser known fairy bells well worth seeking out for its vigorous, spreading nature, *D. viridescens* is a herbaceous, rhizomatous and stoloniferous perennial with upright, sometimes branched stems, 12–32 in.

(30–80 cm) tall. The oval to lance-shaped, midgreen leaves are 2–5 in. (5–12.5 cm) long. Plants can quickly form large, dense colonies. Whitish green, starlike flowers hang singly or in pairs at the stem tips in spring followed by black berries in summer and fall.

Dryas
Rosaceae

Mountain avens are tough, extremely hardy, evergreen, mat-forming perennials from Arctic and mountain habitats that make easy ground covers, especially in cold climates. The flowers are reminiscent of other rose family members, including species of *Rubus*, *Geum*, *Potentilla*, and *Fragaria*, but most have eight petals rather than the typical five.

CULTURE/CARE Easy to grow in full to part sun in moist, average, or dry, well-drained soils, especially with added sand or gravel. Drought tolerant once established, though occasional deep watering is appreciated. Shear plants to rejuvenate, if needed.

USES Small- to medium-scale applications on green roofs, between paving stones, in borders and rock gardens, as an edging plant, as an accent, or to spill over walls. Spreads at a moderate rate. Tolerant of occasional foot traffic. Attractive to pollinators, especially bees and butterflies.

PROPAGATION Cuttings or division of rooted stems

Dryas drummondii
YELLOW MOUNTAIN AVENS, DRUMMOND'S AVENS

Zones 2–9

Moist, frequently calcareous places from sea level to 9800 ft. (3000 m), including sandy and gravelly beaches, flood plains, along streams, in grassy areas, and in alpine habitats such as scree slopes, ridge crests, and glacial moraines, from Alaska to Oregon and east to Quebec.

A creeping, semiwoody, mat-forming subshrub, reaching 1–6 in. (2.5–15 cm) tall and 24 in. (60 cm) or more wide, with small, leathery, evergreen, elliptic to egg-shaped leaves up to 1 in. (2.5 cm) long and half as wide, with rounded, toothed margins, a shiny, crinkled, midgreen upper surface, and a white, hairy underside. Prostrate stems can root as they travel. Solitary, usually nodding flowers never fully open and are up to 1 in. (2.5 cm) wide, with 8–10 yellow petals, golden yellow stamens, and sepals covered in burgundy to black hairs, held on slightly hairy, green to

Dryas octopetala

Dryas drummondii

reddish stems 2–10 in. (5–25 cm) tall, blooming from late spring to late summer. Rounded powder-puff seed heads of white and brown feathery hairs twist when immature and in damp weather.

Dryas octopetala
WHITE MOUNTAIN AVENS, WHITE DRYAD

Zones 2–9

Circumboreal occurring in North America, Europe, and Asia on tundra and in mountains, frequently on dry, exposed, rocky or gravelly sites with calcareous soils.

This tough species is the territorial flower of Canada's Northwest Territories and the national flower of Iceland. It is a creeping, semiwoody, mat-forming

subshrub, 3–6 in. (7.5–15 cm) tall and 24 in. (60 cm) or more wide, with small, leathery, evergreen, oval, oblong, or elliptic leaves up to 1 in. (2.5 cm) long and half as wide, with blunt-toothed margins that roll under, a shiny, midgreen upper surface, and a white, hairy underside. Prostrate stems can root as they travel. Solitary, upward-facing flowers are 1 in. (2.5 cm) across with eight white petals around golden yellow stamens held on slightly hairy, burgundy stems, 1–5 in. (2.5–12.5 cm) tall, from late spring to midsummer. Seed heads have white, feathery hairs resembling disheveled cotton balls. AGM

'Minor': free-flowering dwarf form, 2 in. (5 cm) tall and 8 in. (20 cm) wide

D. ×*suendermannii*: hybrid with *D. drummondii* resembling *D. octopetala* but with somewhat nodding flowers, yellowish in bud opening to creamy white, AGM

Dryopteris
Dryopteridaceae

The wood ferns offer many excellent species for the shade garden. The shorter species with numerous dense fronds, especially those with a slow-creeping rhizomatous habit, make for good ground covers when mass-planted. In addition to those treated here, other uncommon species are worth seeking out, including *D. carthusiana*, *D. championii*, *D. intermedia*, *D. lepidopoda*, *D. pycnopteroides*, and *D. sieboldii*. A number of larger species are suited as specimens in average gardens or mass-planted tall ground covers in large gardens or landscapes, including *D. affinis*, *D.*

Dryopteris cycadina

×*australis*, *D. celsa*, *D. crassirhizoma*, *D. filix-mas*, *D. goldiana*, *D. ludoviciana*, *D. pseudofilix-mas*, *D. tokyoensis*, and *D. wallichiana* and its more compact cultivar 'Hollasic' Jurassic Gold.

CULTURE/CARE Shade to part shade in average to moist soils. Cut back fronds of evergreen species in early spring, if needed, before new growth emerges.

USES Medium-sized to large mass plantings in shaded sites, including under trees and shrubs. Not tolerant of foot traffic. Deer and rabbit resistant.

PROPAGATION Division, spores

Dryopteris cycadina
SHAGGY SHIELD FERN, BLACK WOOD FERN

Zones 5–8
Mountain slopes of broadleaf evergreen forests at 1600–7500 ft. (480–2300 m) throughout China, adjacent Southeast Asian countries, and Japan.

This distinctive fern, also known as *D. atrata*, has dramatic stipes covered in brownish black scales that twist like black, contorting snakes as they unfurl in spring. Fronds are once-pinnate with dentate lobes, emerging light green and aging to midgreen. Plants are 12–24 in. (30–60 cm) tall with a vaselike habit of upward and horizontally spreading fronds. Evergreen in milder zones. AGM

Dryopteris dilatata
BROAD BUCKLER FERN, BROAD WOOD FERN

Zones 4–9
Deciduous and coniferous woodlands, hedgerows, ditches, and open, rocky habitats, usually in evenly moist to poorly drained acidic soils in Northern Europe and North Asia.

A large deciduous to semi-evergreen fern with finely cut, two- to three-pinnate, triangular to lance-shaped fronds, with strongly toothed segments centered with stipes covered in dark brown scales. Typically 24–36 in. (60–90 cm) or more tall, with a wide-spreading habit that can cover a lot of ground. AGM

'Crispa Whiteside': crested with crisped margins, lacy appearance, 24–36 in. (60–90 cm) tall, AGM

'Jimmy Dyce': dwarf form, 12–18 in. (30–45 cm) tall and wide, semi-upright habit and broad, lush pinnae in deep blue and forest green, more semi-evergreen to evergreen in milder climates than other cultivars

'Lepidota Cristata': smaller, crested, parsleylike fronds, 24 in. (60 cm) tall and wide, AGM

Dryopteris erythrosora
AUTUMN FERN, JAPANESE SHIELD FERN

Zones 5–8
Woodland hillsides and forested mountain slopes of Japan, Korea, and China.

A popular species with glossy, semi-evergreen to evergreen, triangular, twice-pinnate, arching fronds, 12–24 in. (30–60 cm) long, slowly spreading into dense colonies. New foliage emerges lustrous copper-red to copper-pink, changing to light green and then dark green. Spore-forming sori on undersides of mature fronds are bright red, aging to copper-red. Sun tolerant with good moisture. Drought tolerant in shade.

'Brilliance': new growth in brighter, longer lasting shades of copper-pink, autumn red tones can develop on mature fronds

var. *koidzumiana*: evergreen, low elevation variety for zones 7–10, often recognized as *D. koidzumiana*, with later emerging, glossy and deep burgundy-red fronds turning slowly to brilliant copper-orange and then to green, holding color until late summer

var. *prolifica*: narrower pinnae with lacy appearance on more arching, bulbil-producing fronds

'Radiance': new growth possibly brighter than 'Brilliance' on larger fronds

Dryopteris dilatata

Dryopteris erythrosora

Dryopteris marginalis

Dryopteris labordei
GOLDEN MIST WOOD FERN

Zones 5–8

Subtropical, broadleaf evergreen forests in China and Japan.

Similar to *D. erythrosora*, with glossy, semi-evergreen to evergreen, triangular, twice-pinnate, arching fronds, 12–24 in. (30–60 cm) long, slowly spreading into dense colonies. New foliage emerges glowing gold to orange-gold, aging to vivid green.

Dryopteris marginalis
LEATHERLEAF WOOD FERN, MARGINAL WOOD FERN

Zones 2–8

Rocky, shaded habitats including crevices and bluffs, forest edges, and road and streambanks in eastern North America from Newfoundland to Georgia, west to Oklahoma and north to Minnesota.

Extremely hardy, evergreen, clumping fern with somewhat glossy, leathery, green to bluish green fronds that are egg- to lance-shaped, twice-pinnate, and arching, 12–36 in. (30–90 cm) long. Tolerant of dry shade.

Duchesnea indica
MOCK STRAWBERRY, FALSE STRAWBERRY

Rosaceae

Zones 3–9

Mountain slopes, meadows, riverbanks and other wet places, and field margins from Afghanistan to Japan south to Indonesia. Naturalized in North America, Europe, and Africa.

Resembling wild strawberry, with veined or pleated, trifoliate leaves with broadly serrated margins, spreading stolons, and edible though flavorless red fruit, *D. indica* differs in having bright yellow flowers, 1 in. (2.5 cm) wide, smaller leaves held closer to the ground, and fruit studded with protruding seeds held upward on erect stems. It forms an indefinitely spreading, herbaceous to evergreen ground cover, 2–4 in. (5–10 cm) tall, with flowers from spring to fall and contrasting fruit from summer onward. Potentially invasive in some regions. Now recognized scientifically as *Potentilla indica*.

CULTURE/CARE Easy to grow in dry to moist soils from full sun to part shade. Can spread aggressively in part shade with rich soil and good moisture. Mow or shear in spring to refresh.

USES Spreads quickly and can cover large areas. May be too vigorous for small applications. Tolerant of moderate foot traffic. Could be used as a lawn alternative. Deer resistant. Attractive to pollinators, especially bees.

PROPAGATION Division, removal of plantlets formed by stolons

Duchesnea indica

Eleocharis radicans
ROOTED SPIKERUSH, MINIATURE RUSH

Cyperaceae

Zones 4–8

Streams, lakes, bogs, moist meadows, and other wet or moist places in curiously disjunct regions of the United States, including California, Texas, Florida, Virginia, and Michigan.

A vigorous, rhizomatous, indefinitely spreading, mat-forming sedge with densely packed, bright green, threadlike leaves, to 3 in. (7.5 cm) tall. Tiny, insignificant flowers and seed heads on thin stems invite comparisons to fiber-optic grass, *Isolepis cernua*. Mats can form domes, or "moguls," when grown in tight spaces.

CULTURE/CARE Part to full shade in wet to evenly moist, moderately fertile soils. Spreads quickly with ample moisture, more slowly in drier sites. Leaves will develop brown tips without adequate water.

USES A lawn alternative for small to medium-sized areas in evenly moist to wet soils, as an edger around ponds, between paving stones, in fairy gardens, and with bonsai. Tolerant of moderate foot traffic.

PROPAGATION Seed, division

Ellisiophyllum pinnatum
ELLISIOPHYLLUM

Plantaginaceae

Zones 7–9

Grasslands, along streams, and in open forests from India and China east to Japan and south to the Philippines and New Guinea.

Vigorous, indefinitely spreading, stoloniferous, evergreen ground cover forming dense mats, 2–3 in. (5–7.5 cm) tall, with midgreen, pinnately dissected and lobed, somewhat fernlike foliage topped with small, starry, pure white, five-petaled flowers with green to greenish yellow throats throughout the summer.

CULTURE/CARE Evenly moist, moderately fertile soil in part sun to shade.

USES Spreads quickly under and around shrubs and perennials, along pathways, between paving stones, and in crevices. Tolerant of occasional foot traffic.

PROPAGATION Division

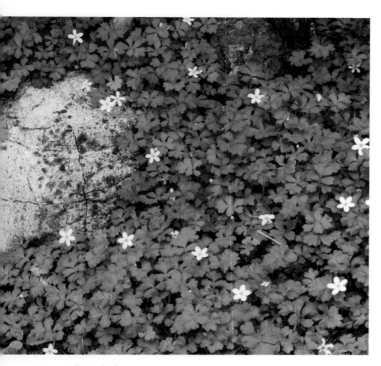

Ellisiophyllum pinnatum

Epilobium
Onagraceae

Better known horticulturally as a member of the genus *Zauschneria*, California fuchsias have been for some time assigned to the genus *Epilobium*, though their distinctiveness remains recognized in their own eponymous section of the genus. Irrespective of taxonomic status, they are valuable perennials or subshrubs, often with wide-spreading habits, with great heat and drought tolerance, offering summer to late season, bright red to orange, trumpet-shaped flowers popular with hummingbirds. Though the genus is generally suited for gardens in milder climates, a few hardier cultivars are available for areas in colder zones.

CULTURE/CARE Full to part sun in well-drained to sharply draining soils of average to poor fertility and average to low moisture. Drought tolerant. In colder, wetter, and higher elevation regions, plant in soils of low fertility and with excellent drainage, preferably on slopes. Shear plants in early spring to maintain shape, if required.

USES Cascading over walls, along sidewalks and driveways, and in xeriscapes, rock gardens, and hell strips, and containers, spreading at a slow to moderate rate. Not tolerant of foot traffic. Deer and rabbit resistant. Attractive to pollinators, especially hummingbirds.

PROPAGATION Cuttings, division, seed

Epilobium canum
CALIFORNIA FUCHSIA

Zones 4–11, depending on cultivar

Dry slopes, ridges, and chaparral, and along seasonal creeks, seeps, and springs in the drier southern parts of its range in western North America, especially California.

This variable perennial or subshrub forms mats or mounds, 3–18 in. (7.5–45 cm) tall and 24–36 in. (60–90 cm) wide, of green to gray, usually hairy, linear, lance-shaped, or egg-shaped leaves, and spreads slowly by rhizomes but is not overly aggressive. Tubular, bright scarlet flowers are produced in profusion through summer and fall.

Epilobium canum subsumes four species of *Zauschneria* as subspecies, which intergrade where their ranges overlap: *Z. californica*, *Z. cana*, *Z. garrettii*, and *Z. arizonica*. Their taxonomy may not as of yet be completely resolved.

> subsp. *angustifolium* (syn. *Z. californica*) cultivars have narrow foliage. The taxonomy of this subspecies remains in question, leaving the exact identities of most cultivars previously assigned to *Z. californica* in question.

> subsp. *canum* (syn. *Z. cana*) is a perennial herb or subshrub with gray, linear to lance-shaped, often clustered leaves with smooth margins.

> subsp. *garrettii* (syn. *Z. garrettii*) is a perennial herb with generally green, broadly egg-shaped leaves with prominent marginal teeth and conspicuous lateral veins.

> subsp. *latifolium* (syn. *Z. arizonica*) is a perennial herb with generally green, lance- to egg-shaped leaves with smooth to lightly toothed margins.

Cultivars are hardy to zone 7 unless otherwise noted.

E. canum subsp. *angustifolium* cultivars

'Carmen's Gray': narrow, silver-gray foliage, scarlet flowers, 8–18 in. (20–45 cm) tall and 24–30 in. (60–75 cm) wide

'Chaparral Silver': narrow, silver-gray foliage, scarlet flowers, 12–18 in. (30–45 cm) tall and 36 in. (90 cm) wide

'Cloverdale': broad, nearly triangular, light olive-green foliage, deep orange to orange-red flowers, 12–24 in. (30–60 cm) tall and 24–36 in. (60–90 cm) wide

Epilobium canum subsp. *garrettii* 'Orange Carpet'

'Dublin' (syn. 'Glasnevin'): one of the earliest to bloom, with gray-green, lance-shaped foliage, scarlet flowers, 8–12 in. (20–30 cm) tall and 18–24 in. (45–60 cm) wide, more common in the UK and rare in the US, probably zone 8, AGM

'El Tigre': linear, gray-green foliage, scarlet flowers, 6–12 in. (15–30 cm) tall and 24–48 in. (60–120 cm) wide, zone 7 or 8

'Everett's Choice': lance-shaped, gray-green foliage, scarlet flowers, 6–12 in. (15–30 cm) tall and 24–48 in. (60–120 cm) wide

'John Bixby': broad, gray-green foliage, large scarlet flowers, 12–18 in. (30–45 cm) tall and 4–5 ft. (1.2–1.5 m) wide, a top garden trial performer

'Marin Pink': broad, gray-green foliage, salmon-pink flowers, 18–24 in. (45–60 cm) tall and 3–5 ft. (1–1.5 m) wide

'Northfork Coral': broad, green foliage, coral to peachy orange flowers, 18 in. (45 cm) tall and 36 in. (90 cm) wide, very hardy to zone 5

'Schieffelin's Choice': lance-shaped, gray foliage, scarlet flowers, 4–8 in. (10–20 cm) tall and 24–36 in. (60–90 cm) wide

'Solidarity Pink': lance-shaped, light green foliage, pale salmon-pink flowers, 8 in. (20 cm) tall and 24 in. (60 cm) wide

'Summer Snow': broad, gray foliage, white flowers, 4–10 in. (10–25 cm) tall and 24 in. (60 cm) wide

'U.C. Hybrid': broad, gray-green foliage, scarlet flowers, 12–18 in. (30–45 cm) tall and 24–36 in. (60–90 cm) wide

E. canum subsp. *canum* and subsp. *garrettii* cultivars

subsp. *canum* 'Calistoga': broad, gray, fuzzy foliage, very red flowers, 12–18 in. (30–45 cm) tall and 3–4 ft. (1–1.2 m) wide

subsp. *garrettii* 'Pwwg01s' Orange Carpet: broad, green, fuzzy foliage, orange to scarlet flowers, 4–6 in. (10–15 cm) tall and 18–24 in. (45–60 cm) wide, selected in Wyoming near the Idaho border, very hardy to zone 4

E. canum subsp. *latifolium* cultivars

'Sierra Salmon': lance-shaped, silvery to blue-green foliage, salmon-pink flowers, 12 in. (30 cm) tall and 24–36 in. (60–90 cm) wide

'Woody's Peach Surprise': lance-shaped, green foliage, pink to peachy pink flowers, 6–8 in. (15–20 cm) tall and 18 in. (45 cm) wide, zone 5

Epilobium septentrionale
HUMBOLDT COUNTY FUCHSIA

Zones 7–11

Dry, sandy, or rocky ledges and serpentine slopes from low to high elevations of the Northern Coast and Outer Northern Coast Ranges of California and southwest Oregon.

Formerly *Zauschneria septentrionalis*, this species is likely the most tolerant of winter wet conditions. The low, deciduous, perennial herb is typically 2–8 in. (5–20 cm) or more tall with prostrate stems often curving upward at the tips. Silver-white to grayish silver, pointed, lance- to egg-shaped leaves are up to 1 in. (2.5 cm) long. Bright, vermillion-orange, trumpet-shaped flowers are up to 1 in. (2.5 cm) long, flared into multiple lobes with exserted (outward protruding) stamens and pistil blooming in summer and fall.

'Select Mattole': dense, spreading mounds of silver to silver-green foliage, 6–12 in. (15–30 cm) tall by 24 in. (60 cm) or more wide, blooming relatively early from midsummer into fall

'Wayne's Silver': similar to 'Select Mattole' but seemingly less hardy, to zone 8

Epimedium
Berberidaceae

Barrenworts are among the most bulletproof and useful perennials for shade, deserving equal status with hellebores, hostas, and ferns. They are tough, reliable, long-lived, and weed-smothering ground covers. Additionally, newly introduced Asian species and their selections and hybrids are offering bolder flower and foliage forms, helping to dispel the utilitarian reputation of the genus.

The small and complex, four-parted spring flowers held in racemes or panicles exhibit an intricacy comparable to milkweeds, toadlilies, and even orchids. The outer protective sepals, usually greenish in color, are shed upon opening. The inner sepals are larger and petal-like, while the petals are usually smaller except in plants with hornlike nectar-producing spurs. Flower structure and floral effect varies depending on the relative sizes of flower parts. Some plants, such as E. ×perralchicum 'Fröhnleiten', resemble a simple flower with large sepals and much reduced petals. Others, such as E. ×versicolor, have petals forming a central cup with small spurs and subtending sepals reminiscent of daffodils. Spurred forms, such as E. ×rubrum, have winglike sepals, and long-spurred plants such as E. grandiflorum create an intricate, spidery effect.

The thick and leathery, compound, evergreen or herbaceous leaves with 3–27 leaflets (depending on species) arise from woody rhizomes during or after flowering, some with dramatic mottlings, flushes, and edges of red, burgundy, or purple. Leaflets can be heart-, lance- or arrow-shaped, some with attractive fall and winter colors of yellow, red, and bronze. Foliage mounds are typically 6–12 in. (15–30 cm) tall. In colder zones, evergreen types may be semi-evergreen or may incur winter damage but should remain attractive well into winter. The annual extension of rhizomes determines whether a plant is clumping or spreading in habit.

Whereas only 20 species were known a few decades ago, about 65 species are currently recognized. Additional possibilities not treated here include E. pauciflorum, E. perralderianum, E. sutchuenense, and E. wushanense, as well as many hybrids.

CULTURE/CARE Easy to grow in part to full shade, and even in part sun in colder regions, in rich, well-drained, slightly alkaline, evenly moist soils. Tolerant of dry shade or periods of drought, acidic conditions, and clay, sandy, and rocky substrates. Shear winter-damaged leaves in early spring before flowers begin to emerge. Undamaged evergreen foliage can remain or be sheared to reveal the flowers.

USES Versatile in a range of soil and light conditions for small to large applications in borders, along pathways, and under trees and shrubs, including at the bases of trunks and among shallow roots. Mass plant clumping species to attain closed coverage. Spreading types do so at a slow rate, especially in dry soils or deep shade, so plant as densely as possible. Not tolerant of foot traffic. Deer and rabbit resistant.

PROPAGATION Division

Epimedium alpinum
ALPINE BARRENWORT

Zones 4–8
Broadleaf deciduous forests and among shrubs from low to moderate elevations in Southeast Europe.

One of the hardiest species, with ½ in. (1.3 cm) wide flowers held below the foliage, with red sepals and pale yellow petals with short spurs on plants 6–12 in. (15–30 cm) tall. Evergreen to semi-evergreen leaves are heart-shaped, emerging with a pink tinge in spring and turning reddish bronze in fall. Spreads relatively quickly, up to 12 in. (30 cm) a year in optimum conditions, into an open ground cover. Tolerant of dry shade.

'Shrimp Girl': shorter, 6–8 in. (15–20 cm) tall, spreading slowly up to 5 in. (12.5 cm) per year, forming a denser cover than the species

Epimedium epsteinii
BARRENWORT

Zones 5–8
Forest margins and streamsides from low to moderate elevations in Hunan, China.

Discovered in 1994, E. epsteinii has the widest sepals in the genus, at nearly ½ in. (1.3 cm) across, the flowers resembling white parachutes with contrasting warm purple to maroon petal cups and curved, spidery spurs. Medium-sized, elongated, dark green, glossy, evergreen leaves emerge with a bronze flush, forming dense mats 6–10 in. (15–25 cm) tall, spreading quickly up to 8 in. (20 cm) a year.

Epimedium grandiflorum var. *higoense* 'Bandit'

Epimedium grandiflorum 'Yubae' with new spring foliage

Epimedium grandiflorum
LONGSPUR BARRENWORT, HORNY GOAT WEED

Zones (4)5–8

Moist, acidic soils and among calcareous rocks in hilly deciduous woodlands in Northwest China, Korea, and Japan.

A popular species with large flowers in diverse colors, *E. grandiflorum* is herbaceous and mostly clump-forming. Leaves with 9–27 spiny edged leaflets form mounds 8–20 in. (20–50 cm) tall, depending on cultivar, and usually almost twice as wide. A first flush of short foliage emerges below the blooming flowers in spring, often followed by a second, taller flush after flowering. The spiderlike flowers are 1–2 in. (2.5–5 cm) wide with a central cup and long spurs in white, yellow, pink, and purple. Intolerant of alkaline soils except for *E. grandiflorum* var. *higoense*. AGM

'Dark Beauty': pink sepals and white petals, chocolate-brown/purple new growth, 12 in. (30 cm) tall

var. *higoense* 'Bandit': pure white flowers, leaves emerging red, becoming green with a red edge and then green, 10–12 in. (25–30 cm) tall

'Lilafee' (syn. 'Lilac Fairy'): lavender-violet sepals and lavender petals with white tips, with chocolate-brown/purple new growth, 14 in. (36 cm) tall

'Nanum': dwarf, 10 in. (25 cm) tall, with medium-sized, pure white flowers, with purple-edged new spring foliage, AGM

'Pierre's Purple': rich wine-purple cups with purple spurs tipped in white, bronze new growth turns green and then lime-green in fall, 15 in. (38 cm) tall

'Purple Pixie': vivid purple sepals and lavender to white petals, with reddish new growth, 12 in. (30 cm) tall

'Queen Esta': early to bloom, with lavender-purple sepals and pale lavender to white petals, purple to bronze new growth, 12 in. (30 cm) tall

'Red Beauty': glowing magenta flowers, reddish new growth, 16 in. (40 cm) tall

'Red Queen': rose-red flowers bloom beneath the large foliage, leaflets up to 6 in. (15 cm) long and 4 in. (10 cm) wide, bronze in spring and yellow overlaid with pink and orange in fall, 14 in. (36 cm) tall

'White Queen': pure white flowers, with a single, annual, flush of leaves edged in red, 14 in. (36 cm) tall, AGM

'Yubae' (syn. 'Rose Queen'): magenta flowers, white spur tips, with purple-bronze new foliage, 18 in. (45 cm) tall, semi-evergreen in milder zones, AGM

Epimedium ×*perralchicum*
BARRENWORT

Zones 4–8

This extremely hardy, drought-tolerant hybrid of *E. perralderianum* and *E. pinnatum* subsp. *colchicum* makes an excellent, vigorous ground cover, to 12 in. (30 cm) tall, spreading 4–6 in. (10–15 cm) per year into thick mats of large, leathery, evergreen leaves with

(20 cm) per year, with evergreen leaves of 3–5 shiny, leathery, deep green, rounded leaflets with wavy margins that emerge reddish brown. Sprays of bright yellow flowers are held above the foliage with large, showy sepals and small, yellow, cupped petals with tiny reddish to brownish spurs. Very drought tolerant. AGM

'Thunderbolt': foliage turns purple-black in autumn, brilliant burgundy in sun, with green veins

Epimedium ×rubrum
BARRENWORT

Zones 4–8
A popular, slowly spreading, evergreen hybrid of *E. alpinum* and *E. grandiflorum* with excellent hardiness, sporting panicles of bicolor flowers with cherry-red sepals and pale yellow to white petals with short spurs and small cups. Spring foliage is dramatically flushed bright red with green veins. Plants are 10–16 in. (25–40 cm) tall, spreading 2–4 in. (5–10 cm) per year.

Epimedium ×versicolor
BARRENWORT

Zones 5–9
Semi-evergreen to evergreen, drought-tolerant hybrid of *E. grandiflorum* and *E. pinnatum* subsp. *colchicum*, 12 in. (30cm) tall and spreading 2–6 in. (5–15 cm) per year. Medium-sized, heart-shaped leaflets are flushed with red or bronze in spring. Short-spurred flowers with central cups resemble little daffodils in shades of pink, red, orange, and yellow.

'Cherry Tart': purple buds reveal pink to salmon-pink sepals, cherry-red spurs, and a lemon-yellow cup, with reddish purple spring foliage

'Cupreum': pale to salmon-pink sepals and lemon-yellow petals, with intense red spring foliage

'Neosulphureum': shorter, tighter, and less spreading than 'Sulphureum', with pale yellow sepals and buttery yellow cupped petals atop bronzed young foliage

'Strawberry Blush': pale pink sepals with darker streaks, and yellow cupped petals with purplish spurs atop burgundy spring foliage

'Sulphureum': pale yellow sepals and buttery yellow cupped petals atop reddish bronze young foliage, to 10 in. (25 cm) tall, spreading 4–5 in. (10–12.5 cm) per year, drought tolerant

Epimedium pinnatum subsp. *colchicum*

slightly wavy margins. Butter-yellow flowers with broad sepals and short reddish spurs are held in bright sprays above the new, red-flushed foliage.

'Fröhnleiten': bold displays atop reddish bronze new foliage with dramatic green veins, 8–10 in. (20–25 cm) tall

'Wisley': leaves slightly rippled and puffed between the lighter veins

Epimedium pinnatum subsp. *colchicum*
LARGE-FLOWERED BARRENWORT,
COLCHIAN BARRENWORT

Zones (4)5–8
Moist, mountainous woodlands of the Caucasus along the Black Sea.
A popular species and an excellent ground cover, to 8–12 in. (20–30 cm) tall and spreading up to 8 in.

Epimedium ×warleyense

BARRENWORT

Zones 4–8

A unique chance hybrid of *E. alpinum* and *E. pinnatum* subsp. *colchicum* from the garden of famed plantswoman Miss Willmott of Warley Place, with small, bright, tangerine-orange, concave sepals and buttery yellow petals with small cups and short spurs that create a luminous effect atop red-flushed, heart-shaped leaflets. Evergreen plants are 8–10 in. (20–25 cm) tall, spreading 5–6 in. (12.5–15cm) per year into somewhat open mats.

'Orangekönigin' (syn. 'Orange Queen'): slightly paler than *E. ×warleyense*, with dark veins, spreads by 2–4 in. (5–10 cm) rhizomes into denser, tighter, better ground-covering clumps

Epimedium ×youngianum

BARRENWORT

Zones 5–8

Deciduous or semi-evergreen, clump-forming hybrid of *E. grandiflorum* and *E. diphyllum*, with flowers variable in size, shape, color, and spur length and leaves of variable size and shape. Most cultivars produce a second flush of foliage each season, and some rebloom.

'Beni-kujaku': unique double-flower form resembling a spidery double hellebore, with petals mimicking the ruffled, pink, white-frosted sepals, 12 in. (30 cm) tall

'Merlin': narrow sepals and large, rounded, spur-less petals, both deep pink with white frosting, with bronze-flushed young foliage, 9–12 in. (23–30 cm) tall

'Milky Way': pure white flowers with long spurs, with spring foliage speckled with deep purple and mature foliage with subtle silver veins, 12 in. (30 cm) tall

'Niveum': pure white, short-spurred or spurless flowers and red-tinged spring foliage, 8–12 in. (20–30 cm) tall

'Roseum': dusky pink to lavender-pink flowers atop bronzy foliage, 8–12 in. (20–30 cm) tall

'Tamabotan': silvery lavender-pink flowers with a ruffled double look, with new foliage tinted bluish purple, 18–20 in. (45–50 cm) tall

'Yenomoto': floriferous, with long-spurred white flowers flushed with lavender, 12 in. (30 cm) tall

Epimedium ×warleyense

Epimedium ×youngianum 'Yenomoto'

Epimedium 'Tama-no-genpei'

Epimedium hybrids

Zones 5–8

The discovery of and breeding with new *Epimedium* species has resulted in many new interspecific and complex multispecies hybrids.

'Amber Queen': gold, lemon-yellow, and orange, spidery flowers with a central cup and long spurs, often reblooming, with spiny leaves mottled with burgundy when young on semi-evergreen clumping plants, 24 in. (60 cm) tall, AGM

'Arctic Wings': spreading evergreen plants with red-mottled new foliage and pure white flowers with yellow centers, 8–12 in. (20–30 cm) tall

'Black Sea': evergreen, glossy, nearly black foliage and small yellow flowers with pale orange veins, 8 in. (20 cm) tall, spreading 3–5 in. (7.5–12.5 cm) per year

'Conalba' Alabaster: pure white, spurless flowers of broad, rounded sepals, and petals occasionally flushed with violet, with light green, deciduous, clumping foliage, 9–12 in. (23–30 cm) tall, vigorous, hardy to zone 4

'Domino': spiky evergreen, clumping foliage, 12–14 in. (30–36 cm) tall, mottled in spring, with large, spidery flowers with long white spurs and a deep, dusky rose cup that may rebloom, AGM

'Enchantress': silver-pink flowers with undulating, evergreen foliage turning deep red in winter, 12 in. (30 cm) tall and slowly spreading 2–4 in. (5–10 cm) per year

'Fire Dragon': yellow cupped petals with long curving yellow to white spurs and pink sepals on spidery flowers, with semi-evergreen, clumping foliage, 20 in. (50 cm) tall

'Flamenco Dancer' (syn. 'Flamingo Dancer'): glowing pink, long-spurred flowers with white frosting, with purple-mottled, semi-evergreen to herbaceous, clumping foliage in spring, 12 in. (30 cm) tall

'Pink Champagne': long white spurs and raspberry-pink cups above purple-speckled new growth, on reblooming, clumping, evergreen plants, 12 in. (30 cm) tall

'Pink Elf': evergreen spreader, 12 in. (30 cm) tall, with deep dusky pink cups and white spurs and sepals

'Spine Tingler': long, evergreen, spiny leaflets infused with chocolate-brown hues when young, with lemon-yellow, spidery flowers, 10 in. (25 cm) tall, clumping

'Tama-no-genpei': long, lavender-pink and white reblooming spurs with deeper pink sepals atop purple-flecked new foliage, on herbaceous, clumping plants, 12–16 in. (30–40 cm) tall

Equisetum scirpoides
DWARF HORSETAIL, DWARF SCOURING RUSH

Equisetaceae

Zones 3–10, perhaps hardier

Circumpolar in dry to wet coniferous forests, peat bogs, fens, swamps, and alpine tundra in mountains and alpine zones.

Though the weedy nature of common horsetail (*E. arvense*) has given the genus a bad name in horticulture, respect is due for these much-maligned plants. After all, horsetails are living fossils and likely the oldest surviving land plants, dating back 375 million years! Some species make interesting horticultural statements, as long as their spreading rhizomatous habit is controlled. The 3–5 ft. (1–1.5 m) tall *E. hyemale* is commonly used as an accent in or adjacent to ponds or in minimalist planting designs but could be used as a tall ground cover for large applications.

The best ground cover, however, is the smallest species, the extremely hardy dwarf horsetail, which forms tightly packed, spreading mats of midgreen, cylindrical, hollow, vertical or curving, leafless, evergreen, wiry stems, jointed with black and white sheaths at the internodes. Plants grow 4–12 in. (10–30 cm) tall,

Equisetum scirpoides

spreading indefinitely from brown rhizomes. Fertile stems are tipped with small black cones.

CULTURE/CARE Full sun to part shade in evenly moist to wet soils or in shallow water. Tolerant of average soils, which reduce the rate of spreading, though some summer irrigation may be required to maintain lushness. Tolerant of exposed, windy, and coastal sites.

USES A useful architectural ground cover around ponds, along streams, or in low-lying, moist sites. Use where its spreading nature is desirable or where hardscape features will restrict its spread. Not tolerant of foot traffic. Deer resistant.

PROPAGATION Division

Erica
Ericaceae

The heaths are low-growing, evergreen, spreading to mounding shrubs with small, needlelike leaves and bell- or urn-shaped flowers borne in racemes at the branch tips. Some cultivars can bloom over long periods between early winter and midspring, while others bloom in summer and fall. Heaths are valuable nectar sources for pollinators in fall, winter, and spring, when fewer plants are blooming.

CULTURE/CARE Full to part sun in evenly moist, average to moderately rich, free-draining soils. Plants can become leggy in overly rich soils. Sandy or gravelly soils that do not become overly dry are fine, but clay soils are best avoided. In hot summer climates, they prefer part sun or dappled shade, and in colder zones, good snow cover or an airy mulch of pine needles are necessary for winter protection to prevent desiccation from low temperatures and wind. More tolerant of heat, humidity, and alkaline soils than *Calluna* species. Encourage a tight structure with a light annual shearing just after flowering, especially when plants are young. Salt tolerant.

USES Mass plantings in small to large areas especially on slopes for erosion control, in coastal gardens, as edgers for borders and pathways, and as companions to dwarf conifers and other acid-loving plants, including the summer heathers (*Calluna* spp.), *Vaccinium* species, and manzanitas (*Arctostaphylos* spp.). Mounds develop at a slow to moderate rate and are extremely effective at suppressing weeds. Not tolerant of foot traffic. Deer and rabbit resistant.

PROPAGATION Cuttings, removal and replanting of rooted stems

Erica carnea
WINTER HEATH, SPRING HEATH

Zones (4)5–9

Coniferous woodlands and rocky slopes in mountainous areas of Central and Southern Europe.

Erica carnea is among the hardiest species, with some reports of survival in zones 3 and 4 with good snow cover. It typically forms carpeting, semiprostrate mounds, 6–9 in. (15–23 cm) tall and 18–24 in. (45–60 cm) wide. Small flowers are up to ¼ in. (6 mm) long but borne in large numbers, presenting bold displays in late winter and early spring. Easy to grow, adaptable, and tolerant of salt and both acidic and mildly alkaline soils.

f. *alba* 'Golden Starlet': white flowers from winter to early spring and bright gold foliage turning lime-green in winter, spreading habit, 6 in. (15 cm) tall by 16 in. (40 cm) wide, AGM

f. *alba* 'Isabell': white flowers from late winter to spring and bright green foliage, erect spreading habit, 6 in. (15 cm) tall by 14 in. (36 cm) wide, AGM

f. *alba* 'Schneekuppe': white flowers from midwinter to early spring and bright green foliage, compact habit, 6 in. (15 cm) tall by 12 in. (30 cm) wide

f. *alba* 'Springwood White': midpink flowers from midwinter to midspring and bright green foliage, spreading habit, 8 in. (20 cm) tall by 24 in. (60 cm) wide, AGM

'Ann Sparkes': deep rose-pink flowers from midwinter to late spring and gold and orange foliage with reddish bronze tips in winter, spreading habit, plants 6–9 in. (15–23 cm) tall by 10 in. (25 cm) wide, possibly hardy to zone 4, AGM

f. *aureifolia* 'Foxhollow': lavender-pink flowers from midwinter to spring, yellow foliage tipped bronze and becoming orange-red tipped in winter, vigorous spreading habit, 6 in. (15 cm) tall by 18 in. (45 cm) wide, AGM

f. *aureifolia* 'Westwood Yellow': shell-pink flowers from midwinter to spring and yellow foliage tinted orange in winter, compact upright habit, 6 in. (15 cm) tall by 14 in. (36 cm) wide, AGM

'Challenger': magenta flowers from midwinter to spring and dark green foliage, 6 in. (15 cm) tall by 18 in. (45 cm) wide, AGM

'March Seedling': deep pink flowers from late winter to late spring and midgreen foliage, 6 in. (15 cm) tall by 20 in. (50 cm) wide, AGM

'Myretoun Ruby': magenta-red flowers from midwinter to spring and dark green foliage, spreading habit, 8 in. (20 cm) tall by 18 in. (45 cm) wide, AGM

Erica carnea f. *alba* 'Schneekuppe'

'Nathalie': deep pink to lavender-pink flowers from midwinter to spring and dark green foliage, compact habit, 6 in. (15 cm) tall by 16 in. (40 cm) wide, AGM

'Pink Spangles': shell-pink flowers from midwinter to spring and midgreen foliage, spreading habit, 6–12 in. (15–30 cm) tall by 18 in. (45 cm) wide, AGM

'Pirbright Rose': shell- or dusky pink to midpink flowers from midwinter to midspring and green foliage tinged red, spreading habit, 6 in. (15 cm) tall by 12 in. (30 cm) wide

'Rosalie': glowing pink flowers from midwinter to midspring and bronzy green foliage, upright spreading habit, 6 in. (15 cm) tall by 16 in. (40 cm) wide, AGM

'Springwood Pink': midpink flowers from midwinter to midspring and bright green foliage, spreading habit, 8 in. (20 cm) tall by 20 in. (50 cm) wide

'Tanja': glowing pink to magenta flowers from late winter to midspring and dark green foliage turning bronzy green in winter, 6 in. (15 cm) tall by 14 in. (36 cm) wide

'Vivellii': lavender-pink to magenta flowers from midwinter to midspring and dark green foliage, bronze-cast in winter, bushy habit, 9 in. (23 cm) tall by 14 in. (36 cm) wide, AGM

'Wintersonne': glowing pink to magenta flowers from late winter to late spring and dark green foliage, reddish brown in winter, 6 in. (15 cm) tall by 18 in. (45 cm) wide, AGM

Erica cinerea

BELL HEATH, TWISTED HEATH

Zones 6–8

Dry, acidic, nutrient-poor soils on moors, heathlands, and coastal dunes in Western Europe from the Faroe Islands to northern Spain.

Less commonly grown than other species with more exacting cultural requirements, *E. cinerea* can nevertheless be one of the showiest of the hardy heaths in appropriate conditions. Bell heath typically grows 6–24 in. (15–60 cm) tall, with an upright habit, and large bell-shaped flowers in shades of glowing pink and magenta, plus whites and deep purples, from mid- to late summer into autumn, with copious amounts of nectar for pollinators. Drought tolerant. Prefers well-drained, acidic soils in full sun. Winter protection in colder regions is important.

f. *alba* 'Celebration': white flowers from midsummer to early fall and bright gold foliage turning lime-green in winter, prostrate habit, 8 in. (20 cm) tall by 16 in. (40 cm) wide

f. *aureifolia* 'Golden Drop': deep lavender-pink flowers from early to late summer and golden to bright orange foliage turning deep orange-red in cool seasons, low spreading habit, 8 in. (20 cm) tall by 18 in. (45 cm) wide

'C.D. Eason': glowing magenta flowers from early summer to early fall and dark green foliage, spreading habit, 9 in. (23 cm) tall by 20 in. (50 cm) wide, AGM

'Pink Ice': rose-pink flowers from midsummer to late fall and dark green foliage, dwarf habit, 6 in. (15 cm) tall by 14 in. (36 cm) wide, AGM

'P.S. Patrick': purple flowers from early summer to early fall and dark green foliage, bushy habit, 10–12 in. (25–30 cm) tall by 18 in. (45 cm) wide

'Stephen Davis': glowing pink to magenta flowers from early summer to early fall and dark green foliage, 8 in. (20 cm) tall by 18 in. (45 cm) wide, AGM

'Velvet Night': purple to magenta flowers from early summer to early fall and dark green foliage, upright habit, 10 in. (25 cm) tall by 24 in. (60 cm) wide, AGM

Erica ×darleyensis
DARLEY HEATH, WINTER HEATH

Zones (5)6–8
Garden origin.

Darley heaths are hybrid crosses that first occurred at Darley Dale Nursery in the United Kingdom. They combine some of the best characteristics of each parent, including the long bloom time and bold colors of *E. carnea* and the abundant flower production, fragrance, and vigorous growth of the Irish heath, *E. erigena*. Size, habit, and hardiness are intermediate, with plants reaching 12–18 in. (30–45 cm) or more tall, with a compact, upright, bushy habit and hardiness to zone 6, possibly 5. Buds form in late summer and can bloom from midfall until spring, with colors deepening as flowers age. Among the easiest heaths to grow with good drought tolerance.

f. *albiflora* 'Silberschmelze' (syn. 'Molten Silver'): grayish white flowers from winter to midspring, broad upright habit, 18 in. (45 cm) tall by 24 in. (60 cm) wide, with midgreen foliage with creamy new growth

'Arthur Johnson': mid- to deep pink flowers from early winter to midspring, open bushy habit, 18 in. (45 cm) tall by 30 in. (75 cm) wide, with medium green foliage and creamy spring new growth, AGM

f. *aureifolia* 'Eva Gold': midpink to magenta flowers from midwinter to midspring, 12 in. (30 cm) tall by 20 in. (50 cm) wide, with golden foliage with bronze highlights, greener in winter

f. *aureifolia* 'Golden Perfect': white flowers from early winter to midspring, compact spreading habit, 16 in. (40 cm) tall by 28 in. (71 cm) wide, with yellow foliage, greenish yellow in winter

f. *aureifolia* 'Mary Helen': pink flowers from late winter to spring, bushy habit, 10 in. (25 cm) tall by 18 in. (45 cm) wide, with yellow to gold foliage, bronzed in winter

Erica cinerea f. *alba* 'Celebration'

Erica ×darleyensis f. *aureifolia* 'Eva Gold'

Erica ×darleyensis 'White Perfection'

'Darley Dale': shell-pink to midpink flowers from late fall to midspring, bushy habit, 18 in. (45 cm) tall by 36 in. (90 cm) wide, with midgreen foliage

'Furzey': lilac-pink to deep pink flowers from early winter to midspring, bushy habit, 16 in. (40 cm) tall by 24 in. (60 cm) wide, with dark green foliage and bright pink new growth, AGM

'Ghost Hills': lilac-pink to deep pink flowers from early winter to midspring, bushy habit, 18 in. (45 cm) tall by 36 in. (90 cm) wide, with light green foliage with creamy new growth, AGM

'Jenny Porter': lilac flowers from midwinter to midspring, spreading habit, 10 in. (25 cm) tall by 24 in. (60 cm) wide, with medium green foliage and creamy new growth, AGM

'J.W. Porter': lilac-pink to midpink flowers from midwinter to midspring, bushy habit, 10 in. (25 cm) tall by 16 in. (40 cm) wide, with dark green foliage and creamy to red new growth, AGM

'Katia' (Winter Belles Series): large white flowers from winter to midspring, bushy habit, 14 in. (36 cm) tall by 32 in. (80 cm) wide, with medium green foliage and creamy new growth

'Kramer's Rote' (syn. 'Kramer's Red'): among the most popular of all heaths, with deep pink to magenta flowers from midwinter to spring, bushy habit, 16 in. (40 cm) tall by 24 in. (60 cm) wide, with dark green foliage with bronze tints in winter, AGM

'Lucie' (Winter Belles Series): large deep pink to magenta flowers from midwinter to spring, bushy habit, 18 in. (45 cm) tall by 24 in. (60 cm) wide, with dark green foliage with bronze tints in winter

'Margaret Porter': lilac-pink to midpink flowers from midwinter to midspring, bushy habit, 10 in. (25 cm) tall by 18 in. (45 cm) wide, with medium green foliage with creamy new growth

'Rubina': lilac-pink to glowing pink flowers from midwinter to early spring, 12 in. (30 cm) tall by 24 in. (60 cm) wide, with dark green foliage, bronzed in winter

'Spring Surprise': light to midpink flowers from early to midspring, broad upright habit, 18 in. (45 cm) tall by 24 in. (60 cm) wide, with dark green foliage

'White Perfection': white flowers from winter to spring, bushy habit, 16 in. (40 cm) tall by 28 in. (71 cm) wide, with bright green foliage, AGM

'Winter Surprise': large rose-pink flowers from early winter to spring, bushy habit, 14 in. (36 cm) tall by 24 in. (60 cm) wide, with dark green foliage

Erigeron
Asteraceae

These relatives of asters and coneflowers have classic daisy-like flowers with greenish yellow to golden yellow centers and distinctively numerous and narrow ray florets in shades of white, pink, or lavender in a single row or overlapping in multiple rows. They are popular with pollinators, especially native bees and butterflies, and are deer resistant.

CULTURE/CARE Easy to grow in full to part sun in average to dry soils. Salt tolerant.

PROPAGATION Division, seed

Erigeron glaucus
BEACH FLEABANE, SEASIDE DAISY

Zones 4–9

Beaches, bluffs, and dunes in coastal Oregon and California.

Dense, rhizomatously spreading mats of thick, leathery, rounded or spoon-shaped, bluish green, evergreen leaves topped with 1–15 white, lavender, or purplish blue daisies on stems to 8 in. (20 cm) tall in late spring.

USES A tough ground cover for poor, dry soils and salty, coastal sites in full sun. Use as an edger for borders and pathways or tumbling over walls and down stairways. Not tolerant of foot traffic.

'Albus': white flowers

'Bountiful': lavender flowers

'Olga': compact habit, large lilac flowers

'Sea Breeze': lavender-pink flowers

'Wayne Roderick': lavender flowers, good heat tolerance

Erigeron glaucus

Erigeron karvinskianus

Erigeron pulchellus var. *pulchellus* 'Lynnhaven Carpet'

Erigeron karvinskianus

MEXICAN FLEABANE, SANTA BARBARA DAISY

Zones 6–10

Open, steep banks, hillsides, cliffs, rock crevices, and open pine–oak forests and thickets in damp positions, at 2950–11,500 ft. (900–3500 m) in Mexico and Central America.

Mounds of crisscrossed, interlocking stems, 6–12 in. (15–30 cm) tall and 12–36 in. (30–90 cm) wide, produce hundreds of small daisy-like flowers constantly from early summer through fall, with golden yellow centers and numerous narrow ray florets that emerge white and deepen to lavender-pink. AGM

USES Mass plant to attain full coverage, interplant with perennials, or combine with other ground covers. Fast-growing plants are seemingly capable of growing in any hot, dry, sunny site with seeds readily colonizing cracks in paving stones and stone walls. A self-seeding annual where not hardy. Not tolerant of foot traffic.

'Lavender Lady': lavender flowers darkening slightly with age

'Moerheimii' (syn. *E.* ×*moerheimii*): more compact and sterile, zone 7 or 8

'Profusion': floriferous selection

'Sea of Blossom' (syn. 'Blütenmeer'): similar to 'Profusion'

Erigeron pulchellus

ROBIN'S PLANTAIN, FLEABANE

Zones (4)5–8

Rocky or open woods, wooded sand dunes, thickets, fields, moist streambanks, and disturbed areas in most of eastern North America.

Spreading by rhizomes and/or stolons, this colony-forming fleabane has relatively large, lightly hairy, gray-green leaves and white to pale violet ray florets around yellow centers, held in small clusters on stems 12–24 in. (30–60 cm) tall in mid- to late spring.

USES Widely adaptable from full sun to shade and tolerant of both moist and dry soils. Protect from full sun in hot summer climates. Not tolerant of foot traffic.

var. *pulchellus* 'Lynnhaven Carpet': dense mats to 6 in. (15 cm) tall, with pale lavender flowers on 12 in. (30 cm) stems

Eriogonum
Polygonaceae

The buckwheats are dryland relatives of better-known garden plants such as fleeceflower (*Persicaria* spp.), creeping wire vine (*Muehlenbeckia axillaris*), rhubarb (*Rheum* spp.), and sorrel (*Rumex* spp.). This genus remains at the fringes of cultivation, but with the growing importance of water-wise and pollinator-friendly plantings, the time has arrived for a larger audience.

Eriogonum is one of the most species-rich genera in North America, having undergone rapid evolution particularly in arid regions in dry, lean, sunny habitats from deserts to mountain peaks. They have evolved closely with many butterfly species for which they are important nectar sources and often requisite larval hosts.

The high species diversity and wide variation within species offers much horticultural potential. Some species may be successful in diverse climate regions, while others may be limited to drier climates or, with less hardy varieties such as E. grande var. *rubescens*, to California and other regions with mild climates.

Perennials, subshrubs, or shrubs, producing attractive umbels of white, yellow, pink, or red flowers atop green, gray-green, bluish green, or silver foliage.

CULTURE/CARE Dry, rocky, lean soils in full sun with good air circulation.

USES Valuable for consistently dry sites such as unirrigated areas, hell strips, dry banks, and rock gardens from small applications to large mass plantings. Not tolerant of foot traffic. Deer and rabbit resistant. Attractive to pollinators, especially bees, butterflies, and hummingbirds.

PROPAGATION Seed

Eriogonum allenii
SHALE BARRENS BUCKWHEAT

Zones 5–10

Rocky shale slopes in oak and pine woodlands in Virginia and West Virginia.

A lush, leafy species with large, oblong, gray-green foliage up to 6 in. (15 cm) long from a central rosette forming mounds 6 in. (15 cm) tall and 20–40 in. (50–100 cm) wide, topped with long-flowering, bright yellow umbels on stems to 16 in. (40 cm) tall, becoming interesting seed heads. Foliage is semi-evergreen, especially in milder climates, developing shades of bronzy orange in fall and winter.

'Little Rascal': short, compact, uniform plants and more attractive umbels

Eriogonum umbellatum
SULFUR FLOWER, SULFUR BUCKWHEAT

Zones 3–8

Diverse dry habitats from British Columbia and Alberta, south to Mexico.

A widespread and incredibly diverse species, with 41 different taxonomic varieties and much potential for horticulture. Long-lived plants form mats or mounds of oblong to elliptic, gray-green to silver, evergreen leaves and showy umbels of bright sulfur-yellow flowers in early summer, frequently developing fiery tones with age.

var. *aureum* 'Psdowns' Kannah Creek: sulfur-yellow flowers in late spring develop orange and orange-red tones with age, with burgundy winter foliage

'Gentle Giant': large plants, 18–24 in. (45–60 cm) tall and up to 28 in. (71 cm) wide, with silver leaves, hardy to zone 4

'Poncha Pass Red': dwarf plants, 4–6 in. (10–15 cm) tall by 12–15 in. (30–38 cm) wide, with gray-green foliage and deep red seed heads in late summer

'Proliferum': compact, dome-shaped plants, 12 in. (30 cm) tall and 18 in. (45 cm) wide, with gray-green leaves with white undersides and a profuse flower display, hardy to zone 4

'Shasta Sulfur': gray-green leaves with white undersides in mounds 12 in. (30 cm) tall by 24 in. (60 cm) wide or larger, with lemon-yellow flowers in spherical clusters on each umbel, hardy to zone 5

Eriogonum umbellatum var. *aureum* 'Psdowns' Kannah Creek

(LEFT) *Eriogonum allenii* 'Little Rascal'

Eriogonum wrightii var. wrightii
SNOW MESA BUCKWHEAT

Zones 4–9

Gravelly or rocky slopes, mixed grasslands, and open woodlands from California to Texas and south into Mexico.

Mounds of spreading and erect stems, 20 in. (50 cm) tall by 18–24 in. (45–60 cm) wide, with small, smooth to fuzzy, silver leaves completely obscured from late summer to late fall by masses of white to pale pink flowers aging to tan.

Erodium
Geraniaceae

These lesser known cranesbill cousins form compact mounds or mats of attractive, often dissected, weed-suppressing foliage and small flowers resembling those of their kin. They can be extremely long-blooming in shades of white, pale yellow, and pink. In addition to the commonly grown species and hybrids, other options include E. absinthoides, E. glandulosum, E. guttatum, and E. ×kolbianum 'Natasha', and hybrids such as E. 'Fran's Delight' and E. 'Stephanie'.

CULTURE/CARE Excellent drainage in full sun. Tolerant of hot, dry sites.

USES Mass plant to form a closed cover for small applications along pathways, at the front of borders, and in rock gardens and troughs. Clumps develop slowly. Not tolerant of foot traffic. Attractive to pollinators, especially bees.

PROPAGATION Seed, division, cuttings

Erodium chrysanthum
SILVER HERONSBILL, YELLOW HERONSBILL

Zones (5)6–9

Open, stony, calcareous habitats of central and southern Greece.

Dense, evergreen tufts or mounds, 6 in. (15 cm) tall by 18 in. (45 cm) wide, of silvery green, twice pinnate, hairy, fernlike leaves with creamy yellow (occasionally pink), lemon-scented flowers from spring until fall, blooming up to nine months in mild climates. Plants are dioecious, requiring plants of both sexes to produce the female's unique beaked fruits.

Erodium manescavii
STORKSBILL, HERONSBILL

Zones 5–9

Grasslands of the western and central Pyrenees.

Lush, green, finely dissected, fernlike leaves up to 12 in. (30 cm) long, in mounds to 18 in. (45 cm) tall and wide. Thin stems emerge continuously from early summer into fall, with 1 in. (2.5 cm) wide, deep pink to magenta flowers, centrally frosted with lavender and lined with dark purple veins.

Erodium reichardii
STORKSBILL, HERONSBILL

Zones 6 or 7–9

Damp, rocky areas in the Balearic Islands.

A compact, diminutive, evergreen to semi-evergreen plant, 2–4 in. (5–10 cm) tall and 10 in. (25 cm) wide, with densely held, rounded green leaves with scalloped edges and long-blooming, solitary white flowers often veined and blushed with pink. A cross with E. corsicum created the commonly grown E. ×variabile hybrids.

'Album': white flowers with pink veins

'Charm': pale pink flowers with dark pink veins

E. ×variabile 'Album': white flowers with pink veins

E. ×variabile 'Bishop's Form': glowing pink double flowers with magenta veins

E. ×variabile 'Flore Pleno': glowing pink flowers with magenta veins and white splotches

E. ×variabile 'Roseum': pink flowers with dark pink veins

Eryngium
Apiaceae

Resembling thistles more than carrots, the sea hollies, with their spiky, true-blue flowers and subtending bracts, are usually accent plants in perennial borders. A few species, however, with thick masses of leathery foliage, can be used as mass-planted ground covers.

CULTURE/CARE Full sun in average to dry, well-drained, poor to moderately fertile soils. Salt tolerant. Eryngium variifolium is tolerant of some winter and spring moisture in well-draining soils.

USES Mass plant for small to medium-sized applications at the front of borders or along pathways. Not tolerant of foot traffic. Deer and rabbit resistant. Attractive to pollinators, especially bees and butterflies.

PROPAGATION Division, root cuttings, seed

Erodium chrysanthum

Erodium ×*variabile* 'Bishop's Form'

Eryngium variifolium

Eryngium bourgatii
MEDITERRANEAN SEA HOLLY

Zones (4)5–9

Dry, stony, open habitats of the Mediterranean Basin from Spain and Morocco to Turkey and Lebanon.

Distinctive in foliage and flower, with low, herbaceous mounds up to 18 in. (45 cm) wide of multidissected, green to blue-green, spiny leaves with silver-white veins topped with branching flowering stems, 18–24 in. (45–60 cm) tall, in mid- to late summer. The thimblelike flower heads are packed with tiny blue flowers and subtended by a collar of spiny, thistlelike bracts up to 2 in. (5 cm) long in shades of blue, silver, and grayish green. Cultivars such as 'Oxford Blue', 'Picos Amethyst', and 'Picos Blue' are popular in the United Kingdom but absent from North America.

Eryngium variifolium
MOROCCAN SEA HOLLY, MARBLE-LEAF SEA HOLLY

Zones (4)5–9

Temporarily flooded habitats (most likely in winter and spring) such as along streams, in fens, and in depressions in the mountainous areas of Morocco.

An evergreen, rosetted perennial, forming low clumps, 10–12 in. (25–30 cm) wide, of shiny, leathery, dark green, serrated, heart-shaped leaves with white veins, held on long stems like spoons. Flowering spikes are 12–16 in. (30–40 cm) tall, with thimblelike heads of tiny lavender-blue to silver-blue flowers subtended by long, narrow, lance-shaped, branching, pointed (and quite menacing!) silver-white bracts.

Erysimum
Brassicaceae

The evergreen perennial wallflowers are ground-hugging mats or mounding subshrubs with racemes of four-petaled, often fragrant flowers in a range of colors that change with age in certain cultivars. Inflorescences can bloom for long periods, elongating high above the foliage, as seed pods form below the blooming tips.

CULTURE/CARE Long-lived and compact in hot, dry situations with poor to moderately fertile soils. Short-lived, leggy, and prone to decline in rich, overly moist soils. Tolerant of salt and coastal situations. Shear unsightly elongated flowering stems to tidy up and encourage rebloom, and shear 1–2 in. (2.5–5 cm) of foliage after flowering to encourage more compact habit. Plants can be rejuvenated with a hard prune usually to 6 in. (15 cm) in spring once new growth has started; plants may not reflush well if too heavily pruned.

USES The slow-growing, mat-forming types are tolerant of light foot traffic and are useful for small applications in rock gardens and crevices and between paving stones. The subshrub forms are not tolerant of foot traffic and should be mass planted in small to large areas in rock gardens and dry gardens, on sunny banks, along roadsides and driveways, and in other dry sites. Deer and rabbit resistant. Attractive to pollinators, especially bees, butterflies, and hummingbirds.

PROPAGATION Cuttings, seed

Erysimum kotschyanum
CREEPING GOLD WALLFLOWER,
ALPINE WALLFLOWER

Zones 4–9
Rocky slopes and screes in alpine regions of Turkey.
A diminutive, long-lived, evergreen stoloniferous species, forming dense mounds or mats, 1–2 in. (2.5–5 cm) tall and 12–24 in. (30–60 cm) wide, of midgreen leaves with jagged edges. Bright lemonyellow, sweet and spicy fragrant flowers emerge from muted deep pink buds in early spring, along with crocuses and forsythias.

Erysimum hybrids

Zones 5, 6 or 7–9
Garden origin.
The majority of subshrubby cultivars are of hybrid origin, likely involving *E. mutabile, E. linifolium, E. cheiri,* and others. They typically form evergreen mounds, 12–24 in. (30–60 cm) tall and wide (unless otherwise stated), with flowers blooming over a long period from early spring until summer, with possible fall rebloom.

'Apricot Twist': purple buds open to fragrant, bright tangerine-orange flowers, zone 6

'Bowles's Mauve': most common cultivar with purple buds and nonfragrant lavender to warm purple flowers, 24–36 in. (60–90 cm) tall and wide, zone 6

'Bowles Me Away': more compact than 'Bowles's Mauve', does not require vernalization to bloom, zone 6

'Constant Cheer': purple buds open to fragrant, orange-coral flowers aging to a warm, light purple, zone 6

Erysistible Series: hardy, compact, well-branched, upright mounds, 16–22 in. (40–56 cm) tall, with large, multicolored flowers changing as they age, includes 'Erysistible Magenta', 'Erysistible Sunset', 'Erysistible Tricolor', and 'Erysistible Yellow', zone 5

Glow Series: hardy, low-growing mats or mounds of dense, ground-hugging foliage, 12 in. (30 cm) or more wide with honey-scented flowers in yellow and orange shades, includes Bright Gold, Coral, Golden, Mango, and Orange, zone 5

'Golden Jubilee': short, mat-forming cultivar resembling a larger *E. kotschyanum,* to 6 in. (15 cm) tall and 8 in. (20 cm) or more wide, with fragrant lemon-yellow flowers, zone 6

'John Codrington': warm purple buds open to fragrant yellow flowers aging to peachy pink on compact plants, 12 in. (30 cm) tall and wide, zone 6

'Variegatum': variegated form of *E. linifolium* from Spain and Portugal forming a bushy subshrub, 18 in. (45 cm) tall and wide, with warm purple buds opening to lavender or coral-rose flowers aging to light purple, zone 7

'Walfrastar' Walberton's Fragrant Star: cream-variegated sport of 'Walfrasun'

'Walfrasun' Walberton's Fragrant Sunshine: muted purple buds open to fragrant golden yellow flowers on mounds 18 in. (45 cm) tall by 24 in. (60 cm) wide, zone 6

'Wenlock Beauty': warm purple buds open to reddish coral flowers, aging to light purple, zone 5

Euonymus fortunei
WINTERCREEPER, FORTUNE'S SPINDLE

Celastraceae

Zones 4 or 5–9
Woodlands, scrub, and forests from low to high elevations over much of East and Southeast Asia including China, Korea, and Japan.
Wintercreeper is an evergreen shrub or vine with thick, leathery, matte to glossy, lance-, egg-, or oval-shaped leaves on stems that can root into the ground or attach to vertical surfaces. A range of variation within wild populations offers three habits for horticulture: low-growing, trailing ground covers; mounding forms wider than they are tall with upright, arching, and horizontal stems; and large, upright, rounded shrubs (not included here). Despite a utilitarian reputation, wintercreepers are durable and

Erysimum linifolium 'Variegatum'

Euonymus fortunei 'Coloratus'

Euonymus fortunei 'Emerald 'n' Gold'

beautiful, offering diverse variegations and hardiness rare for an evergreen species. Flowers are green and inconspicuous. Considered an invasive weed in some regions, such as the eastern United States, but benign in others.

CULTURE/CARE Easy to grow and tough as nails, in sun to shade in a wide range of soil types and moisture regimes. Tolerant of periodic drought.

USES Mounding forms (as well as large upright cultivars such as 'Emerald Gaiety', 'Sarcoxie', and 'Sunspot') can be sheared flat or cloud pruned to maintain lower specimens or left as is as tall ground covers. Trailing cultivars are tolerant of occasional foot traffic and could be used as lawn alternatives, including 'Coloratus', 'Kewensis', 'Minimus', and 'Wolong Ghost'. New plantings grow slowly at first.

PROPAGATION Cuttings

'Canadale Gold': mounding habit, 2–3 ft. (0.6–1 m) tall by 3–4 ft. (1–1.2 m) wide, with green leaves edged in bright yellow, zone 5

'Coloratus': purpleleaf wintercreeper, trailing habit, 12–18 in. (30–45 cm) tall by 6–8 ft. (1.8–2.4 m) wide, with green leaves with lighter veins, flushed red and purple in colder months, zone 4

'Emerald 'n' Gold': mounding habit, 12–24 in. (30–60 cm) tall by 3–4 ft. (1–1.2 m) wide, with small, golden yellow leaves with variable green central markings, zone 5, AGM

'Harlequin': mounding habit, 12–18 in. (30–45 cm) tall by 36 in. (90 cm) wide, with small leaves emerging icy white and developing green speckles, slowly turning green with white speckles

'Hoogi' Golden Harlequin: creamy yellow to gold variegated form of 'Harlequin', zone 5

'Interbolwi' Blondy: mounding habit, 18–24 in. (45–60 cm) tall and wide, possibly wider, with larger, deep green leaves with variable golden yellow centers, zone 5

'Kewensis': trailing habit, 2–4 in. (5–10 cm) tall, spreading indefinitely, with tiny deep green leaves with lighter veins, producing textured carpets, zone 4

'Minimus': similar to 'Kewensis'

'Moonshadow': mounding habit, 24 in. (60 cm) tall by 5 ft. (1.5 m) wide, with larger deep green leaves with variable creamy yellow to golden yellow centers, zone 4

'Roemertwo' Gold Splash: mounding habit, 18–24 in. (45–60 cm) tall and wide, with golden leaves with variable green centers, zone 5

'Tricolor': mounding habit, 12–36 in. (30–90 cm) tall by 3–4 ft. (1–1.2 m) wide, green leaves with creamy white edges, zone 5

'Waldbolwi' Goldy: mounding habit, 18–24 in. (45–60 cm) tall and wide, with golden leaves, zone 5

'Wolong Ghost': trailing habit, 6–10 in. (15–25 cm) tall, spreading indefinitely, with linear, dark green leaves with bold, silver-green veins, zone 4, AGM

Euphorbia
Euphorbiaceae

Spurges are sun-loving, drought tolerant, easy to grow, mounding or rhizomatous perennials with boldly textured, colorful, and sometimes succulentlike foliage, offering distinctive specimens or textured ground covers. Their electric-green to bright yellow flowers provide unusual floral interest over a long season in spring and summer.

In addition to those covered here, several other evergreen species and cultivars offer short, shrubby habits and can, if mass-planted, form effective ground covers for small to large sites, including *E. amygdaloides* 'Purpurea' and 'Waleuphglo' Ruby Glow; short cultivars of *E. characias* such as 'Glacier Blue' and subsp. *wulfenii* 'Shorty'; cultivars of *E. ×martini* including 'Ascot Rainbow', 'Inneuphhel' Helena's Blush, and 'Waleutiny' Tiny Tim; and more complex hybrids such as 'Nothowlee' Blackbird and 'Charam' Red Wing.

CULTURE/CARE Average to dry, well-drained soils in full to part sun except *E. amygdaloides* var. *robbiae*, which prefers part sun to shade, including dry shade. Both *E. myrsinites* and *E. rigida* are drought tolerant, while *E. cyparissias*, *E. amygdaloides* var. *robbiae*, and *E. epithymoides* are somewhat drought tolerant but appreciate more mesic conditions. Remove dried flower heads to the top of the foliage. Cut back old stems to their base when leaves turn brown. Do not remove stems of evergreen species that have not yet bloomed, because they will bloom the following spring. All spurges contain poisonous white latex that should be washed off the skin immediately to avoid possible ill effects. Take care to avoid touching mucous membranes of the eyes, nose, and mouth after working with spurges.

USES Mass plant *E. myrsinites*, *E. rigida*, and *E. epithymoides* in beds, on banks, at the top of walls, and in rock gardens. Plant *E. cyparissias* and *E. amygdaloides* var. *robbiae* in areas contained by hardscape or where their spreading habit is desirable. None are tolerant of foot traffic. Deer and rabbit resistant.

PROPAGATION Seed, division, cuttings

Euphorbia amygdaloides var. *robbiae*
WOOD SPURGE, MRS. ROBB'S BONNET

Zones 5–8
Woodlands in Europe, Turkey, and the Caucasus.

Large, lush, dark green leaves flushed purple beneath and up to 3 in. (7.5 cm) long in whorls surrounding vertical stems, 8–12 in. (20–30 cm) tall, topped with 8 in. (20 cm) inflorescences of small flowers with large and rounded, light green, chartreuse, or yellow bracts. Foliage can develop a purple tone in winter. Unlike the other varieties of the species, var. *robbiae* spreads vigorously via rhizomes, especially in loose, richer soils, forming bold, leafy, ever-expanding colonies. AGM

'Blue Lagoon': hybrid with *E. characias*, mostly resembling and performing like var. *robbiae*, but larger, with bluish green leaves and red-flushed new growth

Euphorbia cyparissias
CYPRESS SPURGE

Zones 4–8
Dunes, coastal headlands and grasslands, and disturbed habitats in Europe.

A small, dainty herbaceous spurge with erect stems 6–12 in. (15–30 cm) tall, spreading quickly and indefinitely by rhizomes to form dense, highly textured mats of narrow, linear, blue-green foliage resembling little conifer trees. Heads of tiny flowers are subtended by electric-green to bright yellow bracts in spring. Considered a noxious weed in some regions and too territorially ambitious by many gardeners.

'Fens Ruby': foliage and stems emerge burgundy in spring, contrasting with the bright flowers, and then turn blue-green with burgundy tints by summer

'Orange Man': electric-green flowers develop orange and orange-red tints

Euphorbia epithymoides
CUSHION SPURGE, CHROME SPURGE

Zones (3)4–8

Rocky hillsides and open, dry woodlands in Central and Southeastern Europe, Asia Minor, and Libya.

Long known as *E. polychroma*, cushion spurge forms attractive herbaceous domes, 18 in. (45 cm) tall and 18–24 in. (45–60 cm) wide, with lush, midgreen foliage topped with showy clusters of glowing chartreuse bracts in early to midspring. Foliage develops gold and red tones in fall.

'Bonfire': red- and burgundy-infused foliage with deep burgundy-red to purple-red fall color and chartreuse flower bracts with flushes of orange

'Candy': blue-green foliage purple-flushed when young

'First Blush': long, narrow, lightly ruffled gray-green leaves and bracts with creamy white edges flushed pink in cool weather, and reddish pink fall color

'Lacy': leaves and bracts gray-green with ruffled, creamy white edges flushed pink in cool weather

Euphorbia epithymoides

Euphorbia amygdaloides var. *robbiae*

Euphorbia epithymoides 'Bonfire'

Euphorbia cyparissias

Euphorbia myrsinites
DONKEYTAIL SPURGE, MYRTLE SPURGE

Zones 5–9
Sunny, rocky places in Southern Europe from the Balearic Islands to Asia Minor.

An evergreen spurge forming clumps, 6–8 in. (15–20 cm) tall and 18–24 in. (45–60 cm) wide, of sprawling, ascending, and prostrate stems covered in spirals of grayish blue to powder-blue, semisucculent, pointed leaves. Flower clusters borne at the stem tips in spring are rounded umbels, with small flowers subtended by chartreuse bracts. Considered invasive in some regions of western North America. Salt tolerant. AGM

Euphorbia rigida
SILVER SPURGE, GOPHER SPURGE

Zones 7–10
Sunny, rocky habitats from the Mediterranean Basin into southwestern Asia.

Resembling the hardier, more common *E. myrsinites* but with narrower, more linear bluish foliage and a more upright habit, with upright stems eventually becoming prostrate, forming textural clumps, 12–24 in. (30–60 cm) tall and up to 36 in. (90 cm) wide. AGM

Euphorbia nicaeensis, which resembles *E. rigida* but is uncommonly cultivated, has been crossed with *E. seguieriana* subsp. *niciciana* to create *E.* 'Blue Haze', which can be mass-planted as a ground cover. This clumping evergreen perennial has narrow, finely textured, lance-shaped, powder-blue foliage on upright and prostrate stems with chartreuse flowers in spring.

Eurybia
Asteraceae

Recent phylogenetic work has moved the North American species of *Aster* into new genera, including *Eurybia*. New names, however, take nothing away from the value of certain species as ground covers. Chief among them are three shade-loving species: *E. divaricata* (white wood aster), *E. macrophylla* (bigleaf aster), and *Symphyotrichum cordifolium* (blue wood aster), which can form extensive colonies and provide uncommon late-season color in the woodland garden.

CULTURE/CARE Easy to grow in average to dryish soils in part sun to shade, though plants remain fresher with reasonable moisture. Stems are more upright in higher light conditions and more arching to lax with less light. Some colonies can be shy to flower, resulting from low fertility, light, or moisture.

USES Shade and woodland gardens under trees and large shrubs, on slopes, and along pathways. *Eurybia divaricata* and its relative *Symphyotrichum cordifolium* are good fillers among other shade plants, with sprawling stems that will intermingle with neighbors. Not tolerant of foot traffic. Deer resistant. Attractive to pollinators, especially bees and butterflies.

PROPAGATION Division

Eurybia divaricata
WHITE WOOD ASTER

Zones 3–8
Dry to mesic, open deciduous and mixed woods, clearings, roadsides, and forest edges in eastern North America from southern Quebec and Ontario through the Appalachians almost to Florida.

Previously known as *Aster divaricatus*, forming dense, rhizomatous, herbaceous colonies, with green to black stems, 12–36 in. (30–90 cm) long, topped with airy clouds of tiny white flowers with yellow centers in late summer and fall. Stems are upright or arching in sun but sprawl and weave into a billowy carpet in shade. Foliage is midgreen and thin with serrated margins.

'Eastern Star': shorter than the species with shiny, mahogany colored to jet-black stems, 18–24 in. (45–60 cm) long

Eurybia macrophylla
BIGLEAF ASTER, LARGE-LEAVED ASTER

Zones 3–8
Moist to dry soils in deciduous, mixed, or coniferous forests, thickets, clearings, and shaded roadsides in much of eastern North America except the Deep South.

Previously known as *Aster macrophyllus*, forming dense, rhizomatous, herbaceous colonies with large, somewhat heart-shaped, rough-textured leaves with serrated edges, to 4–10 in. (10–25 cm) long and 2–6 in. (5–15 cm) wide. Upright to arching stems, 12–36 in. (30–90 cm) tall, with open clusters of violet to bluish lavender or white flowers with yellow centers in late summer and fall.

'Albus': white flowers

Euphorbia myrsinites

Euphorbia rigida

Eurybia divaricata

Eurybia macrophylla

F

Festuca
Poaceae

Fescues are best loved for their mounds of thin, wirelike, textural foliage in tones of greenish blue to powder-blue that can make for a dramatic mass-planted ground cover. They sometimes have a reputation as short-lived plants, but this occurs primarily because of overly moist or overly rich soils. Given full sun and dryish conditions, they can make a bold statement for many years. *Festuca glauca* is the most popular species, though other blue-leaved relatives are available, especially in the North American West, including *F. amethystina*, *F. mairei*, *F. idahoensis*, and *F. californica*.

CULTURE/CARE Full sun in average to dry soils with average to low fertility, even more so for *F. gautieri*; these conditions increase longevity and foliage color intensity. If soils are too moist or rich, plants can fail, usually over the winter but sometimes resulting from continuous summer irrigation. Avoid hot, humid conditions. Though they are drought and salt tolerant, occasional deep watering in summer can maintain freshness. In early spring, comb out dead leaves with your fingers or a leaf rake, or shear back to 2 in. (5 cm). Division may be required every three years in some garden situations if clumps die out in the centers.

USES Mass plant in small to large areas as an edger for pathways or borders or in rock gardens and xeriscapes. *Festuca gautieri* should be planted in rock gardens, troughs, or other areas with excellent drainage. Fescues must be planted closely together to outcompete weeds. Even then, an interplanting with low-growing, trailing, weed-suppressing ground covers is encouraged, such as *Arctostaphylos uva-ursi*; *Sedum spurium*, *S. rupestre* 'Angelina', or *S. tetractinum*; or *Thymus pseudolanuginosus*. Not tolerant of foot traffic. Deer resistant.

PROPAGATION Division, seed

Festuca gautieri
BEARSKIN FESCUE, SPIKY FESCUE

Zones 4–9
Dry, open habitats in the Pyrenees.
Formerly known as *F. scoparia*, this evergreen to semi-evergreen tufted grass forms compact, pincushiony mounds of short, prickly, needlelike, bright green leaves, 2–6 in. (5–15 cm) tall and 12–18 in. (30–45 cm) wide, with flowering stems 6–12 in. (15–30 cm) tall.

Festuca glauca
BLUE FESCUE

Zones (3)4–9
Dry, sunny habitats from Central and Southern Europe to Turkey.
An evergreen to semi-evergreen perennial bunch or tufted grass with thin, needlelike, greenish blue, silver-blue, or powder-blue leaves, radiating in all directions and forming textural mounds, 6–10 in. (15–25 cm) tall and 12–18 in. (30–45 cm) wide. The inflorescences and their stems, to 10–14 in. (25–35 cm) tall, are at first blue, sometimes purple-tinged, aging to tan.

'Blaufuchs' (syn. 'Blue Fox'): greenish blue foliage integrates well with naturalistic plantings

'Blauglut' (syn. 'Blue Glow'): icy blue foliage

'Boulder Blue': powder-blue foliage, slightly more compact than 'Elijah Blue' and possibly tougher and more drought tolerant

'Casca11' Beyond Blue: among the bluest of cultivars, holding color well through summer, known as 'Casblue' Intense Blue in Europe

'Cool as Ice': greenish blue in spring, intensifying to powder-blue in summer, with good heat tolerance

'Elijah Blue': the most popular cultivar, a strong performer with excellent powder-blue to icy blue color held through the season

'Golden Toupee': chartreuse to glowing gold foliage on compact, less vigorous plants

'Pepindale Blue': powder-blue foliage, slightly finer and more silver than 'Elijah Blue'

'Seeigel' (syn. 'Sea Urchin'): compact, dense habit with rigid leaves

'Siskiyou Blue': likely a hybrid with *F. idahoensis*, with longer, more arching foliage than *F. glauca*

Festuca glauca

Ficaria verna 'Coppernob' with *Primula vulgaris*

Ficaria verna

LESSER CELANDINE, FIG BUTTERCUP

Ranunculaceae

Zones 4–8

Along water courses including ditches, streambanks, and pond edges, and in wet meadows, forests, and parks across Europe into North Africa and the Middle East.

A spring ephemeral, previously known as *Ranunculus ficaria*, emerging in late winter to early spring and going dormant by early summer. It produces shiny, heart- or kidney-shaped, dark green leaves about 1 in. (2.5 cm) across in dense mats, 1–4 in. (2.5–10 cm) tall and 6 in. (15 cm) wide, topped with bright yellow, narrow-petaled, starlike buttercups. Bulbils produced in the lower leaf axils allow for quick spread into large colonies. Embraced as a harbinger of spring in its native Europe, it is considered invasive in the Pacific Northwest and eastern North America, where it can carpet average to moist forest floors, excluding native species and leaving ground open to erosion when dormant. The named cultivars are often better behaved.

CULTURE/CARE Full sun to shade in average to moist, fertile soils including seasonally wet or flooded sites. Less moisture will reduce vigor.

USES Beneath deciduous shrubs and trees, around late-emerging perennials such as hostas and ferns or as a marker for late-emerging bulbs or perennials, or in combination with other ground covers. Not tolerant of foot traffic.

PROPAGATION Division of rhizomes, bulbils

Alba Group: white petals with coppery reverses

'Brambling': leaves mottled green, black, and silver

'Brazen Hussy': burgundy-black leaves

'Collarette': tight, green-eyed, yellow pom-pom flowers, subtended by normal single petals, with green leaves marked in burgundy and silver

'Coppernob': coppery yellow-orange flowers fading to almost white around orange centers, with burgundy foliage

'Double Mud': grayish purple buds reveal pale yellow to greenish yellow double flowers, with burgundy-mottled foliage

Flore Pleno Group: double pom-pom flowers, yellow with green centers

'Green Petal': double flowers with irregular green and yellow markings

'Salmon's White': creamy white flowers from bluish purple buds, with lightly silver-mottled leaves

Filipendula
Rosaceae

Meadowsweets are tough, hardy, deer-resistant, clumping perennials. Shorter *Filipendula* species can act as mass-planted ground covers with lush, low mounds of textural foliage topped with frothy flowers on short stems or with tall, see-through stems raising the flowers high above the leaves.

CULTURE/CARE Full sun to part shade for *F. multijuga* in average to evenly moist, fertile soils with afternoon shade in hot summer climates. *Filipendula vulgaris* prefers part shade in average soils and is tolerant of periodic drought.

USES Mass plantings in small to large areas. Not tolerant of foot traffic. Deer and rabbit resistant. Attractive to pollinators, especially bees and butterflies.

PROPAGATION Division, seed

Filipendula multijuga
DWARF MEADOWSWEET, ALPINE DROPWORT

Zones 3–9
Mountains of central and southern Japan.
Formerly known as *F. palmata* 'Nana', dwarf meadowsweet is a clumping, herbaceous perennial with textured, light to midgreen, palmate foliage resembling maple leaves, forming lush clumps, 8–12 in. (20–30 cm) tall and 12 in. (30 cm) or more wide. In early summer, reddish, branching stems, 16–24 in. (40–60 cm) tall, are topped with a finely textured froth of tiny, fragrant, light to glowing pink flowers.

'Kahome': possibly a hybrid with *F. purpurea*, with fragrant, frothy, pink flowers on small plants, 12 in. (30 cm) tall and wide

'Red Umbrellas': hybrid with *F. palmata*, with pink flowers and highly textured palmate leaves, light to midgreen, with central veins flushed dramatically with burgundy, 24–30 in. (60–75 cm) tall and nearly as wide

Filipendula vulgaris
FERN-LEAF DROPWORT

Zones 2–9
Dry, calcareous grasslands and pastures from Europe and northern Africa to Central and North Asia.
Herbaceous perennial with highly dissected, fernlike foliage, 4–10 in. (10–25 cm) long, resembling yarrow, in mounds 12 in. (30 cm) tall and 20 in. (50 cm)

Filipendula 'Kahome'

wide, with 24–36 in. (60–90 cm) tall, leafless, reddish stems branching into numerous white to pink buds that open to frothy white to creamy white flowers. May slowly spread by rhizomes. Crushed foliage smells of wintergreen.

'Multiplex' (syn. 'Flore Pleno'): double flowers

Fragaria
Rosaceae

The beloved strawberry has mid- to deep green, often glossy, trifoliate leaves with serrated edges and prominent veins with small, roselike, single flowers with five white petals around yellow centers in spring. Most significantly, the plants produce tasty, red or sometimes yellowish or white, conical or heart-shaped, aggregate fruits—strawberries—that are grown worldwide in gardens and commercial fields. Their vigorous, stoloniferous habit makes many of them useful, beautiful, edible ground covers.

CULTURE/CARE Full sun to part shade in well-drained soils of average to rich fertility and average to even moisture. Tolerant of short periods of drought. *Fragaria chiloensis* is very drought and salt tolerant. Can be sheared down or mowed in late winter to refresh plants.

USES Small- to medium-scale plantings as a ground cover, lawn alternative, or slope stabilizer. Plants grow and spread quickly, though it may take time for rosettes to provide a closed cover. Tolerant of occasional foot traffic. Deer and rabbit resistant. Attractive to pollinators, especially bees.

PROPAGATION Division of plants or plantlets, seed

Fragaria 'Lipstick'

Fragaria ×*ananassa*
STRAWBERRY, GARDEN STRAWBERRY

Zones 3–9
Garden origin.

A hybrid between the white-fruited South American *F. chiloensis* subsp. *chiloensis* f. *chiloensis* and the North American *F. virginiana* subsp. *virginiana* that occurred by chance in Brittany, France, in the 1750s. The large, sweet fruit of *F.* ×*ananassa* soon replaced that of *F. vesca*, which had been cultivated in France since the early seventeenth century. The main commercial cultivars of garden strawberries could well be used as edible ground covers; however, these hybrids tend to decrease in productivity after a few years and can require replanting. Certain complex hybrids, including *F.* ×*ananassa* 'Frel' Pink Panda and *F.* 'Lipstick', are longer lived with attractive pink flowers. Recent introductions, many of which are seed strains, offer attractive pink or magenta flowers with medium-sized fruit. Their longevity is as yet untested.

Berri Basket Series: everbearing seed strains with pink, deep pink, and white flowers with medium-sized elongated fruit, includes 'Hot Pink', 'Pink', 'Rose', and 'White'

Berries Galore Series: everbearing seed strains with magenta, light pink, and white flowers producing medium-sized, rounded to elongated fruit, includes 'Rose', 'Pink', and 'White'

'Frel' Pink Panda: pink flowers and wild-type fruits on self-infertile plants (*F.* 'Lipstick' is a good pollinator), a strange, complex hybrid resulting from a cross between the garden strawberry and the deep pink-flowered *Comarum palustre* (formerly *Potentilla*), backcrossed five times to the garden strawberry, resulting in 96 percent *Fragaria* genes

'Gasana': pink flowers and medium-sized fruit, everbearing seed strain

'Lipstick': glowing magenta flowers on a self-infertile plant, produces wild-type fruit and was bred similarly to 'Frel' Pink Panda, which makes a good pollinator

'Toscana': magenta flowers and medium-sized fruit, everbearing seed strain

'Tristan': magenta flowers and medium-sized, elongated fruit, everbearing seed strain

'White Carolina' Aloha Berry: everbearing, medium-sized, white fruit called a pineberry because of its subtle pineapple flavor

F. ×*ananassa* 'Variegata': foliage with variable white edges, previously *F. vesca*

Fragaria chiloensis

Fragaria chiloensis
BEACH STRAWBERRY, COASTAL STRAWBERRY

Zones 4–9

Beaches, rocky coastal cliffs and headlands, and scrub along the Pacific Coast of North and South America, usually at low elevations and within the salt-spray zone.

Small, thick, leathery, dark green, shiny, silky-haired, evergreen foliage, with leaflets 1–2 in. (2.5–5 cm) long, on trioecious plants with white flowers that can be male, female, or perfect (both male and female). Plants grow 2–6 in. (5–15 cm) tall, spreading indefinitely. Small, red fruits up to ⅔ in. (1.5 cm) long are white inside. Good drought tolerance. Foliage can develop red tones in cold weather. *Fragaria chiloensis* has been cultivated by the native peoples of Chile for more than 1000 years.

'Chaval': strong, vigorous selection

'Green Pastures': vigorous male selection with larger flowers and possibly larger leaves and more stolons

Fragaria vesca
ALPINE STRAWBERRY, EUROPEAN STRAWBERRY

Zones (3)4–10

Hillsides, meadows, open woodlands, embankments, roadsides, along paths, and in clearings in much of the Northern Hemisphere.

Thin, light to midgreen leaves, with leaflets 2.5 in. (6 cm) long, on stoloniferous plants, 4–8 in. (10–20 cm) tall, with small red fruit up to ¾ in. (2 cm) long.

'Alexandria' (syn. 'Alexandra'): slightly larger fruit on runnerless plants that form robust clumps

'Golden Alexandria' (syn. 'Golden Alexandra'): lime-green to gold-foliaged form of 'Alexandria'

'Mignonette': seed strain with larger fruit

'White Soul': seed strain producing white fruit from runnerless plants

'Yellow Wonder': seed strain producing yellow fruit from runnerless plants

Fragaria virginiana
VIRGINIA STRAWBERRY, SCARLET STRAWBERRY

Zones 3–9

Moist to dry sites in open forests and forest edges, in hedgerows and fields, and along roadsides and railroads across North America.

Thin, light to midgreen or bluish green leaves on leaf stems up to 6 in. (15 cm) long, with leaflets 1–2.5 in. (2.5–6.5 cm) long, often developing red fall color. Stoloniferous plants are 4–8 in. (10–20 cm) tall, spreading indefinitely with trioecious flowers and small, red fruit about ½ in. (1.3 cm) long.

Francoa
Francoaceae

A small group of evergreen to semi-evergreen, rosette-forming species endemic to Chile, attractive in foliage and flower and useful as mass-planted ground covers, though they may spread slightly via short rhizomes. They form dense mounds up to 12 in. (30 cm) tall and 24 in. (60 cm) wide of large basal leaves that are deeply lobed, mid- to dark green, and fuzzy with winged appendages on their leaf stalks. In summer and fall, they are topped by leafless, airy, see-through, upright or arching wands (sometimes branching) of long-blooming, orchidlike, four-petaled pink or white flowers with deep pink markings that move in the breeze.

CULTURE/CARE Easy to grow in humus-rich, consistently moist soils in part sun to part shade. Provide more shade in hot summer climates. Tolerant of short dry periods.

USES Mass-planted dense mounds are impenetrable to weeds, making good substitutes for the more familiar species of *Brunnera*, *Geum*, *Heuchera*, ×*Heucherella*, and *Tiarella*. Not tolerant of foot traffic.

Francoa appendiculata

BRIDAL WREATH, MAIDEN'S WREATH

Zones 6–9

Steep slopes or ravines in thickets or forests in interior valleys and coastal mountains, from low to moderately high elevations in Chile.

Shell-pink to white flowers with deep pink markings on stems 24–36 in. (60–90 cm) tall and rippled, fuzzy, shiny, dark green leaves in mounded rosettes, 12–24 in. (30–60 cm) wide.

Francoa ramosa

BRIDAL WREATH, MAIDEN'S WREATH

Zones 7–10

Partly shaded habitats in Chile.

The longest flowering species with white to sometimes pale pink, unmarked flowers on stems 24–36 in. (60–90 cm) tall and scalloped, fuzzy, shiny, dark green leaves in mounded rosettes, 12–24 in. (30–60 cm) wide.

Francoa sonchifolia

BRIDAL WREATH, MAIDEN'S WREATH

Zones 7–9

Partly shaded habitats in Chile.

Rosy pink flowers with magenta markings on stems 24–32 in. (60–80 cm) tall, and rippled, fuzzy, shiny, dark green leaves in mounded rosettes, 12–18 in. (30–45cm) wide.

'Pink Giant': larger flowers on taller stems to 36 in. (90 cm)

'Rogerson's Form': bright pink flowers on dwarf plants, 12 in. (30 cm) tall

G

Galium odoratum

SWEET WOODRUFF, SWEETSCENTED BEDSTRAW

Rubiaceae

Zones 4–8

Widespread across Europe to Algeria, Asia Minor, and Asia, in woodlands, shaded habitats, and along streams and other moist places.

Sweet woodruff's dainty appearance and disarming moniker belie its hardiness, vigor, and rhizomatous determination, recognized in its German common name, *waldmeister*, or master of the woods. This herbaceous, edible, spreading ground cover forms dense, textural mats of upright stems, whorled with 6–9 narrowly elliptic midgreen leaves, 1–2 in. (2.5–5 cm) long, with clusters of small, pure white, lightly fragrant flowers, each with four reflexed petals, that are borne on stems 4–8 in. (10–20 cm) tall. Also known as bedstraw, it was once used to stuff mattresses and pillows, as the dried leaves, which contain coumarin, smell of vanilla.

CULTURE/CARE Prefers rich, acidic, evenly moist but well-drained soils. Tolerant of sandy and heavier clay soils. Best in part to full shade or morning sun.

USES A general ground cover over small to large areas, as a lawn alternative, between pavers and stepping stones, or at the base of shallowly rooted trees and shrubs, spreading at a moderate rate. It can spread into nearby plantings if left unchecked or not contained by hardscape. Not tolerant of foot traffic. Deer and rabbit resistant.

PROPAGATION Division

Francoa sonchifolia

Galium odoratum

Gaultheria
Ericaceae

Related to heaths and rhododendrons, with evergreen foliage and often edible fruits, this genus is best known for its wintergreen flavoring, from *G. procumbens*, and greenery for floral bouquets, from *G. shallon*. Other uncommon species can also be used as ground covers, including *G. cuneata*, *G. hispidula*, *G. miqueliana*, and *G. nummularioides*.

CULTURE/CARE Light shade in acidic, evenly moist soils rich in organic matter, or other evenly moist but free-draining soils. Flowers and fruit may be reduced in full shade. Rhizomes of *G. procumbens* occur just below the soil surface and will spread more quickly if the top layer is composed of loose, airy, organic matter.

USES *Gaultheria procumbens* spreads at a slow rate and should be planted densely in small applications along pathways, between stonework, and among the roots of trees and shrubs. *Gaultheria shallon* spreads at a moderate rate after establishment in naturalized plantings and under trees and shrubs. Not tolerant of foot traffic. Deer and rabbit resistant.

Gaultheria procumbens
COMMON WINTERGREEN, WINTERBERRY

Zones 3–7

Acidic and/or sandy soils in dry to mesic mixed or coniferous woodlands, powerline rights of way, road banks, old fields, maritime and montane heathlands, and bogs and fens from sea level to high elevations in eastern North America.

A lovely, rhizomatous or stoloniferous, aromatic, evergreen subshrub (semi-evergreen in colder climates) forming mats 3–6 in. (7.5–15 cm) tall. The shiny, broadly elliptic to oval, dark green foliage is 1–2 in. (2.5–5 cm) long, emerging copper-red and developing red and purple tones in winter. White to pinkish, urn-shaped, waxy, nodding spring flowers yield plump, round berries that age to deep red in fall and winter. Leaves and fruit are edible and used for tea and fresh eating, respectively, being the traditional source of wintergreen flavoring because of the presence of methyl salicylate, an anti-inflammatory and topical pain suppressor. AGM

PROPAGATION Division, seed

'Gaulbril' Winter Splash: variably white-variegated and mottled leaves flushed pink

Gaultheria procumbens

Gaultheria shallon

Gaura lindheimeri 'Crimson Butterflies'

'Gaulsidh5' Cherry Berries: extra large berries about double the size of the species

'Gaulsidh11' Berry Cascade: flowers and fruit along the length of the stems rather than just the tips

'Specgp11' Peppermint Pearl: white fruit

'Very Berry': heavily fruiting seed strain

Gaultheria shallon
SALAL

Zones 7–10

Dry to wet forests and bogs from low elevations to montane zones in coastal western North America.

Salal can be used as a tall or sheared ground cover, with its rhizomatous habit, upright stems, and lush, large, dark green foliage. In dry, sunnier positions, it does not grow tall, and it may not achieve a closed cover. In rich and moist soils, it forms spreading, mounded colonies, 3–6 ft. (1–1.8 m) tall. In extreme situations in its native habitat on the West Coast of Vancouver Island, salal can reach 8–10 ft. (2.4–3 m)! It can be kept sheared to any height, however. Purple-black berries are edible and were an important food source of indigenous peoples.

Gaura lindheimeri
BUTTERFLY GAURA, LINDHEIMER'S BEEBLOSSOM

Onagraceae

Zones (5)6–9

Prairies, pinelands, and pond edges in Louisiana, Oklahoma, and Texas.

Traditionally a border perennial, new dwarf cultivars with dense mounds of colorful foliage and flowers can be used as mass-planted ground covers. The dwarf forms are generally 12 in. (30 cm) tall and 18–24 in. (45–60 cm) wide, with woody bases and narrow, linear green leaves often suffused with burgundy. Short, vertical or arching, wandlike stems, 6–12 in. (15–30 cm) long, offer four-petaled pink or white flowers resembling butterflies from late spring through summer. Now known scientifically as *Oenothera lindheimeri*. AGM

CULTURE/CARE Full sun in hot, dry locations with average to thin soils. Occasional watering may be required during periods of drought. May not overwinter reliably in rich soils or in wet winter climates without sharp drainage. Shear lightly after flowering to encourage rebloom.

USES Small to medium-sized areas, especially in unamended and unirrigated sites. Mounds reach full size in one or two years. Not tolerant of foot traffic. Deer and rabbit resistant. Attractive to pollinators, especially bees and butterflies.

PROPAGATION Cuttings, seed

Height measurements include flowers; foliage height is about half to two-thirds of the flower height.

Ballerina Series: green leaves tinted burgundy, 18 in. (45 cm) tall by 14 in. (36 cm) wide, includes 'Baltinblus' Blush, 'Baltincite' White, and 'Baltinrose' Rose

Belleza Series: green leaves, 12–18 in. (30–45 cm) tall by 20 in. (50 cm) wide, includes 'Kleau04263' Dark Pink, 'Kleglo6261' Compact Light Pink, and 'Klegl14844' White Improved

'Crimson Butterflies': burgundy foliage, deep pink flowers, 24 in. (60 cm) tall and wide

Gaudi Series: green leaves tinted burgundy, 12 in. (30 cm) tall by 14 in. (36 cm) wide, includes 'Floragaured' Red, 'Florgaucompi' Pink, and 'Florgaucompro' Rose

'Harrosy' Rosy Jane: white flowers with pink picotee edges, green leaves, 18–24 in. (45–60 cm) tall and wide

'Little Janie': white flowers with pink tips, green foliage tinted burgundy, 18 in. (45 cm) tall by 16 in. (40 cm) wide

'Passionate Rainbow Petite': pink flowers with variegated green, reddish burgundy, white, and pink leaves, 18 in. (45 cm) tall by 20 in. (50 cm) wide

'Sme-2' Passionate Blush: pink flowers, green foliage tinted burgundy, 24 in. (60 cm) tall and wide

'So White': white flowers, green foliage, 24 in. (60 cm) tall and wide

'Whiskers Deep Rose': glowing deep pink flowers, green foliage tinted burgundy, 16 in. (40 cm) tall by 14 in. (36 cm) wide

Gaylussacia brachycera
BOX HUCKLEBERRY, BOX-LEAVED WHORTLEBERRY

Ericaceae

Zones 5–8

Upland and montane woods in the eastern United States from Pennsylvania to Tennessee.

A rhizomatous, evergreen blueberry relative thought to be among the longest living woody plants in the world, with a Pennsylvania colony estimated at 8000–13,000 years old that originally stretched for 6500 ft. (2 km) before a wildfire and construction destroyed 80 percent of it. Plants resemble boxwood with shiny, dark green, elliptic to oval leaves up to 1 in. (2.5 cm) long, with serrated edges on laterally spreading branches, 6–18 in. (15–45 cm) tall. Foliage color can be coppery when young, develop a red cast in full sun in summer, and turn bronzy to reddish purple in winter. Pendulous clusters of bell- or urn-shaped, white and pink–blushed spring flowers become edible, though flavorless, blueberry-like fruit. Clones are self-sterile.

CULTURE/CARE Full sun to part shade in evenly moist, well-drained, organically rich, acidic soils. Very little, if any, maintenance is required.

USES For small to medium-sized areas as a general cover, under larger shrubs and trees, and in naturalistic settings. Growth is somewhat slow to moderate. Stems extend about 6 in. (15 cm) each year. Rhizomes take time to establish and begin spreading. Not tolerant of foot traffic. Attractive to pollinators, especially bees and butterflies.

PROPAGATION Division, cuttings, seed

'Berried Treasure': differences from the species are unclear

Gazania linearis
TREASURE FLOWER

Asteraceae

Zones 4–9

Open grasslands, rocky slopes, along roadsides, and in disturbed areas at high elevations in the Drakensberg Mountains of Southern Africa.

A mat-forming, tap-rooted perennial up to 4 in. (10 cm) tall with narrow leaves, 4–5 in. (10–12.5 cm) long, that are shiny, dark green to gray-green above and white and woolly below. From late spring to fall, 3 in. (7.5 cm) wide flowers with golden centers and bright yellow ray petals, with or without brown bases, open in the morning just above the foliage and close at night. Plants may lose vigor over time but are usually replaced by new seedlings, a trait called "naturalizing" in some regions where reseeding is desirable, or "invasive" in others, such as California, where it is not.

CULTURE/CARE Hot and sunny to part sun locations with average to somewhat nutrient-poor, well-drained soils. Overly fertile sites may encourage lush foliage but poor flowering. Drought tolerant. Rebounds quickly after severe drought.

Gazania linearis 'Colorado Gold'

Gelsemium sempervirens 'Margarita'

USES Sites with marginal, rocky, sandy, or infertile soils including rock gardens, hell strips, dry slopes and banks as a soil stabilizer for erosion control, dry meadows, coastal sites, and at the front of the border. Not tolerant of foot traffic. Attractive to pollinators, especially bees and butterflies.

PROPAGATION Seed

'Colorado Gold': seed strain from open-pollinated crosses of multiple accessions at the Denver Botanic Gardens with greater vigor and hardiness than the parents, basal markings of the ray petals range from none to deep brown or black

Gelsemium sempervirens
CAROLINA JESSAMINE, TRUMPET FLOWER

Gelsemiaceae

Zones 6 or 7–9
Forest edges and clearings, thickets, along roadsides, and in open fields from Virginia south to Florida, west to Texas, and south to Central America.

An evergreen to semi-evergreen vine typically grown in milder climates on trellises and pergolas, with shiny, lance-shaped, dark green, 2–4 in. (5–10 cm) long leaves and masses of strongly fragrant, trumpet-shaped, golden yellow flowers, 1–2 in. (2.5–5 cm) long, held in loose clusters in spring and possibly reblooming in fall. Wiry, reddish brown stems can reach 10–20 ft. (3–6 m) long and, unsupported, can make a billowy, informal, ground-covering mat 12–36 in. (30–90 cm) tall with indefinite spread. All plant parts are poisonous. A rare relative, G. rankinii, the swamp jessamine, is twice-blooming in spring and fall, nonfragrant, and tolerant of wet soils.

CULTURE/CARE Full sun in average to moist, organically rich, well-drained soils for best blooming. Tolerant of part shade, periods of drought, salty seaside locations, and heat and humidity.

USES For medium-sized to large applications on flat ground or on banks and slopes for erosion control, spreading at a moderate rate. Not tolerant of foot traffic. Deer and rabbit resistant. Attractive to pollinators, especially bees, butterflies, and hummingbirds.

PROPAGATION Cuttings, seed

'Margarita': larger, more prominent flowers, one zone hardier than the species, to zone 6

'Pride of Augusta': double flowers

Genista
Fabaceae

Tough, wiry, low-growing shrubs with long, narrow, nearly leafless, green, photosynthetic stems that can be upright, arching, or prostrate, unbranched or branched. Forms dense, textural, mounded thickets of arching, interlocking branches with bright yellow, sometimes fragrant pea flowers in late spring or summer. Some rarer species may be useful, including G. hispanica and G. sagittalis. Others, such as G. tinctoria, are potentially invasive in some regions and have fallen from favor.

CULTURE/CARE Full sun in infertile, dry soils. Low maintenance. Drought tolerant. Shear after blooming if desired.

USES Small to large applications including dry gardens, rocky banks or slopes, rock gardens, hell strips, and other hot, dry sites. Slow to moderate growth rate. Tolerant of occasional foot traffic. Deer and rabbit resistant. Attractive to pollinators, especially bees and butterflies.

PROPAGATION Cuttings, seed

Genista lydia
LYDIAN BROOM, WOADWAXEN

Zones 3–9
Open sites among limestone rocks in Southeast Europe.

Plants with arching stems in mounds 18 in. (45 cm) tall by 48 in. (120 cm) wide, flowering in summer. AGM

'Select' Bangle: longer blooming for up to six weeks, possibly slightly more compact

Genista pilosa
CREEPING BROOM, SILKYLEAF WOADWAXEN

Zones (3)4–9
Open sites in sandy or stony soils or on cliffs in Western and Central Europe.

A bushy, upright shrub to 5 ft. (1.5 m) tall. Cultivars are all derived from prostrate forms.

'Gold Flash': stronger, more pliable stems to withstand breakage from foot traffic, 6–12 in. (15–30 cm) tall and 36 in. (90 cm) wide

'Procumbens': prostrate mats, 4–12 in. (10–30 cm) tall, AGM

'Vancouver Gold': prostrate growth, 3–8 in. (7.5–20 cm) tall by 24–36 in. (60–90 cm) or more wide, blooming from late spring to early summer, sterile

Gentiana
Gentianaceae

Gentians offer a touch of magic for small spaces, with low foliage mats topped with stunning, true-blue, trumpet-shaped flowers. Many species and cultivars are available from specialist nurseries, but only the easiest to grow and most commonly available are treated here. New hybrids such as 'Blue Silk', 'Eugen's Allerbester', 'Shot Silk', and 'Strathmore' are expanding the range and may perhaps lead to more quickly spreading, easier to grow forms.

CULTURE/CARE Best in cool summer climates in moderately rich, well-drained, evenly moist, acidic soils in full sun to part shade. In warmer summer climates, plant in part shade.

USES Small applications in rock gardens, along pathways, and at the front of borders. Not tolerant of foot traffic.

PROPAGATION Seed, division

Gentiana acaulis
TRUMPET GENTIAN, STEMLESS GENTIAN

Zones 3–9
High elevation acidic grasslands, stony areas, and bogs in the alpine of Central and Southern Europe.
Evergreen mats, 1–2 in. (2.5–5 cm) tall and 12 in. (30 cm) or more wide, of lush, shiny, lance-shaped to elliptic, midgreen foliage up to 2 in. (5 cm) long, topped with relatively large, 3 in. (7.5 cm) long, electric–royal blue, upward-facing trumpets with blue-freckled throats striped in green and white in late spring and summer. AGM

Gentiana septemfida
SUMMER GENTIAN, CRESTED GENTIAN

Zones 3–9
Alpine meadows and coniferous forests of Turkey, Iran, and the Caucasus.
Prostrate to ascending stems, 6–12 in. (15–30 cm) long, forming 12–24 in. (30–60 cm) wide mats of

Genista pilosa 'Vancouver Gold'

Gentiana 'Eugen's Allerbester'

Gentiana septemfida

lush, lance-shaped to heart-shaped, midgreen foliage up to 2 in. (5 cm) long. Stem tips and upper leaf axils produce clusters of royal-blue to purplish blue, upward-facing trumpets, 1¾ in. (4.5 cm) long, often with white stripes and dark purple-blue speckling in the throat in summer. *Gentiana septemfida* var. *lagodechiana* is more prostrate with fewer flowers and possibly more tolerant of heat and humidity. AGM

Gentiana sino-ornata
SHOWY CHINESE GENTIAN, AUTUMN GENTIAN

Zones (3)4–9
Mountain grasslands, wet alpine meadows, riverbanks, scrub, and forests at high elevations in Sichuan, Yunnan, and Tibet, China.

Dense, semi-evergreen mats of narrow, light to midgreen, grasslike foliage on trailing stems with ascending tips topped with solitary, upward-facing trumpets to 2⅓ in. (5.5 cm) long, usually in sky-blue to royal-blue (but sometimes purple-pink or pale yellow), with tubes striped in white, pale yellow, or dark purple-blue. AGM

Geranium
Geraniaceae

Cranesbills are one of the most beloved and popular groups of plants in temperate gardening. Although some species are rhizomatous ground covers, others with trailing or mounding habits can be mass-planted to fulfill this function. All have palmate leaves varying in overall size; in the number, degree of dissection, and size of the lobes; and in the relative smoothness or fuzziness of the leaf surface. Most are herbaceous, but some are evergreen to semi-evergreen. The flowers are five-petaled, usually 1–2 in. (2.5–5 cm) wide, and in shades of white, pink, purple, and blue. Some flowers have dark centers and veins. The seed heads, though not particularly showy, resemble a bird's bill, hence the common name.

Most of the hundreds of species, cultivars, and hybrids could be used as ground covers. Those with greater width than height are best. In addition to those treated here, others suitable for ground covers include rarer species such as *G. magniflorum* and its cultivar 'P013s' La Veta Lace, *G. orientalitibeticum*, and *G. platypetalum* 'Turco', along with taller or more upright species such as *G. phaeum* and its cultivars 'Album',

'Lily Lovell', 'Margaret Wilson', and 'Samobor'; *G. psilostemon*; and *G. sylvaticum* and its cultivars 'Album', 'Amy Doncaster', and 'Mayflower'.

CULTURE/CARE Easy to grow in full sun to part shade in average to evenly moist, well-drained, fertile soils. Some species are tolerant of drier conditions and full shade. Plants can be sheared to 2 in. (5 cm) tall or mown after flowering to refresh clumps and encourage rebloom.

USES Small species can be used for small to medium-sized areas along paths, at the front of the border, and in rock gardens, and larger species are useful for medium-sized to large plantings. Relatively fast-growing plants reach mature size within a couple seasons in good conditions. Not tolerant of foot traffic. Deer and rabbit resistant. Attractive to pollinators, especially bees and butterflies.

PROPAGATION Division, seed, cuttings

Geranium ×cantabrigiense
CRANESBILL

Zones 4–8
Garden origin.
These sterile hybrids of two rhizomatous species, *G. macrorrhizum* and *G. dalmaticum*, are among the best ground covers of the genus. Rhizomatous mats, 6–12 in. (15–30 cm) tall and 24 in. (60 cm) or more wide, have aromatic, evergreen to semi-evergreen, glossy, light green foliage developing orange and red tones in fall and winter. White to pink, long-lasting, 1 in. (2.5 cm) wide flowers bloom from late spring to early summer and sporadically thereafter. Tolerant of occasional drought and sandy and clay soils.

'Abpp' Crystal Rose: glowing magenta-pink flowers

'Biokovo': naturally occurring hybrid from Croatia's Biokova Mountains, with longish rhizomes and pink-flushed white flowers with pink stamens, Perennial Plant of the Year 2015

'Cambridge': mauve flowers with pink flushes

'Karmina': lilac-pink to deep pink flowers

'St Ola': similar to 'Biokovo' but possibly more vigorous, offers a white effect with pure white flowers blushed with less pink and with white stamens

'Westray': bright pink flowers, more compact plant

Geranium Cinereum Group
GRAYLEAF CRANESBILL, ASHY CRANESBILL

Zones 5–8, possibly zones 3 and 4

Mountain grasslands and shaded slopes in the Pyrenees Mountains.

Cinereum Group refers to a complex of closely related species and their hybrids from section Subacaulia, whose taxonomic identities have been in flux, at one time all falling under *G. cinereum* and more recently having been split into about 15 different species. Named cultivars could be selections of true *G. cinereum* or hybrids with its related species, depending on the taxonomic treatment. *Geranium* 'Ballerina', for instance, is a hybrid between *G. cinereum* and *G. subcaulescens*, which was once considered a subspecies of *G. cinereum*. The term Cinereum Group is used to contain the ambiguity within the naming of crosses within the section. This group offers compact plants forming mounds or trailing mats, 4–8 in. (10–20 cm) tall by 12–18 in. (30–45 cm) wide, with small, gray-green to bluish green leaves, usually the same size or smaller than the flowers at 1 in. (2.5 cm) wide. Flowers are often detailed with dark centers and veination, blooming multiple times from early summer to fall.

'Ballerina': pale pink flowers with dark purple centers and veins, AGM

'Carol': glowing pink to magenta flowers with dark centers and deep pink veins

Jolly Jewel Series: range of cultivars with unusual bright colors with large, dark centers and strong veination

'Laurence Flatman': whitish to midpink flowers with deep purple centers and veins

'Purple Pillow': purplish magenta flowers with dark purple-pink veins

'Thumbling Hearts': lavender-pink flowers with large dark centers and bold veins

G. subcaulescens 'Giuseppii': brilliant magenta flowers with black centers, AGM

G. subcaulescens 'Splendens': glowing magenta-pink flowers with black centers, AGM

Geranium 'Ballerina'

Geranium himalayense 'Plenum'

Geranium macrorrhizum 'Album'

Geranium dalmaticum
DALMATIAN CRANESBILL

Zones 4–8
Mountains of coastal Croatia.
Masses of 1 in. (2.5 cm) wide, shell-pink, ruffled flowers in early summer just above small, shiny, aromatic, semi-evergreen foliage that turns orange and red in fall, 4–6 in. (10–15 cm) tall and 18 in. (45 cm) or more wide, spreading slowly by rhizomes. AGM

'Album': white flowers sometimes pink-tinged

Geranium himalayense
HIMALAYAN CRANESBILL, LILAC CRANESBILL

Zones 3–8
Subalpine and alpine meadows from Afghanistan to Tibet, China.
Large plants in all respects, with blue to purple-blue summer flowers often more than 2 in. (5 cm) wide atop leaves up to 4 in. (10 cm) across, forming mounds 12–24 in. (30–60 cm) tall by 24–36 in. (60–90 cm) wide.

'Baby Blue': large blue flowers with magenta-purple veins and white centers on compact plants, 12 in. (30 cm) tall by 12–24 in. (30–60 cm) wide

'Derrick Cook': white flowers with warm purple veins

'Gravetye': blue flowers with reddish centers

'Irish Blue': pale silvery blue flowers flushed with pinkish centers

'Plenum' (syn. 'Birch Double'): long-lasting, lavender-blue double flowers

Geranium macrorrhizum
BIGROOT GERANIUM

Zones 3–8
Among limestone rocks, on screes, and in woods and scrub at high elevations from the Southern Alps to the Balkan Peninsula.
Among the best ground-covering Geranium species, forming large, spreading, weed-smothering colonies up to 12 in. (30 cm) tall from fleshy rhizomes and thick, interweaving aboveground stems. The large, aromatic, slightly sticky, semi-evergreen foliage can be 4 in. (10 cm) wide with red tones in autumn. Small, long-lasting, deep pink to white flowers emerge from reddish buds in late spring to early summer with occasional rebloom. Tolerant of heat, humidity, shade, and drought including dry shade.

'Album': white flowers contrast boldly with red sepals

'Bevan's Variety': glowing deep pink flowers

'Czakor': magenta-pink flowers

'Ingwersen's Variety': light lavender-pink flowers

'Spessart': white flowers with a pale pink blush

'Variegatum': variably variegated, grayish green leaves with creamy edges and midpink flowers

'White-Ness': pure white flowers from green buds, AGM

Geranium nodosum
KNOTTED CRANESBILL, PYRENEES GERANIUM

Zones 5–8
Deciduous mountain forests and forest margins from the Pyrenees to the Balkan Peninsula.
Slowly creeping by rhizomes into colonies 8–12 in. (20–30 cm) tall by 20 in. (50 cm) or more wide, with distinctive, shiny, deeply veined, 3–5 lobed leaves. Rose-pink to lavender-pink flowers with purple veins are 1 in. (2.5 cm) wide, with notched petals blooming not profusely but over a long period from late spring to fall. Performs in sun to shade, including dry shade. May reseed.

'Clos du Coudray': violet flowers with darker purple striations and a pale lavender picotee edge

'Silverwood': pure white flowers with green veins

'Svelte Lilac': lavender flowers with purple veins

'Whiteleaf': very similar to 'Clos du Coudray', but possibly with less pronounced striations

Geranium pyrenaicum
MOUNTAIN CRANESBILL

Zones 5–9
Grassland and scrub from Western Europe to the Caucasus.
Small lavender-blue to rose-purple flowers with dark purple veins produced by the hundreds from late spring through fall. The five bilobed, heart-shaped petals give the impression of a ten-petaled flower. Plants have a mounding, sprawling habit, about 12 in. (30 cm) tall by 24 in. (60 cm) wide. They can be short- or long-lived and will readily reseed around the garden. Drought and heat tolerant.

'Bill Wallis': lavender-blue flowers

Geranium renardii

CAUCASIAN CRANESBILL, RENARD CRANESBILL

Zones 4–9

Subalpine meadows of the Caucasus.

A compact species, to about 10 in. (25 cm) tall and 14 in. (36 cm) wide, with rounded, five-lobed, sage-green leaves with rippled teeth and a finely bumpy, felted, textured surface. Pure white flowers with warm purple veins in late spring and early summer. AGM

'Philippe Vapelle': hybrid cross with *G. platypetalum* resembling *G. renardii*, with lavender-blue flowers with purple veins

'Stephanie': hybrid cross with *G. peloponnesiacum* resembling *G. renardii*, with silvery lavender-blue flowers with purple veins

'Tcschelda': pale blue to pale lavender flowers

Geranium sanguineum

BLOODY CRANESBILL

Zones 3–9

Rocky and sandy soils in open habitats, meadows, forest margins, and scrub across most of Europe to northern Turkey and the Caucasus.

Commonly grown for its trailing, textural, rhizomatously spreading mounds, 8–12 in. (20–30 cm) tall and 24 in. (60 cm) wide, with small, lightly hairy, deeply dissected leaves with linear lobes topped with magenta to deep pink 1 in. (2.5 cm) wide flowers from late spring to early summer and intermittently thereafter. Foliage develops red tones in fall. Tolerant of heat, humidity, and clay soils.

'Album': pure white flowers, AGM

'Ankum's Pride': glowing pink flowers, AGM

'Elke': likely a hybrid, with candy-pink flowers, dark pink veins, and a frosted picotee edge

'Elsbeth': violet-magenta flowers

'Glenluce': lavender-pink flowers with deep pink veins

'Max Frei': violet-magenta flowers

'New Hampshire Purple': bright violet-magenta flowers

var. *striatum*: pale pink flowers with pink veins

'Tiny Monster': sterile hybrid with *G. psilostemon* with a vigorous, sprawling habit, 10 in. (25 cm) tall and 24 in. (60 cm) or more wide, with deep lilac-pink flowers from late spring to fall and red and copper foliage in autumn

Geranium renardii

Geranium sanguineum 'Max Frei'

Geranium wallichianum 'Buxton's Variety'

Geranium wallichianum
WALLICH GERANIUM

Zones 5–9

Open broadleaf forests, scrub, and open slopes in the Himalayas from Afghanistan to Bhutan.

A large, sprawling species with trailing stems 24–40 in. (60–100 cm) long on plants 12 in. (30 cm) or more tall, with large, lightly marbled leaves up to 4 in. (10 cm) across. Long-blooming summer flowers have two distinct color zones joined by warm purple veins—the outer in shades of blue, purple-blue, or pinkish purple and the inner in white. Flowers are bluer in cooler temperatures or part shade and more lavender-purple in warmer temperatures and full sun.

'Buxton's Variety': long-blooming, lavender-blue flowers with white centers and warm purple veins

'Crystal Lake': compact habit, long-blooming, icy lavender-blue flowers with prominent warm purple veins

'Noorthava' Havana Blues: compact habit, long-blooming, large, lavender-blue to blue flowers with white centers and warm purple veins atop gold to chartreuse foliage aging to light green

'Rise and Shine': compact habit, long-blooming large flowers, the white center surrounded by a pink halo grading into lavender-blue to blue

Geranium hybrids

Zones 4–8, depending on cultivar
Garden origin.

Countless historical hybrids have been joined by many important additions in recent decades, especially 'Gerwat' Rozanne and similar large-flowered, long-blooming cultivars such as 'Azure Rush', 'Pink Penny', 'Rosetta', and 'Sweet Heidy'. Many of these hybrids provide mounding habits and can be mass-planted, rambling habits that will cover ground and weave into neighbors, or prostrate habits that form thick and attractive mats. These plants represent a selection of the most valuable and distinctive hybrids.

'Ann Folkard': gold to light green foliage, magenta flowers with black centers, rambling to 24 in. (60 cm) tall by 36 in. (90 cm) or more wide, zones (4)5–8, AGM

'Anne Thomson': similar to 'Ann Folkard' but more compact, zones 4–8, AGM

Geranium ×*antipodeum* 'Pink Spice'

×*antipodeum* 'Pink Spice': trailing mounds of small, scalloped, chocolate-brown leaves and multitudes of tiny pink flowers with white-frosted edges, zones 7–9

'Azure Rush': similar to 'Gerwat' Rozanne but more compact with lighter blue flowers, zones 5–8

'Bertie Crug': small, bronze foliage on dense, creeping mounds, 4 in. (10 cm) tall, with deep pink flowers, zones 5–8

'Blogold' Blue Sunrise: golden foliage flushed with orange when young, aging to light green, 16 in. (40 cm) tall by 24 in. (60 cm) wide, lavender-blue flowers from late spring to fall, zones 4–8, AGM

'Blushing Turtle': rose-pink flowers in late spring/early summer with sporadic rebloom, 24 in. (60 cm) tall by 36 in. (90 cm) wide, zones 5–8

'Bremdra' Dragon Heart: large, magenta flowers with black centers from late spring to fall, 18 in. (45 cm) tall, sprawling to 24–36 in. (60–90 cm) wide, zones 5–8

'Bremdream' Dreamland: pale pink flowers from late spring to fall, 12 in. (30 cm) tall, sprawling to 24 in. (60 cm) wide, zones 5–8

'Bremerry' Orkney Cherry: sprawling mats of small, burgundy-brown foliage, 4–10 in. (10–25 cm) tall and 24 in. (60 cm) wide, with small, hot-magenta-pink flowers with lighter centers from late spring to fall, zones 5–8

'Brempat' Patricia: magenta flowers with black centers and veins from spring to fall, 24 in. (60 cm) or more tall and wide, zones 4–8, AGM

'Cheryl's Shadow': trailing mounds 6–10 in. (15–25 cm) tall and 12–18 in. (30–45 cm) wide of small, scalloped, purple, grayish purple, or brownish purple leaves and tiny light pink flowers from late spring to fall, zones 7–10

'Dilys': prostrate stems to 10 in. (25 cm) tall and 36 in. (90 cm) or more wide, with purplish pink flowers from late spring into early summer, zones 4–8, AGM

'Dusky Crûg': pale lavender-pink flowers atop small, bronzy brown foliage on spreading mounds, 18 in. (45 cm) tall and 30 in. (75 cm) wide, zones 4–8

'Eureka Blue': large, long-blooming, blue flowers, 30 in. (75 cm) tall and 36 in. (90 cm) wide, zones 4–8

'Gernic' Summer Skies: mauve-pink double flowers with yellow centers in spring and early summer with sporadic rebloom thereafter, 24 in. (60 cm) tall and wide, zones 5–8

'Gerwat' Rozanne: most popular of all cranesbills, with large, mauve flowers in full sun to blue in part shade with lighter centers, blooming from late spring to fall on mounding and spreading plants, usually 20 in. (50 cm) tall and 24 in. (60 cm) wide, sometimes larger, zones 4–8, AGM, Perennial Plant of the Year 2008

'Lilac Ice': a sport of 'Gerwat' Rozanne with palest lavender flowers

×*magnificum* 'Blue Blood': dark purple-blue summer flowers, 16 in. (40 cm) tall and wide, zones 4–8

'Mavis Simpson': pink flowers with white centers from spring until fall, 24 in. (60 cm) tall by 48 in. (120 cm) wide, zones 6–8, AGM

×*oxonianum* 'Claridge Druce': pale pink flowers all summer, 24 in. (60 cm) or more tall and wide, zones 4–8

×*oxonianum* 'Katherine Adele': new foliage centered with burgundy-red, with small, white flowers with pink veins in spring and periodically through summer, 16 in. (40 cm) tall by 24 in. (60 cm) wide, zones 4–8

×*oxonianum* f. *thurstonianum* 'Southcombe Double': double flowers with many very narrow pink petals, 18 in. (45 cm) tall by 24 in. (60 cm) wide, zones 5–8

'Pink Penny': similar to 'Gerwat' Rozanne with rose-pink flowers with dark veins, zones 4–8

'Rosetta': similar to 'Gerwat' Rozanne with deep pink flowers, zones 4–8

×*riversleaianum* 'Russell Prichard': trailing plants, 12 in. (30 cm) tall by 36 in. (90 cm) wide, with magenta-pink flowers from late spring to fall, zones 6–8, AGM

'Salome': similar to 'Ann Folkard' but more compact, with chartreuse foliage and lavender flowers with purple-black centers and veins from spring to fall, zones 6–9

'Sandrine': similar to 'Ann Folkard' but with much larger flowers and perhaps more vigor, zones 4–9

'Sue Crûg': spreading plants, 12 in. (30 cm) tall by 36 in. (90 cm) wide, with lavender-pink flowers with dark purple centers and veins, each petal with a white central frosting in late spring and reblooming thereafter, zones 5–8

'Sweet Heidy': tricolored flowers of white, pink, and lavender-blue with dark veins, with habit and bloom time similar to 'Gerwat' Rozanne, zones 4–8

Geum
Rosaceae

Easy to grow, evergreen to semi-evergreen, densely mounded perennials forming basal rosettes 6–12 in. (15–30 cm) tall and slightly wider of fuzzy, veined, lobed, palmate, or dissected leaves. Flowers ½–1½ in. (1.3–4 cm) wide, with yellow or orange central stamens and five petals in a range of warm colors, are held loosely on mostly leafless, see-through stems, 12–24 in. (30–60 cm) tall, from mid- to late spring into summer with possible rebloom thereafter. Some species have attractive, round, fuzzy or bristly seed heads.

CULTURE/CARE Full sun to part shade in fertile, average to evenly moist, well-drained soils. Provide afternoon shade in hot summer climates. Avoid wet winter soils (except *G. rivale*) and regions with high summer heat and humidity. *Geum triflorum* is more tolerant of drought and dry soils. Deadhead to encourage rebloom.

USES Mass plant as a weed-suppressing cover for small to medium-sized areas, along paths, at the front of the border, and in lightly shaded areas. Not tolerant of foot traffic. Deer and rabbit resistant. Attractive to pollinators, especially bees.

PROPAGATION Division, seed

Geum coccineum 'Eos'

Geum coccineum
DWARF ORANGE AVENS

Zones 5–9
Mountain meadows from Southeast Europe to Turkey.
Basal mounds of textured, fuzzy foliage to 6 in. (15 cm) tall, with bright orange to deep orange flowers on stems 10–18 in. (25–45 cm) tall.

'Cooky': bright orange flowers lighten with age

'Eos': dark orange flowers produced more sparingly than other cultivars, with golden foliage, protect from full sun

'Koi': dark orange flowers

'Werner Arends': dark orange single to semidouble flowers

Geum rivale
WATER AVENS, PURPLE AVENS

Zones (2)3–8
Full sun to partly shaded swamps, fens, bogs, wet meadows, and moist, rich woods across Europe, Siberia, Canada, and the northern United States.
Clump-forming or rhizomatous, colony-forming plants with small, nodding, bell-shaped flowers with prominent brownish purple sepals around small, creamy to pale pink or peach petals on green to brownish purple stems. Small, attractive, burgundy seed heads.

'Album': ivory-white to palest yellow petals with green sepals and stems

'Leonard's Variety': coppery pink semidouble flowers with burgundy sepals and stems

Geum triflorum
PRAIRIE SMOKE, OLD MAN'S WHISKERS

Zones 3–8
Prairies, grassy openings in dry forests, bluffs, open coniferous forests, and on thin soils over limestone in western North America from the Yukon to California and east to the Great Lakes.
Rhizomatously spreading plant with ferny, pinnate leaves up to 12 in. (30 cm) long, with lobes increasing in size toward the tips. Small, nodding, yellowish, pink, or purple flowers with striking purplish to rose-red sepals on burgundy stems become large, highly ornamental, upward-facing seed heads with long, silky, silver and red hairs up to 2 in. (5 cm) or more long.

Geum hybrids

Zones 5–9
Garden origin.
The most popular cultivated avens are hybrids that typically form basal mounds, 6 in. (15 cm) tall and 6–12 in. (15–30 cm) wide, with flowering stems 12–24 in. (30–60 cm) tall. Of the many cultivars, these are the most commonly grown.

'Beech House Apricot': ruffled yellow petals streaked with apricot-orange

'Blazing Sunset': ruffled scarlet-red double flowers

'Borisii': tangerine-orange flowers

Cocktails Series: excellent hybrids involving *G. rivale, G. coccineum, G. montanum,* and occasionally *G. chiloense,* offering single, semidouble, and double flowers in a wide range of colors

'Alabama Slammer': yellow and orange double flowers with red highlights on dark stems

'Banana Daiquiri': lemon-yellow semidouble flowers

'Citronge': creamy orange flowers

'Cosmopolitan': creamy yellow to palest creamy apricot double flowers edged with rosy pink

'Gimlet': pale yellow semidouble flowers with white-frosted tips

'Mai Tai': single to semidouble flowers on dark stems, opening apricot-infused with reddish pink aging to peachy pink

'Sangria': bright red single to semidouble flowers on dark stems

Geum 'Sangria' (Cocktails Series)

'Sea Breeze': deep orange, wavy single flowers sometimes with extra petals

'Tequila Sunrise': lemon-yellow double flowers tipped with reddish pink on dark stems

'Wet Kiss': red-orange semidouble flowers aging to peachy orange

'Double Bloody Mary': ruffled scarlet red double flowers

'Fire Storm': ruffled bright orange double flowers

'Fireball': larger version of 'Fire Storm'

'Flames of Passion': copper-pink to copper-red, semi-double, lightly ruffled, partly nodding flowers on burgundy stems

'Mango Lassi': yellow double flowers flushed with apricot and light orange

'Mrs. J. Bradshaw': ruffled scarlet-red semidouble flowers

'Pink Fluffy': fringed pink petals

'Prinses Juliana': lightly ruffled tangerine semidouble flowers

'Sunkissed Lime': bright golden foliage and tangerine flowers, more floriferous than 'Eos'

Tempo Series: early and long-blooming, compact plants

'Tngeuto' Tempo Orange: peachy orange single to double flowers

'Tngeutr' Tempo Rose: rose-pink semidouble flowers

'Tngeuty' Tempo Yellow: lemon-yellow semidouble flowers

'Tngeupp' Pretticoats Peach: reblooming, peach, cream, and pale yellow semidouble flowers on compact plants

'Tngeuro' Rustico Orange: long-blooming reddish orange flowers

'Totally Tangerine' (syn. 'Tim's Tangerine'): small, light orange flowers

Glechoma hederacea
GROUND IVY, CREEPING CHARLIE

Lamiaceae

Zones 3–10
Damp, disturbed sites, hedgerows, fields, and woodland margins in Europe and southwestern Asia. Naturalized in much of North America.

A vigorous, stoloniferous, evergreen mint relative with small, broadly toothed, aromatic, slightly hairy, light green, rounded to kidney-shaped leaves, forming dense, spreading mats 6–12 in. (15–30 cm) tall, via square, green to reddish, rooting stems. New leaves can be flushed purple. Small, lavender-purple, tubular axillary flowers appear on upright, leafy stems in spring. Ground ivy is edible and was moved around the world by European settlers for use in teas, stews, and salads.

CULTURE/CARE Easy to grow in full sun (with good moisture) to shade in average to evenly moist soils.

USES Fast-spreading for medium-sized to large areas including slopes and as a lawn alternative. Can grow too quickly for small spaces. Considered invasive in some regions. Tolerant of occasional foot traffic. Deer resistant.

PROPAGATION Division, removal of rooted plantlets or stems

'Variegata': green to grayish green leaves with creamy white edges

Globularia cordifolia
HEART-LEAVED GLOBE DAISY

Plantaginaceae

Zones 4–9
Limestone cliffs and mountain slopes from Central and Southern Europe to Western Turkey.

Low, dark green, evergreen mats, 2 in. (5 cm) tall and 12 in. (30 cm) or more wide, with woody stems and small, glossy, leathery, rounded to spatula-shaped leaves with notched tips, less than 1 in. (2.5 cm) long. Lavender-blue flowers in fuzzy, spherical heads appear in late spring to early summer on stems

Glechoma hederacea

1–4 in. (2.5–10 cm) tall. Various similar species such as *G. meridionalis*, *G. nudicaulis*, *G. repens*, and *G. trichosantha*, and the hybrid 'Blue Eyes', may be available from specialist nurseries. AGM

CULTURE/CARE Full sun with sharp drainage. Drought tolerant.

USES Easy to grow and slowly spreading for small areas in alpine, gravel, or rock gardens, rocky and thin soils, and in troughs and walls. Not tolerant of foot traffic.

PROPAGATION Seed

Gunnera
Gunneraceae

Famed for its most impressive species, *G. manicata* (giant rhubarb), with some of the largest leaves in the plant kingdom, the genus *Gunnera* also includes a handful of charming, diminutive members with small leaves that form prostrate, spreading mats. All species are dioecious or monoecious, with separate male and female flowers on different plants or on the same plant, respectively. Flower spikes are interesting but not showy, except when adorned with orange-red fruit. In addition to those species treated here, other rarer ground-covering species include *G. dentata* and *G. hamiltonii*.

CULTURE/CARE Rich, fertile, evenly moist soils in sun to part shade.

USES Small to medium-sized areas at pond edges, along streams, and in moist, low-lying sites. Not tolerant of foot traffic.

PROPAGATION Division, replanting of rooted stolons, seed

Gunnera magellanica
CREEPING GUNNERA, PIG VINE

Zones 7–9

Damp grassy areas and moist places from sea level to montane elevations of southern and Andean South America.

Prostrate, stoloniferous, indefinitely spreading, semi-evergreen to herbaceous mats, 2–4 in. (5–10 cm) tall, of shiny, kidney-shaped, emerald-green, pleated, 2 in. (5 cm) wide leaves with crenate margins, resembling small Asian fans. Short spikes of simple florets give way to orange-red berries on female plants.

Gunnera magellanica

Gunnera monoica
SOLITARY GUNNERA, CREEPING GUNNERA

Zones 7–10

Moist to wet habitats including wet cliffs, among rocks, and on forest floors in New Zealand.

Dense, creeping, stoloniferous, evergreen mats to 4 in. (10 cm) tall and spreading indefinitely. Midgreen, leathery, kidney- or heart-shaped, smooth to hairy leaves with crenate margins are sometimes copper or bronze flushed. Monoecious plants have spikes with male florets above and female florets below, producing whitish fruit.

Gunnera prorepens
CREEPING GUNNERA

Zones 7–11

Moist to wet places in forests and grasslands from lowlands to subalpine areas in New Zealand.

Dense, creeping, stoloniferous, evergreen mats to 4 in. (10 cm) tall, spreading indefinitely. Midgreen, leathery, oval to spoon-shaped leaves with crenate to smooth margins are often flushed with purple or chocolate-brown, especially in more light. Dioecious with short vertical spikes, 2–4 in. (5–10 cm) tall, of red to orange-red fruit on female plants.

Gymnocarpium dryopteris
OAK FERN

Cystopteridaceae

Zones 2–9

Moist to wet, rocky, coniferous or mixed forests, bog margins, rocky ledges, and talus slopes from sea level to montane zones. Circumboreal across North America, Europe, and Asia.

A delicately beautiful, lacy, creeping, deciduous fern eventually forming open to dense colonies, 6–10 in. (15–25 cm) tall, of individual, light green, twice pinnate, triangular fronds, 2–10 in. (5–25 cm) long, on wiry black stems from long, underground rhizomes.

CULTURE/CARE Rich soils high in organic matter with even moisture and good drainage in shade to part shade.

USES For small areas along pond edges or other moist places, in woodland gardens, and beneath trees and large shrubs. Spreads slowly to moderately. May take time to develop a closed cover. Interplant with *Cyclamen hederifolium*, which emerges when oak fern

Gunnera prorepens

Gymnocarpium dryopteris

Gypsophila cerastioides

goes dormant, or semi-evergreen to evergreen ground covers such as *Ajuga reptans*, *Euonymus* 'Wolong Ghost', and *Vinca minor*. Not tolerant of foot traffic. Deer and rabbit resistant.

PROPAGATION Division, spores

'Plumosum': broader pinnae, producing a fuller look

Gypsophila
Caryophyllaceae

The well-known cottage garden or florist baby's breath (*G. paniculata*)—sidekick to long-stemmed roses everywhere—has a handful of low-growing, mat-forming, mountain-dwelling cousins that make easy ground covers.

CULTURE/CARE Full sun with excellent drainage, especially in winter. Drought and salt tolerant. *Gypsophila cerastioides* is more tolerant of rich soils and moisture. A light shearing after flowering can encourage rebloom.

USES Edgers for small applications along pathways, stairways, or sunny borders, in rock and alpine gardens, troughs, and stone walls. Not tolerant of foot traffic. Deer resistant. Attractive to pollinators, especially bees and butterflies.

PROPAGATION Division, seed

Gypsophila cerastioides
ALPINE BABY'S BREATH

Zones 4–9
Rocky slopes and banks at high elevations in the Himalayas from Bhutan to Pakistan.

A lush, tufted or mat-forming, herbaceous to evergreen ground cover, 4–6 in. (10–15 cm) tall by 8 in. (20 cm) or more wide, with small, rounded, midgreen, hairy leaves and small, white, often purple-lined flowers held in clusters just above the foliage in late spring to summer.

Gypsophila repens
CREEPING BABY'S BREATH

Zones 3–8
Among calcareous rocks and in grasslands in mountainous regions of Central and Southern Europe.

A long-lived, easy to grow, herbaceous alpine forming spreading mats up to 6 in. (15 cm) tall and 24 in.

Gypsophila repens 'Filou White'

(60 cm) or more wide, with 1 in. (2.5 cm) long, grayish green leaves nearly completely obscured in early summer by masses of small, fragrant, white to lavender flowers on short panicles just above the foliage.

'Alba': long-blooming white flowers

'Filou Rose': larger, light to midpink, long-blooming flowers

'Filou White': larger, long-blooming white flowers

'Rosea': rose-pink flowers

Hakonechloa macra
JAPANESE FOREST GRASS, HAKONE GRASS

Poaceae

Zones 5–9
Cool and moist forests, shaded cliffs, and mountainous regions of central Japan.

Distinctive for its elegant habit and shade tolerance, Japanese forest grass is one of the most useful and beautiful garden grasses. This herbaceous, warm-season, slowly spreading, rhizomatous species has graceful foliage up to 10 in. (25 cm) long and ⅜ in. (1 cm) wide that arches into cascading mounds 12–18 in. (30–45 cm) or more tall and 24 in. (60 cm) or more wide. In summer, insignificant, airy flowers occur above or among the foliage, though not always

Hakonechloa macra mass planting in a park in Stockholm, Sweden

in cool summer climates or in shade. Foliage blushes pink or red with summer heat or drought and cool fall weather before turning tan as plants go dormant. AGM

CULTURE/CARE Easy to grow in part sun to part shade, in rich, evenly moist, well-drained soils. Plants can withstand occasional drought. Tolerant of full shade or full sun in cool summer climates or with good moisture. Variegated and golden cultivars may be less sun tolerant and are more compact and slower growing.

USES Mass plant in small to large areas along pathways, in borders, in woodland gardens, and in other partly shaded areas, with a slow to moderate growth rate, especially at first, increasing as plants establish. Not tolerant of foot traffic. Deer resistant.

PROPAGATION Division

'Alboaurea': green leaves variegated with gold and white, AGM

'Albovariegata' (syn. 'Albo Striata'): green leaves variegated with creamy white, larger and more vigorous than other cultivars

'All Gold': foliage is bright gold in sun, lime-green in shade

'Aureola': gold leaves with green stripes, AGM, Perennial Plant of the Year 2009

'Beni-kaze': green leaves develop bolder cherry-red, purple-red, and orange fall color

'Briform' Fubuki: compact leaves boldly variegated with white, cream, and green

'Habsf1007' Sunflare: sport of 'Aureola' with earlier red tints and bold red and burnt-orange fall foliage colors

'Naomi': resembling 'Aureola' with earlier and bolder purple-red fall foliage colors

'Nicolas': green leaves with bold orange-red fall colors

'Stripe it Rich': sport of 'All Gold' with gold and white foliage

'Sunny Delight': larger sport of 'Aureola' with green leaves striped gold

Hebe
Plantaginaceae

A large group of freely branching evergreen shrubs primarily from New Zealand, named after the Greek goddess of youth, with somewhat thickened, evergreen, lance-shaped to oval green, gray-green, burgundy, or silver-blue leaves often held in geometric patterns. Clusters or short spikes of white, pink, lavender, lavender-blue, or purple flowers usually occur in summer. High elevation small-leaved and whipcord species and their cultivars are the hardiest.

In addition to the plants treated here, other small and uncommon species include *H. carnosula*, *H. chathamica*, *H. cupressoides* 'Boughton Dome', and *H. vernicosa*. Additionally, many larger, upright or mounding hebes growing to 24–36 in. (60–90 cm) or more tall and wide can be used as ground covers for parks or large gardens, including 'Western Hills', 'Hinerua', *H. recurva* 'Boughton Silver', or the superlative 30 in. (75 cm) tall by 48 in. (120 cm) wide mounds of *H. odora* 'Purpurea Nana' (syn. *H. anomala*). Hebes have been taxonomically reclassified and are now included in the genus *Veronica*.

Hebe glaucophylla

Hebe ochracea 'James Stirling'

CULTURE/CARE Full sun in average, well-drained soils or light shade in hot summer climates. Tolerant of salt and occasional drought. Pruning is usually not necessary. Trim lightly after flowering if desired. Hardiness improves with free-draining, drier winter soils.

USES Prostrate species can be planted along pathways, as edgers, and on walls. Mass plant mounding species in small to large areas for an undulating ground cover of domes, similar in look to mass plantings of *Calluna* and *Erica* species. Plants grow at a slow to moderate rate. Not tolerant of foot traffic. Attractive to pollinators, especially bees.

PROPAGATION Cuttings

Hebe albicans
WHITE HEBE, NELSON HEBE

Zones 7–10

Mountainous regions at the north end of the South Island, New Zealand.

Thick, silver-blue leaves just over 1 in. (2.5 cm) long on mounded shrubs, 24 in. (60 cm) tall by 36 in. (90 cm) wide. White flowers from purple-pink buds on numerous short spikes up to 2.5 in. (6 cm) long. AGM

'Sussex Carpet' (syn. 'Prostrate Form'): low-growing form, 10–12 in. (25–30 cm) tall by 24–36 in. (60–90 cm) wide

Hebe decumbens
GROUND HEBE

Zones 7–10

Rocky, open sites in dry alpine and subalpine at the north end of the South Island, New Zealand.

Shiny, olive-green leaves with red edges on black, prostrate stems to 6 in. (15 cm) tall and 36 in. (90 cm) or more wide. Very short spikes appear as rounded clusters of white flowers from pink-flushed buds in early summer.

Hebe glaucophylla
BLUE-LEAFED HEBE

Zones 7–10

Scrub and tussock grassland on the northern half of the South Island, New Zealand.

Small, blue-gray, cupped, rounded leaves on compact plants, 18 in. (45 cm) or more tall and 36 in. (90 cm) wide. Clusters or short spikes of white flowers. Sometimes shy to flower.

Hebe ochracea
WHIPCORD HEBE

Zones 7–10

Low alpine at the north end of the South Island, New Zealand.

Olive-green to brownish or orange-tinged, scalelike leaves tightly appressed to the stems on flat-topped, vase- or anvil-shaped plants up to 4 ft. (1.2 m) tall and wide, resembling a juniper or cypress. White flowers in small clusters at branch tips on established plants. More hardy than other species.

'James Stirling': dwarf form, 12 in. (30 cm) tall by 18 in. (45 cm) wide, with bolder gold and orange colors, especially in winter, AGM

Hebe odora
BOXWOOD HEBE

Zones 7–10

Moist, mountainous habitats throughout New Zealand.

A variable species, previously known as *H. buxifolia*, typically with small, glossy, elliptic to oval, cupped, deep green leaves with lighter edges and short spikes or clusters of white flowers in summer. Rounded shrubs reach 3–4 ft. (1–1.2 m) tall and 4–5 ft. (1.2–1.5 m) wide.

'Nana': dwarf, upright mounded form, 8 in. (20 cm) tall and 18 in. (45 cm) wide, with white to lavender flowers

var. *prostrata*: sometimes listed as *H. odora* prostrate form, the carpet hebe forms mats 4 in. (10 cm) tall and up to 3 ft. (1 m) wide, with smaller lance-shaped leaves and lavender-tinged, white flowers

'Summer Frost': low-growing prostrate form, 4 in. (10 cm) tall and up to 3 ft. (1 m) wide, with smaller lance-shaped leaves

Hebe pimeleoides
HEBE

Zones 7–10

Dry, mountainous habitats of the South Island, New Zealand.

Dark, wiry, spreading or ascending stems with small, narrow, lance-shaped, bluish leaves with red margins on openly structured plants, 12–24 in. (30–60 cm) tall and 24–36 in. (60–90 cm) wide, with bluish purple flowers in short spikes in early summer. For complete coverage and weed suppression, under-plant with a low ground cover such as *Ajuga reptans*, *Cymbalaria muralis*, or *Sedum rupestre* 'Angelina'.

'Quicksilver': more intensely blue to silver-blue leaves and black stems, 12 in. (30 cm) tall and 24 in. (60 cm) wide, AGM

Hebe pinguifolia
DISH-LEAVED HEBE

Zones 7–10

Low scrub, grasslands, open rocky mountainsides, and stable screes on the drier eastern side of the Southern Alps on the South Island, New Zealand.

A variable species with wild forms up to 36 in. (90 cm) tall with thick, leathery, overlapping, cupped,

Hebe pimeleoides 'Quicksilver'

Hebe 'Silver Dollar'

oval, gray-green to bluish leaves sometimes with red edges. White flowers in short spikes in early summer.

'Pagei': bluish leaves with red margins and purplish stems, 12 in. (30 cm) tall and 36 in. (90 cm) or more wide, tolerant of a wide range of conditions, AGM

'Sutherlandii': gray-green to silvery green leaves without red edges, 18 in. (45 cm) tall and 24–36 in. (60–90 cm) wide

Hebe hybrids

Zones 7–9
Garden origin.
Many low-growing and mounding hybrids make useful ground covers.

'Bracken Hill': cross of *H. allanii* and *H. pimeleoides* with gray-green leaves and purple flowers on prostrate plants, 6–10 in. (15–25 cm) tall and 24–36 in. (60–90 cm) wide

'Emerald Gem' (syn. 'McKean'): bright green mounds of tiny, green, nearly scalelike leaves and white flowers, 8–12 in. (20–30 cm) tall and 18 in. (45 cm) wide, AGM

'Pretty in Pink': light to midpink flowers and reddish purple new growth that ages to burgundy and then deep green on mounds 12–18 in. (30–45 cm) tall and 36 in. (90 cm) wide

'Red Edge': hybrid involving *H. albicans* with light purple to pink flowers that age to white and rounded, cupped leaves, emerging purplish and aging to gray-green to blue-green with red edges, 24 in. (60 cm) tall and 36 in. (90 cm) wide, AGM

'Silver Dollar': resembles 'Red Edge' but with creamy variegated edges flushed glowing pink in cold weather

'Walter Buccleugh': seedling of 'Youngii' with upright and spreading stems, 12–18 in. (30–45 cm) tall and wide, with burgundy-infused foliage and light purple flowers

'Wingletye': amethyst flowers with gray leaves and black stems forming mats 4–8 in. (10–20 cm) tall by 24–36 in. (60–90 cm) wide, AGM

'Youngii' (syn. 'Carl Teschner'): mats 8 in. (20 cm) tall and 24 in. (60 cm) wide with black stems and small, deep green, shiny leaves, and with violet-purple flowers lightening with age, AGM

Hedera
Araliaceae

Ivies are staple ground covers that offer beauty, versatility, reliability, and vigor. Their lush, attractive, shiny, 3–5 lobed, triangular, evergreen foliage on trailing, rooting stems can quickly cover large areas as maintenance-free, impenetrable, weed-suppressing, indefinitely spreading mats. Unfortunately, some species such as *H. hibernica*, *H. algeriensis*, and some cultivars of *H. helix* have proven invasive, especially in urban forests of northwestern and southeastern North America, Australia, and New Zealand.

Hedera species are dimorphic with distinct juvenile and adult forms. The familiar trailing or climbing, nonflowering juvenile form usually comprises large mats, 4–6 in. (10–15 cm) tall. Where stems find vertical support, they will climb via adventitious roots, developing thick, woody stems and smaller, thicker, unlobed adult foliage with spherical clusters of small, white to green, nectar-rich flowers in fall, followed by black fruit popular with birds.

CULTURE/CARE Full sun to full shade in a variety of soils including dry shade. Tolerant of occasional drought, though regular watering maintains lushness. Almost no maintenance is required except to control spread.

USES Small to large applications, depending on the cultivar, as a lawn alternative, slope stabilizer, or for dense cover in shade. Spreads quickly once established. The wide-ranging, vinelike stems can colonize areas of extreme drought such as under coniferous trees or near building foundations if planted nearby in favorable conditions. Tolerant of occasional foot traffic. Deer and rabbit resistant. Attractive to pollinators, especially bees.

PROPAGATION Cuttings, division of rooted stems

Hedera algeriensis
ALGERIAN IVY

Zones 7–10
Consistently moist soils in the coastal mountains of North Africa.
Similar to *H. hibernica* and *H. helix* but with larger, glossier, triangular leaves up to 6 in. (15 cm) wide with shallow to absent side lobes and occasional bronze winter color. More tolerant of dry periods and salty conditions than most other species. Its cultivars were previously attributed to closely related *H. canariensis*.

'Gloire de Marengo': variegated foliage in shades of blue-green, gray-green, emerald-green, and white on red leaf stalks, AGM

'Marginomaculata': leaves mottled with green and creamy white, flushed pink in winter, on red leaf stalks

'Montgomery': large, dark green leaves

'Tropical Blizzard': variably mottled and flecked with gold and white, recent introduction listed as *H. canariensis* but may eventually join *H. algeriensis*

Hedera colchica
PERSIAN IVY

Zones 6–9

Humid, moist forest floors and up, trees, rocks, and cliffs in Turkey, Iran, the Caucasus, and Afghanistan.

Similar to *H. helix* and *H. hibernica* but with the largest leaves in the genus, up to 10 in. (25 cm) long and 6 in. (15 cm) wide. Aromatic when crushed, leaves are generally heart-shaped with a light gloss and shallow marginal teeth, with undulating, often curling leaf blades, for a wilting or ruffled look. Fastest spreading species in warm climates.

'Dentata Variegata': tricolor foliage of deep blue-green, gray-green, and ivory, AGM

'Sulphur Heart': tricolor foliage of dark green, midgreen, and light green to yellow, AGM

Hedera helix
ENGLISH IVY, COMMON IVY

Zones (4)5–9

Spreading across the ground or vertically (given the opportunity) in forested habitats, on rocks, cliffs, trees, and other vertical structures across most of Europe to Iran and northern Turkey.

Often confused with *H. hibernica*, most *H. helix* in cultivation consists of dainty forms with wiry stems and small leaves on compact, manageable plants made popular by hundreds of cultivars selected for leaf shape, size, and variegation for outdoor and indoor use. *Hedera helix* tends to have smaller leaves, less than 3⅛ in. (8 cm) wide (with many cultivars having leaves only 1–2 in. [2.5–5 cm] across), whereas the robust tetraploid *H. hibernica* has larger leaves, greater vigor, and larger overall size. Certain cultivars of *H. helix* such as 'Baltica', 'California', 'Pittsburgh', and 'Star' have proven invasive; most populations of invasive

Hedera colchica 'Dentata Variegata' in Tofino, BC

Hedera helix 'Oro di Bogliasco'

ivy—83 percent of those tested in the state of Washington, for instance—seem to be *H. hibernica*. Take caution when using *H. helix*, though most small-leaved ornamental cultivars should not pose much risk of invasiveness. Moderately salt tolerant. Some cultivars may not be fully hardy to zone 5.

'Baltica': often confused with *H. hibernica*, with large, dark green leaves turning purplish in winter with white to greenish veins, spreading to 25 ft. (7.5 m) or more—vigorous, aggressive, and invasive in certain regions

'Buttercup': small, butter-yellow new leaves remain bright in sun or turn to lime-green in shade, AGM

'Duckfoot': small green leaves with three rounded lobes, AGM

'Glacier': small, irregularly variegated leaves in blue-green, gray-green, and ivory, AGM

'Goldchild': small green leaves with broad, irregular, yellow to creamy yellow margins, AGM

'Golden Ingot': small blue-green and gray-green mottled leaves with variable yellow margins, AGM

'Green Ripple': small deep green leaves with pointed lobes and a net of light green veins

'Ivalace': dark green, shiny leaves with wavy upward-curled margins

'Needlepoint': small mid- to deep green leaves with five long, narrow lobes

'Oro di Bogliasco' (syn. 'Goldheart'): small to medium-sized, bright yellow leaves with dark green margins and red stems

'Silverdust': small gray-green leaves with creamy variegation

'Teardrop': small, unlobed, heart-shaped green leaves with lighter veins

'Thorndale': large, dark green leaves with lighter veins on vigorous plants

'Yellow Ripple': medium-sized to large, blue-green and gray-green leaves with creamy yellow margins and pointed lobes, the central one lengthened

Hedera hibernica
ATLANTIC IVY, IRISH IVY

Zones 5–11
Forest floors or other shaded or sunny habitats and up cliffs, trees, and walls along the Atlantic and Baltic coasts of Europe from the British Isles and Scandinavia south to Spain and Portugal.

Although English ivy (*H. helix*) has been labeled invasive, the culprit, at least in the U.S. Pacific Northwest, is more often *H. hibernica*, which has been confused with *H. helix* in horticulture. *Hedera hibernica* is a more robust tetraploid, generally larger in all parts with leaves more than 3⅛ in. (8 cm) across, with a honeylike scent when crushed.

'Spetchley': extremely small, triangular or three-lobed, deep green leaves, AGM

Helianthemum hybrids
SUN ROSE, ROCK ROSE

Cistaceae

Zones 5–9
Alkaline grasslands, scrub, chalk downs, and open and sunny locations throughout Europe.

Related to the rock rose (*Cistus* spp.), these smaller, low-growing, evergreen shrubs or subshrubs are 6–12 in. (15–30 cm) tall and up to 36 in. (90 cm) wide, offering almost every color except purples and blues. Flowers are five-petaled, roselike, slightly less than 1 in. (2.5 cm) across, and bloom for only one day, but in a profuse succession lasting up to two months in spring and summer. The simple, linear foliage is green, gray-green, or silvery. Most cultivars have been attributed to *H. nummularium*, but all are hybrids of this or other species such as *H. mutabile*, with flowers changing from deep pink to white as they age.

CULTURE/CARE Full sun in thin, dry, well-drained, rocky or sandy, alkaline soils. Salt tolerant. Provide good winter drainage. Shear after flowering to maintain density.

USES Dry gravel or rock gardens, along pathways, on slopes, at the front of hot borders, or trailing over walls. Spreads at a moderate rate once established. Not tolerant of foot traffic. Deer and rabbit resistant. Attractive to pollinators, especially bees.

PROPAGATION Cuttings

'Annabel': pink double flowers

'Belgravia Rose': rose-pink flowers

'Ben Fhada': bright yellow flowers with orange centers

'Ben Ledi': glowing, deep rose-pink flowers with darker centers

'Ben More': deep orange flowers

'Ben Nevis': tangerine-orange flowers with red centers

'Cheviot': salmon-pink and apricot flowers with yellow centers

Helianthemum 'Annabel'

'Fire Dragon': orange-red flowers, AGM

'Henfield Brilliant': orange-red flowers, AGM

'Mesa Wine': deep wine-red flowers

'Mrs. C.W. Earle' (syn. 'Fireball'): red double flowers, AGM

'Raspberry Ripple': deep raspberry-pink flowers irregularly white-splashed

'Rhodanthe Carneum' (syn. 'Wisley Pink'): soft salmon-pink flowers with yellow centers, AGM

'The Bride': pure white flowers with yellow centers, AGM

'Wisley Primrose': butter-yellow flowers, AGM

Helianthus salicifolius
WILLOWLEAF SUNFLOWER

Asteraceae

Zones 5–9
Limestone prairies and rock outcrops of the South Central United States.

A towering 8 ft. (2.4 m) tall prairie perennial with airy, linear foliage and 2 in. (5 cm) wide, bright yellow daisies with dark centers in fall. Dwarf selections form textural, slowly spreading, rhizomatous mounds. The foliage elegance is lost in the shorter, stubbier cultivars, but they remain valuable for texture and late-season color, sometimes in very late fall in cool summer climates.

CULTURE/CARE Average to alkaline, moderately rich, well-drained soils in full sun. Tolerant of light shade but plants will be more open, will grow taller, and will bloom less.

USES Mass plantings, where clumps will fill gaps slowly between plants. Not tolerant of foot traffic. Deer resistant. Attractive to pollinators, especially bees and butterflies.

PROPAGATION Division

'Low Down': 12–18 in. (30–45 cm) tall and 24 in. (60 cm) or more wide

'Table Mountain': flowering stems reach a uniform height between 12–16 in. (30–40 cm)

Helictotrichon sempervirens
BLUE OAT GRASS

Poaceae

Zones (3)4–8
Grasslands of Central and Southern Europe.

A tough, easy to grow, clumping grass, forming striking, textural mounds, 18–24 in. (45–60 cm) tall and wide, of narrow, linear, steel-blue, evergreen foliage that moves in the breeze. Airy, blue, upright and arching inflorescences, to 36 in. (90 cm) in early summer, turning gold in midsummer. The most reliable blue grass with greater tolerance of richer soils and winter wet than *Festuca* species. AGM

CULTURE/CARE Full sun in average to dry soils. Salt tolerant.

USES Mass plant over small to large areas. Plants may not form a closed cover. For full weed suppression, interplant with a low-spreading ground cover such as *Erodium* spp., *Helianthemum* spp., or *Sedum*

Helictotrichon sempervirens (foreground) with Japanese blood grass (*Imperata cylindrica* 'Rubra')

rupestre 'Angelina' or 'Blue Spruce'. Plants bulk up at a moderate rate. Not tolerant of foot traffic.

PROPAGATION Division

'Saphirsprudel': leaves wider and bluer with better resistance to rust, heat, and humidity

Helleborus
Ranunculaceae

Achievements in hellebore breeding over the past 20 years have elevated the genus to one of the most valuable in the perennial garden, especially in zones 7–9, where hellebores are superlative, but also in zones 5, 6, and colder.

Hellebores are both the first and last perennials of the year to bloom in mild winter climates, particularly in the Pacific Northwest and the United Kingdom. Christmas roses (*H. niger*) bloom from late autumn to late winter, the caulescent hybrids such as *H. ×ballardiae*, *H. ×ericsmithii*, *H. ×nigercors*, and more complex crosses of these with *H. ×hybridus* bloom from midwinter to spring, while *H. ×hybridus* blooms from late winter through spring. In colder climates such as zone 5, the blooming seasons are compressed, with *H. niger* beginning bloom in early spring, followed soon thereafter by the rest of the parade.

No matter the climate, hellebores provide color in the garden when few other perennials can. That they can also be mass-planted to form an evergreen ground cover makes them all the more valuable.

CULTURE/CARE Easy to grow in average to rich, neutral to alkaline soils, though they are tolerant of acidic soils. Grow *H. niger* in part sun to part shade, the caulescent hybrids in full to part sun, and *H. ×hybridus* in part sun to part shade, though they are tolerant of full shade and dry shade and periods of drought. The old foliage of established *H. ×hybridus* plants can be removed before blooming if unsightly or to reveal the flowers. Undamaged foliage of all other hellebores should be left on the plants. Because hellebores are heavy feeders, apply 2–3 in. (5–7.5 cm) of compost each year and slow-release fertilizer in spring to encourage lush foliage and early fall to increase developing flower buds.

USES Mass plant for small to large applications where flowers can be appreciated during the winter and early spring seasons. Young plants bulk up slowly at first. In the interim, interplant with carpeting ground covers to provide coverage. Not tolerant of foot traffic. Deer and rabbit resistant. Attractive to pollinators, especially bees and occasionally hummingbirds.

PROPAGATION Hellebores are not easily propagated. Seed-grown plants of *H. niger* or *H. ×hybridus* can take 2–3 years to reach adolescent bloom. Most caulescent hybrids are sterile and produce no seed. Only *H. ×hybridus* can be divided and then only after clumps are at least 5–10 years old.

Helleborus niger
CHRISTMAS ROSE

Zones (3)4–9

Woods, thickets, and grasslands, usually on calcareous soils, in mountainous areas from southern Germany to northern Italy and east to Austria and Croatia.

Thick, leathery, dark green, palmate leaves with shallowly toothed margins, and pure white, outward-facing, 3 in. (7.5 cm) wide, five-petaled flowers centered with golden stamens. Flowers may flush pink with age. Plants reach 8–12 in. (20–30 cm) tall and 12–18 in. (30–45 cm) wide.

Historical selections such as *H. niger* 'Potter's Wheel' and 'Praecox' lack the vigor, foliage and flower production, and long bloom period of more recent introductions, particularly the Helleborus Gold Collection (HGC). Bloom times are for mild winter climates.

'Coseh 210' HGC Joel: compact habit and lightly fragrant flowers in early winter

'Coseh 220' HGC Jonas: frequently with 6–7 petals per flower in early winter

'Coseh 230' HGC Snow Frills: double flowers with rounded, ruffled inner petals

'Coseh 1000' HGC Jesko: rounded, overlapping petals form cup-shaped flowers in late fall to early winter

'Coseh 1010' HGC Jasper: good vigor, blooms in winter

'Double Fashion' (Winter Magic Series): double flowers with long, narrow, pointed inner petals on vigorous plants

'HGC Jacob': lightly fragrant flowers with narrower, less overlapping petals in early winter

'HGC Josef Lemper': larger, taller plants with large, slightly cupped flowers in early winter, best for landscape plantings

'HGC Joshua': lightly fragrant flowers with overlapping petals in early winter

Helleborus caulescent hybrids
HELLEBORE, SNOW ROSE

Zones (4)5–9

Derived from multiple species native to Central and Mediterranean Europe.

Caulescent hybrids are crosses of *H. argutifolius*, *H. foetidus*, *H. lividus*, and/or *H. niger* that offer mounds of thick, leathery, sun-loving foliage in shades of dark green, gray-green, blue-green, and powder-blue, some with light silver mottling. The 2–3 in. (5–7.5 cm) wide, outward-facing flowers in shades of white, cream, green, dusty rose, and pink top the foliage on multiple closely held stems.

H. ×ballardiae (*H. lividus* × *H. niger*): hybrids with more pink coloration than other caulescent hybrids, especially in cooler weather, with leaves frequently mottled with white and mint-green and flower color that begins white or cream with pink and dusty rose reverses, deepening with age toward dusty rose and then green

'Coseh 700' HGC Cinnamon Snow: pink flowers with cinnamon tones

'Coseh 710' HGC Pink Frost: the pinkest flowers on large, vigorous plants

'Coseh 720' HGC Spring Party: silver-veined foliage and red flower stems with mostly white flowers

'Coseh 800' HGC Snow Dance: heavily blooming white flowers age to cinnamon

'Coseh 810' HGC Merlin: pink flowers, aging to raspberry/chocolate-brown, with dark green foliage

'Coseh 890' HGC Maestro: white to pale pink flowers on red stems, with mottled foliage

'Coseh 930' HGC Mahogany Snow: large, ruffled, white flowers with pink flushes, aging to mahogany-pink

'Coseh 940' HGC Camelot: cream-colored flowers with a hint of yellow overlain with pink

'HGC Love Bug': small, cream-colored flowers with good pink highlights on compact plants with deep green, serrated foliage

'HGC Platinum Rose': cream-colored flowers aging to dark rose, with large, blue-gray leaves

H. ×ericsmithii (*H. ×sternii* × *H. niger*): hybrids with white buds sometimes flushed with dusty rose, opening to large white to cream flowers that age to dusty rose

'Bl to2' Angel Glow (Frostkiss): cream and light pink flowers with blue-gray foliage

Helleborus ×*ballardiae* 'Coseh 710' HGC Pink Frost with *Lysimachia nummularia* 'Aurea'

'Candy Love' Vancouver Medallion (Winter Magic): flowers open creamy white, darkening to yellow-green with a pink blush to rich chocolate-brown; trade name commemorates the 2010 Winter Olympics

'Coseh 730' HGC Champion: pink buds open to large, creamy white flowers

'Coseh 790' HGC Shooting Star: many small white flowers in congested mounds

'Coseh 860' HGC Monte Cristo: creamy white and yellowish flowers with peachy pink reverses on red stems, with blue-gray leaves

'Coseh 980' HGC Marlon: bright white flowers on red stems

'Pirouette' (Frostkiss): pink flowers on leaning stems, with bluish foliage

'Winter Moonbeam' (Frostkiss): large white flowers with striking, deep green foliage with icy white veins, aging to mint-green

H. ×*nigercors* (*H. argutifolius* × *H. niger*): tough hybrid for the landscape, with extra thick, leathery, mid- to dark green or blue-green foliage and large, white to cream-colored flowers with green highlights, aging to green, sometimes with a slight pink flush

'Coseh 750' HGC Ice Breaker Max: large flowers

'Coseh 820' HGC Ice Breaker Fancy: large flowers with pink highlights as they age

'Coseh 830' HGC Ice Breaker Prelude: petals with green centers resembling stars

'Coseh 840' HGC Ice Breaker Pico: flowers with pink highlights on compact plants

'Honeyhill Joy': vigorous plant with dark green, serrated leaves

'Snow Love' (Winter Magic): flowers aging to luminous apple-green, with grayish green foliage

'White Beauty' (Frostkiss): white and cream flowers with dark green foliage

H. ×*sahinii* 'Winterbells' (*H. foetidus* × *H. niger*): rare cross with small, cupped, nodding, creamy white flowers with dusty rose reverses, often blooming for seven months from midwinter onward

Helleborus caulescent/acaulescent hybrids

HELLEBORE, SNOW ROSE

Zones (4)5–9

Crosses of caulescent species and hybrids with the distantly related *H. ×hybridus* (acaulescent group), a feat previously thought impossible, have combined the bold colors of pink, red, purple, and pure white from *H. ×hybridus* with the more upright habit and bold foliage of the caulescent hellebores.

Frostkiss Series: attributed to complex hybrid *H. ×iburgensis* or, alternatively, the Rodney Davey Marbled Group, with large leaves with dramatic veining, at first white in white-flowered cultivars or pink to red in colored cultivars, aging to mint-green, with outward-facing flowers beginning in midwinter

> 'Abcrd01' Penny's Pink: deep pink flowers

> 'Abcrd02' Anna's Red: large red flowers

> 'Epb12' Sally's Shell: midpink and shell-pink flowers

> 'Epb20' Moondance: cupped, white flowers with a chartreuse blush

> 'Epb21' Charmer: large, lavender-red, early blooming flowers on compact plants

> 'Epb25' Glenda's Gloss: bicolor purple and white flowers

> 'Epb29' Dorothy's Dawn: pink flowers

> 'Epb30' Dana's Dulcet: flowers in muted pinks and purples

> 'Epb31' Cheryl's Shine: glowing pink flowers

> 'Epb42' Reanna's Ruby: purple-red flowers with burgundy speckling

> 'Epbrd01' Molly's White: white to ivory-white flowers

> 'Rd06' Bayli's Blush: peach-pink flowers

> 'Rd09' Pippa's Purple: purple-pink flowers

HGC Ice N' Roses Series (*H. ×glandorfensis*): extra large, deep green leaves with large, outward-facing flowers beginning in midwinter on extra large plants

> 'Coseh 4100' Red: red and burgundy-red flowers

> 'Coseh 4200' Rose: midpink flowers brightening toward the centers

> 'Coseh 4500' White: white flowers

> 'Coseh 4600' Barolo: large, deep maroon-red flowers

> 'Coseh 5000' Picotee: white flowers with pink edges

'Walhero' Walberton's Rosemary (*H. niger* × *H. ×hybridus*): profusion of flowers with pointed petals, aging from mid-pink with subtle white veining to glowing pink, and then bright salmon

H. ×lemonnierae 'Lem 100' HGC Madame Lemonnier: largest flowers in the genus, up to 4 in. (10 cm) across, with rounded, overlapping petals in shades of pink and lavender-pink with faint white veining, all aging to deep salmon

Helleborus ×hybridus

HELLEBORE, LENTEN ROSE

Zones (4)5–9

Derived from multiple species native to Mediterranean Europe and Turkey.

Complex hybrids of multiple acaulescent species, including *H. atrorubens*, *H. cyclophyllus*, *H. multifidus*, *H. odorus*, *H. orientalis*, *H. purpurascens*, *H. torquatus*, and *H. viridis*, all of which are good garden plants with small, quiet flowers. Modern hybrids, however, offer a dazzling range of colors in every shade but true-blue, orange, and hot red. They also have large flowers up to 3 in. (7.5 cm) across; single, double, and semidouble (anemone centered) forms; and various detailing including picotee edges, basal flares, speckling, and veining. Thick, leathery, palmate foliage is deep green, with 5–9 or more leaflets forming dense mounds 12–16 in. (30–40 cm) tall and 12–24 in. (30–60 cm) wide. Perennial Plant of the Year 2005

Some hellebores are produced via tissue culture, resulting in uniform plants, but most are grown from seed strains, presenting a range of variability within each strain. The best strains are managed by skilled breeders through controlled crosses and show continual improvement of color range and consistency, detailing, flower size, and symmetry. Open-pollinated or less diligently managed strains offer "entry level" plants for beginners or for budget-conscious mass plantings. These are common and notable hellebores available in North America.

Frostkiss Series: large leaves with dramatic veining

> 'Tutu': tissue-cultured anemone-centered form in shades of warm purple with darker speckling

> 'White Tutu': tissue-cultured anemone-centered form in white with purple speckling

Honeymoon Series: counterpart to the Wedding Party Series with good quality, well-bred, single flowers in a range of color strains, including California Dreaming, French Kiss, New York Night, Paris in Pink, Rio Carnival,

Romantic Getaway, Rome in Red, Sandy Shores, Spanish Flare, Tropical Sunset, and Vegas Nights

Lady Series: entry-level strains including Blue Lady, Blue Metallic Lady, Pink Lady, Red Lady, White Lady, White Lady Spotted, and Yellow Lady

Royal Heritage: entry-level strain of single flowers in mixed colors

Wedding Party Series: counterpart to the Honeymoon Series with good quality, well-bred double flowers in a range of color strains, including Black Tie Affair, Blushing Bridesmaid, Confetti Cake, Dark and Handsome, Dashing Groomsmen, First Dance, Flower Girl, Maid of Honor, Mother of the Bride, Shotgun Wedding, True Love, Wedding Bells, and Wedding Crasher

Winter Jewels Series: excellent strains, with the boldest, most consistent colors, flower detailing, symmetrical shapes, and vigor

> Double strains: Amber Gem, Amethyst Gem, Berry Swirl, Cotton Candy, Double Painted, Double Slate, Fire and Ice, Golden Lotus, Harlequin Gem, Jade

Tiger, Onyx Odyssey, Peppermint Ice, Red Sapphire, Rose Quartz, Sparkling Diamond, and Sun Flare

Single strains: Amethyst Glow, Apricot Blush, Black Diamond, Blue Diamond, Cherry Blossom (anemone centered), Golden Sunrise, Jade Star, Painted, Picotee Pearl (anemone centered), and Ruby Wine

Winter Thrillers Series: various single and double color strains of good quality

Herniaria glabra
RUPTUREWORT, GREEN CARPET

Caryophyllaceae

Zones 5–10
Sandy or dry places across most of Europe and in northern Africa and Western Asia.

A tiny carnation relative with no resemblance to its colorful cousin in flower or foliage, but with a tough, functional nature resembling creeping thyme or

Helleborus 'Abcrdo2' Anna's Red (Frostkiss)

Helleborus ×*hybridus* 'Sparkling Diamond' (Winter Jewels)

Mass planting of *Helleborus* ×*hybridus* at Hidcote Manor Garden, UK

Herniaria glabra (lower right)

Corsican mint. Low, evergreen mats, 1–3 in. (2.5–7.5 cm) tall and 12 in. (30 cm) or more wide, of vibrant green, tiny, oval leaves, sometimes developing bronze tones in winter. Insignificant flowers.

CULTURE/CARE Full sun to light shade in well-drained soils of average moisture. Tolerant of heat and humidity. Provide supplemental water during dry periods.

USES Lawn alternative for small to medium-sized areas, for edging pathways, or between stepping stones. Underplant with small spring- or fall-blooming bulbs or ephemeral perennials or use as a cover for potted shrubs or bonsai. Spreads at a slow to moderate rate. Tolerant of moderate foot traffic. Deer resistant.

PROPAGATION Division, cuttings, seed

'Sea Foam': creamy white to pale yellow margins

Heuchera
Saxifragaceae

Coral bells are among the most beloved, colorful, and ubiquitous of garden perennials, forming mounded rosettes of palmately lobed leaves, either rounded or pointed, with flat or ruffled leaf blades, in practically every foliage color except blue, from a central, woody crown. Mounds are typically 6–8 in. (15–20 cm) tall and 12 in. (30 cm) wide, though both smaller and larger cultivars exist. They are evergreen to semi-evergreen in mild winter climates, herbaceous in colder zones. Though grown more for their foliage, their airy, branched, 12–18 in. (30–45 cm) tall inflorescences of small, pendulous, bell-shaped, white, pink, or red flowers are attractive. They are amenable to a wide range of garden conditions and can act as a mass-planted ground cover.

CULTURE/CARE Average to organically rich, humusy soils with good drainage and average moisture, though longevity can be decreased in soils that are too rich or too moist. If woody stems develop, they can be cut and replanted. In leaner conditions, plants will be less vigorous and more compact though potentially longer lived, requiring less maintenance. Avoid heavy clay and wet winter soils. Coral bells are sometimes considered shade plants, but they require full sun to part shade with more light in cool summer climates. Cultivars with lime-colored foliage should always be protected from hot afternoon sun. Irrigation will increase sun tolerance and reduce leaf scorch. For shadier conditions, use ×*Heucherella* cultivars. Some cultivars are more tolerant of heat and humidity. Good air circulation will minimize fungal diseases in all climates. Deadhead to encourage rebloom.

USES Edgers for borders, along pathways, and mass-planted in small to medium-sized applications to form a colorful, mounded ground cover. Interplant to achieve full coverage with carpeting ground covers such as *Acaena* spp., *Ajuga reptans*, *Cymbalaria muralis*, *Lamium maculatum*, and *Sedum* spp. Not tolerant of foot traffic. Deer and rabbit resistant. Attractive to pollinators, especially bees and hummingbirds.

PROPAGATION Species can be grown from seed; cultivars can be divided or grown from stem cuttings

Heuchera sanguinea
CORAL BELLS

Zones 3–8

Moist, shaded, rocky habitats, cliffs, hills, and alpine areas in the southwestern United States and northern Chihuahua, Mexico.

The original, old-fashioned perennial, named for its bell-shaped, red, deep pink, or white fragrant flowers popular with hummingbirds in late spring and summer on stems 12–18 in. (30–45 cm) tall above lobed, kidney-shaped or rounded, midgreen leaves in mounds 12–18 in. (30–45 cm) wide.

'Leuchtkäfer' (syn. 'Firefly'): bright red flowers

Heuchera villosa 'Autumn Bride'

'Ruby Bells': ruby-red flowers

'Snow Angel': leaves variably mottled in creamy white, with deep pink flowers

'White Cloud': white flowers and silver-veined leaves

Heuchera villosa
MAPLE-LEAVED ALUM ROOT

Zones 3–8

Shaded rocks, ledges, or shallow rocky soils in woodlands across the eastern United States.

Noted for its robust clumps of large, light to mid-green, lightly felted, maple-like foliage and its tall, dramatic, dense or open inflorescences, 8–32 in. (20–80 cm) tall and up to 6 in. (15 cm) wide, of white flowers from late spring to fall. Particularly tolerant of heat and humidity.

'Autumn Bride': large, velvety, light green leaves in mounds 16 in. (40 cm) tall and 24 in. (60 cm) wide, topped with dense, conical inflorescences of creamy white flowers on stems 24 in. (60 cm) tall from late summer until frost

'Palace Purple': breakthrough cultivar that first brought burgundy-colored foliage to coral bells, with large, shiny, smooth, puckered, burgundy leaves with open, airy inflorescences of white flowers, Perennial Plant of the Year 1991

Heuchera 'Tnheunes' Northern Exposure Silver

Heuchera hybrids

Zones 4–9

Hybrids from North American native species usually occurring in rocky habitats, woodlands, prairies, and alpine areas in sun to part shade.

Most *Heuchera* cultivars in horticulture are complex hybrids selected for various ornamental and cultural traits, including leaf size, color, and shape; flower color and floriferousness; plant size and habit; cold hardiness; light requirements; and heat and humidity tolerance. The major parent species are *H. americana*, *H. micrantha*, *H. sanguinea*, and *H. villosa*, with contributions from *H. cylindrica*, *H. pubescens*, *H. pulchella*, *H. richardsonii*, and others, all of which can be grown but have mostly been supplanted by their progeny. Although *H. americana*, *H. pubescens*, and *H. villosa* confer heat and humidity tolerance, *H. sanguinea* provides sun tolerance, *H. americana* provides shade tolerance, and *H. richardsonii* provides cold tolerance, hybrid origin is usually not discussed. The exception has been the promotion of *H. villosa* and *H. americana* genetics for heat and humidity tolerance and *H. richardsonii* for rust resistance and cold tolerance.

These *Heuchera* hybrids, organized by foliage color, represent a selection of distinctive, reliable, and commonly grown cultivars. Other series of interest include the Big Top, Carnival, Dolce, Kira, and Little Cuties.

Black foliage

'Black Pearl' (Primo Series) (*H. villosa* hybrid): large, shiny, ruffled, jet-black foliage with purple undersides, white flowers, in mounds up to 20 in. (50 cm) wide

'Black Taffeta': crisped and ruffled, shiny, purple-black foliage and pink flowers, in mounds up to 16 in. (40 cm) wide

'Mocha' (*H. villosa* hybrid): very large, maple-like, chocolate-brown leaves turning near black in sun, with white flowers, in mounds up to 20 in. (50 cm) wide

'Obsidian': classic black cultivar to judge all others against, with shiny purple-black foliage, great vigor and performance, and white flowers, in mounds to 16 in. (40 cm) wide

'Tnheugb' Grande Black (*H. villosa* hybrid): large, wavy foliage and pink flowers, in mounds 28 in. (70 cm) wide

Burgundy foliage

'Chocolate Ruffles' (likely *H. americana* hybrid): ruffled, shiny, chocolate-brown leaves with purplish flowers, in mounds to 24 in. (60 cm) wide

'Crimson Curls': densely curled, burgundy-red foliage with reddish undersides and masses of white flowers, in mounds up to 18 in. (45 cm) wide

'Melting Fire': ruffled, bright crimson new foliage aging to dark maroon-red in summer, with white flowers, in mounds up to 12 in. (30 cm) wide, seed grown

Green foliage

'Apple Crisp': leaves with silver veil and crispy, ruffled margins, white flowers, in mounds to 12 in. (30 cm) wide

'Berry Timeless': leaves with silver veil, with continuous pink blooms from summer to frost, in mounds to 20 in. (50 cm) wide

'Green Spice': leaves with bold silver veil, dark red veins, bright orange fall color, with white flowers, in mounds to 16 in. (40 cm) wide, good shade tolerance

'Hercules': leaves variably mottled with cream, with bright red flowers, in mounds to 16 in. (40 cm) wide

'Lipstick': resembling *H. sanguinea* 'Firefly', with masses of bright red flowers that bloom repeatedly, but larger with silver-veiled foliage, in mounds to 14 in. (36 cm) wide

'Paris': resembling *H. sanguinea* but with silver-veiled foliage and deep rose-pink flowers, in mounds to 14 in. (36 cm) wide

'Sashay': heavily crinkled leaves with rose-purple undersides produce a bicolor effect, white flowers, in mounds to 16 in. (40 cm) wide

Lime-green foliage

'Citronelle' (*H. villosa* hybrid): sport of 'Caramel', with yellow and lime-green leaves and white flowers, in mounds to 18 in. (45 cm) wide

'Delta Dawn': large, rounded leaves mostly orange-red with a yellow rim in spring and fall and gold to lime-green with bold orange-red veination in summer, yellowish green flowers, in mounds to 12 in. (30 cm) wide

'Lime Marmalade': most sun-tolerant lime-green cultivar with frilly foliage and white flowers, in mounds to 24 in. (60 cm) wide

'Pretty Pistachio' (Primo Series): large, chartreuse leaves age to lime-green, topped with dramatic pink, conical inflorescences up to 4.5 in. (12 cm) wide from summer into fall, in mounds to 32 in. (80 cm) wide

'Red Lightning' (*H. villosa* hybrid): very large, gold to lime-green leaves with bold red veins, white flowers, in mounds to 16 in. (40 cm) wide

'Tiramisu' (*H. villosa* hybrid): similar to 'Delta Dawn' but colors are less bold

'Tnheunel' Northern Exposure Lime (*H. richardsonii* hybrid): lime-green and yellow foliage, reddish flowers, in mounds to 22 in. (56 cm) wide

Orange foliage

'Caramel' (*H. villosa* hybrid): slightly fuzzy foliage in hues of apricot, caramel, and pink, with pink flowers, in mounds to 20 in. (50 cm) wide

'Marmalade': thick, ruffled peach and orange foliage with hot pink undersides, white flowers, in mounds to 18 in. (45 cm) wide

'Peach Crisp': similar to 'Marmalade' and 'Peach Flambé', but more rust resistant, with heavily ruffled peach and amber foliage and white flowers, in mounds to 14 in. (36 cm) wide

'Peach Flambé': bold peach and orange ruffled foliage becoming plum-purple in winter, white flowers, in mounds to 14 in. (36 cm) wide

Heuchera 'Peach Flambé'

'Peachberry Ice' (Primo Series): large, glowing, apricot-orange-pink new leaves muting to pinkish purple with silver veil and bright pink undersides, white flowers, in mounds to 34 in. (86 cm) wide

'Pink Pearls' (*H. villosa* hybrid): large, orange, pink, and reddish foliage, with bold sprays of light pink flowers, in mounds to 12 in. (30 cm) wide

'Southern Comfort' (*H. villosa* hybrid): large, fuzzy, orange, pink, and cinnamon leaves, white flowers, in mounds to 24 in. (60 cm) wide

'Tnheunea' Northern Exposure Amber (*H. richardsonii* hybrid): orange and amber foliage, greenish yellow flowers, in mounds to 20 in. (50 cm) wide

'Zipper' (*H. villosa* hybrid): similar to 'Marmalade' and Peach Flambé', but more rust resistant, large and heavily ruffled, orange and amber foliage and white flowers, in mounds to 12 in. (30 cm) wide

Purple foliage

'Amethyst Myst' (*H. americana* hybrid): warm purple foliage with silver veil, white flowers, in mounds 24 in. (60 cm) across

'Berry Smoothie' (*H. americana* × *H. villosa*): rose-pink foliage with silver veil, white flowers, in mounds 20 in. (50 cm) wide

'Blackberry Ice' Dolce Blackberry Ice (*H. villosa* hybrid): shiny leaves with dark purple veins, silver veil with age, white flowers, in mounds 22 in. (56 cm) wide

'Frosted Violet': warm dark purple leaves, silver veil, light pink flowers, in mounds 24 in. (60 cm) wide

'Midnight Rose': warm to deep purple foliage with pink speckles, white flowers, in mounds 16 in. (40 cm) wide

'Plum Pudding' (likely *H. americana* hybrid): plum-purple foliage with silver veil, white flowers, in mounds 16 in. (40 cm) wide

'Plum Royale': shiny purple leaves with dark purple veins, white flowers, in mounds 14 in. (36 cm) wide

'Rave On': foliage with silver veil, deep pink flowers, in mounds to 14 in. (36 cm) wide

'Silver Scrolls': purple foliage with bold silver overlay, white flowers, in mounds 12 in. (30 cm) wide

'Tnheufp' Forever Purple: glossy, plum- to warm purple, ruffled leaves with dark purple veins, purple-pink flowers, in mounds to 22 in. (56 cm) wide

'Tnheuga' Grande Amethyst (*H. villosa* hybrid): large, wavy, purple-black foliage, pink flowers, mounds 22 in. (55 cm) wide

'Tnheunes' Northern Exposure Silver (*H. richardsonii* hybrid): foliage with bold silver veil, greenish yellow flowers, in mounds to 16 in. (40 cm) wide

'Wild Rose' (Primo Series): large, rosy purple foliage with dark purple veins, pink flowers, in mounds 20 in. (50 cm) wide

Red foliage

'Cherry Cola': reddish brown foliage, showy cherry red flowers, in mounds to 14 in. (36 cm) wide

'Fire Alarm' (*H. villosa* hybrid): large, glossy leaves among the reddest of all in spring and autumn, brownish red in summer, pink flowers, in mounds to 14 in. (36 cm) wide

'Galaxy': large, thick foliage with bright red speckling, aging to reddish purple with pink speckling, white flowers, in mounds to 12 in. (30 cm) wide

'Mahogany Monster' (Primo Series): extra large, glossy, mahogany-red leaves, white flowers, in mounds to 28 in. (71 cm) wide

'Tnheufr' Forever Red: likely the reddest foliage of all, white flowers, in mounds to 14 in. (36 cm) wide

'Tnheuner' Northern Exposure Red (*H. richardsonii* hybrid): red to burgundy-red foliage with serrated edges, greenish yellow flowers, in mounds to 20 in. (50 cm) wide

×*Heucherella* hybrids
FOAMY BELLS

Saxifragaceae

Zones 4–9
Garden origin.

Foamy bells are intergeneric hybrids with the bold foliage colors of *Heuchera* cultivars and the greater shade tolerance, showier flower spikes, leaf lobing, and central leaf markings of *Tiarella* species. Their value is primarily in their shade tolerance, enabling bold displays where heucheras would slowly diminish. They also offer bolder yellows and golds and trailing, stoloniferous forms.

CULTURE/CARE Grow similar to heucheras, but in part sun to part shade. Some may be tolerant of full shade, but test before mass planting. Others may be tolerant of full sun in cooler summer climates. They are not prone to heuchera rust.

USES Use similarly to heucheras. Trailing cultivars will form closed mats over larger areas and trail over walls. Deer and rabbit resistant.

PROPAGATION Division

Following is a selection of the most distinctive, reliable, and commonly grown cultivars, organized by leaf color.

Burgundy foliage

'Onyx': glossy leaves with ruffled surfaces, shy to flower, in mounds to 16 in. (40 cm) wide, tolerant of heat and humidity

'Solar Eclipse': scalloped leaves with lime-green edges, white flowers, in mounds to 16 in. (40 cm) wide

Gold foliage

'Alabama Sunrise': gold spring foliage turns lime-green in summer and pinkish orange in fall, with dark red centers bleeding outward, white flowers, in mounds to 20 in. (50 cm) wide

'Gold Cascade': small, shallowly lobed leaves with red centers, pink flowers, trailing to 24 in. (60 cm) wide

'Gold Zebra': feathery, multilobed foliage boldly flushed with red, white flowers, in mounds to 15 in. (38 cm) wide

'Sunrise Falls': maple-shaped leaves with pointed lobes and delicate red central markings, white flowers, trailing to 30 in. (75 cm) wide

'Yellowstone Falls': lobed gold to lime-green leaves with red central speckling, white flowers, trailing to 48 in. (120 cm) or more wide

Green foliage

'Blue Ridge': shallowly lobed, blue-green leaves with silver veils and burgundy veins, white flowers, in mounds to 18 in. (45 cm) wide

'Bridget Bloom': leaves with subtle burgundy veins, profuse shell-pink flowers, in mounds to 12 in. (30 cm) wide

'Dayglow Pink': leaves with subtle burgundy centers, profuse and showy pink flowers, in mounds to 14 in. (36 cm) wide

'Glacier Falls': ivy-shaped leaves with silver veils and red veins, white flowers, trailing to 28 in. (71 cm) wide

'Kimono': deeply lobed, maple-like leaves with burgundy centers and silver veils, pale pink flowers, in mounds to 12 in. (30 cm) wide

'Tapestry': deeply lobed leaves with bold burgundy veins and silver veils, with profuse, airy, pink flowers, in mounds to 16 in. (40 cm) wide, tolerant of heat and humidity

Orange foliage

'Autumn Cascade': deeply lobed, orange and tan leaves with silver veils and pink undersides, white flowers, trailing to 36 in. (90 cm) wide

'Brass Lantern': palmate, five-lobed, shiny leaves with glowing reddish centers and orange edges, white flowers, in mounds to 24 in. (60 cm) wide

'Copper Cascade': small, coppery orange and tan leaves with darker veins and silver veils, white flowers, trailing to 32 in. (80 cm) wide

'Redstone Falls': reddish orange, copper, and tan foliage, white flowers, trailing to 36 in. (90 cm) wide, tolerant of heat and humidity

'Sweet Tea': large, palmate, glowing cinnamon-orange leaves with red centers, white flowers, in mounds to 28 in. (71 cm) wide

×*Heucherella* 'Sweet Tea' on the High Line, New York City

Purple foliage

'Cracked Ice': deeply multilobed leaves with veils, emerging silver-pink and aging to silver, white flowers, in mounds to 15 in. (38 cm) wide

'Plum Cascade': deeply lobed leaves with silver veils and dark purple veins, long-blooming pink flowers, trailing to 32 in. (80 cm) wide

'Twilight': grayish purple leaves with silver veils and darker veins, white flowers, in large mounds to 24 in. (60 cm) wide

Holcus mollis
CREEPING VELVET GRASS, CREEPING SOFT GRASS

Poaceae

Zones 5–9

Woodland clearings, forest edges, grasslands, and heaths in Europe and Asia.

Rhizomatous, shade-tolerant, herbaceous grass with narrow, upright blades, 20 in. (50 cm) tall. Summer inflorescences are tinged purple.

CULTURE/CARE Average, well-drained soils in full sun to part shade. Shallow rhizomes occur about 2 in. (5 cm) deep and are easy to remove, though any pieces remaining in the soil can resprout from dormant buds. Drought tolerant.

USES Border edges, along pathways, and in woodland gardens. Plant where its spreading habit is desirable or where hardscape will control its spread. Not tolerant of foot traffic.

PROPAGATION Division

'Albovariegatus': white-edged, bluish green blades, 6–8 in. (15–20 cm) tall

Hosta
Asparagaceae

Among the best-known and most beloved of temperate garden plants, with beauty, diversity, ease of growth, hardiness, and longevity, hostas are important for shadier sites as single focal points or mass-planted in bold displays. Native to diverse habitats in Northeast Asia, they exhibit a variety of forms, from small plants to large, hulking mounds. Foliage can be very small to very large, narrow and linear or oval and cordate, and variably ridged, rippled, and puckered. Although *Hosta* species are occasionally cultivated, their hybrids and sports, numbering in the thousands, are most commonly grown. The bold, lush, herbaceous, frequently variegated foliage in shades of white, cream, green, blue-green, and blue is most praised, but the tall scapes of tubular summer flowers in shades of purple, lilac, and white also provide a valuable show. Although most are not fragrant, flowers of *H. plantaginea* and its cultivars and hybrids are sweetly scented.

Some species and cultivars spread via rhizomes into small colonies, but these remain somewhat uncommon. Despite their primarily clumping habit, hostas make excellent mass-planted ground covers. Practically all cultivars of good vigor can be used, though the best candidates are plants with abundant foliage in horizontally spreading mounds wider than they are tall. Small to medium-sized cultivars are best-suited for ground cover applications. Miniatures could be used for small areas, and large or giant hybrid cultivars such as 'Frances Williams', 'Sum and Substance', and 'Empress Wu' may be used in landscapes.

CULTURE/CARE Evenly moist, moderately rich, well-drained soils in part shade to part sun, especially provided morning sun and afternoon shade. Tolerant of full shade but growth will be slower. Some, especially some gold-foliaged cultivars, are tolerant of full sun in cooler summer climates with adequate moisture. Avoid heavy, wet clay and sandy soils. Snails and slugs can damage newly emerging foliage. Apply organic slug pellets, use beer traps, or pick them off by hand, or choose cultivars with thicker, less palatable foliage.

USES Mass plant over small to large areas along pathways, on banks, and beneath shrubs and trees. Hostas bulk up steadily, though a young plant or single-eyed division may take up to five years to reach mature size. Not tolerant of foot traffic. Attractive to pollinators, especially bees and hummingbirds.

PROPAGATION Division

Hosta venusta
HANDSOME PLANTAIN LILY

Zones 3–8
Rocky, often dry sites among grasses or in dense shade with a limited distribution in South Korea. Likely introduced to Japan.

Among the smallest of species, spreading via creeping rhizomes into a low, dense mat of rosettes with small, cordate to elliptic, mid- to deep green leaves up to 1.5 in. (4 cm) long. Plants are 4 in. (10 cm) tall, forming colonies 20 in. (50 cm) or more wide, with light

purple flowers on stems 8–12 in. (20–30 cm) tall in late summer. AGM

'Kinbotan': wavy yellow margins turn lime-green by summer

'Paradise Puppet': hybrid with lightly ruffled and twisted leaves and good vigor

Hosta hybrids
PLANTAIN LILY

Zones 3–9
Garden origin.
Few genera offer such a dizzying array of cultivars as *Hosta*. The selected cultivars presented are vigorous and easy to grow, with dense foliage for small to medium-sized applications. All have foliage under 12 in. (30 cm) tall and are at least twice as wide as tall. Miniature, small, and larger cultivars can also be selected depending on the application.

Blue foliage

'Baby Bunting': densely packed, rounded, heart-shaped leaves, blue-green turning to midgreen, in mounds 10 in. (25 cm) tall by 20 in. (50 cm) wide, AGM

'Blue Mouse Ears': thick, rubbery, rounded, densely packed, cupped leaves, in mounds 6 in. (15 cm) tall by 12 in. (30 cm) wide, with balloonlike buds that open to lavender flowers, AGM

Gold foliage

'Bitsy Gold': linear, lightly rippled, bright yellow leaves, in mounds 7 in. (18 cm) tall by 18 in. (45 cm) wide, may bleach in too much sun

'Cheatin' Heart': oval to cordate, lightly rippled, sun-tolerant leaves emerge chartreuse, aging to muted gold, in mounds 7 in. (18 cm) tall by 15 in. (38 cm) wide

'Fire Island': rounded, sun-tolerant foliage emerges bright yellow, darkening with age atop red petioles, in mounds 10 in. (25 cm) wide by 18 in. (45 cm) tall, AGM

'Gold Drop': chartreuse to golden yellow, sun-tolerant leaves, in mounds 6 in. (15 cm) tall by 12–18 in. (30–45 cm) wide

'Lemon Lime': rounded, somewhat elongated, chartreuse to greenish yellow leaves, in vigorous mounds 10 in. (25 cm) tall by 24 in. (60 cm) wide

Hosta 'Blue Mouse Ears'

Hosta 'Mighty Mouse'

Gold-variegated foliage

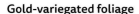

'Autumn Frost': striking foliage with blue centers and broad, golden yellow margins, in mounds 12 in. (30 cm) tall by 24 in. (60 cm) wide

'Cracker Crumbs': shiny, bright yellow leaves with green margins age to chartreuse, in mounds 6 in. (15 cm) tall by 12 in. (30 cm) wide, AGM

'Gaijin': spreading via rhizomes into mats, 6 in. (15 cm) tall by 12 in. (30 cm) or more wide, with small, oval to lance-shaped, midgreen, slightly wavy leaves with narrow yellow margins

'Golden Tiara': rounded, heart-shaped midgreen leaves with yellow to chartreuse margins, in mounds 12–16 in. (30–40 cm) tall by 30–36 in. (75–90 cm) wide, AGM

'Grand Prize': heart-shaped green leaves with broad, bright yellow to creamy yellow margins, in mounds 9 in. (23 cm) tall by 15 in. (38 cm) wide

'Kabitan': lance-shaped yellow leaves turning to chartreuse with green margins, in mounds 10 in. (25 cm) tall by 15 in. (38 cm) wide

'Lakeside Cupcake': rounded, strongly cupped, corrugated, blue-green leaves with yellow centers aging to creamy white, in mounds 5 in. (12.5 cm) tall by 15 in. (38 cm) wide

'Lakeside Dragonfly': long, broadly lance-shaped, tapered and pointed, arching, blue-green leaves with pale yellow margins, in mounds to 12 in. (30 cm) tall by 26 in. (66 cm) wide

'Lakeside Paisley Print': rounded, heart-shaped, rippled, blue-green leaves uniquely variegated with central

feathers of creamy yellow and light green, in mounds 10 in. (25 cm) tall by 20 in. (50 cm) wide

'Little Aurora': golden, puckered, cupped foliage, in mounds 10 in. (25 cm) tall by 20 in. (50 cm) wide

'Mighty Mouse': yellow-edged foliage, sport of 'Blue Mouse Ears' but slower growing

'Rainbow's End': shiny, deep green leaves irregularly variegated with linear, gold to chartreuse patterns, in mounds 10 in. (25 cm) tall by 20 in. (50 cm) wide

'Rainforest Sunrise': rounded, heart-shaped, cupped, corrugated, sun-tolerant, chartreuse to gold leaves with blue-green margins, in mounds 10 in. (25 cm) tall by 24 in. (60 cm) wide

Green foliage

'Cody': shiny, dark green leaves, in mounds 5 in. (12.5 cm) tall by 10 in. (25 cm) wide

'Feather Boa': wavy, pointed leaves emerge yellow to light green, aging quickly to chartreuse (especially in more sun), in mounds 10 in. (25 cm) tall by 20 in. (50 cm) wide

'Hacksaw': long, linear, tapering, heavily rippled, lightly serrated, sun-tolerant, light green leaves held flat in mounds 8 in. (20 cm) tall by 28 in. (71 cm) wide

'Plug Nickel': thick, slightly wavy, shiny, dark green leaves in densely packed mounds 6 in. (15 cm) tall by 12 in. (30 cm) wide

'Teaspoon': rounded, cupped, midgreen leaves on long petioles, in mounds 10 in. (25 cm) tall by 22 in. (56 cm) wide

White-variegated foliage

'Diamond Tiara': sport of 'Golden Tiara' with rounded, heart-shaped, midgreen leaves with white margins, in mounds 12–16 in. (30–40 cm) tall by 30–36 in. (75–90 cm) wide

'Dixie Chick': broadly lance-shaped, shiny leaves with a slight wave and narrow white margins, in mounds 6 in. (15 cm) tall by 15 in. (38 cm) wide

'Ginko Craig': elongated, oval, lightly rippled, midgreen leaves with white margins, in mounds 9 in. (23 cm) tall by 24 in. (60 cm) wide, AGM

'Iced Lemon': rounded, lance-shaped, light green leaves with narrow white margins in low, dense mounds 5 in. (12.5 cm) tall by 11 in. (28 cm) wide

'Raspberry Sundae': light to midgreen leaves with white central variegation and cherry-red petioles and scapes, deep purple flowers, in mounds 9 in. (23 cm) tall by 21 in. (53 cm) wide

'Stiletto': lance-shaped, rippled, midgreen leaves with narrow white margins in tightly packed mounds 12 in. (30 cm) tall by 24 in. (60 cm) wide

'Winsome': dark green leaves with moderately wide creamy white margins, in mounds 10 in. (25 cm) tall by 20 in. (50 cm) wide

Houttuynia cordata
CHAMELEON PLANT, FISH MINT

Saururaceae

Zones 4–10

Moist to wet, shady to sunny habitats from Japan and Korea south through China to Southeast Asia.

A vigorous, rhizomatous, colony-forming, herbaceous perennial with upright stems 8–16 in. (20–40 cm) tall, clothed in heart-shaped, green to blue-green leaves, which can suffocate any competitor be it weed or garden plant. Crushed leaves smell of oranges and taste of fish and are used widely in the cuisines within its native range. Tightly packed summer flower spikes resemble a narrow thimble up to 1 in. (2.5 cm) long, subtended by four showy, white, petal-like bracts.

CULTURE/CARE Average, moist, wet, or even submerged soils in full to part sun. Tolerant of part shade.

USES Areas of poor drainage, pond or stream edges, and along pathways. Spreads quickly and indefinitely if not controlled by maintenance or hardscape features. Not tolerant of foot traffic. Deer and rabbit resistant.

PROPAGATION Division

Houttuynia cordata 'Chameleon'

Houttuynia cordata

'Chameleon': green, red, pink, yellow, and cream foliage on bright red stems, boldest colors in full sun

'Flore Pleno': green foliage often infused with purple with doubled bracts

Humulus lupulus
COMMON HOPS

Cannabaceae

Zones 4–8
River flood plains, forest edges, hedgerows, and sunny, disturbed sites across Europe and western Asia and in much of North America.

In cultivation for more than 1000 years as a flavoring for beer, hops are also grown in gardens as interesting, fast-growing ornamental vines. Without vertical support, hops plants can be used as rambunctious, clambering ground covers. The roughly textured, twining, 15–20 ft. (4.5–6 m) or more long stems are clad in rough, palmate, 3–5 lobed, veined leaves, 5 in. (12.5 cm) long and wide. Herbaceous, rhizomatous, and dioecious, producing female and male flowers on separate plants. Female forms of the European variety are the most commonly available. Flowers are concealed in cone-shaped clusters of pale green bracts.

CULTURE/CARE Easy to grow in sun to part shade in soils of average to medium moisture with average to high fertility. Remove dried stems in autumn once plants have gone dormant.

USES Large, open areas absent of vertical structures, or use to cover or soften unsightly features. Not tolerant of foot traffic.

PROPAGATION Division

Humulus lupulus 'Aureus'

'Aureus': golden foliage turning to chartreuse in shade, AGM

'Bianca': similar to 'Aureus'

'Cascade': popular brewing hops with green leaves and large flower bracts

'Golden Tassels': dwarf, female, golden hops, to 6–10 ft. (1.8–3 m), possibly with better sun tolerance

'Nugget': brewing hops with green leaves

Hydrangea
Hydrangeaceae

Climbing hydrangeas, with their self-clinging stems and creamy white, fragrant flowers, are typically used to cover shaded walls and fences, but without vertical support, they will grow as an unexpected ground cover. At first forming a prostrate, rooting cover, they can eventually grow into billowy, cloudlike masses of foliage and flowers. *Hydrangea anomala* subsp. *petiolaris* is most widely cultivated, but evergreen species expand the utility and aesthetic possibilities of the genus.

CULTURE/CARE Part shade to shade in fertile, well-drained soils. Tolerant of deep shade, dry shade, and part sun with even moisture. Plants require 2–3 years to establish a strong root system before initiating meaningful aboveground growth. Ample water and fertilizer can expedite establishment. First flowering usually occurs 3–7 years after planting, on old wood. Prune only if absolutely required and after flowering.

USES Medium-sized to large applications, especially in part shade to part sun, under large shrubs or trees. Can be used to cover irregular features in the landscape such as rocks, uneven ground, low walls, and tree stumps. Because plants are slow to establish, a fast-spreading, low-growing complementary ground cover could be interplanted to provide coverage and weed suppression while the climbing hydrangea establishes a closed cover. Not tolerant of foot traffic. Attractive to pollinators, especially bees and butterflies. *Hydrangea anomala* subsp. *petiolaris* is salt tolerant.

PROPAGATION Cuttings

Hydrangea anomala subsp. petiolaris
CLIMBING HYDRANGEA

Zones 5–8

Dense to open forests in valleys or on rocky mountain slopes in Japan, China, and adjacent Himalayan countries.

A large, deciduous vine with self-clinging aerial roots from exfoliating, light brown, woody stems, 30–50 ft. (9–15 m) long, with light to midgreen, rounded to oval leaves with pointed tips, up to 3 in. (7.5 cm) long, turning yellow in fall. Flat-topped, creamy white, fragrant, lacecap inflorescences 6–8 in. (15–20 cm) wide are borne in summer. Fertile florets create textured centers surrounded by showy, sterile florets, each with four broad, rounded petals. AGM

var. *cordifolia* 'Brookside Littleleaf': smaller leaves and more compact, with stems 10–12 ft. (3–3.6 m) long,

Hydrangea anomala subsp. *petiolaris* as both ground cover and vine

previously considered a cultivar of *Schizophragma hydrangeoides*

'Mirranda': variegated with irregular golden edges turning to creamy white

'Silver Lining': leaves with blue-green and gray-green centers and irregular ivory-white margins

'Skylands Giant': lacecaps up to 12 in. (30 cm) wide

Hydrangea integrifolia
EVERGREEN CLIMBING HYDRANGEA

Zones 7–10

Woodland floors, tree trunks, and rocky outcrops in dense forests at high elevations in the Philippines and Taiwan, China.

Thick, leathery, somewhat glossy, mid- to deep green, elliptic leaves with smooth edges (often with blunt teeth on young plants), emerging with bronze tones on woody, self-clinging, reddish stems, 30–60 ft. (9–18 m) long. Large, round, white buds break open to reveal irregular, frothy mounds of creamy white, lacy, fertile flowers punctuated with a few small, sterile florets.

'Taiping Shan': clone from Taiwan, China

Hydrangea seemannii
EVERGREEN CLIMBING HYDRANGEA

Zones 7–10

High elevation cloud forests of western Mexico.

Thick, leathery, somewhat glossy, mid- to deep green, rounded, broadly elliptic leaves emerging with golden bronze tones on woody, self-clinging stems 20 ft. (6 m) or more long. Stems are thicker and sturdier than other climbing species, possibly requiring more effort to establish as a prostrate ground cover. Large, round, white buds open to fragrant, lacy domes of creamy white, fertile flowers punctuated with sterile florets with rounded petals.

Hydrocotyle sibthorpioides
PENNYWORT

Araliaceae

Zones (5)6–10

Shaded habitats, including streambanks, forests, and wet and grassy sites from low to high elevations in Japan, China, and Southeast Asia.

Hydrangea seemannii

Hydrocotyle sibthorpioides

Tiny, shiny, kidney-shaped, scallop-edged leaves, ¼–1 in. (6–25 mm) wide on fast-spreading rooting stems, forming mats 1–4 in. (2.5–10 cm) tall. Insignificant flowers.

CULTURE/CARE Part shade to shade in wet to evenly moist soils.

USES Between paving stones and rocks and on walls.

PROPAGATION Division

'Crystal Confetti': bluish green leaves with variable cream-colored edges

Hypericum calycinum

CREEPING ST. JOHN'S WORT, ROSE OF SHARON

Hypericum calycinum 'Brigadoon'

Hypericaceae

Zones 5–9

Grassy areas and open woods in Southeast Europe and Southwest Asia.

This cheerful, yet thuggish, semiwoody, semi-evergreen to deciduous subshrub produces upright stems to 12 in. (30 cm) or more tall, spreading indefinitely via rhizomes into impenetrable mats. Leaves are opposite, midgreen, oval to oblong, 2–4 in. (5–10 cm) long and 1 in. (2.5 cm) wide, often turning purplish in fall. Large, bright yellow summer flowers are 2–3 in. (5–7.5 cm) wide, with five petals and numerous long, yellow stamens. Trailing St. John's wort, *H. cerastioides*, is sometimes grown.

CULTURE/CARE Full sun to part shade, though tolerant of shade and dry shade. Tolerates diverse soil fertility and moisture conditions, including salt, spreading more slowly in suboptimum sites. Flowers occur on new growth and are most numerous in full sun. In cold winter climates, stems may partially die back but remain intact and hold foliage in milder regions. Shear or mow every 1–3 years to refresh.

USES Medium-sized to large areas, especially on slopes for erosion control, in dry sites, and for institutional plantings. Contain vigorous spread with hardscape features. Not tolerant of foot traffic. Deer and rabbit resistant. Attractive to pollinators, especially bees.

PROPAGATION Division

'Brigadoon': gold foliage, less vigorous and prone to burn in full sun

'Crowthyp' Fiesta (North America) or Carnival (Europe): blue-green foliage with broad, irregular, chartreuse or yellow margins aging to creamy yellow flushed pink on new growth

Iberis sempervirens
EVERGREEN CANDYTUFT

Brassicaceae

Zones 3–8

Rocky crevices in high mountains of Southern Europe.

Though of utilitarian reputation, candytuft is tough, reliable, and quite beautiful in bloom. It is a low-growing, evergreen subshrub with woody bases and rooting stems, with shiny, linear, dark green leaves 1 in. (2.5 cm) or more long, forming mounds or mats 6–12 in. (15–30 cm) tall and 18 in. (45 cm) or more wide. Small, four-petaled, bright white flowers in dense, flattened, 2 in. (5 cm) wide clusters can completely smother plants in a white spring carpet.

CULTURE/CARE Easy to grow in full sun in average to dry soils, tolerating periods of drought. Moderately tolerant of salt. Shear plants by one-third after flowering to refresh and encourage compact growth. In cold winter climates, foliage is usually semi-evergreen and benefits from the cover of evergreen boughs or snow to help reduce sun scorch and desiccation.

USES Small to medium-sized areas as a border edger, along pathways, on walls, in rock gardens, and on low slopes. Spreads slowly. Not tolerant of foot traffic. Deer and rabbit resistant. Attractive to pollinators, especially bees and butterflies.

PROPAGATION Cuttings, seed

'Alexander's White': compact, early blooming

'Forte' Snowsurfer: potentially more flowers over a longer period, more vigorous than 'Purity'

'Golden Candy': gold to chartreuse foliage with fewer flowers

'Ib2401' Absolutely Amethyst: hybrid with glowing purple-pink flowers

'Masterpiece': probable hybrid with *I. gibraltarica*, with large, long-blooming, white flowers with pink centers, zones 8–10

'Pink Ice': late-blooming hybrid with *I. gibraltarica* or *I. aurosica*, with deep pink buds and lavender-pink flowers, zones 5–9

'Purity': classic long-bloomer, often reblooming in the fall

'Snow Cone': large flowers

Iberis sempervirens

Impatiens omeiana

Imperata cylindrica 'Rubra'

'Snowflake': dark green foliage, large flowers in broad clusters, AGM

'Sweetie Pie': hybrid with pale lavender to lavender-pink flowers lightening with age, zones 7–9

'Weisser Zwerg' (syn. 'Little Gem'): compact habit

Impatiens omeiana
HARDY IMPATIENS

Balsaminaceae

Zones 6–9

Forests, forest margins, and thickets at moderate elevations in Sichuan, China.

CULTURE/CARE Part shade to shade in rich, average to moist soils.

Handsome, rhizomatous plants, 8–18 in. (20–45 cm) tall, with reddish upright stems topped with whorls of lance-shaped, deep green leaves with yellowish centers. Pouchlike yellow flowers occur in late summer and fall. Colonies spread indefinitely but can be controlled.

USES Woodland and shade gardens, border edges, and along pathways. Not tolerant of foot traffic.

PROPAGATION Division

'Ice Storm': compact plants with green leaves subtly frosted with silver

'Silver Pink': compact plants with deep pink veins and subtle silvering

Imperata cylindrica
JAPANESE BLOOD GRASS

Poaceae

Zones 5–9

Sandy riversides, seashores, and disturbed fields in Asia, Australia, Africa, and Southern Europe.

A very distinctive, rhizomatous, herbaceous warm-season grass with broad, light to midgreen, vertical blades with variable height in wild populations but typically 12–18 in. (30–45 cm) or more tall in its cultivated form, slowly spreading into attractive colonies. Wild plants are considered one of the worst noxious weeds in the world, especially in tropical, subtropical, and warm winter climates, reaching 24–48 in. (60–120 cm) tall and spreading aggressively by rhizome and seed. Luckily, the red-foliaged horticultural form is much more polite. Silvery white flowers are rarely produced in late summer or fall.

CULTURE/CARE Full sun to part shade in well-drained, average to moist, rich to moderately fertile soils. Tolerant of shade, poor soils, and drought. Some believe that the cultivar 'Rubra' could revert to its larger, invasive green form, though this is rarely, if ever, seen. If so, remove the green section.

USES Small to medium-sized applications in borders, between rocks, and for erosion control on slopes, spreading at a slow to moderate rate in cooler summer climates, faster where summers are warmer. Not tolerant of foot traffic. Deer and rabbit resistant.

PROPAGATION Division

'Rubra' (syn. 'Red Baron'): top third to half of leaf blade emerges bright green to yellow, turning purple-red or bright lipstick-red, deepening to burgundy in fall, spreading at a slow to moderate rate, rarely flowering and with no seed

Iris
Iridaceae

Irises, with their colony-forming habit, tightly packed and upright to arching fans of foliage, and rhizomes that dominate the soil horizon at or below the surface, can be useful ground covers that offer beauty and interest while outcompeting weeds and reducing erosion. Additionally, with a wide range of soil moisture tolerances from wet to dry, and light preferences from sun to part shade, they can be valuable throughout the garden. Although the shorter species are the most effective as ground covers, the taller species can be mass-planted as tall ground covers on a landscape scale and allowed to form large, contiguous colonies. These include *I. ensata*, *I. foetidissima*, *I. pallida*, *I. pseudacorus*, *I. sibirica*, *I. unguicularis*, and *I. versicolor*.

CULTURE/CARE *Iris cristata*, *I. japonica*, and *I. tectorum* prefer rich, well-drained, average to evenly moist soils, in part sun to part shade. *Iris cristata* and *I. tectorum* also prefer full sun with good moisture where they may produce more flowers. In more shaded sites, *I. cristata* is tolerant of seasonally dry soils once established. *Iris pumila* prefers full sun and average to dry, well-drained soils but tolerates poor soils. Divide to rejuvenate clumps every 2–3 years if flower production decreases. Protect new growth of all species from slugs. *Iris japonica* and *I. tectorum* can be sheared down in spring, if needed, to refresh clumps.

USES Border edges, along pathways, and for erosion control on slopes. *Iris pumila* and *I. cristata* are best for small applications. *Iris japonica* and *I. tectorum* can be used in small to medium-sized areas. For faster coverage, mass plant and allow clumps to spread into one another over time. None are tolerant of foot traffic. Deer and rabbit resistant. Good for erosion control on slopes.

PROPAGATION Division

Iris cristata
DWARF CRESTED IRIS

Zones 3–9

Rich woods, ravines, bluffs, mountain ledges, streamsides, and rocky hillsides, usually on calcareous soils, in the eastern and southeastern United States.

An excellent, lush, herbaceous ground cover that spreads quickly and indefinitely via runners into large, rhizomatous colonies, about 4–6 in. (10–15 cm) tall, of light green, sword-shaped, nodding blades. In midspring, colonies are topped with small pale to deep violet or bluish violet, 1–2 in. (2.5–5 cm) wide flowers with white and yellow markings on short stems.

'Abbey's Violet': grape-purple flowers with white and orange markings

'Alba': white flowers with gold crests

'Eco Blue Bird': bluish purple flowers with orange crests

'Powder Blue Giant': large, lavender-blue, gold-crested flowers nearly 3 in. (7.5 cm) wide, foliage up to 12 in. (30 cm) tall

'Tennessee White': abundant pure white flowers with gold crests, possibly appearing earlier and lasting longer than other cultivars

'Vein Mountain': white flowers with golden crests surrounded by a light blue ring, 12 in. (30 cm) tall

Iris japonica
JAPANESE IRIS, FRINGED IRIS

Zones 7–9

Forest clearings and margins and wet grasslands in China, Japan, and Myanmar.

Japanese iris is a vigorous, evergreen, rhizomatous species that forms indefinitely spreading colonies up to 10–12 in. (25–30 cm) tall of broad, semiglossy, sword-shaped, midgreen leaves that arch at the tips, for a somewhat subtropical look. The 2 in. (5 cm) wide, fragrant, orchidlike flowers of ruffled petals are held on branching stems and can be pale blue, lavender,

Iris unguicularis

Iris cristata 'Tennessee White'

Iris 'What Again'

or white, with yellow to orange crests and dark blue markings.

'Aphrodite': ivory-white and gray-green variegated foliage, pale blue flowers

'Eco Easter': more reliable to bloom, lavender-blue flowers

'Ledger' (syn. 'Ledger's Variety'): white flowers

'Porcelain Maiden': white flowers with lavender markings

'Skirt Chaser': more reliable to bloom, lavender-blue flowers with royal-purple markings

'Variegata': green leaves variegated with white and yellow, white to pale lavender flowers

Iris pumila
DWARF BEARDED IRIS

Zones 3–9
High elevations and dry continental Eurasian steppe, from Eastern Europe through Ukraine and Turkey to southern Siberia.

Among the smallest of the bearded species, resembling the German or tall bearded iris in miniature, at 8–16 in. (20–40 cm) in height. Flowers are fragrant, held among the foliage, and occur in a variety of colors in the wild. The true species is much less cultivated than its hybrids, which are referred to as the standard dwarf bearded iris class and are crosses between I. pumila and tall bearded irises, offering the same range of flower colors and detailing and the typical upright, swordlike, gray-green foliage.

'Banbury Ruffles': deep violet-blue flowers

'Blue Denim': light blue flowers

'Boo': white standards, blue and white falls

'Cherry Garden': wine-purple flowers

'Fireplace Embers': yellow flowers, maroon falls

'What Again': lavender-blue standards, coppery yellow falls

'Yankee Skipper': deep purple-blue flowers, dark purple markings on the falls

Iris tectorum
JAPANESE ROOF IRIS

Zones (4)5–9
Forest margins, sunny banks, meadows, and damp places in China, Korea, and Japan.

Broad, light to midgreen, sword-shaped foliage in upright or arching fans somewhat resembling I. japonica but hardier. Clumps can be semi-evergreen to evergreen in milder zones, 12–16 in. (30–40 cm) tall, spreading indefinitely. Large lavender-purple flowers can be 6 in. (15 cm) wide.

'Alba': white petals, yellow bases

'Slippery Slope': bluish lavender flowers with purple markings

'Variegata': white and green variegated leaves and pale lavender flowers

'Woolong': vigorous and clumping with lavender-purple flowers

Jasminum
Oleaceae

These much beloved vines and arching, viny shrubs are famous for their masses of perfumed white and pink flowers. Though the nonfragrant, yellow-flowered winter jasmine has been most commonly used as a ground cover, the fragrant species, in the absence of vertical support, can also provide rambunctious, textural, fragrant coverage.

CULTURE/CARE Full sun to part shade in soils of average moisture and fertility. Jasminum nudiflorum is tolerant of poor soils, which will reduce vigor. Jasminum officinale, which blooms on new wood, and J. nudiflorum, which blooms on old wood, can be cut back hard in spring (after flowering for J. nudiflorum) if needed to about 12–24 in. (30–60 cm) to refresh plants or control size.

USES Jasmines are vigorous growers though they require time to reach maximum size. Use on slopes, banks, retaining walls, and to cover medium-sized to large areas where their arching and trailing habits can be assets. Branches can root into the soil, aiding in slope stabilization. Not tolerant of foot traffic. Deer resistant. Attractive to pollinators, especially butterflies and hummingbirds.

PROPAGATION Cuttings, layering

Jasminum nudiflorum
WINTER JASMINE

Zones 6–9

Thickets, ravines, and slopes in western China.

Blooming in late winter and early spring, with bright yellow, nonfragrant, trumpet-shaped flowers when the green stems are devoid of their compound, trifoliate leaves that will emerge later in the season. Plants grow as a sprawling, viny shrub with branches arching in all directions from a central crown, eventually forming mounds up to 4 ft. (1.2 m) tall and 4–7 ft. (1.2–2.1 m) wide, though plants can be kept smaller with hard pruning after flowering. Two less hardy, larger species with similar habits, *J. floridum* (zone 7) and *J. mesnyi* (zone 8), can also be used. AGM

'Aureum': leaves irregularly splashed in yellow, less vigorous

'Mystique': leaves edged in white, less vigorous

'Nanum': rare dwarf, slow-growing form possibly derived from *J. nudiflorum* f. *pulvinatum*

Jasminum officinale
POET'S JASMINE

Zones 6–9

Valleys, ravines, thickets, woodlands, along rivers, and in meadows in China and adjacent Himalayan countries.

A vine that, absent of vertical support, will grow as an informal ground cover with lacey, textural, compound foliage intermingling with nearby plants from a central mound of vigorous, deciduous, trailing stems, 15–20 ft. (4.5–6 m) long and about 6–12 in. (15–30 cm) tall. The profuse late spring bloom of fragrant, white, trumpet-shaped, edible flowers from pink buds can continue intermittently or constantly until frost. Other similar, less hardy species can be used, including *J. beesianum* (zone 7), *J. polyanthum* (zone 8), and *J. ×stephanense* (zone 7).

f. *affine* (syn. 'Grandiflorum'): new foliage flushed burgundy, with large flowers, AGM

'Argenteovariegatum': gray-green leaves with creamy yellow to white margins, AGM

'Aureum' (syn. 'Aureovariegatum'): green leaves with irregular gold splashes

Jasminum nudiflorum

Jasminum officinale 'Frojas' Fiona Sunrise

Jovibarba globifera

'Devon Cream': larger, pale yellow to creamy white flowers said to have a more intense fragrance

'Frojas' Fiona Sunrise: golden foliage in full sun, lime-green in less light, AGM

'Inverleith': deep red new growth fades to deep green, deepest pink to reddish buds open to white flowers with pink reverses, AGM

Jovibarba
Crassulaceae

Rosette-forming, monocarpic succulents closely related to hen and chicks (*Sempervivum* spp.), differing in their greenish yellow to yellow or white flowers, fewer petals, and lack of stolons. Their colonies are either tight clumps, formed through splitting of the rosettes, which makes them difficult to separate, or through the production of small, lightly attached "rollers" that easily separate, roll away, and root. After much taxonomic flux, the genus is now considered to comprise two species, each with various subspecies.

CULTURE/CARE Full sun in well-drained to sharply drained or gravelly soils.

USES Small applications for dry and sunny sites, in rock gardens, along pathways, between paving stones, and in troughs and other containers. *Jovibarba heuffelii* is slow to expand. Not tolerant of foot traffic. Deer and rabbit resistant. Attractive to pollinators, especially bees.

PROPAGATION Division

Jovibarba globifera
ROLLING HEN AND CHICKS

Zones 3–9

Rocky habitats and grasslands, usually in mountainous regions, from Western Russia through Central Europe into France.

Formerly known as *J. sobolifera*, this species has now subsumed *J. allionii*, *J. arenaria*, and *J. hirta* as subspecies, though they are still often sold under their old names. *Jovibarba globifera* forms small spherical rosettes, ⅜–3 in. (1–7 cm) wide, depending on the subspecies, with pointed succulent foliage ranging in color from apple-green to yellowish or grayish green, sometimes with red flushes or red tips. Shy to flower but reproduces readily via pea-sized, easily detached rollers.

Jovibarba heuffelii
JOB'S BEARD, HEN AND CHICKS

Zones 3–9

Mountainous regions of Southeast Europe from Romania to Bosnia-Herzegovina, south to Greece, usually on rocky limestone substrates.

A variable species resembling *Sempervivum* species in form and in its similar range of foliage colors and patterns, including greens, blues, purples, reds, burgundies, and browns. Tightly packed rosettes, 2–5 in. (5–12 cm) wide, form colonies through splitting or via new rosettes within the mother crown. Colonies grow from a carrotlike root, often forming raised mounds with rosettes at lightly skewed angles. Propagation and spread can be very slow. Boasts many uncommonly found cultivars.

Juniperus
Cupressaceae

An exceedingly tough group of coniferous trees and shrubs that grow throughout the Northern Hemisphere, often in exposed and rocky sites, from low elevations to the tallest mountaintops. Indeed, the two tallest tree lines in the Northern Hemisphere are made up of *J. tibetica*, at 16,075 ft. (4900 m) in Tibet, China, and *J. indica*, at 15,580 ft. (4750 m) in Bhutan. Ground-covering cultivars are either derived from naturally prostrate species, subspecies, or varieties, or from chance dwarf forms of species that normally grow as upright trees or shrubs.

In the garden, junipers are among the hardiest, most durable, drought-tolerant, and low-maintenance ground-covering shrubs. Though they may have a reputation as a utilitarian group, closer consideration reveals an abundance of textures, colors, and beautiful features. Some species possess needlelike leaves on young plants, transitioning with age to scalelike leaves, while other species possess only needlelike leaves. This distinction between coarse and prickly needles versus soft and feathery scales can be important both for the textural impact and the comfort of working with these plants in the garden.

Junipers can be monoecious, with male and female cones on the same plant, or dioecious, with separate male and female plants. Some cultivars produce attractive blue or blue-black seed cones resembling blueberries. Various juniper species have long histories of human use of their aromatic parts, but it is the juniper berries, usually harvested from *J. communis*, that are most famous as the primary flavoring of gin.

CULTURE/CARE Easy to grow in full sun in most well-drained conditions from loamy to dry or gravelly soils. Growth rates will be slower in leaner conditions. Drought tolerant once established, rarely requiring supplemental water. Salt tolerant. If appropriate cultivars are selected, pruning will not be required unless plants spread beyond desired boundaries.

USES Small to large applications as a general cover, as a lawn alternative, for foundation plantings, or for erosion control on slopes, spreading at a slow to moderate rate. More pliant plants such as *J. communis* 'Corielagen', *J. procumbens*, or numerous cultivars of *J. horizontalis* are excellent for trailing over walls and around hardscape features including rocks and boulders. Not tolerant of foot traffic. Deer and rabbit resistant.

PROPAGATION Cuttings, layering

Included plants comprise spreading cultivars generally less than 24 in. (60 cm) tall. For large-scale applications, many horizontally spreading cultivars exist in heights of 2–6 ft. (0.6–1.8 m).

Juniperus chinensis
CHINESE JUNIPER

Zones 4–9

Mountainous regions of China, Mongolia, eastern Russia, Myanmar, and Japan.

Variable species grows as an upright shrub or tree up to 60 ft. (18 m) tall across most of its range but as a procumbent shrub in certain regions. Foliage is green to blue-green or grayish, needlelike on young plants, with mixed needlelike and scalelike foliage on mature plants—or entirely scalelike in *J. chinensis* var. *sargentii*. Cultivars offer an informal look in either vase shapes or spreading mounds.

'Paul's Gold': golden scalelike foliage brightest when young on plants with a mounding, arching, spreading habit, 16–20 in. (40–50 cm) tall by 24 in. (60 cm) wide

'San Jose': sage-green foliage, needlelike on young plants, mixed on mature plants held on rigid, irregular branches, 12–18 in. (30–45 cm) tall and 8 ft. (2.4 m) wide

var. *sargentii* (syn. 'Sargentii'): bluish green foliage is scaly on mature plants, 12–24 in. (30–60 cm) tall by 9 ft. (2.7 m) wide

var. *sargentii* 'Glauca': bluish, soft-textured foliage is scaly on mature plants, 18 in. (45 cm) tall by 9 ft. (2.7 m) wide

J. ×*pfitzeriana* 'Daub's Frosted': hybrid with *J. sabina*, with two-toned, needlelike foliage, bright golden yellow when young and blue-green when mature, 12–24 in. (30–60 cm) tall by 8 ft. (2.4 m) wide

Juniperus communis

COMMON JUNIPER

Zones 2–8

Circumpolar and circumboreal in dry and rocky soils in varied habitats including plains, forests, slopes, rock crevices, and summits throughout North America, Europe, and Asia, with populations in mountains as far south as the southern United States and the Atlas Mountains of North Africa.

Said to be the most widespread woody plant in the world, with forms ranging from trees 30 ft. (9 m) tall to prostrate shrubs, a form that is sometimes ecologically induced and sometimes genetically induced, depending on subspecies and variety. Needlelike foliage is dull green to bluish green. Less tolerant of hot, humid regions. Berries are used to flavor gin.

'Corielagen': low spreading, carpeting habit, 12 in. (30 cm) tall by 10 ft. (3 m) wide, with midgreen foliage and pliant red stems that mold to the contours of the ground

var. *depressa* 'Amidak' Blueberry Delight: dark green to bluish green foliage retaining good color into winter, in mounds 12 in. (30 cm) tall by 4 ft. (1.2 m) wide, with abundant seed cones resembling blueberries produced in the presence of a male plant, such as var. *depressa* 'Reedak'

var. *depressa* 'Reedak' Copper Delight: dense, slightly mounding habit, 12–16 in. (30–40 cm) tall by 4–5 ft. (1.2–1.5 m) wide, with light green foliage that turns to coppery bronze in fall, especially on younger growth, pollinator for var. *depressa* 'Amidak'

'Effusa': dull green foliage with silver-white undersides, low spreading habit, 9–12 in. (23–30 cm) tall by 4–6 ft. (1.2–1.8 m) wide

'Green Carpet': low spreader, 4–6 in. (10–15 cm) tall by 4–6 ft. (1.2–1.8 m) wide, with bright green new growth becoming dark green, AGM

'Greenmantle': dense green foliage on low spreading plants, 4 in. (10 cm) tall and 6 ft. (1.8 m) wide

'Mondap' Alpine Carpet: low, dense habit, 8 in. (20 cm) tall by 3 ft. (1 m) wide, with midgreen to slightly bluish green foliage

'Repanda': prostrate habit, 12 in. (30 cm) tall by 6 ft. (1.8 m) wide, with dark green foliage turning bronze in winter, AGM

Wild *Juniperus communis* overlooking Notre Dame Bay near Baytona, Newfoundland

Juniperus horizontalis
CREEPING JUNIPER, ANDORRA JUNIPER

Zones 2–9

Sand dunes, sandy and gravelly soils, prairies, slopes, rock outcrops, and streambanks across much of boreal Canada and the Canadian Rockies, with isolated populations in the northern United States.

A tough, horizontally spreading, mat-forming species up to 24 in. (60 cm) tall by 6 ft. (1.8 m) wide, with blue-green to gray-green feathery foliage often turning reddish purple in fall and winter, especially in colder climates. Foliage is mostly scalelike in adult plants with occasional needlelike foliage. Plants are dioecious. Fruit is uncommon on cultivated plants.

'Bar Harbor': silver-blue foliage with purplish winter tips, ground-hugging habit, 6–12 in. (15–30 cm) tall by 6 ft. (1.8 m) wide, relatively fast growth rate

'Blue Chip': silver-blue foliage with purplish winter tips, 8–12 in. (20–30 cm) tall by 6–8 ft. (1.8–2.4 m) wide

'Gold Strike': bright yellow new foliage fades to chartreuse with coral winter tones, 6 in. (15 cm) tall by 4 ft. (1.2 m) wide

'Golden Carpet': golden foliage with purplish tones in winter, more vigorous than 'Mother Lode', 12 in. (30 cm) tall by 10 ft. (3 m) wide, AGM

'Hughes': silver-blue foliage tinged purple in winter, 12 in. (30 cm) tall by 6–8 ft. (1.8–2.4 m) wide

'Monber' Icee Blue: silver-blue foliage purple-tinged when young and in winter on prostrate plants, 4 in. (10 cm) tall by 8 ft. (2.4 m) wide, with excellent winter color

'Mongeo' Jazzy Jewel: bright green foliage splashed with gold, turning bronzy purple in winter, 24 in. (60 cm) tall by 6 ft. (1.8 m) wide

'Mother Lode': gold foliage turns bronzy in winter, 4–6 in. (10–15 cm) tall by 8–10 ft. (2.4–3 m) wide

'Noslg' Limeglow: bright gold to chartreuse foliage holds color well into summer, resistant to sunburn, turns bronzy in winter on vase-shaped plants with slightly ascending branches, 6–12 in. (15–30 cm) tall by 4 ft. (1.2 m) wide, AGM

'Pancake': grayish blue foliage on extremely prostrate plants, 2–6 in. (5–15 cm) tall by 4 ft. (1.2 m) wide

'Plumosa' (syn. 'Plumosa Compacta'): green to blue-green foliage with purple tones in winter, 24 in. (60 cm) tall by 10 ft. (3 m) wide

'Prince of Wales': low mats, 4–6 in. (10–15 cm) tall by 3–6 ft. (1–1.8 m) wide, of bluish green foliage turning burgundy-purple in winter

'Wiltonii' (syn. 'Blue Rug'): intense silver-blue foliage developing purple tones in winter with excellent, uniform, trailing habit, 6 in. (15 cm) tall by 6–8 ft. (1.8–2.4 m) wide

'Youngstown': bright green to gray-green foliage turning purplish in winter, prostrate habit, 12 in. (30 cm) tall by 6 ft. (1.8 m) wide, with feathery, ascending branches

Juniperus procumbens
JAPANESE GARDEN JUNIPER

Zones 4–9

Shrublands, rocky areas, inland cliffs, and mountain peaks of southern Japan.

A dense and compact, textural, mat-forming species with sharply pointed, needlelike green to blue-green foliage purple-tinged in winter. Slow growth rate. Wild plants are 8–18 in. (20–45 cm) tall by 10–15 ft. (3–4.5 m) wide.

'Green Mound': bright, light green foliage, 8 in. (20 cm) tall by 6 ft. (1.8 m) wide

'Nana': low, dense, and slow-growing with bright green foliage aging to blue-green, purplish in winter, 4–12 in. (10–30 cm) tall by 6–8 ft. (1.8–2.4 m) wide, AGM

Juniperus rigida subsp. conferta
SHORE JUNIPER

Zones 5–9

Coastal areas, including sand dunes, of Japan and Sakhalin Island, Russia.

Dense, prickly, needlelike, green to blue-green, aromatic foliage forming coarsely textured, slowly expanding mats, 8–18 in. (20–45 cm) tall by 6 ft. (1.8 m) wide, often with ascending and arching branches, giving a varied topography. Previously known and still often sold as *J. conferta*.

'All Gold': bright golden yellow to chartreuse foliage becoming bronzy in winter, 12–18 in. (30–45 cm) tall by 8 ft. (2.4 m) wide, AGM

'Blue Pacific': blue-green foliage with better color, density, and form than the species, 6–12 in. (15–30 cm) tall by 6 ft. (1.8 m) wide

'Emerald Sea': emerald-green foliage becoming yellow-green in winter, 6–12 in. (15–30 cm) tall by 6 ft. (1.8 m) wide

'Silver Mist': silvery new foliage ages to blue-green, becoming bronzy in winter, 18–24 in. (45–60 cm) tall by 10 ft. (3 m) wide

Juniperus horizontalis 'Monber' Icee Blue

Juniperus horizontalis 'Mother Lode'

Juniperus procumbens 'Nana'

Juniperus rigida subsp. *conferta* 'Blue Pacific'

Juniperus sabina
SAVIN JUNIPER

Zones 3–8
Mountains of Central and Southern Europe to Siberia.

Widespread and somewhat variable, typically growing in the wild as a small to large, broadly spreading shrub with dull, dark green, aromatic foliage. Juvenile plants have needlelike foliage becoming scalelike in mature plants.

'Arcadia': spreading, mounding, layered form with blue-green, feathery foliage, 12 in. (30 cm) tall by 6–8 ft. (1.8–2.4 m) wide

'Blue Forest': distinctive upturned branches resemble a miniature forest of blue-green trees, 8–12 in. (20–30 cm) tall by 4–5 ft. (1.2–1.5 m) wide, sometimes attributed to *J. horizontalis*

'Buffalo': feathery green foliage with horizontal and ascending branches, 12 in. (30 cm) tall by 8 ft. (2.4 m) wide

'Monard' Moor-Dense: bright green, feathery foliage with compact, layered habit, 8–12 in. (20–30 cm) tall by 6 ft. (1.8 m) wide

'Monna' Calgary Carpet: light to midgreen foliage with low, prostrate habit, 9–12 in. (23–30 cm) tall by 10 ft. (3 m) wide

'Skandia': gray-green, feathery foliage, 12–18 in. (30–45 cm) tall by 8–10 ft. (2.4–3 m) wide

'Tamariscifolia': spreading, mounding form with layered branches of feathery, bluish green foliage, 18 in. (45 cm) tall by 15 ft. (4.5 m) wide

'Tamariscifolia New Blue': foliage brighter blue than 'Tamariscifolia'

Juniperus scopulorum
ROCKY MOUNTAIN JUNIPER,
ROCKY MOUNTAIN RED CEDAR

Zones 3–6
Dry, rocky outcrops, rocky soils, and slopes from British Columbia to New Mexico.

Incredibly long-lived, with scalelike foliage, typically growing as a tree up to 65 ft. (20 m), but with a few excellent dwarf forms.

'Monam' Blue Creeper: mounding, spreading form, with outstanding powder-blue foliage that intensifies in winter, 24 in. (60 cm) tall by 6–8 ft. (1.8–2.4 m) wide

Juniperus squamata 'Blue Star'

'Monoliver' Burly Blue: mounding, spreading form, with elegant blue-gray foliage, denser habit than 'Monam', 24 in. (60 cm) tall by 6–8 ft. (1.8–2.4 m) wide

Juniperus squamata
SINGLESEED JUNIPER, FLAKY JUNIPER

Zones 4–8
Forests, thickets, valleys, and roadsides in mountainous areas of China and the Himalayas.

Highly variable, growing as a large shrub, 7–30 ft. (2.1–9 m) tall, with gray-green, sharp, stiff, needlelike foliage, but offering dwarf cultivars.

'Blue Carpet': silver-blue foliage turns blue-green in winter on vigorous carpets, 12 in. (30 cm) tall by 5 ft. (1.5 m) wide, AGM

'Blue Star': dense, compact, and slow-growing, with bold, powder-blue foliage forming mounds 12–36 in. (30–90 cm) tall by 3–4 ft. (1–1.2 m) wide, AGM

'Floreant': blue foliage with sparks of creamy yellow to creamy white, on dwarf plants 12 in. (30 cm) tall by 16 in. (40 cm) wide

L

Lamium
Lamiaceae

These nonaromatic mint family members have textured, lightly fuzzy foliage that can be silver or green with silver markings, perfect for lighting up shaded areas. Though their pretty yellow, white, or pink flowers and leaves look somewhat delicate, they are tough, hardy plants.

CULTURE/CARE Average to moist soils in part to full shade. *Lamium galeobdolon* is tolerant and *L. maculatum* is somewhat tolerant of dry shade; *L. maculatum* may not tolerate hot, humid summer climates. Extremely vigorous *L. galeobdolon* is difficult to remove once established, becoming potentially aggressive in the garden and invasive in some regions including British Columbia and Washington. *Lamium maculatum* grows at a moderate rate with ever-expanding mats but is not invasive and can be easily controlled.

USES Use *L. galeobdolon* for quick cover of medium-sized to large areas, including near building foundations, hanging over walls, and on slopes for erosion control. *Lamium maculatum* is best for small to medium-sized applications. Not tolerant of foot traffic. Deer and rabbit resistant. Attractive to pollinators, especially bees.

PROPAGATION Division, cuttings

Lamium galeobdolon
YELLOW ARCHANGEL, GOLDEN DEAD-NETTLE

Zones (3)4–9
Widespread in woodlands and shaded habitats of Europe and into Western Asia.

A vigorous, quickly spreading, herbaceous to evergreen perennial with toothed, heart- to arrow-shaped, lightly fuzzy, midgreen leaves, 1–3 in. (2.5–7.5 cm) long, sometimes with variable silver markings. Formerly known as *Lamiastrum galeobdolon*. It spreads via rhizomes and via 12–18 in. (30–45 cm) long rooting stolons, creating a dense, weed-smothering cover, 6–12 in. (15–30 cm) tall, spreading indefinitely and possibly overwhelming small spaces. Soft yellow, hooded, snapdragon-like flowers have subtle orange-red markings and appear in regularly spaced whorls on upright, leafed stems.

Lamium galeobdolon 'Herman's Pride'

'Florentinum' (syn. 'Variegatum'): variegated foliage with a bold silver chevron

'Herman's Pride': clump-forming without stolons, with heavily silver-mottled, more serrated, and elongated leaves

Lamium maculatum
SPOTTED DEAD NETTLE

Zones 3–8
Grasslands and woodlands in moist, fertile soils from sea level to high elevations from Europe and North Africa into Western Asia.
Mat-forming, herbaceous to semi-evergreen perennial, 4–8 in. (10–20 cm) tall, spreading indefinitely at a moderate rate with 1 in. (2.5 cm) long, fuzzy, heart- or arrow-shaped leaves often with silver markings. Hooded, spotted, spring-blooming flowers are typically pink, purplish pink, or white in terminal clusters atop upright, leafy stems.

'Album': white flowers, green leaves with a central silver stripe

'Anne Greenaway': pink flowers, green leaves with a central silver stripe and gold edges

'Aureum': pink flowers, gold leaves with a central silver stripe, slower growing

'Beacon Silver': deep pink flowers, silver leaves edged with green

'Checkin' Pink Chablis: pale pink flowers, silver leaves edged with green

'Chequers': deep pink flowers, green leaves with central silver stripe

'Dellam' Golden Anniversary: similar to but more stable than 'Anne Greenaway'

'Ghost': deep pink flowers, silver leaves edged with green

'Lemon Frost': deep pink flowers, gold leaves with a central silver stripe

'Orchid Frost': pink flowers, silver leaves edged with green

'Pink Pewter': pale pink flowers, silver leaves edged with green

'Purple Dragon': deep lavender-pink flowers, silver leaves edged with green

'Red Nancy': deep lavender-pink flowers, silver leaves edged with green

'Shell Pink': pale pink flowers, green leaves with a central silver stripe

'White Nancy': white flowers, silver leaves edged with green

Larix decidua
EUROPEAN LARCH

Pinaceae

Zones 2–9
Mountains of Central Europe.
Medium-sized to large, deciduous conifer with tufts of soft, gray-green needles turning bright yellow in autumn before they fall. Dwarf prostrate cultivars grafted onto short root stock can be used as ground covers.
CULTURE/CARE Full sun in average, well-drained soils.
USES Specimen for smaller spaces or as a mass planting for large applications. Not tolerant of foot traffic.
PROPAGATION Grafting

'Pendula': somewhat lax, prostrate habit, growing 12 in. (30 cm) or more per year

'Varied Directions': prostrate, branching into fans, growing 12 in. (30 cm) or more per year

Lathyrus latifolius
PERENNIAL PEA, EVERLASTING PEA

Fabaceae

Zones 3–9
Hedgerows, woodland edges, fields, and disturbed meadows from Southern and Central Europe to northwest Africa. Widely naturalized along roadsides, embankments, railways, and in fields and waste places in North America.
A rhizomatous, herbaceous, long-lived perennial resembling the annual sweet pea, with nonfragrant, long-blooming, pink to white summer blooms that make good cut flowers. Winged stems and green to blue-green compound leaves will scramble into thick, rambunctious masses of interlocking, somewhat vining foliage, 12–24 in. (30–60 cm) tall by 3–6 ft. (1–1.8 m) wide. With vertical support, plants can climb to 6–9 ft. (1.8–2.7 m). Considered invasive in some regions. Seed pods and seeds can be toxic in quantity. AGM
CULTURE/CARE Full sun to part shade in average, well-drained soils with moderate moisture. Drought

Lamium maculatum 'Ghost'

Lamium maculatum 'Orchid Frost'

Larix decidua 'Pendula'

Lathyrus latifolius 'Albus'

tolerant once established. Best in cooler summer climates.

USES A vigorous, informal, rambling cover with a cottage garden look for medium-sized to large areas, including slopes and embankments for erosion control or between garden perennials and shrubs as a filler and knitter. Not tolerant of foot traffic. Attractive to pollinators, especially bees and butterflies.

PROPAGATION Division, seed

'Albus': pure white flowers, AGM

Pearl Mix: flowers in a range of pinks and white

'Red Pearl': glowing magenta-pink flowers

'Rosa Pearl': delicate light pink to lavender-pink and white flowers, AGM

'White Pearl': pure white flowers, AGM

Lavandula
Lamiaceae

Lavenders are among the most popular garden plants and are easy to grow, romantic, and beautiful. They are tolerant of heat and drought, they support pollinators, and they have edible and fragrant foliage and flowers for food flavorings and perfumes. Small, semi-evergreen to evergreen, semiwoody to woody shrubs have green, gray-green, or silver foliage and wands of blue, purple, pink, or white early summer flowers. Typically planted in herb gardens or borders, they can be mass-planted to form excellent ground covers.

CULTURE/CARE Full sun in dry, lean soils, especially sandy or gravelly sites, with neutral to alkaline pH. Tolerant of slightly acidic and salty soils. Avoid rich soils, clay soils, and wet winter soils that will encourage sprawling growth and decrease longevity. Lavenders may not perform in hot and humid summer regions, though the lavandins (*L. ×intermedia*) will show more tolerance for these conditions. To help maintain a compact habit, shear plants lightly in early spring as plants break dormancy and again after flowering.

USES Mass plant on walls, along pathways, as foundation plantings, as a low hedge (especially the *L. ×intermedia* cultivars), on slopes, and as specimens in rock gardens and borders. Plants reach full size in 2–3 years. Not tolerant of foot traffic. Deer and rabbit resistant. Attractive to pollinators, especially bees and butterflies.

PROPAGATION Cuttings, seed

Lavandula angustifolia and its hybrids
ENGLISH LAVENDER, LAVANDIN

Zones 5–9

Rocky grasslands, coastal and inland cliffs, and mountain peaks, often on calcareous soils, in Spain, France, and Italy.

English lavender, *L. angustifolia*, is the classic species of gardens, kitchens, sachets and potpourris, and of the famous Mediterranean fields and perfume factories. Plants form rounded mounds, twice as wide as they are tall and, in flower, as wide as they are tall. Linear, gray-green, 2 in. (5 cm) long foliage is evergreen in mild climates, semi-evergreen to deciduous in the coldest zones. Flower spikes are held above the foliage on mostly naked stems over a long period beginning in early summer.

Lavandula ×chaytoriae is a hybrid of *L. angustifolia* and *L. lanata*. Hardiness can vary greatly depending on cultivar.

Lavandins, *L. ×intermedia*, are sterile hybrids of *L. angustifolia* and *L. latifolia*, usually forming large mounds, 24–36 in. (60–90 cm) or more tall and wide, with larger flowers and longer, more easily harvested stems beginning to bloom in midsummer. Commonly grown for commercial purposes with their strong fragrance and copious production of aromatic oils, though the higher camphor content results in a lower quality oil less suited for the kitchen and perfume. Less hardy than *L. angustifolia* but more tolerant of heat, humidity, and acidic soils.

L. angustifolia cultivars

'Arctic Snow': white flowers, gray-green foliage, compact, 20 in. (50 cm) tall and wide

Ellagance Series: compact, first-year blooming, seed-grown series with gray-green, fragrant foliage, 12–14 in. (30–35 cm) tall and wide

'Ellagance Ice': white flowers with a pale blue blush

'Ellagance Pink': light pink flowers

'Ellagance Purple': dark purple-blue flowers

'Ellagance Sky': light violet-blue flowers

'Ellagance Snow': pure white flowers that resist blushing pale blue, especially in cool temperatures

'Folgate': excellent early blooming oil producer and culinary lavender with sweetly fragrant, vibrant violet-blue flowers and gray-green foliage, 18–24 in. (45–60 cm) tall and wide, AGM

Lavandula angustifolia at Chantecler Gardens, Queenstown, New Zealand

'Hidcote': classic lavender, with fragrant, dark purple flowers, gray-green foliage, 16–20 in. (40–50 cm) tall and wide, AGM

'Hidcote Superior': seed-grown cultivar with deep purple flowers, considered an improvement on 'Hidcote', with better flowers on more uniform, compact plants, to 16 in. (40 cm) tall and wide

'Lavang 21' Violet Intrigue: long, fragrant, vibrant violet-blue spikes with possible rebloom, gray-green foliage, 18–24 in. (45–60 cm) tall and wide

'Martha Roderick': fragrant violet flowers, gray-green foliage, 18–24 in. (45–60 cm) tall and wide

'Mini Blue': dwarf, first-year blooming, seed-grown, compact plants, 10–12 in. (25–30 cm) tall and wide, with gray-green foliage and fragrant, vibrant violet-blue flowers

'Momparler' Platinum Blonde: gray-green foliage with creamy margins, blue flowers on long spikes, 24 in. (60 cm) tall and wide, zone 6

'Munstead': classic with fragrant, lavender-blue flowers, gray-green foliage on compact plants, 12–18 in. (30–45 cm) tall and wide

'Rosea' (syn. 'Jean Davis'): soft pink flowers with a fruity, clean flavor, popular for culinary uses, gray-green foliage, 18 in. (45 cm) tall and wide

'Schola' Blue Cushion: dwarf, compact plants, 12–16 in. (30–40 cm) tall and wide, with fragrant, violet-blue flowers fading to light blue and gray-green foliage

'Silver Mist': among the most silvery foliage, 16–20 in. (40–50 cm) tall and wide, with fragrant, violet-blue flowers

'SuperBlue': fragrant, deep violet-blue flowers, on compact plants 12 in. (30 cm) tall and wide, good winter hardiness and heat and humidity tolerance

'Thumbelina Leigh': compact and floriferous, blooming up to three times a year, 12–18 in. (30–45 cm) tall and wide, with chubby, fragrant, violet-blue spikes

L. ×chaytoriae hybrid

'Sawyers': silver foliage, light purple to purple-blue flowers, good fragrance, 24 in. (60 cm) tall and wide, zone 6, AGM

L. ×intermedia hybrids

'Alba': pure white flowers on short spikes 2–3 in. (5–7.5 cm) long, may rebloom, AGM

'Edelweiss': pale pink buds open to intensely fragrant, white flowers, with gray-green foliage

'Fred Boutin': silver-gray to near white leaves, with violet flower spikes on long stems, perhaps not as fragrant as other lavandins

'Gros Bleu': one of the darkest lavandins, with 4 in. (10 cm) long, purple, often reblooming flower spikes close to the color of 'Hidcote', on plants more compact than 'Grosso' with a sweeter fragrance and less camphor, and gray-green foliage

'Grosso': strong fragrance with likely the highest oil content of the lavandins, grown commercially in France, with violet flower spikes up to 6 in. (15 cm) long and gray-green foliage

'Niko' Phenomenal: reliable cultivar with good winter survival and minimal dieback, blooms a little earlier than other lavandins, often reblooming in late summer, with violet-blue flower spikes up to 5 in. (15 cm) long, gray-green foliage, good heat and humidity tolerance

'Provence': commercially grown for oil production in France, milder and sweeter than other lavandins and sometimes used for culinary purposes, with good heat and humidity tolerance, light violet flower spikes up to 3 in. (8 cm) long, gray-green foliage

Lavandula stoechas
SPANISH LAVENDER, FRENCH LAVENDER

Zones 6 or 7–10

Dry hills, garigue shrublands, and open woodlands on both granite- and limestone-derived soils over most of Mediterranean Europe and the western half of Mediterranean Africa.

Called Spanish lavender in North America and French lavender in Europe, *L. stoechas* is immediately recognizable by its winglike sterile bracts in shades of pink, purple, or white atop each inflorescence. Beneath are the true flowers—small, purple-red to dark purple trumpets on short, stubby, four-sided spikes atop naked stems, blooming earlier than English lavender and reblooming throughout the season. Plants are mounded to upright with fragrant, fuzzy, gray-green to silver foliage. Hardiness varies between cultivars. Claims to zone 6 may be overstated, at least for many regions. However, sharp drainage will greatly increase overwintering success. Oils are used medicinally and in insect repellants, soaps, and perfumes but are considered of lower quality than English lavender oils. Leaves are used in potpourri.

'Anouk': gray-green foliage, dark purple flowers, lavender-pink bracts, compact, 18 in. (45 cm) tall and 24 in. (60 cm) wide, zone 6 or 7

Lavandula 'Ibpr910-2' The Princess

'Bentley' With Love: gray-green foliage, deep magenta-pink flowers, long and delicate glowing pink bracts, 20 in. (50 cm) tall and wide, early to bloom with good repeat bloom, zone 6

'Ghostly Princess' (*L. pedunculata* × *L. stoechas*): striking silver foliage, warm purple flowers, pale pink bracts, 18–24 in. (45–60 cm) or more tall and wide, zone 7

'Ibpr910-2' The Princess (*L. pedunculata* × *L. stoechas*): gray-green foliage, warm purple flowers, glowing pink bracts, 18–24 in. (45–60 cm) or more tall and wide, early flowering with repeat bloom throughout summer, zone 7

Javelin Forte Series: large flowers on strong, well-branched plants in shades of purple, pink, and white, zone 7

Madrid and New Madrid Series: well-branched, floriferous plants in a variety of colors, zone 7

Madrid Lavish Series: multiple bracts throughout the inflorescence in a variety of colors, zone 7

'Otto Quast': gray-green foliage, dark purple flowers, lavender-pink bracts, 24 in. (60 cm) or more tall and wide, zone 7

'Silver Anouk': silver foliage, dark purple flowers, lavender-pink bracts, compact, 18 in. (45 cm) tall and 24 in. (60 cm) wide, zone 6 or 7

subsp. *stoechas* f. *leucantha* 'Snowman': compact British cultivar seemingly yet undiscovered in North America, with pure white flowers and white bracts with green veins, 12 in. (30 cm) tall and wide, zone 6 or 7

subsp. *stoechas* f. *rosea* 'Kew Red': gray-green foliage, reddish purple flowers, light pink bracts with reddish purple veins, 18–24 in. (45–60 cm) tall and wide, zone 7

Leptinella
Asteraceae

Mat-forming, rhizomatous, evergreen to herbaceous perennials from the Southern Hemisphere, the commonly cultivated species are from New Zealand, with soft, feathery or fernlike, compound leaves and yellowish to greenish buttonlike inflorescences that hardly resemble their aster and daisy cousins. Textural carpets reach just 1–2 in. (2.5–5 cm) tall but can spread indefinitely.

CULTURE/CARE Easy to grow in average, well-drained soils with even moisture in full sun to part shade. Avoid full sun in hot summer climates. Intolerant of drought.

USES Small to medium-sized applications as a lawn alternative, between paving stones, at the front of the border, along stairways, and in containers, spreading at a moderate to fast rate. Tolerant of light to moderate foot traffic. Deer resistant.

PROPAGATION Division

Leptinella gruveri
MINIATURE BRASS BUTTONS

Zones 7–10

Evenly moist habitats including salt marshes, seepages, and permanently damp fields from coastal to mountainous regions of New Zealand.

Mosslike habit with tiny, hairless, fernlike, bright green leaves forming dense, semi-evergreen to ever-green mats not more than a ½ in. (1.3 cm) tall. Prefers shade to part shade and reliable moisture. The name *L. gruveri* doesn't exist in the flora of New Zealand, even as a synonym. The proper name may be *L. dioica* 'Minor'.

Leptinella potentillina
VERDIGRIS BRASS BUTTONS,
CHATHAM BRASS BUTTONS

Zones (4)5–10

Coastal regions, especially near seepages, in damp fields, on sand dunes, and in damp and sandy hollows around Auckland and in the Chatham Islands, New Zealand.

Resembles *L. squalida* with large, feathery leaves forming mats 2 in. (5 cm) tall but bright green with a verdigris cast like the weathered copper of the Statue of Liberty. Develops bronze tones in summer.

Leptinella pusilla
PURPLE BRASS BUTTONS

Zones 5–9

Open sites on gravel or sand, in open tussock grass-land, and in the shade of rock outcrops from coastal to subalpine regions in New Zealand.

Similar to *L. squalida* but with leaves more dissected and feathery, with tones of light gray-green, purplish bronze, and coppery brown. Good drought tolerance.

Leptinella squalida
BRASS BUTTONS

Zones 4–10

Coastal to alpine areas, at riversides, on cobble and sand beaches, in short tussock grassland, and in alpine herbfields in New Zealand.

The most commonly grown brass buttons, form-ing tight mats of light green to gray-green, feathery foliage, 2 in. (5 cm) tall. Drought tolerant once established.

'Platt's Black': older leaves change from gray-green to near black, purple-gray, and bronze

Leucanthemum ×superbum
SHASTA DAISY

Asteraceae

Zones 4–9

Garden origin.

Thick, almost succulent, dark green foliage and masses of yellow-centered, white summer daisies growing as upright border perennials, except for 'Car-pet Angel Daisy', which forms low spreading mats.

CULTURE/CARE Easy to grow in full sun in soils of average moisture and average to rich fertility. Drought tolerant once established.

USES Small- to medium-scale plantings along border edges and pathways. Not tolerant of foot traffic. Deer and rabbit resistant.

PROPAGATION Division, cuttings

'Carpet Angel Daisy': shaggy, double, anemone-type, summer daisies with drooping ray florets and ruffled white and yellow centers on compact, prostrate plants, with mats 3–4 in. (7.5–10 cm) tall and 20 in. (50 cm) wide, and flowers that sit just above the foliage

Leymus arenarius
BLUE LYME GRASS

Poaceae

Zones 4–9

Coastal areas, including sand dunes, of Western and Northern Europe.

A rhizomatous, semi-evergreen, cool-season grass with thick, blue-green to powder-blue, upright to arch-ing blades 24 in. (60 cm) tall, forming dense, vigorous, indefinitely spreading colonies. Blue inflorescences reach 36 in. (90 cm) tall, turning straw-colored with age. *Leymus condensatus* and its cultivar 'Canyon Prince' are similar yet larger and less hardy but can be used similarly.

CULTURE/CARE Full sun in well-drained, dry to moist soils of low to good fertility. Salt tolerant. Can be overly aggressive in gardens if not controlled or corralled by hardscape. Shear foliage in spring to refresh plants.

Leptinella potentillina

Leptinella squalida 'Platt's Black'

Leucanthemum ×*superbum* 'Carpet Angel Daisy'

Leymus arenarius in Madeira Park, BC

Libertia peregrinans

USES Medium-sized to large applications as a tall ground cover, especially on slopes, in dry, sunny sites, and for erosion control. Not tolerant of foot traffic. Deer and rabbit resistant.

PROPAGATION Division

'Blue Dune': bright blue foliage

'Findhorn': more compact with good blue foliage

Libertia peregrinans
NEW ZEALAND IRIS

Iridaceae

Zones 8–10

Sandy, peaty, or pumice-based soils on dunes, in swales, at the margins of swamps, and in bogs throughout New Zealand.

A rhizomatous, evergreen perennial with stiff, vertical fans of narrow, pointed, sword-shaped, green and orange leaves forming dense, slowly expanding colonies, 12–18 in. (30–45 cm) tall, thick enough to serve as an unusual but useful ground cover. Though sometimes shy to flower, mature plants can produce branched inflorescences of small, pure white, lightly fragrant, 1 in. (2.5 cm) wide, iris-like flowers from late spring through summer.

CULTURE/CARE Full to part sun in average to moist, moderately fertile soils. Drought tolerant once established. Moderate levels of stress from drought, heat, or cold will intensify the orange foliage coloration.

USES Small to medium-sized applications along pathways, at the front of the border, and as a low foundation planting. Stunning when backlit by early morning or late evening sun. Spreads at a slow to moderate rate. Not tolerant of foot traffic. Deer and rabbit resistant.

PROPAGATION Division

Lindernia grandiflora
SAVANNAH FALSE PIMPERNEL, BLUE MONEYWORT

Linderniaceae

Zones (6)7–10
Pinelands, marshes, and swamps in Georgia and Florida.
Creeping, indefinitely spreading, herbaceous to evergreen mats, 1–4 in. (2.5–10 cm) tall, of trailing stems of tiny, tear-shaped, midgreen leaves. Small purple-blue and white tubular flowers with three large lower lobes and two small upper lobes attract small pollinators from spring to fall.
CULTURE/CARE Average, moist, or wet soils in sun to part shade.
USES Along pathways, between stepping stones, at the edge of waterways or ponds, along stairways, between rocks, as a lawn alternative, and trailing over walls. Grows quickly. Tolerant of light to moderate foot traffic.
PROPAGATION Cuttings

Linnaea borealis
TWINFLOWER

Caprifoliaceae

Zones 2–8
Circumboreal in coniferous forests, along trails, in forest openings, on forest edges, and in taiga and tundra from sea level to montane zones. Three subspecies occur in North America: *americana*, widespread across North America except the South Central and southeastern United States; *longiflora*, in the Pacific Northwest and British Columbia; and *borealis*, in the Yukon and Alaska and across Asia to Europe.
This favorite of Carl Linnaeus bears his name as a tribute to his fundamental contributions to biology. It is a charming, low-growing, evergreen, semiwoody species, spreading into semiclosed mats via prostrate, rooting stems that give rise to short, leafy, vertical shoots, 1–4 in. (2.5–10 cm) tall, of small, leathery, rounded, scalloped, midgreen leaves topped in late spring or summer with a pair of nodding, sweetly fragrant, pale pink, funnel-shaped flowers.
CULTURE/CARE Grows naturally in the duff and moss layers atop very thin and rocky soils or sometimes over deeper, richer soils with roots descending to access moisture and nutrients below. For success in the garden, these conditions should be emulated in part sun to part shade. Drought tolerant once established.

Linnaea borealis in the wild, Saturna Island, BC

USES Small-scale plantings in special locations, including shady rock gardens, along pathways and stairways, beneath conifers, and on shallow slopes. Occasional foot traffic is tolerated. Deer resistant.
PROPAGATION Division, removal of rooted stems

Liriope
Asparagaceae

Clumps or spreading colonies of narrow, linear, arching or upright, somewhat leathery, evergreen foliage resembling dark green sedges or grasses. Purple summer flowers reveal allegiances not to graminoids but to the asparagus family, including lily of the valley (*Convallaria majalis*), Solomon's seal (*Polygonatum* spp.), false Solomon's seal (*Maianthemum* spp.), and black mondo grass (*Ophiopogon planiscapus* 'Nigrescens'). Rhizomes resemble small potatoes.
CULTURE/CARE Widely adaptable from sand to clay and full sun to shade, though protect *L. muscari* from full sun in hot summer climates. Tolerant of heat, humidity, periods of drought, dry shade, and root competition from shallowly rooted trees. *Liriope spicata* is

salt tolerant. If leaves are damaged in winter, trim tips with scissors, shear, or mow plants down just before active growth resumes.

USES Easy and adaptable for edging borders, pathways, or driveways; as a foundation plant; for erosion control on slopes; and as a lawn alternative including at the base of trees. Clumping *L. muscari* bulks up at a somewhat slow rate. Mass plant for full coverage over small to large areas. *Liriope spicata* can spread aggressively and *L. minor* moderately by rhizomes. *Liriope spicata* is best for medium- to large-scale applications, while *L. minor* is best for small- to large-scale areas. Hardscape features can control spread. Both *L. muscari* and *L. spicata* are potentially invasive in the southeastern United States. *Liriope minor* is tolerant of foot traffic. Deer and rabbit resistant.

PROPAGATION Division

Liriope minor
LILYTURF

Zones 5–10

Forests, shady hillsides, and grassy slopes from middle to high elevations in China and Japan.

Low growing, rhizomatous species with leaves 3–8 in. (7.5–20 cm) long and lavender flowers on stems shorter than the foliage in late summer.

'Nonomonnrj' NoMo: spreading mats, 2–3 in. (5–7.5 cm) tall, tolerant of drought and heat, effective lawn alternative that requires less summer irrigation than turf grass and little maintenance except mowing in early spring to remove brown tips and application of slow release fertilizer

Liriope muscari
BLUE LILYTURF, MONKEY GRASS

Zones (5)6–10

Forests, bamboo forests, scrub, shady and moist ravines, and on slopes from lowlands to montane areas in China and Japan.

Leaves 12–24 in. (30–60 cm) long and ½–1 in. (1.3–2.5 cm) wide in clumps, 12–24 in. (30–60 cm) tall and wide. Spikes of lavender, lavender-blue, or dark purple, six-petaled, summer flowers resemble the grape hyacinth (*Muscari* spp.) on 6–8 in. (15–20 cm) tall, upright stems followed by shiny, round fruit aging from green to black. Herbaceous in cold winter climates, evergreen in milder zones. AGM

'Big Blue': deep lavender-blue flowers with thick, robust foliage, 18–24 in. (45–60 cm) tall

'Gold-banded' (syn. 'Gold Band'): shorter, broad, yellow-edged leaves, 12–18 in. (30–45 cm) tall

'Lirf' Isabella: narrow foliage, pink flowers, 16 in. (40 cm) tall

'Majestic': deep lavender flowers

'Monroe White': pure white flowers, dark green foliage, 18 in. (45 cm) tall

'Okina': leaves emerge pure white, slowly developing striations of dark green, becoming fully dark green by autumn, 12 in. (30 cm) tall

'Pee Dee Ingot': gold foliage in sun, chartreuse in shade, 12–18 in. (30–45 cm) tall

'Royal Purple': dark purple flowers

'Silvery Sunproof': lighter green leaves with creamy white to yellow edges, good sun tolerance, said to bloom profusely

'Super Blue': showy, vibrant violet-blue flowers with stems on large plants to 20 in. (50 cm) tall

'Variegata': variegated with creamy yellow edges, 12–18 in. (30–45 cm) tall

Liriope spicata
CREEPING LILYTURF

Zones 4–10

Forests, grassy slopes, and moist places from lowlands to montane areas of China, Japan, Korea, and Vietnam.

Vigorously spreading, rhizomatous species with leaves 12–16 in. (30–40 cm) long and ¼ in. (6 mm) wide, forming dense colonies 10–16 in. (25–40 cm) tall, spreading indefinitely. Spikes of light purple or white, six-petaled flowers, less showy than *L. muscari*, arise among the foliage in late summer on upright stems, followed by shiny, round fruit aging from green to black. Evergreen in mild regions but with tip dieback or fully herbaceous in colder zones.

'Gin-ryu' (syn. 'Silver Dragon'): white-striped leaves, possibly zone 5

Liriope muscari

Liriope muscari 'Variegata'

Liriope spicata (foreground)

Lithodora diffusa

LITHODORA

Boraginaceae

Zones (5)6–8

Scrub, pine woodlands, and sandy coastal areas in Spain.

A popular ground cover with drifts of small, five-lobed, ½ in. (1.3 cm) wide flowers in shades of cobalt-blue, royal-blue, sky-blue, and white in mid-spring with intermittent rebloom through summer. Evergreen subshrub forms mats 4–6 in. (10–15 cm) or more tall and 24–36 in. (60–90 cm) wide with small, linear, dark green, hairy leaves.

CULTURE/CARE Full sun to part shade. Avoid full sun in hot summer climates. Well-drained, evenly moist, moderately fertile, acidic soils. Alkaline soils can cause yellowish leaves and shift blue flowers toward purple.

USES Walls, terraces, stairways, along pathways, and on slopes for small to medium-sized applications. Moderate growth rate. Not tolerant of foot traffic. Deer resistant. Attractive to pollinators, especially bees and butterflies.

PROPAGATION Cuttings

'Alba': white flowers

'Crystal Blue': sky-blue flowers

'Grace Ward': cobalt-blue flowers, AGM

'Heavenly Blue': royal-blue flowers, AGM

'Litgs' Gold 'n Sapphires: royal-blue flowers, gold foliage, with good sun tolerance

'Star': white flowers with blue stars

'White Star': blue flowers with white stars

Lonicera

Caprifoliaceae

The genus *Lonicera* includes many woody vines and shrubs but is best known for its climbing species and hybrids that adorn walls and trellises with clusters of beautiful, tubular, often fragrant flowers. The genus is lesser known for its shrubby components, some of which make good ground covers. In the absence of vertical structures, the vining species can also be used as large, rambling, ground-covering masses, 8–24 in. (20–60 cm) tall. In addition to the common vining

Lithodora diffusa 'Star'

Lithodora diffusa

Lithodora diffusa 'Litgs' Gold 'n Sapphires

honeysuckles, many other species can be used, including *L. acuminata*, *L. alseuosmoides*, *L. ×americana*, *L. henryi*, *L. ×tellmanniana*, and *L. tragophylla*.

CULTURE/CARE Rich, well-drained soils with good moisture in full sun to part shade, with more flowers in more light. Moderately salt tolerant, especially *L. pileata*, which, along with *L. sempervirens*, is drought tolerant.

USES Vining species grow quickly on banks, slopes, and walls, and can be used to cover unsightly garden features such as rocks and stumps for medium-sized to large applications. Dwarf cultivars are suitable for smaller spaces. Shrubby species grow at a moderate pace and can be used for foundation plantings and border edges for small to large applications. Deer and rabbit resistant. Attractive to pollinators, especially hummingbirds.

PROPAGATION Cuttings

Lonicera crassifolia
CREEPING HONEYSUCKLE

Zones 7–8
Streamsides, rocky cliffs, crevices, and moist forest margins in montane areas of Yunnan, Sichuan, and adjacent Chinese provinces.

A little-known evergreen, trailing species with small, shiny, dark green, rounded, almost succulent leaves that show off the small, unscented flowers that are deep pink in bud, opening into white and pink trumpets, the white aging through yellow to light orange. Blue-black berries persist into winter against purplish and reddish foliage. Stems grow 36 in. (90 cm) or more long on plants 3–4 in. (7.5–10 cm) tall and 3–6 ft. (1–1.8 m) wide.

Lonicera japonica
JAPANESE HONEYSUCKLE

Zones (4)5–9
Scrub, open forests, mountain slopes, rocky places, and roadsides throughout China, Japan, and Korea.

Semi-evergreen to evergreen twining vine with stems up to 33 ft. (10 m) long of midgreen oval leaves and small, strongly vanilla-scented flowers opening white and aging to yellow, followed by black fruit, though usually only in warmer zones where plants can become invasive. There it can clamber up and

Lonicera crassifolia at the Miller Garden, Seattle

Lonicera japonica var. *repens*

Lonicera japonica 'Halliana' along a riverbank in Zaragoza, Spain

overwhelm trees and shrubs or form matlike mono-cultures that can outcompete native plants, a trait that recommends it as a ground cover to control weeds where it is not invasive.

'Aureoreticulata': small green leaves with golden yellow-netted veins, less vigorous, with stems 10–15 ft. (3–4.5 m) long, AGM

'Halliana': white flowers aging to creamy yellow, on stems 33 ft. (10 m) long, semi-evergreen in mild climates

'Hall's Prolific': large, free-flowering selection from 'Halliana', flowering earlier, longer, and more profusely, with white flowers aging to creamy yellow, semi-evergreen in mild climates, AGM

'Mint Crisp': leaves variably speckled in creamy yellows

var. *repens* (syn. 'Purpurea'): purple-red stems and green leaves flushed with purple when young, with deep pink buds that open to white flowers, aging to yellow flushed pink on the outside, less vigorous than 'Hall's Prolific' or 'Halliana' and possibly a little less hardy, AGM

Lonicera periclymenum
EUROPEAN HONEYSUCKLE, DUTCH HONEYSUCKLE

Zones 5–8

Scrubland, woodlands, or hedgerows throughout Western Europe into Morocco, absent in calcareous soils.

A large, vigorous, deciduous, twining species with stems 23 ft. (7 m) or more long, with showy clusters of large, fragrant flowers in shades of creamy white, yellow, pink, and red followed by red fruit. Fragrance is stronger at night.

'Belgica': deep pink buds reveal pink-flushed flowers with white interiors, aging to creamy yellow on stems 20–25 ft. (6–7.5 m) long, AGM

'Graham Thomas': long and profuse blooming, large, fragrant flowers opening creamy white and aging to deep yellow on stems 12 ft. (3.6 m) long, AGM

'Honey Baby': dwarf hybrid of 'Belgica Select' and *L. japonica* 'Halliana', with large clusters of fragrant white flowers aging to yellow on stems 3–5 ft. (1–1.5 m) long

'Honeybush': dwarf cultivar with stems 3 ft. (1 m) long, fragrant flowers with deep pink buds opening to white, with plum-purple foliage in fall

'Inov86' Peaches and Cream: compact plants with stems to 6 ft. (1.8 m) long and pink and purple buds opening to fragrant white flowers, aging to deep yellow

'Inov205' Chic & Choc: compact, dwarf plants growing as a shrub, 20 in. (50 cm) tall and wide, pink and purple buds open to fragrant white flowers aging to deep yellow

'Scentsation': profuse, large, fragrant flowers open creamy white aging to yellow over a long period, followed by red berries on stems 10 ft. (3 m) long

'Serotina': vigorous plants with blue-green leaves on purple stems, 10–20 ft. (3–6 m) long, with intensely fragrant flowers in shades of purple-red to glowing pink and creamy white to creamy yellow, followed by red berries, AGM

L. ×italica 'Sherlite' Harlequin: first introduced as L. periclymenum and later revealed to be L. etrusca × L. caprifolium, with rose-pink and yellow fragrant flowers and foliage with creamy white margins on stems to 10–12 ft. (3–3.6 m) long

Lonicera pileata
BOX-LEAF HONEYSUCKLE, PRIVET HONEYSUCKLE

Zones 5–9
Slopes and open forests in China.
A dense, tough, deciduous to evergreen shrub with small, oval, midgreen leaves resembling boxwood on arching to spreading, rooting branches, 12–24 in. (30–60 cm) tall by 8 ft. (2.4 m) wide. Small, fragrant, trumpet-shaped, creamy white spring flowers produce small, translucent, royal-purple berries in fall and winter.

'Royal Carpet': straighter, more horizontally spreading branches

Lonicera sempervirens
TRUMPET HONEYSUCKLE, SCARLET HONEYSUCKLE

Zones 4–9
Roadsides, streambanks, thickets, and forest edges in the southeastern United States.
A vigorous, deciduous, twining vine with stems 10–15 ft. (3–4.5 m) or more long, bright red flowers in late spring, and red berries in fall. Typically nonfragrant, a few cultivars may be lightly scented. Can be evergreen in zones 8–9.

Lonicera pileata 'Royal Carpet'

Lonicera sempervirens

'Honey Coral': dwarf cultivar, stems 4–6 ft. (1.2–1.8 m) or more long, with red flowers over an extended bloom period

'Magnifica': red flowers age to orange with light orange interiors, good fragrance, on stems 6–12 ft. (1.6–3.6 m) long

'Major Wheeler': likely the best red cultivar, long-blooming from late spring through summer, on stems 6–12 ft. (1.6–3.6 m) long

'Mandarin': hybrid of *L. tragophylla* and *L.* ×*brownii* 'Dropmore Scarlet', with unscented, mandarin-orange flowers with light orange interiors, AGM

f. *sulphurea* 'John Clayton': bright yellow, lightly fragrant flowers with good rebloom and fall berry production, on stems 6–12 ft. (1.8–3.6 m) long

L. ×*brownii* 'Dropmore Scarlet': hybrid of *L. hirsuta* × *L. sempervirens* with orange-red flowers, zone 3 or 4

L. ×*heckrottii* 'Gold Flame': hybrid of *L. sempervirens* × *L.* ×*americana* with large, fragrant flowers in shades of rose-pink, white, and deep yellow on stems 10–15 ft. (3–4.5 m) long, zone 5, AGM

Luzula
Juncaceae

The grasslike or sedgelike wood rushes are a cosmopolitan genus of about 140 species, yet only a couple of them are commonly cultivated, both hailing from Europe. Among the least-known of the graminoids, they are reliable, tough, and attractive, with evergreen to semi-evergreen, rhizomatous or stoloniferous habits and flattened, hairy-edged leaves.

CULTURE/CARE Part sun to shade in moist, fertile, neutral to acidic soil. Tolerant of full sun with good moisture. Tolerant of short periods of drought.

USES Mass plant the slowly expanding clumps for good coverage over small to medium-sized areas along pathways, in woodland gardens, and beneath large shrubs or trees. Not tolerant of foot traffic. Deer and rabbit resistant.

PROPAGATION Division, seed

Luzula nivea
SNOWY WOOD RUSH

Zones 4–9
Mountain woodlands and scrub in southwestern and Central Europe.

Semi-evergreen to evergreen, slowly expanding clumps, 12–16 in. (30–40 cm) tall and wide, of light to midgreen leaves, 8–12 in. (20–30 cm) long and ¼ in. (6 mm) wide, margined with copious white, silky hairs. Showy clusters of white to off-white flowers top 20–28 in. (50–71 cm) tall stems in spring into summer and can be dried for flower arrangements.

'Lucius': seed strain not much different from the species

Luzula sylvatica
GREATER WOOD RUSH

Zones 4–9
Moist and acidic soils on streambanks, rock ledges, and slopes, and in open woodlands and fields across Europe to the Caucasus.

Slowly spreading, semi-evergreen to evergreen clumps, 12–16 in. (30–40 cm) tall and 12–24 in. (30–60 cm) wide, of light to midgreen leaves, 4–12 in. (10–30 cm) long and ½ in. (1.5 cm) wide, margined with scattered white hairs. Flower clusters top 12–32 in. (30–80 cm) tall stems like chestnut-brown fireworks. Clumps expand slowly by short stolons.

'Aurea': light green foliage brightens to glowing gold in winter

'Hohe Tatra': similar to 'Aurea', AGM

'Marginata': green leaves with thin white to cream edges, AGM

'Solar Flair': seed strain similar to 'Aurea'

'Starmaker': seed strain with good form and even flowering

'Taggart's Cream': foliage emerges in striking white, aging to green

Lysimachia
Primulaceae

Golden creeping Jenny, *L. nummularia* 'Aurea', is one of the most popular of all ground covers. Other relatives also offer prostrate ground-covering forms. For larger spaces, a number of upright, vigorous, rhizomatous species of 24–36 in. (60–90 cm) tall can form dominant colonies as tall ground covers, including *L. ciliata* and its cultivar 'Firecracker', *L. clethroides*, *L. lanceolata* var. *purpurea*, and *L. punctata* and its cultivars 'Alexander' and 'Walgoldalex' Golden Alexander.

CULTURE/CARE Average, moist, or wet soils of average to rich fertility in full sun to part shade.

Luzula sylvatica 'Marginata'

Lysimachia congestiflora 'Persian Chocolate'

Lysimachia japonica var. *minutissima*

Lysimachia nummularia 'Aurea' may need protection from hot afternoon sun, especially in drier conditions. Gold and burgundy foliage is more intense in more light.

USES Fast growers for use along pathways, between flagstones, beside ponds, on walls, as lawn alternatives for small areas, and in any other moist locations. Both *L. nummularia* and *L. japonica* are tolerant of occasional foot traffic. Deer and rabbit resistant. Attractive to pollinators, especially bees.

PROPAGATION Division, cuttings

Lysimachia congestiflora
CREEPING JENNY, DENSE-FLOWERED LOOSESTRIFE

Zones (6)7–9

Ditches, roadsides, banks of rice paddies, and damp forest margins throughout China and the Himalayan countries into Southeast Asia.

A vigorous, prostrate, herbaceous to evergreen perennial spreading via branching, rooting stems into mats 3–6 in. (7.5–15 cm) tall and spreading indefinitely with rounded, light to midgreen leaves up to 1.5 in. (4 cm) long. Clusters of cupped, five-petaled, starlike, bright yellow flowers bloom from late spring to midsummer.

'Midnight Sun': chocolate-brown foliage on red stems

'Outback Sunset' (syns. Walkabout Sunset, Waikiki Sunset): green and golden yellow to lime-green variegated foliage

'Persian Chocolate': chocolate-brown foliage on red stems

Lysimachia japonica var. *minutissima*
MINIATURE CREEPING JENNY,
DWARF CREEPING JENNY

Zones 5–9

Grassy banks, ditches, streamsides, thickets, and open areas in China, Korea, Japan, Indonesia, and the Himalayan countries.

An uncommon species resembling *L. nummularia* in miniature, forming mats 1–2 in. (2.5–5 cm) tall and spreading indefinitely but with much smaller, darker green, oval leaves and starlike, bright yellow flowers in early summer. Herbaceous to evergreen, depending on climate.

Lysimachia nummularia
CREEPING JENNY, MONEYWORT

Zones 4–9

Wet and moist habitats including banks, ditches, meadows, shorelines, broadleaf forests, and rocky ridges across Europe into Turkey and Russia.

A vigorous, prostrate, herbaceous to evergreen perennial with branching, rooting stems forming mats 1–2 in. (2.5–5 cm) tall and spreading indefinitely with rounded, light to midgreen, slightly shiny leaves up to 1 in. (2.5 cm) long. Cupped, five-petaled, bright yellow flowers bloom in early summer. Potentially invasive in some regions.

'Aurea' (syn. 'Goldilocks'): gold foliage in sun, lime-green in part shade, AGM

Lysimachia nummularia 'Aurea', Wisley Gardens, UK

Magnolia laevifolia
MICHELIA, MAGNOLIA

Magnoliaceae

Zones (7)8–10

Thickets and in the understories of pine forests in mountainous regions of Southwest China.

An upright, broad-leaved, evergreen shrub or small tree, formerly known as *Michelia yunnanensis*, 8–13 ft. (2.4–4 m) tall, with rounded, elliptic, shiny, dark green leaves up to 4 in. (10 cm) long. Lower leaf surfaces and flower buds are covered in velvety, chestnut-brown indumentum. Buds form in late winter, opening in spring to 3 in. (7.5 cm) wide, ivory-white, star-shaped, sweetly lemon-scented flowers, each with 6–12 narrow petals. The prostrate cultivar 'Free Spirit' can be used as a ground cover.

CULTURE/CARE Sun to part shade in evenly moist, well-drained soils. Protect from cold winter winds.

USES Medium-sized to large applications including foundation plantings, in large landscapes, as a specimen, and in shrub borders. Plants grow at a slow to moderate rate. Not tolerant of foot traffic.

PROPAGATION Cuttings

'Free Spirit': prostrate, horizontally spreading form, 24 in. (60 cm) tall and 6–8 ft. (1.8–2.4 m) wide, though mature plants may reach 36 in. (90 cm) tall, with upward-facing flowers, each with 6–7 slightly overlapping petals

Mahonia
Berberidaceae

These beautiful and stately evergreen shrubs from Asia and North and Central America offer a few western North American species suitable as ground covers. They have dark green, compound leaves with holly-shaped leaflets and bright yellow winter or spring flowers, followed by sour, yet edible, grapelike blue fruit. Their yellow inner bark, wood, and roots were a traditional source of dye for native peoples.

CULTURE/CARE Tough, versatile, and able to grow in all light conditions and most soil types. Best in full sun to part shade in average to moist, acidic, well-drained soils with good fertility, but tolerant of sand, clay, full shade, and drought, including dry

Magnolia laevifolia 'Free Spirit'

Mahonia aquifolium 'Compacta'

Mahonia nervosa in full sun with developing winter color

shade. Plants in full sun will be lighter green, possibly turning yellowish with too much sun and drought.

USES Foundation plantings, for erosion control on slopes, for dry shade beneath coniferous trees, in shrub borders, and along pathways over small to large areas. Not tolerant of foot traffic. Deer and rabbit resistant. Attractive to winter and early spring pollinators.

PROPAGATION Division, cuttings, seed

Mahonia aquifolium
OREGON GRAPE

Zones 5–9

Average to dry, open or closed, rocky woods and coniferous forests from low to high elevations from southern British Columbia and Alberta south to Idaho and Oregon.

An upright, multistemmed, slowly rhizomatous shrub, typically 6–8 ft. (1.8–2.4 m) tall, but with dwarf forms useful as ground covers. Glossy, prickly leaves up to 10 in. (25 cm) long have 5–11 leaflets. New foliage is flushed bronzy red. Mature foliage can develop reddish tints in full sun and burgundy tones in winter. Lightly fragrant, yellow, early spring flowers in large terminal clusters are followed by blue, grapelike fruit in summer and fall.

'Apollo': compact dome, 18–24 in. (45–90 cm) tall by 36 in. (90 cm) wide, with light orange-yellow flowers, AGM

'Compacta': compact dome, 24–36 in. (45–90 cm) tall by 4 ft. (1.2 m) wide

'Smaragd': compact dome, 18–24 in. (45–90 cm) tall by 36 in. (90 cm) wide, possibly with improved winter color

Mahonia nervosa
DULL OREGON GRAPE, CASCADE MAHONIA

Zones 5–10

Average to dry or moist open slopes, shady canyons, and shady coniferous forests from low to high elevations from southern British Columbia to Southern California.

A low, evergreen shrub, 24 in. (30 cm) tall by 36–48 in. (90–120 cm) wide, spreading slowly by underground rhizomes with 9–19 evergreen, leathery, holly-shaped leaflets in each compound leaf and an inflorescence of clustered spikes, each up to 8 in. (20 cm) long, of fragrant, bright yellow spring flowers becoming blue, grapelike fruit in late summer. Foliage can develop plum colors in full sun and red tints in winter.

Mahonia repens
CREEPING OREGON GRAPE

Zones (4)5–9

Dry, rocky slopes and open forests from middle to high elevations across much of the western half of the United States into Alberta and British Columbia.

A low, rhizomatous, evergreen shrub or shrublet, 12 in. (30 cm) or more tall and up to 36 in. (90 cm) wide, with 3–7 muted midgreen to blue-green, relatively thin, holly-shaped leaflets on each compound leaf. Clusters of fragrant, bright yellow spring flowers become grapelike blue fruit in late summer. Foliage can develop striking tones of purple, red, and orange in winter.

Maianthemum
Asparagaceae

These relatives of the better-known Solomon's seal (*Polygonatum* spp.) are North American woodlanders with terminal clusters or spikes of starlike flowers rather than pendulous, axillary bells. Best known for the large *M. racemosum*, with its impressive clumps of arching foliage, a few smaller rhizomatous species make excellent ground covers for shaded sites. Formerly included in the genus *Smilacina*.

USES Woodland gardens, beneath trees and shrubs, on slopes, and near ponds and watercourses, spreading slowly at first but accelerating once established. Salt tolerant. Not tolerant of foot traffic.

CULTURE/CARE Part shade to shade (or morning sun) in fertile, average to moist, well-drained soils. Best in cooler summer climates. May not tolerate heat and humidity. Somewhat tolerant of dry shade.

PROPAGATION Division, seed

Maianthemum canadense
CANADA MAYFLOWER, WILD LILY OF THE VALLEY

Zones 3–9

Average to moist coniferous, deciduous, and mixed forests and clearings across most of Canada (except the West Coast) and the North Central and eastern United States.

Midgreen, elongated, heart-shaped, almost clasping leaves, 1–4 in. (2.5–10 cm) long and 1–2 in. (2.5–5 cm) wide, 2–3 per stem on stems 2–10 in. (5–25 cm) tall, forming open to dense, rhizomatously spreading colonies that can fill the understory. Short spikes of small, white, starlike, late spring flowers become spherical, brown-mottled, greenish fruits, slowly turning bright red through summer.

Maianthemum dilatatum
FALSE LILY OF THE VALLEY

Zones 3–9

Average to wet forests, shaded slopes, and streambanks from sea level to montane zones from Japan and the Kamtchatka Peninsula to Alaska and Northern California, mostly west of the Cascades and Coast mountains.

A sister species to *M. canadense* but taller and with larger foliage. Midgreen, heart-shaped leaves, 2–5 in. (5–12.5 cm) long and wide, usually two per 4–14 in. (10–36 cm) tall stem, forming open to dense, rhizomatously spreading colonies that can dominate the understory. Short spikes of white, starlike, late spring flowers become spherical, brown-mottled, greenish fruits, slowly turning bright red through summer. Known as *Maianthemum bifolium* subsp. *kamtschaticum* in the United Kingdom.

Maianthemum stellatum
STAR-FLOWERED FALSE SOLOMON'S SEAL

Zones 3–8

Average to moist or sometimes dry forests, streambanks, clearings, and meadows from sea level into the lower alpine across most of North America except Texas and the southeastern states.

Reminiscent of a miniature false Solomon's seal (*M. racemosum*) with upright to arching stems with 5–11 alternating lance-shaped, midgreen leaves, 2–6 in. (5–15 cm) long and ¾–1½ in. (2–4 cm) wide, on stems 8–24 in. (20–60 cm) tall, forming open to dense, rhizomatously spreading colonies. Open terminal clusters of white, starlike, late spring flowers become purple- or burgundy-striped greenish fruits, turning to deep red through summer.

Mahonia repens in full sun with developing winter color

Maianthemum canadense in the wild in Birchy Bay, Newfoundland

Maianthemum dilatatum in the wild in Pacific Rim National Park Reserve, BC

Maianthemum stellatum in the wild near Musgrave Harbour, Newfoundland

Marrubium

Lamiaceae

Horehounds come from hot, xeric, Mediterranean habitats and are well suited to tough conditions, offering textural, spreading mounds of attractive silver-felted foliage. They are related to Jerusalem sage (*Phlomis* spp.), a fact revealed by their (albeit less attractive) floral show with regularly spaced clusters on square stems. *Marrubium globosum* is sometimes grown in addition to the species mentioned.

CULTURE/CARE Extremely drought tolerant for unirrigated sites with infertile, rocky or sandy soils in full, hot sun. Avoid hot and humid climates. Mostly grown for their foliage, the flowering stems can be removed at any time or left for pollinators. Plants can also be sheared to the ground to refresh. Foliage is semi-evergreen to evergreen in milder climates.

USES Hot, dry, wind-exposed sites such as rock gardens, dry slopes, sunny pathways, hell strips, and terraces. Grows at a moderate to fast rate. Not tolerant of foot traffic. Deer and rabbit resistant. Attractive to pollinators, especially bees.

PROPAGATION Division, cuttings

Marrubium globosum

Marrubium bourgaei

GREEN HOREHOUND

Zones 7–10
Stony mountain slopes and screes up to 7875 ft. (2400 m) in Turkey.
The only form of *M. bourgaei* in cultivation is 'All Hallows Green'. Plants are entirely covered in dense, yellowish indumentum, in mounds 4–12 in. (10–30 cm) tall and 24–36 in. (60–90 cm) wide of scalloped, oval or spatula-shaped, lime-green leaves. Vertical stems, 18–24 in. (45–60 cm) tall, hold evenly spaced clusters of off-white to greenish flowers in mid- to late summer.

Marrubium bourgaei 'All Hallows Green'

Marrubium incanum

SILVER HOREHOUND

Zones 6–9
Rocky places in Italy, the Balkan States, and Bulgaria.
Vigorous plants entirely covered in dense, woolly-white indumentum, forming more vertical mounds, 24 in. (60 cm) tall and wide, of scalloped, egg-shaped, silver leaves. Regularly spaced clusters of off-white flowers occur on vertical or sprawling stems, 18 in. (45 cm) tall, in mid- to late summer.

Marrubium incanum

Marrubium rotundifolium

Marrubium rotundifolium
SILVER EDGED HOREHOUND,
SILVERHEELS HOREHOUND

Zones 4–9

Sunny, limestone slopes from moderate to high elevations in the mountains of Turkey.

Vigorous, very hardy plants, entirely covered in dense, woolly-white indumentum, forming mounds, 10 in. (25 cm) tall and 36 in. (90 cm) wide, of rounded, felted leaves that are gray-green above and silver beneath, with upward curving edges outlining each leaf in a scalloped silver margin. Clusters of off-white flowers occur at regular intervals along vertical or sprawling stems, 12–18 in. (30–45 cm) tall, in mid- to late summer.

Marrubium supinum
SCALLOP SHELL MARRUBIUM,
SCALLOP SHELL HOREHOUND

Zones (6)7–10

Mountain slopes of Spain, Morocco, Algeria, and Tunisia.

Velvety, aromatic plants entirely covered in dense, woolly-white indumentum, forming mounds, 4–12 in. (10–30 cm) tall and 24 in. (60 cm) wide, of crinkled, kidney-shaped to heart-shaped, scalloped leaves, gray-green above and silver beneath, with edges curving upward, outlining each leaf in silver. Clusters of small pink to lilac flowers with white edges occur at regular intervals along vertical stems, 18–24 in. (45–60 cm) tall, in mid- to late summer.

Mazus
Mazaceae

This valuable genus of cute, very low-growing, mat-forming species once included in the figwort family (Scrophulariacae) with garden favorites such as foxgloves and cape fuchsia (*Phygelius* spp.) has been moved into its own little family, Mazaceae, with just three genera. The tubular, nearly 1 in. (2.5 cm) long flowers flare into upper two-lipped and lower three-lipped lobes. The flowers, held singly or in small clusters, are oriented horizontally, facing in all directions and resembling a crowd of little cartoon characters engaged in myriad exciting conversations.

CULTURE/CARE Full sun to part shade in fertile, average, moist, or wet soils. Tolerant of hot, humid summers. Intolerant of drought.

USES Vigorous growers for between stepping or paving stones, along pathways, near ponds and watercourses, and as a lawn alternative over small to medium-sized areas. Tolerant of foot traffic. Deer resistant. Attractive to pollinators, especially butterflies.

PROPAGATION Division

Mazus radicans

Mazus radicans
FRECKLED MAZUS, MOTLEY MAZUS

Zones 6–9
Damp places and along bog and watercourse edges in the subalpine of the South Island, New Zealand.

An uncommon cousin to the better known *M. reptans*, hailing from a different continent entirely, the freckled mazus is a herbaceous to evergreen, low-growing, mat-forming plant, 1–2 in. (2.5–5 cm) tall, forming a dense carpet, spreading indefinitely by creeping, rooting stems above and below the soil surface, with hairy, green to tan-green, burgundy speckled, tongue-shaped leaves, 1–2 in. (2.5–5 cm) long. White summer flowers can be marked with purple and yellow.

Mazus reptans 'Albus'

Mazus reptans
CREEPING MAZUS

Zones 5–9
Moist places in the Himalayas.
A low-growing, mat-forming, herbaceous to evergreen plant, 1–2 in. (2.5–5 cm) tall, spreading indefinitely by creeping, rooting stems and forming a dense carpet of plants with light to bright green, oval leaves, 1 in. (2.5 cm) long, with broadly toothed edges. Each lavender to bluish lavender late spring flower has a white patch spotted with yellow, orange, or red.

'Albus': pure white flowers with yellow spots

Meehania cordata

Meehania cordata
MEEHAN'S MINT, CREEPING MINT

Lamiaceae

Zones 4–8
Rich woods on flats and slopes in the East Central United States.

A lovely, underused, herbaceous, stoloniferous, square-stemmed, mint relative forming slowly spreading mats, 1–4 in. (2.5–10 cm) tall, of fuzzy, light green, heart-shaped leaves with scalloped edges. Lavender to lavender-blue, trumpet-shaped flowers with a four-lobed hood and a two-lobed lip marked with white blotches and small hairs bloom on short spikes in late spring to early summer when many spring-blooming ground covers are done. Two rare Asian cousins could also be useful: *M. montis-koyae* and *M. urticifolia* and its variegated cultivar 'Wandering Minstrel'.

CULTURE/CARE Part sun to shade in fertile, average to moist, well-drained soils. Tolerant of dry shade.

USES Shade or woodland gardens, along pathways, and at the front of borders, especially in moist soils. Not tolerant of foot traffic. Deer resistant. Attractive to pollinators, especially bees.

PROPAGATION Division, cuttings

Mentha
Lamiaceae

Mints hardly need an introduction, being among the best known and most enjoyed herbs. Their garden reputation also precedes them—even nongardeners know they can spread profusely. Common culinary mints are vigorous, rhizomatous or stoloniferous, colony formers, 12–24 in. (30–60 cm) tall with indefinite spread, and useful as tall ground covers. These include ginger or basil mint (*M. ×gracilis*), spearmint (*M. spicata*), apple and pineapple mint (*M. suaveolens*), peppermint (*M. ×piperita*), mojito mint (*M. ×villosa*), and related lemon balm (*Melissa officinalis*). Two species treated here, pennyroyal (*M. pulegium*) and Corsican mint (*M. requienii*), are more conventional, low ground covers.

CULTURE/CARE Full sun to part shade in fertile, evenly moist, well-drained soils. *Mentha requienii* can be intolerant of full sun in hot summer climates and dislikes drought. In mild, wet winter climates such as the Pacific Northwest, it seems to require free-draining, sandy soils to overwinter well.

USES Use *M. pulegium* along pathways and border edges. *Mentha requienii* is tolerant of light foot traffic and is best between stepping stones and pavers or as a lawn alternative for small applications. Both grow at a moderate rate. Deer and rabbit resistant. Attractive to pollinators, especially bees and butterflies.

PROPAGATION Division

Mentha pulegium
PENNYROYAL

Zones 6–10
Moist meadows and sandy soils along watercourses in the Mediterranean Basin.

A popular culinary, medicinal, and insecticidal herb in Greek, Roman, and Medieval times, though hardly known nowadays, perhaps because the leaves can be mildly toxic if ingested. Aromatic foliage is similar to spearmint or peppermint with a similar habit but in miniature and with a slower growth rate. Vertical and horizontal stems expand into semi-evergreen mats of light to midgreen leaves with summer spikes, 6–12 in. (15–30 cm) tall, of clustered lavender flowers. Potentially invasive in California.

'Nana': foliage mats, 1–4 in. (2.5–10 cm) tall, with short flower spikes

Mentha requienii
CORSICAN MINT, CREEPING MINT

Zones 6–9

Wet meadows and wetland edges from middle to high elevations on the islands of Corsica and Sardinia.

One of the lowest of all ground covers, not more than 1 in. (2.5 cm) tall (but usually less), forming dense, flat, spreading, herbaceous to evergreen mats of tiny, round, bright green leaves that release an intense, minty fragrance when crushed. Corsican mint is the source of flavoring for crème de menthe liqueur. Tiny lavender flowers appear in summer. May self-seed in good conditions.

Microbiota decussata
SIBERIAN CARPET CYPRESS, RUSSIAN ARBORVITAE

Cupressaceae

Zones 2–7

Mountainous areas of southeastern Siberia near China and North Korea.

A tough, extremely cold-tolerant, low-growing, evergreen conifer forming mats 8–12 in. (20–30 cm) tall and eventually 10–12 ft. (3–3.6 m) wide. Resembles the layered, horizontal, low-growing junipers, but with the soft, feathery, scalelike, dull green foliage of hedging cedars such as *Thuja plicata*, flushing purple-bronze or coppery in fall and winter. AGM

CULTURE/CARE Full to part sun in well-drained, average to moist soil. Tolerant of infertile soils, exposed sites, part shade, and some drought once established. Rarely requires pruning but can be trimmed lightly.

USES Use like juniper ground covers for mass plantings on flats or slopes, along pathways and road-ways, against foundations, and as an alternative to sun-loving junipers in shadier conditions. Spreads at a moderate rate. Not tolerant of foot traffic. Deer and rabbit resistant.

PROPAGATION Cuttings

'Condavis' Fuzzball: vase-shaped habit, 12–24 in. (30–60 cm) tall by 36 in. (90 cm) wide

'Condrew' Drew's Blue: blue-green foliage turning maroon in winter

'Gold Spot': some fans golden yellow

'Jakobsen': upright form, 6–12 in. (15–30 cm) tall by 36–48 in. (90–120 cm) wide, for smaller spaces

'Prides' Celtic Pride: uniform growth habitat, resistant to tip dieback

Microbiota decussata

Mitchella repens

Mitchella repens
PARTRIDGE BERRY, TWINBERRY

Rubiaceae

Zones (2)3–8
Dry to moist woods, along streambanks and bogs, and on knolls and sandy slopes in eastern Canada and the eastern half of the United States.

A dainty, creeping, semiwoody evergreen species with trailing, rooting stems of small, dark green, shiny, round to oval leaves with a pale greenish to whitish midrib and veins, in mats 1–2 in. (2.5–5cm) tall, spreading indefinitely yet slowly. Small, fragrant, hairy, four-lobed, trumpet-shaped, white spring flowers emerge from pink-flushed buds in pairs. Curiously, the fertilized ovaries of the two flowers fuse into one edible, yet tasteless, orange-red fruit with two darker red spots, persisting through winter.

CULTURE/CARE Part shade to shade. As with other forest floor species such as *Cornus canadensis* and *Linnaea borealis*, *Mitchella* species appreciate a layer of primarily organic matter (duff) atop humus-rich, well-drained soils.

USES Small-scale ground cover for shady pathways and naturalized settings. Tolerant of occasional foot traffic. Deer and rabbit resistant.

PROPAGATION Cuttings, seed

f. *leucocarpa*: white fruit

Mitella breweri
BREWER'S MITREWORT, BREWER'S BISHOP'S CAP

Saxifragaceae

Zones 5–9
Moist mountain meadows, woods, and forests into the subalpine from British Columbia and Alberta, south to the Sierra Nevada range of Central California and Nevada.

These little-known saxifrage relatives from North America and Asia are quietly beautiful compared to their louder cousins in the genus *Heuchera*. They are smaller but similar in habit, with mounds of lobed, kidney-shaped, mid- to dark green, herbaceous to evergreen basal foliage, 1–3 in. (2.5–7.5 cm) wide, with white or brown hairs and a slight luster. Airy, vertical flowering stems 6–12 in. (15–30 cm) tall produce up to 60 small, distinctive, cupped, greenish yellow flowers with dissected, skeletal petals that appear fuzzy from a distance. Shiny, jet-black seeds self-seed gently from green cups, filling in the gaps of the

Mitella breweri

dense, rhizomatous, slowly spreading colonies. *Mitella diphylla* and *M. ovalis* are occasionally cultivated.

CULTURE/CARE Part shade to shade in evenly moist, well-drained soils.

USES Small applications in shady sites along pathways and stairways, between paving stones, and in woodland settings. Not tolerant of foot traffic.

PROPAGATION Division, seed

Monardella macrantha
SCARLET MONARDELLA

Lamiaceae

Zones 6–10
Partially shaded habitats in chaparral, woodlands, and forests in mountainous areas of California and Baja California, Mexico.

Low, partially open to dense evergreen mats of shiny, dark green, lightly aromatic leaves on rhizomatous plants, 3–4 in. (7.5–10 cm) tall and 12–18 in. (30–45 cm) or more wide, with clusters of purple-red buds subtended by purple-red bracts, opening to brilliant red, nearly 2 in. (5 cm) long, upward-facing, trumpet-shaped flowers famous for attracting hummingbirds in late spring through summer.

CULTURE/CARE Full sun to part shade in dry, hot locations with excellent drainage, including rock gardens, gravelly and sandy areas, exposed sites, and infertile soils. Can be short-lived without sharp drainage. Appreciates afternoon shade in hot summer climates. Somewhat drought tolerant.

USES Small applications in rock gardens, troughs, walls, and other dry and rocky sites, spreading at a

Monardella macrantha subsp. *macrantha* 'Marian Sampson'

moderate rate. Not tolerant of foot traffic. Deer and rabbit resistant. Attractive to pollinators, especially hummingbirds.

PROPAGATION Cuttings, division

subsp. *macrantha* 'Marian Sampson': the best form with vigor, disease resistance, and a free-flowering habit

Muehlenbeckia
Polygonaceae

Two similar *Muehlenbeckia* species differ mainly in size and vigor. Though neither, like many New Zealand plants, has showy flowers, both are valuable for the textural effect of their thick, interwoven mats of wiry stems and tiny leaves.

CULTURE/CARE Full sun to part shade in average to moist, well-drained soils. Tolerant of salt (especially *M. complexa*), periods of drought, infertile soils, and exposed sites.

USES Medium-sized to large applications as fillers in shrub borders, on slopes for erosion control, and in coastal gardens, spreading at a moderate to fast rate. *Muehlenbeckia axillaris* could be used as a lawn alternative. Tolerant of occasional foot traffic. Deer and rabbit resistant.

PROPAGATION Cuttings or removal of rooted stems, division

Muehlenbeckia axillaris
CREEPING WIRE VINE, CREEPING POHUEHUE

Zones 6–10

Montane habitats in the Australian Alps and Tasmania and in rocky areas and along riverbeds in New Zealand.

A vigorous, prostrate, horizontally spreading and rhizomatous, evergreen, semiwoody species, 2–6 in. (5–15 cm) tall and 36 in. (90 cm) or more wide, with long, red-brown to black, wiry, rooting stems with

Muehlenbeckia axillaris

Mukdenia rossii 'Karasuba'

small, dark green, rounded leaves to ⅜ in. (1 cm) wide. Inconspicuous flowers swell into an interesting, milky white, translucent structure that holds the dry, black fruit. Often sold with the cultivar names 'Nana' and 'Little Leaf', though it is unclear if these differ from the species. *Muehlenbeckia complexa* and M. *axillaris* have frequently been confused in horticulture, and these cultivar names may have been applied to differentiate M. *axillaris* from its larger counterpart when the species identities were unclear.

'Tricolor': foliage variably mottled with white and pink, aging to green

Muehlenbeckia complexa
WIRE VINE, MAIDENHAIR VINE

Zones 7–10
Coastal, lowland, and montane forests and forest edges, and sand dunes, rocky places, and coastal scrub throughout New Zealand.

A vigorous, horizontally sprawling, clambering, or climbing, evergreen to semi-evergreen, semiwoody species, 12–24 in (30–60 cm) tall, spreading or climbing to 7–20 ft. (2.1–6 m) or more, with long, brown, wiry rooting stems with small, dark green, rounded leaves, 1 in. (2.5 cm) or more wide. Flowers and fruit similar to M. *axillaris*. Mass-planted in a large space, plants can form undulating, mounded hummocks.

Mukdenia rossii
MUKDENIA

Saxifragaceae

Zones 4–9
Rocky slopes and ravines on the Korean Peninsula and adjacent Chinese provinces.

Herbaceous perennial spreading slowly by compact rhizomes into small colonies, 12 in. (30 cm) tall and 12–18 in. (30–45 cm) wide, with light green, fan- or maple-shaped leaves, 4–6 in. (10–15 cm) wide, flushing burgundy in summer in bright light. Branched flowering stems, 8–16 in. (20–40 cm) tall, precede the foliage in early spring with white, starry flowers.

CULTURE/CARE Part sun to shade in fertile, evenly moist, well-drained soils. Tolerant of full sun in cooler climates with good moisture. In hot summer climates, provide more shade.

USES Small areas along pathways, in woodlands, and as an edger for shade borders. Not tolerant of foot traffic.

PROPAGATION Division

'Karasuba' (syn. 'Crimson Fans'): new leaves bronze-tinted, fading to green and then flushing bold red in summer, deepening to fiery red by fall, with bolder colors in more light

×*Mukgenia* 'Flame' (Nova Series): intergeneric hybrid of 'Karasuba' with *Bergenia*, intermediate in characteristics between both parents, with flowers that resemble those of *Mukdenia* but dark pink to fuchsia on less branched stems, roughly oval, leathery, and somewhat shiny leaves have pointed tips and toothed edges, turning bright red in summer and fall before going winter dormant

N

Nassella tenuissima
MEXICAN FEATHER GRASS, ANGEL'S HAIR GRASS

Poaceae

Zones 6–10

Dry habitats in the mountains of West Texas and New Mexico into Mexico. Disjunct to Argentina and Chile.

Formerly *Stipa tenuissima*, this distinctive, textural, cool-season grass with wispy, flowing, bright green, hairlike foliage forms irregular fountains, 16–24 in. (40–60 cm) tall by 24 in. (60 cm) wide, that move in the slightest breeze. Shiny, tan-colored flowers appear in summer. Persistent foliage can remain partially green year-round or turn mostly tan in summer and/or winter. Impressive when mass-planted for a closed cover.

CULTURE/CARE Full sun in fertile to poor, average to dry, well-drained soils. Provide good winter drainage. Very tolerant of drought and infertility. Somewhat salt tolerant. May gently self-seed in most regions. Potentially invasive in Mediterranean climates such as California and Australia. In early spring, rake out old foliage or comb with fingers.

USES Mass plant over small to large areas, along pathways and roadsides, as a low foundation planting, in park and institutional plantings, and at the front or midborder. Clumps bulk up at a moderate rate. Not tolerant of foot traffic. Deer and rabbit resistant.

PROPAGATION Division, seed

'Wind Whispers': up to 12 in. (30 cm) taller than the species, with foliage somewhat more robust and upright, possibly one zone less hardy

Nepeta racemosa
CATMINT

Lamiaceae

Zones 3–9

Sunny, open sites in the Caucasus, Turkey, Iran, and Iraq.

Nassella tenuissima at the Denver Botanic Gardens

Nepeta 'Early Bird'

A cousin of *N. cataria*, or catnip, the go-to recreational drug of the feline world, *N. racemosa* and other species can also affect some cats. This herbaceous, mounding perennial has hairy, textured, rounded to oblong, aromatic, gray-green foliage with heart-shaped bases and scalloped edges on horizontal, ascending, and upright stems, 12 in. (30 cm) tall by 18 in. (45 cm) wide. Long-blooming spikes bear many small violet, lavender, or lavender-blue trumpets flaring into smaller upper and larger lower lips often with dark detailing. *Nepeta* ×*faassenii*, from hybrid crosses with *N. nepetalla*, is similar but sterile and often larger, typically 12–24 in. (30–60 cm) tall and 24–36 in. (60–90 cm) wide. Flowers and leaves are edible. AGM

CULTURE/CARE Full to part sun in fertile to poor, average to dry, well-drained soils. Tolerant of drought, shallow and rocky soils, and salt. Shear flower stems or whole plants after flowering to encourage rebloom.

USES Small to medium-sized applications along pathways or roadways, in traffic medians, parking lots, rock gardens, and for edging borders, growing at a moderate rate. Not tolerant of foot traffic. Deer and rabbit resistant. Attractive to pollinators, especially bees and hummingbirds.

PROPAGATION Division, cuttings, seed

Plants denoted as "hybrid" are likely the result of more complex crosses but are similar in habit to *N. racemosa*.

'Alba': white flowers

'Cat's Pajamas': hybrid with vibrant deep blue flowers that cover stems from the ground up, 14 in. (36 cm) tall by 20 in. (50 cm) wide

'Dropmore' (syn. 'Dropmore Hybrid'): hybrid with bright blue flowers, bred in northern Manitoba and possibly hardy to zone 2

'Early Bird': hybrid, earlier blooming with violet-blue flowers

'Felix': freely reblooming, deep lilac-blue flowers

'Little Titch': compact mounds, 8–10 in. (20–25 cm) tall, good rebloom

'Psfike' Little Trudy: dwarf hybrid, 10 in. (25 cm) tall by 16 in. (40 cm) wide, with compact, somewhat dense spikes of deep lavender-purple flowers

'Purple Haze': hybrid with dense spikes of purple-blue flowers resembling *Agastache* 'Blue Fortune', on low plants 8 in. (20 cm) tall by 30 in. (75 cm) wide

'Six Hills Giant': large hybrid plants, 36 in. (90 cm) tall by 36 in. (90 cm) or more wide

'Snowflake': white flowers

'Walker's Low': one of the most popular cultivars, larger than the species, to 24–30 in. (60–80 cm) tall, with vibrant, violet-blue flowers, AGM, Perennial Plant of the Year 2007

N. ×*faassenii* hybrids involving *N. nepetella*

'Blue Wonder': deep violet-blue flowers, compact, 12 in. (30 cm) tall

'Cat's Meow': dense flower spikes of vibrant violet-blue on more upright stems, 20 in. (50 cm) tall

'Kit Kat': compact plants, 16 in. (40 cm) tall

'Kitten Around': vibrant violet-blue flowers nearly from top to bottom on the stems, in mounds 14 in. (36 cm) tall and 22 in. (56 cm) wide

'Limelight': slow-growing, somewhat lax, dwarf form, 10 in. (25 cm) tall by 24 in. (60 cm) wide with gold to lime-green foliage

'Novanepjun' Junior Walker: sterile, dwarf form of 'Walker's Low', 16 in. (40 cm) tall and 36 in. (90 cm) wide, with lavender-blue flowers

'Purrsian Blue': good, controlled habit, vibrant blue flowers on dense spikes, in mounds 18 in. (45 cm) tall and 30 in. (75 cm) wide

O

Oenothera
Onagraceae

Old-fashioned evening primroses have many valuable attributes, including heat and drought tolerance, low water and nutrient requirements, a long bloom period with showy flowers, ease of growth, and a popularity with pollinators.

CULTURE/CARE Average to dry, well-drained soils in full sun, preferring hot, dry sites and performing well in infertile sandy or gravelly soils.

USES Mass-planted in rock gardens, border and pathway edges, or hell strips and other hot and dry sites. Moderate growth rate. Not tolerant of foot traffic. Deer and rabbit resistant. Attractive to pollinators, especially bees, butterflies, and moths.

PROPAGATION Seed

Oenothera kunthiana
KUNTH'S EVENING PRIMROSE

Zones 5–10
Open woodlands, hillsides, and washes from Arizona to Texas and south to Central America.

Low-growing, mounding to prostrate, herbaceous perennial, 18–24 in. (45–80 cm) tall by 12 in. (30 cm) wide, with broadly lance-shaped leaves up to 4 in. (10 cm) long and 1.5 in. (4 cm) wide, and white to light pink, four-petaled, lightly fragrant flowers opening in the mornings in late spring. Can be short-lived but can readily self-seed.

'Glowing Magenta': deep magenta-pink flowers on compact plants 6–12 in. (15–30 cm) tall and 12 in. (30 cm) wide, resembles an annual impatiens

Oenothera macrocarpa
MISSOURI EVENING PRIMROSE, OZARK SUNDROPS

Zones 3–8
Hilly, dry, calcareous prairies, barrens, and limestone glades and outcrops, often in sandy or gravelly soils, in the Central and South Central United States.

A species formerly known as *O. missouriensis*, which has also subsumed *O. fremontii* and *O. incana* as subspecies, is a sprawling, herbaceous to evergreen, rhizomatous perennial, 10–16 in. (25–40 cm) tall and 18–36 in. (45–90 cm) wide, with red stems, dark green

Oenothera kunthiana 'Glowing Magenta'

Oenothera macrocarpa subsp. *incana* 'SilverBlade'

lance-shaped leaves, and numerous four-petaled, lightly fragrant, canary-yellow flowers, 3–5 in. (7.5–12.5 cm) wide, in late spring through fall, opening in the afternoon and closing the next morning, flushing reddish orange as they fade. Four-winged, 4 in. (10 cm) long seed pods are considered ornamental by some and used in dried floral arrangements. AGM

subsp. *fremontii* 'Lemon Silver': narrow silver-green to silver-blue foliage, compact habit, 6–8 in. (15–20 cm) tall

subsp. *fremontii* 'Shimmer': very narrow silver-blue foliage, compact habit, 6–8 in. (15–20 cm) tall

subsp. *fremontii* 'Silver Wings': seed strain similar to 'Lemon Silver' and 'Shimmer'

subsp. *incana* 'Silver Blade': broad silver to silver-green leaves, 4–8 in. (10–20 cm) tall and 16–24 in. (40–60 cm) wide

Oenothera speciosa
WHITE EVENING PRIMROSE, PINK EVENING PRIMROSE

Zones 4–9

Rocky prairies, open woodlands, slopes, roadsides, meadows, plains, and disturbed areas in the Central to South Central United States (but naturalized throughout the country) and into Mexico.

Formerly *O. berlandieri*, with fragrant, four-petaled, cupped, 2–3 in. (5–7.5 cm) wide, white flowers from spring into summer, opening in the evening and closing in the morning, flushing pink as they fade. Clumps of erect to sprawling, herbaceous stems, 10–24 in. (25–60 cm) tall, spread aggressively by rhizomes to 24 in. (60 cm) or more wide. Foliage is narrow, lance-shaped, and midgreen. For a similar rhizomatous spreader with an upright habit, yellow flowers, and taller stems to 30 in. (75 cm), use *O. fruticosa* and its more compact cultivar 'Fyrverkeri' (syn. 'Fireworks').

'Siskiyou': clear pink flowers, more compact, 10–12 in. (25–30 cm) tall, spreading steadily but less aggressively

'Turner01' Twilight: leaves with purple-bronze central markings, especially when young, clear pink flowers

Omphalodes
Boraginaceae

These relatives of forget-me-nots and brunnera have similar true-blue flowers. They are valuable early spring-blooming ground covers that overlap with hellebores and early spring bulbs such as *Corydalis solida*, crocuses, early narcissus and tulips, erythroniums, and trilliums.

CULTURE/CARE Evenly moist, well-drained soils in part shade.

USES Small to medium-sized areas beneath trees and shrubs, including among exposed roots, along pathways, and on the edges of shady borders, spreading at a moderate rate. Tolerant of sandy and clay soils. Not tolerant of drought or foot traffic. Deer and rabbit resistant.

PROPAGATION Division, seed

Omphalodes cappadocica
CAPPADOCIAN NAVELWORT

Zones 6–9

Woodlands of Turkey and adjacent Georgia.

Tufted, stoloniferous, slowly creeping, semi-evergreen to evergreen perennial, 6–10 in. (15–25 cm) tall and 16 in. (40 cm) wide, with slightly shiny, mostly smooth, midgreen, veined, oval to heart-shaped, 3–4 in. (7.5–10 cm) long leaves with pointed tips. Small flowers are similar to forget-me-nots, bright midblue to purple-blue with a white starlike eye, in small, loose clusters in early to midspring. AGM

'Cherry Ingram': larger vibrant blue flowers, AGM

'Joy Skies': rich sky-blue flowers

'Lilac Mist': palest lilac or lilac-blue flowers

'Parisian Skies': warm purple flowers aging to purplish blue and then rich sky-blue

'Starry Eyes': midblue flowers with white edges flushed lilac-pink when young

Omphalodes cappadocica 'Starry Eyes'

Omphalodes verna

Onoclea sensibilis

Omphalodes verna
BLUE-EYED MARY, CREEPING NAVELWORT

Zones 6–9

Shaded sites, mountain forests, and scrublands from sea level to high elevations in Central and Southeast Europe.

Stoloniferous, mat-forming, herbaceous to evergreen perennial, 4–8 in. (10–20 cm) tall and spreading indefinitely, with rough, midgreen, veined, oval, 1–3 in. (2.5–7.5 cm) long leaves with pointed tips. Small flowers are similar to forget-me-nots, bright blue (sometimes emerging violet) with a white to yellowish starlike eye in small, loose clusters in early to midspring.

'Alba': white flowers

'Elfenauge': pale icy blue flowers

'Grandiflora': flowers about twice the size of the species

Onoclea sensibilis
SENSITIVE FERN, BEAD FERN

Onocleaceae

Zones 2–10

Moist habitats including open swamps, thickets, marshes, and low woods in sun and shade across North America east of the Great Plains.

A beautiful and distinctive rhizomatous species, named sensitive fern because its fronds turn brownish yellow and go dormant with the first autumn frost, despite, ironically, hardiness to zone 2. It grows 12–24 in. (30–60 cm) tall, spreading indefinitely with both sterile and fertile fronds not in a rosette but at intervals along the rhizome. Sterile fronds emerge in spring from fiddleheads with coppery red stems and copper-flushed leaf blades, becoming light green and once-pinnate with lobed or rippled edges. Vertical fertile fronds emerge in late summer, persist over winter, and release spores in spring from beadlike structures.

CULTURE/CARE Consistently moist, well-drained, fertile, neutral to acidic soils in full to part shade or in sun with ample moisture, though leaves can become yellowish. Tolerant of average moisture in shade. Spreads readily in loose, moist soils and slowly in compact or drier soils.

USES Woodland and shade gardens and near ponds and streams. Not tolerant of foot traffic. Deer and rabbit resistant.

PROPAGATION Division

Ophiopogon
Asparagaceae

These grasslike cousins of lilyturf (*Liriope* spp.) from temperate and tropical Asia are more closely related to lilies than graminoids, a fact revealed by their starlike or bell-shaped flowers producing spherical, pea-sized, blue or purple fruit. From their ranks comes the popular black mondo grass (*O. planiscapus* 'Nigrescens'), with thick, arching, linear foliage like narrow strips of black plastic. In addition to other more easily found cultivars from *O. jaburan* and *O. japonicus*, additional species are sometimes available, including *O. clarkei* and *O. intermedius*.

CULTURE/CARE Full sun to full shade in evenly moist, well-drained soils. Tolerant of periods of drought once established. Protect from hot afternoon sun in hot summer climates. Winter burn or browning can occur in colder zones. Trim or shear in spring to refresh. *Ophiopogon japonicus* is moderately salt tolerant.

USES Border or pathway edges, low foundation plantings, between paving stones, and beneath bonsai. Mass plant in small to medium-sized areas. Rhizomatous species are slow to fill in. Interplant with mat-forming ground covers to provide faster coverage. Combine *O. planiscapus* 'Nigrescens' with a contrasting foliage to make it visible against dark soil. Dwarf cultivars are tolerant of light foot traffic. *Ophiopogon japonicus* 'Nanus' and *O. planiscapus* 'Nigrescens' could be used as small- to medium-scale lawn alternatives. Deer and rabbit resistant.

PROPAGATION Division

Ophiopogon jaburan
GIANT MONDO GRASS, BLUE SNAKE'S BEARD

Zones (6)7–10
Shaded habitats of Japan and Korea.
Large species, 12–18 in. (30–45 cm) tall and 18–24 in. (45–60 cm) wide, with arching, evergreen, leathery, linear, dark green blades in clumping mounds. White, pendulous flowers on the underside of arching spikes resemble toothbrushes, later producing dark blue spherical fruit.

'Hocf' Crystal Falls: better resistance to winter damage and disease, possibly hardy to zone 6

'Vittatus' (syn. 'Variegatus'): foliage irregularly striped in green and white

Ophiopogon japonicus
DWARF MONDO GRASS

Zones (6)7–9
Moist, shady habitats including forests, dense scrub, ravines, slopes, streamsides, and cliffs from low to high elevations throughout China, Japan, and Korea.
Arching evergreen perennial, 6–12 in. (15–30 cm) tall, with narrow, linear, leathery, dark green blades in slowly expanding rhizomatous mounds. White or purplish flowers are held on short spikes within the foliage, followed by spherical, royal- to dark blue fruit. Some cultivars, especially the dwarfs, can be shy to

Ophiopogon japonicus 'Nanus'

bloom. Widely cultivated in China for its medicinal tuberous roots.

Dwarf cultivars remain confused in horticulture because of nomenclatural issues, plasticity of plant characters in different growing conditions, and the fact that 'Nanus' likely includes numerous clones.

'Gyoku-ryu': very dwarf, compact, 2–3 in. (5–7.5 cm) tall, may be synonymous with 'Super Dwarf'

'Haku Ryu Ko' (syns. 'Little Tabby', 'Pamela Harper'): 6 in. (15 cm) tall and 8–12 in. (20–30 cm) wide, with creamy white margins and occasional inner stripes

'Kigimafukiduma' (syn. 'Silver Mist'): narrow, variegated foliage with white margins and inner stripes, 6 in. (15 cm) tall and 8–12 in. (20–30 cm) wide

'Kyoto' (syns. 'Kioto', 'Kyoto Dwarf'): very dwarf, compact, and similar to 'Gyoku-ryu' but slightly larger, to 3–4 in. (7.5–10 cm) tall

'Nanus' (syn. 'Minor'): dwarf, slower spreading cultivar (or possibly a group of different dwarf clones) forming tight mounds to about 3–4 in. (7.5–10 cm) tall and 4–6 in. (10–15 cm) wide; 'Nanus', the North American cultivar, is likely synonymous with 'Minor' in the United Kingdom and mainland Europe

Ophiopogon planiscapus
MONDO GRASS

Zones (5)6–9

Open and forested slopes in Japan.

Arching to upright evergreen perennial, 6–12 in. (15–30 cm) tall, with dark green, leathery, linear blades slightly wider than some other species in slowly expanding, rhizomatous mounds. White, sometimes purple-tinged, bell-shaped flowers are held on short spikes within the foliage followed by spherical, dark purple to purple-black fruit.

'Nigrescens' (syns. 'Arabicus', 'Black Dragon', 'Ebknizam' Ebony Knight): unmistakable, with true jet-black foliage (with green bases when young), 6–8 in. (15–20 cm) tall, flowers often purplish or pinkish; seeds can produce green-leaved plants so remove fruit in fall to avoid black and green bicolor colonies, AGM

'Nigrescens Nana': resembles *O. japonicus* 'Nanus' but with jet-black foliage, very slow growing

'Yapard' Black Beard: no observable difference from 'Nigrescens'

Ophiopogon planiscapus 'Nigrescens'

Opuntia
Cactaceae

Prickly pears are native to North America and the Caribbean and include a number of extremely hardy species that can be used as bold and distinctive ground covers. *Opuntia fragilis* and *O. humifusa* are among the best, but other horizontally spreading, colony-forming species including *O. basilaris*, *O. macrorhiza*, *O. phaea-cantha*, *O. polyacantha*, and *O. polyacantha* var. *erinacea* and their cultivars can also be useful.

CULTURE/CARE Full to part sun in sharply draining, rocky, gravelly, or sandy soils. In wet winter climates, overhead protection from rain can minimize rot and brown spotting. Salt tolerant.

USES Small applications in arid, unirrigated sites. On their own, prickly pears may not make good weed suppressors because they spread slowly and their menacing thorns can deter gardeners more than weeds. Combine with other mat-forming, drought-tolerant plants such as *Sedum* and *Delosperma* spp. to achieve a closed cover. Not tolerant of foot traffic (nor are feet tolerant of them!). Deer and rabbit resistant. Attractive to pollinators, especially bees.

PROPAGATION Separation of pads, seed

Opuntia fragilis

Opuntia fragilis
BRITTLE PRICKLY PEAR, FRAGILE PRICKLY PEAR

Zones 2–9

Dry, grassy, sandy, or gravelly slopes, knolls, and flats from low to high elevations, from British Columbia to Ontario and most of the western United States.

This smallest and hardiest prickly pear reaches the 58th parallel north in British Columbia and Alberta, forming decumbent, evergreen mats, 2–8 in. (5–20 cm) tall, spreading slowly to 12–24 in. (30–60 cm)

Intriguing, slow-growing, gray-green, 4 in. (10 cm) wide rosettes of leaves with soft, white, spiny tips and 4–12 in. (10–30 cm) tall spikes of greenish yellow flowers. Overwintering domes of crowded, tightly packed, inward-pointing, overlapping leaves expand in spring into an open dome of outward-pointing, fleshy, rounded, linear to oblong leaves. Intermediate forms in fall resemble an alien maw, or, if the summer leaves persist into winter, an otherworldly starfish.

Osteospermum barberae var. *compactum*

HARDY AFRICAN DAISY

Asteraceae

Zones 4–9
Drakensberg Mountains of South Africa and Lesotho.

Best known for the nonhardy, colorful hybrids of seasonal containers and hanging baskets, *O. barberae* is a breathtaking five zones hardier than its pampered zone 9 cousins. It forms a dense mound or mat, 12 in. (30 cm) tall and 24 in. (60 cm) or more wide, of rich green, aromatic, oblong to lance-shaped leaves with occasional broad teeth. Silvery lavender-pink, daisy-like flowers with dark centers bloom over a long period from late spring through summer. Sometimes considered synonymous with *O. jucundum*.

CULTURE/CARE Full to part sun in average to dryish, well-drained soils of reasonable fertility. Provide good drainage in wet winter climates. Tolerant of periods of drought once established, though occasional watering keeps plants fresh.

USES Along driveways and walkways, on banks and slopes, atop walls, and at the front of the border. Not tolerant of foot traffic. Deer and rabbit resistant. Attractive to pollinators, especially bees and butterflies.

PROPAGATION Cuttings

'Avalanche': vigorous, disease-resistant, floriferous hybrid with *O. jucundum*, with pure white flowers on wide mats; 'Snow Pixie' is a similar cultivar in the United Kingdom though its relative hardiness is uncertain

'Po05s' Purple Mountain: vibrant, deep lavender-magenta flowers

'Po06s' Lavender Mist: possibly a hybrid, with flowers that open white, flushing lavender at the tips, spreading toward the center, sometimes less vigorous than 'Avalanche' and 'Po05s' Purple Mountain

Osteospermum 'Avalanche'

Othonna capensis

LITTLE PICKLES

Asteraceae

Zones 5 or 6–9
Dry, rocky flats in the Little Karoo, South Africa.

Succulent aster family member resembling a sedum or ice plant, forming spreading mats, 1 in. (2.5 cm) tall and 12 in. (30 cm) or more wide, of cylindrical, succulent, 1 in. (2.5 cm) long, green to blue-green leaves flushing purplish under stress. Small, solitary, ½ in. (1.3 cm) wide, yellow summer daisies open from pink buds on stems 1–3 in. (2.5–7.5 cm) tall.

CULTURE/CARE Full sun in well-drained to sharply drained soils, especially important in wet winter climates. Avoid rich soils to encourage a tight, compact habit.

USES Rock gardens, border edges, walls, and between paving stones, spreading at a slow to moderate rate. Not tolerant of foot traffic.

PROPAGATION Division, seed

Oxalis
Oxalidaceae

A large, nearly cosmopolitan genus of approximately 570 species, popular for their beautiful flowers and shamrock-shaped foliage. Most species used as ground covers are rhizomatous, but others arise from bulbs. Some, such as *O. depressa*, *O. tetraphylla* 'Iron Cross', and *O. triangularis*, are commonly grown as seasonal or container specimens but can be used as ground covers where hardy.

CULTURE/CARE Part to full shade, except *O. adenophylla* and *O. articulata*, which prefer full sun to light shade. All prefer average to fertile, evenly moist but well-drained soils, particularly important for *O. adenophylla*, which can overwinter better in frozen winter conditions in colder zones than wet soils in milder zones. *Oxalis oregana* is a vigorous spreader best planted where it has space to grow or where it can be contained by hardscape.

USES Habit and rate of spread varies greatly by species. *Oxalis adenophylla* is suitable for small applications or accents in sunny areas, between paving stones, and in rock gardens. The others can be used for edging borders and pathways, in woodlands, and beneath trees, with *O. articulata*, *O. griffithii*, and *O. magellanica* suitable for small to medium-sized applications and *O. oregana* suitable for medium-sized to large applications. *Oxalis magellanica* and *O. oregana* could be used as lawn alternatives. Not tolerant of foot traffic except for perhaps *O. magellanica*. Deer and rabbit resistant.

PROPAGATION Division

Oxalis adenophylla
SILVER SHAMROCK, CHILEAN OXALIS

Zones 4–10
High elevation talus slopes and rocky plains in the Andean alpine of Chile and Argentina.

Extremely hardy and herbaceous, noted for its striking, silver to silver-green, ½–1 in. (1.3–2.5 cm) wide, pleated leaves, each with up to 20 leaflets, forming a polite clump or slowly spreading colony, 4 in. (10 cm) tall and 4–6 in. (10–15 cm) or more wide. Showy white, 1 in. (2.5 cm) wide, summer flowers flushed pink at the tips have a dark red, central eye. May go summer dormant in hot summer climates. AGM

Oxalis articulata
PINK WOOD SORREL, WINDOWBOX WOOD SORREL

Zones 5–10
Shady habitats in Brazil, Paraguay, Uruguay, and Argentina. Naturalized in parts of the United States, Europe, and Australia.

Often sold as *O. crassipes*, this evergreen to herbaceous species blooms almost continuously from late spring to fall, with showy, pink to rich rose-pink flowers up to ¾ in. (2 cm) wide, with darker throats, in clusters of 5–10. Lush, bright green, shamrock-shaped leaves, ½–1 in. (1.3–2.5 cm) wide, form polite clumps or slowly spreading colonies, 8 in. (20 cm) tall and 18 in. (45 cm) or more wide. Flowering may decrease or stop in high temperatures.

'Alba': white flowers

'Rosea': bright pink, showy flowers

Oxalis griffithii
WOOD SORREL

Zones 6–9
Moist to dry, shady places in mixed, deciduous, or coniferous forests and thickets from middle to high elevations in China, adjacent Himalayan countries, Korea, Japan, and the Philippines.

A rare species resembling *O. oregana* in flower and foliage, but with lightly puckered, slightly shiny leaves on plants 2–8 in. (5–20 cm) tall. White flowers with lilac to pink veins bloom from spring to fall. Evergreen to semi-evergreen and clumping to slowly spreading via short rhizomes.

'Pink Charm' (syn. Pink Double Flower form): semidouble to double rosy pink flowers

'Snowflake' (syn. Double Flowered form): semidouble to double white flowers

Oxalis magellanica
WHITE OXALIS, SNOWDROP WOOD SORREL

Zones 7–9, possibly hardier
Along streams, rivers, and ponds in coastal to mountain forests, occasionally into the alpine in New Zealand, Australia, and Patagonian Chile and Argentina.

Diminutive, semi-evergreen to herbaceous, dense to open, spreading mats, 1–2 in. (2.5–5 cm) tall, of tiny,

Oxalis triangularis

Oxalis articulata 'Rosea'

Oxalis magellanica

shamrock-shaped, mid- to dark green leaves, ⅛–¼ in. (3–6 mm) wide, topped with larger white flowers, ½–1 in. (1.3–2.5 cm) wide. Spreads via rhizomes at a slow to moderate rate.

'Nelson': white double pom-pom flowers

Oxalis oregana
REDWOOD SORREL

Zones 6–9

Moist, coniferous, deciduous, and mixed forest floors and streambanks at low to moderate elevations from southern British Columbia to Northern California.

Vigorously spreading, rhizomatous, evergreen to herbaceous perennial, 2–6 in. (5–15 cm) tall, spreading quickly and indefinitely into lush mats of bright green, shamrock-shaped leaves less than 1–2 in. (2.5–5 cm) wide, comprising three heart-shaped leaflets joined at their bases, sometimes lightly silvered at their centers. Small, solitary, five-petaled flowers can appear,

Oxalis oregana

usually intermittently, from spring to fall in shades of deep pink, light pink, or white with pink stripes. *Oxalis oregana* is a sister species to the similar though smaller *O. montana* (formerly *O. acetosella* subsp. *montana*) of eastern North America and *O. acetosella* of Eurasia, though these species are uncommon in cultivation.

'Klamath Ruby': dark green leaves with subtle silvering in the center of each leaflet and dramatic purple-red undersides and stems, tending toward evergreen, with white flowers with pink stripes, good heat tolerance

'Select Pink': glowing pink flowers with yellow centers and evergreen foliage resembling *O. oregana* f. *smalliana*

'Wintergreen': deep green, evergreen leaves with silver centers and large pink flowers; plants sold as "evergreen form" could be this cultivar or a similar selection

'Xera's Blush': silver-pink to lavender-pink flowers with yellow centers, good heat tolerance

Pachyphragma macrophyllum
LARGE-LEAVED PACHYPHRAGMA,
CAUCASIAN PENNYCRESS

Brassicaceae

Zones (4)5–9
Wet beech forests up to 6200 ft. (1890 m) in the Caucasus, Iran, and Turkey.
Rounded, scalloped, lightly ruffled, slightly shiny, midgreen leaves, up to 4 in. (10 cm) wide, form evergreen to semi-evergreen rosettes, 16 in. (40 cm) tall and 24–36 in. (60–90 cm) wide, sometimes red-flushed in winter. Clusters of bright white, four-petaled flowers emerge after the snowdrops in early spring, blooming for a month or more, followed by heart-shaped fruit. May politely reseed into colonies.
CULTURE/CARE Prefers full sun to part shade in spring and more shade in summer in average to evenly moist, well-drained, woodland soils. Tolerant of dry shade and diverse soils, including sand and clay. Can go semidormant in hot summer climates.
USES Under trees and shrubs in woodland and shade gardens. Not tolerant of foot traffic.
PROPAGATION Seed

Pachysandra
Buxaceae

Few would connect this utilitarian ground cover with two of the most commonly cultivated shrubs—boxwood (*Buxus* spp.) and sweet box (*Sarcococca* spp.)—but all belong to the boxwood family. They indeed share similar traits: toughness, reliability, evergreen habit, and the early to midspring flowering of inconspicuous, often fragrant, white flowers. *Pachysandra terminalis* is one of the most popular and reliable of all shady ground covers. Its lesser known Chinese and American cousins, *P. axillaris* and *P. procumbens*, offer some interesting variations.
CULTURE/CARE Part to full shade in average to fertile, well-drained soils of medium moisture. *Pachysandra terminalis* and *P. procumbens* are tolerant of deep shade and part sun but can bleach in too much light. Drought tolerant once established. *Pachysandra terminalis* is salt tolerant.
USES Under large trees or shrubs, on slopes, along pathways and border edges, as a low foundation planting, and in difficult shaded areas. Plants can be slow to establish. Plant as densely as budget will allow to attain full coverage quickly, or interplant with another fast-spreading ground cover. Not tolerant of foot traffic. Deer and rabbit resistant. Attractive to pollinators, especially bees.
PROPAGATION Division, cuttings

Pachysandra axillaris
PACHYSANDRA

Zones 6–9
Forests and thickets from moderate to high elevations in southern China.
Evergreen ground cover, 6–18 in (15–45 cm) tall, with relatively large, shiny, egg-shaped to oblong, pointed, broadly toothed leaves emerging light green and becoming mid- to dark green on ascending, reddish stems. Fragrant, axillary, downward-curving spikes of red tepals and white stamens emerge in spring, often repeating in fall. Spreads by rooting stems at or below the soil surface at a moderate rate once established.

'Windcliff Fragrant': most common form cultivated in North America, blooming in spring and fall, 6–12 in. (15–30 cm) tall

Pachysandra procumbens

ALLEGHENY SPURGE

Zones 5–9

Rich woodlands of the southeastern United States.

Attractive whorls of oval, broadly toothed, blue-green leaves variably marbled with purple and silver form dense, indefinitely spreading colonies, 8–12 in. (20–30 cm) tall, by long rhizomes, spreading more slowly than *P. terminalis*. Herbaceous in colder zones and semi-evergreen to evergreen in milder zones. Small, white, fragrant early spring flowers on bottlebrush-like spikes rise from the base of plants to peek through the overwintered leaves before the new flush of foliage.

'Angola': heavily patterned olive-green leaves with silvery green centers and mottling

Pachyphragma macrophyllum

Pachysandra procumbens

Pachysandra terminalis

JAPANESE SPURGE, PACHYSANDRA

Zones 4–9

Shady, damp areas in forests from middle to high elevations in China and Japan.

Reliable and impenetrable, forming dense, evergreen, rhizomatous colonies of matte to slightly glossy, mid- to dark green, narrowly fan shaped, broadly toothed leaves, 2–4 in. (5–10 cm) long, in whorls atop fleshy stems, 6–10 in. (15–25 cm) tall, spreading indefinitely. Small, white early spring flowers on 1–2 in.

Pachysandra axillaris 'Windcliff Fragrant', Seattle

Pachysandra terminalis 'Variegata'

(2.5–5 cm) long bottlebrush-like spikes form at the tips of old stems followed by new foliage.

'Cutleaf': foliage with deeply dissected teeth resembling Italian parsley

'Green Carpet': more compact, to 6–8 in. (15–20 cm) tall, with deeper green, glossier leaves

'Green Sheen': extremely glossy, deep green leaves

'Variegata' (syn. 'Silver Edge'): gray-green to blue-green foliage with variably variegated creamy white edges and pale silver markings

Packera
Asteraceae

This primarily North American genus, whose members were formerly included within the genus *Senecio*, offers two species grown for their mats of spreading, herbaceous to semi-evergreen, basal foliage and yellow, daisy-like flowers. They are tolerant of full sun to shade and a variety of soil types, allowing for mass or repeated plantings that connect different areas of the garden. This and their quick growth rate have made them popular, especially within their native range, as tough, easy to grow, native, weed-suppressing ground covers.

CULTURE/CARE Full sun to part shade in well-drained, moist to somewhat dry soils. Tolerant of periods of drought. Plants grown in sun will require more moisture. *Packera obovata* is more tolerant of dry soils, heat, and sun. Both *P. aurea* and *P. obovata* grow quickly in moist conditions and bloom well even in shade. Remove flowering stems when desired to improve appearance or retain for light reseeding.

USES In a variety of light and soil conditions over small to large areas, including under trees and large shrubs, beside water features, along pathways, in borders, in woodlands, and on slopes for erosion control. Not tolerant of foot traffic. Deer and rabbit resistant. Attractive to pollinators, especially bees and butterflies.

PROPAGATION Division, seed

Packera aurea
GOLDEN GROUNDSEL, GOLDEN RAGWORT

Zones 3–9

Common throughout the eastern half of North America in damp or swampy places, in woodlands and meadows, along water courses, and in sandy or gravelly soils from sea level to moderate elevations.

Tough, rhizomatous perennial, previously known as *Senecio aureus*, with heart- or kidney-shaped, toothed, midgreen basal leaves, 2–3 in. (2.5–7.5 cm) long and wide, on long leaf stems in dense, spreading mats, 4–6 in. (10–15 cm) tall. Flat-topped clusters of golden yellow daisy-like flowers occur from late spring to early summer on nearly leafless stems, 12–24 in. (30–60 cm) tall.

Packera aurea

Packera obovata
ROUNDLEAF GROUNDSEL, ROUNDLEAF RAGWORT

Zones 3–9

Moist meadows and rocky areas in open deciduous woodlands, along watercourses, and on rocky wooded hillsides from sea level to high elevations, from Ontario and Quebec through the eastern and South Central United States.

Tough stoloniferous and rhizomatous perennial with rounded, oval, or egg-shaped, toothed, midgreen basal leaves, 2–4 in. (5–10 cm) long, in dense, spreading mats, 4–6 in. (10–15 cm) tall. Flat-topped clusters of golden yellow daisy-like flowers on nearly leafless stems, 10–20 in. (20–50 cm) tall, begin blooming slightly later than but overlap with *P. aurea*.

Parahebe
Plantaginaceae

This genus of small, evergreen subshrubs, related to the genus *Hebe* and now included in the genus *Veronica*, are grown in mild winter regions for their evergreen foliage, long bloom period, and tough demeanor. Less common species are occasionally available, including *P. linifolia* and its cultivar 'Blue Skies', *P. lyallii* and its cultivar 'Snowcap', and the hybrid *P.* 'Snow Clouds'.

CULTURE/CARE Sun to part shade in average to moist, well-drained soils. *Parahebe perfoliata* is tolerant of drought and infertile soil. It blooms on old wood. Trim *P. perfoliata* only as needed and only after flowering. Deadheading can encourage late summer rebloom. *Parahebe catarractae* can be sheared hard after flowering or in spring.

USES On slopes and walls, along pathways and border edges, in mass and foundation plantings over small to medium-sized areas. Not tolerant of foot traffic.

PROPAGATION Cuttings, seed

Parahebe catarractae
PARAHEBE

Zones 7–10

Along water courses in sand and silt, on cliffs, and in rocky places including landslide debris from sea level to mountainous areas across New Zealand.

Compact, evergreen, woody-based subshrub, 12–16 in. (30–40 cm) tall and 24 in. (60 cm) wide, of upright and trailing, rooting, maroon stems with shiny, dark green, lance-shaped, serrated, 1–4 in. (2.5–10 cm) long leaves. Small terminal spikes hold small flowers up to ½ in. (1.3 cm) wide in shades of light purple, purple-blue, or white, with a reddish magenta central ring flaring into thin veins. Blooms occur from late spring through summer and often into the fall.

'Delight': lavender to lavender-blue flowers

'Miss Willmott': white flowers

Parahebe perfoliata
DIGGER'S SPEEDWELL

Zones 7–10

Mountains of Southeast Australia.

Distinctive evergreen subshrub, forming graceful to slightly rambunctious mounds, 12–24 in. (30–60 cm) tall and 36 in. (90 cm) wide, with trailing, ascending, and upright semiwoody stems with opposite pairs of heart-shaped, clasping, blue-green foliage resembling that of eucalyptus. Nodding terminal spikes of small lavender to lavender-blue flowers are produced on old wood in spring and summer, often reblooming in the fall. Can be herbaceous in cold winters.

Parahebe perfoliata

Parathelypteris novae-boracensis
NEW YORK FERN, TAPERING FERN

Thelypteridaceae

Zones 4–8

Canopy openings in deciduous or mixed woodlands; in swamps, streams, and wooded ravines; and on ridge tops and mountain benches from sea level to higher elevations throughout eastern North America.

The marsh fern family has undergone much rearrangement, especially between the genera *Parathelypteris*, *Phegopteris*, and *Thelypteris*, all of which offer beautiful, rhizomatous species useful as ground covers. New York fern, formerly a species in genus *Thelypteris*, has graceful, airy, twice-pinnate, light green, herbaceous, sterile fronds, 12–24 in. (30–60 cm) long, with rounded pinnae tips and blades tapering toward the base, turning golden yellow in fall. Fertile fronds are similarly shaped but larger and more upright. Fronds emerge along vigorously spreading rhizomes that can quickly form large colonies. A rare, related, usually shorter Asian species, *P. beddomei*, also spreads quickly.

CULTURE/CARE Evenly moist to wet, fertile, soils, appreciating acidic conditions, in part sun to full shade. Plants spread more slowly with less moisture. Use hardscape features to control spread.

USES For medium-sized to large areas including shaded, wet sites, and woodland or wild gardens. Not tolerant of foot traffic. Deer and rabbit resistant.

PROPAGATION Division

Parthenocissus
Vitaceae

A popular genus of large, hardy, self-clinging, deciduous vines grown for their lush green foliage and brilliant fall color, *Parthenocissus* can be dramatic when grown into large trees and is famous as cladding for old stone and brick buildings, especially on the campuses of storied British and American universities and on the brick outfield walls of Chicago's Wrigley Field. In fact, the planting of *P. tricuspidata* (Boston ivy) at Harvard, Yale, Princeton, and other northeastern U.S. universities inspired the term "Ivy League." Though likely planted because of its established history of cultivation, it is ironic that Boston ivy is actually from China, Korea, and Japan and was used when its cousin, *P. quinquefolia* (Virginia creeper), was

growing wild in nearby fields and forests across much of eastern North America.

Without vertical support, *Parthenocissus* species can make good ground covers. Inconspicuous greenish or reddish flowers give rise to small clusters of blue-black or black fruit resembling small grapes (which reveal their familial connections), which are often obscured by the foliage until the leaves are dropped in autumn.

CULTURE/CARE Tough and easy in full sun to part shade in most well-drained soils of average to moderate moisture. Tolerant of full shade, dry soils, and salty soils. Best fall color is attained in full sun.

USES Medium-sized to large areas, 4–8 in. (10–20 cm) tall and spreading quickly and indefinitely via rooting stems. Use on large flat areas, on slopes for erosion control, or to cover unsightly landscape features such as stumps, rock piles, or unattractive hardscaping. Not tolerant of foot traffic. Deer and rabbit resistant.

PROPAGATION Cuttings

Parthenocissus henryana
SILVERVEIN CREEPER

Zones 6–9

Moist, rocky cliffs or rocky areas in valleys and on hillsides from low to moderately high elevations in Central and South Central China.

The most beautiful species, *P. henryana*, is a large, deciduous vine with toothed, palmately compound, silver-veined and purple-flushed leaves with five elliptic leaflets, up to 4 in. (10 cm) long and 2 in. (5 cm) wide, with purple to burgundy undersides. Light shade enhances spring and summer leaf colors, though best purple and bright red fall colors are achieved in full sun. Somewhat more restrained than other species, with stems up to 35 ft. (10.5 m) long. AGM

Parthenocissus quinquefolia
VIRGINIA CREEPER, WOODBINE

Zones 3–9

Open woods, ravines, rocky banks and ledges, thickets, fencerows, roadsides, and waste places across most of eastern North America.

Large, deciduous vine with serrated, palmately compound leaves with five elliptic leaflets up to 5 in. (12.5 cm) long and 2 in. (5 cm) wide on stems 30–50 ft. (9–15 m) long. Foliage is purplish in spring, midgreen in summer, and purple and crimson-red in fall.

Parthenocissus henryana as a ground cover

Parthenocissus tricuspidata growing on a wall

Passiflora 'Incense'

var. *engelmannii*: slower growing with smaller leaves turning reddish bronze in fall

'Monham' Star Showers: leaves variably variegated and splattered with white and cream, pink-flushed in cool weather

'Troki' Red Wall: burgundy new growth in spring, bright red in fall

'Yellow Wall': golden yellow fall foliage

Parthenocissus tricuspidata
BOSTON IVY, JAPANESE IVY

Zones 4–8

Shrubby habitats, cliffs, and rocky hillsides from low to moderately high elevations in eastern China, Korea, and Japan. Naturalized in the northeastern United States and Ontario.

Dark green, palmate leaves, 4–8 in. (10–20 cm) wide, usually with three lobes and toothed margins, resemble grape or maple leaves on stems 30–50 ft. (9–15 m) long. Foliage is purple and bright red in autumn. Potentially invasive in some regions.

'Fenway Park': golden sport found either on a building near the fabled home of the Boston Red Sox or within the stadium on the outfield wall known as the "Green Monster," with yellow-green foliage in sun, lime-green in shade, and fall colors of red, orange, and yellow

'Lowii': compact, slower growing, with smaller, crinkled leaves with more lobes, turning crimson red in fall on stems 6–8 ft. (1.8–2.4 m) long

'Veitchii': smaller leaves with shallower lobes, emerging bronze-purple in spring, AGM

Passiflora incarnata
MAYPOP, PURPLE PASSIONFLOWER

Passifloraceae

Zones 5–11

Open woodlands, savannas, prairies, dunes, riverbanks, and disturbed areas in a variety of often infertile and dry soils throughout the South Central and eastern United States.

Of the mostly tropical passionflowers, *P. incarnata* is the hardiest, growing as a vigorous vine, 6–8 ft. (1.8–2.4 m) or more long, with palmate, deeply three-lobed, serrate, light to midgreen leaves, 3–5 in. (7.5–12.5 cm) wide. The incredibly intricate, 3 in. (7.5 cm) wide, fragrant, fringed, lavender and white summer flowers with purple detailing become green-ish yellow, egg-shaped, edible fruits in fall. Plants are self-fertile and herbaceous, freezing to the ground in most zones, or deciduous, maintaining semiwoody stems in subtropical zones. Without vertical support, maypop will grow as a ground cover, 6–12 in. (15–30 cm) tall. Indeed, it is grown this way in open fields for harvesting for medicinal purposes. Its zone 7 hardy cousin, *P. caerulea*, the hardy blue passion-flower, may also be used as a ground cover.

CULTURE/CARE Full to part sun in almost any evenly moist to dryish, well-drained soil. Overwinter-ing success can be improved by burying stems 4–6 in. (10–15 cm) deep on initial planting and mulching the base of plants with fallen leaves.

USES Fast-growing ground cover for medium-sized areas including flat ground or slopes or to cover unsightly garden features. Not tolerant of foot traffic. Attractive to pollinators, especially bees.

PROPAGATION Cuttings, seed

'Incense': hybrid with *P. cincinnata*, with deeper lavender flowers and good fragrance, zone 6

Paxistima
Celastraceae

Reminiscent of boxwood (*Buxus* spp.), two North American *Paxistima* species, one eastern and one western, remain uncommon in cultivation because of production challenges and sensitivity to garden conditions. In appropriate conditions, they are attrac-tive, evergreen shrubs, useful as ground covers, with special interest for native plant gardeners.

CULTURE/CARE Organically rich, evenly moist, well-drained soils in part shade or in rocky to sandy soils in more sun. Tolerant of full sun and dry shade. *Paxistima canbyi* is tolerant of salt and may prefer alka-line soils. *Paxistima myrsinites* is more likely to prefer acidic conditions. Growth is slow. Pruning is usually not required.

USES Mass plant on small to moderate scales in native plant or rock gardens or on slopes for erosion control. Not tolerant of foot traffic.

PROPAGATION Cuttings

Paxistima canbyi

Paxistima canbyi
CANBY'S MOUNTAIN LOVER, CLIFF GREEN

Zones 3–7
Shaded open woods and wooded slopes in moist organic soils, to full sun on limestone cliffs and uplands in gravelly soils from low to moderate ele-vations in the Appalachians in the central eastern United States.

Considered threatened or endangered in some states, it is a dense, low-growing, prostrate, spreading, rooting evergreen shrub with shiny, lance-shaped or narrowly oblong, finely serrated, deep green leaves turning bronzy in cold weather, 12 in. (30 cm) tall and 3–4 ft. (1–1.2 m) or more wide. Inconspicuous axillary greenish to reddish flowers become white fruit.

Paxistima myrsinites
OREGON BOX, OREGON BOXLEAF

Zones 3–8
Shaded forests, mesic to dry slopes, and open rocky outcrops from low to high elevations in western North America.

Moderately dense to dense, low-growing, layered, prostrate, spreading to ascending, evergreen shrub resembling box-leaf honeysuckle (*Lonicera pileata*), with shiny, oval, finely serrated, dark green leaves on plants 8–24 in. (20–60 cm) or more tall and 24–36 in. (60–90 cm) wide. Inconspicuous, fragrant, reddish axillary flowers become white fruit.

Pennisetum
Poaceae

Best known for the annual purple fountain grass, *P. ×advena* (syn. *P. setaceum*) 'Rubrum', many perennial *Pennisetum* species and cultivars are valuable in gardens, with fine foliage and arching inflorescences that resemble foxtails. These clumping, warm-season grasses break dormancy in midspring into arching mounds that can be mass-planted to form effective ground covers. In addition to the hardier species, other less hardy and less common cousins include *P. massaicum* 'Red Bunny Tails', *P. thunbergii* 'Red Buttons', and *P. villosum*.

CULTURE/CARE Full sun to part shade in average to moist, well-drained soils. Best flowering occurs in full sun. Tolerant of periods of drought and wet soils. Shear to the ground in early spring before new growth appears.

USES Mass plant for erosion control on slopes, and for foundation plantings, border edges, rock gardens, large-scale mass plantings, and rain gardens, bulking up at a moderate rate. Not tolerant of foot traffic. Deer resistant.

PROPAGATION Division, seed

Pennisetum alopecuroides
DWARF FOUNTAIN GRASS, CHINESE FOUNTAIN GRASS

Zones 5–9

Grassy hills, roadsides, and field margins from sea level to high elevations in China and Japan through Southeast Asia to Australia.

Graceful, clumping, dense, textural mounds, 12–24 in. (30–60 cm) tall and wide, of narrow, arching, linear, midgreen leaves, about ¼–½ in. (6–12 mm) wide, turning to golden yellow in fall and fading to tan from winter to spring. Arching, silvery white to pinkish flower spikes rise to 12 in. (30 cm) above the foliage in mid- to late summer, turning brown and then tan and persisting into late fall or early winter. May require protection in zone 5. Use sterile cultivars where potentially invasive.

'Burgundy Bunny': compact mound, 16 in. (40 cm) tall and wide, with deep red summer leaf tips expanding into bright red fall color

'Cassian's Choice' (syn. 'Cassian'): resembles 'Hameln' but usually larger, to 24 in. (60 cm) tall and wide, with bold orange and red fall color and potentially greater hardiness, AGM

Pennisetum alopecuroides 'Hameln'

'Desert Plains' Prairie Winds: large plants, 3–4 ft. (1–1.2 m) tall in flower, with smoky purple spikes above reddish summer leaf tips, expanding into bright gold, orange, and red fall color

'Foxtrot': large plants with foliage to 4 ft. (1.2 m) tall and pinkish flower spikes to 5 ft. (1.5 m) tall

'Ginger Love': early blooming, dark red flower spikes, 2–3 ft. (0.6–1 m) tall

'Hameln': compact, 12–24 in. (30–60 cm) tall and wide, with short flower spikes within or just above the foliage

'JS Jommenik' Lumen Gold: compact mounds, 18 in. (45 cm) tall and wide, emerging bright gold in spring, softening to lemon-yellow or light green through summer

'Little Bunny': very compact mounds, 12 in. (30 cm) tall and wide, with short flower spikes

'Little Honey': compact sport of 'Little Bunny' with cream-edged foliage, 6–12 in. (15–30 cm) tall and wide

'Moudry': large plants with broad leaves and purple-black flower spikes, can reseed aggressively in some regions

'National Arboretum': similar to 'Moudry' but may flower more consistently

'Piglet': intermediate between 'Little Bunny' and 'Hameln', with mounds 12 in. (30 cm) or more tall and wide

'Red Head': large, reddish spikes up to 4 ft. (1.2 m) tall, atop mounds, 3 ft. (1 m) tall and wide

'Tift H18' Praline: sterile tetraploid, 16 in. (40 cm) tall and wide, with large, long-blooming, pinkish spikes, 30 in. (75 cm) tall

'Tift Pa5' Hush Puppy: long-blooming, sterile tetraploid with slender foliage and pink plumes, 30 in. (75 cm) tall

'Tift Pa17' Etouffée: long-blooming, sterile tetraploid with light pink earlier blooming plumes, 42 in. (106 cm) tall

'Tift Pa18' Cayenne: long-blooming, dark red to blackish, sterile plumes on stems 24–36 in. (60–90 cm) tall

'Tift Pa19' Jambalaya: long-blooming, sterile tetraploid with maroon plumes becoming silver-pink

f. *viridescens*: similar to 'Moudry'

Pennisetum orientale
ORIENTAL FOUNTAIN GRASS

Zones 5–9
Open, sunny habitats including rock outcrops, woodlands, shrublands, steppe, and deserts from India and Nepal to North Africa.

Pennisetum orientale 'Karley Rose'

Resembles *P. alopecuroides* but widespread and variable in the wild, 1–6 ft. (0.3–1.8 m) tall, often with 12 in. (30 cm) flower spikes. In cultivation, plants are typically 18–24 in. (45–60 cm) tall and wide, with green to gray-green foliage, topped in mid- to late summer by arching, pinkish plumes held about 12 in. (30 cm) above the foliage, which turns golden yellow in fall and tan in winter.

'Karley Rose': deeper pink, fuller plumes bloom over a longer period atop darker foliage

'Tall Tails': large plants, 4–5 ft. (1.2–1.5 m) tall in flower, with 9 in. (23 cm) long, arching, pink-flushed white plumes

Penstemon
Plantaginaceae

Penstemon is the largest genus of flowering plants endemic to North America, with approximately 250 species of perennials and subshrubs with upright spikes of showy, colorful, tubular flowers popular in gardens for their beauty and usefulness to pollinators. Less recognized are their adaptations to dry, sunny habitats and the mounding or mat-forming species that make good small-scale ground covers for dry conditions. In addition to the species treated here there are many less common options—mostly for dry, sunny sites—including *P. caespitosus, P. davidsonii* var. *menziesii* 'Microphyllus', *P. fruticosus* 'Purple Haze', *P. heterophyllus* and its cultivars 'Heavenly Blue' and 'Margarita BOP', *P. newberryi, P. procerus, P. rupicola,* and *P. virgatus* 'Blue Buckle'.

CULTURE/CARE Full to part sun in average to dry soils, including rocky and sandy sites. Avoid overly rich or moist soils. Shear spent flower spikes to encourage rebloom.

USES Rock gardens, xeriscapes, dry slopes, border edges, and along driveways and pathways. Not tolerant of foot traffic. Deer resistant. Attractive to pollinators, especially bees, butterflies, and hummingbirds.

PROPAGATION Cuttings, seed

Penstemon hirsutus var. *pygmaeus*
DWARF HAIRY BEARDTONGUE

Zones 3–9

Dry woods, rocky fields, rock outcrops, and bluffs, often in calcareous soils, in eastern North America.

Easy to grow low mounds or mats, 8 in. (20 cm) or more wide, of thick, dark green leaves with tubular, pink to lavender, white-throated flowers on upright stems, 8 in. (20 cm) tall, in early summer. Evergreen to semi-evergreen with bronze to reddish winter foliage.

Penstemon linarioides var. *coloradoensis*

BLUEMAT PENSTEMON, COLORADO NARROW-LEAF BEARDTONGUE

Zones 4–10

Foothills, open coniferous woodlands, and semi-desert to high elevations in Colorado, New Mexico, and Arizona.

Light lavender, lavender-blue, or light blue tubular flowers with white markings on the lower lobes in late spring and early summer on stems 12 in. (30 cm) tall, atop silvery, evergreen, linear foliage. Growing 12–16 in. (30–40 cm) wide in the wild, plants can reach 24–36 in. (60–90 cm) wide with good moisture and drainage.

'Po14s' Silverton: lavender-blue to light blue flowers, good silvery foliage

Penstemon pinifolius
PINELEAF PENSTEMON

Zones 4–9

Plains, deserts, rocky areas, and open coniferous woodlands into high elevations in southern New Mexico and eastern Arizona.

Penstemon pinifolius

Distinctive, small, very fine, linear, needlelike evergreen leaves form low, textural mounds, 12 in. (30 cm) tall and 18 in. (45 cm) or more wide, that resemble a dwarf conifer. Small, narrow, bright orange-red, tubular flowers are produced in great numbers over a long period in late spring and summer. AGM

'Luminous': compact, 8–10 in. (20–25 cm) tall, with bright orange flowers with yellow throats

'Mersea Yellow': bright lemon-yellow flowers

'Po19s' SteppeSuns Sunset Glow: bright orange flowers with yellow throats

Persicaria
Polygonaceae

Fleece flowers are not as common in North American gardens as they are in European ones, perhaps owing to confusion, as plants of genus *Persicaria* used to be within the genus *Polygonum*—the invasive knotweeds. Or perhaps the somewhat coarse foliage of some species can be reminiscent of roadside weeds. A number of useful trailing species, however, have quite attractive foliage, plus impressively long-lasting floral displays, with spherical or pokerlike inflorescences that provide a structural contrast to other flower types. Other taller species with larger leaves and mounding habits, such as *P. bistorta*, can be used as mass-planted ground covers for landscape settings. Other options include *P. amplexicaulis* and its many cultivars, including 'Alba', 'Blackfield', 'Blotau' Taurus, 'Firetail', 'Golden Arrow', and 'Rosea'; *P. campanulata*; *P. microcephala* 'Red Dragon'; *P. runcinata* 'Purple Fantasy'; *P. virginiana* var. *filiformis* and its cultivars 'Painter's Palette' and 'Brushstrokes'; and *P. virginiana* Variegated Group.

CULTURE/CARE Full sun to part shade in average to evenly moist, fertile soils.

USES The trailing species (*P. affinis*, *P. capitata*, and *P. vacciniifolia*) can be used in rock gardens, along pathways, as edgers, or trailing over walls or containers for small to medium-sized applications. *Persicaria affinis* and *P. vacciniifolia* are tolerant of occasional foot traffic. *Persicaria bistorta* and other mounding species can be mass-planted as tall ground covers over small to large areas. Deer and rabbit resistant. Attractive to pollinators, especially bees and butterflies.

PROPAGATION Division

Persicaria affinis
HIMALAYAN BISTORT, KNOTWEED

Zones (3)4–8

Grassy slopes, wet meadows, streambanks, and rocky areas at high elevations from Tibet, China, through adjacent Himalayan countries to Pakistan.

A tough, herbaceous to semi-evergreen, weed-smothering ground cover forming low, dense mats, 4–6 in. (10–15 cm) tall, spreading indefinitely with leathery, slightly shiny, deep green, lance-shaped to elliptic, 2–4 in. (5–10 cm) long leaves with whitish undersides. Successively emerging, pokerlike spikes, 8–12 in. (20–30 cm) tall, of tightly packed white to pale pink flowers age to rose-pink, pinkish red, and deep red, later drying to brown and persisting into winter atop bronze-flushed leaves.

'Border Jewel': similar to 'Superba'

'Darjeeling Red': flowers aging to darker brick-red with larger, more reddish fall foliage, AGM

'Donald Lowndes': pale pink flowers age to deep pink, AGM

'Superba' (syn. 'Dimity'): vigorous grower with pale pink flowers aging to red, with good red to brownish winter foliage, AGM

Persicaria bistorta
EUROPEAN BISTORT, MEADOW BISTORT

Zones 3–9

Hilly grasslands, moist meadows, wooded swamps, and forest edges from moderate to high elevations from China and Japan to Europe.

Herbaceous to semi-evergreen, clumping to slowly expanding perennial from thick, twisted rhizomes with somewhat coarse, broadly lance-shaped to narrowly oval, 8 in. (20 cm) long, midgreen leaves with heart-shaped bases, forming basal mounds, 12–24 in. (30–60 cm) tall and wide. Soft baby-pink to lavender-pink flowers in tight, poker-like spikes top leafless stems, 24–36 in. (60–90 cm) tall, in late spring through summer. Now known scientifically as *Bistorta officinalis*.

subsp. *carnea*: more compact with narrower leaves and deeper pink flowers on more spherical spikes

'Hohe Tatra': brighter pink flowers emerging slightly later from reddish buds on more compact plants

'Superba': slightly larger in all respects than the species with more profuse bloom, AGM

Persicaria capitata
PINK-HEADED PERSICARIA, PINK BUBBLE PERSICARIA

Zones 7–10

Mountain slopes and shaded valleys at moderate to high elevations from China into the Himalayas and Southeast Asia.

Fast-growing, trailing, branching, herbaceous to semi-evergreen mats, 2–4 in. (5–10 cm) tall, spreading indefinitely, with reddish stems rooting at the nodes. Pointed, oval, gray-green to bluish green leaves with a brownish chevron are flushed bronzy red when young and more red in sun when mature. Small, spherical pom-pom heads of tightly packed, soft pink flowers appear singly or in pairs at the stem tips from late spring into summer.

Persicaria vacciniifolia
BLUEBERRY-LEAVED FLEECE FLOWER, CREEPING FLEECE FLOWER

Zones 4–9

In thickets on mountain slopes and in rocky areas at high elevations in the Himalayas.

Uncommon, trailing, branching, rooting, herbaceous, 2–4 in. (5–10 cm) tall, indefinitely spreading

Persicaria affinis

Persicaria capitata

Persicaria vacciniifolia

Petasites frigidus var. palmatus 'Golden Palms'

mats with rusty orange stems and pointed, elliptic, dark green, glossy leaves that turn bright red and gold in fall. Small, light pink, 8 in. (20 cm) tall spikes appear in summer. AGM

Petasites frigidus var. palmatus
ARCTIC SWEET COLTSFOOT, ARCTIC BUTTERBUR

Asteraceae

Zones 2–10

Streambanks, fens, swamps, roadside ditches and embankments, and forests at low to moderately high elevations from Alaska to California and across Canada into the Great Lakes and the U.S. Northeast.

These dramatic, large-leaved, rhizomatous, fast-spreading, herbaceous perennials are revered as

the edible *fuki* of Japan, particularly P. *japonicus* subsp. *giganteus*, its variegated cultivar 'Nishiki-buki' (syn. 'Variegatus'), and more rarely the purple-flushed P. *japonicus* f. *purpureus*. With foliage up to 3–4 ft. (1–1.2 m) wide on stalks 3–5 ft. (1–1.5 m) tall, they can also be used as a ground cover in large landscapes and parks.

For smaller spaces, P. *frigidus* var. *palmatus* has entire to toothed, smooth to woolly, starfish-shaped, palmate, 16–20 in. (40–50 cm) wide leaves with 5–11 deep lobes (themselves often variably lobed) on stems 12–18 in. (30–45 cm) tall. Foliage is preceded in early spring by unusual, tight to open heads of fuzzy white flowers of disc florets elongating over time. Other smaller species are sometimes grown, including P. *albus*, P. *fragrans*, P. *hybridus*, and P. *paradoxus*.

CULTURE/CARE Full sun to part shade in average to moist, fertile soils. Provide even moisture in full sun and afternoon shade in hot summer climates. May go summer dormant in overly dry conditions. Can spread vigorously in moist soils, more slowly with less moisture. Contain spread with hardscape features. Protect young foliage from slugs.

USES Pond edges, along water courses, or in shaded woodland or wild gardens. Not tolerant of foot traffic.

PROPAGATION Division

'Golden Palms': lime-green in shadier conditions or golden yellow with red edges and a reddish flush in bright light, discovered in the wild at a moderate elevation in the Pacific Northwest and listed as zone 6, but may be hardier

Peucedanum ostruthium
PEUCE MASTERWORT

Apiaceae

Zones 5–9
Woodlands, damp places, and mountain meadows of Central and Southern Europe.

Palmately lobed, slightly shiny, toothed, herbaceous, midgreen leaves forming clumps or slowly spreading mounds, 6–12 in. (15–30 cm) tall and 12–24 in. (30–60 cm) wide, topped with white-flowered summer umbels on stems 18–24 in.

(45–60 cm) tall. Resembles the thuggish bishop's weed (*Aegopodium podagraria*), but with slightly larger leaves and a well-behaved, nonaggressive habit. Now known scientifically as *Imperatoria ostruthium*.

CULTURE/CARE Part sun to shade in fertile, evenly moist soil.

USES Mass plant in small to medium-sized areas including woodland gardens and border edges, and beneath deciduous trees and shrubs. Not tolerant of foot traffic. Deer resistant.

PROPAGATION Division, seed

'Daphnis': well-behaved substitute for *Aegopodium podagraria* 'Variegatum', with slightly larger gray-green leaves edged with yellow and maturing to creamy white

Phegopteris decursive-pinnata
JAPANESE BEECH FERN

Thelypteridaceae

Zones 4–10
Along watercourses and in low mountains and forests from sea level to moderate elevations in China, Japan, Korea, and northern Vietnam.

The marsh fern family has undergone much rearrangement, especially between the genera *Parathelypteris*, *Phegopteris*, and *Thelypteris*, all of which offer beautiful, rhizomatous species useful as ground covers. Japanese beech fern, formerly a species

Phegopteris decursive-pinnata

of *Thelypteris*, is an excellent ground cover fern with graceful, narrowly lance-shaped, toothed, once- to twice-pinnate, bright green, herbaceous to evergreen fronds, 12–24 in. (30–60 cm) long, with lighter green undersides and blades tapering toward the base. Fronds arise in clusters along short, spreading rhizomes, forming colonies at a reasonable, nonaggressive rate. Two related North American species, the terrestrial and lithophytic *P. connectilis* and the terrestrial *P. hexagonoptera*, also spread by rhizomes and are useful as ground covers.

CULTURE/CARE Average to evenly moist, fertile soils in part sun to shade. Tolerant of dry periods. Plants spread more slowly with less moisture. Tolerant of heat and humidity.

USES Shaded, moist sites in woodland or wild gardens. Not tolerant of foot traffic. Deer and rabbit resistant.

PROPAGATION Division

Phemeranthus calycinus
FAMEFLOWER, ROCK PINK

Montiaceae

Zones 5–10

Rocky or sandy habitats including rocky glades, hilly prairies, and barren savannas, usually on or near rock outcrops, from low to higher elevations in the South Central United States.

Short, herbaceous, succulent mounds or mats, 2–4 in. (5–10 cm) tall and 6–12 in. (15–30 cm) wide, produce rounded, linear, green to blue-green, 2–3 in. (5–7.5 cm) long leaves sometimes flushed pink. Pink to magenta, five-petaled, 1 in. (2.5 cm) wide, cupped to starry, dark yellow–centered flowers bloom in cymes atop wiry, 8 in. (20 cm) stems in late spring and summer, opening only in the afternoon. Can self-seed readily, forming large colonies. Formerly known as *Talinum calycinum*.

CULTURE/CARE Full sun in average to dry, well-drained, rocky or sandy soils. Good drainage is essential. Avoid wet winter soils.

USES Small applications in rock gardens, on green roofs, and in other dry, sunny sites. Fast growing but may not form a closed cover depending on conditions. Effective in combination with *Sedum* and *Delosperma* spp. Not tolerant of foot traffic. Attractive to pollinators, especially bees and butterflies.

PROPAGATION Seed

Phlomis russeliana
JERUSALEM SAGE, TURKISH SAGE

Lamiaceae

Zones 4–9

Open woods and woodland openings in Turkey and Syria.

Widely considered a midborder summer perennial, for much of the other three seasons it exists as low mounds or mats of evergreen, weed-suppressing foliage. Bold, fuzzy, textural, aromatic, heart-shaped, gray-green, 6–8 in. (15–20 cm) long leaves form mounds 12–16 in. (30–40 cm) tall, spreading slowly by rhizomes into dense colonies. The architectural flowering stems, 24–36 in. (60–90 cm) tall, are square, with similar yet smaller, narrower leaves subtending evenly spaced, whorled clusters of creamy yellow, hooded flowers. Dry brown flower stems provide winter interest. Other shrubby species could be used as tall ground covers for larger sites, such as *P. chrysophylla*, *P. italica*, *P. lanata*, and *P. fruticosa* and its hybrid with *P. russeliana*, *P.* 'Edward Bowles'. AGM

CULTURE/CARE Full to part sun in average to dry, moderately fertile, well-drained, sandy soils. Tolerant of light shade and dry conditions. Avoid wet soils.

USES Mass-planted in the front, middle, or back of borders and in water-wise gardens. Spreads at a slow to moderate rate. Not tolerant of foot traffic. Deer and rabbit resistant. Attractive to pollinators, especially bees and butterflies. Birds are attracted to the seeds.

PROPAGATION Division, seed

Phlomis russeliana

Phlox
Polemoniaceae

Tall garden phlox, *P. paniculata*, and the moss phlox, *P. subulata*, are old cottage garden favorites that hail from a large group native to diverse North American habitats, from woodlands and prairies to mountain tops and alpine tundra. There are phlox for every garden situation in the sunny border, the shady woodland, the rock garden, and the alpine house, including many ground covers. Their beautiful, brightly colored flowers are often fragrant and attract pollinators. *Phlox glaberrima* 'Morris Berd' and subsp. *triflora* 'Triple Play' are sometimes grown.

CULTURE/CARE *Phlox douglasii*, *P. subulata*, and *P. ×procumbens* prefer full sun in humusy, average to moderately moist, sandy or gravelly soils with good drainage. Tolerant of salt, heat, and periods of drought. Protect from afternoon sun in hot summer climates. Shear plants by half after flowering to encourage denser growth and possible rebloom. *Phlox divaricata* and *P. stolonifera* appreciate part shade to shade in organically rich, evenly moist, well-drained soils and are tolerant of periods of drought. *Phlox divaricata* is susceptible to powdery mildew usually after flowering, and *P. stolonifera* is also susceptible, though less so, and plants recover more quickly. Provide good air circulation, avoid water stress during periods of high humidity, and trim back spent flowering stems, which also helps to avoid self-seeding. If mildew still occurs, grow plants in combination with other ground covers or plant around later emerging perennials such as hostas, astilbes, and ferns.

USES *Phlox divaricata* and *P. stolonifera* are best in woodlands, native gardens, shaded rock gardens, along pathways, and as border edgers. Not tolerant of foot traffic. Use *P. douglasii*, *P. subulata*, and *P. ×procumbens* in rock gardens, as border edgers, on walls and slopes, and along stairways and pathways. *Phlox subulata* could be used as a lawn alternative. Deer and rabbit resistant. Attractive to pollinators, especially butterflies and hummingbirds.

PROPAGATION Division, cuttings, seed

Phlox divaricata
WOODLAND PHLOX, BLUE PHLOX

Zones 3–8

Rich woods and woodland openings, partly shaded fields, floodplains, and along streams across eastern North America.

Phlox divaricata 'Blue Moon'

Charming, shade-loving, herbaceous to semi-evergreen species forming low, loose, indefinitely spreading mats via short rhizomes or rooting stems of midgreen, lance-shaped or elliptic, 2 in. (5 cm) long foliage. Five-petaled, notched (subsp. *divaricata*) or unnotched (subsp. *laphamii*), lilac, rose, or blue, lightly fragrant, pinwheel-like flowers bloom from midspring into early summer in loose clusters on glandular, sticky stems, 12–16 in. (30–40 cm) tall. Similar to *P. stolonifera* but slower spreading, more fragrant, and blooming 1–2 weeks earlier on taller stems. Plants could be described as "semi-ephemeral," with foliage gradually declining through summer, sometimes made worse by powdery mildew. AGM

These are the best-performing cultivars from the phlox trials at the Mt. Cuba Center botanical garden in Delaware.

'Blue Elf': light blue to purplish blue flowers, 6 in. (15 cm) tall, foliage holds well after flowering

'Blue Moon': likely the best cultivar overall, with lavender-blue flowers on 16 in. (40 cm) stems

'Charleston Pink': pink to lavender-pink flowers, 12 in. (30 cm) tall

'Clouds of Perfume': lavender-blue flowers similar to 'Blue Moon' with good fragrance, 12 in. (30 cm) tall

subsp. *laphamii* (syn. 'Laphamii'): lavender-blue flowers on 18 in. (45 cm) stems

subsp. *laphamii* 'Chattahoochee': lavender-blue flowers with a warm purple eye, 6–12 in. (15–30 cm) tall, AGM

'London Grove Blue': vigorous plants with blue to lavender-blue flowers, 14 in. (36 cm) tall

'May Breeze': palest blue to nearly white flowers give a white effect, 16 in. (40 cm) tall

'Tinian Sprite': vigorous plants with pink to lavender-pink flowers, 10 in. (25 cm) tall

'White Perfume': white flowers, 12 in. (30 cm) tall

Phlox douglasii
TUFTED PHLOX, COLUMBIA PHLOX

Zones 3–8

Dry habitats including sagebrush scrub, forest openings, slopes, and mountainous, rocky areas at high elevations, from British Columbia and Montana southwest to California and New Mexico

Western North American counterpart to the eastern *P. subulata* of similar form and bloom time, with evergreen, mosslike cushions of linear foliage, 4 in. (10 cm) tall, and masses of colorful spring flowers. Some cultivars may be hybrids of *P. douglasii* (or its western cousin, *P. diffusa*) and *P. subulata* (or its eastern cousins, *P. bifida* and *P. nivalis*). They can be listed as *P. douglasii*, *P. ×douglasii* or *P.* Douglasii Group. Even more complicated is that *P. douglasii* is now known as *P. caespitosa* subsp. *caespitosa*! Another interesting western species is *P. kelseyi* and its cultivars 'Lehmi Midnight' and 'Lehmi Purple'.

'Boothman's Variety': broad, overlapping, light lavender petals with a purple eye, AGM

'Crackerjack': deep magenta-pink flowers, AGM

'Eva': broad, overlapping, soft mauve petals

'Ice Mountain': pure white flowers

'Ochsenblut': deepest magenta-pink to almost red flowers with red eyes

'Red Admiral': bold rose-red flowers with red eyes, AGM

'Waterloo': deep pink flowers with red eyes

'White Admiral': white flowers with yellow eyes

Phlox stolonifera
CREEPING PHLOX

Zones 5–9

Deciduous woods and woodland openings, shaded rocky slopes, and streambanks in the Appalachians.

Shade-loving, herbaceous to evergreen species quickly forming low, dense, indefinitely spreading mats via short rhizomes and long stolons of midgreen, oblong to oval, 2–3 in. (5–7.5 cm) long foliage. Lovely, five-petaled, lightly fragrant, lavender-blue, pink, or white pinwheel flowers appear in loose clusters in late spring to midsummer on stems 6–10 in. (15–25 cm) tall. Similar to *P. divaricata* but denser and faster spreading with better weed suppression, holds foliage better after flowering, is more resistant to powdery mildew, and has less fragrant flowers on shorter stems, blooming 1–2 weeks later. Perennial Plant of the Year 1990

Most of these are the best-performing cultivars from the phlox trials at the Mt. Cuba Center botanical garden in Delaware.

'Blue Ridge': light blue flowers, 8 in. (20 cm) tall, AGM

'Bruce's White': white flowers, 8 in. (20 cm) tall, not as vigorous or strong

'Fran's Purple': vigorous, mildew-resistant plants, light purple to bluish purple flowers, 8 in. (20 cm) tall

'Home Fires': deep pink flowers, 12 in. (30 cm) tall, good mildew resistance

'Margie': lavender to light blue flowers, 8 in. (20 cm) tall

'Pink Ridge': deep pink flowers similar to 'Home Fires', 10 in. (25 cm) tall

'Sherwood Purple': vigorous, fairly mildew-resistant plants, light purple to bluish purple flowers, 12 in. (30 cm) tall

'Weesie Smith': vigorous plants, blue to lavender-blue flowers, 10 in. (25 cm) tall

Phlox stolonifera 'Home Fires'

Phlox subulata
MOSS PHLOX, CREEPING PHLOX

Zones 3–9

Dry, rocky or sandy habitats including open woodlands and slopes in eastern North America.

Tough, old-fashioned ground cover forming creeping, mosslike, semi-evergreen to evergreen mats, 4–6 in. (10–15 cm) tall and 24 in. (60 cm) or more wide, with pointed, linear, 1 in. (2.5 cm) long, dark green leaves. Plants are nearly completely covered by clusters of fragrant pinwheel flowers in midspring, each with five notched petals in shades of purple, deep pink, pink, and white. Other similar eastern species include *P. bifida* and its cultivars 'Snowmass' and 'Top Notch' and *P. nivalis*.

'Amazing Grace': white flowers with deep pink eyes

'Bavaria': white flowers with blue eyes

Bedazzled Series: moderately spreading hybrids with star-shaped, notched petals that bloom a week before *P. subulata*, zone 4

'Crimson Beauty': deep pink flowers with red eyes

'Emerald Cushion Blue': lavender-blue flowers with lavender eyes, plants sold as 'Emerald Blue' and 'Emerald Cushion' are likely identical

'Emerald Pink': midpink flowers

'Eye Candy': light lavender-pink flowers with warm purple eyes

'Eye Caramba': midpink flowers with red eyes

'Eye Shadow': rosy purple flowers with dark purple eyes

'Fort Hill': rosy pink to lavender-pink flowers with deep pink eyes

'McDaniel's Cushion': bright rosy pink flowers with deep pink eyes, AGM

Mountainside Collection: slowly spreading, lower growing hybrids blooming 1–2 weeks before *P. subulata*, zone 4

'North Hills': white flowers with lavender blush, purple eyes

'Purple Beauty': light purple flowers with purple eyes

'Red Wings': reddish pink flowers with red eyes, AGM

Rocky Road Series: compact, floriferous, moderately spreading hybrids with good drought tolerance in a range of colors, zone 4

'Ronsdorfer Schöne' (syns. 'Beauty of Ronsdorf', 'Ronsdorfer Beauty'): deep pink flowers with red eyes

'Scarlet Flame': reddish pink flowers with red eyes

'Snowflake': pure white flowers

Phlox subulata 'Violet Pinwheels'

Spring Series: earlier blooming plants of good habit in a range of colors, formerly Early Spring Series

Spring Bling Series: moderately spreading hybrids with large flowers, blooming two weeks or more before *P. subulata*, zone (3)4

Sprite Series: low, mounding to very slowly spreading hybrids blooming one week later than *P. subulata*, tolerant of part shade

'Tamaongalei' (syn. 'Candy Stripe'): pink petals with white edges and red eye

'Violet Pinwheels': lower growing, mounding to slowly spreading hybrid with small, violet purple flowers, zone 4

'White Delight': pure white flowers

Phlox ×procumbens
HYBRID CREEPING PHLOX, TRAILING PHLOX

Zones 5–9

Garden origin.

Hybrids of mosslike, sun-loving *P. subulata* and lush, green, shade-loving *P. stolonifera* are intermediate in size and habit, resembling a larger, lusher *P. subulata* with evergreen mats of lance-shaped, midgreen foliage covered in flowers with rounded, almost overlapping petals over a long period from early to late spring. Somewhat susceptible to powdery mildew in shady conditions.

Paparazzi Series: early flowering plants with good heat and humidity tolerance in a range of colors, named after famous personalities, including Jagger, Levine, Adele, Paris, Britney, Miley, Lindsay, Angelina, and Gaga

'Pink Profusion': deep lavender-pink flowers with purple eyes and white halos

'Variegata': variegated leaves with creamy white edges, rose-pink flowers, less vigorous

Phuopsis stylosa
CAUCASIAN CROSSWORT, LARGE-STYLED CROSSWORT

Rubiaceae

Zones 5–8

Hillsides and deciduous woodlands in the Caucasus, Turkey, and Iran.

Unusual, vigorous, easy to grow herbaceous ground cover for challenging sites, resembling the spheres of ornamental onions (*Allium* spp.) atop finely textured foliage. Dense, spreading mats, 6–8 in. (15–20 cm) tall and 12–24 in. (30–60 cm) or more wide, have bright green, pointed, linear, whorled leaves on square stems, creating an informal, billowy look. Dome-shaped, pincushiony terminal clusters appear in late spring and summer with tiny, light to bright pink, tubular, five-lobed flowers with long, protruding styles. Foliage and flowers smell skunky, like cannabis.

CULTURE/CARE Average to moderately moist, well-drained soils in full sun to part shade. Tolerant of poor soils and drought. Not tolerant of heat and humidity. Shear plants after flowering if reseeding is not desired and to encourage compactness and rebloom.

USES Rock gardens, walls, slopes, border edges, hell strips, and other difficult or disturbed sites. Not tolerant of foot traffic. Deer and rabbit resistant. Attractive to pollinators, especially bees.

PROPAGATION Seed, division, cuttings

'Purpurea': slightly larger, with more purple flowers

×*Phylliopsis*
Ericaceae

Zones 5–9

Hybrids of different species of the circumboreal genus *Phyllodoce* and the Oregon endemic *Kalmiopsis leachiana*.

Intergeneric hybrid resembling heath (*Erica* spp.) and heather (*Calluna* spp.) but with lusher, greener foliage and relatively large flowers. Low-growing, evergreen, spreading mounds, 6–12 in. (15–30 cm) tall and 12–24 in. (30–60 cm) or more wide, of linear, round-tipped, deep green leaves produce flushes of large, sideways-facing, urn-shaped, pink flowers in spring, summer, and often fall.

CULTURE/CARE Similar to heaths and heathers. Full to part sun in fertile, average, to evenly moist but well-drained, gritty, acidic soils.

USES Alpine and rock gardens, as an edger along borders and pathways, and on slopes for erosion control, spreading at a slow to moderate rate. Not tolerant of foot traffic.

PROPAGATION Cuttings

×*P.* 'Coppelia': lavender-pink flowers, 12 in. (30 cm) tall and wide (*Phyllodoce empetriformis* × *Kalmiopsis leachiana*)

×*P. hillieri* 'Pinocchio': purplish pink flowers on dense plants, 6–12 in. (30–45 cm) tall by 18 in. (45 cm) wide (*Phyllodoce brewerii* × *Kalmiopsis leachiana*)

×*P. hillieri* 'Sugar Plum': pink flowers, 6–12 in. (15–30 cm) tall by 12–24 in. (30–60 cm) wide (*Phyllodoce caerulea* × *Kalmiopsis leachiana*)

Phuopsis stylosa

×*Phylliopsis hillieri* 'Sugar Plum'

Physalis alkekengi var. *franchetii*
CHINESE LANTERN

Solanaceae

Zones 3–9
Disturbed sites, plains, forests, and mountain slopes from moderate to moderately high elevations from Europe to China.

A popular, seasonally decorative plant for the fall, especially around Halloween, with bright orange, papery, inflated, lantern-shaped calyces that hide the ripening orange-red, edible fruit within. The distinctive fruit of this relative of tomatillo (*P. philadelphica, P. ixocarpa*) and cape gooseberry (*P. peruviana*) are preceded by small, white, insignificant, axillary flowers in summer on vertical stems, 12–24 in. (30–60 cm) tall, with midgreen, pointed, oval, 2–3 in. (5–7.5 cm) long leaves with rippled margins. Plants are herbaceous and can spread by seed or aggressively by rhizomes into large patches that can overrun garden beds but make for a dense, upright ground cover.

CULTURE/CARE Easy to grow in full to part sun in average to evenly moist, well-drained soils.

USES In areas contained by hardscape features such as driveways, buildings, and walkways. Not tolerant of foot traffic. Deer resistant.

PROPAGATION Division, seed

'Zwerg': dwarf plants, 8 in. (20 cm) tall

Physalis alkekengi var. *franchetii*

Picea
Pinaceae

The genus *Picea* includes 35 species of coniferous trees from temperate and boreal regions of the Northern Hemisphere, with distinctive, four-sided needles held with persistent, peglike stem structures. Though all species grow naturally as tall, upright trees, a number of low, vigorous, horizontally spreading cultivars are useful as ground covers. Denser, slow-growing, and mounding or globe-shaped cultivars often derived from witch's brooms tend to be as wide as or somewhat wider than they are tall. Though not treated here, these forms can be mass-planted in small spaces.

Spreading or dwarf conifers are often high-grafted onto rootstocks 3–6 ft. (1–1.8 m) tall to create globe, nest, or weeping standards. Low-grafts on short rootstocks will make the best ground covers. Or, for some creative topography, look for a weeping cultivar on a midrange height rootstock, 1–3 ft. (0.3–1 m) tall, and allow the descending branches to spread across the ground.

In addition to species treated here, *P. omorika* 'Kamenz' or 'Pancake' and *P. orientalis* 'Ferny Creek Prostrate' can be used as ground covers.

CULTURE/CARE Easy to grow in average to evenly moist, well-drained, fertile, acidic soils in full sun. Tolerant of periods of drought. *Picea pungens* is tolerant of part shade and intolerant of heat and humidity, and *P. abies* is more tolerant of heat and humidity than other conifers and does well into zone 8. Both are moderately salt tolerant.

USES Specimens for small spaces or mass-planted over medium-sized to larger gardens, parks, and landscape settings. Many cultivars are striking when placed to flow around rocks, down slopes, and over walls. Not tolerant of foot traffic. Deer and rabbit resistant.

PROPAGATION Grafting

Picea abies
NORWAY SPRUCE

Zones 3–8
Mountainous regions of Central, Eastern, and Northern Europe.

A large, conical forest conifer widely planted in parks and gardens and used as a Christmas tree and for forestry in Europe and North America. Generally a vigorous species, with ½–1 in. (1.3–2.5 cm) long, blunt-tipped, green needles, light green when young

Picea abies 'Nidiformis'

Picea pungens 'Glauca Procumbens'

and quadrangular in cross section, surrounding the orange-brown twigs. The cones are the longest of any spruce, to 4–7 in. (10–17.5 cm). Dwarf and horizontally spreading cultivars are useful as ground covers.

'Elegans': nest type with slightly ascending, densely held branches, 24 in. (60 cm) tall and 4 ft. (1.2 m) wide in 10 years, growing 3–5 in. (7.5–12.5 cm) per year, to 4 ft. (1.2 m) tall over time

'Formanek': prostrate plants, 6–12 in. (15–30 cm) tall and 3–6 ft. (1–1.8 m) wide, growing 3–6 in. (7.5–15 cm) per year, with branches that flow like water across the ground, around rocks, and over walls

'Frohburg': somewhat lax, ascendant branches, 12–24 in. (30–60 cm) tall and 10 ft. (3 m) wide, growing 8–12 in. (20–30 cm) per year

'Gold Drift': golden version of 'Reflexa'

'Nidiformis': nest type, 12–24 in. (30–60 cm) tall and 3–4 ft. (1–1.2 m) wide in 10 years, can reach 8 ft. (2.4 m) tall and 10–12 ft. (3–3.6 m) wide after 30 years

'Pendula': undulating ground cover with decumbent branches, 12–24 in. (30–60 cm) or more tall and 8–10 ft. (2.4–3 m) wide, growing 6–12 in. (15–30 cm) or more per year

'Procumbens': slightly ascending branches, 16 in. (40 cm) tall and 36 in. (90 cm) wide in 10 years, growing 2–4 in. (5–10 cm) per year, eventually to 10 ft. (3 m) wide

'Reflexa': spreading plants, 12 in. (30 cm) tall and 4 ft. (1.2 m) wide in 10 years, growing 12 in. (30 cm) per year

'Repens': cultivar from at least 1898, to 18 in. (45 cm) tall and 4–5 ft. (1.2–1.5 m) wide in 10 years, growing 3–5 in. (7.5–12.5 cm) per year

Picea pungens
BLUE SPRUCE, COLORADO SPRUCE

Zones 2–8

A high-elevation Rocky Mountain species from moist, mountainous habitats from Montana and Idaho to New Mexico.

Large, conical forest conifer widely planted in parks and gardens for its striking, stiff and bristly, green, bluish green, or silver-blue, 1.5 in. (4 cm) long needles surrounding the stems along horizontal branches, often held to the ground even on mature trees. Cones are 4 in. (10 cm) long.

'Dietz Prostrate': silver-blue needles on horizontally spreading plants to 12 in. (30 cm) tall and 3 ft. (1 m) wide in 10 years, eventually 12–16 in. (30–40 cm) tall and 8–10 ft. (2.4–3 m) wide, growing 6–12 in. (15–30 cm) per year

'Glauca Pendula': silver-blue needles on sprawling, billowing, horizontally spreading plants, 12–24 in. (30–60 cm) tall and 8–10 ft. (2.4–3 m) wide, growing 12 in. (30 cm) per year

'Glauca Procumbens' (syn. 'Procumbens'): silver-blue needles on undulating, horizontally spreading plants, 24 in. (60 cm) tall and 10 ft. (3 m) wide, growing 6–8 in. (15–20 cm) per year

'Glauca Prostrata': silver-blue needles, 12–24 in. (30–60 cm) tall and 6–10 ft. (1.8–3 m) wide, growing 6–12 in. (15–30 cm) per year, may produce a leader that can be removed if desired

'Mesa Verde': green needles on uniform, nest-type plants, 24 in. (60 cm) tall and 8 ft. (2.4 m) wide, growing 3–6 in. (7.5–15 cm) or more per year

Pinus mugo
MUGO PINE, DWARF MOUNTAIN PINE

Pinaceae

Zones 2–8
High mountain habitats from the Iberian Peninsula to Eastern Europe.

A highly variable pine, from large trees, to multi-stemmed, mounded shrubs often wider than they are tall, and even as low, prostrate specimens. The compact, mounding or shrubby forms useful as ground covers are mostly derived from *P. mugo* subsp. *mugo* and its cultivars in the Pumilio Group. Bright green, 1–3 in. (2.5–7.5 cm) long needles are held two per bundle. Oval to conical, warm brown, 2.5 in. (6 cm) long cones age to gray-brown.

CULTURE/CARE Full sun in average to evenly moist, well-drained, fertile soils. Tolerant of dry conditions and sandy, clay, and salty soils but not of poor drainage. Prefers cool summer climates, resenting heat and humidity.

USES As a specimen ground cover for small spaces or mass-planted over medium-sized to large areas in large gardens, parks, and landscape settings. Not tolerant of foot traffic. Deer and rabbit resistant.

PROPAGATION Grafting

Pinus mugo offers many mounding or globose forms that are generally as wide as or somewhat wider than they are tall. These can be mass-planted as a general cover but are not treated here, with preference to more prostrate forms. The habit of pine cultivars and their usefulness as ground covers will be determined by the height of the grafting root stock.

'Green Creeper': short needles on slow-growing, prostrate plants, 8 in. (20 cm) tall and 30 in. (75 cm) wide in 10 years

'Prostrata': prostrate plants, 12–24 in. (30–60 cm) tall and 3–6 ft. (1–1.8 m) wide

'Spilled Milk': slow-growing, prostrate plants with white terminal buds, 8 in. (20 cm) tall and 30 in. (75 cm) wide in 10 years

'Valley Cushion': dense, slow-growing TRUdwarf cultivar, 12 in. (30 cm) tall and 4 ft. (1.2 m) wide, growing 3–5 in. (7.5–12.5 cm) per year

Various other *Pinus* species offer prostrate or spreading cultivars.

'Albyn' (syn. 'Albyn Prostrata'): *P. sylvestris* cultivar, very prostrate, 12 in. (30 cm) tall and 6 ft. (1.8 m) wide, growing 6 in. (15 cm) per year, with pairs of thick, twisted, shiny, bluish green, 2 in. (5 cm) long needles, zones 2–8

'Glauca Pendula': *P. flexilis* cultivar, bluish green, 4 in. (10 cm) long needles with silver bands in bundles of five on irregular, undulating branches, 24 in. (60 cm) tall and 8 ft. (2.4 m) wide, growing 4–6 in. (10–15 cm) per year, zones 4–9

'Hillside Creeper': *P. sylvestris* cultivar, very prostrate, 12 in. (30 cm) tall and 6–10 ft. (1.8–3 m) wide, growing 8–12 in. (20–30 cm) per year, with gray-green to yellow-green needles, zones 2–8

'Hornibrookiana': *P. nigra* cultivar, compact, spreading mounds, 12–24 in. (30–60 cm) tall and 4–6 ft. (1.2–1.8 m) wide, with pairs of stiff, dark green, 2–3 in. (5–7.5 cm) long needles, salt tolerant, zones 4–8

'Mount Hood Prostrate': *P. thunbergii* cultivar, 12 in. (30 cm) tall and 4 ft. (1.2 m) wide in 10 years, growing 6 in. (15 cm) or more per year, with pairs of long, midgreen needles, salt tolerant, zones 5–8

'Pendula': *P. densiflora* cultivar, pairs of midgreen, 4 in. (10 cm) long needles, 12–24 in. (30–60 cm) tall and 6 ft. (1.8 m) or more wide, growing 6–8 in. (15–20 cm) or more per year, strongly weeping and good for slopes or cascading over walls, zones 4–8

'Schoodic': *P. banksiana* cultivar, dense, prostrate plants, 24 in. (60 cm) tall and 4 ft. (1.2 m) wide, growing 3–5 in. (7.5–12.5 cm) per year with pairs of short, bright green needles and plentiful cones, good for banks or trailing over walls, zones 2–8

'Uncle Fogy': *P. banksiana* cultivar, vigorous, wide-spreading plants, 24 in. (60 cm) tall and 12–15 ft. (3.6–4.5 m) wide, with pairs of olive-green needles and wildly undulating branches, growing 12–18 in. (30–45 cm) per year, zones 2–8

Pleioblastus pygmaeus
PYGMY BAMBOO

Poaceae

Zones 5–10
Forest floors in Japan.

The word "bamboo" strikes fear in gardeners' hearts, but the reason for their fear—bamboo's legendary spreading habit—can be useful for covering ground. Pygmy bamboo are relatively short, rhizomatous, and shade-tolerant. *Pleioblastus pygmaeus*, also known as *Sasa pygmaea* and *Arundinaria pygmaea*, is a quickly spreading, running species, 12–18 in. (30–45 cm) tall, with bright green, lance-shaped, 5 in. (12.5 cm) long leaves with minute hairs on the undersides held at

Pinus mugo 'Valley Cushion'

Pleioblastus pygmaeus 'Distichus'

intervals along the slender culms. Evergreen in mild climates, it may turn brown in winter in colder regions.

Other species typically reaching 24–48 in. (60–120 cm) tall can be used as larger ground covers, including *P. argenteostriatus*, its form *pumilus*, and its cultivar 'Akebono'; *P. variegatus* and its cultivars 'Fortunei' (syn. *P. fortunei*) and 'Tsuboii'; and *P. viridistriatus*. They can be sheared annually to maintain shorter cover.

CULTURE/CARE Part sun to shade in average to moist, fertile, well-drained soils, including a range of soil types. Plants can be overly aggressive where not managed or controlled by hardscape. The Missouri Botanical Garden Plant Finder states, "fertilizing this plant may be tantamount to throwing gasoline on a fire." Indeed, less-fertile and drier sites will slow its rate of spread. Shear plants after winter if foliage needs a refresh. Spring shearing every 1–3 years can help control height. In Japan, *P. pygmaeus* and *P. pygmaeus* 'Distichus' are often clipped or mowed regularly to maintain turflike mats only a few inches tall.

USES Small to large applications including on slopes for erosion control, under trees and large shrubs, and as a lawn alternative. Contain using hardscape features. When sheared to the height of a lawn, plants are tolerant of light foot traffic. Deer resistant.

PROPAGATION Division

'Distichus' (syn. *P. distichus*): tough, erect stems with fernlike or palmlike, somewhat congested fans of foliage at the culm tips, often with five leaves on each side of the culm, possibly slightly hardier than the species

var. *pygmaeus* 'Mini': sometimes listed as *P. distichus*, 8–12 in. (20–30 cm) tall

'Wooster's Dwarf': perhaps the shortest of all running bamboos, 2–6 in. (5–15 cm) tall

Podophyllum peltatum

MAYAPPLE

Berberidaceae

Zones 3–8

Mixed and deciduous, moist to dryish forests, fields, moist banks, and along water courses throughout the eastern half of the United States and into southern Ontario and Quebec.

These rhizomatously spreading, colony-forming, herbaceous shade perennials emerge from spring soils like closed umbrellas that open to reveal broad, midgreen, palmately lobed leaves, 6–16 in. (15–40 cm) wide, with smooth or toothed margins. Leaves, solitary on young plants and in opposite pairs on mature plants, hide a waxy, cupped, pendulous, fragrant, white (sometimes pink), 6–9 petaled flower attached at the fork of the leaf pedicels in spring. Flowers become fleshy, pendulous, egg-shaped, green fruit, ripening to yellow or sometimes orange or maroon. Colonies reach 12–18 in. (30–45 cm) tall, spreading indefinitely at 2–8 in. (5–20 cm) per year. Plants go dormant in summer. Most Asian relatives, including *P. delavayi*, *P. pleianthum*, *P. versipelle*, and *Sinopodophyllum hexandrum*, plus hybrids *P.* 'Kaleidoscope' and *P.* 'Spotty Dotty', are primarily clumping or very slowly spreading and can be mass-planted in small areas for a bold, attractive cover.

CULTURE/CARE Part to full shade in fertile, evenly moist, well-drained soils. Tolerant of periods of drought and drier conditions, though this may hasten summer dormancy.

USES Woodland and shade gardens, especially under trees and large shrubs. Not tolerant of foot traffic. Deer and rabbit resistant.

PROPAGATION Division, seed

Polygala chamaebuxus

SHRUBBY MILKWORT, BOX-LEAVED MILKWORT

Polygalaceae

Zones 5–8

Forested slopes, rocky ridges, and open meadows in the mountains of Western and Central Europe.

Dense, dwarf, slowly spreading, suckering, mat-forming, evergreen subshrub, 4–8 in. (10–20 cm) tall and 24 in. (60 cm) wide. Thick, leathery, deep green, oval to broadly lance-shaped leaves resemble boxwood (*Buxus* spp.). Solitary or paired, pealike, fragrant, creamy white or magenta flowers with yellow stigma lobes bloom in the upper leaf axils from late winter to late spring and sporadically in fall. Known scientifically as *Polygaloides chamaebuxus*. AGM

CULTURE/CARE Part sun to part shade in humus-rich or peaty, well-drained, sandy or gritty, moisture-retentive soils in cool summer climates. Tolerant of full sun with good moisture and periods of drought. Resents heat and humidity.

USES Slow to very slow spreader for small applications between paving stones, along pathways and border edges, and in rock gardens. Not tolerant of foot traffic. Deer resistant.

PROPAGATION Cuttings, division

'Grandiflora' (syns. var. *rhodoptera*, 'Rhodoptera'): magenta to purple-pink and yellow flowers, AGM

'Kamniski': similar to 'Grandiflora' but more robust, to 10 in. (25 cm) tall, with flowers located farther from narrower foliage

Polygonatum

Asparagaceae

Though less celebrated than hostas or ferns, Solomon's seals are among the most reliable of shade plants. Extremely hardy and easy to grow, their arching stems, pointed oval leaves, and pendulous flowers strike a distinctive pose. Their slow, rhizomatously spreading habit also makes them useful as ground covers, with *P. humile* and *P. odoratum* best suited to the job. The lavender-flowered *P. hookeri* is sometimes also grown. Other larger species, 3–4 ft. (1–1.2 m) tall, produce clumps that can become ground covers for large applications, including *P. biflorum* (syn. *P. commutatum*) and its rare cousin *P. pubescens* from North America, and the Eurasian *P. multiflorum* and its cross with *P. odoratum*, *P. ×hybridum*. The genus also rewards the collector with many rare, distinctive options such as the burgundy-leaved *P. ×hybridum* 'Betberg' and *P. mengtzense* f. *tonkinense*, *P. prattii* with lavender flowers, *P. lasianthum* 'Kon Chiri Shima' with golden foliage, and *P. punctatum*, which is evergreen in milder zones.

CULTURE/CARE Easy to grow in moist, humus-rich, well-drained soils in part to full shade. Tolerant of part sun with ample moisture, though foliage may turn yellowish.

USES Small to medium-sized applications under trees and shrubs, in woodland gardens, and along pathways for *P. humile*, spreading at a slow rate. Mass plant for faster coverage. The arching stems of *P. odoratum* will form a closed, weed-suppressing canopy long before the rhizomes meet. Not tolerant of foot traffic. Deer and rabbit resistant.

PROPAGATION Division

Podophyllum peltatum growing through *Liriope spicata*

Podophyllum 'Spotty Dotty'

Polygala chamaebuxus 'Grandiflora'

Polygonatum hookeri

Polygonatum humile
DWARF SOLOMON'S SEAL

Zones 4–8

Forests and grassy slopes from middle to higher elevations in China, Mongolia, Siberia, and Japan.

Herbaceous, creeping, rhizomatous perennial, 8–10 in. (20–25 cm) tall, with glossy, light to midgreen, linear-veined, upward-facing leaves perpendicular to the erect stems. Solitary or paired, pendulous, tubular, green and white flowers appear in the upper leaf axils in spring, sometimes followed by blue-black berries in fall.

'Prince Charming': hybrid, often listed as *P. biflorum nanum* but likely derived from *P. biflorum* × *P. humile*, resembling more the former parent but with intermediate characteristics, forming dense, vigorous colonies with short, upright-arching, blue-green stems, 12 in. (30 cm) tall, with narrower, broadly lance-shaped, blue-green leaves with silvery undersides

'Shiro-shima-fu': leaves heavily streaked and flecked with creamy white

Polygonatum odoratum
FRAGRANT SOLOMON'S SEAL,
SCENTED SOLOMON'S SEAL

Zones 3–9

Widespread from Morocco and Europe through Russia and China to Japan in shaded habitats, including forests and slopes, from low to high elevations.

Graceful, arching stems of alternating, elliptic to oval leaves, 2–4 in. (5–10 cm) long and 1–2 in. (2.5–5 cm) wide, with pendulous, cylindrical, bell-shaped, white and green, fragrant flowers descending from the leaf axils in mid- to late spring, sometimes producing blue-black fall berries. Dense colonies, 12–24 in. (30–60 cm) tall, spread slowly but indefinitely. Golden yellow fall color. Though the soil remains exposed below the foliage, the deep shade and thick rhizomes exclude most weeds. Often confused with *P. odoratum* in the trade, *P. falcatum* is generally less vigorous with narrower leaves and offers a few interesting cultivars, including 'Tiger Stripes', 'Silver Lining' (syn. silver striped), and 'Wedding Bells'.

'Angel Wing' (syn. 'Carlisle'): broad leaves with variable white edges and streaks on red stems aging to green

'Byakko': white leaf bases and green tips

Polygonatum humile

Polygonatum odoratum var. *pluriflorum* 'Variegatum'

Polygonum aubertii

'Dai Koga': bold golden leaves with green edges

'Double Stuff': broad, white leaf edges and streaks on red stems

'Fireworks': leaves variably yet boldly streaked with creamy white and yellow on red stems

'Flore Pleno': double hose-in-hose flowers

'Koryu': variable, raised, central ridge on each leaf

var. *pluriflorum* 'Jinguji': red stems

var. *pluriflorum* 'Variegatum': leaves variably edged and streaked with white, stems tinged reddish, Perennial Plant of the Year 2013

'Ruby Slippers': red stems, leaves with silvery undersides

'Silver Wings': dwarf form, 12 in. (30 cm) tall, silver leaf undersides

'Spiral Staircase': large, closely set leaves with good silver undersides on slightly twisting stems

P. ×*hybridum* 'Striatum' (syn 'Grace Barker'): hybrid with *P. multiflorum* with more heavily white-streaked leaves than var. *pluriflorum* 'Variegatum' on slower growing plants

Polygonum aubertii
SILVER LACE VINE

Polygonaceae

Zones 4–8

Slopes and thickets in valleys from moderate to high elevations in China.

An extremely vigorous, deciduous, twining, semiwoody vine now known as *Fallopia baldschuanica*, with stems 20–30 ft. (6–9 m) or more long, growing 10–15 ft. (3–4.5 m) per year once established. Arrow-shaped leaves, 1–2 in. (2.5–5 cm) long and about 1 in. (2.5 cm) wide, emerge red-flushed, turning to bright green. Masses of small, fragrant, creamy white flowers in copious panicles cover the vine from summer into fall. Without vertical support it will grow as a rambunctious, billowing ground cover, 12–24 in. (30–60 cm) or more tall, spreading widely via long stems and bulking up via spreading rhizomes.

CULTURE/CARE Full sun to part shade in well-drained, average to fertile soils with even moisture. Tolerant of periods of drought and diverse soil types. Dry, infertile soils will reduce vigor. Chop stems 12–36 in. (30–90 cm) from the crown in early spring to control size.

USES Medium-sized to large areas, including slopes for erosion control and to cover unsightly features such as stumps or ugly hardscape. Few species can cover ground as quickly. Not tolerant of foot traffic. Deer and rabbit resistant. Attractive to pollinators, especially bees.

PROPAGATION Division of rhizomes, cuttings, seed

Polypodium
Polypodiaceae

These epiphytic and lithophytic, summer deciduous to evergreen ferns present intriguing ground cover options for specialized applications, with fronds emerging along thick, hairy or scaly rhizomes. Species can also grow terrestrially in shallow soils over large rocks or on rocky ground or steep banks. Summer dormancy aids survival in summer-dry habitats. Emergence begins with fall rains with wintergreen plants in growth until the following summer.

CULTURE/CARE Part sun to shade in any thin, sharply drained, evenly moist soil that mimics native habitats. Very drought tolerant when dormant. *Polypodium scouleri* is drought tolerant but usually evergreen year-round. Summer-dormant species can maintain fronds through summer with even moisture, though new growth mostly emerges in fall and spring. Larger fronds are produced in deeper shade.

USES Small to medium-sized applications in any rocky or thin soils in cool, shaded rock gardens, on and in walls, along stairways, over and between rocks, on stumps and logs, and in living walls and green roofs, spreading slowly. Not tolerant of foot traffic. Deer resistant.

PROPAGATION Division, spore

Polypodium cambricum
SOUTHERN POLYPODY, WELSH POLYPODY

Zones 6–10

Well-drained, often calcareous, rocky substrates including steep slopes and road banks, rock outcrops, cliffs, and quarries, and in castle or mortared walls, especially if built of limestone, usually in proximity to coasts in Southern and Western Europe, North Africa, and the Canary Islands, Azores, and Madeira.

Somewhat lush, tropical-looking colonies, 12–18 in. (30–45 cm) tall, spreading via creeping rhizomes with slightly shiny, leathery, once-pinnate, oblong to triangular fronds, 12–20 in. (30–50 cm) or more long, with long, pointed or blunt-tipped, rippled pinnae with yellow sori on the reverses. Though rare in North America, *P. cambricum* and its many cultivars can be found at specialist nurseries in Europe.

'Cambricum': pinnae with sharply toothed edges, AGM

'Conwy': pinnae tips with long, narrow, sharp cresting

'Grandiceps Fox': broad fronds with branched, lacy cresting at the tips, AGM

'Richard Kayse': one of the earliest of all named cultivars, found in 1668 in South Wales, with spiky, serrated pinnae, for a lacy effect, AGM

'Whilharris': spiky, serrated pinnae giving a ruffled, lacy effect, AGM

'Whitley Giant': hybrid, resembles *P. cambricum*, but larger growing with long, rippled, mostly evergreen fronds 16 in. (40 cm) long

Polypodium glycyrrhiza
LICORICE FERN

Zones 5–9
Rocks, logs, trees (especially *Acer macrophyllum* in the Pacific Northwest), and in thin, moss-covered soils from low to moderate elevations from coastal Alaska to California, with disjunct populations in Idaho and Arizona.

Lance-shaped to triangular, once-pinnate fronds, 6–12 in. (15–30 cm) or more long, with pointed to blunt-tipped pinnae cut nearly to the stem. Edible rhizomes have a sweet licorice flavor and were used by native peoples. Among the most reliable living wall

species in the Pacific Northwest. Two other similar North American species are occasionally grown: the zone 3 hardy rock polypody, *P. virginianum*, from most of eastern North America, and the California polypody, *P. californicum*, from California and Baja California, Mexico, hardy to zone 8.

'Longicaudatum': lush in habit with overlapping lateral pinnae and a long terminal pinna, AGM

Polypodium scouleri
SCOULER'S POLYPODY

Zones 7–10
Coastal rocks, trees, and logs, often in the salt spray and fog zones on bluffs, rock outcrops, and in forests, from full sun to full shade, from British Columbia to Guadalupe Island in Baja California, Mexico.

Distinctive, thick, leathery, evergreen, oblong to triangular fronds, 2–8 in. (5–20 cm) or more long, with broad, round-tipped, shiny pinnae producing round, rusty orange sori on the reverses. Rhizomes are smooth, thick, and white. Plants are drought tolerant, usually remaining evergreen year-round. Best in cool summer climates.

Polypodium vulgare
COMMON POLYPODY

Zones 3–8
A lithophyte or epiphyte that grows in shaded to semishaded locations often among moss on trees, rocks, old walls, cliffs, and in rocky soils, widely

Polypodium cambricum 'Richard Kayse'

Polypodium glycyrrhiza at the Miller Garden, Seattle

distributed across Europe through Russia to Northwest China.

Derived from an ancient hybridization, likely between *P. sibiricum* and *P. glycyrrhiza*, and subsequent chromosome doubling. Resembles licorice fern with edible but bittersweet rhizomes. Many cultivars have been selected but remain rare.

'Bifidocristatum': terminal pinna divided into two lacy, branching, crested tips

'Uulong Island': more tolerant of heat and humidity

P. ×mantoniae 'Cornubiense': hybrid with *P. interjectum*, with lacy, twice-pinnate fronds with serrated edges often mixed with regular once-pinnate fronds, AGM

Polystichum
Dryopteridaceae

This large genus of beautiful temperate and subtropical species is found on every continent except Australia and Antarctica, offering some of the most important and useful garden ferns. Their small to large, vaselike habits with ascending to arching fronds make impressive specimens or effective tall, mass-planted ground covers. In addition to those treated here, many less common species could be used, including *P. aculeatum*, *P. rigens*, *P. xiphophyllum*, and *P. braunii* and its hybrid with *P. proliferum*, *P. ×dycei*.

CULTURE/CARE Part to full shade in fertile, evenly moist, well-drained soils. Tolerant of dry shade once established, especially *P. aculeatum*, *P. acrostichoides*, *P. munitum*, and *P. setiferum*. Tolerant of deep shade and part sun with even moisture. Remove brown or winter-damaged fronds in early spring before new foliage emerges.

USES Mass plant as a general cover or foundation planting or on slopes for erosion control. Most bulk up at a slow to moderate rate. Not tolerant of foot traffic. Deer and rabbit resistant.

PROPAGATION Division, spores

Polystichum acrostichoides
CHRISTMAS FERN

Zones 3–9

Dry to moist, shady woodlands, rocky slopes, ravines, and streambanks from low to high elevations across most of the eastern United States into Canada.

Once-pinnate, somewhat thick and leathery, dark green, upright to arching, lance-shaped fronds on dark brown to black stipes with light brown scales, reminiscent of *P. munitum*, though smaller, with a subtle luster on slightly rippled pinnae with a triangular lobe at their bases. Fertile, spore-producing pinnae are smaller than sterile pinnae on the same frond. Evergreen, even in colder zones, providing fronds for Christmas decorating, growing to 12–24 in. (30–60 cm) tall and wide. Tolerant of dry shade. Seems to have a mutual exclusion agreement with its western relative, *P. munitum*, as each normally robust species tends to grow poorly in the other's native territory.

Polypodium scouleri in the wild, Ucluelet, BC

Polystichum acrostichoides

Polystichum luctuosum
FROSTED ROCK FERN, MOURNING SHIELD FERN

Zones 6–9
Evergreen forests at moderate to high elevations in South Africa.

Taxonomists consider *P. luctuosum*, previously regarded as endemic to Southern Africa, to include the widespread Asian *P. tsussimense*, with the only real morphological and horticultural difference being a pewter-gray patina on plants of African origin.

Polystichum makinoi
MAKINOI'S HOLLY FERN

Zones 5–9
Moist forest habitats in China, Japan, Bhutan, and Nepal.

Elegant, midsized fern with shiny, olive-green, evergreen, twice-pinnate, arching, triangular fronds with subtle purplish midribs and stipes with tan-colored scales. Plants reach 24 in. (60 cm) tall and wide. Tolerant of heat and humidity.

Polystichum munitum
WESTERN SWORD FERN

Zones (4)5–9
Abundant in average to moist coniferous and mixed forests, from sea level to high elevations, from British Columbia to California, primarily within and west of the major mountain chains but also occurring across southern British Columbia into Idaho and Montana.

Large, impressive fern with once-pinnate, somewhat thick and leathery, midgreen, erect to ascending, lance-shaped fronds on stipes with cinnamon-colored to nearly black scales, reminiscent of *P. acrostichoides* though larger, the serrated pinnae with a triangular lobe at their bases resembling a sword hilt. Evergreen, 24–36 in. (60–90 cm) or more tall and wide, and tolerant of dry shade. Tends not to grow well in eastern North America; use *P. acrostichoides* in its place. AGM

Polystichum makinoi

Polystichum munitum

Polystichum polyblepharum with new and overwintered fronds

Polystichum neolobatum
ASIAN SABER FERN, LONG-EARED HOLLY FERN

Zones 5–9

Broadleaf forests from moderate to high elevations in Japan, China, and neighboring Himalayan countries.

Tough, leathery, evergreen, midsized fern with glossy and almost silvery, midgreen, twice-pinnate, arching to somewhat horizontal, lance-shaped fronds on stipes with mid- to dark brown scales. Plants reach 24–30 in. (60–75 cm) tall and wide. Strong fronds resist breaking from heavy winter snow and wind.

Polystichum polyblepharum
TASSEL FERN

Zones 5–9

Mountain forests at low elevations in eastern China, Korea, and Japan.

Stately, leathery, evergreen, midsized fern with glossy, mid- to dark green, twice-pinnate, arching, feathery, lance-shaped fronds with overlapping pinnae on stipes with cinnamon to black scales. Vase-shaped plants reach 24–30 in. (60–75 cm) tall and wide. Distinctive croziers contort before straightening and unfurling. AGM

Polystichum setiferum
SOFT SHIELD FERN

Zones 6–9

Woodlands and steep slopes from low to high elevations in Southern and Western Europe into North Africa, the Canary Islands, Azores, and Madeira.

Large, semi-evergreen to evergreen fern with lance-shaped, twice-pinnate, bright green, somewhat glossy, feathery fronds, 24–36 in. (60–90 cm) long, with serrated, bristly pinnae and cinnamon-colored scales along the stipe and midrib. Tolerant of dry shade. Great morphological variation within P. setiferum has long fascinated pteridophiles with a range of forms classified into different groups, which come relatively true from spore. Some superior cultivars are propagated vegetatively. Historically, more than 300 cultivars have been described. Though most are no longer cultivated, many remain available for contemporary gardens. In addition to the groups and cultivars treated here, more options can be found from the Acutilobum,

Congestum, Cristatum, Plumosodivisilobum, and Plumosum groups. AGM

Divisilobum Group: further divided pinnae give an extra lacy, filigree appearance on more or less prostrate, straight or curving fronds, includes 'Herrenhausen', which is more compact with excellent lacy, prostrate fronds, AGM

Plumosomultilobum Group: four times pinnate with very fine, overlapping pinnae, giving a congested, fuzzy look, resembling bright green moss on triangular, arching to spreading to almost horizontal fronds

Pulcherrimum Group: includes the popular 'Bevis', with dark green, feathery, lance-shaped, tapering, erect to arching fronds, AGM

Polystichum setiferum with a *Pulmonaria* cultivar

Polystichum tsussimense
KOREAN ROCK FERN

Zones 6–9

Broadleaf evergreen forests on slopes and streambanks from low to high elevations in China, northwest India, Korea, Japan, and Vietnam.

Most taxonomists consider the Asian P. *tsussimense* synonymous with the South African P. *luctuosum*, which, because of the rules of precedence in botanical nomenclature, makes the latter the official name for this multicontinental species, a distribution not uncommon for ferns with their light, easily dispersed spores. By whatever name, this is a small fern with leathery, matte to somewhat glossy, mid- to dark green, evergreen, twice-pinnate, ascending, lance-shaped to triangular fronds with black veins, forming vase-shaped plants, 12–18 in. (30–45 cm) tall and wide. Fronds are commonly used in floral arrangements and for boutonnieres. In horticulture, P. *luctuosum* tends to refer to South African plants with a pewter-gray patina and P. *tsussimense* to the green Asian form. AGM

'K Rex': nearly twice the size with somewhat shinier fronds, 18–24 in. (45–60 cm) long

Potentilla
Roseaceae

These old-fashioned, clumping or spreading, herbaceous to sometimes semi-evergreen cottage garden plants have excellent hardiness, toughness, and drought tolerance. Their strawberry-like leaves usually have five smooth to fuzzy, veined leaflets with serrated edges. Clumping forms resemble avens (*Geum* spp.), with low mounds topped with tall, airy, mostly leafless stems of single, 1 in. (2.5 cm) wide flowers in mostly hot colors, each with five heart-shaped petals. Many of the hundreds of Northern Hemisphere species make good garden plants, including many not treated here: P. *cinerea*, P. *cuneata* (syn. *Sibbaldia parviflora*), P. *eriocarpa*, P. *megalantha*, P. *nevadensis*, P. *recta* var. *sulphurea*, P. *rupestris*, and P. ×*hopwoodiana*.

CULTURE/CARE Easy to grow in average to moist, well-drained soils in full to part sun. Tolerant of periods of drought. Best in cool summer climates. Plants may resent the heat and humidity of hot summer regions. Provide afternoon shade to reduce stress.

USES Mass plant clumping forms as a general cover or as an edger for pathways and borders. Use spreading species as a border edger, between paving stones,

trailing over walls, and in rock gardens. Clumping forms are not tolerant of foot traffic, though spreading forms can tolerate some. Use either form for small to medium-sized areas. Deer resistant. Attractive to pollinators, especially bees.

PROPAGATION Division, seed

Potentilla atrosanguinea
RUBY CINQUEFOIL, HIMALAYAN CINQUEFOIL

Zones 5–8

Lower mountain slopes, forests, thickets, sandy riverbanks, and ditches at high elevations in Nepal, Pakistan, and Tibet, China.

Low mounds, 12–24 in. (30–60 cm) wide, of somewhat glossy, dark green, tripartite, palmate leaves with serrated edges, outlined in white from the tomentose undersides visible at the edges. Velvety, blood-red flowers on hairy, 18–24 in. (45–60 cm) tall stems appear in midspring, possibly reblooming in fall.

Cultivars noted as hybrids were formerly considered P. *atrosanguinea* or are of unknown or undeclared parentage.

'Arc-en-ciel': hybrid, semidouble red flowers with variable yellow highlights at the petal tips

var. *argyrophylla*: yellow flowers with orange to red centers

var. *argyrophylla* 'Scarlet Starlit': scarlet to crimson-red flowers

'Esta Ann': hybrid, yellow flowers with red eyes

'Gibson's Scarlet': hybrid, bright scarlet-red flowers with dark centers

'Melton Fire': hybrid, pink to apricot-pink flowers with deep pinkish red centers

'Monsieur Rouillard': hybrid, deep red semidouble flowers with variable yellow petal tips

'Volcan': hybrid, velvety red double flowers

'William Rollison': hybrid, semidouble orange flowers with yellow centers

Potentilla crantzii
ALPINE CINQUEFOIL

Zones 3–9

Meadows, slopes, coastlines, and rocky areas including outcrops, cliffs, and ledges, usually on calcareous soils, from sea level to higher elevations from Asia and Europe to Greenland and Nunavut in Canada.

Dark green, semi-evergreen, slightly glossy, mostly smooth or slightly hairy, palmate leaves with 3–5 leaflets with serrated edges on ascending to horizontally spreading stems, forming a mound or mat, 4–6 in. (10–15 cm) tall by 10 in. (25 cm) wide. Plants can spread via rhizomes and rooting stems. Yellow flowers often with a subtle orange eye are borne in late spring, just above the foliage or on stems up to 10 in. (25 cm) tall. Provide excellent drainage.

'Pygmaea': the primary cultivated form, compact and refined like the species in miniature, 1–4 in. (2.5–10 cm) tall and spreading slowly into mats

Potentilla 'Arc-en-ciel'

Potentilla nepalensis
NEPAL CINQUEFOIL

Zones 5–8, possibly hardier
Meadows, pastures, and cultivated areas in the Himalayas from Pakistan to Nepal.

Low, 12–24 in. (30–60 cm) wide clumps of somewhat glossy, dark green, hairy, palmate leaves with five leaflets with serrated edges. Red to deep pink summer flowers with darker centers on hairy, reddish, 12–24 in. (30–60 cm) tall stems.

'Helen Jane': bright midpink flowers with reddish centers on compact plants, 12 in. (30 cm) tall

'Miss Willmott': deep pink to salmon-pink flowers with reddish centers, 12–18 in. (30–45 cm) tall

'Ron McBeath': glowing, deep pink flowers with reddish centers on compact plants, 12 in. (30 cm) tall

'Shogran': bright pink flowers with reddish centers on dwarf plants, 8 in. (20 cm) tall

Potentilla nepalensis 'Ron McBeath'

Potentilla neumanniana
SPRING CINQUEFOIL, SPOTTED CINQUEFOIL

Zones 4–8
Roadsides, dry meadows, and talus slopes from France east to the Black Sea.

Dark green, slightly glossy, palmate leaves with five leaflets with serrated edges on horizontally spreading, rooting stems in mounds or mats, 2–4 in. (5–10 cm) tall by 12 in. (30 cm) or more wide, topped with yellow spring flowers.

'Nana': compact, 2–3 in. (5–7.5 cm) tall, spreading slowly into a prostrate mat

Potentilla neumanniana 'Nana'

Potentilla thurberi
SCARLET CINQUEFOIL

Zones 5–9

Coniferous and oak woodlands, forests, dry grassy slopes, streambanks, and moist meadows at high elevations from the U.S. Southwest into Mexico.

Low, 12–24 in. (30–60 cm) wide clumps of somewhat glossy, dark green, smooth to hairy, palmate, serrated leaves of five leaflets with or without cottony reverses. Red flowers with darker centers bloom throughout summer on hairy stems 12–24 in. (30–60 cm) tall.

'Monarch's Velvet': deep red flowers

Potentilla tridentata
THREE-TOOTHED CINQUEFOIL

Zones 1–8

Dry, acidic soils along rocky or gravelly shorelines, shale outcrops, mixed forests, dry meadows, and alpine tundra from the Northwest Territories, Alberta, and the Central United States to Greenland.

Evergreen, rhizomatous plants with dark green, glossy, smooth-edged, palmate leaves with three blunt-tipped, three-toothed leaflets in mounds or mats, 3–6 in. (7.5–15 cm) tall by 12–16 in. (30–40 cm) wide. Pure white, starry flowers with long stamens are borne in late spring and summer just above the foliage or on stems up to 12 in. (30 cm) tall. Deep red fall color. Now known scientifically as *Sibbaldiopsis tridentata*.

'Minima': dwarf, 3 in. (7.5 cm) tall

'Nuuk': good, compact selection from Greenland

'White Cloud': new foliage emerges white, maturing to cream and then light green with dark veins

Potentilla ×*tonguei*
TRAILING HYBRID CINQUEFOIL

Zones 4–9

Garden origin.

Low, trailing hybrid likely derived from a cross of the mounding *P. nepalensis* and the trailing *P. anglica*, 4–8 in. (10–20 cm) tall and 12–24 in. (30–60 cm) wide, with glossy, dark green, smooth, palmate, serrated leaves of five leaflets. Apricot-colored flowers with red centers bloom just above the foliage from early to late summer. AGM

Pratia
Campanulaceae

A blue star creeper by any name would be just as cute and useful. The saga of scientific names for this popular ground cover is long and tumultuous and includes the genera *Solenopsis*, *Laurentia*, *Isotoma*, and now *Pratia*, all of which are still in use in horticulture with preference for the latter two. In fact, the saga continues, as *Pratia* is now known scientifically as *Lobelia*! By whatever name, the vigorous mats of tiny foliage and charming, starry flowers are easy to love and easy to grow.

CULTURE/CARE Evenly moist soils in part sun to part shade. Tolerant of full sun with good moisture. Appreciates cooler conditions where it will grow verdantly.

USES Small to medium-sized areas along pathways and stairways, between stepping stones, trailing over walls, and as a lawn alternative. Spreads at a moderate to fast rate especially in good conditions. Tolerant of light foot traffic. Deer and rabbit resistant.

PROPAGATION Division

Potentilla ×*tonguei*

Pratia angulata

Pratia pedunculata

Pratia angulata
WHITE STAR CREEPER

Zones 6–10
Common in damp habitats throughout New
Zealand.
Similar in most respects to the more popular blue
star creeper except with white flowers, often with
subtle purple veining on the petal reverses. Known
scientifically as *Lobelia angulata*.

'Treadwellii' (syn. var. *treadwellii*): larger flowers

Pratia pedunculata
BLUE STAR CREEPER

Zones 5–9
Damp lowland and montane areas in southern Australia, including Tasmania, and in New Zealand.
Often sold as *Isotoma fluviatilis* and recently
renamed *Lobelia pedunculata*, forming charming,
herbaceous to semi-evergreen, stoloniferous and
rhizomatous mats, 2–4 in. (5–10 cm) tall, spreading
indefinitely at a moderate to fast rate. Tiny, bright
green, often dentate, oblong to elliptic leaves are
topped by sky-blue, nearly symmetrical star-shaped
flowers from mid- to late spring through much
of summer.

'Alba': white flowers

'Celestial Spice': similar to 'County Park' with deeper blue
flowers

'County Park': darker blue petals with a dark blue
central vein

Primula
Primulaceae

This diverse, long-cultivated genus of hundreds of species and thousands of cultivars occupies a prominent
place in the hearts and minds of those who garden
in temperate climates, with rosettes of coarse, often
tongue-shaped, foliage and attractive flowers in every
rainbow color. Larger species, especially *P. denticulata*, *P. florindae*, and the candelabra-flowered section
Proliferae, are long-lived and easy to grow, with larger
leaves. All this, plus the tendency of some species
to self-seed, make various *Primula* species useful as
ground covers for small to medium-sized areas. There
are also rhizomatous, colony-forming species, though
they are rare.
CULTURE/CARE Part sun to part shade in fertile,
evenly moist to wet, well-drained soils. Tolerant of full
sun with good moisture, especially in cool summer
climates.

USES Partly shaded rock gardens, between stepping stones, and along pathways, watercourses, and border edges, bulking up fairly quickly to full size. Interplanting with a fast-spreading, low-growing, carpeting ground cover will help achieve a closed cover. Not tolerant of foot traffic. Deer resistant.

PROPAGATION Division, seed

Primula denticulata
DRUMSTICK PRIMROSE

Zones 3–9

Moist meadows, grassy slopes, among shrubs, and in open forests from middle to high elevations across the Himalayas from Afghanistan to Myanmar and China.

This distinctive, easy to grow primrose offers a spherical challenge to the ornamental onion (*Allium* spp.), with rounded heads of lightly fragrant, yellow-eyed flowers in shades of white, pink, purple, lavender, and lavender-blue on erect stems, 12 in. (30 cm) tall, from early to late spring. Herbaceous rosettes comprise oblong, tongue-shaped, finely serrated, 6–8 in. (15–20 cm) long leaves. AGM

var. *alba*: pure white flowers

Ronsdorf Hybrids: mix of colors

'Rubin': glowing deep pink to fuchsia flowers

Primula florindae
GIANT COWSLIP, TIBETAN PRIMROSE

Zones 3–9

Moist to wet soils in coniferous forests from middle to high elevations in Tibet, China.

Rosettes of midgreen, coarse-textured, paddle-shaped leaves with heart-shaped bases on long petioles, together measuring 12–18 in. (30–45 cm) long. Open umbels of 15–30 trumpet-shaped, sweetly fragrant, yellow flowers resemble irregularly exploding fireworks in late spring to early summer on 12–36 in. (30–90 cm) stems. AGM

'Ray's Ruby': ruby-red to orange-red flowers, similar strains denoted as "orange-flowered" and "red-flowered" also exist

Primula denticulata

Primula florindae

Primula sieboldii

CHERRY BLOSSOM PRIMROSE, SIEBOLD PRIMROSE

Zones 4–9

Wet, shaded habitats in forests, open woodlands, and grasslands in Northeast China, Korea, Russia, and Japan.

Slowly spreading, rhizomatous species with fuzzy, light green, pointed, oblong, slightly lobed and toothed leaves with heart-shaped bases on long petioles, together 4–8 in. (10–20 cm) long. Large and outward-facing rose-pink, lavender, or white spring flowers in umbels of 5–15 atop 5–10 in. (12.5–25 cm) tall stems have distinctly heart-shaped petals tipped with two rounded lobes. Hundreds of cultivars have been selected for flower color and extra dissection of the petal tips extending to extremely lacy, multidissected, snowflake-shaped forms. *Primula cortusoides*, also from section Cortusoides, is sometimes grown. AGM

Most cultivars are offered only by specialty nurseries.

'Geisha Girl': lavender-pink flowers with white streaks radiating from the eye toward the lacy petal tips

'Ice Princess': white and pale lavender-blue flowers with lacy petal tips

'Lacy Lady': white flowers with vivid pink edges and lacy petal tips

'Late Snow': pure white flowers with extra lacy petal tips

'Snowdrop': pure white flowers with ruffled petals

'Snowflake': pure white flowers with lacy petal tips

Primula section Primula

PRIMROSE

Zones 3 or 4–9

Moist habitats, meadows, pastures, and woodlands in Europe and Southwest Asia.

Some of the most beloved species belong to this section, including the classic common primrose, *P. vulgaris* and its myriad cultivars, the hybrid 'Wanda' derived from crosses with *P. juliae*, and the cowslip, *P. veris*, a favorite wildflower in the United Kingdom.

Primula elatior (oxlip) is similar to *P. veris* but with larger, lighter yellow flowers, zones 4–8, AGM.

Primula juliae (carpet primrose) is a tiny species primrose with small, smooth, finely toothed, kidney- or heart-shaped leaves less than 1 in. (2.5 cm) long and often flushed reddish or bronze, with solitary, yellow-eyed, rose-purple to magenta flowers just above

Primula juliae

Primula 'Guinevere'

the foliage. Notable for its rhizomatous habit, forming small, long-lived colonies and its extensive contributions to the breeding of larger, more robust hybrids including 'Wanda', referred to variously as *P.* ×*juliana*, *P.* ×*pruhonicensis*, Wandas, Julianas, Juliana Hybrids, or Pruhonicians. Slowly spreading into small, ground-hugging, 12–24 in. (30–60 cm) wide colonies.

Hybrids involving *P. juliae*

'Guinevere': pale pink flowers with yellow and orange eyes, bronze-red sepals, stems, and leaves, AGM

'Jay-Jay': intense magenta-red flowers with starry yellow eyes

'Kinlough Beauty': rose-pink flowers with starry yellow eyes with orange halos

'Lady Greer': fragrant, creamy white flowers with yellow eyes flushing pink with age, and pale, dusty lavender sepals, AGM

'Wanda': magenta-purple flowers with starry yellow eyes, AGM

Primula 'Jay-Jay'

Primula vulgaris 'Francisca'

Wanda Group: burgundy foliage, flowers in a full range of colors, including 'Wanda Blue Shades', 'Wanda Dark Pink', 'Wanda Lilac Colors', 'Wanda Pink with Eye', 'Wanda Raspberry Red Shades', 'Wanda Velvet Red Shades', 'Wanda White', and 'Wanda Yellow'

Primula veris (cowslip) has loose umbels of sweetly fragrant, cone-shaped, yellow flowers, perched atop fuzzy, 6 in. (15 cm) long leaves often with whitish undersides, zones 3–8. AGM

'Sunset Shades': mix of red and orange flowers

Primula vulgaris (common primrose), the most beloved species, offers hundreds of cultivars with dark green, ruggedly textured, 4–6 in. (10–15 cm) long leaves topped with solitary single or double, edible flowers in tight bouquets just above the foliage in a range of colors. Though similar to the short-lived *P.* ×*polyanthus* hybrids of supermarkets, *P. vulgaris* is long-lived in appropriate conditions, zones 4–8.

Primula veris 'Sunset Shades'

Primula Belarina Series mix

Belarina Series: double flowers bloom over a long period on vigorous plants

> 'Kerbelbut' Buttercup: golden yellow flowers
>
> 'Kerbelchamp' Pink Champagne: creamy flowers turning pink
>
> 'Kerbelcob' Cobalt Blue: royal-blue flowers
>
> 'Kerbelcrem' Cream: creamy white flowers
>
> 'Kerbelil' Lively Lilac: white flowers with striking lilac-pink detailing
>
> 'Kerbelnec' Nectarine: yellow flowers with peach and red tones
>
> 'Kerbelpice' Pink Ice: white and pink flowers
>
> 'Kerbelpicotee' Amethyst Ice: bluish purple flowers with thin white edges
>
> 'Kerbelred' Valentine: rich, deep red flowers

'Francisca': ruffled, apple-green flowers last for months, AGM

Prima Belarina Series: larger flowers than the Belarina Series

> 'Kerbelcarmen' Carmen: carmine-red flowers
>
> 'Kerbelchab' Blue Champion: royal-blue flowers
>
> 'Kerbelgoldie' Goldie: deep golden flowers

Primula section *Proliferae*

CANDELABRA PRIMROSE

Zones 4 or 5–9

Moist to wet habitats in the mountains of Sichuan and Yunnan, China, and Japan (*P. japonica*).

Like *P. denticulata*, candelabra primroses are distinctive, with erect, 12–24 in. (30–60 cm) tall stems, featuring evenly spaced, tiered whorls of outward-facing flowers from mid- to late spring into early summer, each budded whorl emerging upward from the one below. Herbaceous rosettes comprise oblong, tongue-shaped, toothed, midgreen, 4–12 in. (10–30 cm) long, almost lettuce-like leaves.

Primula beesiana (Bee's primrose, candelabra primrose): sometimes considered a subspecies of *P. bulleyana*, with lavender-pink to rose-pink fragrant flowers with yellow eyes and orange-red rings, in 2–4 or more whorls on stems 8–14 in. (20–35 cm) tall, zones (4)5–9, AGM

Primula ×*bulleesiana* (candelabra primrose): hybrid of *P. beesiana* and *P. bulleyana* with orange, yellow, apricot, lavender, purple, pink, salmon, and white flowers, zones 4–9

Primula bulleyana

Primula bulleyana (Bulley's primrose): light orange fragrant flowers from dark orange to coral red buds, in 5–7 whorls on stems 8–24 in. (20–60 cm) tall atop large, 12 in. (30 cm) long leaves, zones 5–9, AGM

Primula japonica (Japanese primrose): red, magenta, pink, or white flowers with red or purple eyes, in up to six whorls, on stems 12–24 in. (30–60 cm) tall above 10 in. (25 cm) long leaves, zones 4–9

> 'Alba': white flowers with yellow eyes
>
> 'Apple Blossom': shell-pink flowers with red eyes
>
> 'Miller's Crimson': crimson-red flowers, AGM
>
> 'Postford White': white flowers with yellow eyes, AGM

Primula poissonii (Poisson's primrose): daintier inflorescences with fewer yet larger fragrant, lavender-pink flowers with yellow eyes and red rings, in 2–6 whorls on stems 8–16 in. (20–45 cm) tall atop rosettes of smaller leaves, 4–8 in. (10–20 cm) long, zones 4–9

Primula pulverulenta (powdered primrose, candelabra primrose): similar to *P. japonica* in shades of rose-purple to reddish pink with red or purple eyes, in 3–4 whorls on white-powdered stems (which may resemble powdery mildew) 12–18 in. (30–45 cm) tall, zones 5–9, AGM

Prostanthera cuneata
ALPINE MINT BUSH

Lamiaceae

Zones 7–10

Among low shrubs and granite rocks at subalpine elevations in Southeast Australia, including Tasmania.

Dense, evergreen shrub with tiny, dark green, mint- or herb-scented leaves, to 24 in. (60 cm) tall and 5 ft. (1.5 m) wide. Small, lobed, tubular, orchidlike white flowers, sometimes flushed with lavender and speckled with dark pink and yellow, appear in late spring and summer.

CULTURE/CARE Full sun to part shade in well-drained soils. Drought tolerant once established.

USES Specimen, foundation planting, or mass-planted in shrub borders or in landscapes. Not tolerant of foot traffic. Deer resistant. Attractive to pollinators, especially bees and butterflies

PROPAGATION Cuttings

Prostanthera cuneata

Prunella grandiflora
LARGE-FLOWERED SELF-HEAL, HEAL-ALL

Lamiaceae

Zones 4–8

Widespread across most of Europe into Central and Western Asia, in meadows and on moist slopes in forests and scrub from low to high elevations.

Not widely embraced because of its weedy cousin, P. vulgaris, this species is a showy herbaceous to semi-evergreen perennial worthy of a place in the garden. Sprawling mats, 6–12 in. (15–30 cm) or more tall and 24–36 in. (60–90 cm) or more wide, spread via stolons and rhizomes with oval to lance-shaped, mid- to deep green, 2–4 in. (5–10 cm) long leaves, sometimes with irregular teeth or side lobes. Tubular, hooded, snapdragon-like, 1 in. (2.5 cm) long, summer flowers in shades of blue, purple, pink, or white emerge from darker buds in compact, terminal, 2–3 in. (5–7.5 cm) tall spikes on fuzzy, square stems.

CULTURE/CARE Full sun to part shade in average to moist, fertile, well-drained soils. Shear or mow after flowering to refresh, maintain good habit, and avoid self-seeding, which can introduce plants of differing characteristics.

USES Small to medium-sized areas as a general cover or along paths, stairways, and border edges, spreading at a moderate rate. Not tolerant of foot traffic. Deer and rabbit resistant. Attractive to pollinators, especially bees and butterflies.

PROPAGATION Division, seed, cuttings

'Alba': white flowers

Bella Series: compact seed strains, 6–8 in. (15–20 cm) tall, in violet-blue ('Bella Blue') and rose-pink ('Bella Deep Rose')

Prunella grandiflora 'Loveliness'

'Binsumdaz' Summer Daze: hybrid with *P. laciniata* with lobed leaves and pink flowers on 12–14 in. (30–35 cm) stems

'Freelander Blue': seed strain of purple-blue flowers

Lacy Series: compact seed strains 6–8 in. (15–20 cm) tall in blue ('Lacy Blue') and rose-pink ('Lacy Deep Pink')

Loveliness Series: full range of colors

'Blue Loveliness': blue flowers

'Loveliness': pale lavender-blue flowers

'Pink Loveliness': pink flowers

'White Loveliness': white flowers

'Pagoda': compact seed strain, 6 in. (15 cm) tall, in a variety of colors

'Rubra': deep pink flowers

Pterocephalus depressus
MOROCCAN PINCUSHION FLOWER,
CARPETING PINCUSHION FLOWER

Caprifoliaceae

Zones 5–9

Open habitats at high elevations in the Atlas Mountains, Morocco.

Related to the other pincushion flower (*Scabiosa* spp.), which is obvious by comparison with the occasionally cultivated *P. perennis*, which resembles a mat-forming scabious with pincushion-like flower heads of small, tubular flowers on short stems above the dense foliage. The relationship is less obvious in the more common *P. depressus*, with dusty rose to lavender-pink late spring and summer flowers from

Pterocephalus depressus

muted purple buds in heads that sit mostly within or slightly above the tight, semi-evergreen to evergreen, 2 in. (5 cm) tall, indefinitely spreading mats of tiny, lobed or dissected, gray-green leaves. Attractive, fuzzy, grayish seed heads follow the flowers.

CULTURE/CARE Full sun in average to dry, free-draining soils, especially in gravel, or in hot, dry sites with infertile soils.

USES Rock gardens, xeriscapes, between pavers, along stairways, and as an edger. Tolerant of light foot traffic. Deer resistant. Attractive to pollinators, especially bees and butterflies.

PROPAGATION Division, seed

Pulmonaria
Boraginaceae

Zones 3 or 4–8

Woodlands, forests, scrub, and other semishaded habitats in Europe and Western Asia.

Classic cottage garden favorites for shaded gardens, admired for their velvety, elliptic to lance-shaped, silver-spotted or mottled, deep green foliage and early to midspring cymes of true-blue, lavender, pink, red, or white flowers that often change color with age. Plants are herbaceous to semi-evergreen, either clumping or often slowly spreading via short rhizomes into mounds of horizontal foliage, 6–10 in. (15–25 cm) tall and 12–24 in. (30–60 cm) wide. Flowering stems often precede the foliage, which expands during and after bloom.

Most cultivars are hybrids of five species. *Pulmonaria angustifolia* has narrow, 6–12 in. (15–30 cm) long, deep green leaves and pink buds opening to violet and then blue flowers; *P. longifolia* is similar with spotted leaves. *Pulmonaria officinalis* has elongated, heart-shaped, spotted leaves and red or pink buds opening to violet flowers, aging to blue. *Pulmonaria rubra* has unspotted, elliptic to oblong leaves and pinkish red flowers, and *P. saccharata* has heavily spotted, 4–12 in. (10–30 cm) long, elliptic leaves with pink buds opening to violet and then blue flowers.

CULTURE/CARE Part to full shade in fertile, evenly moist, well-drained soils. Tolerant of dry shade. Foliage can scorch in sun. Can be susceptible to powdery mildew, though newer cultivars are more resistant. Remove flower stems after bloom if needed.

USES Mass plant as a general cover for small to medium-sized areas along pathways and border edges or under deciduous shrubs. Plants spread very slowly.

Pulmonaria 'Ocupol' Opal

Pulmonaria 'Trevi Fountain'

Not tolerant of foot traffic. Deer and rabbit resistant. Attractive to pollinators, especially bees.

PROPAGATION Division

'Blue Ensign': solid green foliage, bright blue flowers from pink buds, AGM

'Dark Vader': reddish pink buds, deep pink flowers turning violet and then blue, with elliptic, spotted leaves, good heat and humidity tolerance, and mildew resistance

'Diana Clare': wine-purple flowers turning blue, mostly silver leaves intensify with time, with good heat and humidity tolerance, AGM

'Excalibur': mostly silver foliage with a green edge, coral-red flowers turning violet and then blue, good mildew resistance

'High Contrast': boldly mottled silver foliage, coral-red flowers turning violet and then blue, with good heat and humidity tolerance and mildew resistance

'Little Star': compact with lightly silver-spotted leaves, heavy flowering with deep pink flowers turning bright blue, AGM

'Majesté': mostly silver, green-edged leaves, pink flowers turning violet and then blue

'Moonshine': boldly spotted foliage, with pale pink flowers turning bluish white, with good heat and humidity tolerance and mildew resistance

'Ocupol' Opal: heavily silver-mottled foliage, pale pink flowers turning palest blue and then white, AGM

'Raspberry Splash': bright raspberry-pink flowers turning violet, with narrow, silver-spotted leaves on large plants, with good heat and humidity tolerance and mildew resistance

'Shrimps on the Barbie': coral-red buds opening to glowing deep pink flowers, with silver-spotted foliage on large plants with good heat and humidity tolerance and mildew resistance

'Silver Bouquet': bold silver foliage, coral-red flowers turning pink, violet, and blue, with good heat and humidity tolerance and mildew resistance

'Sissinghurst White': older cultivar with silver-spotted leaves and palest pink buds opening to white flowers, AGM

'Trevi Fountain': pink buds turning violet and then cobalt-blue, silver-spotted leaves with good heat and humidity tolerance and mildew resistance, AGM

P. longifolia cultivars

'Bertram Anderson': older cultivar with long, spotted leaves and brilliant blue flowers from pink buds

subsp. *cevennensis*: extremely long, narrow leaves up to 24 in. (60 cm) with silver spots

P. rubra cultivars

'David Ward': broad leaves with a white margin, coral-red flowers

'Redstart': coral-red flowers, green leaves

P. saccharata cultivar

'Mrs Moon': older cultivar with lightly spotted leaves and pink flowers turning bright blue

Pulsatilla vulgaris
EUROPEAN PASQUE FLOWER

Ranunculaceae

Zones 4–8
Calcareous grasslands and grassy slopes across much of Europe.

Harbingers of spring across the Northern Hemisphere, *P. vulgaris* is most commonly grown, but a similar species, *P. patens*, known as the eastern pasque flower or prairie crocus, is an admired wildflower across Eurasia and much of North America. Pasque flowers can be mass-planted to form an attractive, textural ground cover with showy flowers and seed heads.

This herbaceous perennial emerges as the snow melts, with soft, silver-haired, 4–6 in. (10–15 cm) tall stems, and large, nodding, outward-facing to upright, cupped, six-petaled, violet flowers embossed with bright yellow stamens. These precede or emerge with the deeply divided, silky, midgreen foliage that becomes mounds, 8–12 in. (20–30 cm) tall and 12–18 in. (30–45 cm) wide. Flowers produce attractive spherical seed heads of silver-pink, feathery threads on stems 12 in. (30 cm) tall.

CULTURE/CARE Full to part sun in fertile, gritty, average to moderately moist, well-drained soils. Intolerant of poor drainage. Tolerant of periods of drought in cool summer climates. Somewhat resentful of heat and humidity.

USES Mass plant as a general cover for small to medium-sized areas in rock gardens and border edges, and to punctuate areas of lower growing ground covers. Plants bulk up at a moderate rate. Not tolerant

Pulsatilla vulgaris red-flowered

of foot traffic. Deer and rabbit resistant. Attractive to pollinators, especially bees.

PROPAGATION Division, seed

'Alba': white flowers

'Blaue Glocke' (syn. 'Violet Bells'): seed strain of violet-purple flowers

subsp. *grandis*: large violet flowers, sometimes recognized as *P. grandis*

subsp. *grandis* 'Papageno': double-flowered seed strain with dissected, fringed petals in shades of purple, violet, red, pink, and white, young plants often with single flowers

Heiler hybrids: mixed seed strain includes red, violet, pink, cream, and white flowers

'Perlen Glocke' (syn. 'Pearl Bells'): seed strain of soft pink to pale salmon-pink flowers

red-flowered (syn. var. *rubra*): deep crimson-red to burgundy-red flowers

'Röde Klokke' (syns. 'Red Bells', 'Rote Glocke'): seed strain of deep crimson-red to burgundy-red flowers

Pyrrosia lingua
TONGUE FERN

Polypodiaceae

Zones 7b–10
Forest epiphytes and lithophytes of low to moderately high elevations in China, Japan, Korea, India, Myanmar, and Vietnam.

This rare, evergreen relative of the polypody fern (*Polypodium* spp.) offers a bold statement for small spaces, with thick, stiff, leathery, linear, midgreen fronds, 6–12 in. (15–30 cm) or more long and 1–3 in. (2.5–7.5 cm) wide, resembling lightly undulating tongues with cinnamon-colored, felted undersides. Plants are 8–16 in. (20–40 cm) or more tall and 24–36 in. (60–90 cm) wide, slowly spreading via long, furry, horizontal creeping rhizomes above, at, or just below the soil surface from which leaves arise individually. Related species, including *P. hastata, P. polydactyla*, and *P. sheareri*, are clumping to excruciatingly slow spreading.

CULTURE/CARE Part to full shade in sharply draining and/or shallow, fertile soils with high organic content, or as an epiphyte or lithophyte. Fastest growth is achieved with regular moisture. Tolerant of periods of drought, especially in shade.

USES On stumps or logs, on moss-covered rocks, between rocks, in shaded rock gardens, or on steep slopes, walls, or vertical surfaces. Not tolerant of foot traffic.

PROPAGATION Division

'Eboshi': variably twisting fronds

'Futaba Shishi': fronds with forked, crested tips

'Hiryu': fronds with serrated edges

'Ogon Nishiki': variably striped with light green to chartreuse bands, brightest on young fronds

'Tachiba Koryu': blue-green fronds with heavily rippled margins

Pyrrosia lingua 'Hiryu'

R

Ranunculus repens
CREEPING BUTTERCUP

Ranunculaceae

Zones 4–9
Wet meadows, pastures, and woodlands in Europe, North Africa, and Asia.

To be very clear, this is an invasive weed of lawns and borders across most of the United States and Canada. Some forms, however, are occasionally cultivated. This herbaceous to semi-evergreen, stoloniferous perennial spreads quickly and indefinitely, especially with good moisture, into large, dense mats, 2–6 in. (5–15 cm) tall, topped with typical buttercup flowers in spring and summer. Compound leaves of three multi-lobed leaflets have variable lighter green markings.

CULTURE/CARE Full sun to part shade in average, moist, or wet soils. Growth is slower with less moisture. Very strongly rooting and difficult to remove from borders, lawns, and crowns of perennials.

USES Border edges, along pathways or in wet, shaded sites where other options are lacking but especially where hardscape will control spread. Named cultivars are apparently slower growing. Tolerant of light foot traffic. Deer resistant.

PROPAGATION Division

'Buttered Popcorn': striking light green, chartreuse, to golden foliage with a bold, variable, silver overlay

var. *pleniflorus* (syn. 'Flore-Pleno'): sterile, bright yellow, double pom-pom flowers with green centers

Raoulia australis
NEW ZEALAND SCAB PLANT, SCABWORT

Asteraceae

Zones 5–9
Rocky and stony subalpine habitats including open ground, scree slopes, and stony riverbeds on the South Island, New Zealand.

This strange and wonderful aster family genus brings us "vegetable sheep." A handful of species, especially *R. eximia* and *R. mammilaris*, from New Zealand's high alpine, form tightly packed, billowy shrubs of tiny silver-white leaves that, from a distance, resemble sheep on the mountainside. Most commonly cultivated

Ranunculus repens 'Buttered Popcorn'

Raoulia australis

Reineckea carnea

is *R. australis*, a prostrate, evergreen, mat-forming species vying for the title of lowest of all ground covers, often less than ½ in. (1.3 cm) tall, spreading slowly but indefinitely. Tiny gray-green to silver-white leaves emerge from rooting stems with tiny, greenish to mustard-yellow summer flowers without ray florets. Also sometimes grown are the similar but slightly larger *R. haastii*, *R. hookeri* and *R. tenuicaulis*, which resemble flat, green, mossy mats.

CULTURE/CARE Full sun and sharp drainage, especially in winter. Best in cool summer climates with mild winters. Often described as drought tolerant but serious drought can kill plants, at least in pots. More likely, they require average to even moisture with sharp drainage, with some tolerance of periods of drought once established.

USES Rock and scree gardens and troughs. Grows slowly. Tolerant of occasional foot traffic.

PROPAGATION Division

Reineckea carnea
FALSE LILYTURF

Asparagaceae

Zones (5)6–9

Dense forests and shady, moist slopes from low to high elevations in China and Japan.

Lovely, rhizomatous, semi-evergreen to evergreen woodlander forming dense, spreading mats of upright to arching, lance-shaped, light to midgreen, slightly glossy, 6–12 in. (15–30 cm) long leaves in loose fans, reminiscent of *Liriope* or *Carex* species. Spikes of dark pink buds open to small, fragrant, light pink, lily-like flowers on pink to reddish stems in summer, blooming profusely within or at the colony's leading edge, sometimes followed by red berries.

CULTURE/CARE Easy to grow and vigorous in average to moist, fertile soils in part to full shade. Tolerant of dry shade once established. Clip or shear in early spring to refresh if needed.

USES Small applications for woodlands, border and pathway edges, and under deciduous or evergreen shrubs or trees, spreading at a slow rate. Not tolerant of foot traffic.

PROPAGATION Division

'Variegata': rare variegated form with variably white-striped leaves

Rhodiola
Crassulaceae

This genus of herbaceous succulents from cold climates of the Northern Hemisphere is closely related to, and sometimes included within, the genus *Sedum*. Plants grow in mounds or spreading mats of upright to leaning stems, with whorls of gray-green to bluish green foliage. They are the only members of the stonecrop family with separate male and female plants.

CULTURE/CARE Full sun in average to dry, well-drained to sharply draining soils, including sandy or gravelly substrates. Drought tolerant once established.

USES Small applications in rock gardens, troughs, and along border edges and pathways, bulking up at a slow to moderate rate. Not tolerant of foot traffic. Deer and rabbit resistant. Attractive to pollinators, especially bees and butterflies.

PROPAGATION Division, cuttings, seed

Rhodiola pachyclados
AFGHANI SEDUM, GRAY STONECROP

Zones 4–9

Open sites among rocks in the mountains of Pakistan and Afghanistan.

Rosettes of blue-green, spatula-shaped, shallowly trilobed leaves on upright to spreading stems in mats 2–6 in. (5–15 cm) tall and 8–12 in. (20–30 cm) or more wide, often remaining evergreen in mild winter climates. Like the lady's mantle (*Alchemilla* spp.), its foliage can hold individual water droplets to nice effect. White, starlike, summer to fall flowers are held between or just above the rosettes. Often sold as *Sedum pachyclados*.

Rhodiola rosea
ROSE ROOT, GOLDEN ROOT

Zones 1–7

Moist, rocky ledges and talus slopes of coastal cliffs from sea level to high elevations in boreal and Arctic regions of Europe, Asia, and North America.

More popular in herbal medicine than gardens, but extremely hardy and useful as a small ground cover. Blue-green, lightly toothed, elliptic leaves sometimes with reddish margins on vertical to leaning stems in clumping mounds or domes, 4–12 in. (5–30 cm) tall and 8–12 in. (20–30 cm) or more wide. Terminal clusters of sulphur to deep yellow summer flowers develop into red seed heads.

Rhus
Anacardiaceae

These super hardy relatives of the cashew are tough and reliable shrubs useful for challenging sites and erosion control on slopes. They also are beneficial to pollinators.

CULTURE/CARE Easy to grow in full sun to part shade in dry to moderately moist, well-drained soils of poor to average fertility. Salt tolerant.

USES General cover for medium-sized to large areas, including large gardens and parks, naturalistic settings, areas of infertile soil, and on slopes for erosion control. Tolerant of periods of drought and clay and rocky soils. Not tolerant of foot traffic. Deer and rabbit resistant. Attractive to pollinators, especially bees and butterflies.

PROPAGATION Cuttings, seed

Rhodiola pachyclados

Rhodiola rosea in the wild, Straight Shore, Newfoundland

Rhus aromatica
FRAGRANT SUMAC

Zones 3–9

Open, rocky woods, glades, prairies, valley bottoms, thickets, and roadsides and other disturbed ground in the eastern half of North America.

Dense, deciduous, suckering, mounding shrub, 24–48 in. (60–120 cm) or more tall, spreading to 10 ft. (3 m) or more wide, with upright, ascending, and horizontal branches. Shiny, trifoliate, midgreen to blue-green leaves smell citrusy when crushed and have variably toothed and lobed, pointed, oval leaflets that turn shades of orange, red, and purple in fall. Dense clusters of greenish yellow male or female flowers, usually on the same plant, on naked stems in early to midspring become bright red, hairy, summer fruits popular with birds.

'Gro-Low': dense, low-growing form, 12–24 in. (30–60 cm) tall and 8 ft. (2.4 m) or more wide

Rhus trilobata
THREE-LEAF SUMAC, SKUNKBUSH SUMAC

Zones (3)4–8

Dry, rocky sites including foothills, canyons, and slopes across most of the western half of North America.

Low, spreading, branching, deciduous shrub similar to *R. aromatica* with trifoliate leaves with reddish pedicels on mounds 3 ft. (1 m) tall and 8 ft. (2.4 m) wide. Leaves smell pungent or skunklike when crushed. Yellowish to bright green flowers in spring become sticky, tart, edible, reddish berries. Foliage turns yellow, orange, and red in autumn.

'Autumn Amber': golden yellow autumn foliage

Rohdea japonica
JAPANESE SACRED LILY

Asparagaceae

Zones (5)6–9

Moist forests and grassy slopes at moderate to high elevations in Southeast China and Japan.

A tough and attractive, yet little-known, evergreen, clumping perennial with thick, shiny, arching, deep green, subtropical leaves, 8–12 in. (20–30 cm) long and about 2 in. (5 cm) or more wide, forming slow-growing clumps, 8–12 in. (20–30 cm) tall and 12–24 in. (30–60 cm) wide. Strange, conelike spikes of waxy, pale yellow flowers bloom within the foliage, becoming tightly packed clusters of showy orange-red fruit. Rare variegated cultivars are sometimes available.

CULTURE/CARE Part to full shade in average to moist, fertile, well-drained soils. Tolerant of deep shade and dry shade. Said to survive in zone 5 but herbaceous.

USES Mass plant to achieve a closed cover for small to medium-sized applications in woodland gardens, along pathways, at the base of trees, and under shrubs. Plants bulk up slowly. Not tolerant of foot traffic. Deer resistant.

PROPAGATION Division, seed

Rhus trilobata 'Autumn Amber'

Rohdea japonica

Rosa
Rosaceae

Zones 2, 3, or 4–9, depending on cultivar

Open to partly shaded habitats including forest openings and edges in the Northern Hemisphere.

Roses are one of the most beloved of all garden plants, immortalized in art, literature, religion, politics, folklore, and popular culture for hundreds, if not thousands, of years. Most famous as cut flowers, roses have also long been used for fragrance in perfumes, potpourris, and soaps and as a flavoring for foods. Most roses grow as upright or arching herbaceous shrubs. Some shrub roses grow as mounds as wide or wider as they are tall, a habit useful to create mass-planted ground covers.

CULTURE/CARE Easy to grow in full to part sun in fertile, average to evenly moist, well-drained soils. Black spot and powdery mildew susceptibility can vary widely with cultivar and climatic conditions.

USES As a general cover over small to large areas in gardens, parks, and institutional plantings, and on slopes for erosion control. Not tolerant of foot traffic. Attractive to pollinators, especially bees.

PROPAGATION Cuttings, grafting

Many rose cultivars could be used as ground covers. In addition to those treated here, cultivars in the slightly larger Knock Out Series grow 3–4 ft. (1–1.2 m) tall and wide, and some of the Parkland Series roses, such as R. 'Morden Blush', R. 'Morden Fireglow', R. 'Morden Ruby', and R. 'Winnipeg Parks', typically reach 3 ft. (1 m) tall and wide. Some uncommon cultivars would also make excellent ground covers, including R. 'Korimro' Grouse, R. 'Korweirim' Partridge, and R. 'Kordapt' Pheasant, which reach 12 in. (30 cm) tall and up to 10 ft. (3 m) wide, and R. lucieae (syns. R. wichuraiana, R. wichurana), at 12–18 in. (30–45 cm) tall and 6–15 ft. (1.8–4.5 m) wide.

Drift Series: disease-resistant, repeat-blooming, compact, 12–18 in. (30–45 cm) tall and 24–36 in. (60–90 cm) wide, blooming from late spring until fall

'Meidrifora' Coral Drift: semidouble, glowing coral-pink flowers

'Meigalpio' Red Drift: semidouble, deepest pink, almost red, flowers

'Meiggili' Peach Drift: semidouble flowers aging from light peachy orange to pink with a central yellow glow

'Meijocos' Pink Drift: glowing deep pink single flowers, white central glow, AGM

'Meimirrote' Apricot Drift: double apricot-pink flowers

'Meisentmil' Lemon Drift: semidouble lemon-yellow flowers

'Meiswetdom' Sweet Drift: double midpink flowers

'Meizorland' White Drift: double ivory to pure white flowers

'Novarospop' Popcorn Drift: yellow buds open to creamy yellow to creamy white double blooms

Flower Carpet Series: disease-resistant, repeat-blooming, 24–32 in. (60–80 cm) tall and 24–36 in. (60–90 cm) or more wide, blooming from late spring until fall

'Deseo' Sunset: single bright orange flowers, central white glow

'Noa168098f' Pink Supreme: semidouble bright pink flowers

'Noa83100b' Scarlet: semidouble orange-red flowers, AGM

'Noa97400a' Amber: orange buds open to light peachy orange semidouble flowers, aging to shell-pink

'Noafeuer' Ruby: semidouble red flowers

'Noala' Coral: single peachy orange flowers, wider mounds to 3 ft. (1 m), AGM

'Noalesa' Gold/Yellow: double lemon-yellow flowers

'Noamel' Appleblossom: double light pink flowers, wider mounds to 3 ft. (1 m)

'Noare' Red: deep red single flowers, wider mounds to 4 ft. (1.2 m), AGM

'Noaschnee' White: semidouble white flowers, AGM

'Noason' Sunshine: deep yellow buds open to semidouble yellow flowers, aging to creamy white, AGM

'Noasplash' Pink Splash: semidouble white flowers variably striped with dark pink

'Noatraum' Pink: semidouble glowing dark pink flowers, AGM

Meidiland Series: disease-resistant, repeat-blooming ground cover and upright shrub roses blooming from late spring through fall, 18–24 in. (45–60 cm) tall and 4–6 ft. (1.2–1.8 m) wide

'Meibonrib' Magic: pink semidouble flowers

'Meicoublan' White: double white flowers

'Meineble' Red: single red flowers with white centers

'Meipsidue' Fire: double dark red flowers, slightly more compact

Rosa 'Noa97400a' Amber (Flower Carpet Series)

Rosa 'Noatraum' Pink (Flower Carpet Series)

Rosa 'Noare' Red (Flower Carpet Series)

Oso Easy Series: disease-resistant, repeat-blooming shrub roses, some with good spreading forms, blooming from late spring until fall

'Chewground' Fragrant Spreader (Scented Carpet in Europe): single pink flowers with white centers, 12–24 in. (30–60 cm) tall and 5–6 ft. (1.5–1.8 m) wide

'Chewmaytime' Paprika: orange semidouble flowers with yellow centers, 12–24 in. (30–60 cm) tall and 3–4 ft. (1–1.2 m) wide

'Chewpeadventure' Mango Salsa: orange-pink semidouble flowers, 12–36 in. (30–90 cm) tall and 2–4 ft. (0.6–1.2 m) wide

'Horcoherent' Peachy Cream: peachy orange semidouble flowers with yellow centers, 12–36 in. (30–90 cm) tall and 3–4 ft. (1–1.2 m) wide

'Hormeteorie' Strawberry Crush: peachy pink semidouble flowers, 12–36 in. (30–90 cm) tall and 2–4 ft. (0.6–1.2 m) wide

'Meiriftday' Double Pink: midpink semidouble flowers, 18–24 in. (45–60 cm) tall and wide

'Scrivjean' Honey Bun: double flowers aging through pink, yellow, and cream, 24–36 in. (60–90 cm) tall and 3–4 ft. (1–1.2 m) wide

'Zlemarianneyoshida' Petit Pink: pink double flowers, 18–30 in. (45–75 cm) tall and 30–42 in. (75–105 cm) wide

Rosmarinus officinalis
ROSEMARY

Lamiaceae

Zones (7)8–9

Dry, open sites among scrub and rocks throughout the Mediterranean Basin of Europe and North Africa into Western Asia, though absent from the Middle East.

Rosemary is among the best-known and appreciated of the culinary herbs and is used in a wide range of dishes, particularly in Mediterranean cuisine. It is typically an upright, evergreen shrub, 24–48 in. (60–120 cm) tall and not quite as wide, with thick, linear, needlelike, aromatic, gray-green leaves and violet to light blue, two-lipped flowers in spring and summer. Various prostrate and semiprostrate forms can make good ground covers in regions with mild winter climates.

CULTURE/CARE Full sun in lean to rocky, freely draining soils of low to average fertility. Drought and

Rosmarinus officinalis Prostratus Group

salt tolerant. Hardiness is improved with excellent drainage.

USES As a general cover for small to medium-sized sites and trailing over walls and containers and along stairways. Plants grow at a moderate rate. Not tolerant of foot traffic. Deer and rabbit resistant. Attractive to pollinators, especially bees.

PROPAGATION Cuttings, seed

'Blue Lagoon': semiprostrate form with upright and trailing branches and deep blue flowers, 12–24 in. (30–60 cm) tall and 24–36 in. (60–90 cm) wide

'Blue Rain': prostrate form with long, trailing stems and a long bloom period, 12 in. (30 cm) tall and 24 in. (60 cm) or more wide

'Bonnie Jean': semiprostrate form, 12–24 in. (30–60 cm) tall and 36–48 in. (90–120 cm) wide, with good hardiness

'Haifa': prostrate form, 4–6 in. (10–15 cm) tall and 24–36 in. (60–90 cm) wide, with cascading habit

'Huntington Carpet': large prostrate to semiprostrate form, 12–24 in. (30–60 cm) tall and 4–8 ft. (1.2–2.4 m) wide

'Lockwood de Forest': large prostrate to semiprostrate form, 12–24 in. (30–60 cm) tall and 6–8 ft. (1.8–2.4 m) wide

Prostratus Group: prostrate to semiprostrate forms, 6–24 in. (15–60 cm) tall and 24–48 in. (60–120 cm) wide

'Renzels' Irene: prostrate to semiprostrate form, 6–24 in. (15–60 cm) tall and 3–4 ft. (1–1.2 m) wide, with good cascading habit

'Wilma's Gold': prostrate form with gold leaves and light blue flowers, 8 in. (20 cm) tall and 24–36 in. (60–90 cm) wide

Rosularia chrysantha
TURKISH HEN AND CHICKS

Crassulaceae

Zones 5–9

Open, rocky mountain habitats in Turkey.

Despite plants that greatly resemble hen and chicks (*Sempervivum* spp.), the genus *Rosularia* is more closely related to the genus *Sedum*, forming colonies of small, succulent rosettes that differ in often having white or yellow (sometimes pink), tubular flowers, and some species' rosettes do not die after flowering. Monocarpic *R. chrysantha* forms dense colonies of light green, 1 in. (2.5 cm) wide rosettes with soft, short, silvery hairs topped with large, bell-shaped, creamy white summer flowers on pinkish stems. Rosettes can flush orange in winter. Other rarer species can also be used, including *R. aizoon*, *R. muratdaghensis*, *R. platyphylla*, *R. sedoides* var. *alba*, *R. sempervivum*, and *R. sempervivum* subsp. *glaucophylla*.

CULTURE/CARE Full to part sun in gritty, sharply draining soils of average to low fertility. Avoid full sun in hot summer climates and protect from winter wet. Attractive to pollinators, especially bees.

USES Small applications, growing at a slow to moderate rate in rock gardens and troughs, between stones and pavers, in walls, and along stairways. Not tolerant of foot traffic. Deer and rabbit resistant.

PROPAGATION Division of rosettes

Rubus
Rosaceae

Well known as the source of blackberries and raspberries, with suckering, upright or arching, woody "canes" and deciduous foliage, the genus *Rubus* also offers a few species useful as ground covers, including two that are unusual in being evergreen trailing plants, forming a dense, impenetrable cover.

CULTURE/CARE *Rubus arcticus* prefers moist, acidic soils high in organic matter in full sun to part shade. *Rubus rolfei* and *R. tricolor* prefer full sun to shade in well-drained, average to fertile soils, though *R. rolfei* is more tolerant of hot sun, sandy and clay soils, and periods of drought once established. Runners of both can be pruned to control spread.

USES *Rubus rolfei* and *R. tricolor* are fast-spreading but easy to control as general covers for small to large areas, on rock walls, and on slopes for erosion control. Deer resistant, tolerant of occasional foot traffic, and potentially useful as lawn alternatives. *Rubus arcticus* is useful for small areas as a general cover or beneath shrubs or trees and especially for permaculture and edible gardens. Not tolerant of foot traffic. Attractive to pollinators, especially bees.

PROPAGATION Division, cuttings

Rubus arcticus
ARCTIC RASPBERRY, ARCTIC BRAMBLE

Zones 2–8

Circumboreal in damp meadows, swamps, moist forests, and along streambanks.

Resembling a miniature raspberry, with upright, thornless, semiwoody stems, 6–12 in. (15–30 cm) tall, suckering via rhizomes into deciduous to herbaceous colonies, 12–24 in. (30–60 cm) or more wide. Textured tripartite leaves are prominently veined, toothed, and slightly shiny. In early summer, 1 in. (2.5 cm) wide, white or pink to magenta flowers with 5–8 petals produce deep red to purplish edible fruits with a sweet-tart flavor.

subsp. *stellarcticus* or subsp. ×*stellarcticus* 'Anna', 'Beata' (syn. 'Beta'), 'Sofia' (syn. 'Sophia'), and 'Valentina': hybrids 6 in. (15 cm) tall with heavier crops, more fragrant flowers, and good fall color bred from *R. arcticus* subsp. *arcticus* for good fruit flavor and aroma and *R. arcticus* subsp. *stellatus* for vigor, flower fragrance, and uniform red fruit color, requires two different cultivars for cross-pollination

Rubus rolfei

CREEPING RASPBERRY,
CREEPING TAIWANESE BRAMBLE

Zones 6–9

Forests and forest clearings from moderate to high elevations in the mountains of Taiwan, China.

Tough, vigorous, evergreen, weed-smothering, trailing ground cover, also known as *R. calycinoides* and *R. pentalobus*, with 3–5 lobed, heavily textured, somewhat shiny, leathery leaves, 1–2 in. (2.5–5 cm) long and wide, mid- to dark green above and lighter green beneath, on long, fuzzy, rusty brown, rooting, intermingling, and trailing stems, in mats 4–10 in. (10–25 cm) tall, spreading indefinitely. Foliage can develop tones of orange and pink in winter. Occasional white flowers produce edible yet not very flavorful raspberry-like golden fruit.

'Emerald Carpet' (syn. 'Formosan Carpet'): most common form grown, with burgundy tones in cool seasons

'Golden Quilt': golden yellow to chartreuse new foliage ages to dark green with reddish cool-season color

'Sonya's Parasol': creamy white variegation

Rubus tricolor

CHINESE BRAMBLE

Zones 6–9

Slopes, forests, and thickets from moderate to high elevations in Sichuan and Yunnan, China.

Resembling the more familiar *R. rolfei*, but larger in habit, with grapelike leaves up to 4 in. (10 cm) long. Similarly tough, vigorous, weed-smothering, trailing, and evergreen with heart-shaped to triangular, textured, veined, glossy, leathery leaves dark green above and whitish below, with variably lobed and toothed margins. Long, rooting, intermingling stems covered in rusty brown bristles form mats 6–12 in. (15–30 cm) tall, spreading indefinitely. Foliage can flush with burgundy when young, have burgundy edges when mature, and develop red tones in winter. Occasional white flowers produce edible yet not very flavorful raspberry-like bright red fruit.

'Betty Ashburner': less vigorous hybrid with *R. rolfei*, with lobed leaves, good burgundy tinting, and orange-yellow fruit

Rubus rolfei

Rubus tricolor cascading down a wall

Rumex sanguineus var. *sanguineus*

Rumex sanguineus var. sanguineus
BLOODY DOCK, RED-VEINED DOCK

Polygonaceae

Zones 5–8

Fields, ditches, clearings, disturbed ground, and forests in Europe, North Africa, and Central Asia.

Distinctive, herbaceous to semi-evergreen, taprooted perennial forming rosettes of broadly lance-shaped to oblong, 4–6 in. (10–15 cm) long, midgreen leaves with bold, deep red to purplish red veins, in clumps 6 in. (15 cm) tall and 12 in. (30 cm) or more wide. Young, edible leaves make a striking addition to salads. Non-ornamental, vertical stalks of tiny, star-shaped, greenish flowers arise in early summer, later turning red. Can self-seed to form colonies.

CULTURE/CARE Full to part sun in well-drained soils of moderate moisture and fertility. Flower stems can be removed to maintain aesthetics or preserved to encourage self-seeding, which is usually gentle but can be more aggressive under some conditions.

USES Mass plant in small areas, especially in permaculture and edible gardens, bulking up and self-seeding at a moderate rate. Not tolerant of foot traffic. Deer resistant.

PROPAGATION Seed, division

Ruschia pulvinaris
CREEPING SHRUBBY ICE PLANT

Aizoaceae

Zones 6–10

Eastern Cape of South Africa.

Related to the genus *Delosperma* with similar linear, blue-green, succulent foliage on woody stems in dense mats, 4 in. (10 cm) tall and 12 in. (30 cm) or more wide. Bright magenta-pink flowers of many linear petals surrounding yellow centers occur from late spring into summer.

CULTURE/CARE Full sun in dry, lean, free-draining soil. Tolerant of drought, heat, and humidity. Resents wet winter conditions.

USES Small to medium-sized applications including rock gardens, troughs, walls, gravelly and thin soils, dry slopes, and along pathways, spreading at a moderate rate. Not tolerant of foot traffic. Deer resistant. Attractive to pollinators, especially bees.

PROPAGATION Cuttings, seed

S

Sagina subulata
IRISH MOSS, SCOTCH MOSS

Caryophyllaceae

Zones 4–8

Dry to wet, sandy or gravelly soils along streams and in grasslands, fields, and rocky places across most of Europe.

Recipient of the award for most mosslike flowering plant, forming dense, prostrate, semi-evergreen to evergreen, indefinitely spreading, bright green mats, scarcely 1–2 in. (2.5–5 cm) tall, sometimes forming slight mounds. Small, pointed, awl-shaped leaves and tiny, white, five-petaled, starlike spring flowers are held on thin, creeping, interweaving stems.

CULTURE/CARE Evenly moist but free-draining, rich soils in part sun (especially morning sun) to part shade, resenting both drought and waterlogged soils including clay. Tolerant of full sun with good soil moisture in cooler summer climates. Stress in hot, humid summer climates, especially in bright light, may cause browning.

USES Excellent between paving and stepping stones, along pathways and stairways, and in cracks, crevices, and spaces between rocks. Good as a lawn alternative for small to medium-sized spaces. Spreads at a moderate to fast rate. Tolerant of light to moderate foot traffic. Deer and rabbit resistant.

PROPAGATION Division, seed

'Aurea': Scotch moss, golden yellow in bright light, lime-green in shadier conditions

Sagina subulata

Salix
Salicaceae

Best known for the weeping willow (*S. babylonica*) that so elegantly graces the banks of ponds and rivers, nearly 400 other *Salix* species of deciduous shrubs and trees can be found in the Arctic, boreal, alpine, and temperate zones of the Northern Hemisphere, usually in moist soils. Shrubby species can be large and upright, arching and mounding, or prostrate. Large, upright forms are generally unsuitable as ground covers unless mass-planted and coppiced annually to maintain a lower cover in large landscapes. Suitable plants include *S. purpurea* 'Gracilis' (syn. 'Nana') and 'Pendula' and *S. integra* 'Flamingo', 'Hakuro-nishiki', and 'Pendula'. Mounding plants such as *S. lapponum* and *S.* 'Mark Postill' are usually wider than they are tall, useful as specimens or mass plantings over medium-sized to large areas. Many slow-growing, prostrate Arctic and alpine species are useful for small applications especially in colder climates. Other species could also be useful, including *S. apoda*, *S. herbacea*, *S. myrtilloides* 'Pink Tassels', *S. petrophila*, *S. reticulata*, *S. retusa*, *S. serpyllifolia*, and *S. uva-ursi*.

Willows are dioecious, with male and female catkins on separate plants. The silky, silvery pussy willows are a crowd-pleaser, in colors of white, green, pink, tan, brown, or black. Some have attractive colorful branches, especially in winter.

CULTURE/CARE Full sun to part shade in evenly moist, coarse, free-draining soil. Tolerant of clay with adequate drainage. Many are salt tolerant.

USES Alpine gardens, troughs, or moist, rocky, or gravelly sites. Not tolerant of foot traffic.

PROPAGATION Cuttings, layering

Salix lindleyana
CREEPING HIMALAYAN WILLOW,
LINDLEY'S WILLOW

Zones 4–8
High elevation rocky alpine slopes in the Himalayas from Pakistan to China.

Excellent ground cover with dark green, glossy, elliptic leaves on reddish stems forming dense, vigorous mats, 4–6 in. (10–15 cm) tall and 24–36 in. (60–90 cm) or more wide, resembling *Cotoneaster* spp. Catkins are deep red with yellow anthers.

Salix nakamurana var. yezoalpina
CREEPING ALPINE WILLOW, YEZO WILLOW

Zones 4–8
Steep, rocky, exposed mountain slopes of Hokkaido, Japan.

Spreads beautifully over and around rocks with prostrate, reddish brown to olive-brown, rooting branches, 6–24 in. (15–60 cm) tall and 3–6 ft. (1–1.8 m) or more wide. Erect, pure white, 2 in. (5 cm) long male catkins have yellow stamens in late winter and early spring, soon followed by 2 in. (5cm) long and wide, heart-shaped leaves covered in silky silver hairs when young, later revealing attractive, netted veins and then bright yellow fall color sometimes with red highlights.

Salix repens
CREEPING WILLOW

Zones 4–9
Dunes, sandy shores, wet heathlands, grasslands, and hills of Europe, Asia Minor, and Siberia.

Variable, prostrate or mounding forms, 12–24 in. (30–60 cm) tall and 5–10 ft. (1.5–3 m) wide, with 1–2 in. (2.5–5 cm) long, oval leaves, gray-green above and grayish white below, on brown to reddish or purplish brown stems. Fuzzy white catkins are up to 1.5 in. (4 cm) long.

var. *argentea* (syn. 'Argentea'): commonly grown silver-leaf form

'Boyd's Pendulous': weeping form, male clone, with silvery green leaves with white undersides, 12 in. (30 cm) tall and 36 in. (90 cm) or more wide

'Bridal Rice': silvery blue-green leaves, 18 in. (45 cm) tall and 4–8 ft. (1.2–2.4 m) wide

'Iona': dwarf male clone, with gray-green, narrowly oval leaves on reddish stems, 4–6 in. (10–15 cm) tall and 18 in. (45 cm) wide

'Voorthuizen': female clone, with dark green foliage with silver undersides on red stems, 6 in. (15 cm) tall and 4 ft. (1.2 m) wide

Salix ×grahamii 'Moorei'
MOORE'S WILLOW

Zones 4–8
Moors of Scotland.

Naturally occurring complex hybrid resembling *Cotoneaster* spp., with dense, glossy, dark green leaves on low, cinnamon-red, trailing stems, 12 in. (30 cm) tall and 36 in. (90 cm) or more wide. 'Moorei' is a female clone.

Salix nakamurana var. yezoalpina

Salix repens var. argentea

Salvia officinalis 'Icterina'

Salvia officinalis
COMMON SAGE, CULINARY SAGE

Lamiaceae

Zones (4) 5–9

Open, rocky places, usually in thin, calcareous soils in the Western Mediterranean regions of Europe and North Africa.

A popular garden plant, long valued for its ornamental and aromatic properties, grows as a semi-evergreen to evergreen, mounding shrub, 12–24 in. (30–60 cm) tall and wide, with branching, woody stems and oblong, paddle-shaped, gray-green, rough-textured leaves with hairy, whitish undersides. Spikes of fragrant, two-lipped, purple to purple-blue flowers emerge from darker calyces in late spring and summer. Variegated cultivars are usually less aromatic

but can still be used in the kitchen. Beyond this culinary species, *S. daghestanica* is sometimes grown for its fuzzy, silver mats.

CULTURE/CARE Full to part sun in average to poor, rocky soils with good winter drainage. Drought tolerant. Heat and lower soil fertility can increase longevity and aromatic intensity.

USES Mass plant as a general cover of repeating mounds over small to large areas or along pathways, sidewalks, or driveways. Not tolerant of foot traffic. Deer and rabbit resistant. Attractive to pollinators, especially bees and butterflies.

PROPAGATION Cuttings, seed

'Albiflora': white flowers

'Berggarten': larger, nicely aromatic leaves, AGM

'Berggarten Variegated': sport of 'Berggarten' with slightly narrower leaves and variable, creamy white edges

'Grower's Friend' (syn. 'Garden Gray'): rarely, if ever, flowers, highly aromatic with reddish stems

'Icterina': broad leaves with variable golden yellow edges, AGM

'Mildred Faye's Rainbow': new leaves emerge purplish fading to gray-green, revealing variable cream and light green variegation

'Nazareth': silver leaves, compact habit

'Purpurascens': purplish new leaves, AGM

'Silver Sabre': broader white edges than 'Tricolor', more compact

'Tricolor': variable white-edged leaves flushed pink and purple when young

'Woodcote': two-tone pale green and dark green leaves

Sanguinaria canadensis
BLOODROOT, CANADA PUCCOON

Papaveraceae

Zones 3–8

Moist to dry woods and thickets, often in floodplains or on slopes near water, throughout the eastern half of the United States and adjacent southern Canada.

Treasured woodland native with thick, reddish, branching rhizomes at or just below the soil surface, with all plant parts exuding a poisonous, orange-red sap when cut. Solitary, starlike, pure white, 8–12 petaled, 1–2 in. (2.5–5 cm) wide flowers with yellow stamens bloom for a week or two in early spring, though individual flowers may bloom for only one or two days if pollinated. Each flower is cupped by a small, young, gray-green leaf that expands during and after flowering into a deeply scalloped, 5–7 lobed, kidney- or heart-shaped blade up to 10 in. (25 cm) across. Seeds are collected and distributed by ants that eat the attached elaiosome. Attractive mounds, 6–12 in. (15–25 cm) or more tall, can slowly form spreading colonies. Though considered a spring ephemeral, plants can resist dormancy until mid- to late summer.

CULTURE/CARE Evenly moist, well-drained soils in part shade to shade. Tolerant of winter wet locations. Consistent moisture delays summer dormancy.

USES Small applications in woodlands, shade gardens, and along pathways. Not tolerant of foot traffic. Deer and rabbit resistant.

PROPAGATION Division, seed

f. *multiplex* (syn. 'Multiplex'): longer lasting, fully double flowers with large leaves

f. *multiplex* 'Plena' (syn. 'Flore Pleno'): longer lasting, fully double sterile flowers with smaller leaves, AGM

pink-flowered (syns. 'Rosea', 'Roseum'): pale pink flowers possibly from multiple introductions of pink-flowered forms

'Snow Cone': fertile, long-blooming, and semidouble flowers with 18–25 petals

'Venus': pink buds open to white flowers with pink reverses, may have been sold as 'Rosea' or 'Roseum'

Santolina
LAVENDER COTTON, COTTON LAVENDER

Asteraceae

Evergreen, mounding, often aromatic, semiwoody Mediterranean shrubs with small, simple or pinnate, green or silver leaves topped with apetalous, buttons of disc florets in shades of white, cream, or yellow in summer, on nearly leafless stems above the foliage mound.

CULTURE/CARE Full sun in free-draining, rocky or gravelly, infertile soils. Provide excellent winter drainage. Tolerant of drought, alkalinity, and salt. Intolerant of high humidity. Plants can splay open, especially when older and in flower. Avoid rich soils. Shear plants lightly in early spring and again after flowering to encourage branching and a tighter habit. Can be herbaceous in cold winter climates.

USES Mass plant over small to medium-sized areas as a general cover, an edger for pathways and borders, on slopes for erosion control, and as specimens in rock gardens. Mounds expand at a moderate rate. Not tolerant of foot traffic. Deer and rabbit resistant. Attractive to pollinators, especially bees and butterflies.

PROPAGATION Cuttings, seed

Sanguinaria canadensis f. *multiplex*

Santolina chamaecyparissus 'Lambrook Silver'

Santolina chamaecyparissus
LAVENDER COTTON, GROUND CYPRESS

Zones 6–9

Dry, rocky, often calcareous banks and slopes from Spain to the Balkans.

Silver-gray, textural mounds, 18–24 in. (45–60 cm) tall and 36 in. (90 cm) wide, of small, rough-textured, pinnately divided, aromatic leaves. Bright yellow, ¾ in. (2 cm) wide, solitary, buttonlike, summer flowers bloom on nearly leafless, felted stems 6 in. (15 cm) above the foliage.

'Lambrook Silver': large cultivar, 30 in. (75 cm) tall with intense silver foliage

'Lemon Queen': soft yellow to ivory flowers

'Nana': compact mounds, 12 in. (30 cm) tall and 12–24 in. (30–60 cm) wide, AGM

'Pretty Carroll': compact mounds, 16 in. (40 cm) tall and wide, AGM

'Small-Ness': very compact mounds, 8 in. (20 cm) tall and 16 in. (40 cm) wide

Santolina pinnata subsp. neapolitana
GREEN SANTOLINA,
ROSEMARY-LEAVED LAVENDER COTTON

Zones 8–10

Dry, open sites in Campania, Italy.

Green to gray-green, textural mounds, 18–24 in. (45–60 cm) tall and 36 in. (90 cm) wide, of small,

Santolina rosmarinifolia

rough-textured, pinnately divided, aromatic leaves with a fine, feathery texture. Lemon-yellow, ¾ in. (2 cm) wide, solitary, buttonlike, summer flowers bloom on nearly leafless stems 6 in. (15 cm) above the foliage. AGM

'Edward Bowles': palest yellow to creamy white flowers

'Sulphurea': creamy yellow flowers

Santolina rosmarinifolia
HOLY FLAX

Zones 6–9

Open, sandy and stony habitats from low to high elevations in Portugal, Spain, Algeria, and Morocco.

Green to blue-green, textural mounds, 24 in. (60 cm) tall and 36 in. (90 cm) wide, of small, rough-textured, pinnately divided, aromatic leaves. Creamy yellow to yellow, ¾ in. (2 cm) wide, solitary, buttonlike summer flowers bloom on nearly leafless stems, 6 in. (15 cm) above the foliage.

'Lemon Fizz': gold foliage in sun, lime-green in less light, compact plants 18 in. (45 cm) tall, AGM

'Morning Mist': silver-green foliage

subsp. *rosmarinifolia* 'Primrose Gem': pale yellow flowers, AGM

Saponaria ocymoides
ROCK SOAPWORT

Caryophyllaceae

Zones 3–8

Sunny slopes and rocky, often calcareous areas from foothills to high elevations from Spain to the Alps.

Extremely hardy, vigorous, old-fashioned, semi-evergreen perennial forming compact carpets of bright green leaves topped in prolific clusters of small, fragrant, bright pink, five-petaled flowers from fused, tubular, reddish sepals in late spring and summer. Plants reach 4–8 in. (10–20 cm) tall and up to 12–24 in. (30–60 cm) wide. AGM

CULTURE/CARE Average to poor soils in full to part sun. Tolerant of clay with good winter drainage and drought. To avoid gentle reseeding, shear after flowering, which also encourages compact growth.

USES Small to medium-sized areas in rock gardens, between stepping stones, along pathways, on slopes, and atop walls. Grows quickly. Tolerant of occasional foot traffic. Deer resistant. Attractive to pollinators, especially bees and butterflies.

PROPAGATION Cuttings, seed, division

'Bressingham' (syn. 'Bressingham Pink'): small, floriferous hybrid for the rock garden, 2 in. (5 cm) tall, AGM

'Snow Tip': white flowers

S. ×*empergii* 'Max Frei': hybrid of *S. cypria* and *S. intermedia*, forming mats or mounds 6–12 in. (15–30 cm) tall and 24 in. (60 cm) wide, covered in pink flowers over a long period from early summer to midfall

Sarcococca hookeriana
HIMALAYAN SWEET BOX

Buxaceae

Zones 6–9

Moderate to high elevation forests from Central China through the Himalayas to Afghanistan.

Evergreen shrub with lance-shaped, 2–3 in. (5.–7.5 cm) long, dark green, glossy foliage on suckering stems and small, white and red, fringed apetalous flowers with a sweet, heady perfume from midwinter to early spring. Clustered axillary flowers are male near the stem tips and female lower down, producing shiny black berries. The best ground cover is *S. hookeriana* var. *humilis*, 12–24 in. (30–60 cm) tall, spreading slowly into dense weed-suppressing colonies. Much larger plants, *S. hookeriana* var. *hookeriana* and var. *digyna* are 3–5 ft. (1–1.5 m) tall, suckering with time into ground-covering colonies; var. *digyna* differs in its purplish stems and narrower leaves up to 4 in. (10 cm) long. Other species grow to similar heights, such as *S. confusa*, *S. ruscifolia*, and *S. saligna*, though the first two are not suckering.

CULTURE/CARE Easy to grow in part shade to shade or morning sun in rich, evenly moist, well-drained soil. Tolerant of periods of drought and of sandy or clay soils with good drainage. Avoid hot afternoon sun. Does not require pruning.

USES Though slow to establish, plants can form large colonies in woodland or shade gardens, along pathways, as foundation plantings and informal low hedges, and in large park or institutional plantings. Mass plant as tightly as budget allows, or interplant

Saponaria 'Bressingham'

Sarcococca hookeriana

with a low, fast-spreading species to provide coverage in the interim. Not tolerant of foot traffic. Deer and rabbit resistant.

PROPAGATION Division, cuttings

var. *digyna* 'Purple Stem': dark wine-purple stems, 24–36 in. (60–90 cm) or more tall

var. *humilis* 'Sarsid 1' Fragrant Valley: more vigorous spreader with larger, narrower leaves reminiscent of var. *digyna* on stems 18 in. (45 cm) tall

var. *humilis* 'Sarsid 2' Fragrant Mountain: larger, wider, glossier, darker green leaves on stems 24–36 in. (60–90 cm) tall

'Pmoore03' Winter Gem: hybrid of 'Purple Stem' and var. *humilis*, 12–24 in. (30–60 cm) tall, with larger leaves and bold red sepals

Sasa veitchii
KUMA BAMBOO

Poaceae

Zones 6–9
Woodlands and damp sites in Central and southern Japan.

Vigorous, low-growing running bamboo with large, broadly lance-shaped to oblong, midgreen leaves up to 8 in. (20 cm) long on upright to slightly arching, 2–5 ft. (0.6–1.5 m) tall stems. Leaf margins usually dry out to a nearly white, pale straw color by fall, giving a distinctive variegated look. Evergreen in zones 7 and higher.

CULTURE/CARE Full sun to part shade in average to rich soils of average to good moisture. Provide afternoon shade in hot summer climates. In full sun, stems typically reach 24–36 in. (60–90 cm) and in shade 4–5 ft. (1.2–1.5 m). Shear to the ground before new spring growth to refresh clumps if needed. Plants will grow back to the same height. Or shear after the new spring growth emerges and plants will reflush into a low ground cover, 12 in. (30 cm) or more tall, depending on conditions. Plants can spread aggressively if not contained.

USES Medium-sized to large applications where its spread is an asset or can be contained by hardscape. Excellent on slopes for erosion control. Not tolerant of foot traffic.

PROPAGATION Division

Satureja douglasii
YERBA BUENA

Lamiaceae

Zones (6)7–10
Average to dry, coniferous forests and shrublands from sea level to montane zones from southern British Columbia to California.

Aromatic, herbaceous mats, 2 in. (5 cm) tall and 36 in. (90 cm) or more wide, of small, bright green, egg-shaped to rounded leaves with bluntly toothed or scalloped edges on trailing stems and solitary, tubular, lobed, axillary, white to light purple flowers. Still primarily offered as *S. douglasii*, though botanists have now transferred it into the genus *Micromeria* via *Clinopodium* (or vice versa). *Satureja montana* and *S. spicigera* remain in the genus and are also occasionally grown as ground covers.

Sasa veitchii, Naritasan Shinshoji Temple, Japan

Satureja douglasii

CULTURE/CARE Rich, moist soils. Tolerant of full sun in cool summer climates with good soil moisture. Prefers part shade to shade in hotter climates.

USES Small to medium-sized applications between stepping stones, along pathways, and trailing over walls, expanding at a moderate to fast rate. Tolerant of limited foot traffic. Deer resistant.

PROPAGATION Cuttings, division

'Indian Mint' GrowFlow: improved, uniform, dense, trailing habit with good branching and dark green leaves

Saxifraga
Saxifragaceae

Hundreds of species have been used to develop a few thousand *Saxifraga* cultivars and hybrids, most of which form small cushions or buns, best suited to the alpine garden and trough. The more vigorous alpine types such as *S. paniculata*, an encrusted saxifrage, can function as a small-scale ground cover. Otherwise, excellent options include *S. stolonifera* and the London Pride and Mossy Groups, which are tough, easy to grow, and evergreen, offering a succulent aesthetic for shadier conditions where most succulents fear to tread.

CULTURE/CARE *Saxifraga stolonifera* and the London Pride Group prefer part shade, shade, or morning sun in evenly moist soils. They are tolerant of periods of drought between deep waterings and dry shade. Mossy Group cultivars are amenable to a variety of well-drained yet moisture-retentive soil types, from humus-rich to clay. Grow in full sun in cool summer climates, light shade in hotter regions.

USES Edgers for borders and pathways, between paving stones, along stairways, and in shaded rock gardens. *Saxifraga stolonifera* spreads at a moderate to fast rate. The London Pride and Mossy Groups spread at a slow to moderate rate. None are tolerant of foot traffic. Deer and rabbit resistant.

PROPAGATION Division, seed

Saxifraga **London Pride Group**
LONDON PRIDE SAXIFRAGE

Zones 4, 6 or 7–9
Shaded habitats in Western and Southern Europe.
London Pride Group refers to the various cultivars, often hybrids, of three of the four species of section Gymnopera, all of which cross easily: *S. hirsuta*,

S. spathularis, and *S. umbrosa*. They are evergreen, rosette-forming species of shaded habitats with short to long petioles holding thick, leathery, somewhat semisucculent, rounded to oblong, mid- to deep green leaves with scalloped or toothed edges, spreading into tight mats by rhizomes or stolons. Each has value in the garden, as does the section's fourth species, *S. cuneifolia* and its cultivar 'Variegata'. All produce relatively tall, 10–20 in. (25–50 cm), often branched flower stems of small white flowers with yellow basal spots, often with red or pink speckles.

These cultivars are now listed as members of the London Pride Group, most without specific epithet or hybrid names because their parentage is often confused or obscure. The bracketed names suggest their most likely affinities.

'Aureopunctata' (syns. *S. umbrosa* 'Variegata', *S. ×urbium* 'Variegata'): [×*urbium*] variegated form with variable golden splotches

'Clarence Elliott' (syn. 'Elliott's Variety'): [*S. umbrosa*] similar to or the same as 'Primuloides', zone 6 or 7, AGM

'Dentata': [×*polita*] long, narrow petioles with rounded, sharply toothed leaf blades, often erroneously attributed to *S. ×geum*, which is similar but with smaller and shallower dentation, zone 6

'Miss Chambers' (syn. 'Chambers Pink Pride'): similar to *S. ×urbium* but with red-flowering stems and pink flowers, zone 7

'Primuloides' (syn. *S. ×urbium* var. *primuloides*): [*S. umbrosa*] small, dark green rosettes, leaves with smooth margins, light pink flowers on stems 6 in. (15cm) tall

×*urbium*: dark green, spoon-shaped leaves with scalloped to broadly toothed edges in large rosettes, zone 4 or 5, AGM

Saxifraga **Mossy Group**
MOSSY SAXIFRAGE, ROCKFOIL

Zones (3)4–8
Garden origin of primarily European species.
The Mossy Group includes *S. ×arendsii* and various similar plants from more complex hybridization. Indeed, many cultivars sold as *S. ×arendsii* are from more complex crosses. The mossy saxifrages are evergreen with small, midgreen, semisucculent, palmate leaves in congested rosettes forming spreading, rooting, mosslike colonies, 12 in. (30 cm) wide. Small, five-petaled flowers are borne in late spring and early summer, ranging from ½ to 1½ in. (1.3 to 4 cm) wide in shades of white, pink, or red, often with lighter or

Saxifraga 'Dentata'

Saxifraga 'Primuloides'

Saxifraga 'Aureopunctata'

Saxifraga Mossy Group

darker colors at the centers. Branching flower stems vary from just 2–3 in. (5–7.5 cm) above the foliage to 8–12 in. (20–30 cm), depending on cultivar.

The mossy saxifrages have come in and out of favor during the 150 or so years since they entered Western horticulture, enjoying a particular boom of breeding and collecting in the first few decades of the twentieth century and another uptick in interest late in the century with the growing interest in perennials. Recent new breeding may encourage renewed interest.

Only a few of the more than 100 cultivars currently in cultivation are widely available. *Saxifraga* ×*arendsii* crosses are noted; others are more complex hybrids.

Alpino Early Series: [×*arendsii*] vigorous, early blooming, with large flowers, 6–10 in. (15–20 cm) tall, 2–4 weeks before the Touran Series

> Early Carnival: deep pink flowers
>
> Early Magic Salmon: pale pink flowers
>
> 'Saxz0007' Early Lime: white flowers with lime-green eyes
>
> 'Saxz0001' Early White: white flowers
>
> 'Saxz0008' Early Pink Heart: pink flowers with dark pink eyes
>
> 'Saxz0009' Early Pink: pink flowers
>
> 'Saxz0010' Early Picotee: white to pale pink flowers with dark pink striations at the tips

'Apple Blossom': introduced around 1900, with pink buds that open to pink flowers, lightening to white, producing a bicolor effect on dark stems to 6 in. (15 cm) tall

'Blütenteppich' (syn. 'Flower Carpet'): [×*arendsii*] introduced around 1911, with dark pink buds that open to pink flowers, lightening to pale pink on dark stems to 5 in. (12.5 cm) tall

'Findling': pure white flowers with lime-green centers atop stems 2–5 in. (5–12.5 cm) tall on vigorous, floriferous plants

Highlander Series: vigorous, uniform plants, stems 2–6 in. (5–15 cm) tall

> 'Highlander Red Shades': deep red flowers lightening with age
>
> 'Highlander Rose Shades': pink flowers lightening with age
>
> 'Highlander White': white flowers

'Peter Pan': from 1939, with deep reddish pink flowers that fade with age, with palest pink to white eyes, 2 in. (5 cm) tall

'Purpurmantel' (syn. 'Purple Robe'): from 1911, vigorous and long-blooming, deep pink flowers lightening slightly with age, 4–6 in. (10–15 cm) tall

'Purpurteppich' (syn. 'Purple Carpet'): vigorous plants introduced in 1930, with mid- to pale pink flowers, 6–10 in. (15–20 cm) tall

'Schneeteppich' (syn 'Snow Carpet'): floriferous plants introduced in 1930, with green-eyed, pure white flowers, 6–10 in. (15–20 cm) tall

Touran Series: long-blooming flowers, later than the Alpino Series, 4–8 in. (10–20 cm) tall

> 'Rocklarwhi' Large White: large white flowers with lime-green eyes
>
> 'Rocklet' Scarlet: red flowers
>
> 'Rocklime' Limegreen: white to light green flowers with bright green eyes
>
> 'Rockred' Deep Red: burgundy-red flowers
>
> 'Rockrose' Neon Rose: bright pink flowers
>
> 'Rockwhite' White: white flowers
>
> 'Saxz0003' Early White: [×*arendsii*] early blooming white flowers
>
> 'Saxz0004' White Improved: [×*arendsii*] white flowers
>
> 'Saxz0006' Red: [×*arendsii*] red flowers

'Triumph': [×*arendsii*] large, blood-red flowers on stems 4–6 in. (10–15 cm) tall, plants in cultivation are not always true to name

Saxifraga stolonifera
STRAWBERRY BEGONIA, STRAWBERRY SAXIFRAGE

Zones 7–10

Forests, meadows, scrub, and shaded rocky sites in China, Korea, and Japan.

Rosettes of large, heart- to kidney-shaped, sage-green leaves, 3–5 in. (7.5–12.5 cm) across, sometimes veined with silver or mint-green, with deep red undersides and scalloped to irregularly toothed margins, topped with white hairs. Forms low, dense mats by thin, hairlike stolons. Branched flower stems produce up to 60 showy, orchid-like, five-petaled flowers with three white to pale pink, small upper petals with yellow and deep pink spots and two white larger lower petals. AGM

'Cuscutiformis': bold silver veining

'Harvest Moon': small golden leaves with thin red edges, can burn in full sun but turn light green in too much shade

'Kinki Purple': leaves flushed with purple, especially when young, with silvery veins becoming mint-green

'Maroon Beauty': leaves flushed with reddish burgundy, especially when young, with silvery veins becoming mint-green

'Tricolor': grayish leaves with white margins flushed pink, less vigorous

Saxifraga stolonifera

Schizophragma
Hydrangeaceae

Similar to climbing hydrangea (*Hydrangea anomala* subsp. *petiolaris*) with self-clinging stems and fragrant, creamy white flowers, hydrangea vines are typically used to cover shaded walls via self-clinging aerial roots, but without vertical support, they can make for unique, deciduous ground covers at first growing as prostrate, rooting mats and later billowing into a cloudlike mass of foliage and flowers. Now known scientifically as *Hydrangea*.

CULTURE/CARE Part shade to shade in fertile, well-drained soils. Tolerant of deep shade, dry shade, part sun with even moisture, and salt. Plants focus on root establishment in the first 1–3 years before initiating meaningful aboveground growth of 1–3 ft. (0.3–1 m) per year. Ample water and fertilizer can expedite establishment. First flowering can begin 2–3 years after planting. Flowers are borne on old wood. Prune only if absolutely required.

USES Medium-sized to large applications, especially under large shrubs or trees or to cover unsightly features such as rocks, uneven ground, low walls, and tree stumps. Interplant a fast-spreading, low-growing, ground cover for coverage and weed suppression during establishment. Not tolerant of foot traffic. Attractive to pollinators, especially bees and butterflies.

PROPAGATION Cuttings

Schizophragma elliptifolium
CHINESE HYDRANGEA VINE

Zones 6–9

Open forests and thickets on ridges and mountain slopes at moderate to high elevations in western China.

Medium-sized to large plants with reddish brown, woody stems reported to reach 10–12 ft. (3–3.6 m) long in cultivation, with red leaf stems holding dark green, elliptic, smooth-margined leaves, 3–5 in. (7.5–12.5 cm) long, turning yellow in fall. Flat-topped to domed, creamy white, lacecap inflorescences up to 8 in. (20 cm) wide are borne in summer with lacy centers of fertile florets surrounded by sterile florets, each with a single, large, showy, elliptic sepal.

'Monhart' Lacy Hearts: gray-green foliage variably variegated with ivory-white edges and pale gray-green markings

'Monlabahe' Red Rhapsody: shiny, reddish new growth

Schizophragma hydrangeoides var. *concolor* 'Moonlight'

Scleranthus uniflorus

Schizophragma hydrangeoides
JAPANESE HYDRANGEA VINE

Zones 5–9
Damp woods and thickets in mountains through-out Japan.

Large plants with exfoliating, reddish brown, woody stems, 30–50 ft. (9–15 m) long, with red petioles holding mid- to dark green, toothed, heart-shaped, 3–5 in. (7.5–12.5 cm) long leaves, turning yellow in fall. Flat-topped, creamy white, fragrant, lacecap inflorescences up to 10 in. (25 cm) across are borne in summer with lacy centers of fertile florets surrounded by showy, solitary, teardrop- to heart-shaped sepals.

var. *concolor* 'Moonlight': foliage overlaid with silver, AGM

'Minsens' Rose Sensation: larger, deeper pink sepals than 'Roseum'

'Roseum': pink sepals, deep green foliage, AGM

Schizophragma integrifolium
CHINESE HYDRANGEA VINE

Zones 6–9
Dense to open forests in valleys and on mountain slopes, sparse hillsides, and rocky cliffs at low to high elevations in Central and western China.

Large plants with brown, woody stems up to 30 ft. (9 m) long, holding shiny, elliptic leaves with smooth to lightly toothed margins, 3–8 in. (8–20 cm) long, that turn yellow in fall. Large, flat-topped to domed, fragrant, creamy white, lacecap inflorescences up to 12 in. (30 cm) wide are borne in summer with lacy centers of fertile florets surrounded by showy, usually solitary, egg-shaped to elliptic sepals.

var. *fauriei* 'Plooster' Windmills: formerly a variety of *S. integrifolium*, now elevated to *S. fauriei*, with sepals of sterile flowers on very long stems

Scleranthus uniflorus
NEW ZEALAND MOSS, KNAWEL CUSHION

Caryophyllaceae

Zones 7–10
Open, sunny habitats including dunes in New Zealand.

Evergreen, mosslike, weed-suppressing mounds or smooth to undulating mats of tiny, tightly packed, hard, needlelike, lime-green foliage, 1–2 in. (2.5–5 cm) tall and 12–24 in. (30–60 cm) or more wide. Foliage can develop gold to rusty orange tones under heat, cold, or water stress. Though related to the showy, well-loved pinks (*Dianthus* spp.), *S. uniflorus* flowers have evolved to be tiny, inconspicuous, and greenish white, traits common in the kiwi flora, produced among the foliage in summer. *Scleranthus biflorus* is closely related but hardy to zone 9.

CULTURE/CARE Well-drained to gritty or sandy but evenly moist soil in full to part sun, with some drought tolerance once established.

USES Excellent between stepping stones or patio stones or rocks, edging borders or pathways, and in rock gardens or alpine troughs, spreading at a slow rate. Tolerant of light foot traffic. Deer resistant.

PROPAGATION Division

Scutellaria
Lamiaceae

Tenacious and drought tolerant, these poorly known herbaceous perennials or subshrubs with low spreading or mounding habits are useful as mass-planted ground covers. Snapdragon-like flowers come in a variety of colors. In addition to those presented, other species worth seeking out include *S. alpina* and *S. pontica*.

CULTURE/CARE Full sun in average to dry, free-draining soils, especially gravelly and infertile soils. Tolerant of light shade, heat, humidity, and drought, once established. Shear lightly after flowering to encourage rebloom.

USES Mass plant along pathways and border edges, on slopes, in the rock garden, and atop walls. Growth rate is moderate. Not tolerant of foot traffic. Deer and rabbit resistant. Attractive to pollinators, especially bees and butterflies.

PROPAGATION Seed, cuttings

Scutellaria resinosa
STICKY SKULLCAP, RESINOUS SKULLCAP

Zones 4–8
Rocky or sandy soils in prairies from the Central United States into Northern Mexico.

Compact, durable, herbaceous plants with a woody base, forming dense, spreading mounds, 4–10 in. (10–25 cm) tall and 16 in. (40 cm) wide, of upright and ascending stems with very small, lightly pubescent, resinous, oval to round, gray-green foliage. Blooms from late spring into summer with small, two-lipped, bluish violet flowers with white markings.

'Smoky Hills': deep purple to purple-blue flowers on larger, longer lived plants

Scutellaria scordiifolia
SKULLCAP

Zones 5–10
Deciduous and coniferous forests, marshy grasslands, and grassy slopes from sea level to high elevations in China, Japan, Mongolia, and Russia.

Tough, easy to grow, long-lived, herbaceous perennial forming attractively textured mounds, 12–16 in. (30–40 cm) tall and 16–20 in. (40–50 cm) wide, of upright stems covered in small, shiny, green leaves and

Scutellaria resinosa 'Smoky Hills'

long-blooming purple to blue flowers with white markings on the lower lip from summer to fall.

'Pat Hayward' Sky's Edge: violet-blue flowers

Scutellaria suffrutescens
CHERRY SKULLCAP, MEXICAN SKULLCAP

Zones (6)7–9
Open, sunny habitats in northeastern Mexico.

Compact, durable, herbaceous plant with a woody base, forming dense, spreading mounds or mats, 4–8 in. (10–20 cm) tall and 16 in. (40 cm) wide, with small, glossy, oval, gray-green foliage. Blooms from early summer into fall with small, pink to reddish pink flowers resembling a small heath or heather (*Erica* or *Calluna* spp.).

'Texas Rose': dark pink flowers

Sedum
Crassulaceae

These beautiful, easy to grow, extremely hardy leaf succulents primarily from sunny and/or dry Northern Hemisphere habitats are among the best ground covers for areas of full to part sun, offering a diverse range of foliage and flowers from hundreds of species and their cultivars. Evergreen to herbaceous foliage in a wide range of shapes, sizes, and colors are topped with clusters of starry, typically five-petaled flowers in white, yellow, pink, magenta, and red. Their popularity has continued to grow with increased interest in succulents, container gardening, water-wise plantings, and green roofs.

Such has been the explosion of interest that a vast palette is now available in horticulture. Beyond the most common species treated here, enthusiasts and professionals may also consider *S. aizoon* 'Euphorbioides', *S. anacampseros*, *S. glaucophyllum*, *S. hispanicum*, *S. humifusum*, *S. lydium*, *S. middendorffianum* and its cultivar 'Striatus', *S. montanum* subsp. *orientale*, *S. nevii*, *S. palmeri*, *S. ochroleucum* and its cultivar 'Red Wiggle', *S. oreganum*, *S. sediforme* and its cultivar 'Turquoise Tails', *S. selskianum* and its cultivars 'Goldilocks' and 'Spirit', *S. sichotense*, *S. stefco*, and *S. stoloniferum*.

Recent taxonomic revisions have separated certain groups from the genus *Sedum*: the roseroots into *Rhodiola*, the upright and semi-upright species into *Hylotelephium*, and the ground-covering species into *Petrosedum* or *Phedimus* or remaining in *Sedum*. The traditional nomenclature is retained here with notes to their new names.

CULTURE/CARE Full to part sun in average to free-draining, thin or gravelly soils. Shade-tolerant species are noted in their descriptions. Plants may resent overly moist soils and high humidity. Most are salt tolerant.

USES Between stones and pavers, in rock gardens, on walls and green roofs, in living walls, at the edges of borders, and along driveways and sidewalks, generally spreading at a slow to moderate rate. Not tolerant of foot traffic. Deer and rabbit resistant. Attractive to pollinators, especially bees and butterflies.

PROPAGATION Division, cuttings, seed

Sedum acre
GOLD MOSS STONECROP, BITING STONECROP

Zones (2)3–9
Dry, rocky sites, beaches, banks, roadsides, sandy meadows, and waste places in Europe and North Africa.

Dense, fast-spreading, mosslike, finely textured evergreen mats, 2–4 in. (5–10 cm) tall and 12 in. (30 cm) or more wide, of tiny, overlapping, tightly packed, triangular, light green leaves. Small clusters of golden yellow, starry, early to midsummer flowers

less than ½ in. (1.3 cm) wide can completely cover plants for 1–2 months. Tolerant of part shade.

'Aureum': new golden foliage creates contrasting tips

'Elegans': new creamy white foliage creates contrasting tips

'Golden Queen': similar to 'Aureum'

'Minus': dwarf, 1–2 in. (2.5–5cm) tall

'Oktoberfest': creamy white flowers

Sedum album
WHITE STONECROP

Zones 3–8
Walls, dry banks, crevices, rocky seashores, and meadows across most of Europe into North Africa.

Open to dense, fast-spreading, finely textured evergreen mats, 2–4 in. (5–10 cm) tall and 12–24 in. (30–60 cm) or more wide, of very small, shiny, plump, green to reddish leaves, usually developing deeper red and burgundy tones with drought, heat, or cold stress. Small clusters of white, starry flowers about ¼ in. (6 mm) wide open in early summer to midsummer, often completely covering the plant. Plants can spread quickly by easily dislodged, rooting leaves or by seed. Shear after flowering to avoid reseeding. Tolerant of part shade. *Sedum stefco* is similar.

'Athoum': larger form with more rounded, oval, flattened leaves

'Black Pearl': purple-bronze foliage under stress

'Coral Carpet': free-flowering white to pale pink flowers, with completely red foliage from fall to spring

'Faro Form': compact, 1–2 in. (2.5–5 cm) tall, with good red foliage highlights

subsp. *teretifolium* var. *micranthum* 'Chloroticum': compact, 1 in. (2.5 cm) tall, with light to midgreen leaves year-round

subsp. *teretifolium* var. *micranthum* 'Green Ice': olive-green foliage year-round

subsp. *teretifolium* var. *micranthum* 'Orange Ice': orange-tinted foliage with stress

subsp. *teretifolium* var. *micranthum* 'Red Ice': foliage with red tones with stress

subsp. *teretifolium* var. *murale*: purple-red foliage under stress, with light pink flowers, possibly confused within horticulture

Sedum acre

Sedum album subsp. *teretifolium* var. *micranthum* 'Green Ice'

Sedum album 'Coral Carpet'

Sedum dasyphyllum

CORSICAN STONECROP

Zones 5–9

Among rocks and on rock walls from Southern Europe to North Africa.

Diminutive stonecrop for small applications with small, thick, rounded, silver-blue, sometimes pubescent foliage in dense mounds or mats, 2 in. (5 cm) tall and 8 in. (20 cm) wide. Easily dislodged leaves can root to form new plants, developing pink to purplish tones with heat or cold stress. Upward-facing, white summer flowers emerge from pale pink buds. *Sedum dasyphyllum* subsp. *dasyphyllum* var. *macrophyllum* has larger, hairless leaves. Requires good drainage.

Sedum dasyphyllum

Sedum divergens
OLD MAN'S BONES, CASCADE STONECROP

Zones (2)3–9
Rocky habitats of western North America from sea level to high elevations.

Distinctive evergreen mats, 2–4 in. (5–10 cm) tall and 12 in. (30 cm) or more wide, for small applications, with upright and ascending stems tightly packed with shiny, opposite, plump, midgreen leaves often flushing red with heat or cold stress. Clusters of starry, yellow, early summer flowers are not produced profusely. Tolerant of part shade and some moisture. Best in cooler summer climates.

Sedum forsterianum
ROCK STONECROP

Zones 4–9
Cliffs, rocky outcrops, screes, sandy habitats, and moist forests in Western Europe and Morocco.

Textural, evergreen stonecrop resembling S. rupestre with finer, needlelike, more numerous, glaucous leaves in spreading mats, 4–6 in. (10–15 cm) tall and 12–18 in. (30–45 cm) wide. Older foliage can develop deep pink tones with heat or cold stress. Clusters of yellow flowers bloom on 10 in. (25 cm) stems in summer. Tolerant of part shade and some soil moisture. Also known as Petrosedum forsterianum.

'Antique Grill': blue-green foliage developing bold reddish tones in cool weather

subsp. elegans 'Silver Stone': seed strain with silver-blue to blue-green leaves

'Oracle': seed strain with silver-blue to blue-green leaves

Sedum hybridum
MONGOLIAN STONECROP, SIBERIAN STONECROP

Zones 3–9
Rocky crevices on forested slopes at middle to moderately high elevations in Siberia and Mongolia.

Related to and resembling S. kamtschaticum, with lush, vigorous mats of upright to ascending stems, 4–6 in. (10–15 cm) tall and 12 in. (30 cm) or more wide, with relatively large, flattened, midgreen leaves with toothed tips. Differs in having somewhat wider, semi-evergreen to evergreen leaves flushing orange to red in colder seasons. Clusters of starry, bright

yellow summer flowers may rebloom in fall. Tolerant of shade and very tolerant of drought. Also known as Phedimus hybridus.

'Czar's Gold': seed strain with red stems but less winter color

'Immergrünchen': foliage with bold red and orange tones

Sedum kamtschaticum
ORANGE STONECROP, RUSSIAN STONECROP

Zones 3–9
Rocky habitats at middle to moderately high elevations in Japan, Korea, China, and Siberia.

Also known as Phedimus kamtschaticus, forming lush, vigorous, herbaceous mats of upright to ascending stems, 4–6 in. (10–15 cm) tall and 12 in. (30 cm) or more wide, with relatively large, flattened, midgreen leaves with toothed tips. Clusters of starry, bright yellow summer flowers develop orange to rusty brown centers. Foliage briefly turns bright pink or orange before winter dormancy. Very drought tolerant. Similar plants include S. selskianum and its cultivars 'Goldilocks' and 'Spirit', and S. sichotense. AGM

var. ellacombianum: bright green foliage, AGM

var. ellacombianum 'Boogie Woogie' (Rock 'N Grow Series): variegated sport of 'Little Miss Sunshine', with cream margins

var. ellacombianum 'Cutting Edge': serrated with broad, gold to light yellow leaf margins

var. ellacombianum 'Little Miss Sunshine': compact, vigorous, to 20 in. (50 cm) wide with dark green foliage

var. kamtschaticum 'Variegatum': cream- to pale yellow-edged leaves, AGM

'Sweet and Sour': nearly white new foliage develops green central veins, turning completely green by summer

'Takahira Dake': older form, to 6 in. (15cm) tall, with good flowering

'The Edge': serrated leaves with thin, light yellow margins

'Weihenstephaner Gold' (syn. 'Bailey's Gold'): red stems and more heavily toothed leaves turn beet-red in fall, flower centers turn orange-red as they age, S. middendorffianum and its cultivar 'Striatus' are similar

'Yellow Brick Road': floriferous hybrid likely involving S. kamtschaticum but blooming a few weeks later

Sedum divergens

Sedum forsterianum 'Antique Grill'

Sedum kamtschaticum var. *ellacombianum*

Sedum kamtschaticum var. *kamtschaticum* 'Variegatum'

Sedum makinoi
JAPANESE STONECROP, MAKINO STONECROP

Zones (6)7–9

Alpine rock crevices and rocky, shaded, moist forest habitats in eastern China and Japan.

Resembling baby's tears (*Soleirolia soleirolii*), with quite small, rounded to spatulate, midgreen leaves, evergreen in mild climates, on trailing, green to reddish stems in compact mats, 1–2 in. (2.5–5 cm) tall and 12 in. (30 cm) wide. Yellow flowers are shy to bloom. Unusual in preferring part sun to part shade and even soil moisture.

'Limelight': light green to chartreuse foliage develops bronze tones in cool weather

'Ogon': golden foliage in more sun, chartreuse in more shade, can burn with sun or drought stress

Sedum makinoi 'Ogon'

'Salsa Verde': shiny, dark green, notched leaves flushing red with sun and heat

'Variegatum': gray-green foliage with white edges

Sedum rupestre 'Angelina'

Sedum sexangulare

Sedum rupestre
SPRUCE-LEAVED STONECROP,
CROOKED STONECROP

Zones 3–9

Rocky and sandy habitats including slopes, meadows, and waste places across much of Western, Central, and Mediterranean Europe.

Vigorous, easy to grow, and tolerant of full sun to part shade, forming somewhat open to tightly closed, textural, evergreen mats of prostrate, ascending, and upright stems, 4–6 in. (10–15 cm) tall and 12–24 in. (30–60 cm) or more wide, with needlelike, green to blue-green leaves sometimes turning reddish in winter. Rooting stems can break off to create new colonies. Flat-topped clusters of yellow, 6–7 petaled flowers are borne on stems 6–12 in. (15–30 cm) tall. Also known as *S. reflexum* and *Petrosedum rupestre*. *Sedum ochroleucum* is similar, and its cultivar 'Red Wiggle' develops bright red winter foliage.

'Angelina': among the most popular of stonecrops, shy to bloom, with golden foliage in full sun that flushes orange with stress, lime-green in part shade; *S. mexicanum* 'Lemon Ball' Lemon Coral looks very similar but is hardy only to zone 8

'Angelina's Teacup': compact form of 'Angelina' from the SunSparkler Series

'Blue Spruce': blue-green to powder-blue foliage flushing purple with stress

'Gold Form' (syn. 'Grosegold') Prima Angelina: said to be denser, more compact, and more vivid than 'Angelina'

'Green Spruce': green foliage

Sedum sexangulare
TASTELESS STONECROP, WATCH CHAIN STONECROP

Zones 3–9

Rocky and sandy habitats and waste places from Eastern and Central Europe to adjacent Asia.

Adaptable, easy to grow, evergreen staple of green roofs, very similar to *S. acre* but with the small, cylindrical leaves positioned geometrically on six sides of the stem, forming dense, fast-spreading, mosslike, finely textured, light green mats, 2–4 in. (5–10 cm) tall and 12 in. (30 cm) or more wide, sometimes flushing bronze in winter. Small clusters of small, golden yellow, starlike flowers can completely cover plants for 1–2 months in early to midsummer. Tolerant of drought and part shade.

'Golddigger': gold to chartreuse foliage

Sedum spathulifolium
PACIFIC STONECROP, BROADLEAF STONECROP

Zones 5–9

Coastal cliffs, ledges, crevices, on moss-covered rocks, in gravelly soils, and in forest openings from British Columbia to Southern California.

Popular and beautiful, with striking foliage in tight, evergreen mats, 2–3 in. (5–7.5 cm) tall and 12 in. (30 cm) or more wide, of ascending and upright stems with whorls of thick, flattened, spatula-shaped, gray-green to silver-white leaves, often with reddish highlights, especially on older foliage. Scattered to plentiful clusters of bright yellow flowers are produced just above the foliage. Prefers full sun to part shade.

Sedum spathulifolium 'Cape Blanco'

Sedum spathulifolium 'Purpureum'

Sedum 'Silver Moon'

Sometimes finicky outside its native range, likely because of freezing and wet winter soils.

'Cape Blanco' (syn. 'Capo Blanco'): powder-white to gray-green foliage sometimes tinged pink, AGM

'Carnea' (syn. 'Carneum'): silver-white rosettes, outer leaves flushed reddish to purplish

'Purpureum': silver-white rosettes, outer leaves flushed with reddish purple, larger rosettes and habit than 'Cape Blanco', AGM

'Silver Moon': hybrid with *S. laxum*, with silvery foliage flushed pink and red

Sedum spurium

TWO-ROW STONECROP, CAUCASIAN STONECROP

Zones 3–9

Among rocks in moist, montane, and alpine habitats of the Caucasus.

Popular and easy to grow stonecrop, also known as *Phedimus spurius*, with excellent vigor and ease of growth in full sun to part shade. Dense mats, 4 in. (10 cm) tall and 12–24 in. (30–60 cm) or more wide, of upright and ascending stems with flattened, shallowly toothed leaves in opposite pairs that are semi-evergreen to evergreen in mild climates, herbaceous in colder zones. Flat-topped clusters of white or light to dark reddish pink flowers deepen with age just above the foliage.

'Album Superbum': green foliage with sporadic white flowers

'Bronze Carpet': early darkening, bronze foliage with mid- to deep pink flowers

'Elizabeth': red-edged and burgundy-flushed foliage with midpink flowers

'Fool's Gold': similar to 'Tricolor' with broader variegated margins on longer, narrower leaves

'Fuldaglut' (syns. 'Blaze of Fulda', 'Fulda Glow'): green foliage edged and flushed with red to burgundy, especially in sun, with mid- to deep pink flowers

'Green Mantle': green foliage with sporadic white flowers

'John Creech': vigorous, bright green, more evergreen foliage with mid- to bright pink flowers

'Pink Jewel': green foliage with pink flowers

'Purpurteppich' (syn. 'Purple Carpet'): reddish burgundy–tinged foliage with deep pink flowers

'Red Carpet': bright red foliage with midpink flowers

'Roseum': similar to 'John Creech'

'Royal Pink': similar to 'John Creech'

'Ruby Mantle': similar to 'Red Carpet' with larger foliage and reddish pink flowers

'Schorbuser Blut' (syn. 'Dragon's Blood'): green foliage flushing burgundy in full sun with midpink to reddish pink flowers, similar to 'Fuldaglut' with narrower stems and smaller leaves, AGM

'Summer Glory': seed strain with green foliage and dark pink flowers

'Tricolor': variegated foliage with creamy edges flushed pink, with light pink flowers

'Voodoo': seed strain with red foliage and mid- to deep pink flowers

Sedum spurium 'Ruby Mantle'

Sedum spurium 'Schorbuser Blut'

Sedum spurium 'Tricolor'

Sedum takesimense 'Nonsitnal' Atlantis

Sedum ternatum

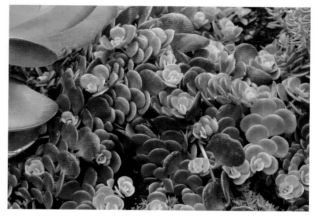

Sedum tetractinum

Sedum takesimense

ULLEUNGDO STONECROP

Zones 4–9

Endemic to Ulleungdo Island and nearby islets, South Korea.

Thick, light to deep green, glossy, pointed, lance- to diamond-shaped leaves with deep marginal serrations, somewhat resembling *S. kamtschaticum*, on upright and ascending stems with terminal clusters of bright yellow summer flowers. Plants are semi-evergreen to evergreen in milder climates, 6–8 in. (15–20 cm) tall and 12 in. (30 cm) wide. Also known as *Phedimus takesimensis*.

'Gold Carpet': darker green, thicker, shorter foliage

'Nonsitnal' Atlantis: broad, creamy white margins with deep green centers on wider, more rounded leaves flushing pink in cool weather

Sedum ternatum

WOODLAND STONECROP,
THREE-LEAVED STONECROP

Zones 3–9

Shaded and forested habitats, including rocky slopes, rock outcrops, streambanks, bluffs, and cliffs from low to high elevations in eastern North America.

Whorled trios of rounded, spoon-shaped, green leaves in mats 3–6 in. (7.5–15 cm) tall and 12–18 in.

(30–45 cm) wide, topped with white, four-petaled, star-like spring flowers with purplish stamens. Unusual in its preference for moist, part sun to part shade conditions, it can decline in full sun, especially in hot summer climates or where moisture is inadequate.

'Larinem Park': larger, more robust and floriferous

Sedum tetractinum

CHINESE STONECROP

Zones 5–8

Among rocks and along streams in eastern China.

Distinctive, vigorous, relatively large, disc-shaped, shiny, mid- to dark green, evergreen leaves on long, trailing stems, 3–4 in. (7.5–10 cm) tall and 12–18 in. (30–45 cm) or more wide, developing coral to copper tones with heat and sun through summer into autumn. Yellow flowers are produced sporadically. Tolerant of moderately moist soils and part shade. Excellent for containers and walls.

'Coral Reef': deeper coral-red tones

Sedum (syn. *Hylotelephium*) species, cultivars, and hybrids

STONECROP

Zones 2 or 3–9 for all cultivars except the SunSparkler Series, zones (3)4–9

Garden origin unless otherwise noted.

These various *Sedum* species, cultivars, and hybrids, some now considered species of *Hylotelephium*, have upright, ascending, or trailing stems with flattened, oval or rounded leaves about 1 in. (2.5 cm) wide, usually forming low, dense, clumping, herbaceous mounds, 4–6 in. (10–15 cm) tall and 6–12 in. (15–30 cm) wide. Stems are often upright at first, later sprawling into mats or domes with terminal flower clusters in late summer and fall. Mass plant to achieve an attractive, closed cover.

'Bertram Anderson': classic old hybrid, similar to S. 'Vera Jameson' but more prostrate with gray-blue foliage deepening to plum-purple, deep rose-colored flowers, AGM

'Lidakense': *S. cauticola* cultivar, Japanese species with grayish foliage flushed with reddish purple, pink flowers, AGM

'Misebaya-nakafu' (syn. 'Mediovariegatum'): *S. sieboldii* cultivar, Japanese species with arching stems of blue-gray foliage, the species edged in pink and the cultivar with a variable creamy to golden yellow central thumbprint, more open habit than other cultivars with pink flowers, foliage turns to pink, red, orange, and yellow in fall, AGM

Rock 'N Round Collection: dome-shaped mounds of bluish foliage, 10–12 in. (25–30 cm) tall and 16–20 in. (40–50 cm) wide, blooming in late summer and fall

> 'Bundle of Joy': white flowers
>
> 'Popstar': bright salmon-pink flowers
>
> 'Pride and Joy': pink flowers
>
> 'Pure Joy': light lavender-pink flowers
>
> 'Superstar': bright rosy pink flowers

'Rosenteppich' (syn. 'Rose Carpet'): *S. ewersii* var. *homophyllum* (syn. *S. cyaneum*) cultivar, Asian species with blue-gray foliage, deep pink flowers

'Sakhalin': *S. cyaneum* cultivar, with blue-gray leaves flushed with purple, bright pink flowers

SunSparkler Series: mounding cultivars with bold foliage and good flowering on plants typically 4–6 in. (10–15 cm) tall and 12–18 in. (20–45 cm) wide

> 'Cherry Tart': cherry-red to burgundy-red foliage, bright pink flowers

'Cosmic Comet': bluish foliage and profuse, glowing raspberry-pink flowers

'Dazzleberry': progressively deepening blue-gray to purple-gray foliage, raspberry-pink flowers

'Dream Dazzler': purple foliage with hot pink edges, bright pink flowers

'Firecracker': burgundy to purplish red foliage, bright pink flowers

'Lime Twister': lime-green to bluish green leaves edged in yellow to creamy yellow, light pink flowers

'Lime Zinger': apple-green leaves with a reddish edge, soft pink flowers

'Plum Dazzled': dark purple foliage, cherry-red flowers

×*Sedoro* 'Blue Elf': intergeneric hybrid with *Orostachys* sp., with steel-blue to grayish purple foliage, dark pink flowers

'Wildfire': purple-red foliage with pinkish red edges, pink flowers

'Turkish Delight': *S. ussuriense* cultivar, Korean species with burgundy-black foliage and carmine-red flowers

'Vera Jameson': classic old hybrid, similar to S. 'Bertram Anderson' but more upright, with gray-green leaves flushed purple, dusky pink flowers, AGM

Selaginella
Selaginellaceae

This peculiar and ancient group of primitive, prehistoric plants whose origins date back 400 million years is appreciated for its interesting forms and textural foliage, some members resembling mosses and others ferns. They are considered "fern allies" from a related division of the plant evolutionary tree that, like ferns, reproduce by spores. Leaves are scalelike, bright to dark green, and usually on branching stems. A primarily tropical genus, some species such as resurrection plants (*S. lepidophylla*) occur in deserts, with others from temperate and alpine regions.

CULTURE/CARE Rich, moist to wet soils in part to full shade or morning sun. Tolerant of deep shade.

USES Small to midsized applications between stepping stones and patio stones; along pathways, stairways, and border edges; on walls; in terrariums; and as a lawn alternative (*S. kraussiana* and *S. uncinata*), spreading at a slow to fast rate depending on species. Tolerant of light foot traffic. Deer and rabbit resistant.

PROPAGATION Division, spore

Sedum 'Bertram Anderson'

Sedum sieboldii

Sedum 'Pride and Joy' (Rock 'N Round Series)

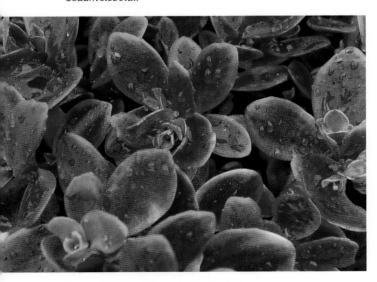

Sedum 'Wildfire' (Sunsparkler Series)

Sedum 'Dream Dazzler' (Sunsparkler Series)

Selaginella braunii

Selaginella braunii
ARBORVITAE FERN, BRAUN'S SPIKEMOSS

Zones 6–9

Rock crevices, usually on limestone, at low to higher elevations in China and Malaysia.

Fernlike species with bright to dark green, semi-evergreen to evergreen, stiff, lacy, triangular fronds of tiny, scalelike leaves resembling cedar (*Thuja* spp.), arising from slowly spreading, creeping rhizomes, 12–18 in. (30–45 cm) tall and 24–36 in. (60–90 cm) wide. In cold weather, foliage can develop orange-pink, bronze, and brown tones.

Selaginella kraussiana 'Aurea' with Sempervivum cultivars

Selaginella kraussiana
KRAUSS' SPIKEMOSS, KRAUSS' CLUBMOSS

Zones 6–10

Streambanks, moist cliffs, waterfalls, and forest margins in the Azores, Canary Islands, and parts of South and East Africa.

Billowy, dense, semi-evergreen to evergreen, mosslike mats, 2–6 in. (5–15 cm) tall, spreading at a moderate rate to 12–18 in. (30–45 cm) wide via feathery, fanlike, branching, rooting stems covered in tiny, scalelike, bright green leaves. Can be weedy in greenhouses and in some mild climate regions, including the United Kingdom, New Zealand, and Australia.

'Aurea': golden in sun, chartreuse in shade

'Brownii': pin-cushion spikemoss, with truncated, frilly, fan-shaped branches in rounded, compact cushions

'Gold Tips': vibrant green foliage, emerging with golden tips

Selaginella moellendorffii
GEMMIFEROUS SPIKEMOSS

Zones 7–10

On rocks and in rock crevices from low to higher elevations in China, Japan, the Philippines, and Vietnam.

Resembling a cross between a cedar (*Thuja* spp.) and a fern, with semi-evergreen to evergreen, bright green, lacy, textural fronds flushing russet to pinkish colors in cold weather, in mounds 4–8 in. (10–20 cm) tall and 12 in. (30 cm) wide, from slowly creeping rhizomes. Fronds produce tiny plantlets or gemmae that dislodge to expand colonies.

Selaginella uncinata
PEACOCK SPIKEMOSS, BLUE SPIKEMOSS

Zones 6–10

Damp soils on shrubby riverbanks and in forests from low to middle elevations in China.

Mosslike species with short, feathery, branching stems covered in shiny, scalelike leaves on long, creeping, rooting, stolonlike stems, forming diffuse to dense mats, 3–6 in. (7.5–15 cm) tall and 12–24 in. (30–60 cm) wide. New foliage is blue-green to iridescent blue, aging to midgreen with coppery tones in cold weather.

Sempervivum
Crassulaceae

Popular, hardy, colony-forming, succulent rosettes, 1–6 in. (2.5–15 cm) wide, for hot and sunny gardens and containers, usually surrounded by young plants produced via short stolons. The many species and thousands of cultivars vary in rosette dimensions, leaf shape and size, degree of leaf blade and margin ciliation, and foliage colors and color patterns, including light to midgreens, blue-greens, pinks, lavenders, reds, burgundies, and occasionally yellows and oranges, all of which can change with the seasons, often becoming bolder in colder months. The Chick Charms Collection attempts to address this vast diversity. It is a trial and marketing program that has evaluated hundreds of existing cultivars to identify those with the greatest beauty and garden performance. These cultivars have been "reintroduced" with new trademarked names along with a few new cultivars.

Sempervivum species are monocarpic. Mature rosettes elongate from their centers into leafy stems, 6–12 in. (15–30 cm) tall, topped with clusters of starlike, pink to red or occasionally yellowish to whitish flowers. Though the flowering plant dies after setting seed, other rosettes will expand into the space. Other species are sometimes grown, including *S. ciliosum*.

CULTURE/CARE Full sun with excellent drainage including shallow, thin, gravelly, or sandy soils. Avoid wet soils, especially in winter. Bright light enhances colors. Most vegetative growth occurs in spring and fall. Salt and extremely drought tolerant.

USES Small to medium-sized applications along pathways, stairways, and border edges; in walls and living walls; on green roofs; and between stepping stones spreading at a slow rate. Not tolerant of foot traffic. Deer and rabbit resistant. Attractive to pollinators, especially bees.

PROPAGATION Division of plantlets, seed

Sempervivum arachnoideum
COBWEB HEN AND CHICKS

Zones (3)4–9

Low to high elevations in mountainous Central, Southern, and Eastern Europe.

Small, tight, distinctive rosettes in dense mats, with heavily ciliated leaf margins with white interconnecting hairs that resemble a spider's web. The small, underlying leaves can be green to gray-green, developing tones of red and burgundy. Flowers are pink. AGM

'Cebenense': larger, light green, heavily offsetting rosettes up to 3 in. (7.5 cm) wide, developing pink to reddish tones with moderate to heavy white webbing

Chick Charms Collection

> 'Emily' Cotton Candy: small, tightly packed, light to midgreen rosettes with burgundy highlights and silver webbing

> subsp. *tomentosum* Fringed Frosting: extra woolly webbing, AGM

'Cobweb Buttons': light green, boldly webbed rosettes, 2–3 in. (5–7.5 cm) wide, developing reddish tones

'Forest Frost': light green rosettes with light to moderate webbing

'Spumanti': light green rosettes flushed red with moderate webbing

subsp. *tomentosum* 'Stansfieldii': small, light green rosettes flushed with red and covered in heavy webbing

Sempervivum arachnoideum

Sempervivum species and cultivars

HEN AND CHICKS, HOUSELEEK

Zones 3–9

Mostly of garden origin.

Thousands of cultivars have been selected from 40–50 different *Sempervivum* species and their hybrids. The most commonly grown are treated here.

'Black': burgundy-black foliage with green bases

'Blue Boy': powdery gray-blue rosettes developing reddish tips, with lavender central blush and/or rusty tones in winter

'Bronco': large green rosettes with burgundy tips in summer, all turning reddish in winter, AGM

'Carmen': large, bright green rosettes with red tips in summer, all turning reddish to purplish in winter

Chick Charms Collection

'Aglow' Bing Cherry: orange-burgundy foliage in summer, deepening to cherry-burgundy in winter

'Citrus Sunrise': leaves variegated with cream, red, and green through winter, brightening to orange-red with creamy yellow edges in summer

'Dakota' Autumn Apple: green rosettes with red tips, turning glowing red in winter

'Director Jacobs' Berry Bomb: large, deep burgundy-red rosettes in summer and pink, green, and gray in winter

'Fashion Diva' Strawberry Kiwi: large rosettes of rich burgundy-red leaves with bright green bases

'Gold Nugget': green tones flushed with red in summer that brighten to lime-green, and then bright golden yellow with red highlights in winter

'Hordubal' Butterscotch Baby: tan-yellow leaves with bright red tips

'Jeanne d'Arc' Cinnamon Starburst: narrow, pointed, white-fringed leaves in rosettes with apple-green centers and red outer foliage

Key Lime Kiss: *S. globiferum* subsp. *allionii*, with small, tightly clustered, light green rosettes

'Killer' Cranberry Cocktail: deep burgundy leaves with bright green tips

'Mrs Giuseppi' Mint Marvel: *S. calcareum* cultivar, with large blue-green rosettes of foliage with rich burgundy tips

'Neptune' Silver Suede: green, pink, and reddish leaves overlain with fine, silver hairs

'Pacific Blue Ice' Berry Blues: large blue-gray rosettes flushed burgundy in winter

'Pacific Devils Food' Chocolate Kiss: large reddish burgundy-brown rosettes

'Prairie Sunset' Plum Parfait: large purplish burgundy rosettes

'Reinhard' Appletini: midgreen leaves with burgundy-black tips

'Rocknoll Rosette' Cherry Berry: bright cherry-red rosettes in summer, turning green with red highlights in winter

Sempervivum 'Citrus Sunrise' (Chick Charms)

Sempervivum 'Emerald Empress'

'Ruby Heart' Watermelon Ripple: large rosettes of rich red leaves mottling toward blue-green tips

'Soft Line' Sugar Shimmer: pale green rosettes with pale pink tips overlain with silver-white hairs

'Urmina' Cosmic Candy: garnet-red rosettes with green centers and white marginal hairs

'Commander Hay': bright to purplish red leaves with apple-green tips and finely fringed leaf margins

'Desert Bloom': gray-green to tawny green rosettes, flushing pink and lavender in summer, deepening to reddish or purplish tones in winter

'Emerald Empress': midgreen leaves can develop tones of lavender, pink, and bronze

'Green Wheel': midsized to large, apple-green rosettes with numerous, densely packed, small, pointed leaves with marginal ciliate hairs

'Hopewell': large apple-green rosettes turning reddish burgundy in winter

'Icicle': bright green central leaves and reddish outer leaves with white marginal hairs, particularly at the leaf tips, forming tufts

'Jade Rose': green rosettes can flush burgundy, red, and rust, especially at the center, with white ciliate margins

'Jubilee': narrow green and red leaves with marginal ciliate hairs

'Kalinda': green leaves often flushing red at their bases in winter

'Lavender and Old Lace': large gray-green rosettes flushing lavender and pink with short, marginal ciliate hairs

'More Honey': large green rosettes developing orange-red outer leaves flushing burgundy in winter

'Moss Rose': green rosettes flushing pink and red with ciliate margins

'Oddity': peculiar cultivar with tubular green leaves tipped with burgundy

'Pekinese': light green leaves covered in white hairs

'Red Beauty': gray-green leaves tipped with red, especially in winter

'Red Heart': green to blue-green rosettes with a central pink and red flush, turning mostly red in winter

'Rita Jane': large olive-green rosettes flushed pink and edged in purple, AGM

'Red Rubin' (syn. 'Rubin'): burgundy-red rosettes with olive-green centers

'Silver King': silver-green to mint-green rosettes with reddish to purplish centers, especially in winter

'Silverine': silver-green leaves flushed with red and purple

'Sir William Lawrence': grayish green rosettes with burgundy tips

'Spring Beauty': lightly cobwebbed apple-green rosettes, flushed pink in winter

'Sunset': *S. tectorum* cultivar, with apple-green rosettes with burgundy tips, turning completely red in winter

'Tederheid': distinctive tawny gold, olive-green, and apple-green rosettes, turning burgundy-red in winter

Sempervivum 'Gold Nugget' (Chick Charms)

Sempervivum 'Sir William Lawrence'

Silene uniflora
SEA CAMPION

Caryophyllaceae

Zones 4–9

Seaside habitats, especially coastal cliffs, from Iceland to Western Europe.

Semi-evergreen mats or cushions, 2–4 in. (5–10 cm) tall, of small, pointed, lance-shaped, gray-green foliage produce five-petaled white flowers from dusky pink, inflated, fused calyces in late spring and summer on short stems. Sometimes short-lived but can reseed.

CULTURE/CARE Full sun with excellent drainage. Drought tolerant. Attractive to pollinators, especially bees and butterflies.

USES Small applications in rock gardens, along pathways, and at border edges. Not tolerant of foot traffic.

PROPAGATION Division, seed

'Druett's Variegated': blue-green leaves with variable creamy white margins

Silene uniflora

Soleirolia soleirolii
BABY'S TEARS, MIND-YOUR-OWN-BUSINESS

Urticaceae

Zones (7)8–10

Low elevations in mainland Italy, Sicily, Sardinia, Corsica, and the Balearic Islands.

Creeping, evergreen to semi-evergreen, mosslike mats of branching, interlocking, rooting stems form carpets, 1–2 in. (2.5–5cm) tall, spreading indefinitely with small, rounded, bright green leaves and insignificant white spring flowers. Traditionally a house and terrarium plant, it is hardy to zone 8, possibly zone 7.

CULTURE/CARE Part shade to shade in rich, evenly moist, well-drained soils. Intolerant of full sun and drought. May be overly vigorous in some situations but not difficult to control.

USES Quickly spreading as an underplanting for larger perennials and shrubs, and along pathways, between pavers, on walls, among rocks, and as a lawn alternative for small applications. Tolerant of occasional foot traffic.

PROPAGATION Division

'Aurea': golden leaves in brighter light, chartreuse in more shade

'Variegata': gray-green leaves with creamy white edges, can revert to green

Soleirolia soleirolii

Speirantha gardenii

Speirantha gardenii
CHINESE LILY OF THE VALLEY

Asparagaceae

Zones 5–8

Broadleaf forests in hills and along streams at middle elevations in eastern China.

A lone species, formerly known as *S. convallarioides*, in a monotypic genus, slowly spreading by rhizomes with midgreen, broadly lance-shaped, pointed leaves, somewhat resembling *Convallaria majalis* (lily of the valley) but narrower and evergreen. Colonies reach 6–10 in. (15–25 cm) tall and 12–24 in. (30–60 cm) wide. Fragrant, starlike, bright white spring flowers bloom on upright spikes within or poking through the new foliage.

CULTURE/CARE Part shade to shade in rich, evenly moist soil.

USES Small applications in woodlands, beneath shrubs and trees, and along pathways and border edges, spreading at a slow rate. Not tolerant of foot traffic. Deer and rabbit resistant.

PROPAGATION Division

Stachys
Lamiaceae

Stachys is a classic genus of spreading ground covers, best known for *S. byzantina* with its large fuzzy, silver leaves. It also has some lesser known yet interesting and beautiful clumping relatives that can be mass-planted as ground covers. These lack the silver-felted foliage but provide green, textural leaves in tough, weed-smothering mounds, with much showier flower displays and good hardiness. *Stachys lavandulifolia* and its cultivar 'P020s' Summer Frost Pink Candy are sometimes grown.

CULTURE/CARE *Stachys byzantina* prefers average to dry, well-drained soils in full sun with afternoon shade in hot summer climates. Tolerant of drought and salt. Often intolerant of high humidity, which can encourage foliar fungal damage. Some gardeners remove flowering stems for aesthetic preferences. *Stachys macrantha*, *S. officinalis*, and *S. spathulata* prefer rich soils with even moisture in full to part sun. Intolerant of heat and humidity. Somewhat drought tolerant once established.

USES *Stachys byzantina* can be used along pathways and border edges, in unirrigated areas, and possibly as a lawn alternative in small to midsized areas. Mass plant *S. macrantha*, *S. officinalis*, and *S. spathulata* as general covers or border edgers over small to midsized areas. None are tolerant of foot traffic. Deer and rabbit resistant. Attractive to pollinators, especially bees and butterflies.

PROPAGATION Division, seed

Stachys byzantina
LAMB'S EARS, WOOLLY BETONY

Zones (3)4–8

The Caucasus of Turkey, Armenia, and Iran.

Every child's first ground cover has thick, felted, silver-white, pointed, elliptic leaves that resemble and feel like a soft animal's ear. They are typically 4 in. (10 cm) long and 1 in. (2.5 cm) or more wide, in striking mats, 4–6 in. (10–15 cm) tall, spreading at a moderate rate via creeping, rooting stems. Evergreen to semi-evergreen in milder climates. Fuzzy, upright, 6–12 in. (15–30 cm) tall spikes with reduced leaves and tightly packed, fuzzy, white buds reveal tubular, two-lipped, lavender-pink flowers in late spring and early summer.

'Big Ears' (syns. 'Countess Helen von Stein', 'Helen von Stein', 'Helene von Stein'): leaves 8–10 in. (20–25 cm) long in mats 8 in. (20 cm) tall, rarely flowers, possibly more tolerant of heat and humidity

'Cotton Boll' (syn. 'Sheila McQueen'): sterile flowering stems produce fuzzy clusters but no flowers, more tolerant of heat and humidity

'Fuzzy Wuzzy': seed strain with dense, silver-gray leaves

'Primrose Heron': yellowish to chartreuse leaves in spring becoming silver-green in summer and yellow-green in fall

'Silky Fleece': dwarf seed strain with much smaller foliage and mats 2–3 in. (5–7.5 cm) tall

'Silver Carpet': rarely flowers

Stachys byzantina 'Silver Carpet'

Stachys macrantha 'Superba'

Stachys officinalis 'Hummelo'

Stachys macrantha

BIG BETONY

Zones 3–8

Alpine meadows of the Caucasus region.

Handsome, dense mounds, 12 in. (30 cm) tall by 18–24 in. (45–60 cm) wide, of rounded, arrow-shaped to ovate, midgreen leaves with cordate bases and scalloped margins with textural, veined surfaces. Large, showy, tubular, two-lipped, lavender-pink to bright pink flowers in whorls on upright stems above the foliage in late spring to early summer. Previously known as *S. grandiflora*. Sometimes placed in genus *Betonica*.

'Morning Blush': pink-flushed white flowers

'Superba': bright purplish pink flowers, AGM

Stachys officinalis

WOOD BETONY, COMMON HEDGENETTLE

Zones 4–9

Dry grasslands, meadows, hedgerows, banks, heaths, and open woods across much of Europe east to the Caucasus and Western Asia and south to North Africa.

Attractive, dense mounds, 8–12 in. (20–30 cm) tall by 18–24 in. (45–60 cm) wide, of paddle-shaped, midgreen, semi-evergreen leaves with long petioles, cordate bases, and broadly toothed to scalloped margins with shiny, textural surfaces. Showy, tubular, two-lipped, rose-pink to fuchsia flowers in tight, upright spikes, 12 in. (30 cm) above the foliage in early to midsummer. Previously known as *S. monieri* and *S. densiflora*. Sometimes placed in the genus *Betonica*.

'Densiflorus': smaller, more compact rosettes flowering at 8–10 in. (20–25 cm) tall with bright rose-pink to fuchsia blossoms

'Hummelo': bright fuchsia-pink flowers, AGM, Perennial Plant of the Year 2019

'Pink Cotton Candy': similar to 'Hummelo' with light to midpink flowers

'Wisley White': white flowers

Stachys spathulata

DWARF BETONY, MINIATURE BETONY

Zones (4)5–8

Grasslands at low to moderately high elevations in Southern Africa.

Dwarf, dense, rhizomatous, slowly spreading clumps, 2–4 in. (5–10 cm) tall by 12 in. (30 cm) wide, of paddle-shaped, ground-hugging, midgreen leaves with broadly toothed to scalloped margins and shiny, textural surfaces. Evergreen to semi-evergreen in milder climates. Showy, tubular, two-lipped, bright lavender-pink flowers bloom in tight, upright spikes, 4–6 in. (10–15 cm) above the foliage in early to midsummer. Previously known as *S. minima*.

Stephanandra incisa 'Crispa'

Stephanandra incisa

LACE SHRUB, CUTLEAF STEPHANANDRA

Rosaceae

Zones 4–9

Thickets from low to moderate elevations on mountain slopes, often along streams, in China, Japan, and Korea.

Tough, easy to grow, versatile, mounding, deciduous shrub with bright green, 2–3 in. (5–7.5 cm) long, maple-like leaves on arching, cinnamon-brown stems. Loose, nonshowy clusters of small, white to yellowish, starlike flowers occur in late spring. Spreads by underground suckers and by rooting stems, especially in moist soils. Foliage turns shades of yellow, orange, and occasionally reddish or purplish in autumn before falling to reveal an attractive winter architecture. Now known scientifically as *Neillia incisa*.

CULTURE/CARE Full sun to shade in soils of average fertility and average to good moisture. Drought tolerant once established.

USES Spreads quickly for medium-sized to large applications in parks or other large spaces, as a foundation planting, and for erosion control on slopes. Not tolerant of foot traffic. Deer and rabbit resistant.

PROPAGATION Cuttings, division of suckers, separation of rooted stems

'Crispa': likely the only form in cultivation, more compact, 12–24 in. (30–60 cm) or more tall and 48 in. (120 cm) or more wide, with deeply incised leaves

Stylophorum

Papaveraceae

A poppy family genus from shady habitats of eastern North America and China, with interesting lobed foliage and long-blooming, bright yellow, four-petaled flowers that lighten the shade garden. Species contain colored sap.

CULTURE/CARE Easy to grow in moist to dry soils in part shade to shade. Tolerant of dry shade, especially *S. lasiocarpum*, and clay. Will self-seed lightly to moderately around the garden. *Stylophorum diphyllum* may go dormant with excessive summer heat or drought.

USES Neither plant mentioned here spreads vegetatively, but both reproduce readily from seed, especially in moist, shady sites, forming attractive colonies beneath shrubs and trees. Plants may reseed where not desired but are easy to remove. Not tolerant of foot traffic. Deer and rabbit resistant.

PROPAGATION Seed, division

Stylophorum diphyllum

CELANDINE POPPY, WOOD POPPY

Zones 4–9

Moist, deciduous woods, thickets, cedar barrens, and occasionally in fields or on shaded dunes from low to moderate elevations in eastern North America.

Bright yellow, poppylike flowers with darker yellow stamens bloom throughout spring and rebloom in summer above fuzzy, green to blue-green, pinnately lobed leaves with silvery undersides on plants 12–18 in. (30–45 cm) tall and 12 in. (30 cm) wide. Tolerant of all but the driest conditions in shade and part shade. Stems contain bright yellow sap that was used traditionally as a dye by native peoples.

Stylophorum diphyllum

Stylophorum lasiocarpum
CHINESE CELANDINE POPPY

Zones 6–9

Forest understories and openings and in ditches at moderate to higher elevations in Central China.

Chinese species with large, bright yellow, poppy-like flowers centered with darker yellow stamens, blooming from midspring to fall. Unusual light green foliage is broadly and irregularly serrated and pinnately lobed, increasing in size toward a large terminal lobe, sometimes on purplish midribs. Mounds reach 18 in. (45 cm) tall and wide. Contains yellow sap in the flower stems, orange sap in the leaves, and red sap in the roots.

Symphoricarpos ×chenaultii
CHENAULT CORALBERRY, SNOWBERRY

Caprifoliaceae

Zones 4–8

Garden origin.

Hybrid of *S. orbiculatus* and *S. microphyllus* forming a tough, medium-sized to large, deciduous, suckering and layering shrub with arching, rooting stems with mid- to dark green, elliptic, 1 in. (2.5 cm) long leaves. White to pink, bell-shaped flowers are followed by pink-flushed white berries in fall, persisting into winter.

CULTURE/CARE Easy to grow in full sun to part shade in well-drained soils of average moisture. Tolerant of full shade and diverse soil types and moisture regimes, including both wet soils and drought. Prune in early spring if needed to encourage a compact habit and increase fruit and flower production.

USES Medium-sized to large applications in parks and institutional plantings and on slopes for erosion control, spreading at a fast rate. Not tolerant of foot traffic. Deer resistant.

PROPAGATION Division of suckers, layering

'Hancock': dwarf, 18–24 in. (45–60 cm) tall, spreading to 8–12 ft. (2.4–3.6 m) wide, with green to bluish green leaves, pink flowers, and pink berries

Symphyotrichum
Asteraceae

This genus includes various North American asters, previously included within the genus *Aster*. Some can be used as ground covers, where their late-season color offers both function and beauty to the garden and nourishment for pollinators.

CULTURE/CARE *Symphyotrichum cordifolium* prefers dry to moist, well-drained soils, from full sun to part shade, while *S. ericoides* prefers average to dry soils in full to part sun and is tolerant of drought, clay, and shallow, rocky soils. Good air circulation will help minimize fungal issues for both species.

USES Use *S. cordifolium* in shaded sites, where stems are more lax, including borders and woodlands, and under large shrubs and trees for small to large applications. Use *S. ericoides* for small to medium-sized applications on walls, as a companion for evergreens, and in rock gardens and other dry sites in full to part sun. Neither is tolerant of foot traffic. Both are deer resistant and attractive to pollinators, especially bees and butterflies.

PROPAGATION Division, cuttings, seed

Symphyotrichum cordifolium
COMMON BLUE WOOD ASTER,
HEART-LEAVED ASTER

Zones 3–9

Open wooded slopes and bluffs, forest edges and clearings, streambanks, roadsides, and swampy areas in central and eastern North America.

Shade-tolerant, rhizomatously spreading aster similar to *Eurybia divaricata* (syn. *Aster divaricatus*) but larger, growing on stems 24–36 in. (60–90 cm) long from cordate, hairy, toothed basal leaves, with clouds of hundreds of small, pale blue flowers with yellow and orange-red centers in late summer and fall. Stems are upright or arching in sun but sprawl and weave into a billowy ground cover in shade. Formerly known as *Aster cordifolius*.

'Avondale': prolific bloomer

'Little Carlow': hybrid with *S. novi-belgii*, with larger, 1 in. (2.5 cm) wide, lavender-blue flowers

'Silver Spray': white flowers

Stylophorum lasiocarpum

Symphoricarpos ×chenaultii 'Hancock'

Symphyotrichum cordifolium

Symphyotrichum ericoides var. *prostratum* 'Snow Flurry'

Symphyotrichum ericoides

HEATH ASTER

Zones 3–9

Open, dry to moist, sandy or gravelly soils on prairies, dunes, roadsides, hills, in glades and fields, and along watercourses from near sea level to high elevations across most of North America.

Formerly *Aster ericoides*, the extremely late-blooming heath aster has small, stiff, linear to lance-shaped, needlelike, green to gray-green leaves on upright, arching, and/or procumbent stems, 12–36 in. (30–90 cm) long, covered in late summer and fall with hundreds, if not thousands, of small, densely packed, white daisies with yellow centers, turning orange-red with age.

'Bridal Veil': upright stems become arching and cascading with time, forming mounds 24 in. (60 cm) tall and 24–48 in. (60–120 cm) wide, hybrid cross of var. *prostratum* 'Snow Flurry' with an unknown pollen parent

'First Snow': arching and prostrate stems in mounds, 12–24 in. (30–60 cm) tall by 36–48 in. (90–120 cm) wide

var. *prostratum* 'Snow Flurry': excellent ground cover with rigid, stiffly prostrate stems forming a carpet of plants, 4–8 in. (10–20 cm) tall and 24–48 in. (60–120 cm) wide, resembling a low-growing juniper before flowering, AGM

Symphytum grandiflorum
LARGE-FLOWERED COMFREY

Boraginaceae

Zones 4–8

Woodlands in the Caucasus. Naturalized in Europe. Tough and easy, yet rarely grown, rhizomatous, semi-evergreen ground cover with coarsely textured, elliptic to egg-shaped, mid- to dark green, 6 in. (15 cm) long leaves in dense, spreading mats. Pendulous clusters of creamy yellow to white flowers bloom just above the foliage in midspring.

CULTURE/CARE Part sun to part shade in organically rich soils of average moisture. Tolerant of drought and full shade. Difficult to remove once established, as pieces of rhizome can resprout.

USES Shaded borders, woodlands, beneath shrubs, and along pathways, spreading at a moderate to fast rate. Not tolerant of foot traffic. Deer resistant. Attractive to pollinators, especially bees.

PROPAGATION Division, root cuttings

'All Gold': golden foliage, now considered *S. ibericum*

'Goldsmith': hybrid of unknown origin, resembling a larger, clumping *S. grandiflorum* with leaves edged with golden yellow and white, and blue flowers from reddish buds

'Hidcote Blue': hybrid sometimes attributed to *S. grandiflorum*, spreading vigorously by rhizomes into mats 12–18 in. (30–45 cm) tall and 24 in. (60 cm) or more wide, with pendulous, bluebell-like flowers opening blue and white from red buds

'Hidcote Pink': similar to 'Hidcote Blue' with red buds opening to pink and white

'Wisley Blue': blue flowers

Symphytum grandiflorum

T

Tanacetum densum subsp. amani
PARTRIDGE FEATHER

Asteraceae

Zones 4–9

Open and rocky habitats of southeastern Turkey. Striking evergreen subshrub for hot, sunny, dry locations with soft, featherlike, highly dissected, silver-white foliage forming textured mats, 4–6 in. (10–15 cm) tall and 18–24 in. (45–60 cm) or more wide. Topped with late spring and summer clusters of bright yellow, buttonlike flowers on short stems. Silver lace tansy, *T. haradjanii*, is similar but hardy only to zone 8.

CULTURE/CARE Full sun in dry, sandy, or gravelly, free-draining soils. Drought tolerant. Intolerant of humidity and winter wet. Provide a mulch of gravel or pine needles to protect foliage from winter humidity. Plants resprout densely after a hard prune.

USES Small to medium-sized sites such as rock gardens, between rocks, and on shallow slopes, spreading at a slow rate. Not tolerant of foot traffic. Deer and rabbit resistant. Attractive to pollinators, especially bees and butterflies.

PROPAGATION Seed, cuttings

Taxus cuspidata
JAPANESE YEW

Taxaceae

Zones 4–8

Broad, columnar, evergreen tree or shrub with linear, pointed, dark green, 1 in. (2.5 cm) long needles, sometimes yellowish beneath and tinged yellowish to reddish in winter.

CULTURE/CARE Full sun to part shade in average to evenly moist, well-drained soils. Tolerant of shade. Intolerant of wet soils.

USES Shrub borders, as a specimen ground cover in smaller spaces, and for erosion control on slopes, spreading at a slow rate. Not tolerant of foot traffic. Rabbit resistant.

PROPAGATION Seed, cuttings

'Monloo' Emerald Spreader: compact, dense, spreading, slow-growing plants, 30 in. (75 cm) tall and up to 9 ft. (2.7 m) wide, more layered and spreading in shade

Tanacetum densum subsp. *amani*

Taxus cuspidata 'Monloo' Emerald Spreader in the shade

Tellima grandiflora

Tellima grandiflora
FRINGECUPS, BIGFLOWER TELLIMA

Saxifragaceae

Zones 4–8

Moist forests, streambanks, and thickets from low to higher elevations in western North America from Alaska to Northern California.

Closely related to and resembling *Heuchera* species in form, foliage, and inflorescence, with 10 in. (25 cm) tall and 12 in. (30 cm) wide basal mounds of large, fuzzy, lobed, lightly toothed, midgreen leaves, each to 4 in. (10 cm) wide. Airy, one-sided flower stems, 18–24 in. (45–60 cm) tall, have small, fragrant, cupped, whitish green flowers with reflexed, dissected petals aging to pink. Evergreen in mild winters. Spreads slowly by rhizome and readily by self-seeding.

CULTURE/CARE Easy to grow in part shade to shade in evenly moist soils.

USES Woodland gardens, shaded wildflower meadows, borders, and near water features. Can quickly expand colonies via self-seeding. Not tolerant of foot traffic. Deer and rabbit resistant. Attractive to pollinators, especially bees, butterflies, and hummingbirds.

PROPAGATION Seed, division

'Purpurteppich': reddish flower stems, pink-rimmed green flowers, and purple-veined and blushed leaves in summer, becoming purple-red in winter

Teucrium
Lamiaceae

Uncommonly grown mint family member in North America, despite a long history of herbal and ornamental use in Europe, the genus includes more than 170 species, primarily from the Mediterranean, conveying tolerance of heat, drought, and exposed sites. In addition to the species treated here, *T. ackermannii* and *T. pyrenaicum* are particularly suited to the xeriscape garden.

CULTURE/CARE Full sun in well-drained soils of average to low moisture. *Teucrium aroanium* prefers grittier soils. Somewhat tolerant of drought, poor soils, and light shade. Shear in early spring to refresh plants and encourage a compact habit.

USES Small applications as a facer for buildings and walls, as a semiformal hedge, in rock gardens, and along walkways and border edges, growing at a moderate rate. Not tolerant of foot traffic. Deer and rabbit resistant. Attractive to pollinators, especially bees and butterflies.

PROPAGATION Cuttings, division

Teucrium aroanium
GRAY CREEPING GERMANDER

Zones 5–10
Sunny, rocky habitats in Greece.
Uncommon, woody, stoloniferous, evergreen subshrub with rooting stems covered in narrow, linear to oblong, aromatic, gray-green leaves, forming mounds or mats 2–3 in. (5–7.5 cm) tall and 24 in. (60 cm) or more wide, topped with clusters of fragrant, magenta-pink, tubular, two-lipped flowers in late spring and summer.

Teucrium chamaedrys
GROUND GERMANDER, COMMON GERMANDER

Zones 4–9
Sunny, dry habitats, waste places, old walls, and rock outcrops, usually on calcareous soils, across most of Europe into Morocco and Algeria.
Long a component of European horticulture, particularly in herbal and physic gardens and in knot gardens, maintained as a more formal element. Evergreen to semi-evergreen subshrub forming clumps or mounds, 8–18 in. (20–45 cm) tall and 18–24 in. (45–60 cm) wide, of upright and ascending stems with shiny, aromatic, ¾ in. (2 cm) long, dark green, oaklike leaves with spikes of tubular, two-lipped, pink to purplish pink flowers in late spring and summer.

f. *albiflora*: white flowers

'Prostratum' (syn. 'Nanum'): compact, floriferous, 6–8 in. (15–20 cm) tall, with a vigorous, rhizomatous habit, often referred to as creeping germander

'Summer Sunshine': likely a sport of 'Prostratum', with golden foliage turning chartreuse by summer

'Tickle Pink': deeper green foliage and deeper pink flowers, compact habit, 12 in. (30 cm) tall by 24 in. (60 cm) wide

Thymus
Lamiaceae

The creeping thymes are quintessential, easy to grow, low-maintenance ground covers for sun, offering drought tolerance, durability, versatility, colorful flowers, and aromatic foliage. Most are evergreen to semi-evergreen and bloom in early to midsummer, with clusters of tiny, tubular, two-lipped, pink to

Teucrium aroanium

Teucrium chamaedrys

Thymus citriodorus

purple-pink or white flowers. Their mounding cousins, lemon and common thyme, enjoy similar conditions, offering heavily scented foliage for culinary uses. Other species worth searching out include *T. comosus*, caraway thyme (*T. herba-barona*), *T. longicaulis*, juniper leaf thyme (*T. neiceffii*), and lavender-scented thyme (*T. thracicus*).

CULTURE/CARE Full to part sun in free-draining sandy or gravelly soils of average to poor fertility and average to low moisture. Avoid moist, rich soils and winter wet. *Thymus serpyllum* is salt tolerant. Shear lemon and common thyme in early spring to maintain compactness.

USES Creeping thymes are tolerant of light foot traffic as a lawn alternative or can be planted among rocks, between pavers, along border edges and walkways, and in walls and containers, spreading at a moderate to fast rate. Mass plant mounding thymes to achieve coverage in similar locations. Deer and rabbit resistant. Attractive to pollinators, especially bees and butterflies.

PROPAGATION Cuttings, seed, division

Thymus citriodorus
LEMON THYME

Zones 5–9

Likely from non-Mediterranean Europe.

Evergreen subshrub valued for its edible, aromatic, lemon-scented foliage but also useful as a mounding ground cover resembling common thyme (*T. vulgaris*) in size and habit. Upright and ascending, 4–12 in. (10–30 cm) tall, green to reddish stems spread 12–18 in. (30–45 cm) wide, topped by pale pink to pale lavender-pink flowers. Once thought to be a naturally occurring hybrid of *T. pulegioides* and *T. vulgaris* called *T. ×citriodorus*, recent DNA evidence suggests true species status.

Some of these cultivars are sometimes considered hybrids. Cultivars 'Lemon Frost' and 'Lime' are more similar in habit to and may eventually be assigned to *T. pulegioides*.

'Argenteus': silver-edge thyme, creamy white margins and good scent, often listed as *T. vulgaris*

'Lemon Frost': white flowers on creeping plants, 2–4 in. (5–10 cm) tall and 12–18 in. (30–45 cm) wide

'Lime': bright green, lime-scented leaves on prostrate plants, 2–4 in. (5–10 cm) tall and 12–18 in. (30–45 cm) wide

'Silver King': boldly variegated with creamy white margins, broader than 'Silver Queen', on more lax plants, 4–6 in. (10–15 cm) tall and 12 in. (30 cm) wide

'Silver Queen': midgreen, strongly aromatic leaves with creamy white margins on upright plants, 8–12 in. (20–30 cm) tall and 12–18 in. (30–45 cm) wide, AGM

'Tm95' Orange Spice (syn. 'Spicy Orange'): needle-shaped, orange-scented foliage and pale pink flowers

Thymus pseudolanuginosus
WOOLLY THYME

Zones (4)5–9

Open, sunny habitats from the Iberian Peninsula to Scandinavia, including Great Britain and Iceland.

Vigorous, fast-spreading, prostrate, hairy, evergreen, mat-forming subshrub with tiny, rounded to elliptic, nonaromatic, gray-green foliage and green to reddish, wiry, branching stems with sparse pale pink to lavender-pink flowers. Excellent as a general cover, along pathways, on walls, between stones, or as a flat to undulating lawn alternative, ½–2 in. (1.3–5 cm) tall, spreading indefinitely. Known scientifically as either *T. polytrichus* subsp. *britannicus* or *T. praecox* subsp. *britannicus*.

Thymus pseudolanuginosus

Thymus pulegioides 'Aureus'

Thymus pulegioides
BROAD-LEAVED THYME, LEMON THYME

Zones 4–9

Dry grasslands, hills, rocky outcrops, gravelly and sandy places, waste ground, and roadsides, usually on calcareous soils, across most of Europe.

Creeping, evergreen subshrub, somewhat similar to *T. serpyllum* in habit but larger overall, with larger and lusher foliage. Forms spreading mounds or mats, 12–24 in. (30–60 cm) wide, of upright, ascending, prostrate, reddish stems, 4–8 in. (10–20 cm) tall, topped with pink to lavender-pink flowers. Edible, lemon-scented foliage can be used for culinary purposes.

The gold-leaved cultivars were previously attributed to *T. citriodorus*, but DNA testing places them here.

'Archer's Gold': chartreuse to golden or variably gold-splashed leaves, brightest in winter and spring

'Aureus': green leaves with golden edges, strong scent, AGM

'Bertram Anderson' (syn. 'Anderson's Gold'): lightly aromatic, bright gold to chartreuse foliage brightest in winter and spring, AGM

'Foxley': strongly aromatic, dark green leaves with creamy white margins and pink new growth

Thymus serpyllum and similar hybrids
CREEPING THYME, BRECKLAND THYME

Zones 4–9

Rocky hills, sandy heaths, rock outcrops, riverbanks, meadows, and roadsides across most of Europe excluding the Mediterranean.

Prostrate, creeping, evergreen to semi-evergreen, variably hairy subshrub with tiny, oblong to elliptic, dark green to gray-green, glossy, aromatic leaves on wiry, branching, green to reddish stems. Usually blooms profusely with pink, lavender, magenta, purple, or white flowers in late spring to early summer on upright stems, 2–4 in. (5–10 cm) tall. Excellent as a general cover or lawn alternative, 2–3 in. (5–7.5cm) tall and 12–24 in. (30–60 cm) or more wide. Historically confused with *T. praecox*, whose cultivars have mostly been transferred to *T. serpyllum* or designated as hybrids. Current taxonomic work suggests that true *T. praecox* is not actually commonly cultivated.

var. *albus* (syn. 'Albus'): white flowers

'Annie Hall': pale pink to lilac-pink flowers

'Elfin': extremely compact, spreading dwarf with tightly packed, miniature foliage and lavender-pink flowers; a more compact UK form, which is slower growing, forms hummocks or cushions and flowers only sparsely, is sometimes sold in North America as "True UK Clone"

'Goldstream': dark green foliage flecked with gold

'Magic Carpet': seed strain with bright magenta-pink flowers and lemon-scented foliage

'Minor' (syn. 'Minus'): similar to 'Elfin', very dense, compact, and low-growing with tiny leaves

'Pink Chintz': light salmon-pink flowers, slightly hairy, dark green foliage, AGM

'Purple Carpet': North American selection with bright lavender-purple flowers, still usually attributed to *T. praecox* and not synonymous with the European *T. praecox* 'Purpurteppich'

'Russetings': European cultivar with bright lavender-pink flowers and aromatic foliage

'Snowdrift': white flowers

The exact parentage of these hybrid cultivars is generally unknown but probably involves *T. serpyllum*.

'Bressingham': clear to bright pink flowers with aromatic, hairy leaves

Coccineus Group: deep magenta to magenta-red flowers, AGM

'Doone Valley': dark green, lemony leaves irregularly splashed with gold, especially in cooler seasons, with lavender-pink flowers

Thymus serpyllum var. *albus*

Thymus 'Doone Valley'

Thymus 'Hartington Silver'

Thymus serpyllum 'Elfin'

Thymus Coccineus Group

'Hartington Silver' (syn. 'Highland Cream'): boldly variegated dark green leaves with pale yellow to creamy white margins and mid- to pale pink flowers

'Pink Ripple': shell-pink flowers on lemon-scented plants, 3–6 in. (7.5–15 cm) tall

'Ruby Glow': glowing magenta flowers

'Purpurteppich' (Coccineus Group): common European cultivar with bright magenta-pink flowers

Thymus vulgaris
COMMON THYME, GARDEN THYME

Zones 5–11
Dry hills, among rocks, and in maquis, always on clay or calcareous soils in the western Mediterranean Basin.

Common culinary thyme forms spreading mounds, 12–18 in. (30–45 cm) wide, of upright and ascending stems, 6–12 in. (15–30 cm) tall, with tiny, linear to elliptic, gray-green leaves with under-rolled margins and pale pink to pale lavender-pink flowers. Evergreen in milder climates.

'Compactus': compact form

'Dot Wells': strongly aromatic, flavorful foliage

'English Wedgewood': sweeter, milder foliage with yellow to light green centers and dark green edges

'Orange Balsam': orange-scented foliage

'Peter Davis': likely a hybrid, with early pink to mauve flowers, often listed as *T. richardii* or *T. nitidus*

'Pinewood': hybrid resembling *T. vulgaris* with pine-scented foliage

'Silver Posie': likely a hybrid, with ivory-white edged leaves tinged pink in cool weather on reddish stems

'Sparkling Bright': possibly a hybrid, with brightly variegated creamy white edges

Tiarella cordifolia
FOAMFLOWER

Saxifragaceae

Zones 3 or 4–9
Open to shady, dry to swampy, deciduous woods and along shady streams from low to higher elevations in eastern North America.

Dependable, hardy, shade-loving coparent with *Heuchera* of genus ×*Heucherella*, with less dramatic

Thymus 'Silver Posie'

Tiarella cordifolia 'Brandywine'

foliage but showier floral displays. Shallowly lobed, lightly glossy, wrinkled, sometimes fuzzy, midgreen, maple-like leaves up to 4 in. (10 cm) wide are sometimes veined with burgundy and remain evergreen in mild winter climates, often flushed red to burgundy. Mounds 6–10 in. (15–25 cm) tall and 6–12 in. (15–30 cm) or more wide can be clumping or quickly spreading via stolons into dense colonies. Showy flower spikes, 12–18 in. (30–45 cm) tall, carry white to pink buds opening to starry white flowers with long stamens in spring. *Tiarella wherryi*, previously considered a distinct, clumping species, is now considered a synonym, though the name may still identify nonstoloniferous clones in horticulture. An uncommon Asian species, *T. polyphylla* and its seed strain 'Filigran', are also worth growing. AGM

CULTURE/CARE Evenly moist, well-drained, average to rich soils in part shade to shade. Tolerant of dry shade.

USES Mass plant clumping cultivars in woodlands, along pathways and border edges, and beneath shrubs and trees. Stoloniferous cultivars spread quickly into lush mats for woodlands or to fill in between larger perennials and among exposed or shallow tree roots. Not tolerant of foot traffic. Deer and rabbit resistant.

PROPAGATION Division, seed

This palette of foamflowers comprises plants derived from *T. cordifolia* as well as hybrids involving this and other species.

'Brandywine': vigorous, with some short runners, a long bloom time, and good burgundy fall and winter color

'Oakleaf': five-lobed, maple-like leaves, brilliant burgundy winter color, with pink buds and white flowers

River Series: cultivars with excellent hardiness, perhaps to zone 3, and variable, stoloniferous habits

> 'Delaware': large, heart-shaped leaves with shallow lobes and burgundy veins, vigorous, to 18 in. (45 cm) wide in one season, with pink buds and white flowers

> 'Lehigh': five-lobed leaves with burgundy centers, with peachy pink buds and white flowers

> 'Octoraro': best of the series for use as a ground cover, spreading quickly to 24–36 in. (60–90 cm) wide, with pink buds and white flowers, foliage lightly marked with burgundy

> 'Susquehanna': white buds and flowers, foliage more burgundy marked with age, on vigorous plants spreading to 24 in. (60 cm) wide in one season

> 'Wissahickon': shiny foliage, slowly spreading plants to 8 in. (20 cm) wide in one season, blooming from spring into midsummer

'Running Tapestry': vigorous spreader with heart-shaped, burgundy-speckled leaves and white buds and flowers

Tiarella hybrids

'Crow Feather': deeply cut, burgundy-centered leaves, with excellent winter colors of pink, red, purple, and black on mounding plants

'Elizabeth Oliver': dissected leaves with burgundy centers on clumping plants

'Iron Butterfly': pink buds and white, lightly fragrant flowers, with deeply dissected, burgundy-veined leaves turning purplish bronze in winter on clumping plants

'Jeepers Creepers': deeply cut leaves with bold burgundy centers, with large white flowers on creeping plants

'Pacific Crest': deeply cut leaves with bold burgundy centers spreading quickly via long stolons, member of the American Trails Series, with cultivars that may no longer be in active cultivation but include 'Appalachian Trail', 'Cascade Creeper', 'Happy Trails', 'Oregon Trail', and 'Sunset Ridge'

'Pink Skyrocket': bold shrimp-pink buds and white flowers, with deeply dissected leaves with burgundy centers turning burgundy to black in winter, on clumping plants, AGM

'Spring Symphony': deeply dissected leaves with burgundy centers on clumping plants, heavy flowering with pink buds and white flowers, AGM

'Sugar and Spice': shiny, corrugated, dissected foliage with burgundy centers on clumping plants, with pink buds that open to pink flowers aging to white

'Tntiasl' Sylvan Lace: deeply cut leaves with rounded lobes and burgundy centers on clumping plants

Tinantia pringlei
SPOTTED WIDOW'S TEARS

Commelinaceae

Zones 7–11
Mountains of northeastern Mexico.
Tinantia pringlei resembles its relative, the houseplant spiderwort (*Tradescantia* spp.), with purple stems clothed in clasping, lance-shaped, slightly thickened, olive-green leaves with variable purple speckling, forming mounds 12 in. (30 cm) tall and 24 in. (60 cm) wide. Small, lavender, three-petaled flowers bloom all summer long. May reseed.

CULTURE/CARE Part sun to part shade in soils of average moisture and fertility.

Tinantia pringlei

USES Small applications along border edges and pathways and on walls. Not tolerant of foot traffic.

PROPAGATION Cuttings

'Panther': good speckled form

Tolmiea menziesii
PIGGYBACK PLANT, PICKABACK PLANT

Saxifragaceae

Zones 6–9

Moist, coniferous forests from low to middle elevations, especially along streams, mainly west of the Coast and Cascade mountain ranges from Alaska to Northern California.

Related to genera *Heuchera* and *Tiarella*, *Tolmiea menziesii* forms small evergreen to semi-evergreen mounds, 12 in. (30 cm) tall and wide, of hairy, toothed, heart-shaped, midgreen leaves up to 4 in. (10 cm) wide, with 5–7 shallow lobes. Small plantlets can form at the top of petioles, "piggybacking" on the leaf blade, and can drop to the soil to form extensive colonies. Flowers occur in late spring and summer on open, 12–24 in. (30–60 cm) tall spikes, consisting of small, nodding, brownish, reddish, or purplish tubes ending in reflexed, threadlike petals with orange stamens.

CULTURE/CARE Evenly moist to wet, average to rich soils in part shade to shade. Somewhat drought tolerant.

USES Mass plant in woodland and shade gardens between larger perennials, beneath large shrubs and trees, and along pathways. Not tolerant of foot traffic. Deer and rabbit resistant.

PROPAGATION Seed, division, separation of plantlets

'Cool Gold': light green to greenish gold foliage

'Taff's Gold': green leaves irregularly spotted with gold and gold leaves spotted with green

Trachelospermum
Apocynaceae

Valuable climbers and ground covers for mild winter regions, with attractive dark green foliage and lovely fragrant flowers. They are not related to true jasmines (*Jasminum* spp.) from the olive family but to oleander (*Nerium oleander*), milkweed (*Asclepias* spp.), and periwinkle (*Vinca* spp.), a fact revealed by their milky sap.

CULTURE/CARE Fertile, average to evenly moist, well-drained soils in full sun to light shade. Provide afternoon shade in hot summer climates. Slow to establish. May take a few years for appreciable new growth and blooms. Shear in spring to encourage compact growth, if needed.

USES Medium-sized to large applications across flat ground, over protruding tree roots, and on slopes for erosion control, spreading at a slow to moderate rate. Not tolerant of foot traffic. Deer resistant. Attractive to pollinators, especially bees.

PROPAGATION Cuttings, division of rooted stems

Trachelospermum asiaticum
ASIAN STAR, ASIATIC JASMINE

Zones 7–11

Dense to open montane forests and brush, often attached to trees, from low to middle elevations in China, India, Thailand, Korea, and Japan.

Evergreen, self-clinging, twining, woody vine with thick, leathery, somewhat shiny, dark green, elliptic to oval leaves up to 2 in. (5 cm) long, which can take on reddish tones in winter. Clusters of ¾ in. (2 cm) wide, white pinwheels of sweetly fragrant flowers age to yellow in late spring and summer. Unsupported plants are less likely to flower but will trail into a ground cover 6–12 in. (15–30 cm) tall and 10 ft. (3 m) or more wide. AGM

'Ft01' Flat Mat: more prostrate selection

'Golden Memories': gold to chartreuse foliage

'Ogon-nishiki': coppery orange new growth fades to gold with green markings

'Shirofu Chirimen': slow-growing, with pink new foliage aging to cream and green, rarely flowers

'Theta': very narrow leaves emerge coppery, turning green to reveal whitish veins, and flushing bronze and red in colder seasons

Trachelospermum jasminoides
STAR JASMINE, CONFEDERATE JASMINE

Zones (7)8–11

Sunny forest edges and openings, and shrubby areas, from low to middle elevations in China, Vietnam, Korea, and Japan.

Evergreen, self-clinging, twining, woody vine with thick, leathery, somewhat shiny, dark green, elliptic to

Trachelospermum asiaticum

Trachelospermum jasminoides 'Tricolor'

Trachystemon orientalis

oblong leaves up to 4 in. (10 cm) long, often emerging purplish and flushing red in winter. Clusters of almost 1 in. (2.5 cm) wide, white, sweetly fragrant pinwheel flowers bloom in late spring and summer. Unsupported plants will trail into a ground cover, 12–18 in. (30–45 cm) tall and 12 ft. (3.6 m) or more wide. AGM

'Madison': abundant blooms, said to be hardy to zone 7

'Pink Showers': pink flowers

'Selbra' Star of Toscana: creamy white, deep yellow-centered flowers aging to light yellow

'Tricolor': new pink leaves age to variable white and green variegation, becoming mostly green

'Variegatum': dark green to gray-green leaves variably marked in cream, AGM

'Waterwheel': slow-growing, with very fine, narrow, white-veined leaves, flushing dark red to purplish in winter

'Wilsonii': deep green leaves with whitish veins and purple tones, flushing vibrant red in winter

Trachystemon orientalis
EARLY FLOWERING BORAGE, ABRAHAM-ISAAC-JACOB

Boraginaceae

Zones (5)6–9
Southern end of the Black Sea from Bulgaria through Turkey to the Caucasus.

Rhizomatous, herbaceous borage relative for shade, forming dense mats, 12–18 in. (30–45 cm) tall and 24–36 in. (60–90 cm) or more wide. Blooms emerge in early spring before the foliage on hairy, branched, purplish stalks with panicles of downward-facing, royal-blue to purple-blue flowers with white throats and reflexed and curled petals. Coarse, corrugated, bristly, heart-shaped, midgreen leaves have 6–12 in. (15–30 cm) petioles and 12 in. (30 cm) blades.

CULTURE/CARE Moist, fertile, well-drained soils in part shade to shade. Tolerant of dry shade, especially in cool summer climates, plus deep shade and sun with even moisture.

USES Weed-smothering ground cover for midsized to large applications in woodlands, on slopes, and beneath shrubs and trees, including among shallow tree roots, spreading at a moderate rate. Not tolerant of foot traffic. Deer resistant. Attractive to pollinators, especially bees.

PROPAGATION Division, root cuttings

Trifolium repens
WHITE CLOVER, DUTCH CLOVER

Fabaceae

Zones 4–9

Meadows, lawns, paths, waste ground, roadsides, and shorelines across Europe and North Africa into Central Asia.

Variable species well known as a weed in lawns introduced to temperate regions, mostly for its value as a nitrogen-fixing and forage crop. In horticulture, numerous compact, prostrate, less vigorous ornamental cultivars are useful as spreading mats, 2–4 in. (5–10 cm) tall, with prostrate, rooting stems and small, bright green, shamrock-shaped, mostly trifoliate foliage with mint-green chevrons. White flowers age to pink in globose flower heads in late spring and summer. Leaves and flowers are edible.

CULTURE/CARE Full sun to part shade in average to moist, well-drained soils. Tolerant of dryish and infertile soils. Trim or mow to refresh foliage if needed. Plants can be overvigorous in small spaces or can crowd out smaller, less vigorous plants.

USES Along pathways and border edges, between paving stones, and as a lawn alternative, growing at a fast rate. Tolerant of some foot traffic. Attractive to pollinators, especially bees.

PROPAGATION Division

4 Luck Series: cultivars with 3–4 leaflets

'Coco Mint': burgundy leaves with green bases

'Green Glow': emerald-green leaf bases and mint-green tips

'Red Green': burgundy-black leaf bases and mint-green tips overlain with red speckling

'Red Stripes': emerald-green leaf bases and mint-green tips overlain with red feathering

Trifolium repens 'Atropurpureum'

'Atropurpureum' (syns. 'Purpurascens Quadrifolium', 'Purpurascens', Pentaphyllum', Dark Dancer): often called black-leaved clover, each leaf with 3–4 maroon leaflets with green edges; listed synonyms are currently used in horticulture, but it is unclear if the cultivars are identical and, if so, which name is valid

'Dragon's Blood': tripartite leaves, leaflets with emerald-green bases and silvery to mint-green tips overlain with a central, blood-red, feathery mark

'Isabella' Limerick: tripartite leaves with glowing maroon-red leaflets with green bases and pink flowers

var. *pipolina*: micro clover with tiny foliage, mix with turf grass or use on its own as a lawn alternative

Tsuga
Pinaceae

Large forest trees of North America and Asia, characterized by finely textured needles, a pyramidal habit, a drooping leader, and a preference for even moisture. Important as specimens for large gardens and parks and in forestry for timber and pulp production. Some species offer dwarf, prostrate, or horizontally spreading forms useful as ground covers when grafted onto a low rootstock.

CULTURE/CARE Full sun to part shade in well-drained soils of average to medium moisture. Provide afternoon shade in hot, humid summer climates. Protect from drying winds. Intolerant of drought.

USES Dwarf cultivars can be used as specimens or mass-planted over medium-sized to large areas, growing at a slow to moderate rate. Use as a general cover, on slopes, on walls, or among rocks. Not tolerant of foot traffic.

PROPAGATION Grafting

Tsuga canadensis
CANADIAN HEMLOCK, EASTERN HEMLOCK

Zones 3–7

Moist woods and slopes, rocky hillsides and ridges, and wooded ravines at moderate elevations from Nova Scotia to Minnesota south to Alabama.

Dense, elegant, pyramidal conifer that can reach 100 ft. (30 m) tall. Small, dark green needles about ½ in. (1.3 cm) long have two white stomatal bands on their undersides, presented on flattened, spreading branches as two opposite rows with a row of smaller needles on top, along with small, light brown cones.

Tsuga canadensis 'Pendula'

'Cole's Prostrate': prostrate to weeping mounds or mats, 6–12 in. (15–30 cm) tall and 4–5 ft. (1.2–1.5 m) wide, growing 3–5 in. (7.5–12.5 cm) per year, with dark green needles contrasting with silver-white bark

'Gracilis': horizontally spreading branches with dark green needles, 24 in. (60 cm) tall and 4 ft. (1.2 m) wide, growing 1–3 in. (2.5–7.5 cm) per year

'Jeddeloh': bird's nest hemlock with bright green needles on horizontally spreading branches, 24 in. (60 cm) tall and 4 ft. (1.2 m) wide, growing 3–5 in. (7.5–12.5 cm) per year, AGM

'Pendula': larger weeping cultivar, typically 4–5 ft. (1.2–1.5 m) tall and 8–10 ft. (2.4–3 m) wide, but can be maintained at 2–3 ft. (0.6–1 m) tall with pruning, grows 12–15 in. (30–38 cm) per year

Tsuga heterophylla

WESTERN HEMLOCK

Zones 6–9

Sea level to middle elevation montane forests in a coastal band from Alaska to Northern California and in the Canadian Rockies and the northern United States.

Elegant, pyramidal conifer with a distinctive drooping leader can reach up to 150 ft. (45 m) tall in cultivation but is much taller in the wild. Small, shiny, dark green needles are variable in size, ¼–¾ in. (6–20 mm) long, with two white stomatal bands on the underside of each leaf. Brown cones are pendulous.

'Thorsen's Weeping': emerald-green needles on prostrate branches, 4 in. (10 cm) tall and 5 ft. (1.5 m) wide, growing 3–6 in. (7.5–15 cm) per year

U

Umbilicus oppositifolius

LAMB'S TAIL, GOLD DROP

Crassulaceae

Zones 5–9

Wet crevices, banks, and rocky woods in shaded mountain areas of the Caucasus.

Like a lush ground cover sedum dreaming of becoming a golden chain tree, *U. oppositifolius*, formerly known as *Chiastophyllum oppositifolium*, has large, succulent, ovate, scalloped leaves, 1–2 in. (2.5–5 cm) long and nearly as wide, with pendulous panicles of bright yellow, rounded buds that barely seem to open on brownish red, 6–8 in. (15–20 cm) stems, from midspring into summer. Plants, 4–6 in. (10–15 cm) tall and 12 in. (30 cm) or more wide, can flush red with summer stress or winter cold and remain evergreen in milder zones. AGM

CULTURE/CARE Part sun to part shade in evenly moist, well-drained soils.

USES Shaded rockeries, border edges, walls, or containers. Spreads at a slow to moderate rate. Not tolerant of foot traffic.

PROPAGATION Division

'Jim's Pride' (syn. 'Frosted Jade'): leaves with variable creamy white edges

'Solar Yellow': seed strain seemingly not much different from the species

Umbilicus oppositifolius

V

Vaccinium
Ericaceae

Best known for the commercial tallbush blueberry (*V. corymbosum*), this genus offers a number of other tough, extremely hardy, ground-covering shrubs that provide beauty and function plus valued fruits such as cranberries, wild blueberries, and lingonberries. Flowers and fruit are also much appreciated by pollinators and wildlife.

CULTURE/CARE Full to part sun in organically rich, acidic, evenly moist but well-drained soils. Tolerant of poor soils, drought, and part shade, though may produce less fruit. Possibly intolerant of heat and humidity in hot summer climates, except *V. crassifolium*. *Vaccinium macrocarpon* is tolerant of wet soils, and *V. angustifolium* and *V. vitis-idaea* are salt tolerant. Stems of *V. angustifolium* can be sheared back every few years to refresh plants.

USES Mass plant to achieve good, timely coverage. Use in cool-climate gardens, exposed sites, among rocks, along pathways, and in edible gardens. *Vaccinium macrocarpon* is tolerant of occasional foot traffic and could be used as a lawn alternative. *Vaccinium vitis-idaea* is deer resistant. Attractive to pollinators, especially bees, and birds for the fruit.

PROPAGATION Cuttings, layering, division, seed

Vaccinium angustifolium
LOWBUSH BLUEBERRY

Zones 2–8
Headlands, rock outcrops, dry and sandy areas, pine or peaty barrens, bogs, regenerating forests, and abandoned pastures from sea level to high elevations in most of eastern North America except the U.S. Southeast.

Widespread, ecologically adaptable, culturally and economically important, low-growing shrub that produces wild blueberries harvested for homemade jams, jellies, and pies and commercially from planted fields and managed wild populations. Plants, 4–12 in. (10–30 cm) or more tall and 12–24 in. (30–60 cm) wide, form extensive semi-open to dense colonies from spreading rhizomes with deciduous, green to blue-green, elliptic, 1.5 in. (4 cm) long leaves with fine marginal serrations, turning crimson, scarlet,

Vaccinium angustifolium

and purple in fall. Pendulous, urn-shaped, waxy, white spring flowers with a tinge of pink become pale green fruit, ripening through pink, purple, and finally blue when ripe and sweet in summer. Self-fertile but pollination from another clone can increase fruit production.

'Burgundy': burgundy new growth, with abundant light blue fruit and excellent fall color

'Top Hat': hybrid with *V. corymbosum*, the tallbush and common cultivated blueberry, 24 in. (60 cm) tall and wide

Vaccinium crassifolium
CREEPING BLUEBERRY

Zones 6–10
Coastal plains, pine barrens, disturbed sites, and open habitats from Georgia to Virginia.

Creeping, evergreen mat, 3–12 in. (7.5–30 cm) tall and 4–6 ft. (1.2–1.8 m) wide, with prostrate and ascending, spreading, wiry, reddish stems clad in oval to broadly lance-shaped, glossy, dark green leaves emerging bronze-flushed. Clusters of pink, bell-shaped spring flowers sometimes become purplish black fruit.

'Well's Delight': low-growing, 3–8 in. (7.5–20 cm) tall, with smaller leaves

Vaccinium macrocarpon 'Hamilton'

Vaccinium vitis-idaea

Vaccinium macrocarpon
AMERICAN CRANBERRY

Zones 1–8

Bogs, swamps, shorelines, and headlands from sea level to high elevations in most of eastern North America, except the U.S. Southeast.

The Thanksgiving cranberry is a low-growing, woody, evergreen subshrub from constantly moist habitats, growing 2–6 in. (5–15 cm) or more tall and 12–24 in. (30–60 cm) wide, with wiry, prostrate to ascending stems and small, elliptic leaves with slightly downcurved margins, bluish green undersides, and a burgundy flush in winter. Axillary, nodding, white to pink, self-fertile late spring to early summer flowers are not bell-shaped but have tightly appressed stamens and pistils with four often curled, strongly reflexed petals. Relatively large, pink to red fruit ripen in autumn.

'Ben Lear': early ripening with large burgundy-red fruit, very productive

'Early Black': early ripening, large purple-red fruit and burgundy winter foliage

'Hamilton': compact, dwarf mounds, 4 in. (10 cm) tall by 6 in. (15 cm) wide, with good burgundy winter color

'Lohzam' Lo-Hugger: fruit lasts well into winter among red-bronze winter foliage

'Pilgrim': late-ripening, very large, bright red fruit

'Stevens': commercial cultivar producing large, deep red fruit

'WSU': productive with large, bright red fruit

Vaccinium vitis-idaea
LINGONBERRY, PARTRIDGEBERRY

Zones 2–8

Widespread and circumboreal across the northern half of North America and northern Eurasia in boreal taiga, beneath jack pine; in muskegs, bogs, and tundra; and on rocky barrens, heaths, headlands, cliffs, and mountain summits.

Tough, widespread, ecologically adaptable, low-growing evergreen shrub with fruit harvested for homemade jams, jellies, and pies, and sometimes grown commercially, especially in Northern Europe. Dense colonies, 4–18 in. (10–45 cm) tall, expand via upright to creeping stems that may also spread underground. Small, oval, glossy green foliage is reddish when young. Terminal clusters of pendulous, bell-shaped, waxy, white and pink-tinged spring flowers become pale green fruit, ripening to bright red in late summer and fall. Self-fertile but pollination from another clone can increase fruit production.

'Erntesegen': vigorous and very productive, with large, mildly flavored, light red fruit

Koralle Group: commercially important, vigorous plants produce an abundance of intense, tart fruit, AGM

'Meliro' Miss Cherry: bushy, compact, ornamental, and productive

'Red Candy': bushy, compact, ornamental, and productive

'Red Pearl': large, mild-flavored fruit ripening earlier than Koralle Group

Valeriana supina
DWARF VALERIAN

Caprifoliaceae

Zones 4–9

Screes and other rocky sites, and along streams at high elevations in the European Alps, often on calcareous soils.

Uncommon, herbaceous to semi-evergreen, dense, creeping, rhizomatous mats, 4 in. (10 cm) tall and 24 in. (60 cm) or more wide, with aromatic, oval, bright green leaves on rooting stems. Rounded clusters of fragrant, pale lavender-pink, late spring flowers are held just above the foliage.

CULTURE/CARE Full to part shade in varied, well-drained soil types.

USES Rockeries and alpine gardens, along pathways and border edges, and beneath deciduous trees and shrubs, spreading at a moderate to fast rate. Not tolerant of foot traffic. Attractive to pollinators, especially bees and butterflies.

PROPAGATION Division, seed

Vancouveria
Berberidaceae

Three rhizomatous species named for eighteenth-century navigator and explorer George Vancouver resemble their Eurasian cousins in the genus *Epimedium*, with attractive foliage and small, intriguing flowers for the woodland garden. Their delicate, nodding, parachute-like flowers have reflexed petals and stamens appressed around the pistil, blooming in airy sprays for short periods in spring.

CULTURE/CARE Part shade to shade in average to rich, evenly moist, well-drained, sandy or clay-based soils. Somewhat drought tolerant once established, especially *V. chrysantha*. Possibly intolerant of heat and humidity in hot summer climates.

USES Woodland gardens, along pathways, and between and beneath deciduous and coniferous trees and shrubs. Clumping at first, later spreading at a slow to moderate rate. Not tolerant of foot traffic. Deer and rabbit resistant.

PROPAGATION Division

Vancouveria chrysantha
GOLDEN INSIDE-OUT FLOWER,
SISKIYOU INSIDE-OUT FLOWER

Zones 6–9

Dry forests and chaparral in the Siskiyou and Klamath mountain ranges of Southern Oregon and Northern California.

Colonies of evergreen to semi-evergreen, rhizomatously spreading plants, 8–12 in. (20–30 cm) tall, with compound, lobed foliage and leaflets that resemble a duck's foot, emerging orange to reddish and aging to bright and then dark green. Yellow flowers have orange stamens on burgundy stems.

Vancouveria hexandra
WHITE INSIDE-OUT FLOWER,
AMERICAN BARRENWORT

Zones 5–9

Moist, mixed, and coniferous forests from low to high elevations, from Washington to Northern California west of the Cascades.

Mostly herbaceous, rhizomatously spreading, 12–18 in. (30–45 cm) tall, white-flowered colonies with compound, lobed foliage and leaflets that resemble a duck's foot, emerging bright green and aging to dark green, turning yellow in autumn.

Vancouveria planipetala
REDWOOD IVY, INSIDE-OUT FLOWER

Zones 6–9

Coast redwood and other coastal forests from the Siskiyou and Klamath mountain ranges of Southern Oregon to Big Sur in Central California.

Evergreen, rhizomatous, 8–12 in. (20–30 cm) tall colonies with tiny white flowers and compound, lobed, shiny, somewhat leathery foliage emerging bronze-orange and aging to dark green. Possibly herbaceous in colder zones.

Verbena
Verbenaceae

Few garden annuals or perennials produce as many flowers as verbenas, the trailing vervains, now known scientifically as genus *Glandularia*. From midspring until frost, their sprawling and interlacing stems are topped with showy clusters of small, tubular flowers

Vancouveria hexandra

Vancouveria planipetala

Verbena canadensis 'Homestead Purple'

in a range of bold colors. Though technically hardy in many regions, they can be short-lived, especially in wet winter soils. If ever a case were to be made to plant annual ground covers, the vervains would be top candidates.

CULTURE/CARE Easy to grow in full sun in free-draining soils of average to low fertility and average to low moisture, performing well in drought, heat, and rocky soils. Intolerant of winter wet, especially in overly rich, moist soils. Shear to refresh during the growing season and in early spring. May reseed.

USES Mass plant as a general cover over small to medium-sized areas and along stairways, pathways, and border edges, on slopes, in rock gardens, and spilling over walls. Spreads at a moderate to fast rate. Not tolerant of foot traffic. Deer resistant. Attractive to pollinators, especially bees, butterflies, and hummingbirds.

PROPAGATION Seed, cuttings

Verbena bipinnatifida
PRAIRIE VERBENA, PLAINS VERBENA

Zones (4)5–8

Open grassy areas, prairies, and disturbed sites in the Central and southern United States.

Similar to *V. canadensis* but smaller, growing to 4–6 in. (10–15 cm) tall and 12–18 in. (30–45 cm) wide, with more dissected foliage and pink, lavender, and purple flowers.

'Valley Lavender': vibrant purple flowers

Verbena canadensis
ROSE VERBENA, ROSE VERVAIN

Zones 6–10

Prairies of low to moderate moisture, limestone and sandstone glades, meadows, rocky and open woods and wooded bluffs, on dry and disturbed sites, and along roadways across the Central and eastern United States.

Dense, spreading clumps, 6–12 in. (15–30 cm) tall and 24–36 in. (60–90 cm) wide, of somewhat glossy, textured, lance-shaped, scalloped to lobed, 3–4 in. (7.5–10 cm) long midgreen foliage on trailing and ascending, interlacing, pubescent, rooting stems. Evergreen in mild winter climates. Round flower clusters, 1–2 in. (2.5–5 cm) wide, hold lightly fragrant, tubular, red, magenta, purple, pink, or white blooms, flared into five notched petals, opening from the outside inward from spring to fall.

'Blue Princess': hybrid with nicely fragrant lavender flowers, zone 7

'Homestead Purple': lavender-purple to magenta-purple flowers

'Homestead Red': bright red flowers

'Lapis Lazuli Blue': hybrid with bluish purple flowers, zone 7

'Snow Flurry': white flowers

'Texas Appleblossom': hybrid with light pink flowers lightening to white with a white eye, zone 7

Verbena peruviana
PERUVIAN VERBENA

Zones 6–10
Dry mountainous areas, roadsides, and pastures of Peru, Argentina, and Brazil.
Similar to *V. canadensis* but smaller in all respects, with prostrate stems, 2–3 in. (5–7.5 cm) tall and 12–16 in. (30–40 cm) wide, and bright red flowers with white eyes.

Veronica
Plantaginaceae

Best known for the spiked speedwell, *V. spicata*, with its upright inflorescences of purple-blue, pink, or white flowers, this genus contains about 500 species, many of which are low-growing and mat-forming. Some offer the classic upright spikes, but more often flowers are held in tight to loose clusters or very short spikes. In addition to those treated here, other less common species include *V. allionii* and its cultivar 'Blue Pixie', *V. armena*, *V. montana* and its cultivar 'Corinne Tremaine', and *V. oltensis*.
CULTURE/CARE Most prefer full sun to part sun in average to dry, well-drained soils of average fertility. Many show salt tolerance.
USES Rock gardens, hell strips, between stepping stones and pavers, and along pathways, stairways, and border edges. *Veronica liwanensis*, *V. pectinata*, *V. repens*, and *V. whitleyi* make good lawn alternatives and are tolerant of light foot traffic. Plants spread at a slow to moderate rate depending on the species. Deer and rabbit resistant. Attractive to pollinators, especially bees and butterflies.
PROPAGATION Division, layering, cuttings, seed

Veronica gentianoides
GENTIAN SPEEDWELL

Zones 3–9
Damp, open habitats including grasslands and alpine meadows, and in forests to high elevations in Turkey, Iran, Ukraine, and Western Russia.
Relatively large, glossy, oblong to elliptic, midgreen leaves form rosettes spreading via rhizomes into lush mats. Evergreen in mild winter climates. Upright, 12–16 in. (30–40 cm) tall, early summer spikes with much reduced stem leaves produce white, light blue, or deep blue flowers, sometimes reblooming with deadheading. Useful for small applications in evenly moist, well-drained soils. Tolerant of light shade. Intolerant of drought.

'Barbara Sherwood': powder-blue flowers, AGM

'Tissington White': large white to palest blue flowers with delicate light blue veins

'Variegata': variegated with cream to white margins

Veronica spicata subsp. incana
SILVER SPEEDWELL, WOOLLY SPEEDWELL

Zones (3)4–8
Steppe and meadows of Eastern Europe and Russia.
Striking plants, formerly *V. incana*, grow as mounds or mats, 6 in. (15 cm) tall, spreading slowly to 12–24 in. (30–60 cm) wide, via short, horizontal, sometimes rooting stems with distinctive, 2 in. (5 cm) long, semi-evergreen, densely hairy, silver-white to gray-green, lance-shaped leaves with serrated edges. Upright, tapering spikes of purple-blue flowers are 12–18 in. (30–45 cm) tall in early summer. Plant in hot, dry spots with well-drained or gravelly soils. Likely intolerant of humid summer heat. Provide good winter drainage. AGM

'Pure Silver': bold silver foliage, more tolerant of hot and humid conditions and heavier, moister soils

'Silbersee' (syn. 'Silver Sea'): bold silver foliage and compact habit

Veronica liwanensis
TURKISH SPEEDWELL

Zones 3–9
River valleys, dry steppe, and rock crevices at moderate elevations in the mountains of Turkey.

Veronica spicata subsp. *incana*

Veronica liwanensis

Veronica 'Tidal Pool'

Flat, dense, evergreen, rooting mats, 1–2 in. (2.5–5 cm) tall and 18–24 in. (45–60 cm) or more wide, studded with small, erect, truncated spikes of white-eyed, bright cobalt-blue flowers in spring, aging to lavender-purple. Small, shiny, oval, dark green leaves with lightly serrated margins can develop purple tones in heat and sun. Excellent drought tolerance. Provide good drainage. Tolerant of light shade and salt. May appreciate afternoon shade in hot summer climates.

Cultivars are hybrids with *V. pectinata*, with foliage resembling *V. liwanensis*.

'Blue Reflection': blue flowers

'Po18s' Snowmass: white flowers with blue eyes

'Reavis' Crystal River: light blue flowers

Veronica pectinata
WOOLLY SPEEDWELL

Zones (3)4–9

Steppe, dry and rocky habitats, olive groves, and oak and pine forests from Bulgaria into Asia Minor.

Woolly, gray-green, deeply serrated to pinnatifid foliage in flat, dense, evergreen, rooting mats, 2 in. (5 cm) tall and 18–24 in. (45–60 cm) or more wide, with masses of white-eyed, true-blue flowers fading to lavender in short, dense, erect spikes over a long period from early spring into summer. Drought and salt tolerant. Tolerant of a wide range of well-drained soils.

'Rosea': pink flowers

'Tidal Pool': hybrid of *V. armena* and *V. pectinata* 'Rosea', with white-eyed, cobalt-blue to lavender-blue flowers, smooth leaves, and excellent vigor

Veronica petraea
SPEEDWELL

Zones 4–9
Rocky places, including scree slopes, in the Caucasus.

Uncommon species forming lush, semi-evergreen mats with a looser, more open habit, 4 in. (10 cm) tall and spreading indefinitely by prostrate and ascending, rooting stems, topped with short, open spikes of white-eyed, lavender-blue flowers with purple veins in mid- to late spring with occasional rebloom in summer and fall. Rounded to egg-shaped, broadly toothed, midgreen leaves flush bronze when young and reddish to purplish in cold weather.

'Madame Mercier': light blue to lavender-blue flowers with purple veins

'Waterperry Blue': purportedly a hybrid but much resembles V. petraea, mounding to mat-forming, 4–6 in. (10–15 cm) tall and 16 in. (40 cm) wide, evergreen in milder climates, salt tolerant

'Whitewater': white-flowered sport of 'Waterperry Blue'

Veronica prostrata
PROSTRATE SPEEDWELL, CREEPING SPEEDWELL

Zones 4–8
Steppe, open grasslands, and pastures across most of mainland Europe.

Low-growing, semi-evergreen mats, 4 in. (10 cm) tall, spreading indefinitely by prostrate, rooting stems, topped with upright, 8 in. (20 cm) tall spikes of light to deep blue flowers in late spring and early summer, with occasional rebloom in summer and fall. Linear to egg-shaped, midgreen leaves are 1.5 in. (4 cm) long, with smooth to toothed margins. Salt tolerant. AGM

'Aztec Gold': bright blue flowers with gold foliage in sun and chartreuse in less light, said to have a better habit and foliage color than 'Trehane'

'Dick's Wine' Twilight Lilac (syn. 'Wine'): lavender-pink flowers

'Heavenly Blue': sapphire-blue flowers

'Lilac Time': lavender-pink flowers

'Spode Blue': light blue flowers, AGM

'Trehane': gold to chartreuse foliage with dark blue flowers

'Verbrig' Goldwell: green leaves with golden yellow margins and bright blue flowers

Veronica repens
CREEPING SPEEDWELL

Zones 3–9
Moist, middle altitude mountain habitats in France, Spain, and Morocco.

Dense, low-growing, evergreen mats, 1–2 in. (2.5–5 cm) tall, spreading indefinitely by prostrate, rooting stems covered in short, truncated spikes of white flowers in mid- to late spring. Oval to rounded leaves are light to midgreen. Prefers average to moist soils.

'Sunshine': gold to chartreuse foliage, sometimes shy to flower

Veronica umbrosa
SPEEDWELL

Zones 4–9
Alpine habitats of Ukraine, the Caucasus, and Western Asia.

More open and airy, semi-evergreen mounds or mats, 4–6 in. (10–15 cm) tall and 12–24 in. (30–60 cm) wide, with rooting stems and small, shiny, lance-shaped to rounded, midgreen leaves with lightly serrated margins, flushing purple in winter. Burgundy-stemmed spikes of loosely held, white-eyed, midblue to lavender flowers appear in mid- to late spring, reblooming sporadically through summer. Salt tolerant. Previously known as V. peduncularis.

'Georgia Blue': likely the only cultivar named for the Republic of Georgia, not the state, with rich blue flowers

Veronica whitleyi
WHITLEY'S SPEEDWELL

Zones 3–9
Possibly of horticultural origin.

Hairy, gray-green, deeply serrated to pinnatifid, feathery foliage in dense, evergreen, rooting mats, 2–4 in. (5–10 cm) tall and 18–24 in. (45–60 cm) wide, covered with masses of white-eyed, true-blue to lavender-blue flowers in short, dense spikes in mid- to late spring, reblooming in summer and fall. Tolerant of heat, humidity, and drought.

Veronica 'Whitewater'

Veronica 'Waterperry Blue'

Veronica repens

Veronica prostrata 'Verbrig' Goldwell

Veronica umbrosa 'Georgia Blue'

Vinca
Apocynaceae

Among the most popular ground covers for shade because of their vigor, ease of growth, durability, beauty, and impenetrable, weed-smothering mats—not to mention that *V. minor* is evergreen even in zone 4. *Vinca major* is also commonly used in containers and hanging baskets. Unfortunately, both species are invasive in numerous regions. They should be avoided in gardens close to natural areas. In urban and suburban gardens, away from natural spaces, they could be safely used. Variegated and gold cultivars of *V. minor* are somewhat less vigorous.

CULTURE/CARE *Vinca major* prefers full sun to part shade. *Vinca minor* prefers part sun to part shade and is tolerant of sun with good moisture but can become bleached and lack vigor. Both species appreciate average to moist, well-drained soils and are tolerant of deep shade and periods of drought.

USES Woodland gardens, along pathways, cascading over walls, on banks and slopes for erosion control, and as a lawn alternative, especially *V. minor*. Plants spread quickly once established. Tolerant of occasional foot traffic. Deer and rabbit resistant. Attractive to pollinators, especially bees and butterflies.

PROPAGATION Division, layering, cuttings

Vinca major
GREATER PERIWINKLE, BIG LEAF PERIWINKLE

Zones (6)7–9
Scrub and forested habitats of western and central Mediterranean Europe.

Vigorous, even rambunctious, evergreen ground cover forming dense mats, 12–18 in. (30–45 cm) tall, and spreading indefinitely via sprawling, intertwining, nonflowering, rooting shoots, 24–36 in. (60–90 cm) or more long. Oval, egg-shaped or lance-shaped, mid- to dark green, leathery leaves, 2–4 in. (5–10 cm) long and 1 in. (2.5 cm) wide, with fine marginal hairs. Solitary, axillary, 2 in. (5 cm) wide, upward-facing, funnel-shaped, lilac-blue flowers have a central white star and five wedge- to diamond-shaped petals often tilted counterclockwise, resembling a whirligig. Blooms in early spring and intermittently thereafter.

'Expoflora': broadly variegated creamy white to pale yellow margins around dark, light, and gray-green mottled centers

Vinca major 'Maculata'

Vinca major 'Variegata' trailing over a wall

Vinca minor

Viola 'Silver Samurai'

'Maculata': variegated with variable gold centers and green margins

var. *oxyloba*: starlike flowers with narrow petals

'Variegata': dark green leaves with creamy white margins, AGM

'Wojo's Jem': variegated leaves with variable creamy white to pale yellow centers

Vinca minor
DWARF PERIWINKLE, CREEPING MYRTLE

Zones 4–8

In fields and within and at the edges of woodlands and forests across most of Europe east to the Baltic States, Crimea, and Turkey, excluding Great Britain and Scandinavia.

Vigorous, evergreen ground cover forming dense mats, 4–6 in. (10–15 cm) tall, spreading indefinitely via sprawling, intertwining, nonflowering, rooting shoots, 12–24 in. (30–60 cm) long. Oblong to oval, shiny, dark green, leathery leaves, 1 in. (2.5 cm) long and ½ in. (1.3 cm) wide. Solitary, axillary, 1 in. (2.5 cm) wide, upward-facing, funnel-shaped, lilac-blue flowers have a central white star and five wedge-shaped petals often tilted counterclockwise, resembling a whirligig. Blooms profusely in early spring and intermittently thereafter.

'24 Carat': chartreuse to gold foliage darkens to green

f. *alba* (syn 'Alba'): white flowers

f. *alba* 'Alba Variegata': white flowers, variable creamy yellow to yellow leaf margins

f. *alba* 'Gertrude Jekyll': white flowers

'Argenteovariegata': variegated with creamy white margins, AGM

'Atropurpurea': warm purple flowers, AGM

'Azurea Flore Pleno': semidouble blue flowers, AGM

'Bowles's Variety': violet-blue flowers, AGM

'Illumination': gold foliage with narrow green margins

'Parvin' Moonlit: double blue flowers, leaves with creamy yellow edges and mottled interiors

'Ralph Shugert': leaves with narrow white margins, AGM

Viola
Violaceae

These dainty, somewhat old-fashioned relatives of the larger flowered winter pansies have a long history of cultivation. The fragrant flowers of V. *odorata*, for instance, were very popular in the nineteenth and early twentieth centuries. These ground covers can be used in part shade and morning sun, where their ability to self-seed lightly to moderately is an asset for expanding and enhancing coverage. The edible, bilaterally symmetrical flowers have five rounded to oval petals—two upper petals, two lateral petals, and a lower petal—usually with white and yellow throats. Hundreds of species grow primarily in the temperate Northern Hemisphere. Many not commonly in cultivation and not treated here can also be used, including *V. cucullata*, *V. glabella*, *V. palustris*, and *V. blanda*.

CULTURE/CARE Fertile, evenly moist, well-drained soils in part sun to part shade. Many species are tolerant of periods of drought and full sun in cooler summer climates. Shear hard to refresh clumps as needed.

USES Small to medium-sized applications, between and beneath deciduous shrubs and trees, around late-emerging perennials, in woodland gardens, and along pathways, spreading at a slow to moderate rate. Not tolerant of foot traffic. Deer resistant.

PROPAGATION Seed, division

Viola corsica

Viola corsica
CORSICAN VIOLET

Zones 3–8
Mountains of mainland Italy, Corsica, and Sardinia.
Resembles the better-known *V. cornuta* and its many hybrids, but plants are much hardier; more tolerant of sun, heat, and drought; and typically longer lived, lasting 5–10 years and reseeding gently to freely into colonies over time. Blooms profusely over a long period from early spring to late fall, with fragrant, 1 in. (2.5 cm) wide, lavender and purple flowers with yellow centers and dark purple veins and a white glow on the triangular lower petal. Plants reach 6–8 in. (15–20 cm) tall and 12 in. (30 cm) wide.

Viola odorata

Viola grypoceras var. exilis
CYCLAMEN-LEAVED VIOLET

Zones 3–8
Grassy slopes and thickets, from low to moderately high elevations in China, Korea, and Japan.
Semi-evergreen to herbaceous ground cover with striking silver-gray and dark green, heart-shaped leaves with red undersides, resembling cyclamen, forming dense clumps, 2–6 in. (5–15 cm) tall and 8–12 in. (20–30 cm) wide, via procumbent stems. Small lavender to pink flowers are produced shyly to freely in spring and can readily self-seed.

'Sylettas': exceptionally bold silver variegation

Viola riviniana Purpurea Group

Viola odorata
SWEET VIOLET, ENGLISH VIOLET

Zones 4–9

Forest edges and clearings, fields, and hedgerows, especially on calcareous soils, across large areas of Europe and Asia.

Sweet violet has enjoyed many periods of popularity, from the ancient Greeks to the Napoleonic era to Victorian England. French and British breeding work created many cultivars that are much less appreciated now than in previous eras. This herbaceous to evergreen, stoloniferous species has mid- to dark green, somewhat glossy, kidney- to heart-shaped leaves with scalloped edges in rosettes 6–10 in. (15–25 cm) tall and 12–18 in. (30–45 cm) wide. Beautifully fragrant, typically lavender-purple or white flowers are borne in early spring. Plants also spread by seed.

'Alba': white flowers

'Alba Plena': double white flowers

'Blue Remington': hybrid with large purple-blue flowers

'Coeur d'Alsace': hybrid with rose-pink flowers

'Duchesse de Parme': hybrid with double bluish lavender flowers with a strong fragrance

'Königin Charlotte' (syn. 'Queen Charlotte'): hybrid with purple flowers with a strong fragrance

'Reine des Neiges': hybrid with palest blue flowers aging to white

Rosea Group: pink flowers

'Royal Robe': hybrid with royal-purple flowers

'White Czar': hybrid with white flowers with a green central glow

Viola riviniana **Purpurea Group**
COMMON DOG VIOLET, WOOD VIOLET

Zones 3–9

Woods and woodland edges, hedgerows, heaths, pastures, and rocky mountain habitats on a wide range of soil types throughout Eurasia and northwest Africa.

Previously thought to be *V. labradorica*, the species commonly in cultivation is actually a purple-leaved selection of *V. riviniana* referred to as Purpurea Group. Small, herbaceous to evergreen, 2–6 in. (5–15 cm) tall and 3–6 in. (7.5–15 cm) wide, basal rosettes produce somewhat glossy, heart-shaped, 1 in. (2.5 cm) wide, burgundy-infused dark green leaves with scalloped edges and reddish undersides. Small lavender flowers can bloom continuously from spring to fall in cool summer climates or take a summer break in hot summer climates. Plants can reseed readily, creating a semiclosed to closed cover over time.

Viola sororia
COMMON BLUE VIOLET, COMMON MEADOW VIOLET

Zones 3–8

Moist to mesic prairies, thickets, pastures, disturbed sites, open woodlands, and within and along streams or lakes from sea level to high elevations across Canada and the western and northern United States.

Herbaceous, mid- to dark green, oval to heart-shaped, smooth to pubescent leaves with scalloped edges are produced in basal rosettes, 4–8 in. (10–20 cm) tall and 6–12 in. (15–30 cm) wide. Violet to purple spring flowers with dark veins radiating from white and yellow centers sometimes rebloom in late summer and fall. Spreads slowly by short rhizomes. Self-seeds freely.

'Albiflora': white flowers with yellow centers and purple veins, AGM

'Dark Freckles': palest purple flowers with dark purple speckles

'Freckles': white flowers with purple speckles

'Priceana' (syn. var. *priceana*): often called Confederate violet, with white to pale purple flowers with dark purple veins

'Rubra': reddish purple flowers

Viola sororia 'Dark Freckles'

Viola walteri
PROSTRATE BLUE VIOLET, WALTER'S VIOLET

Zones 6–8

Rich woodlands, high floodplains, and rocky ledges in low to high elevations from Texas to Virginia south to Florida.

Trailing, procumbent, sometimes rooting stems form dense mats, 3–5 in. (7.5–12.5 cm) tall and 10–16 in. (25–40 cm) or more wide, of small, often cupped, heart-shaped green leaves with a silver overlay. Small lavender flowers bloom from spring to fall. Good drought tolerance.

'Silver Gem': silver leaves with gray-green veins and reddish undersides; though unrelated, two similar hybrids, V. 'Dancing Geisha' and V. 'Silver Samurai', also have dramatic silvered leaves, albeit with sharply serrated margins.

Viola walteri 'Silver Gem'

Waldsteinia
Rosaceae

Quietly attractive with a reputation for ease of growth, toughness, and low maintenance, these semi-evergreen to evergreen species have somewhat shiny, smooth to sparsely hairy, trifoliate leaves with wedge-shaped, toothed leaflets in handsome basal mounds. Small clusters of bright golden yellow, five-petaled spring flowers with deeper yellow stamens are held just above the foliage. Dry fruits are non-ornamental and inedible. Sometimes placed in the genus *Geum*, but differing in being stoloniferous and/or rhizomatous versus clumping and preferring part shade versus sun.

CULTURE/CARE Easy to grow in average to moist, well-drained soils in part sun to part shade. Tolerant of diverse soil types, periods of drought, and full sun with good moisture. *Waldsteinia fragarioides* is salt tolerant. Likely intolerant of heat and humidity in hot summer climates.

USES Woodland and shade gardens, beneath deciduous shrubs and trees, along pathways and stairways, on slopes, and as a lawn alternative, spreading at a slow to moderate rate. Tolerant of occasional foot traffic. Deer and rabbit resistant. Attractive to pollinators, especially bees.

PROPAGATION Division, seed

Waldsteinia fragarioides
APPALACHIAN STRAWBERRY,
COMMON BARREN STRAWBERRY

Zones 4–8

Moist to dry hardwood or mixed forests from sea level to moderate elevations in northeastern North America.

Slowly spreading, rhizomatous mounds, 3–6 in. (7.5–15 cm) tall and 6–12 in. (15–30 cm) wide, form nonaggressive colonies with clusters of 3–8 flowers, each less than 1 in. (2.5 cm) wide, in early to midspring. Foliage can flush bronze in winter. Sometimes recognized as *Geum fragarioides*. The similar *W. lobata*, the Piedmont barren strawberry, is sometimes grown.

Waldsteinia ternata

Waldsteinia ternata

BARREN STRAWBERRY, SIBERIAN WALDSTEINIA

Zones 3–8

Moist forests in Central and Eastern Europe, disjunct by 3000 miles (5000 km) to northeastern China, eastern Russia, and Japan.

Most commonly cultivated and most effective as a ground cover, with stoloniferous and rhizomatous mounds, 4–6 in. (10–15 cm) tall and 12–18 in. (30–45 cm) wide, forming nonaggressive colonies over time. Yellow flowers up to 1 in. (2.5 cm) wide bloom in small clusters of 1–3 in mid- to late spring. Sometimes recognized as *Geum ternatum*. The similar Eastern European *W. geoides* is sometimes grown.

Woodwardia
Blechnaceae

Two of the three North American *Woodwardia* species are rhizomatous ferns of wet habitats that can be useful as tall ground covers in moist to wet situations.

CULTURE/CARE Part sun to shade in rich, average to moist or wet soils. Despite hailing from wet habitats, both species presented here do well in average garden conditions with reasonable moisture, especially in shade, though they will spread more slowly with less water. Tolerant of full sun with ample moisture as well as deep shade.

USES Medium-sized to large applications in native and woodland gardens and in moist sites. Not tolerant of foot traffic. Deer and rabbit resistant.

PROPAGATION Division, spore

Woodwardia areolata

Woodwardia areolata
NETTED FERN, NET-VEINED CHAIN FERN

Zones 3–9

Acidic bogs, swamps, seeps, and wet woods from sea level to moderate elevations from eastern Texas to Florida, north to Nova Scotia.

Herbaceous, rhizomatous fern with light to midgreen, somewhat glossy or waxy, lightly serrated, arching, sterile fronds, 12–24 in. (30–60 cm) long and 4–8 in. (10–20 cm) wide, with netted veins, the alternating, lance-shaped pinnae cut not quite to the stipe, creating a webbed look. Fronds emerge pink in spring from bronzy fiddleheads. Fertile summer fronds produce spores in chainlike rows along very narrow, linear pinnae. Can spread into large colonies over time via shallow, branching rhizomes. Sometimes recognized scientifically as *Lorinseria areolata*.

Woodwardia virginica
VIRGINIA FERN, AMERICAN CHAIN FERN

Zones 3–9

Acidic bogs, swamps, marshes, and roadside ditches, avoiding calcareous soils, at low elevations mainly on the Eastern Coastal Plain from eastern Texas to Florida, north to Nova Scotia and inland to the Great Lakes.

Relatively large, herbaceous, rhizomatous fern with midgreen, leathery, somewhat glossy, upright to arching, sterile and fertile fronds, 12–36 in. (30–90 cm) long and 6–12 in. (15–30 cm) wide, with black to reddish petioles and alternating, lance-shaped pinnae nearly twice pinnate, the pinnules lobed and cut nearly to the midvein. New fronds flushed gold to coppery or red, turning bronze in fall. Can spread quickly into large colonies via long, ropelike rhizomes. Sometimes recognized scientifically as *Anchistea virginica*.

X

Xanthorhiza simplicissima
YELLOWROOT

Ranunculaceae

Zones 3–9

Shaded streambanks, moist woods, thickets, and rocky ledges from sea level to moderate elevations in the southeastern United States with disjunct populations to Maine.

Uncommon and unusual deciduous subshrub belonging to the buttercup family, with foliage resembling celery. Upright, woody stems, 24–36 in. (60–90 cm) tall, are topped with glossy, bright green, 3–5 times compound foliage and very small, starry, purple-brown or burgundy flowers on numerous arching sprays in spring, followed by star-shaped fruit. Foliage develops yellow, orange, and reddish purple tones in fall, aging to tan and often persisting into winter. Roots and stems are deep yellow beneath the surface, spreading widely and indefinitely by long rhizomes.

CULTURE/CARE Full sun to shade in organically rich, average to moist soils. Tolerant of diverse soil types and dry conditions. Shear colonies to the ground every few years to control height and increase density. Control spread with maintenance or hardscape barriers.

USES Medium-sized to large applications, beneath large trees and shrubs, and on slopes for erosion control, spreading at a moderate to fast rate, especially in moist soils. Not tolerant of foot traffic.

PROPAGATION Division, stem or root cuttings, seed

A mass planting of *Geranium* 'Gerwat' Rozanne between *Miscanthus sinensis* in the Bressingham Garden at the Gardens at Elm Bank, Wellesley, Massachusetts

Resources

Alpine Garden Society Plant Encylopaedia: encyclopaedia.alpinegardensociety.net

The American Iris Society Iris Encyclopedia: wiki.irises.org

Biodiversity Information System, Argentina: sib.gob.ar

Bluestem Nursery database: bluestem.ca

Chileflora, information on native Chilean plants: chileflora.com

Calflora, information on wild California plants: calflora.org

California Native Plant Society, Calscape: calscape.org

Casa Flora, wholesale nursery: casaflora.com

Catalogue of Life: catalogueoflife.org

Center for Invasive Species and Ecosystem Health, Invasive and Exotic Species of North America: invasive.org

Clearview Horticultural Products, wholesale nursery: clearviewhort.com

E-Flora BC, Electronic Atlas of the Flora of British Columbia: eflora.bc.ca

eFloras database: efloras.org

Euro+Med PlantBase, information resource for Euro-Mediterranean plant diversity: emplantbase.org/home.html

Flora of China: efloras.org/flora_page.aspx?flora_id=2

Flora of North America: efloras.org/flora_page.aspx?flora_id=1

Gardenia, gardener's resource: gardenia.net

Heaths & Heathers Nursery: heathsandheathers.com

Heritage Perennials database: perennials.com

Hoffman Nursery, wholesale nursery: hoffmannursery.com

International Geraniaceae Group, Cultivar Register: geraniaceae-group.org/society/cultivar-register

Invasive Plant Atlas of the United States: invasiveplantatlas.org

The Jepson Herbarium, Jepson Flora Project database: ucjeps.berkeley.edu/eflora

Khumbula Indigenous Garden database of indigenous South African flora: kumbulanursery.co.za

Midwest Groundcovers, wholesale nursery: midwestgroundcovers.com

Missouri Botanical Garden Plant Finder: missouribotanicalgarden.org/plantfinder/plantfindersearch.aspx

The Morton Arboretum plant database: mortonarb.org/trees-plants/search-trees/search-all-trees-and-plants

National Collection of Erysimums: erysimums.onesuffolk.net

National Gardening Association plants database: garden.org

NatureGate database, Finland: luontoportti.com

nzflora database of New Zealand plants: nzflora.info

Perennial Resource: perennialresource.com

Phoenix Perennials and Specialty Plants: phoenixperennials.com

Plant Lust: plantlust.com

Royal Horticultural Society, RHS Plant Finder: rhs.org.uk/plants

San Marcos Growers plant database: smgrowers.com

The Saxifrage Society, Saxbase online database of saxifrages: saxbase.org/plants/saxbase/default.asp

Stepables: stepables.com

Taranaki Educational Resource—Research, Analysis, and Information Network, New Zealand: https://sur.ly/i/terrain.net.nz

Tela Botanica network, France: tela-botanica.org

Three Rivers Rain Garden Alliance: raingardenalliance.org/planting/plantlist

Andreoletti, Jessica. n.d. The Vermont Rain Garden Manual: "Gardening to Absorb the Storm." uvm.edu/seagrant/sites/default/files/uploads/publication/VTRainGardenManual_Full.pdf.

Bell, Neil, and Heather Stoven. 2017. "Evaluating Manzanita: Ongoing study shows this western native shrub to be drought tolerant, great for pollinators, and overall well suited for Northwest landscapes." *Digger*, diggermagazine.com/evaluating-manzanita.

Bitner, Richard L. 2007 *Conifers for Gardens: An Illustrated Encyclopedia*. Portland, Oregon: Timber Press.

Boland, Todd. 2011. Groundcover Cotoneasters... Multipurpose Shrubs. davesgarden.com/guides/articles/view/915#b.

Bonine, Paul. 2012. Hardy Fragrant Jasmine: Romantic Poet's Jasmine Woos Gardening Hearts in Cascadia. *Pacific Horticulture*, pacifichorticulture.org/articles/romantic-poets-jasmine-woos-gardening-hearts-in-cascadia.

Bourne, Val. 2003. How to grow: *Anthemis. The Telegraph*, telegraph.co.uk/gardening/howtogrow/3313033/How-to-grow-Anthemis.html.

Briggs, Helen. 2019. Biodiversity: The Best Plants for Attracting Insects to Gardens. *BBC News*, bbc.com/news/science-environment-50663818.

Buchan, Ursula. 2004. Get Shorty. *The Telegraph*, telegraph.co.uk/gardening/gardenprojects/3321355/Get-shorty.html.

CAB International. 2019. *Hedera helix* (ivy). CABI Invasive Species Compendium, cabi.org/isc/datasheet/26694.

Clark, Patterson. 2013. Ivy: You say *helix*, I say *hibernica. Washington Post*, washingtonpost.com/wp-srv/special/metro/urban-jungle/pages/130219.html.

Clean Water Campaign. n.d. Rain Gardens for Home Landscapes. cfpub.epa.gov/npstbx/files/cwc_raingardenbrochure.pdf.

Curley, Louise. 2015. Gardens: a celebration of sweet violets. *The Guardian*, theguardian.com/lifeandstyle/2015/mar/07/gardens-celebration-of-sweet-violets.

Curto, Michael, and David Fross. 2006. A Sedge by Another Name. *Pacific Horticulture*, pacifichorticulture.org/articles/a-sedge-by-another-name.

Darke, Rick. 2005. *Amsonia* in cultivation. *The Plantsman*, 4(2): 72–75.

Dawson, John, and Rob Lucas. 2000. *Nature Guide to the New Zealand Forest*. Auckland, New Zealand: Godwit/Random House.

DeBaggio, Thomas, and Arthur O. Tucker. 2009. *The Encyclopedia of Herbs: A Comprehensive Reference to Herbs of Flavor and Fragrance*. Portland, Oregon: Timber Press.

Deputy, Jay, and David Hensley. 1998. Mondo Grass. Ornamentals and Flowers-28. Cooperative Extension Service, University of Hawaii, ctahr.hawaii.edu/oc/freepubs/pdf/OF-28.pdf.

Ellis, Barbara W. 2007. *Covering Ground: Unexpected Ideas For Landscaping with Colorful, Low-Maintenance Ground Covers*. North Adams, Massachusetts: Storey Publishing.

Finn, Chad. E., Jorge B. Retamales, Gustavo A. Lobos, and James F. Hancock. 2013. The Chilean Strawberry (*Fragaria chiloensis*): Over 1000 Years of Domestication. *HortScience* 48(4) 418–421.

Fross, David, and Dieter Wilken. 2006. *Ceanothus*. Portland, Oregon: Timber Press.

Gardenia. n.d. Salt Tolerant Solutions. gardenia.net/plants/solutions/salt-resistant.

Guest Shadrack, Kathy, and Michael Shadrack. 2010. *The Book of Little Hostas: 200 Small, Very Small, and Mini Varieties*. Portland, Oregon: Timber Press.

Harrington, Rebecca. 2016. Grass takes up 2% of the land in the continental US. *Business Insider*, businessinsider.com/americas-biggest-crop-is-grass-2016-2.

Harris, James G., and Melinda Woolf Harris. 2001. *Plant Identification Terminology: An Illustrated Glossary*. Utah: Spring Lake Publishing.

Hatch, Laurence C. 2014. International Liriope and Ophiopogon Cultivar Register. *Ornamentals Quarterly*, nanopdf.com/download/international-liriope-and-ophiopogion-cultivar-register_pdf#.

Hawke, Richard G. 1994. A Performance Report of Cultivated Yarrows (*Achillea*). Plant Evaluation Notes 5, Chicago Botanic Garden, chicagobotanic.org/downloads/planteval_notes/no5_yarrow.pdf.

Hawke, Richard. 2012. If you're not growing Geums, you're missing out. *Fine Gardening* 144: 45–51.

Hawke, Richard. 2015. An Evaluation Study of Plants for Use on Green Roofs. Plant Evaluation Notes 38, Chicago Botanic Garden, chicagobotanic.org/downloads/planteval_notes/no38_green-roofplants.pdf.

Heger, Mike. 2017. Perennials Tolerant of Salty Conditions. ambergatehc.com/plant-lists/salt-tolerant-perennials.

Hinkley, Daniel J. 1999. *The Explorer's Garden: Rare and Unusual Perennials*. Portland, Oregon: Timber Press.

Hoffman, M. H. A., ed. 2016. *List of Names of Perennials*. The Netherlands: Naktuinbouw.

Hoffman, M. H. A., ed. 2016. *List of Names of Woody Plants*. The Netherlands: Naktuinbouw.

Horvath, Brent. 2014. *The Plant Lover's Guide to Sedums*. Portland, Oregon: Timber Press.

Ken's Gardens. n.d. Deer and Rabbit Resistant Plants. kensgardens.com/wp-content/uploads/2016/02/deer-rabbit-resistant.pdf.

Locklear, James H. 2011. *Phlox: A Natural History and Gardener's Guide*. Portland, Oregon: Timber Press.

MacKenzie, David S. 1997. *Perennial Ground Covers*. Portland, Oregon: Timber Press.

McGregor, Malcolm. 2008. *Saxifrages: A Definitive Guide to the 2000 Species, Hybrids & Cultivars*. Portland, Oregon: Timber Press.

McMahan, Linda R. n.d. English Ivy is an invasive weed in Pacific Northwest. Oregon State University Extension Service, extension.oregonstate.edu/gardening/node/948.

Metcalf, Lawrie. 2009. *Know Your New Zealand Native Plants*. Auckland, New Zealand: New Holland Publishers.

Miehe, Georg, Sabine Miehe, Jonas Vogel, Sonam Co, and La Duo. 2007. Highest Treeline in the Northern Hemisphere Found in Southern Tibet. *Mountain Research and Development* 27(2): 169–173.

O'Brien, Bart. 2007. Enjoying Zauschnerias. *Pacific Horticulture*, pacifichorticulture.org/articles/enjoying-zauschnerias.

Perkins, Karen. Garden Vision Epimediums 2017 catalog. epimediums.com/wp-content/uploads/2017/01/GVEcatalog.pdf.

Phillips, Roger, and Martyn Rix. 1991. *The Random House Book of Perennials*. 2 vols. New York: Random House.

Pojar, Jim, and Andy MacKinnon. 2016. *Plants of Coastal British Columbia including Washington, Oregon & Alaska*. Vancouver: Lone Pine Publishing.

Rawson, Donald A. 2019. Rhizomatous Hostas. hostalists.org/hosta_list_rhih.php.

Ribbens, Eric. 2008. *Opuntia fragilis*: Taxonomy, distribution, and ecology. *Haseltonia* 14: 94–110.

Richards, John. 2003. *Primula*. Portland, Oregon: Timber Press.

Rudy, Mark R. 2003. An Evaluation Report on Barrenworts for the Shade Garden. Plant Evaluation Notes 20, Chicago Botanic Garden, chicagobotanic.org/downloads/planteval_notes/no20_barrenworts.pdf.

Rudy, Mark R. 2004. Fall-Blooming Anemones. Plant Evaluation Notes 25, Chicago Botanic Garden, chicagobotanic.org/downloads/planteval_notes/no25_anemones.pdf.

Salmon, John T. 1991. *Native New Zealand Flowering Plants*. Auckland, New Zealand: Reed Books.

Salmon, John T. 1999. *A Field Guide to the Alpine Plants of New Zealand*. Auckland, New Zealand: Random House.

Schmid, W. George. 2002. *An Encyclopedia of Shade Perennials*. Portland, Oregon: Timber Press.

Schmid, W. George. 2010. *H. venusta* (Baker) T. Nakai 1911. The Hosta Library, hostalibrary.org/species/pdf/venusta.pdf.

Southern California Salinity Coalition. 2007. Choose salt-tolerant plants. watereuse.org/salinity-management/cp/cp_7.html.

Urbaniak, Linda. 2006. *Gaultheria. Pacific Horticulture* 67(4), pacifichorticulture.org/articles/gaultheria.

Wagner, Warren L., Peter C. Hoch, and Peter H. Raven. 2007. Revised Classification of the Onagraceae. *Systematic Botany Monographs* vol. 83, repository.si.edu/bitstream/handle/10088/7611/bot_Wagner_et_al_2007-Onagraceae-sm.pdf?sequence=1&isAllowed=y.

Photo Credits

All photos are by the author, except for the following:

Garden World, pages 287 (bottom left), 395 (left)

Chris M. Hansen, pages 397 (bottom left and bottom right), 400 (left), 401 (left)

Alasdair MacGregor, page 100 (top)

Lew Matthews, Matthews Botanics, page 299 (top)

North Creek Nurseries, pages 138 (left), 212 (right), 213 (left), 230 (bottom), 267 (bottom), 270 (middle), 326, 336, 339

Plant Select / Dan Johnson, pages 321, 430 (top)

Plant Select / Panayoti Kelaidis, page 102 (top)

Plant Select / David Winger, page 425 (top right)

Proven Winners®, pages 192, 397 (top right)

Howard Rice, page 360 (bottom right)

Schreiner's Gardens, page 270 (bottom)

Anthony Tesselaar, page 371

Walters Gardens, pages 100 (bottom), 102 (bottom), 109, 263 (left), 340

Index

GARY LEWIS has had a lifelong interest in plants and gardening. He holds a Bachelor of Science in Conservation Biology and a Masters of Science in Botany (Plant Ecology), both from the University of British Columbia. His retail and mail-order nursery, Phoenix Perennials, located in Richmond, BC, offers more than 5000 different plants a year. In 2017 it won the Retail Sales Award from the Perennial Plant Association. Gary has written for various garden magazines including *Fine Gardening* and has been a frequent guest on local and regional radio and television stations in British Columbia. He speaks regularly to garden clubs around British Columbia and the Pacific Northwest and has presented at professional conferences across North America. In 2013, he was selected as Communicator of the Year by the British Columbia Landscape & Nursery Association and in 2014 was named as one of Canada's Top 10 Horticultural Professionals under 40 by *Greenhouse Canada* magazine. He has served on the board of directors for the Perennial Plant Association and is a committee member of Great Plant Picks. Gary is an avid traveler and has led garden and botanical tours to Australia, New Zealand, South Africa, and various European countries.